Fodor's 92
New York
City

Fodor's Travel Publications, Inc.
New York and London

's Travel Publications, Inc.

ernational and Pan-American
shed in the United States by
Inc., a subsidiary of Random
ultaneously in Canada by Ran-
Toronto. Distributed by Ran-

*r portions of this book may be
t written permission from the
publishers.*

ISBN 0-679-02070–1

Grateful acknowledgement is made to the following for permission to reprint previously published material: Sterling Lord Literistic, Inc.: Excerpt from NEW YORK PROCLAIMED by V.S. Pritchett. Copyright © 1965 by V.S. Pritchett. Reprinted by permission of Sterling Lord Literistic. Inc.

"What Makes New Yorkers Tick," by Calvin Trillin. Copyright © 1990 by Calvin Trillin. Originally appeared in *TIME*. Reprinted by permission.

Fodor's New York City

Editor: Paula Rackow
Contributors: Michael Adams, Laura Broadwell, Karen Cure, Theodore Fischer, Tara Hamilton, Jane Hershey, Ann LaForge, David Laskin, John Mariani, Peter D. Meltzer, Denise Lewis Patrick, Penelope Papailias, Marcy Pritchard, Craig Seligman, Susan Spano Wells
Art Director: Fabrizio La Rocca
Cartographer: David Lindroth
Illustrator: Karl Tanner
Cover Photograph: Francesco Ruggeri

Design: Vignelli Associates

Special Sales

Fodor's Travel Publications are available at special discounts for bulk purchases (100 copies or more) for sales promotions or premiums. Special editions, including personalized covers, excerpts of existing guides, and corporate imprints, can be created in large quantities for special needs. For more information write to Special Marketing, Fodor's Travel Publications, 201 East 50th St., New York, NY 10022; or call 800/800–3246. Inquiries from the United Kingdom should be sent to Fodor's Travel Publications, 20 Vauxhall Bridge Rd., London, England SW1V 2SA.

MANUFACTURED IN THE UNITED STATES OF AMERICA
10 9 8 7 6 5 4 3 2 1

Contents

Foreword *vi*

Highlights '92 *vii*

Fodor's Choice *xi*

Introduction *xviii*

1 Essential Information *1*

Before You Go *2*

Visitor Information *2*
Tour Groups *2*
Package Deals for Independent Travelers *3*
Tips for British Travelers *3*
When to Go *4*
Festivals and Seasonal Events *5*
What to Pack *8*
What It Will Cost *9*
Cash Machines *9*
Traveling with Film *10*
Traveling with Children *10*
Hints for Disabled Travelers *12*
Hints for Older Travelers *13*
Further Reading *15*

Arriving and Departing *17*

By Plane *17*
By Car *20*
Car Rentals *21*
By Train *22*
By Bus *22*

Staying in New York *23*

Important Addresses and Telephone Numbers *23*
Telephones *23*
Rest Rooms *24*
Crime *24*
Opening and Closing Times *24*
Changing Money *25*
Getting Around *25*
Guided Tours *30*

2 Portraits of New York City *33*

"The New York Babel," by V.S. Pritchett *34*
"What Makes New Yorkers Tick," by Calvin Trillin *39*

3 Exploring Manhattan *43*

Orientation *44*

Exploring *46*

Highlights for First-time Visitors *46*
Tour 1. Rockefeller Center *46*
Tour 2. Midtown from Fifth to Park Avenues *52*
Tour 3. Across 42nd Street *55*
Tour 4. Murray Hill to Union Square *60*
Tour 5. Museum Mile *66*
Tour 6. The Upper East Side *72*
Tour 7. Central Park *77*
Tour 8. The Upper West Side *83*
Tour 9. Columbia University and Environs *90*
Tour 10. Harlem *94*
Tour 11. Chelsea *98*
Tour 12. Greenwich Village *102*
Tour 13. The East Village *109*
Tour 14. SoHo and TriBeCa *113*
Tour 15. Little Italy *119*
Tour 16. Chinatown *121*
Tour 17. Wall Street and the Battery *123*
Tour 18. The Seaport and the Courts *131*

Manhattan For Free *134*

What to See and Do with Children *136*

Off the Beaten Track *138*

4 Exploring the Other Boroughs *141*

Brooklyn *142*

Tour 19. Brooklyn Heights *142*
Tour 20. Park Slope *149*

Queens *153*

Tour 21. Long Island City and Astoria *153*
Tour 22. Flushing *157*

The Bronx *159*

Tour 23. Fordham and the Zoo *159*

Staten Island *163*

Tour 24. Snug Harbor and Richmondtown *163*

What to See and Do with Children *165*

Off the Beaten Track *166*

5 Sightseeing Checklists *168*

6 Sports, Fitness, Beaches *178*

7 Shopping *188*

8 Dining *216*

9 Lodging *253*

10 The Arts *273*

11 Nightlife *294*

12 Excursions from New York City *308*

Montauk, New York *309*
Old Lyme, Connecticut *314*
Hyde Park, New York *316*

Index *320*

Maps and Charts

New York City Area *xiv–xv*
World Time Zones *xvi–xvii*
Manhattan Address Locator *26*
Manhattan Subways *28*
Manhattan Neighborhoods *45*
Tours 1–3: Midtown *48–49*
Tour 4: Murray Hill to Union Square *61*
Tours 5 and 6: Museum Mile, Upper East Side *67*
Tour 7: Central Park *79*
Tours 8 and 9: Upper West Side, Columbia *85*
Tour 10: Harlem *96*
Tour 11: Chelsea *100*
Tours 12 and 13: Greenwich Village and the East Village *104*
Tours 14–16: SoHo, TriBeCa, Little Italy, Chinatown *116–117*
Tours 17 and 18: Lower Manhattan *124–125*
The Five Boroughs *144–145*
Tour 19: Brooklyn Heights *146*
Tour 20: Park Slope *151*
Tour 21: Long Island City and Astoria *154*
Tour 22: Flushing *158*
Tour 23: Fordham and the Bronx Zoo *161*
Tour 24: Staten Island *164*
Manhattan Shopping Highlights *190*
SoHo Shopping *191*
57th Street/5th Avenue Shopping *192*
West Side Shopping *195*
Madison Avenue Shopping *197*
Manhattan Dining *222–223*
Midtown East Dining *233*
Manhattan Lodging *257*
Theater District *279*
Tri-State Area *310*

Foreword

While every care has been taken to ensure the accuracy of the information in this guide, the passage of time will always bring change, and consequently, the publisher cannot accept responsibility for errors that may occur.

All prices and opening times quoted here are based on information supplied to us at press time. Hours and admission fees may change, however, and the prudent traveler will avoid inconvenience by calling ahead.

Fodor's wants to hear about your travel experiences, both pleasant and unpleasant. When a hotel or restaurant fails to live up to its billing, let us know and we will investigate the complaint and revise our entries where the facts warrant it.

Send your letters to the editors of Fodor's Travel Publications, 201 E. 50th Street, New York, NY 10022.

Highlights'92 and Fodor's Choice

Highlights '92

New York City has been hit hard by the nationwide recession. Indeed, not since the near-bankruptcy days of 1975 has the city faced a fiscal crisis of such magnitude. Coupled with the state's financial troubles, Mayor Dinkins's drastic cuts in the city's cultural budget could mean that several arts institutions would have to close down their premises, or a major part of them. Among the museums, performing arts centers, and other popular institutions that would be devastated by such cuts are the Central Park Zoo, New York Botanical Garden, Brooklyn Academy of Music, Brooklyn Museum, City Center, The Museum of the City of New York, and Wave Hill. Also imperiled at press time (summer 1991) are experimental performance spaces such as P. S. 122 and the Kitchen, which, along with the "establishment" organizations, contribute to New York's reputation as a cultural capital. In order to survive the shrinkage in city and state arts allocations, institutions will inevitably tighten their belts with reduced hours, higher admission prices, and fewer or less ambitious productions and exhibitions, so visitors are advised to call ahead or check local magazines and newspapers for the most current information.

Despite the predictions of a cultural Dark Age, expansions and renovations of museums and other institutions continue apace. The **Brooklyn Museum** will complete its $31-million renovation by fall 1992. The **Pierpont Morgan Library** was on schedule in October 1991 when it opened J. P. Morgan's mansion around the corner as part of the museum, linked to the original library by an indoor garden court. Delays have plagued the renovation of the **Solomon R. Guggenheim Museum,** which is currently slated to reopen in fall 1992 with a 50% increase in gallery space. An annex to the landmark Frank Lloyd Wright building in the form of a tower, by architectural firm Gwathmey Siegel, is bound to prove controversial. The Guggenheim is also planning to open a SoHo outpost in a six-story brick building at Broadway and Prince Street; the office and additional exhibition space, to be designed by Arata Isozaki, will occupy 2½ floors.

Fossil fans who flock to the **American Museum of Natural History** to see the dinosaurs will be disappointed to learn that the Hall of Early Dinosaurs will be closed until February 1993, and that the Hall of Late Dinosaurs (which contains the much-beloved *Tyrannosaurus rex*) will be closing in February 1992 for nearly three years.

The long-awaited museum devoted to the Holocaust opens in late 1992 as **A Living Memorial to the Holocaust—Museum of Jewish Heritage.** The museum, located between First and Second Place at Battery Park City, follows the Jewish experience from before World War II through immigration to the United States after the war. Just south of Battery Park City, the **South Garden** should be open for your strolling pleasure by summer 1992. The 3½-acre garden, a series of 18 outdoor "rooms" containing such features as a serpentine garden and a rapids pool, was designed by painter Jennifer Bartlett. (The garden is adjacent to **Pier A,** one of the last remaining Victorian piers in New York. Developers are planning to turn the turn-of-the-century tin firehouse there into a sort of small-scale South Street Seaport, with a mix of shops and restaurants. It's not expected to open until at least 1993).

Film buffs are celebrating the arrival of a new theater at Lincoln Center devoted to "noncommercial" movies, both old and new. Called the **Walter Reade Theater** and located on 65th Street between Amsterdam Avenue and Broadway, the auditorium, which opened in the fall, holds daily screenings. Important anniversaries abound at Lincoln Center. The 1992-93 season is the **New York Philharmonic's** "celebration season," marking the 150th anniversary of the orchestra. With Kurt Masur, the new musical director, at the helm, the Philharmonic is planning many special events to mark the anniversary. During its 1991-92 season, the **Metropolitan Opera** is celebrating the 25th anniversary of the company's move to its Lincoln Center theater with several new productions and the world premiere of John Corigliano's *Ghosts of Versailles*. Culture mavens will not only be watching Kurt Masur but also Andre Bishop, who will be succeeding Gregory Mosher as the **Lincoln Center Theater's** artistic director in January 1992.

Two zoos that have been inaccessible will be reopening. The **Queens Zoo** (in Flushing Meadows Corona Park) will be back in action in the spring of 1992 with a new focus on North American animals in their natural habitat. The **Prospect Park Zoo** is scheduled to reopen in late 1992 as a children's zoo, after an extensive renovation.

Brooklyn has been designated by the New York State Department of Economic Development as its official "I Love New York" destination for the spring of 1992. With the Fund for the Borough of Brooklyn as coordinator, numerous special events are being planned, including boroughwide walking and dining tours of Brooklyn, a regatta in Sheepshead Bay, and a performing arts festival.

Tennis bums have long complained about the dearth of courts in New York, but the $150-million expansion of the **National Tennis Center** at Flushing Meadows Corona Park in Queens should improve matters. Scheduled to begin in 1992, the two-year construction is expected to face opposition and a barrage of reviews because it entails the use of existing parkland. **Madison Square Garden** has undergone a major renovation: The old Felt Forum at the Garden has been reincarnated as the 5,600-seat Forum, a multi-use theater that will host concerts, comedy revues, family and theatrical shows, boxing, trade shows, and conventions.

The recession—and AIDS—have given New York's fashion industry its share of hard knocks, but a rash of store openings belies that predicament. In February 1991, **Henri Bendel** took up residence at 712 Fifth Avenue, behind the restored facades of the landmark Rizzoli and Coty buildings. The fall of 1991 sees the opening of **Galeries Lafayette** in Bonwit Teller's old 57th Street location. The first U. S. outpost of the famous French fashion store, it will showcase—naturally—French and other European designs. **Barney's,** the fashion store of choice among New York's trendiest, is expected to open a branch store by late 1992 on Madison Avenue between 60th and 61st streets.

Among the new hotels that have opened recently are **Embassy Suites** and the **Rihga Royal,** both reviewed in Chapter 9. There are other new properties that, though not ready for full review at press time, should be available to accommodate visitors by early or mid-1992. The Times Square rejuvenation continues with a 315-room **Ramada Rennaissance,** to be located on the triangle formed by Broadway, Seventh Avenue, and 47th Street. Also open is the 638-room **Hotel Macklowe** at 145 West 44th Street, which along with elegant rooms in the expensive range, features a theater, high-tech meeting facilities, and a well-received restaurant called Charlotte.

I. M. Pei is designing what might be New York's most expensive hotel on 57th Street between Madison and Park avenues: the 400-room **Regent of New York.** Until it opens, though, the stunningly restored **St. Regis,** which was unveiled in September 1991, claims that honor: Double rooms start at $350 a night. Central Park South's **Essex House,** now a Nikko Hotel, should be receiving guests as a deluxe property. Downtown, **Marriott** has opened a new 507-room Financial Center hotel near the Vista. Prices are in the upper end of the expensive category.

In anticipation of the 1992 Democratic Convention, the **Sheraton Center,** which, with the Hilton, is hosting the delegates, is getting a major remodeling. The nearby Sheraton City Squire is following suit, and will be renamed the **Sheraton Manhattan Hotel.**

Boutique hotels continue to proliferate. The newly restored **Hotel Wales** on Madison Avenue at 92nd Street, a 90-year-old, 92-room Beaux Arts-style building, has emerged as a moderately priced, European-style property. Lastly, the Guggenheim's new satellite museum in SoHo will have a hotel for a neighbor. Opening in April 1992, the **Mercer Hotel** will occupy a 103-year-old Romanesque Revival building at Mercer and Prince streets, with 78 luxury rooms, a restaurant, and small stores.

Fodor's Choice

No two people will agree on what makes a perfect vacation, but it's fun and helpful to know what others think. We hope you'll have a chance to experience some of Fodor's Choices yourself while visiting New York City. For detailed information about each entry, refer to the appropriate chapters within this guidebook.

Views

The lower Manhattan skyline, seen from the Brooklyn Heights Promenade

The vista of skyscrapers ringing Central Park, best viewed from the reservoir's northwest corner

A moonlit look at the harbor from the Staten Island Ferry

The sun setting over New Jersey and the lights of Manhattan snapping on one by one, from the World Trade Center's observation deck, 107 stories up

Architecture

The Woolworth Building, the Flatiron Building, the Empire State Building, and the World Trade Center's twin towers—each, in its time, the world's tallest building

The Chrysler Building, whose Art Deco chrome spire pierces the sky

The Dakota, grande dame of apartment buildings

The unbroken front of cast-iron beauties along Greene Street in SoHo

The graceful town houses along St. Luke's Place in the West Village

The Cathedral of St. John the Divine, and immense Gothic cathedral still abuilding

Museums

The Pierpont Morgan Library, and Morgan's personal library within

The dioramas at the American Museum of Natural History

The secluded Lehman Pavilion, among other delights at the Metropolitan Museum of Art

The medieval Cloisters, especially its unicorn tapestries

The American Museum of the Moving Image, with a foray into Queens for film lovers

Holidays and Seasonal Events

The lighting of the Christmas tree in Rockefeller Plaza

Cherry blossoms in bloom at the Brooklyn Botanical Garden

The Ninth Avenue Food Fair, a gluttonous early-May street feast

Late August afternoons when the Mets are playing at Shea and, a boardwalk's stroll away, the U. S. Open at Flushing Meadows

The San Gennaro Festival, on Little Italy's streets in September

The inflating of giant balloons the night before Macy's Thanksgiving Day Parade, on West 77th Street

Entertainment

Whatever is onstage at Playwrights' Horizons, on Theatre Row

Jazz into the wee hours at the Blue Note

Standing-room tickets for the Metropolitan Opera, obtainable the Sunday before the performance

A Woody Allen or Martin Scorsese movie, viewed along with a hometown New York audience

Standing in line at the TKTS booth—an afternoon's entertainment in itself

Restaurants

The Four Seasons *(Very Expensive)*

Le Bernardin *(Very Expensive)*

Lutèce *(Very Expensive)*

Felidia *(Expensive)*

Le Cirque *(Expensive)*

Smith & Wollensky *(Expensive)*

La Columbe D'Or *(Moderate)*

Mesa Grill *(Moderate)*

Shun Lee Palace *(Moderate)*

Union Square Café *(Moderate)*

Katz's Delicatessen *(Inexpensive)*

Shopping

Ralph Lauren's Polo store, in a superbly renovated East Side town house

Zabar's, an outstanding food store and cultural institution

Barneys New York for men's and women's clothing

The Enchanted Forest, a special SoHo toy store

An auction at Sotheby's

Hotels

The Mark *(Very Expensive)*

The Pierre *(Very Expensive)*

Le Parker Meridien *(Expensive)*

The Mayfair Regent *(Expensive)*

The United Nations Plaza *(Expensive)*

The Algonquin *(Moderate)*

The Paramount *(Inexpensive)*

Street Life

Itinerant musicians playing at either end of the subway shuttle between Times Square and Grand Central Terminal

The steps of the New York Public Library, weekdays at lunchtime

Lincoln Center's central plaza, just before an 8 PM concert

Central Park's Mall, Bethesda Terrace, and Conservatory Water on weekend afternoons

Quintessentially New York

Browsing among the melon-squeezers on a Saturday morning at the Union Square Greenmarket.

Catching sight of a dog-walker, leashed to a tangle of pooches, in Central Park

Schmoozing in the Garment District, as wheeled racks of ready-to-wear hurtle past

Watching the frenzy on the floor of the New York Stock Exchange

Gallery-hopping along West Broadway in SoHo on a Saturday afternoon (if you like trendoid crowds)

Going to a deli restaurant for a pastrami-on-rye, garlic pickles, and an egg cream

Spotting celebrities—anywhere and everywhere

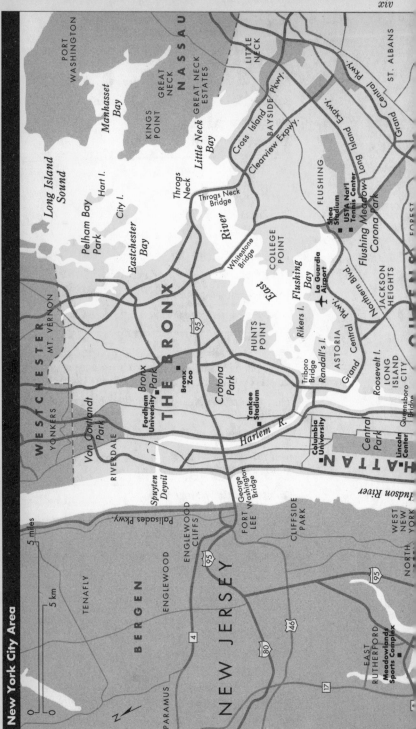

New York City Area

0 ____ 5 miles

0 ____ 5 km

PORT
WASHINGTON

Manhasset
Bay

Long Island Sound

KINGS
POINT

GREAT NECK
ESTATES

GREAT
NECK

LITTLE
NECK

NASSAU

LITTLE
NECK

ST. ALBANS

Grand Central Pkwy.

Pelham Bay
Park

Hart I.

City I.

Eastchester
Bay

Throgs
Neck

Throgs Neck
Bridge

River

Cross Island Pkwy.

BAYSIDE Pkwy.

Clearview Expwy.

Long Island Expwy.

FLUSHING

Shea
Stadium

USTA Nat'l
Tennis Center

Flushing Meadow
Corona Park

FOREST

MT. VERNON

WESTCHESTER

YONKERS

Whitestone
Bridge

COLLEGE
POINT

THE BRONX

95

Fordham
University

Bronx
Park

Bronx
Zoo

Crotona
Park

HUNTS
POINT

Rikers I.

Flushing
Bay

La Guardia
Airport

East

Nothern Blvd.

JACKSON
HEIGHTS

Grand Central Pkwy.

QUEENS

Van Cortlandt
Park

RIVERDALE

Spuyten
Devil

Yankee
Stadium

Harlem R.

Triboro
Bridge

Randall's I.

ASTORIA

Roosevelt I.

LONG
ISLAND
CITY

George
Washington
Bridge

Columbia
University

Central
Park

Lincoln
Center

MANHATTAN

Queensboro
Bridge

FORT
LEE

Palisades Pkwy.

ENGLEWOOD
CLIFFS

CLIFFSIDE
PARK

Hudson River

WEST
NEW
YORK

TENAFLY

ENGLEWOOD

BERGEN

NEW JERSEY

95

4

NORTH

80

PARAMUS

46

EAST
RUTHERFORD

Meadowlands
Sports Complex

17

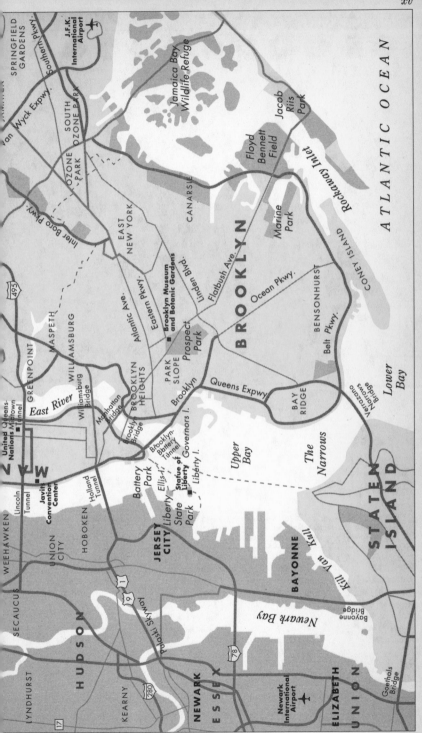

World Time Zones

Numbers below vertical bands relate each zone to Greenwich Mean Time (0 hrs.).
Local times frequently differ from these general indications,
as indicated by light-face numbers on map.

Algiers, **29**

Anchorage, **3**

Athens, **41**

Auckland, **1**

Baghdad, **46**

Bangkok, **50**

Beijing, **54**

Berlin, **34**

Bogotá, **19**

Budapest, **37**

Buenos Aires, **24**

Caracas, **22**

Chicago, **9**

Copenhagen, **33**

Dallas, **10**

Delhi, **48**

Denver, **8**

Djakarta, **53**

Dublin, **26**

Edmonton, **7**

Hong Kong, **56**

Honolulu, **2**

Istanbul, **40**

Jerusalem, **42**

Johannesburg, **44**

Lima, **20**

Lisbon, **28**

London (Greenwich), **27**

Los Angeles, **6**

Madrid, **38**

Manila, **57**

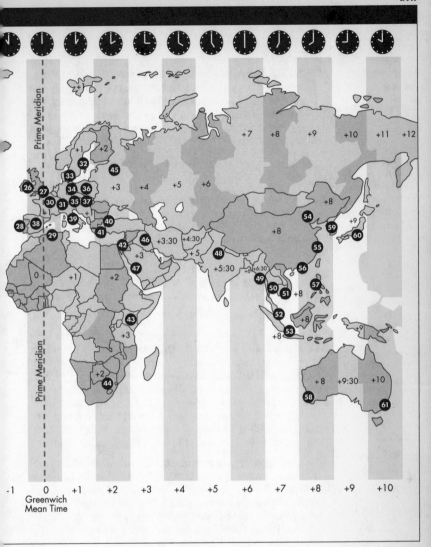

Mecca, **47**
Mexico City, **12**
Miami, **18**
Montreal, **15**
Moscow, **45**
Nairobi, **43**
New Orleans, **11**
New York City, **16**

Ottawa, **14**
Paris, **30**
Perth, **58**
Reykjavík, **25**
Rio de Janeiro, **23**
Rome, **39**
Saigon, **51**

San Francisco, **5**
Santiago, **21**
Seoul, **59**
Shanghai, **55**
Singapore, **52**
Stockholm, **32**
Sydney, **61**
Tokyo, **60**

Toronto, **13**
Vancouver, **4**
Vienna, **35**
Warsaw, **36**
Washington, DC, **17**
Yangon, **49**
Zürich, **31**

Introduction

by Michael Adams

Senior writer for the business travel magazine Successful Meetings, *Michael Adams finally moved to his home town, New York City, 12 years ago.*

In 1925, the youthful songwriting team of Richard Rodgers and Larry Hart wrote "Manhattan," arguably the loveliest city anthem ever. "We'll have Manhattan, the Bronx, and Staten Island, too," it promises, drawing its images from the merry scramble that was the city more than 60 years ago: "sweet pushcarts," "baloney on a roll," a subway that "charms," Brighton Beach, Coney Island, and the popular comedy *Abie's Irish Rose*. "We'll turn Manhattan into an isle of joy," coos the refrain.

Several decades later, in 1989, an album called simply *New York*, by aging enfant terrible rocker Lou Reed, views the same city with glasses fogged by despair and cynicism: Drugs, crime, racism, and promiscuity reign in what Reed considers to be a sinkhole of "crudity, cruelty of thought and sound." His voice brittle with weary irony, he sings, "This is no time for celebration." Manhattan's "sweet pushcarts" now apparently overflow with deadly vials of crack.

So, whom to believe—Lou or Larry?

The truth of the matter is slippery, for New York has long been a mosaic of grand contradictions, a city for which there has never been—nor ever will be—a clear consensus. Hart himself took the city to task in another song, "Give it Back to the Indians," whose lyrics count off a litany of problems that still exist: crime, dirt, high prices, traffic jams, and all-around urban chaos. Yet for all that, millions live here, grumbling but happy, and millions more visit, curious as cats to find out what the magnificent fuss is all about.

I was in eighth grade in suburban Detroit when I first really became aware of New York. A friend's Manhattan-born mother still subscribed to the Sunday *New York Times*, and at their house I'd pore over the "Arts and Leisure" section, as rapt as an archaeologist with a cave painting. The details of what I read there have blurred, but I remember vividly the sensation I felt while reading: a combined anticipation and nostalgia so keen it bordered on pain. Although I had never been there, I was homesick for New York.

It's my home now, yet I can still understand and appreciate the impulse that draws visitors here. In a city so ripe with possibilities, we are all more or less visitors.

I think of this on an uncharacteristically warm day in late March, as I and fellow New Yorkers escape from the hives of offices and homes to celebrate spring's first preview. We unbutton our jackets, leave buses a stop or two before our usual destinations, quicken our resolve to visit that new exhibit at the Met or jog around the Central Park Reservoir. A jubilant sense of renewal infects us all, and I overhear one happy fellow saying to a friend, "I felt just like a tourist yesterday."

Whenever I get the New York blues, the best tonic for me is to glimpse the city through the eyes of a visitor. One day, after subway construction had rerouted me well out of my usual path, I found myself in the grimy Times Square station—hardly the place for a spiritual conversion. As usual I had that armor of body language that we New Yorkers reflexively assume to protect ourselves from strangers bent on (1) ripping us off, (2) doing us bodily harm, (3) converting us, (4) making sexual advances, or (5) being general pains-in-the-butt just for the hell of it. But that day, tucked away in a corner, was a group of musicians—not an uncommon sight in New York—playing the guitar, organ, and accordion with gusto and good spirits behind a homemade sign that dubbed them the "Argentinian Tango Company." Like many street musicians in Manhattan, they were *good*, but I was only half listening, too intent on cursing the city. Just as I passed the band, however, I noticed four teenagers drawn to the music—visitors surely, they were far too open and trusting to be anything else. Grinning as widely as the Argentinians, they began to perform a spontaneous imitation of flamenco dancing—clapping hands above their heads, raising their heels, laughing at themselves, and only slightly self-conscious. Passersby, myself included, broke into smiles. As I made my way to the subway platform, buoyed by the impromptu show, I once again forgave New York. This minor piece of magic was apology enough.

I wonder whether that was the moment one of those teenagers happened to fall in love with the city. It *can* happen in a single moment, to a visitor or to a longtime resident. Perhaps it hits during a stroll through Riverside Park after a blanketing snowfall, when trees have turned to crystal and the city feels a hush it knows at no other time; or when you turn a corner and spy, beyond a phalanx of RVs and a tangle of cables and high-beam lights, the filming of a new movie.

That moment could also come when the house lights begin to dim at the Metropolitan Opera, and the gaudily sparkling chandeliers make their magisterial ascent to the ceiling; or when you first glimpse the magnificently bright Prometheus statue in Rockefeller Center, gleaming like a giant present under the annual Christmas tree as dozens of skaters cut swirls of seasonal colors on the ice below. You may even be smitten in that instant when, walking along the streets in the haze of a summer afternoon, you look up above the sea of anonymous faces to see—and be astonished by—the lofty rows of skyscrapers, splendid in their arrogance and power. At times like these it is perfectly permissible to stop for a moment, take a breath, and think, "Wow! *This is New York!*" We who live here do it every so often ourselves.

For some, of course, that special moment comes with a happy shock of recognition when they spot a street or building made familiar by movies or television, anything from *I Love Lucy* to *On the Waterfront*. At the Empire State Building, who can help but remember King Kong's pathetically courageous swing from its pinnacle? Or at the brooding Dakota, the chilling destiny created for Rosemary's baby within those fortresslike walls? In the mind's eye, Audrey Hepburn is eternally pairing diamonds and a doughnut as she wends her swank way down Fifth Avenue to have breakfast at Tiffany's. And the miniature park on Sutton Place will always be where Woody Allen and Diane Keaton began their angst-ridden *Manhattan* love affair, with the 59th Street bridge gleaming beyond and Gershwin music swelling in the background.

There's a moment of sudden magic when a New York stereotype, seen so often on screen that it seems a joke, suddenly comes to life: when a gum-cracking waitress calls you "hon," or a stogie-sucking cabbie asks, "How 'bout them Yankees, Mac?" There's also the thrill of discovering one of New York's cities-within-the-city: Mulberry Street in Little Italy; Mott Street in Chinatown; Park Avenue's enclave of wealth and privilege; SoHo and TriBeCa, with their artistic types dressed in black from head to toe; or Sheridan Square, the nexus of the city's prominent lesbian and gay communities. The first glimpse of a landmark could begin the visitor's infatuation, too: frenetic Grand Central Station, abustle with suburban commuters; the concrete caverns of Wall Street, throbbing with power and ambition; or the Statue of Liberty, which neither cliché nor cheap souvenir can render common.

As you ready yourself to take on New York's contradictions, prepare to wonder and to exult. Here, on a single day, you might catch a glimpse of Jacqueline Onassis—she's been known to stop at Burger Heaven and have lunch at the counter—or Rollerena, the gloriously tacky drag-queen-cum-fairy-godmother on roller skates, who waves her magic wand to bestow blessings on select public events. Here you can eat sumptuously at a hot dog stand or at a world-celebrated gourmet shrine.

Excess and deprivation mingle here: As a limousine crawls lazily to take its pampered passengers to their luxe destination, it rolls past a threadbare beggar seeking the warmth that steams from the city's belly through an iron grate. It's a ludicrously bright cartoon and a sobering documentary, New York—almost too much for one city to be. It's maddening and it's thrilling; monstrous, yet beautiful beyond parallel.

And I envy anyone their first taste of it.

1 Essential Information

Before You Go

Visitor Information

The **New York Convention and Visitors Bureau** (2 Columbus Circle, New York, NY 10019, tel. 212/397–8222) provides a wealth of free information, including brochures, subway and bus maps, an up-to-date calendar of events, listings of hotels and weekend hotel packages, and discount coupons for Broadway shows. **The New York Division of Tourism** (1 Commerce Plaza, Albany, NY 12245, tel. 518/474–4116 or 800/225–5697) offers a free series of "I Love New York" booklets listing attractions and tour packages available in New York City.

Tour Groups

Thanks to their bulk buying power, tour operators can almost always get you better prices on air and ground transportation, hotels, and sightseeing than you can get on your own. The trade-off is that they require you to march to the beat of a tour guide's drum rather than your own. If not having to deal with the details sounds relaxing to you, an escorted tour is probably a good idea. If you yearn to have more freedom or to delve into a particular area of interest, check into an independent or special-interest tour.

When considering a tour, be sure to find out (1) exactly what expenses are included—particularly tips, taxes, side trips, meals, and entertainment; (2) the ratings of all hotels on the itinerary and the facilities they offer; (3) the cancellation policies for both you and the tour operator; (4) the number of travelers in your group; and (5) if you are traveling alone, the additional cost of single, instead of double, accommodations. Many tour operators request that packages be booked through a travel agent; there is generally no additional charge for doing so.

General-Interest Tours

Bixler Tours (Box 37, Hiram, OH 44234, tel. 216/569–3222 or 800/325–5087) offers four-night tours to New York City during the spring and fall, including Broadway shows and accommodations at the Waldorf-Astoria.

Talmage Tours (1223 Walnut St., Philadelphia, PA 19107, tel. 215/923–7100) has a variety of one- and two-day tours scheduled around popular Broadway shows.

Special-Interest Tours

Multi-Ethnic, Historic

The Lower East Side Tenement Museum (97 Orchard St., New York, NY 10002, tel. 212/431–0233) offers Sunday tours from April to November through old Jewish and Italian communities. Other tours trace the experiences of Jewish, Irish, Italian, Chinese and German immigrants.

Doorway to Design (1441 Broadway, Suite 338, New York, NY 10018, tel. 212/221–1111 or 718/339–1542) can arrange visits to unique private homes and loft spaces and private creative design firms, as well as neighborhood shopping and walking tours.

Music

Dailey-Thorp (315 W. 57th St., New York, NY 10019, tel. 212/307–1555) offers excellent programs, including the best of opera, ballet, and other performing arts, along with a walking tour of the city.

Theater **Broadway Theatours, Inc.** (71 Broadway, New York, NY 10006, tel. 212/425–6410 or 800/843–7469) and **Sutherland Travel Service, Inc.** (370 Lexington Ave., New York, NY 10017, tel. 212/532–7732 or 800/221–2442) offer hotel/theater packages.

Seasonal **Gadabout Tours** (700 E. Tahquitz Way, Palm Springs, CA 92262, tel. 619/325–5556 or 800/952–5068) and **Mayflower Tours** (1225 Warren Ave., Downers Grove, IL 60515, tel. 708/960–3430 or 800/323–7604) offer special Thanksgiving tours.

Maupintour (Box 807, Lawrence, KS 66044, tel. 913/843–1211 or 800/255–4266) has both Thanksgiving and Christmas tours.

Package Deals for Independent Travelers

Americantours International East (350 5th Ave., Suite 718, New York, NY 10018, tel. 212/695–2841) offers two- and five-night packages, including roundtrip airport transfers from JFK, dinner at Windows on the World, and a half-day sightseeing tour of lower Manhattan. The five-night package also includes tickets to a Broadway show and admission to the Empire State Building.

GoGo Tours (69 Spring St., Ramsey, NJ 07446, tel. 201/934–3500 or 800/821–3731) gives you three days in New York City with choice of hotel and sightseeing package.

Allied Tours (165 W. 46th St., New York, NY 10036, tel. 212/869–5100) offers a large selection of preferred hotel rates in all categories of properties.

SuperCities (1212 6th Ave., 9th floor, New York, NY 10036, tel. 212/921–5800 or 800/633–3000) offers a variety of packages with a minimum two-night stay. Some include dinner; others include both dinner and a show.

Amtrak (tel. 800/USA–RAIL) offers rail/hotel packages as well as an independent New York theater package.

Several major airlines also provide air/accommodations packages. Contact **American Fly AAway Vacations** (tel. 800/443–7300); **Continental Grand Destinations** (tel. 713/821–2100 or 800/634–5555); **Delta Airlines** (tel. 800/872–7786); **United Vacations** (tel. 312/952–4000 or 800/328–6877).

Tips for British Travelers

Government Tourist Office Contact the **State of New York Division of Tourism** (2 Cinnamon Row, Plantation Wharf, York Place, London SW11 3TW, tel. 071/978–5275) for brochures and tourist information.

Passports and Visas You will need a valid, 10-year passport (cost £15) to enter the United States. You do not need a visa if you are staying for less than 90 days and have a return ticket on a major airline. There are some exceptions to this, so check with your travel agent or with the **United States Embassy** (Visa and Immigration Department, 5 Upper Grosvenor St., London W1A 2JB, tel. 071/499–3443). No vaccinations are needed for entry into the United States.

Customs Entering the United States, you may bring 200 cigarettes, 50 cigars, or 2 kilograms tobacco; 1 liter of alcohol; duty-free gifts up to a value of $100. Be careful not to take in meat or meat products, seeds, plants, fruits, etc. Absolutely avoid illegal drugs.

Returning to the United Kingdom, you may take home, if you are 17 or older: (1) 200 cigarettes, 100 cigarillos, 50 cigars, or

250 grams of tobacco; (2) 2 liters of table wine and (a) 1 liter of alcohol over 22% by volume (most spirits), (b) 2 liters of alcohol under 22% by volume (fortified or sparkling wine), or (c) 2 more liters of table wine; (3) 60 milliliters of perfume and 250 milliliters of toilet water; and (4) other goods up to a value of £32, but no more than 50 liters of beer or 25 lighters.

Insurance   We recommend that to cover health and motoring mishaps, you insure yourself with **Europ Assistance** (252 High St., Croydon, Surrey CR0 1NF, tel. 081/680–1234). It is also wise to take out insurance to cover lost luggage (if your current homeowners' policies don't cover such loss). Trip-cancellation insurance is also a good idea. **The Association of British Insurers** (Aldermary House, 10–15 Queen St., London EC4N 1TT, tel. 071/248–4477) will give you comprehensive advice on all aspects of holiday insurance.

Tour Operators   The on-again, off-again price battle over transatlantic fares has meant that most tour operators now offer excellent budget packages to the United States. Among those you might consider as you plan your trip are:

Albany Travel (Manchester) Ltd. (Central Buildings, 211 Deansgate, Manchester M2 5QR, tel. 061/833–0202).
American Airplan (Airplan House, Churchfield Rd., Waltonon-Thames, Surrey KT12 2TJ, tel. 0932/231422 for information, 0932/246347 for brochures).
American Travel Centre (77 Victoria St., Windsor, Berkshire SL4 1EH, tel. 0753/831300).
Cosmosair plc (Ground Floor, Dale House, Tiviot Dale, Stockport, Cheshire SK1 1TB, tel. 061/480–5799).
Jetsave (Sussex House, London Rd., East Grinstead, Sussex RH19 1LD, tel. 0342/312033).
Speedbird Holidays (Pacific House, Hazelwick Ave., Crawley, W. Sussex RH10 1NP, tel. 0293/611611).
Thomas Cook Ltd. (Box 36, Thorpe Wood, Peterborough PE3 6SB, tel. 0733/332333).

Airfares   Airlines flying to New York include **British Airways, TWA, Continental,** and **Virgin Atlantic.** At press time, a low-season return APEX fare was anywhere from £419 and up. If you are flexible with your travel dates, Virgin Atlantic offers a Late Saver fare from £349, but it can only be booked three days before departure.

Thomas Cook Ltd. can often book you on cut-price flights. Call the Cook branch nearest you and ask about their Flightsavers program. Be sure to call at least 21 days in advance of when you want to travel.

Also check out the small ads in magazines such as *Time Out* and in the Sunday papers, where flights are offered for as low as £199 return.

When to Go

At one time, it seemed New York's cultural life was limited to the months between October and May, when new Broadway shows opened, museums mounted major exhibitions, and formal seasons for opera, ballet, and concerts held sway. Today, however, there are Broadway openings even in mid-July, and a number of touring orchestras and opera and ballet companies visit the city in summer. In late spring and summer, the streets and parks are filled with ethnic parades, impromptu sidewalk concerts, and performances under the stars. With the exception of regular closing days and a few holidays (such as Christmas, New Year's Day, and Thanksgiving), the city's museums are open year-round. The parks are always free, so in winter you can cross-country ski, in summer you can swim or sunbathe, and in summer and fall you can watch migrating birds make their semiannual New York visits.

Climate Although there's an occasional bone-chilling winter day, with winds blasting in off the Hudson, snow is hardly ever a problem in the city (the skyscrapers trap enough heat to melt most snowfalls). Summer is the only unpleasant time of year here, especially the humid, hot days of August, when many Manhattanites vacate the island for summer homes. Most hotels are air-conditioned, but if you're traveling in the summer and choosing budget accommodations, it's a good idea to ask whether your room has an air conditioner. Air-conditioned stores, restaurants, and museums provide respite from the heat; so do the many green expanses of parks. Subways and buses, however, do not always have functioning air-conditioning, and subway stations can be as hot as saunas (but considerably dirtier).

Because the metropolitan area's water needs are so enormous, occasional summer droughts may entail strict conservation, with the result that air-conditioning is cut back, grass goes unwatered, fountains stand dry, and restaurants serve water only upon request.

The following table shows each month's average temperatures for New York City—the daily highs and lows, expressed in both Fahrenheit and centigrade:

Jan.	41F	5C	May	70F	21C	Sept.	76F	24C
	29	- 2		54	12		61	16
Feb.	43F	6C	June	81F	27C	Oct.	67F	19C
	29	- 2		63	17		52	11
Mar.	47F	8C	July	85F	29C	Nov.	56F	13C
	34	1		70	21		43	6
Apr.	61F	16C	Aug.	83F	28C	Dec.	43F	6C
	45	7		68	20		31	- 1

The city's weather is highly variable, however, so, shortly before your trip, check New York weather reports in your local newspaper. Current weather information for more than 750 cities around the world may be obtained by calling WeatherTrak information service at 900/370–8728 (cost: 95¢ per minute). A taped message will tell you to dial the three-digit access code for the destination in which you're interested. The code is either the area code (in the United States) or the first three letters of the foreign city. For a list of all access codes, send a stamped, self-addressed envelope to Cities (9B Terrace Way, Greensboro, NC 27403). For more information, call 800/247–3282.

Festivals and Seasonal Events

When it comes to special events, New York is indeed, as one bank's slogan puts it, "the city that never sleeps." Here is a list of some of the more important or unusual events projected to take place throughout the year; for more up-to-date information, pick up a copy of *New York* magazine, the *Village Voice*, or the Friday edition of The *New York Times* upon your arrival in the city; contact the New York Convention and Visitors Bureau (*see* Visitor Information, above); or contact the event sponsor noted at the end of some listings.

Dec. 31–Jan. 1: New Year's Eve is marked by the famous countdown in Times Square; expect throngs of somewhat unruly revelers waiting for the ball to drop. Fireworks and a midnight run are held in Central Park.

Jan.: Ice Capades makes its regular winter appearance at Madison Square Garden. Tel. 212/465–6741.

Jan. 9–19: The National Boat Show, at the Jacob K. Javits Convention Center, gives the public a look at all sorts of seaworthy vessels and related equipment. Tel. 212/684–6622.

Jan.: The Winter Antiques Show, an exhibition of 17th- and 18th-century furniture, paintings, and statues, is held at the Seventh Regiment Armory, Park Avenue at 67th Street. Tel. 212/439–0300.

Feb.: The Chinese New Year crackles with fireworks and energy as the Chinatown community prepares for and celebrates the lunar New Year.

Feb.: The Westminster Kennel Club Dog Show showcases top-of-the-line pooches at Madison Square Garden. Tel. 212/465–6741.

Feb.: The Millrose Games, an international track-and-field competition, is held at Madison Square Garden. Tel. 212/465–6741.

Early Mar.: The International Cat Show, at Madison Square Garden, displays favorite breeds along with varieties you've never heard of. Tel. 212/465–6741.

Mar.: Big East Basketball Championships at Madison Square Garden provide some exciting basketball action, with the Big East colleges usually in the national rankings. Tel. 212/465–6741.

Mar. 5–9: Artexpo NY is held at the Jacob K. Javits Convention Center. Tel. 800/225–4569.

Mar. 17: St. Patrick's Day Parade, a classic parade down Fifth Avenue, reflects the vitality of the Irish and Irish-American sector of the city's population.

Mar. 23: Greek Independence Day Parade breaks out along Fifth Avenue from 62nd to 79th streets.

Mid-Mar.–Apr.: Ringling Bros. Barnum & Bailey Circus brings its three-ring act to Madison Square Garden. Tel. 212/465–6741.

Apr.–June: The New York City Ballet (tel. 212/870–5570) and **American Ballet Theatre** (tel. 212/362–6000) launch the spring season with performances at Lincoln Center.

Apr.–Oct.: The major-league baseball season sees the Yankees play their home games at Yankee Stadium in the Bronx, while the Mets hold court at Shea Stadium, Queens.

Apr. 19: Easter Parade, with all its finery, takes place along Fifth Avenue from 49th to 59th streets. Tel. 212/397–8222.

Late Apr.: The Cherry Blossom Festival is in full bloom at the Brooklyn Botanic Garden. Tel. 718/622–4433.

May: Brooklyn Heights Promenade Art Show lines the Promenade with artists and their works, with the panorama of Manhattan across the river as a spectacular backdrop.

May: Ukrainian Festival, held on 7th Street between Second and Third avenues, is a refreshingly homespun event with what is probably the best food of any of the street fairs. Tel. 212/228–6840.

May: Martin Luther King, Jr., Parade marches down Fifth Avenue in memory of the civil rights leader.

May 16–17: The Ninth Avenue International Food Festival features food and merchandise from 32 countries. Tel. 212/581–7217.

May 23–25, 30–31: Washington Square Art Show is celebrated in Greenwich Village. Tel. 212/982–6255.

June–July: Metropolitan Opera performs free on weekday evenings in parks throughout the five boroughs.

June 14: Welcome Back to Brooklyn Day is a gala celebration from noon to 5 along Eastern Parkway from Grand Army Plaza to Washington Avenue.

June 4–14: Feast of St. Anthony, a 10-day festival, spills over from SoHo to Little Italy. Tel. 212/777–2755.

Early June: Museum Mile Festival takes over Fifth Avenue from 82nd to 105th streets, with an evening of free or reduced admission to all 10 museums there.

June 14: Puerto Rican Day Parade proceeds down Fifth Avenue with floats, marching bands, and merrymakers. Tel. 212/665–1600.

Late June: Lesbian and Gay Pride Day Parade runs down Fifth Avenue to Washington Square.

Late June: JVC Jazz Festival features vintage stars and newcomers at venues all around town.

July 4: Independence Day is celebrated with fireworks and street fairs at various locations.

Early–mid-July: American Crafts Festival is held on weekends at Lincoln Center. Tel. 212/877–2011.

July–Aug.: Shakespeare in the Park presents two free productions at the Delacorte Theater in Central Park. Tel. 212/598–7100.

July–Aug.: Summergarden Concerts are performed free by Juilliard School students at the Museum of Modern Art. Tel. 212/708–9480.

July–Aug.: The New York Philharmonic chips in with free concerts in various city parks. Tel. 212/360–1333.

Mid-July–Aug.: Mostly Mozart Festival presents a distinguished series of classical concerts at Avery Fisher Hall in Lincoln Center. Tel. 212/874–2424.

Late July: The New York Track and Field Games bring an international roster of competitors to Wein Stadium, Columbia University. Tel. 212/860–4455.

July–Nov.: New York City Opera performs at the New York State Theater in Lincoln Center. Tel. 212/870–5570.

Mid–Aug.: Harlem Week presents a series of workshops, street fairs, gospel festivals, and cultural events. Tel. 212/427–7200.

Late Aug.: Festival of the Americas brings Latin festivities to Sixth Avenue, otherwise known as Avenue of the Americas.

Late Aug.–Sept.: Lincoln Center Out-of-Doors hosts a variety of cultural events on the complex's plazas.

Late Aug.–early Sept.: U.S. Open Tennis Championships bring world-class excitement to the National Tennis Center in Flushing Meadows, Queens. Tel. 718/271–5100.

Sept. 3–7: Caribbean Festival brings a touch of carnival to Eastern Parkway in Brooklyn. Tel. 718/773–4052.

Sept. 5–7, 12–13: Washington Square Art Fair makes its second yearly appearance. Tel. 212/982–6255.

Mid-Sept.: New York Is Book Country transforms Fifth Avenue into a reader's paradise.

Mid-Sept.: Feast of San Gennaro, a popular, somewhat overcrowded 10-day extravaganza in Little Italy, features games, vendors, and fabulous food. Tel. 212/226–9546.

Sept. 25–Oct. 11: New York Film Festival features an eclectic mix of new and notable international films at Lincoln Center's Alice Tully Hall. Tel. 212/877–1800, extension 489.

Sept.–Apr.: Metropolitan Opera (tel. 212/362–6000) and **New York Philharmonic** (tel. 212/874–2424) hold their seasons at Lincoln Center (the Philharmonic's lasts till May).

Early Oct.: Brooklyn Heights Promenade Art Show returns to the Promenade for an autumn exhibition.

Early Oct.–mid-Dec.: Next Wave Festival showcases contemporary performance works at the Brooklyn Academy of Music. Tel. 718/636–4100.

Oct. 4: Pulaski Day Parade commemorates Polish hero Casimir Pulaski in a festive event up Fifth Avenue.

Oct. 12: Columbus Day Parade gives New York's Italian-Americans a chance to strut their stuff.

Oct. 16–21: The International Antique Dealers Show, a vetted exhibition of antique furniture, porcelain, and other decorative objets d'art, is held at the Seventh Regiment Armory, Park Avenue at 67th Street. Tel. 212/439–0300.

Oct.–Apr.: New York Rangers Hockey cuts the ice at Madison Square Garden. Tel. 212/465–6741.

Oct. 31: Halloween Parade, New York's most outrageous parade, is held in Greenwich Village.

Nov.–Apr.: New York Knicks Basketball should make for an interesting season at Madison Square Garden. Tel. 212/465–6741.

Early Nov.: New York City Marathon starts at the Verazzano Bridge in Staten Island and proceeds through all five boroughs. Tel. 212/860–4455.

Nov. 26: Macy's Thanksgiving Day Parade sends giant balloons and a sleigh-borne Santa from Central Park West at 77th Street to Broadway and 34th Street.

Mid-Nov.–Jan.: Christmas Spectacular, a musical performance featuring the high-kicking Rockettes, hits the Radio City Music Hall stage. Tel. 212/247–4777.

Late Nov.–early Jan.: Lord & Taylor and **Saks Fifth Avenue** present animated window displays.

Dec.–early Jan.: The New York City Ballet's *Nutcracker* performances are a seasonal fixture at Lincoln Center. Tel. 212/870–5570.

What to Pack

New York City has many restaurants that require men to wear jackets and ties. For sightseeing and casual dining, jeans and sneakers are acceptable just about anywhere in the city. Sneakers seem to be the universal walking shoe; you'll even see businesspeople in button-down office attire lacing them on for the sprint from one appointment to another.

An extra pair of glasses, contact lenses, or prescription sunglasses is always a good idea; it is important to pack any prescription medicines you use regularly, as well as any allergy medication you may need.

Pack light, because porters and luggage trolleys can be hard to find at New York airports.

Carry-on Luggage Passengers on U.S. airlines are limited to two carry-on bags. For a bag you wish to store under the seat, the maximum dimensions are 9″ × 14″ × 22″. For bags that can be hung in a closet or on a luggage rack, the maximum dimensions are 4″ × 23″ × 45″. For bags you wish to store in an overhead bin, the maximum dimensions are 10″ × 14″ × 36″. An airline can adapt the rules to circumstances, so on a crowded flight you may be allowed only one carry-on bag. In addition to carryons, you may bring aboard a handbag (pocketbook or purse); an overcoat or wrap; an umbrella; a camera; a reasonable amount of reading material; an infant bag; and crutches, a cane, braces, or other prosthetic device. Infant/child safety seats can also be brought aboard if parents have purchased a ticket for the child, or if there is space in the cabin.

Foreign airlines generally allow only one piece of carry-on luggage in tourist class, in addition to handbags and bags filled with duty-free goods. Passengers in first and business class are allowed to carry on one garment bag as well. Call your airline to find out its current policy.

Checked Luggage Luggage allowances vary slightly from airline to airline. Many carriers allow three checked pieces, but some allow only two, so check before you go. In all cases, check-in luggage cannot weigh more than 70 pounds per piece or be larger than 62 inches (length + width + height).

What It Will Cost

There's no doubt that New York is an expensive city to visit. Hotel rooms with views of Central Park can easily run as high as $250 a night; dinner for two at a *moderate* restaurant, plus orchestra seats at a Broadway show, can set you back $200 (*see* Chapters 8, 9, and 10). While these estimates may daunt the cost-conscious traveler, there's no cause for despair. New Yorkers themselves know how to find bargains; they comb discount clothing outlets, grab food at corner delis, walk just about everywhere, and attend free concerts and plays in the parks. You, too, can moderate the cost of your visit if you do as they do (*see* Manhattan for Free in Chapter 3 and Discount Tickets in Chapter 10).

Hotel taxes add up to 21¼%. The customary tipping rate is 15%–20% for taxi drivers and waiters (*see* Chapter 8 for further tipping advice), and bellhops are usually given $2 in luxury hotels, $1 elsewhere. Hotel maids should be tipped around $1 per day of your stay.

Cash Machines

Virtually all U.S. banks now belong to a network of Automatic Teller Machines (ATMs) that dispense cash 24 hours a day. There are eight major networks in the United States, the largest of which are Cirrus, owned by MasterCard, and Plus, affiliated with Visa. Some banks belong to more than one network. Each network has a toll-free number you can call to locate its machines in a given city: the Cirrus number is 800/424–7787; the Plus number is 800/843–7587. Note that "cash cards" are not issued automatically—they must be requested at your local bank.

Cards issued by Visa, American Express, and MasterCard can also be used in the ATMs, but the transaction fees are usually higher than those on bank cards (and there is a daily interest charge on the "loan"). All three companies issue directories of national and international outlets that accept their cards. You can pick up a Visa or MasterCard directory at your local bank; for an American Express directory, call 800/CASH–NOW (this number can also be used for general inquiries). Contact your bank for information on fees and the amount of cash you can withdraw on any given day. Although each bank levies a charge when you withdraw money with a charge or credit card, using your American Express, Visa, or MasterCard at an ATM can be cheaper than exchanging money in a bank because of variations in exchange rates.

Express Cash allows American Express cardholders to withdraw up to $1,000 in a seven-day period (21 days overseas) from their personal checking accounts at ATMs worldwide. Gold card members can receive up to $2,500 in a seven-day period (21 days overseas). Every transaction carries a 2% fee with a minimum charge of $2 and a maximum of $6. Call 800/CASH–NOW to receive an application to link your accounts or locate Express Cash machines in New York City.

Traveling with Film

If your camera is new, shoot and develop a few rolls of film before leaving home. Pack some lens tissue and an extra battery for your built-in light meter. Invest about $10 in a skylight filter and screw it onto the front of your lens; it will protect the lens and reduce haze.

Film doesn't like hot weather. If you're driving in summer, don't store film in the glove compartment or on the shelf under the rear window. Put it behind the front seat on the floor, on the side opposite the exhaust pipe.

On a plane trip, never pack unprocessed film in check-in luggage; if your bags are X-rayed, you can say good-bye to your pictures. Always carry undeveloped film with you through security and ask to have it inspected by hand. (It helps to isolate your film in a plastic bag, ready for quick inspection.) Inspectors at American airports are required by law to honor requests for hand inspection; abroad, you'll have to depend on the kindness of strangers.

The machines used in U.S. airports are safe for scanning film anywhere from five to 500 times, depending on the speed of the film. After five scans, however, you may be asking for trouble. If your film gets fogged and you want an explanation, send it to the National Association of Photographic Manufacturers (550 Mamaroneck Ave., Harrison, NY 10528), which will try to determine what went wrong, at no charge.

Traveling with Children

There are many free and exciting activities for children in the Big Apple (*see* What to See and Do with Children in Manhattan in Chapter 3, What to See and Do with Children in the Other Boroughs in Chapter 4, Toys in Chapter 7, and The Arts for Kids in Chapter 10). Several local publications, including the *Village Voice*, *New York* magazine, and the Friday edition of the *New York Times*, offer up-to-date calendars of happenings for children, as does *New York Family*, a magazine published nine times a year by New York Family Publications (420 E. 79th St., Suite 9E, New York, NY 10021, tel. 212/744–0309).

Another good source of information is the monthly *Big Apple Parents' Paper* published by Buffalo Bunyip, Inc. (928 Broadway, Suite 709, New York, NY 10010, tel. 212/533–2277).

Publications *Family Travel Times,* a newsletter published 10 times a year, also offers ideas for having fun with children, though not all data is specific to the New York City area. (To order the newsletter, contact Travel with Your Children, 80 8th Ave., New York, NY 10011, tel. 212/206–0688). A $35 yearly subscription includes access to back issues and twice-weekly opportunities to call in for specific information. Send $1 for a sample issue.

Great Vacations with Your Kids, by Dorothy Jordon and Marjorie Cohen, offers complete advice on planning a trip with children (from toddlers to teens), with a special section on New York City vacations ($12.95 from E.P. Dutton. To order, call 800/331–4624).

Kids and Teens in Flight is a U.S. Department of Transportation brochure about children flying alone. To order a free copy, call 202/366–2220.

Home Exchange Exchanging homes is a low-cost way to enjoy a vacation in another part of the country. **Vacation Exchange Club, Inc.** (Box 820, Haleiwa, HI 96712, tel. 800/638–3841) specializes in domestic home exchanges. The club publishes three directories a year, in February, April, and August, and updated late listings throughout the year. Annual membership, which includes your listing in one book, a newsletter, and copies of all publications (mailed first class), costs $50. **Loan-a-Home** (2 Park Ln., Apt. 6E, Mount Vernon, NY 10552, tel. 914/664–7640) is popular with the academic community on sabbatical and businesspeople on temporary assignment. There's no annual membership fee or charge for listing your home, however the directory and supplement cost $35.

Getting There On domestic flights, children under two not occupying a seat travel free. Various discounts apply to children two to 12 years of age. If you want to be sure your infant is secure and traveling in his or her own safety seat, you must buy baby a separate ticket and bring your own infant car seat. (Check with the airline in advance; certain seats aren't allowed.) Some airlines allow babies to travel in their own car seats at no charge if there's a spare seat available, otherwise safety seats will be stored and the child will have to be held by a parent. If you opt to hold your baby on your lap, do so with the infant outside the seatbelt so he or she won't be crushed in case of a sudden stop. For the booklet *Child/Infant Safety Seats Acceptable for Use in Aircraft,* write to the **Federal Aviation Administration,** APA–200, 800 Independence Ave. SW, Washington, DC 20591, tel. 202/267–3479.

Also inquire about special children's meals or snacks. See the February 1990 and 1992 issues of *Family Travel Times* for "TWYCH's Airline Guide," which contains a rundown of the children's services offered by 46 airlines.

Baby-sitting You can usually make child-care arrangements through your
Services hotel's concierge or housekeeper. New York City agencies in-

clude **Babysitters' Guild** (60 E. 42nd St., Suite 912, New York, NY 10165, tel. 212/682–0227), with a multilingual staff that can take your children on sightseeing tours; **Gilbert Child Care Agency** (25 W. 39th St., Suite 700, New York, NY 10018, tel. 212/757–7900); and the **Avalon Registry** (250 W. 57th St., Suite 723, New York, NY 10107, tel. 212/245–0250).

Around Town Children under age 6 travel free on subways and buses; children age 6 and older must pay full fare. Clean rest rooms are often difficult to find; your best bet is to use the washrooms at museums, department stores, hotels, and restaurants while you are there.

If you find you need a stroller once you get here, ask your hotel concierge to find one for you, or contact **AAA-U-Rent** (861 Eagle Ave., Bronx, NY 10456, tel. 212/923–0300 or 212/665–6633).

Hints for Disabled Travelers

Many buildings in New York City are now wheelchair-accessible. The subway is still hard to navigate, however; people in wheelchairs do better on public buses, most of which "kneel" to facilitate getting on and off. For brochures and further information, contact the **Mayor's Office for People with Disabilities** (52 Chambers St., Office 206, New York, NY 10007, tel. 212/566–0972).

The Information Center for Individuals with Disabilities (Fort Point Pl., 1st floor, 27–43 Wormwood St., Boston, MA 02210, tel. 617/727–5540; VTDD 617/727–5236) offers useful problem-solving assistance, including lists of travel agents who specialize in tours for the disabled.

Moss Rehabilitation Hospital Travel Information Service (1200 W. Tabor Rd., Philadelphia, PA 19141, tel. 215/456–9600; TDD 215/456–9602) provides information on tourist sights, transportation, and accommodations in destinations around the world for a small fee.

Travel Industry and Disabled Exchange (TIDE, 5435 Donna Ave., Tarzana, CA 91356, tel. 818/368–5648), for a $15 per person annual membership fee, provides a quarterly newsletter and information on travel agencies and tours.

Mobility International USA (Box 3551, Eugene, OR 97403, tel. 503/343–1284) is an internationally affiliated organization with 500 members. For a $20 annual fee, it coordinates exchange programs for disabled people around the world and offers information on accommodations and organized study programs.

The Society for the Advancement of Travel for the Handicapped (26 Court St., Penthouse Suite, Brooklyn, NY 11242, tel. 718/858–5483) offers access information. Annual membership costs $45; $25 for senior travelers and students. Send $2 and a stamped, self-addressed envelope for a list of tour operators who arrange travel for the disabled.

Greyhound-Trailways (tel. 800/752–4841; TDD 800/345–3109) will carry a disabled person and companion for the price of a single fare. **Amtrak** (tel. 800/USA–RAIL; TDD 800/523–6590; in PA, TDD 800/562–6960) requests 48 hours' notice to provide redcap service, special seats, or wheelchair assistance at stations that are equipped to provide these services. All handicapped passengers are entitled to a 25% discount on regular coach fares. A special children's handicapped fare is also available, offering qualifying kids ages 2–11 a 25% discount on already discounted children's fares. However, it is wise to check the price of excursion tickets first. These often work out to be much cheaper than reductions for the disabled on regular tickets. For a free copy of *Access Amtrak*, a guide to its services for elderly and handicapped travelers, write to Amtrak Customer Relations, 60 Massachusetts Ave. NE, Washington, DC 20002).

Publications The New York Division of Tourism (1 Commerce Plaza, Albany, NY 12245, tel. 518/474–4116 or 800/225–5697) offers the *I Love New York Travel and Adventure Guide,* which includes ratings of various facilities' accessibility. The New York State Parks Department (State Parks, Albany, NY 12238, tel. 518/474–0456) provides information on handicapped facilities in the *Guide to New York State Parks, Historic Sites and Programs.*

The Itinerary (Box 2012, Bayonne, NJ 07002, tel. 201/858–3400) is a bimonthly travel magazine for the disabled. Call for a subscription ($10 for one year, $20 for two); it's not available in stores.

Travel for the Disabled, by Helen Hecker, is a handbook of travel resources that includes advice on all modes of transportation and lists more than 500 access guides for specific destinations around the world ($9.95). *Wheelchair Vagabond,* by John G. Nelson, contains valuable information for independent travelers planning extended trips in a car, van, or camper ($9.95 paperback, $14.95 hardcover). *The Directory of Travel Agencies for the Disabled,* by Helen Hecker, can lead you to agencies both at home and at your destination that will provide information on resources for travelers with special needs ($19.95). These publications are available through your local bookstore or directly from the publisher (Twin Peaks Press, Box 129, Vancouver, WA 98666, tel. 800/637–2256). Add $2 shipping for one book; $1 each additional book.

Access to the World: A Travel Guide for the Handicapped, by Louise Weiss, provides general information on transportation, hotels, travel agents, tour operators, and travel organizations. It is available at your local bookstore or from Henry Holt & Co. for $12.95 plus $2.50 shipping (tel. 800/247–3912; the order number is 0805 001417).

Hints for Older Travelers

The **American Association of Retired Persons** (AARP, 1909 K St. NW, Washington, DC 20049, tel. 202/662–4850) has two programs for independent travelers: (1) the Purchase Privilege Program, which offers discounts on hotels, airfare, car rentals, and sightseeing; and (2) the AARP Motoring Plan, provided by Amoco, which furnishes emergency aid (road service) and trip-routing information for an annual fee of $33.95 per person or married couple. The AARP also arranges group tours and cruises at reduced rates through **AARP Travel Experience from American Express** (Box 5850, Norcross, GA 30091, tel. 800/927–0111). AARP members must be at least 50 years old. Annual dues are $5 per person or per couple.

If you're planning to use an AARP or other senior-citizen identification card to obtain a reduced hotel rate, mention it at the time you make your reservation rather than when you check out. At participating restaurants, show your card to the maître d' before you're seated; discounts may be limited to certain menus, days, or hours. For a free list of hotels and restaurants that offer discounts, call or write the AARP and ask for the "Purchase Privilege" brochure, or call the AARP Travel Service. When renting a car, remember that economy cars, priced at promotional rates, may cost less than the cars that are available with your ID card.

National Council of Senior Citizens (925 15th St. NW, Washington, DC 20005, tel. 202/347–8800) is a nonprofit advocacy group with some 5,000 local clubs across the country. Annual membership is $12 per person or per couple. Members receive a monthly newspaper with travel information and an ID for reduced rates on hotels and car rentals.

Mature Outlook (6001 N. Clark St., Chicago, IL 60660, tel. 800/336–6330), a subsidiary of Sears, Roebuck & Co., is a travel club for people over 50 years of age, offering discounts at Holiday Inns and a bimonthly newsletter. Annual membership is $9.95 per person or couple. Instant membership is available at participating Holiday Inns.

Elderhostel (75 Federal St., 3rd floor, Boston, MA 02110, tel. 617/426–7788) is an innovative educational program for people 60 or over (only one member of a traveling couple has to qualify). Participants live in dormitories on some 1,200 campuses around the world. Mornings are devoted to lectures and seminars; afternoons to sightseeing and field trips. The fee for a trip includes room, board, tuition (in the United States and Canada), and round-trip transportation (overseas). Special scholarships are available for those who qualify financially in the United States and Canada.

Saga International Holidays (120 Boylston St., Boston, MA 02116, tel. 800/343–0273) specializes in group travel for people over 60. A selection of variously priced tours allows you to choose the package that meets your needs.

September Days Club (tel. 800/241–5050) is run by the moderately priced Days Inns of America. The $12 annual membership fee for individuals or couples over 50 entitles them to reduced car rental rates and to reductions of 15%–50% at 95% of the chain's more than 350 motels.

The **Golden Age Passport** is a free lifetime pass to all parks, monuments, and recreation areas run by the federal government. Permanent U.S. residents 62 and over may pick them up in person at any of the national parks that charge admission. The passport covers the entrance fee for the holder and anyone accompanying the holder in the same private (noncommercial) vehicle. It also provides a 50% discount on camping, boat launching, and parking (lodging is not included). Proof of age is necessary.

Greyhound-Trailways (tel. 800/752–4841) offers special fares for senior citizens, subject to date and destination restrictions. **Amtrak** (tel. 800/USA–RAIL) requests 48 hours' notice to provide redcap service, special seats, or wheelchair assistance at stations that are equipped to provide these services. Elderly passengers are entitled to a 25% discount on regular coach fares. However, it is wise to check the price of excursion tickets first. These often work out to be much cheaper than senior citizen discounts on regular tickets. For a free copy of *Access Amtrak*, a guide to its services for elderly and handicapped travelers, write to Amtrak (Customer Relations, 60 Massachusetts Ave. NE, Washington, DC 20002).

Publications ***The International Health Guide for Senior Citizen Travelers,*** by Dr. W. Robert Lange, MD, and ***The Senior Citizens Guide to Budget Travel in the United States and Canada,*** by Paige Palmer, are available for $4.95 and $3.94, respectively, plus $1 for shipping, from Pilot Books (103 Cooper St., Babylon, NY 11702, tel. 516/422–2225).

The Discount Guide for Travelers Over 55, by Caroline and Walter Weintz, lists helpful addresses, package tours, reduced-rate car rentals, etc., in the United States and abroad. To order, send $7.95 plus $1.50 shipping and handling to NAL/Cash Sales (Bergenfield Order Dept., 120 Woodbine St., Bergenfield, NJ 07621, tel. 800/526–0275).

Further Reading

Many a famous writer has set down his or her impressions of this fascinating city. Some of the best full-length accounts are *Christopher Morley's New York*, a mid-1920s essay recently republished; *Cecil Beaton's New York*, a 1938 volume with photographs; *New York Proclaimed* by V. S. Pritchett, also lavishly illustrated; *Brendan Behan's New York*, a highly personal memoir written in 1964; *Walker in the City* by Alfred Kazin; and *Apple of My Eye*, a 1978 account of writing a New York guidebook, by Helene Hanff. Perhaps the best of all is E. B. White's 1949 essay *Here Is New York*, recently reissued.

The early history of New York is wittily told in the classic *Knickerbocker's History of New York*, by Washington Irving. For a fine historical introduction to the city, find the heavily illustrated *Columbia Historical Portrait of New York*, by John Kouwenhoven. *You Must Remember This*, by Jeff Kisseloff, is an oral history of ordinary New Yorkers early in this century.

Imperial City by Geoffrey Moorhouse is an insightful, no-holds-barred recent portrait. *Fiorello H. La Guardia and the Making of Modern New York* by Thomas Kessner is a recent biography of the charismatic Depression-era mayor. *The Power Broker* by Robert Caro is a fascinating biography of Robert Moses, one of the city's most influential parks commissioners. Robert Daley's *Prince of the City* is a true-life drama of New York police corruption. Highly critical accounts of the city's recent politics can be found in *The Streets Were Paved with Gold* by Ken Auletta, *The Rise and Fall of New York City* by Roger Starr, and *City for Sale* by Jack Newfield and Wayne Barrett.

Theater lovers may want to read *Act One*, the autobiography of playwright Moss Hart. *The Kingdom and the Power* by Gay Talese offers a behind-the-scenes look at The *New York Times;* life at one of the city's most venerable magazines is recounted in *Here at the New Yorker* by Brendan Gill.

AIA Guide to New York City, by Elliot Willensky and Norval White, is the definitive guide to the city's many building styles; Paul Goldberger's *The City Observed* describes Manhattan building by building. *City: Rediscovering the Center* by William H. Whyte illuminates urban street life and the use of public space, principally in New York. John Kieran's *A Natural History of New York* explores the wildlife of the city's parks.

Perhaps because so many writers have lived in New York City, there is a wealth of fiction set here. Jack Finney's *Time and Again* is a delightful time-travel story illustrated with 19th-century photos; *Winter's Tale* by Mark Helprin uses surreal fantasy to create a portrait of New York's past. Novels set in 19th-century New York include Henry James's *Washington Square*, Edith Wharton's *The Age of Innocence*, and Stephen Crane's *Maggie, A Girl of the Streets*. O. Henry's short stories depict the early years of this century, while Damon Runyon's are set in the raffish underworld of the 1930s and 1940s. F. Scott Fitzgerald (*The Beautiful and Damned*, 1922), John Dos Passos (*Manhattan Transfer*, 1925), John O'Hara (*Butterfield 8*, 1935), and Mary McCarthy (*The Group*, 1938) also wrote about this city. J. D. Salinger's *Catcher in the Rye* (1951) partly takes place here, as does Thomas Pynchon's *V* (1965). Truman Capote's 1958 novella *Breakfast at Tiffany's* is a special favorite of many New Yorkers.

More current New York novels include *Bonfire of the Vanities* by Tom Wolfe, *The Mambo Kings Play Songs of Love* by Oscar Hijuelos, and *People Like Us* by Dominick Dunne. For portraits of gay life, try Larry Kramer's *Faggots*, David Leavitt's *The Lost Language of Cranes*, Sarah Schulman's *After Delores* and *People in Trouble*, and John Weir's *The Irreversible Decline of Eddy Socket*. The downtown scene is depicted in Tama Janowitz's *Slaves of New York* and Jay McInerney's *Bright Lights, Big City*.

The black experience in Harlem has been chronicled in Ralph Ellison's *Invisible Man*, James Baldwin's *Go Tell It On the Mountain*, and Claude Brown's *Manchild in the Promised Land*. For a portrait of Harlem during the 1920s, there's *When Harlem Was In Vogue* by David Levering Lewis. The history of New York's Jewish population can be traced through such books as *World of Our Fathers* by Irving Howe, *Call It Sleep* by Henry Roth, *The Promise* by Chaim Potok, *Enemies, A Love Story* by Isaac Bashevis Singer, and *Our Crowd* by Stephen Birmingham.

Francine Prose's *Household Saints* is a fictional portrait of life in Little Italy; *The New Chinatown* by Peter Kwong is a recent study of the community across Canal Street. Kate Simon's memoir *Bronx Primitive*, Laura Cunningham's autobiographical *Sleeping Arrangements*, and E. L. Doctorow's novel *World's Fair* are set in the Bronx. Betty Smith's touching prewar novel *A Tree Grows in Brooklyn* is counterbalanced by the searing 1960s portrait of Hubert Selby Jr.'s *Last Exit to Brooklyn*. Bernard Malamud's *The Assistant* is another portrait of Brooklyn neighborhoods.

Mysteries set in New York City range from Dashiell Hammett's urbane 1933 novel *The Thin Man*, to Rex Stout's series of Nero Wolfe mysteries (continued by Robert Goldsborough) to more recent picks: *While My Pretty One Sleeps* (Mary Higgins Clark), *A Ticket to the Boneyard* (Lawrence Block), and *Unorthodox Practices* (Marissa Piesman).

To get children psyched up for a New York trip, give them *Eloise* by Kay Thompson, *Harriet the Spy* by Louise Fitzhugh, or *Stuart Little* by E. B. White.

Arriving and Departing

By Plane

Airports Virtually every major U.S. and foreign airline serves one or more of New York's three airports: **LaGuardia Airport** and **John F. Kennedy International Airport,** both in the borough of Queens, and **Newark International Airport** in New Jersey.

Airlines U.S. carriers serving the New York area include America West (tel. 800/247–5692); American (tel. 800/433–7300); Continental (tel. 800/525–0280); Delta (tel. 800/221–1212); Midway (tel. 800/621–5700); Northwest (tel. 800/225–2525); Pan Am (tel. 800/442–5896); TWA (tel. 800/221–2000); United (tel. 800/241–6522); and USAir (tel. 800/428–4322).

When choosing a flight, be sure to distinguish among (a) *nonstop flights*—no stops or changes of aircraft; (b) *direct flights*—one or more stops but no change of aircraft; and (c) *connecting flights*—at least one change of aircraft and possibly several stops as well.

Smoking Smoking is banned on all scheduled routes within the 48 contiguous states; within the states of Hawaii and Alaska; to and from the U.S. Virgin Islands and Puerto Rico; and on flights of under six hours to and from Hawaii and Alaska. The rule applies to the domestic legs of all foreign routes but does not affect international flights.

On a flight where smoking is permitted, you can request a nonsmoking seat during check-in or when you book your ticket. If the airline tells you there are no seats available in the nonsmoking section on the day of the flight, insist on one: Department of Transportation regulations require U.S. carriers to find seats for all non-smokers, provided they meet check-in time restrictions.

Lost Luggage Luggage loss is usually covered in comprehensive travel insurance packages that include personal accident, trip cancellation, and sometimes default and bankruptcy protection. Several companies offer comprehensive policies:

Access America, Inc., a subsidiary of Blue Cross-Blue Shield (Box 11188, Richmond, VA 23230, tel. 800/334–7525 or 800/284–8300).

Near Services (450 Prairie Ave., Suite 101, Calumet City, IL 60409, tel. 708/868–6700 or 800/654–6700).

Travel Guard International, underwritten by Transamerica Occidental Life Companies (1145 Clark St., Stevens Point, WI 54481, tel. 715/345–0505 or 800/782–5151).

Carefree Travel Insurance (Box 310, 120 Mineola Blvd., Mineola, NY 11501, tel. 516/294–0220 or 800/323–3149).

Luggage Insurance Airlines are responsible for lost or damaged property only up to $1,250 per passenger on domestic flights, or $9.07 per pound ($20 per kilo) for checked baggage and $400 per passenger for unchecked baggage on international flights. If you're carrying valuables, either take them with you on the airplane or purchase additional insurance for lost luggage. Some airlines will issue additional insurance when you check in, but many do not. One that does is American Airlines. Rates for domestic and international flights are $2 for every $100 valuation, with a maximum of $5,000 valuation per passenger.

Insurance for lost, damaged, or stolen luggage is available through travel agents or directly through various insurance companies. Two companies that issue luggage insurance are:

Tele-Trip (Box 31685, 3201 Farnam St., Omaha, NE 68131, tel. 800/228–9792), a subsidiary of Mutual of Omaha, which operates sales booths at airports and also issues policies through travel agents. Tele-Trip will insure checked or hand luggage through its travel insurance packages. Rates vary according to the length of trip.

The Travelers Corporation (Ticket and Travel Dept., 1 Tower Sq., Hartford, CT 06183, tel. 203/277–0111 or 800/243–3174) insures checked or carry-on luggage for a $500–$2,000 valuation per person for a maximum of 180 days. Rates for up to five days for a $500 valuation are $10; for 180 days, $85. Both companies offer the same rates on domestic and international flights. Check the travel pages of your local newspaper for the names of other companies that insure luggage.

Before you go, itemize the contents of each bag in case you need to file an insurance claim. Be certain to put your home address on each piece of luggage, including carry-on bags. If your luggage is stolen and later recovered, the airline must deliver the luggage to your home free of charge.

Between the Airports and Manhattan
LaGuardia Airport

Taxis cost $14–$20 plus tolls (up to $2.50) and take 20–40 minutes. Group taxi rides to Manhattan are available at taxi dispatch lines just outside the baggage-claim areas during most travel hours (except on Saturdays and holidays). Group fares range from $8–$9 per person (plus a share of tolls) depending on your destination. Call 718/784–4343 for more information.

Carey Airport Express buses (tel. 718/632–0500) depart for Manhattan every 20 minutes from 5:30 AM to 1 AM (weekends 6 AM–1 AM). It's a 20- to 30-minute ride to 42nd Street and Park Avenue, directly opposite Grand Central Terminal. The bus continues from there to the Port Authority Bus Terminal, the New York Hilton, Sheraton City Squire, Crown Plaza Holiday Inn, and Marriott Marquis hotels. Other midtown hotels are a short cab ride away. The bus fare is $8.50 ($10 to the hotels); pay the driver. **The Gray Line Air Shuttle Minibus** (tel. 212/757–6840) serves major Manhattan hotels directly to and from the airport. The fare is $11 per person; make arrangements at the airport's ground transportation center or use the courtesy phone.

The most economical way to reach Manhattan is to ride the Q-33 bus (there are no luggage facilities on this bus) to either the Roosevelt Avenue–Jackson Heights station, where you can catch the E or F subway, or the 74th Street–Broadway station (it's the same station), where you can catch the No. 7 subway. Allow 90 minutes for the entire trip to midtown; the total cost is two tokens ($2.30 at press time). You can use exact change for your bus fare but will have to purchase a token to enter the subway.

JFK International Airport

Taxis cost $24–$30 plus tolls (up to $2.50) and take 35–60 minutes.

Carey Airport Express buses (tel. 718/632–0500) depart for Manhattan every 30 minutes from 5 AM to 1 AM, from all JFK terminals. The ride to 42nd Street and Park Avenue (Grand Central Terminal) takes about one hour. The bus continues from there to the Port Authority Bus Terminal, the New York Hilton, Sheraton City Squire, Crown Plaza Holiday Inn, and Marriott Marquis hotels; it's a short cab ride to other midtown hotels. The bus fare is $11 ($12 to the hotels); pay the driver. **The Gray Line Air Shuttle Minibus** (tel. 212/757–6840) serves major Manhattan hotels directly from the airport; the cost is $14 per person. Make arrangements at the airport's ground transportation counter or use the courtesy phone.

New York Helicopter (tel. 800/645–3494) offers daily flights between the airport and the heliport at East 34th Street and First Avenue. Planes leave from TWA International Terminal A at 8:30 AM, 10 AM, and every half hour between 2 PM and 7:30 PM. The one-way fare is $62 per person; reservations are recommended.

The cheapest but slowest means of getting to Manhattan is to take the Port Authority's free shuttle bus, which stops at all terminals, to the Howard Beach subway station, where you can catch the A train into Manhattan. Alternatively, you can take the Q-10 bus (there are no luggage facilities on this bus) to the Union Turnpike–Kew Gardens station, where you can catch the E or F subway, or to the Lefferts Boulevard station, where you can catch the A subway. Allow at least two hours for the trip; the total cost is one token ($1.15 at press time) if you use the shuttle or two tokens ($2.30) if you use the Q-10. You can use exact change for your fare on the Q-10, but you will need to purchase a token to enter the subway.

Newark Airport **Taxis** cost $28–$30 plus tolls ($3) and take 20–45 minutes. "Share and Save" group rates are available for up to four passengers between 8 AM and midnight; make arrangements with the airport's taxi dispatcher.

NJ Transit Airport Express buses (tel. 201/460–8444) depart every 15–30 minutes for the Port Authority Bus Terminal, at Eighth Avenue and 42nd Street. From there it's a short cab ride to midtown hotels. The ride takes 30–45 minutes. The fare is $7; buy your ticket inside the airport terminal.

Olympia Airport Express buses (tel. 212/964–6233) leave for Grand Central Terminal, Penn Station, and 1 World Trade Center (next to the Vista hotel) about every 20 minutes from 6:15 AM to midnight. The trip takes 35–45 minutes to Grand Central and Penn Station, 20 minutes to WTC. The fare is $7.

The Gray Line Air Shuttle Minibus (tel. 212/757–6840) serves major Manhattan hotels directly to and from the airport. You pay $16 per passenger; make arrangements at the airport's ground transportation center or use the courtesy phone.

New York Helicopter (tel. 800/645–3494) offers flights every hour from 2 PM to 7 PM. The 10-minute flight from the Continental terminal to the heliport at East 34th Street and 1st Avenue costs $62; connecting flights to JFK International Airport are free of charge.

Passengers arriving in Newark can also take New Jersey Transit's **Airlink buses,** leaving every 20 minutes from 6:15 AM to 2 AM, to Penn Station in Newark. The ride takes about 20 minutes; the fare is $4. From there they can catch **PATH Trains** (tel. 201/963–2558 or 212/466–7649), which run to Manhattan 24 hours a day. The trains run every 10 minutes on weekdays, every 15–30 minutes on weeknights, every 20–30 minutes on weekends, and stop at the World Trade Center and at five stops along Sixth Avenue—Christopher Street, 9th Street, 14th Street, 23rd Street, and 33rd Street. The fare is $1.

By Limousine Car services must be licensed by the New York City Taxi and Limousine Commission and can pick up riders only by prior arrangement. It is recommended that passengers call at least 24 hours in advance for reservations. The following companies are among those that serve all three metropolitan airports:

A-Marquis Limousine Service (tel. 212/466–6332); **Airway Express Limousine and Car Service** (tel. 800/528–8989); **All State Car and Limo** (tel. 212/741–7440); **Carey Limousines** (tel. 212/599–1122); **Carmel Car and Limousine Service** (tel. 212/662–2222); **Eastside Limo Service** (tel. 212/744–9700); **Exec-U-Ride Ltd.** (tel. 212/279–1710); **La Limousine** (tel. 212/736–0484); **London Towncars** (tel. 212/988–9700); **New York Continental Limousine Inc.** (tel. 212/617–0212); **Silver Bay Limousine Service** (tel. 718/472–0183); **Wall Chauffeured Limousine Service** (tel. 212/695–7266); **Wheels of New York** (tel. 212/465–1630).

Airline Ticket Offices Many airlines have ticket offices in convenient midtown and lower-Manhattan locations. American, Continental, Delta, Eastern, Northwest, Pan Am, TWA, United, USAir, and Virgin Atlantic, for example, all have offices at the **Airlines Building** (100 E. 42nd St.). Offices are generally open weekdays 8–7 and weekends 9–5, but hours vary among carriers.

Ticket offices are also clustered in three other Manhattan locations: the New York Hilton Hotel at 1335 Sixth Avenue (American, Continental, and Eastern); the Sherry Netherland Hotel at 1 East 59th Street (American, Continental, Delta, Pan Am, TWA, United, and USAir); and 1 World Trade Center (American, British Airways, Continental, Delta, Eastern, Lufthansa, Northwest, Pan Am, Swissair, TWA, United, and USAir). Many foreign carriers have ticket offices along Fifth Avenue north of 50th Street.

By Car

The **Lincoln Tunnel** (I–495), **Holland Tunnel,** and **George Washington Bridge** (I–95) connect Manhattan with the New Jersey Turnpike system and points west. The Lincoln Tunnel comes into midtown Manhattan; the Holland Tunnel into lower Manhattan; and the George Washington Bridge into northern Manhattan. Each of the three arteries requires a toll ($4 for cars) eastbound into New York, but no toll westbound.

The **Bayonne Bridge** connects Route 440 in Staten Island with Route 440 in New Jersey; a $4 toll for cars is collected southbound into New York. The **Outerbridge Crossing** and **Goethals Bridge** connect Staten Island with the New Jersey Turnpike and points west. The Outerbridge Crossing, which also feeds into the Garden State Parkway, comes into southern Staten Island, the Goethals Bridge into the northern part of the borough. Both bridges are linked through Route 278 to the Verrazano-Narrows Bridge into southern Brooklyn. The Goethals and Outerbridge require a toll ($4 for cars) eastbound into

New York, but no toll westbound. The Verrazano requires a toll of $5 for cars westbound only.

From Long Island, the **Midtown Tunnel** (I–495) and **Triborough Bridge** (I–278) are the most direct links to Manhattan. Both require tolls ($2.50 for cars) in both directions.

From upstate New York, the city is accessible via the **New York (Dewey) Thruway** (I–87) (toll) to the **Major Deegan Expressway** (I–87) through the Bronx and across the **Triborough Bridge** (toll), or via the **Taconic State Parkway** to the **Saw Mill River Parkway** into upper Manhattan.

From New England, the **Connecticut Turnpike** (I–95) connects with the **New England Thruway** (I–95) (toll) and then the **Bruckner Expressway** (I–278). Take the Bruckner to the **Triborough Bridge** (toll) or to the **Cross Bronx Expressway**, which enters upper Manhattan on the west side.

Manhattan has two major north–south arteries that run the length of the island. The **West Side Highway** skirts the Hudson River from Battery Park (where it's known as West Street) through midtown (it then becomes the Henry Hudson Parkway north of 72nd Street) and past the George Washington Bridge. Both the Holland and Lincoln tunnels enter Manhattan just a few blocks east of this route; the Cross Bronx Expressway connects with the Henry Hudson Parkway in northern Manhattan at the George Washington Bridge. **Franklin D. Roosevelt Drive** (FDR Drive) runs along the East River from Battery Park into upper Manhattan, where it becomes Harlem River Drive north of 125th Street. Both the Queens Midtown Tunnel (East 36th Street) and the Queensboro Bridge (East 59th Street) can be entered a few blocks west of FDR Drive, which connects with the Triborough Bridge at East 125th Street.

Be forewarned: The deterioration of the bridges linking Manhattan, especially those spanning the East River, is a serious problem, and repairs will be ongoing for the next few years. Don't be surprised if a bridge is all or partially closed.

Driving within Manhattan can be a nightmare of gridlocked streets and predatory motorists. Free parking is difficult to find in midtown, and violators may be towed away literally within minutes. All over town, parking lots charge exorbitant rates—as much as $15 for two hours in some neighborhoods. If you do drive, don't plan to use your car much for traveling within Manhattan.

Car Rentals

If you find you absolutely need a car—perhaps for a weekend escape or because Manhattan is part of a longer trip—you'll have to sort out Manhattan's confusing array of car-rental possibilities. Although rates were once cheaper out of Newark airport, that is no longer the case; prices charged by national firms are the same at Newark, Kennedy, and LaGuardia, as well as at Manhattan rental locations. For a subcompact, expect to pay $50–$80 per day, with unlimited mileage. Companies with multiple Manhattan and airport locations include **Avis** (tel. 800/331–1212); **Budget** (tel. 800/527–0700); **Dollar** (tel. 800/800–4000); **Hertz** (tel. 800/654–3131); **National** (tel. 800/ 328–4567); and **Thrifty** (tel. 800/367–2277). Some regional budget companies, such as **Rent-A-Wreck** (tel. 212/721–0080), offer lower rates. If you are flying into LaGuardia or Kennedy, you might look into some local Queens agencies with lower rates, such as **ABC** (tel. 800/247–6110) or **Universal** (tel. 718/786–0786). **Sunshine Rent-A-Car** (tel. 212/989–7260) is good for budget rentals in Greenwich Village.

Whomever you rent from, get a reservation number and ask whether there is free mileage and whether you must pay for a full tank of gas even if you don't use it.

By Train

Amtrak (tel. 800/872–7245) offers frequent service within the Northeast Corridor, between Boston and Washington, DC. Trains arrive at and depart from **Pennsylvania Station** (31st–33rd Sts., between 7th and 8th Aves.). Amtrak trains serve Penn Station from the Southeast, Midwest, and Far West. Penn Station also handles **Long Island Railroad** trains (tel. 718/217–5477), with service to and from all over Long Island, and **New Jersey Transit** trains (tel. 201/460–8444), with frequent service from the northern and central regions of New Jersey. Amtrak trains from Montreal and upstate New York and the *Lake Shore Limited* train from Chicago also leave from Penn Station.

Metro-North Commuter Railroad (tel. 212/532–4900) serves the northern suburbs and Connecticut from Grand Central Terminal as far east as New Haven. The other Metro-North Manhattan stop is at 125th Street and Park Avenue in East Harlem—not a good place to get off the train unless you are visiting this neighborhood.

PATH Trains (tel. 212/466–7649) run 24 hours a day to New York City from terminals in Hoboken, Jersey City, Harrison, and Newark, New Jersey; they connect with seven major New Jersey Transit commuter lines at Hoboken Station, Broad Street Station (Newark), and Penn Station (Newark). PATH trains stop in Manhattan at the World Trade Center and along Sixth Avenue at Christopher Street, 9th Street, 14th Street, 23rd Street, and 33rd Street. They run every 10 minutes on weekdays, every 15–30 minutes on weeknights, and every 20–30 minutes on weekends. The fare is $1.

By Bus

All long-haul and commuter bus lines feed into the **Port Authority Terminal,** a mammoth multilevel structure that occupies a nearly 2-square-block area between 40th and 42nd streets and Eighth and Ninth avenues. Though it was recently modernized and is fairly clean, large numbers of vagrants make the terminal an uncomfortable place to spend much time. Especially with night arrivals, plan to move through the terminal swiftly. Beware of hustlers trying to help you hail a cab on Eighth Avenue—they will demand a tip for performing this unnecessary service and can be hostile and aggressive if crossed.

For information on any service into or out of the Port Authority Terminal, call 212/564–8484. Some of the individual bus lines serving New York include **Greyhound-Trailways** (consult local information for a number in your area); **Adirondack** and **Pine Hill Trailways** from upstate New York (tel. 914/339–4230 or 212/947–5300); **Bonanza Bus Lines** from New England (tel. 800/556–3815); **Martz Trailways** from northeastern Pennsylvania (tel. 800/233–8604); **New Jersey Transit** from around New Jersey (tel. 201/460–8444); **Peter Pan Bus Lines** from New England (tel. 413/781–2900); and **Vermont Transit** from New England (tel. 802/862–9671).

The **George Washington Bridge Bus Station** is located at Fort Washington Avenue and Broadway between 178th and 179th streets in the Washington Heights section of Manhattan. Six bus lines, serving northern New Jersey and Rockland County, New York, make daily stops there from 5 AM to 1 AM. The terminal connects with the 175th Street station on the A subway, making it slightly more convenient for travelers going to and from the Upper West Side.

Staying in New York

Important Addresses and Telephone Numbers

Tourist Information
New York Convention and Visitors Bureau. The main office is at 2 Columbus Circle (tel. 212/397–8222) and is open weekdays 9–6, weekends 10–6.

Emergencies
Dial 911 for **police, fire,** or **ambulance** in an emergency.

Deaf Emergency Teletypewriter (tel. 800/342–4357), for medical, fire, and ambulance emergencies.

Doctor
Doctors On Call, 24-hour house-call service (tel. 212/737–2333). Near midtown, 24-hour emergency rooms are open at **St. Luke's-Roosevelt Hospital** (58th St. at 9th Ave., tel. 212/523–6800) and **St. Vincent's Hospital** (7th Ave. and 11th St., tel. 212/790–7997).

Dentist
The **Dental Emergency Service** (tel. 212/679–3966; after 8 PM, tel. 212/679–4172) will make a referral.

24-Hour Pharmacy
Kaufman's Pharmacy (Lexington Ave. and 50th St., tel. 212/755–2266).

Hotlines
The New York Telephone Company lists important emergency and community services numbers in the front of its white-pages directory. Here are some numbers that may come in handy:

Better Business Bureau of Metropolitan New York (tel. 212/533–6200).

Crime Victims' Hotline (tel. 212/577–7777).

NYC On Stage (tel. 212/768–1818) provides up-to-the-minute information on tickets for theater, music, and dance performances.

Sex Crimes Report Line (tel. 212/267–7273).

For updates on bridge and tunnel construction, call 212/566–2525 (bridges and tunnels crossing the East River) and 800/221–9903 (those linking New York and New Jersey).

Telephones

There are more than 58,000 public telephones in New York City, nearly 25,000 of which are in Manhattan. A visitor should never have to hunt more than three or four blocks before finding a coin-operated phone. If you're making a brief call—and don't mind the cacophonous sound of traffic or subways rumbling in the background—street phones are probably your best bet. If you want to consult a directory or make a more leisurely call, pay phones in the lobbies of office buildings or hotels (some of which take credit cards) are a better choice.

The area code for Manhattan and the Bronx is 212; for Brooklyn, Queens, and Staten Island, it's 718. Pay telephones cost 25¢ for the first three minutes of a local call (this includes calls between 212 and 718 area codes); an extra deposit is required for each additional minute.

Rest Rooms

Public rest rooms in New York run the gamut when it comes to cleanliness. Facilities in Penn Station, Grand Central Terminal, and the Port Authority bus terminal are often quite dirty and are inhabited by homeless people. Rest rooms in subway stations are even more filthy and are often downright unsafe.

As a rule, the cleanest bathrooms are in midtown department stores such as Macy's, Lord & Taylor, and Bloomingdale's, or in the lobbies of large hotels. Public atriums, such as the Citicorp Center and Trump Tower, also provide good public facilities. Restaurants, too, have rest rooms, but usually just for patrons. Be aware that cinemas, Broadway theaters, and concert halls have limited amenities, and there are often long lines before performances, as well as during intermissions.

Crime

Despite New York's bad reputation in this area, most people live here for years without being robbed or assaulted. Nevertheless, travelers make particularly easy marks for pickpockets and hustlers, so caution is advised. Someone who appears to have had an accident at the exit door of a bus may flee with your wallet or purse if you attempt to give aid; the individual who approaches you with a complicated story is probably playing a confidence game and hopes to get something from you. Keep jewelry and valuables out of sight on the street and do not venture down deserted blocks in out-of-the-way neighborhoods, especially after dark. Beware of strangers jostling you in crowds. Women should never hang their purse on a chair in a restaurant or on a hook in a rest-room stall. Men are advised to carry wallets in their front pants pockets rather than in their hip pockets.

Opening and Closing Times

New York is very much a 24-hour city. Its subways and buses run around the clock, and plenty of services are available at all hours and on all days of the week. To compensate for being open at odd times, however, many businesses close during what one would expect to be their normal workweek, so it's always a good idea to check ahead.

Banks are open weekdays 9–3 or 9–3:30, although a few branches in certain neighborhoods may stay open late on Friday or are open on Saturday mornings.

Post offices are generally open weekdays 10–5 or 10–6. The main post office on Eighth Avenue between 31st and 33rd streets is open daily 24 hours.

Museum hours vary greatly, but most of the major ones are open Tuesday–Sunday and keep later hours on Tuesday or Thursday evenings.

Stores are normally open Monday–Saturday 10–5 or 10–6. Major department stores usually have late hours at least one evening a week. In business districts, stores may open earlier, while in neighborhoods such as the Village and SoHo, they open later and close later. Many stores in residential neighborhoods are open on Sundays.

Changing Money

Foreign travelers visiting New York can exchange foreign currency and traveler's checks at a number of offices around Manhattan. Large banks—Bank Leumi, Chase Manhattan, Chemical, Citibank, and Manufacturers Hanover Trust, for example—accommodate travelers during weekday business hours. Other companies provide exchange services up to seven days a week and often quote rates over the phone. They include:

American Express Travel Service, with nine Manhattan locations including: 822 Lexington Avenue, tel. 212/758–6510; Bloomingdale's, 59th Street and Lexington Avenue, tel. 212/705–3171; 150 E. 42nd Street, tel. 212/687–3700; 374 Park Avenue, tel. 212/421–8240; American Express Tower, 200 Vesey Street, tel. 212/640–5130; and Macy's Herald Square, 151 W. 34th Street, tel. 212/695–8075. Hours vary among locations.
Chequepoint USA, 551 Madison Avenue, tel. 212/980–6443. Open weekdays 8–6, weekends 10–6.
Freeport Currencies, 132 W. 45th Street, tel. 212/730–8339. Open weekdays 9–6, weekends 10–5. At 49 W. 57th Street. Open weekdays 9–7, weekends 10–6.
Harold Reuter & Co., Pan Am Building, 200 Park Avenue, Room 332 East, 3rd floor, tel. 212/661–0826. Open weekdays 8–5. At Abraham & Straus, 32nd Street and Sixth Avenue, 6th floor, tel. 212/268–8517. Open Mon.–Sat., 10–6, Sun. 11–6.
New York Foreign Exchange, 61 Broadway, Suite 805, tel. 212/248–4700. Open weekdays 9–5.
People's Foreign Exchange, 500 Fifth Avenue (at 42nd Street), Suite 200, tel. 212/983–4727. Open daily 9–6.
Thomas Cook Currency Service (tel. 212/757–6915) has branches at 630 Fifth Avenue in Rockefeller Center; 1 Herald Center at 33rd Street and Sixth Avenue; 41 E. 42nd Street; and 29 Broadway. Open weekdays 9–5, Saturdays 10–3.

Getting Around

On Foot The cheapest, sometimes the fastest, and usually the most interesting way to explore this city is by walking. Because New Yorkers by and large live in apartments rather than in houses, and travel by cab, bus, or subway rather than by private car, they end up walking quite a lot. As a result, street life is a vital part of the local culture. On crowded sidewalks, people gossip, snack, sunbathe, browse, buy drugs, cement business deals, make romantic rendezvous, encounter long-lost friends, and fly into irrational quarrels with strangers. It's a wonderfully democratic hubbub. Also sharing the streets, however, are increasing numbers of panhandlers, some aggressive, many homeless.

Manhattan Address Locator

To locate avenue addresses, take the address, cancel the last figure, divide by 2, add or subtract the key number below. The answer is the nearest numbered cross street, approximately. To find addresses on numbered cross streets, remember that numbers increase east or west from 5th Ave., which runs north–south.

Ave. A... *add 3*

Ave. B...*add 3*

Ave. C...*add 3*

Ave. D...*add 3*

1st Ave....*add 3*

2nd Ave....*add 3*

3rd Ave....*add 10*

4th Ave....*add 8*

5th Ave.

Up to 200...*add 13*

Up to 400...*add 16*

Up to 600...*add 18*

Up to 775...*add 20*

From 775 to 1286... *cancel last figure and subt. 18*

Ave. of the Americas...*subt. 12*

7th Ave....*add 12*

Above 110th St... *add 20*

8th Ave....*add 9*

9th Ave....*add 13*

10th Ave....*add 14*

Amsterdam Ave. ...*add 59*

Audubon Ave. ...*add 165*

Broadway (23–192 Sts.)...*subt. 30*

Columbus Ave. ...*add 60*

Convent Ave....*add 127*

Central Park West... *divide house number by 10 and add 60*

Edgecombe Ave. ...*add 134*

Ft. Washington Ave. ...*add 158*

Lenox Ave....*add 110*

Lexington Ave....*add 22*

Madison Ave....*add 27*

Manhattan Ave. ...*add 100*

Park Ave....*add 34*

Park Ave. South ...*add 8*

Pleasant Ave....*add 101*

Riverside Drive... *divide house number by 10 and add 72 up to 165 Street*

St. Nicholas Ave. ...*add 110*

Wadsworth Ave. ...*add 173*

West End Ave. ...*add 59*

York Ave....*add 4*

The typical New Yorker, if there is such an animal, walks quickly, dodging around cars, buses, bicycle messengers, construction sites, and other pedestrians. Yet although the natives seem hurried and rude, they will often cheerfully come to the aid of a lost pedestrian, so don't hesitate to ask passersby for directions.

Before you start out, keep a few simple rules in mind: Above 14th Street, the city is planned along a grid, with Fifth Avenue marking the dividing line between east and west. The streets, numbered from 1 to 220, are straight lines running east to west. The avenues—from First to Twelfth—run north to south. Below 14th Street, however, chaos reigns (*see* Orientation in Chapter 3).

By Subway The 244-mile subway system operates 24 hours a day and, especially within Manhattan, serves most of the places you'll want to visit. It's cheaper than a cab and, during the workweek, often faster than either cabs or buses. The trains have finally been rid of their graffiti (some New Yorkers, of course, perversely miss the colorful old trains) and sleek new air-conditioned cars predominate on many lines. The New York subway deserves much of its negative image, however. Many trains are crowded, dirty, and noisy, and even occasionally unsafe. Although trains are scheduled to run frequently, especially during rush hours, you never know when some incident somewhere on the line may stall traffic indefinitely. Unsavory characters lurk around certain stations, and panhandlers frequently work their way through the cars. Don't write off the subway—millions ride it every week without incident—but stay alert at all times.

The subway fare is $1.15. Reduced fares are available for handicapped people and senior citizens during nonrush hours. You must use a token to enter; they are sold at token booths that are *usually* open at each station. It's advisable to buy several tokens at one time to prevent waiting in line later (it always seems the lines are longest just as your train is roaring into the station). A token permits unlimited transfers within the system.

This book's subway map covers the most-visited parts of Manhattan. Maps of the full subway system are posted on many trains and at some stations, but don't rely on finding one when you need it. You may be able to pick up free maps at token booths, too, but they are often out of stock. Make sure the map you refer to is up-to-date—lengthy repair programs can cause reroutings that last long enough for new "temporary" maps to be printed.

For route information, ask the token clerk or a transit policeman. Call 718/330–1234 (a local call, 25¢ from pay phones) for information from 6 AM to 9 PM daily. And don't hesitate to ask a fellow rider for directions: Once New Yorkers realize you're "harmless," most bend over backward to b῀ helpful.

Most midtown stops are crowded until fairly late at night, so for safety's sake, stay among the crowds on the center of the platforms. Avoid empty or nearly empty cars. During off-peak hours, try to ride in the same car as the conductor: It will stop near a line of light bulbs mounted above the edge of the plat-

Manhattan Subways

86th St Bway ①②③⑨

79th St Bway

72nd St Bway

66th St/Bway Lincoln Center

86th St Central Park W

81st St Museum of Natural History

Ⓐ Ⓑ Ⓒ Ⓓ

CENTRAL PARK

④⑤⑥ 86th St Lexington Ave

77th St Lexington Ave

68th St Lexington Ave

63rd St Lexington Ave TRAMWAY Ⓑ Ⓠ

Ⓡ Ⓝ

Roosevelt Island

QUEENS

59th St Columbus Circle

50th St./8th Ave.
50th St./7th Ave.

42nd St 8th Ave

57th St.

Ⓓ

5th Ave 60th St

53rd St./7th Ave.
47th-50th Sts.
49th St.

5th Ave

5th Ave 42nd St

Ⓢ Ⓓ Ⓕ

59th St Lexington Ave

Lexington Ave/53rd St.

Lexington Ave 52nd St.

Queensboro Bridge

Ⓔ Ⓕ 23rd St Ely Ave

Times Sq

Penn Station

34th St 8th Ave

23rd St 8th Ave

14th St 8th Ave

Ⓐ Ⓒ
Ⓔ

①②③⑨

34th St 8th Ave

28th St

Ⓑ Ⓓ Ⓡ Ⓝ Ⓕ Ⓠ

18th St
Ⓛ

Grand Central

34th St Herald Sq

28th St

23rd St

6th Ave

33rd St Park Ave S

④⑤⑥ 28th St Park Ave S

23rd St Park Ave S

3rd Ave

Vernon Blvd Jackson Ave

⑦

Queens-Midtown Tunnel

Ⓛ

Lincoln Tunnel

14th St Union Sq

8th St/Astor Pl

1st Ave

Christopher St Sheridan Sq

W 4th St

Bleecker St Lafayette St

Houston St Varick St

Prince

Spring

Spring

2 Ave/E Houston St

Ⓜ Ⓙ Ⓩ

Williamsburg Br.

Delancey St/Essex St
Delancey St/Spring St
Grand/Christie

E. B'way

Holland Tunnel

Canal St Varick St

Franklin St Varick St.

Chambers St

Chambers St Varick St

Cortland St World Trade Center

Rector St Greenwich St

Rector/Trinity Pl

①⑨ South Ferry

Canal B'way

City Hall B'way

Park Pl

Fulton

Broad/Wall

②③

Ⓜ Ⓝ Ⓡ

Whitehall

④⑤

Manhattan Bridge

Brooklyn Bridge

Ⓐ Ⓒ

Ⓕ BROOKLYN

Ⓓ Ⓑ Ⓠ

York St

Fulton

High St

Clark

Borough Hall

Jay St Borough Hall

Subway Lines

▬▬▬ BMT

───── IND

▬ ▬ ▬ IRT

Brooklyn-Battery Tunnel

form. When disembarking from a train, stick with the crowd until you reach the comparative safety of the street.

By Bus Most buses follow easy-to-understand routes along the Manhattan grid. Routes go up or down the north–south avenues, or east and west on the major two-way crosstown streets. Most bus routes operate 24 hours, but service is infrequent late at night. Buses are great for sightseeing, but traffic jams—a potential threat at any time or place in Manhattan—can make rides maddeningly slow.

Bus fare is the same as subway fare: $1.15, at press time, in coins (no pennies; no change is given) or a subway token. When you get on the bus you can ask the driver for a free transfer coupon, good for one change to an intersecting route. Legal transfer points are listed on the back of the slip. Transfers have time limits of at least two hours, often longer. You cannot use the transfer to enter the subway system.

Guide-A-Rides, which consist of route maps and schedules, are posted at many bus stops in Manhattan and at major stops throughout the other boroughs. Each of the five boroughs of New York has a separate bus map, and they are scarcer than hens' teeth. They are occasionally available in subway token booths, but never on buses. The best places to obtain them are the Convention and Visitors Bureau at Columbus Circle or the information kiosks in Grand Central Terminal and Penn Station.

By Taxi Taxis are usually easy to hail on the street or from a taxi rank in front of major hotels. You can tell if a cab is available by checking its rooftop light; if the center panel is lit, the driver is ready to take passengers. Taxis cost $1.50 for the first ⅕ of a mile, 25¢ for each ⅕ of a mile thereafter, and 25¢ for each 75 seconds not in motion. A 50¢ surcharge is added to rides begun between 8 PM and 6 AM. There is no charge for extra passengers. Taxi drivers also expect a 15% tip. Barring performance above and beyond the call of duty, don't feel obliged to give them more.

To avoid unhappy taxi experiences, try to have a general idea of where you want to go. A few cab drivers are dishonest; some are ignorant; some can barely understand English. If you have no idea of the proper route, you may be taken for a long and costly ride.

By Trolley The Manhattan Neighborhood Trolley, a 1900 vintage red-and-green car seating 30 passengers runs daily, 12 PM–6 PM, making stops every hour at South Street Seaport, Battery Park, the World Trade Center, the World Financial Center, City Hall Park, Chatham Square in Chinatown, Grand Street in Little Italy, and Orchard Street on the Lower East Side. Tickets, which are valid for boarding and reboarding all day, cost $4 for adults, $3 for senior citizens and children under age 12, and may be purchased from a tour guide on board, who provides a running narration, or in advance, at the Seaport, at major hotels, or by mail (Manhattan Neighborhood Trolley, Box 1053, Knickerbocker Station, New York, NY 10002, tel. 212/677–7268).

By Limousine If you want to ride around Manhattan in style, you can rent a chauffeur-driven car from one of many limousine services. Companies usually charge by the hour or offer a flat fee for sightseeing excursions. The Manhattan yellow pages provides a full listing of limousine operators, but here are several recommended companies: **A-Marquis Limousine Service** (tel. 212/466–6332); **All State Car and Limo** (tel. 212/741–7440); **Bermuda Limousine International** (tel. 212/249–8400); **Carey Limousines** (tel. 212/599–1122); **Carmel Car and Limousine Service** (tel. 212/662–2222); **Concord Luxury Limousine** (tel. 212/230–1600); **Eastside Limo Service** (tel. 212/744–9700); **Exec-U-Ride Ltd.** (tel. 212/279–1710); **Gordon's Limousine Service** (tel. 212/921–0081); **La Limousine** (tel. 212/736–0484); **London Towncars** (tel. 212/988–9700); **New York Continental Limousine Inc.** (tel. 212/617–0212); **Silver Bay Limousine Service** (tel. 718/472–0183); **Wall Chauffeured Limousine Service** (tel. 212/695–7266); **Wheels of New York** (tel. 212/465–1630).

Guided Tours

Orientation Tours The most pleasant way to get a crash orientation to Manhattan is aboard a **Circle Line Cruise**. Once you've finished the three-hour, 35-mile circumnavigation of Manhattan, you'll have a good idea of where things are and what you want to see next. Narrations are as interesting and individualized as the guides who deliver them. *Pier 83, west end of 42nd St., tel. 212/563–3200. Fare: $15 adults, $7.50 children under 12. Operates early Mar.–Dec., Tues.–Sun.*

For a shorter excursion, the **TNT Express,** a hydroliner, will show you the island of Manhattan in 75 minutes. *Pier 11, 2 blocks south of South Street Seaport, tel. 212/244–4770. Fare: $15 adults, $13 senior citizens, $8 children under 12, children under 5 free. Boats depart weekdays and Sat. 12 noon and 2 PM.*

At South Street Seaport's Pier 16 you can take two- or three-hour voyages to New York's past aboard the iron cargo schooner *Pioneer* (tel. 212/669–9416). You can take 90-minute tours of New York Harbor aboard the sidewheeler *Andrew Fletcher* or the re-created steamboat *DeWitt Clinton*.

Gray Line (900 8th Ave. at 53rd St., tel. 212/397–2600 or 212/397–2620) offers a number of standard city bus tours, plus cruises and day trips to Brooklyn and Atlantic City. **Short Line Tours** (166 W. 46th St., tel. 212/354–5122) offers some 20 different tour options.

Island Helicopter (heliport at E. 34th St. and East River, tel. 212/683–4575) offers four fly-over options, from $36 (for 7 miles) to $89 (for 35 miles). From the West Side, **Liberty Helicopter Tours** (heliport at W. 30th St. and Hudson River, tel. 212/465–8905) has three tours ranging from $55 to $99.

Special-Interest Tours **Backstage on Broadway** (tel. 212/575–8065) puts you in a Broadway theater setting and lets you mingle with show people. Reservations are mandatory. **Art Tours of Manhattan** (tel. 609/921–2647) provides an inside view of museum and gallery exhibits. **Gallery Passports** (tel. 212/288–3578) takes you to galleries and museums as well as artists' studios and lofts in Manhattan. **SoHo Art Experience** (tel. 212/219–0810) offers tours of SoHo's architecture, galleries, shops, and artists' lofts. **Doorway to Design** (tel. 212/221–1111) tours fashion and interior design showrooms as well as artists' private studios. **Harlem Your Way!** (tel. 212/690–1687), **Harlem Spirituals, Inc.** (tel. 212/302–2594), and **Penny Sightseeing Co., Inc.** (tel. 212/410–0080), offer bus and walking tours and Sunday gospel trips to Harlem. **Brooklyn Connoisseur's Choice Tours** (tel. 718/857–7811) organizes a tour of the Brooklyn Museum and Brooklyn Botanic Garden.

Walking Tours **Sidewalks of New York** (Box 1660, Cathedral Station, New York, NY 10025, tel. 212/517–0201) hits the streets from various thematic angles—Historic Church tours, Ye Old Tavern tours, Celebrity Home tours, Final Resting Places of the Rich and Famous tours. These walks are offered on weekends, both days and evenings, year-round. Tours last 2–2½ hours and cost $10; no reservations are required. Weekday tours are available by appointment. **Adventure on a Shoestring** (300 W. 53rd St., New York, NY 10019, tel. 212/265–2663) is an organization dating from 1963 that explores New York neighborhoods. Tours are scheduled periodically for $5 per person. The **Municipal Art Society** (tel. 212/935–3960) operates a series of bus and walking tours. The **Museum of the City of New York** (tel. 212/534–1672) sponsors Sunday afternoon walking tours. The **Urban Park Rangers** (tel. 212/427–4040) offer weekend walks and workshops, most of them free, in city parks. The **92nd Street Y** (tel. 212/996–1105) often has something special to offer on weekends and some weekdays. **The Streets Where We Lived** is a multi-ethnic historic walking tour given by The Lower East Side Tenement Museum (tel. 212/431–0233). Other knowledgeable walking-tour guides include **Michael Levin** (tel. 212/924–7187), **Michael George** (tel. 212/975–4114), **Joyce Gold** (tel. 212/242–5762), **Arthur Marks** (tel. 212/673–0477), **Ginter-Gotham Urban History** (tel. 212/496–6859), and **Peter Salwen** (tel. 212/873–1944).

The most comprehensive listing of tours offered during a particular week is published in the "Other Events" section of *New York* magazine's "Cue" listings.

Self-Guided The **New York Convention and Visitors Bureau's** "I Love New
Walking Tours York Visitors Guide and Map" is available at the bureau's information center (2 Columbus Circle, tel. 212/397–8222). Walkers in Brooklyn can pick up two maps—"Brooklyn on Tour" and "Downtown Brooklyn Walking Tours"—as well as a handy "Brooklyn Neighborhood Book," all free of charge, at the public affairs desk of the Brooklyn Borough President's office (209 Joralemon St., 3rd floor). All three are available by mail, at $5 each, from the Fund for the Borough of Brooklyn (16 Court St., Suite 1400 W, Brooklyn, NY 11241, tel. 718/855–7882).

The **Municipal Art Society of New York** has prepared a comprehensive "Juror's Guide to Lower Manhattan: Five Walking Tours" for the benefit of jurors who are often required to kill time while serving in downtown courthouses. Along with an explanation of the New York jury system, the pamphlet includes tours of lower Manhattan and Wall Street, the City Hall district, Chinatown and Little Italy, South Street Seaport, and TriBeCa. Nonjurors can purchase copies at Urban Center Books (457 Madison Ave. at 51st St., tel. 212/935–3595).

A free "Walking Tour of Rockefeller Center" pamphlet is available from the information desk in the lobby of the GE building (30 Rockefeller Plaza).

2 Portraits of New York City

The New York Babel

by V. S. Pritchett

One of the great living masters of English prose, V. S. Pritchett expounds delightfully on his impressions of the city in New York Proclaimed. *Here are some choice passages from the book.*

If Paris suggests Intelligence, if London suggests Experience, then the word for New York is Activity. York itself is an almost intolerably famous name, but adding New to it was one of the lucky prophetic insights of nomenclature, for newness, from day to day, was to be the moral essence of the place. There is no place where newness is so continuously pursued.

What is not naturally active in New York soon has to turn to and become so. There is not an inactive man, woman, or child in the place. It might be thought that a contemplative, passive New Yorker, one who is inhabited by his feelings and his imaginings, who lives in an inner world, or was born torpid, must be immune to the active spirit. This is not so in New York, where states like passivity, contemplation, vegetativeness, and often sleep itself are active by prescription. Pragmatism sees to that. The prime example is the bum or derelict. There he lies asleep or drunk on the doorstep or props himself against a wall in the Bowery, an exposed, accepted, but above all an established figure of a 51st state. In a city where all activity is specialized, he has his specialty: he must act in protest against activity, which leads him from time to time on a chase for alcohol, a smoke, or a coin as persistent as a salesman's, but in solitude. Virginia Woolf used to ask where Society was; the notion was metaphysical to her. But Skid Row exists as a recognized place. You go there when the thing comes over you. You graduate in dereliction. You put in a 20-hour day of internal fantasy-making in your studied rejection of the New York norm. The Spanish mendicant has his rights and takes his charity with condescension; the bum grabs with resentment. He is busy. You have upset his dream. The supremely passive man in theory, he will stop in the middle of the street as he crosses the Bowery, holding up his dirty hand at the traffic, and scream in the manner of madness at the oncoming driver. Screaming like that—and New York is dotted with screamers on a scale I have seen in no other city in the world, though Naples has its share—reveals the incessant pressure of the active spirit.

For ourselves who are trying to settle first what we see before our eyes, this active, practical spirit has curious manifestations. New York City is large, but Manhattan is small in extent, so small that a large part of its population has to be pumped out of it every night by bridges and tunnels. Despite the groans about the congestion of its traffic, it is easy to dash from one end to the other of the island and to drive fast all around it. And most people do dash. The only real difficulty is in the downtown tangle of named streets in old New York; the grid has settled the rest. The grid is an unlovely system. It is not originally American: Stuttgart and Berlin hit upon this method of automatically extending cities in the 17th century. By the 18th century Europe had discovered that cities must be designed before they are extended: mere pragmatism and planning will not do. It absolutely will not do if left to engineers, soldiers, or what are called developers. The makers of the New York grid confused the idea that parallel lines can be projected into infinity without meeting, with the idea of design. The boredom this has inflicted upon the horizontal life of Manhattan has turned out to be endurable to the primarily active man who is impatient of the whole idea of having neighbors. The striping, unheeding avenues of the grid have given one superb benefit. They cut through long distances, they provide long vistas that excite the eye, and these are fine where the buildings are high, if they are featureless where the buildings are low. No other city I can think of has anything like the undulating miles that fly down Park Avenue from 96th Street to Grand Central, blocked now though it is by the brutal mass of the Pan Am Building—a British affront to the city and spoken of as a revenge for Suez—or the longer streak of Madison. These two avenues impress most as a whole, other avenues in part, by their assurance as they cleave their way through the cliffs.

Of course, being a stranger, you have been living it up, for if you want a night city, this is preeminently the one. There is a large fluorescent population of pale faces—who is that old man sitting alone in the Automat at this late hour? Where are all those taxis streaking to endlessly through the night? You have been listening to the jazz in Birdland perhaps, listening to the long drumming that says "Encroach, encroach, encroach, encroach, overcome, come!" or to that woman with the skirling voice which is shoving, pushing, and struggling cheerfully to get all her energy out of her body and into her mouth as she sings what is really the theme song of the city: "And it's good. It's all good, good, good." She was wired in to some dynamo.

Those words never fade from the mind. In sleep you still hear them. You are a receiving station for every message Babel sends out day and night. The sirens of the police cars, the ambulances and fire engines, mark the hours, carrying the mind out to fantasies of disaster. I say "fantasies," for surely all these speeding crews are studiously keeping alive the ideal of some ultimate dementia while the rest of us sleep. New York demands more than anything else that one should never fail to maintain one's sense of its drama; even its social manners, at their most ceremonious, have this quality. Where the crowds of other cities are consolidating all day long, filling up the safes and cellars of the mind, the New York crowd is set on the pure function of self-dispersal. A couple of cops idling through the night in a police car will issue their noise as if it were part of the uniform and to keep up their belief in their own reality and in the sacred notion of the Great Slaying or the Great Burglarization. Then there is light traffic on the highways, with its high, whipping, cat-gut whine. On 104th Street on the West Side I used to have the sensation of being flayed alive all night by knives whipping down Riverside Drive; it was not disagreeable. City life is for masochists. On many other avenues the trucks bulldozed the brain. There were bursts of noctambulist shouting off Madison and 60th at 3 or 4; followed by the crowning row of the city, the clamor of the garbage disposers, successors to Dickens's gentlemanly swine, that fling the New York garbage cans across the pavement and grind the stuff to bits on the spot. Often I have sat at my window to watch these night brutes chew up the refuse. The men have to rush to keep up with its appetite. As a single producer of shindy this municipal creature is a triumph.

The only way of pinning some sort of identity onto the people is to think of them as once being strangers like yourself and trace them to their districts. The man who used to bring my breakfast, saying, every morning, "Lousy day," was a 115th Street Puerto Rican, of five years' standing. You learn to distinguish. You know where the Ukrainians, the Sephardic Jews, early and late Italians, degrees of Irish, live. You build up a map of the black and Puerto Rican pockets. You note the Germans are at 86th Street and yet the Irish are there, too; that, at the bottom, on East End Avenue, the neighborhood has become suddenly fashionable. The Greenwich Village Italians are pretty fixed; the several Harlems have established their character, for they have stuck to their district for 60 years, which must be a record for New York. You know the Greeks are on Ninth Avenue. The Lower East Side, now largely transformed, is Jewish and Puerto Rican. But large groups break away; poor give place to poorer. Sometimes poor give place to rich. In Sutton Place they cleared the poor away from that pleasant little cliff on the East River. But one must not understand these quarters as being the old parishes or the ancient swallowed-up villages of European cities, though they were sometimes the sites of farms. Topographically they are snippings of certain avenues and cross streets. For the avenues stripe the city and the groups live on a block or two along or across the stripe. One would have to analyze New York street by street, from year to year, to know the nuances of racial contact.

Statistics deceive, but it is clear that the oldest American stock of Dutch, British, and German, though dominant in wealth and traditional influence, is a small minority in New York. The question no one can answer is how far the contents of the melting pot have really melted and whether a new race has yet been created. For a long time the minorities resist, huddle into corners. Some foreign groups of New Yorkers melt slowly or not at all. O. Henry in his time called Lower Manhattan "Bagdad-on-the-Subway," think-

ing then of the unchanging Syrians and Armenians around
Rector Street, but they have almost vanished. The Ukrainians still have their shops and churches near Avenue A. The
Russian Orthodox priest walks down the street. The Poles
shout from their windows or sit on the cagelike fire escapes
east of Greenwich Village. Slowly these people, no doubt,
merge; but the tendency for social classes to be determined
by race is marked. Many groups of Orthodox Jews remain
untouched. Over in Williamsburg you see a sect wearing
beards, the men in black hats and long black coats, their
hair often long, with curls at the ears, walking with a long
loping shuffle as if they traveled with knees bent. They look
like a priesthood, and the boys, curled in the same way,
might be their acolytes. You will meet them with their
black cases of treasure between their feet, standing on the
pavement outside the diamond markets of 47th Street.

The foreign are tenacious of their religions—there
must be more Greek Orthodox and Russian Orthodox
churches than in any other city outside of Europe—
and of their racial pride. The old Romanian who cleans your
suit has never seen Romania, but he speaks with his old accent; as one looks at his settled, impersonal, American face,
one sees the ghost person of another nation within its out-
lines, a face lost, often sad and puzzled. The Italian cop
stands operatically in the full sun at the corner of Union
Square; the nimble Greek with his four pairs of hands in the
grocer's has the avidity of Athens under that slick, standard air of city prosperity. It occasionally happens that you
go to restaurants in New York kept by the brother-in-law or
uncle, say, of the man who has the founding place in London, Naples, or Paris; you fall into family gossip, especially
with Italians, who are possibly more recent but who are
still entangled in the power politics of the European family
system. I once talked to an Irish waiter who rushed away
into the bar crying, "D'ye see that bloody Englishman? He
knows me father." I didn't, but I did know that his father
was a notorious leader of one of those "columns" of the
I.R.A. in the Irish Civil War.

In this quality of being lost and found there is the mixture of
the guilt, the sadness, the fading mind of exile with the ex-
cited wonder at life which is an essential New York note.
New York tolerance allows the latitude to civilization. People are left alone and are less brutally standardized than in
other cities. "Clearly"—these foreigners tell you with res-
ignation—"this is not Europe. But"—they suddenly
brighten, tense up, and get that look of celebration in their
eyes—"it is New York." That is to say, the miracle. Although New Yorkers of all kinds curse the city for its expense and its pressures, and though all foreigners think it is
the other foreigners who make it impossible, they are mad
about the place. There is no place like it in the world. And
although a Londoner or a Parisian will think the same about
their cities, here the feeling has a special quality: that of a

triumphant personal discovery of some new thing that is getting bigger, richer, higher, more various as every minute of the day goes by. They have come to a ball. And this is felt not only by the New Yorker with the foreign strain, but also by the men and women who come in from the other states, drawn by its wealth but even more by the chances, the freedom, and the privacy that a metropolis offers to human beings. Its very loneliness and ruthlessness are exciting. It is a preemptive if not a literal capital. Scott Fitzgerald speaks of his wife Zelda coming up because she wanted "luxury and largeness beyond anything her world provided," and that precisely describes the general feeling of many a newcomer.

What Makes New Yorkers Tick

by Calvin Trillin

Calvin Trillin, who considers himself a "resident out-of-towner" in Manhattan for 30 years, writes regularly for The New Yorker *and* The Nation. *His most recent book is* Enough's Enough (and Other Rules of Life). "What Makes New Yorkers Tick" *originally appeared in* TIME *in September 1990.*

In the first place, we have more weird-looking people in New York City than can be found in any other American city. Also, more rich people. We have so many rich people that I once came to the conclusion that other cities were sending us the rich people they wanted to get rid of ("Listen, if Frank down at the bank doesn't quit talking about how much his Jaguar cost, we're just going to have to put him in the next shipment to New York"). Some of the weird-looking people and some of the rich people are the same people. Why would a rich person want to look weird? As we New Yorkers like to say: Go know.

When I moved to New York, back in 1961, I remember saying that 90% of the people walking along the street in Manhattan would be interviewed in any other town, and the other 10% would be arrested. It's got a lot weirder since then.

Of course, it's got weirder everywhere since then. But someone in a silly getup in Houston or Cleveland or Denver has to be aware that everyone is looking at him. If a 300-lb. man costumed as Eleanor of Aquitaine walks onto a crosstown bus in New York carrying both an attaché case and a rib roast, the other passengers might glance up for a second, but then they'd go back to their tabloids. If you asked the driver why he didn't seem to be registering such a sight, he'd say, "Hey whadaya—kidding? I seen a million guys like that. You think I'm some kinda farmer or something?"

So if you're making a list of how New Yorkers differ from other Americans—even other city dwellers—write "funny looking" near the top. Also write "jaded" or maybe "blasé": New Yorkers have seen a million guys like that no matter what the guy is like. We've seen everything. We've seen everybody. We are not impressed. The common response of New Yorkers to the presence of the President in their city is not excitement but irritation: His motorcade is going to tie up traffic. He may think he's in town to address the United Nations or raise money at one of those fat-cat banquets at the Waldorf, but as far as New Yorkers are concerned, he is there to cause them aggravation. And why, as a matter of fact, is the United Nations in New York? Also to cause aggravation, this time by taking up a lot of curb space with diplomatic-plate-only parking zones. In the minds of true New Yorkers, an awful lot that happens in the world happens to cause them aggravation. In fact, "aggravation," in that particular usage, is basically a New York word. I know there are people who think it's a Yiddish word—nobody thinks it's an English word—but a Yiddish word and a New York word are the same thing. It's true that you can detect an Italian bounce to some New York phrases, and it's true that white students at expensive Manhattan private schools are as likely as Harlem teenagers to shout "Yo!" when they come across a friend, but I think the basic structure and inflection of the language New Yorkers speak owe their greatest debt to Yiddish. The only purely New York word I can think of—cockamamie—sounds Yiddish, even though it isn't. It means ridiculous or harebrained and is commonly used in such phrases as "another one of the mayor's cockamamie schemes."

A scheme thus classified was launched some years ago by the then mayor, Edward Koch, who had come back from China smitten with the idea of bicycle transportation. He had protective strips of concrete installed to create a bicycle lane up Sixth Avenue. As someone who schlepps around (as we say here) on an old Raleigh three-speed, I was pathetically grateful for the bike lane myself: I suppose that shows that no matter how long I live in New York, I am, at heart, an out-of-towner. The cabdrivers, of course, hated it ("He likes China so much, he shoulda stood in China"). Some storekeepers hated it. But who complained most bitterly about the bike lanes? The bicyclers. The true New York bicyclers complained that the bike lane was full of pedestrians and garment-center pushcarts and people who schlepped around on Raleigh three-speeds. And slush. "It's October," I said to the bicycler who made that complaint: "there's no slush in October." "When there's slush," he said, "the bike lane will have slush."

The bike-lane episode reminds me that you'd better put "contentious" near the top of that list, right under "funny looking." (Not just "funny looking" come to think of it, but also "funny": New York is the only city I've ever been in where almost everyone you meet on the street considers himself a comedian—a fact brought home to me a couple of years ago when a panhandler near my subway stop said to me, "Can you spare some change? I'd like to buy a few junk bonds.") In the matter of contentiousness, I once tried to indicate the difference between New York and the Midwest, where I grew up, by saying that in the Midwest if you approach someone who is operating a retail business and ask him if he has change for a quarter, he is not likely to call you a fascist. He is certainly not going to say, "G'wan—get lost." He would never say, "Ya jerky bastard, ya."

New Yorkers are not polite. If you asked a New York cabdriver why he wasn't more polite, he might say something like "Polite! Where do you think you are—Iowa or Indiana or one of them?" New York cabdrivers do not usually bother to distinguish among states that begin with *I*.

Earlier this year, some booster organization in New York got the idea of launching a campaign to make New Yorkers more polite. Talk about cockamamie ideas! What are they—crazy? Do they think this is Illinois or Idaho or someplace? In the first place, the whole idea of a booster organization is as foreign to New York as Girl Scout cookies. (Yes, I know that thousands of Girl Scout cookies are sold every year in places like Queens and Staten Island. You think I'm a farmer or something?) I have never heard of a New York Chamber of Commerce. If it exists, I suspect it spends most of its time putting out press releases about aggravations. Also, telling New Yorkers not to be rude is the equivalent of telling Neapolitans not to talk with their hands: it could render us speechless.

I don't think there's anything particularly surprising about the level of rudeness in New York. A lot of it is just show. New York has been portrayed in so many books and movies and stand-up acts that the stock characters know how to behave badly. They've all read their press clippings. The Jewish deli waiter knows what to say to an out-of-towner who asks if he could get a pastrami sandwich ("When I'm ready, I'll get" or "Listen, the pastrami here I wouldn't wish on Arafat"). The Irish cop knows how to act like an Irish cop who does not go overboard in showing respect to the citizenry. Some of the newer stock characters, like the Korean greengrocer and the Indian news dealer, aren't certain how to act yet—there haven't been enough movies about them—but when they do get it all hardened into a New York shtick, I rather doubt that they're going to sound like the flight attendant of the month.

Also, I believe rudeness tends to vary in direct proportion to the size of the city, so it's only natural that the largest city is the rudest. It isn't just that the little daily irritations tend to build up in a large city faster than they do in a small town; it's the anonymity. In a small town, what you shout at someone who makes a sudden turn in front of you without a signal is limited in nastiness by the realization that you might find yourself sitting beside that person the next day at the Kiwanis lunch or the PTA meeting. If the town is small enough, the chance that you'll never see the offending party again is nonexistent. That puts a sort of governor on your behavior. In New York, the odds are almost the opposite; you are almost certainly not going to see that person again. The governor is removed. Knowing that, you might do a lot worse than "Ya jerky bastard, ya."

Not you? Yes, you. Right at the top of the list you should write down that there's nothing genetic about any of this. New Yorkers weren't born that way. A lot of New Yorkers weren't even born in New York. Some of them were born on farms. I was born in Kansas City. If you moved to New York, you'd be a New Yorker, and you'd act like a New Yorker. You'd only glance for a moment at the guy costumed as Eleanor of Aquitaine. You'd scheme to get the last seat on the subway car. You'd become a comedian. You might even use harsh language with taxi drivers. You wouldn't behave that way? Well, how about Mother Teresa?

Mother Teresa! Right. In Calcutta, Mother Teresa is probably an absolute pussycat, but if she moved to New York, she'd be a New Yorker. A couple of years ago, I started to use a true story about Mother Teresa to illustrate how all New Yorkers, living in what I believe could be considered a rather challenging environment, find themselves trying to get a little edge. Around 1987, Mayor Koch was briefly hospitalized with a slight stroke, and a few days later he got a surprise visit from Mother Teresa, who happened to be in town to establish a hospice. She told him he had been in her prayers, and he took the occasion to say that New York was grateful for her presence and that she should let him know if there was any way he could be of assistance. She said that as a matter of fact, there was one thing he might do. It would be helpful at the hospice to have a reserved parking spot. So envision this scene: here is Mother Teresa, perhaps a saint, making a sick call on a man who has just had a stroke—and she's trying to hustle him for a parking spot. You've got to say it's a tough town.

3 Exploring Manhattan

Manhattan is, above all, a walker's city. Along its busy streets there's something else to look at every few yards. Attractions, many of them world-famous, are crowded close together on this narrow island, and because it has to grow up, not out, new layers are simply piled on top of the old. The city's character changes every few blocks, with quaint town houses shouldering sleek glass towers, gleaming gourmet supermarkets sitting around the corner from dusty thrift shops, and soot-smudged warehouses inhabited at street level by trendy neon-lit bistros. Many a visitor has been beguiled into walking a little farther, then a little farther still—"Let's just see what that copper dome and steeple belongs to . . ."—and ending up with a severe case of blisters. So be warned: Wear your most comfortable shoes, preferably sneakers, and take time along the way to stop and rest.

Our walking tours cover a great deal of ground, yet they only scratch the surface. If you plod dutifully from point to point, nose buried in this book, you'll miss half the fun. Look up at the tops of skyscrapers and you'll see a riot of mosaics, carvings, and ornaments. Go inside an intriguing office building and study its lobby decor; read the directory to find out what sorts of firms have their offices there. Peep around corners, even in crowded midtown, and you may find fountains, greenery, and sudden bursts of flowers. Find a bench or ledge to perch on, and take time just to watch the street life. New York has so many faces that every visitor can discover a different one.

Orientation

The map of Manhattan bears a Jekyll-and-Hyde aspect. The rational, Dr. Jekyll part prevails above 14th Street, where the streets form a regular grid pattern, imposed in 1811. Consecutively numbered streets run east and west (crosstown), while broad avenues, most of them also numbered, run north (uptown) or south (downtown). The chief exceptions are Broadway (which runs on a diagonal from East 14th to West 79th streets) and the thoroughfares that hug the shores of the Hudson and East rivers.

Fifth Avenue is the east–west dividing line for street addresses: in both directions, they increase in regular increments from there. For example, on 55th Street, the addresses 1–99 East 55th Street run from Fifth, past Madison, to Park (the equivalent of Fourth) avenues, 100–199 East 55th would be between Park and Third avenues, and so on; the addresses 1–99 West 55th Street are between Fifth and Sixth avenues, 100–199 West 55th would be between Sixth and Seventh avenues, and so forth. Above 59th Street, where Central Park interrupts the grid, West Side addresses start numbering at Central Park West, an extension of Eighth Avenue. Avenue addresses are much less regular, for the numbers begin wherever each avenue begins and increase at different increments. An address at 552 Third Avenue, for example, will not necessarily be anywhere near 552 Second Avenue. New Yorkers themselves cannot master the complexities of this system, so in their daily dealings they usually include cross-street references along with avenue addresses (as far as possible, we follow that custom in this book). New Yorkers also rely on the handy

Manhattan Neighborhoods

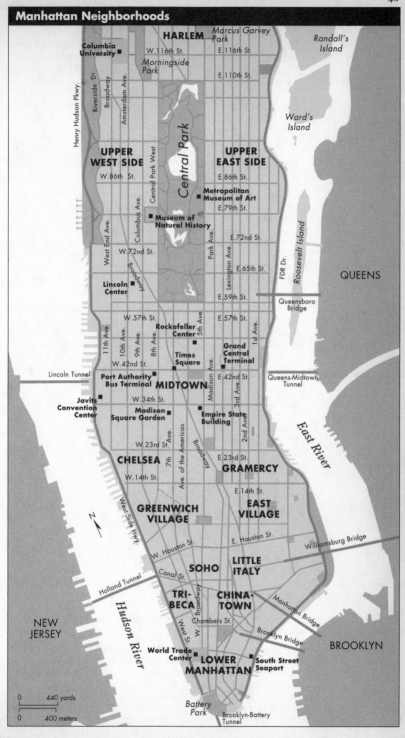

HARLEM
Marcus Garvey Park
Randall's Island

Columbia University
W.116th St.
E.116th St.

Morningside Park
E.110th St.

Henry Hudson Pkwy.
Riverside Dr.
Broadway
Amsterdam Ave.

UPPER WEST SIDE
Central Park
UPPER EAST SIDE

Ward's Island

W.86th St.
E.86th St.

Central Park West
Columbus Ave.
West End Ave.

Metropolitan Museum of Art
E.79th St.

Museum of Natural History

Park Ave.
Lexington Ave.

E.72nd St.

W.72nd St.
E.65th St.

FDR Dr.
Roosevelt Island

QUEENS

Lincoln Center
E.59th St.

Broadway

Queensboro Bridge

W.57th St.
W.57th Ave.

11th Ave.
10th Ave.
9th Ave.
8th Ave.

Rockefeller Center
5th Ave.

Grand Central Terminal

1st Ave.

Times Square
E.57th St.

W.42nd St.
Port Authority Bus Terminal
MIDTOWN
Madison Ave.
E.42nd St.
3rd Ave.

Lincoln Tunnel
Queens-Midtown Tunnel

Javits Convention Center
W.34th St.
Madison Square Garden
Empire State Building
2nd Ave.

East River

W.23rd St.

CHELSEA
Ave. of the Americas
Broadway
E.23rd St.
GRAMERCY

7th Ave.
W.14th St.
E.14th St.

West Side Hwy.
GREENWICH VILLAGE
EAST VILLAGE

W. Houston St.
E. Houston St.
Williamsburg Bridge

SOHO
LITTLE ITALY

Holland Tunnel
Canal St.

TRI-BECA
CHINA-TOWN

Manhattan Bridge

NEW JERSEY
Hudson River
West St.
Broadway
Chambers St.
Brooklyn Bridge

World Trade Center
LOWER MANHATTAN
South Street Seaport

BROOKLYN

0   440 yards

0   400 meters

Battery Park
Brooklyn-Battery Tunnel

Manhattan Address Locator (*see* Chapter 1), found in the front of the local phone book.

Below 14th Street—the area that was already settled before the 1811 grid was decreed—Manhattan streets reflect the disordered personality of Mr. Hyde. They may be aligned with the shoreline or they may twist along the route of an ancient cow path. Below 14th Street you'll find West 4th Street intersecting West 11th Street, Greenwich Street running roughly parallel to Greenwich Avenue, Leroy Street turning into St. Luke's Place for one block and then becoming Leroy again. There's an East Broadway and a West Broadway, both of which run north–south and neither of which is an extension of plain old Broadway. Logic won't help you below 14th Street; only a good street map and good directions will.

You may also be confused by the way New Yorkers use "uptown" and "downtown." These terms refer both to locations and to directions. Uptown means north of wherever you are at the moment; downtown means to the south. But Uptown and Downtown are also specific parts of the city (and, some would add, two very distinct states of mind). Unfortunately, there is no consensus about where these areas are: Downtown may mean anyplace from the tip of Lower Manhattan through Chelsea; it depends on the orientation of the speaker.

A similar situation exists with "East Side" and "West Side." Someone may refer to a location as "on the east side," meaning somewhere east of Fifth Avenue. A hotel described as being "on the west side" may be on West 42nd Street. But when New Yorkers speak of the East Side or the West Side, they usually mean the respective areas above 59th Street, on either side of Central Park. Be prepared for misunderstandings.

Exploring

Highlights for First-time Visitors

Rockefeller Center, Tour 1
Times Square, Tour 3
The United Nations, Tour 3
The Metropolitan Museum of Art, Tour 5
Central Park, Tour 7
The American Museum of Natural History, Tour 8
The Statue of Liberty, Tour 17
The World Trade Center, Tour 17
South Street Seaport, Tour 18
The Brooklyn Bridge, Tour 19

Tour 1: Rockefeller Center

Numbers in the margin correspond with points of interest on the Midtown map.

When movies and TV shows are set in Manhattan, they often start with a panning shot of Rockefeller Center, for no other city scene—except perhaps the downtown skyline—so clearly says "New York." Begun during the Great Depression of the 1930s by John D. Rockefeller, this 19-building complex occupies nearly 22 acres of prime real estate between Fifth and Seventh avenues and 47th and 52nd streets. Its central cluster of buildings are smooth shafts of warm-hued limestone, stream-lined with glistening aluminum, but the real genius of the complex's design was its intelligent use of public space: plazas, concourses, and street-level shops that create a sense of community for the nearly quarter of a million human beings who use it daily. Restaurants, shoe-repair shops, doctors' offices, barbershops, banks, a post office, bookstores, clothing shops, variety stores—all are accommodated within the center, and all parts of the complex are linked by underground passageways.

Rockefeller Center helped turn midtown into New York City's second "downtown" area, which now rivals the Wall Street area in the number of its prestigious tenants. The center itself is a capital of the communications industry, containing the headquarters of a TV network (NBC), several major publishing companies (Time-Warner, McGraw-Hill, and Simon & Schuster), and the world's largest news-gathering organization, the Associated Press.

In many ways, Rockefeller Center is the heart of New York City. Close to the majority of hotels, this is a logical first stop for any visitor to the city.

Let's begin the tour with a proud symbol of the center's might: the huge statue of Atlas supporting the world that stands sentry before the **International Building** (5th Ave. between 50th and 51st Sts.). The building, with a lobby inspired by ancient Greece and fitted with Grecian marble from the island of Tenos, houses many foreign consulates, international airlines, and a passport office from which lines of last-minute applicants overflow onto Fifth Avenue throughout the summer.

One block south on Fifth Avenue, between 49th and 50th streets, you'll come to the head of the **Channel Gardens,** a promenade with six pools surrounded by flowerbeds filled with seasonal plantings, conceived by artists, floral designers, and sculptors—10 shows a season. They are called the Channel Gardens because they separate the British building to the north from the French building to the south (above each building's entrance is a coat of arms bearing that country's national symbols). The French building contains among other shops the **Librairie de France,** which sells French-language books, periodicals, and records; its surprisingly large basement contains a Spanish bookstore and a foreign dictionary store.

At the foot of the Channel Gardens is perhaps the most famous sight in Rockefeller Center (if not all of New York): the great gold-leaf statue of the fire-stealing Greek hero **Prometheus,** sprawled on his ledge above the **Lower Plaza.** A quotation from Aeschylus is carved into the red granite wall behind, and 50 jets of water spray around the statue. The plaza's trademark ice-skating rink is open from late September through April; the rest of the year, it becomes an open-air café. In December the plaza is decorated with an enormous live Christmas tree. On the Esplanade above the Lower Plaza, flags of the United Nations' members alternate with flags of the states.

The backdrop to the Lower Plaza is the center's tallest tower, the 70-story **GE Building** (formerly the RCA Building until GE acquired RCA in 1986), occupying the block bounded by Rockefeller Plaza, Avenue of the Americas (which New Yorkers call Sixth Avenue), and 49th and 50th streets. The block-long

Tours 1-3: Midtown

Columbus Circle

Carnegie Hall

Grand Army Plaza

W. 57th St.
W. 56th St.
W. 55th St.
W. 54th St.
W. 53rd St.
W. 52nd St.
W. 51st St.

Ninth Ave.

THEATER DISTRICT

W. 50th St.

Radio City Music Hall

W. 49th St.
W. 48th St.
W. 47th St.
W. 46th St.
W. 45th St.
W. 44th St.
W. 43rd St.
W. 42nd St.
W. 41st St.
W. 40th St.
W. 39th St.
W. 38th St.

Eighth Ave.

Port Authority Bus Terminal

Times Square

Seventh Ave.

Broadway

Avenue of the Americas (Sixth Ave.)

Bryant Park

Fifth Ave.

Algonquin Hotel, **26**
American Craft Museum, **9**
AT&T World Headquarters, **18**
Bryant Park, **24**
Chrysler Building, **29**
Daily News Building, **30**
Duffy Square, **23**

Ford Foundation Building, **31**
GE Building, **3**
General Motors Building, **16**
Grand Central Terminal, **28**
IBM Building, **17**
International Building, **1**
ICP Mid-Town, **25**
Lever House, **19**
Lower Plaza, **2**

McGraw-Hill Building (1221 6th Ave.), **6**
Museum of Modern Art, **10**
Museum of Television and Radio, **11**
New York Public Library, **27**
The Plaza, **15**
Radio City Music Hall, **4**
St. Bartholomew's Church, **21**

St. Patrick's Cathedral, **12**
St. Thomas Church, **13**
Seagram Building, **20**
Time & Life Building, **8**
Times Square, **22**
Trump Tower, **14**
1211 6th Ave., **5**
1251 6th Ave., **7**
United Nations Headquarters, **32**

street called Rockefeller Plaza, officially a private street (to maintain that status, it closes to all traffic on one day a year), is often choked with celebrities' black limousines, for this is the headquarters of the NBC television network. From this building emanated some of the first TV programs ever; the "Today" show has been broadcast from here since 1952, and a shot of this building is included in the opening credit sequences of "Saturday Night Live" and "Late Night with David Letterman," both taped here.

One way to see what goes on inside is to request free tickets to one of the three live-audience shows taped in Manhattan at NBC (besides "Saturday Night" and "Letterman," there's also the syndicated "Donahue") by sending a postcard to NBC Tickets (30 Rockefeller Plaza, New York, NY 10112). Unfortunately, "Letterman" is usually booked for a year and a half in advance, "Donahue" for about six months, but both shows have standby waiting lists; "Saturday Night" uses a lottery system. Another way to get behind the scenes is to spend $7.25 to take a tour of the NBC studios: One leaves every 15 minutes, 9:30–4:00, Monday through Saturday, and on Sundays during the summer; Thursdays 9:30–8.

You can also buy a T-shirt, ashtray, Frisbee, or other paraphernalia bearing the logos of your favorite NBC programs at a boutique in the magnificent black granite lobby. As you enter the building from Rockefeller Plaza, look up at the ceiling mural above the entrance: Wherever you stand, the figure seems to be facing you. Take time also to study the allegorical murals above the entrance on Sixth Avenue. The old rooftop observation deck is, unfortunately, closed now, but you can take an elevator to the 65th floor to enjoy the spectacular view with drinks or a meal at the **Rainbow Room** (*see* Chapter 8).

Escalators in the GE Building will take you down to the marble catacombs that connect the various components of Rockefeller Center. There's a lot to see down under: restaurants in all price ranges, from the chic American Festival Cafe to McDonald's; a historical exhibit; a post office and clean public rest rooms (scarce in midtown); and just about every kind of store. To find your way around, consult the strategically placed directories or obtain the free "Shops and Services Guide" at the GE Building information desk (where you can also pick up a brochure for a self-guided walking tour). *Center*, a free bimonthly magazine containing articles about Rockefeller Center, a calendar of events, and capsule descriptions of its restaurants, is available in the lobbies of most of the complex's buildings.

NBC isn't the only network headquartered in Manhattan. CBS is located in a black monolith, popularly called Black Rock, at Sixth Avenue and 53rd Street. ABC, once a close neighbor, has now moved its main office to 66th Street on the West Side.

Across 50th Street from the GE Building is America's largest ❹ indoor theater, the 6,000-seat **Radio City Music Hall.** Home of the fabled Rockettes chorus line (which actually started out in St. Louis in 1925), Radio City was built as a movie theater with a stage suitable for live shows as well. Its days as a first-run movie house are long over, but after an announced closing in 1978 Radio City has had an amazing comeback, producing concerts, awards presentations, and special events, along with its own Christmas and Easter extravaganzas. On most days you can tour the premises (tel. 212/632–4041 for prices and availability).

Later additions to Rockefeller Center include Sixth Avenue's skyscraper triplets—the first between 47th and 48th streets, the second, the **McGraw-Hill Building,** between 48th and 49th streets, and the third between 49th and 50th streets—and their cousin immediately to the north, the **Time & Life Building,** between 50th and 51st streets. All have street-level plazas, but the most interesting is McGraw-Hill's, where a 50-foot steel sun triangle points to the seasonal positions of the sun at noon and a pool demonstrates the relative size of the planets.

Time Out   For supercasual eating when the weather is good, the **Sixth Avenue food vendors** near Rockefeller Center offer the best selection in the city. These "à la cart" diners offer far more than trite hot dogs—there's a truly international menu of tacos, falafel, souvlaki, tempura, Indian curry, Afghani kofta kebabs, or Caribbean beef jerky. Food carts are licensed and inspected by the Department of Health, and the price is right: No dish is more than $5, and most cost much less.

Fifty-third Street between Sixth and Fifth avenues is a mini-Museum Row. The **American Craft Museum** spotlights the work of contemporary American and international craftspersons working in clay, glass, fabric, wood, metal, or paper. *40 W. 53rd St., tel. 212/956–3535. Admission: $3.50 adults, $1.50 students and senior citizens. Open Tues. 10–8, Wed.–Sun. 10–5.*

The **Museum of Modern Art** (MOMA) is a bright and airy six-story structure built around a secluded sculpture garden. All the important movements of art since 1880 are represented here, and the collection includes not only painting and sculpture but also photography, architecture, decorative arts, drawings, prints, illustrated books, and films. After only a quick look-see, you'll be able to drop terms such as Cubism, Surrealism, Abstract Expressionism, Minimalism, and Post-Modernism as though you'd known them all your life. Some of the world's most famous paintings are displayed on the second floor: Van Gogh's *Starry Night,* Picasso's *Les Demoiselles d'Avignon,* Matisse's *Dance.* The superstars of American art appear on the third floor: Andrew Wyeth, Andy Warhol, Jackson Pollock, Frank Stella, and Mark Rothko, to name but a few. Leave time to sit outside in the Sculpture Garden, and don't miss the classic office furniture and Paris subway entrance gate in the fourth-floor Architecture and Design Collection. Afternoon and evening film shows, mostly foreign films and classics, are free with the price of admission; tickets are distributed in the lobby on the day of the performance, and often they go fast. Programs change daily; call 212/708–9500 for a schedule. *11 W. 53rd St., tel. 212/708–9400. Admission: $7 adults, $4 students, $4 senior citizens, under 16 free. Pay what you wish Thurs. 5–9. Open Fri.–Tues. 11–6, Thurs. 11–9.*

One block south, the **Museum of Television and Radio** presents special screenings, usually retrospectives of the work of a particular radio or TV star or of an era in TV and radio history. Visitors can also explore items from the museum's stupendous collection of more than 25,000 TV shows, 10,000 commercials, and 15,000 radio programs. *25 W. 52nd St., tel. 212/752–7684.*

Suggested donation: $4 adults, $3 students, $2 senior citizens and under 13. Open Tues. noon–8, Wed.–Sat. noon–5.

Tour 2: Midtown from Fifth to Park Avenues

Numbers in the margin correspond with points of interest on the Midtown map.

The stretch of Fifth Avenue upward from Rockefeller Center glitters with world-famous shops, but the rents are even higher along East 57th Street, a parade of very exclusive smaller shops and upmarket art galleries (*see* Chapter 7). The area is also studded with handsome churches—relics of an era when this was a district of millionaires' mansions—as well as some of the most striking skyscrapers of the later 20th century.

The string of stores begins right across the street from Rockefeller Center's Channel Gardens (*see* Tour 1, above), with no less than **Saks Fifth Avenue** (5th Ave. and 50th St.), the flagship of the national department store chain. On the next block is Gothic-style **St. Patrick's,** the Roman Catholic Cathedral of New York. Dedicated to the patron saint of the Irish—then and now one of New York's principal ethnic groups—the white marble and stone structure was begun in 1858, consecrated in 1879, and completed in 1906. Among the statues in the alcoves around the nave is a striking modern interpretation of the first American-born saint, Mother Elizabeth Seton. From outside, catch one of the city's most photographed views: the ornate white spires of St. Pat's against the black glass curtain of **Olympic Tower,** a multiuse building of shops, offices, and luxury apartments.

Cartier, Inc. displays its wares in a jewel box of a turn-of-the-century mansion on the southeast corner of 52nd Street and Fifth Avenue; similar houses used to line this street, many of their occupants were parishioners of **St. Thomas Church** (5th Ave. at 53rd St.), an Episcopal institution that has occupied the site since 1911. The impressive huge stone reredos behind the altar holds the statues of more than 50 apostles, saints, martyrs, missionaries, and church figures.

On the northwest corner of Fifth Avenue and 54th Street, you'll see the imposing bulk of the **University Club,** a granite palace built by New York's leading turn-of-the-century architects McKim, Mead & White, for this exclusive midtown men's club, one of several that only recently have begun accepting women members. Pick out the crests of various prestigious universities above its windows. On two other corners of this intersection you'll find two branches of the **Gucci** leather and clothing enterprise.

Fifth Avenue Presbyterian Church, a grand brownstone church (1875), sits on the northwest corner of Fifth Avenue and 55th Street. **Steuben Glass** occupies a ground-floor showroom in the green-glass tower at Fifth Avenue and 56th Street; across the street, **Harry Winston** (718 5th Ave.) has a spectacular selection of fine jewelry. Next door is the recently relocated designer fashion store **Henri Bendel** (712–716 5th Ave.); the René Lalique art-glass windows from 1912 on the facade can be viewed at close range from balconies ringing the four-story atrium. Despite its Fort Knox–like Art Deco entrance, **Tiffany & Co.** (727 5th Ave. at 57th St.) is less intimidating and perhaps somewhat less expensive than you may fear. One quintessential New York movie, *Breakfast at Tiffany's*, opens with Audrey Hepburn, dressed in an evening gown, emerging from a yellow cab at dawn to stand here window-shopping with a coffee and Danish.

⑭ A more recent addition to Manhattan's list of attractions is **Trump Tower,** on Fifth Avenue between 56th and 57th streets, an exclusive 68-story apartment and office building named for its developer, Donald Trump. The grand Fifth Avenue entrance leads into a glitzy six-story shopping atrium paneled in pinkish-orange marble and trimmed with lustrous brass. A fountain cascades against one wall, drowning out the clamor of the city. In further contrast to the real world, every inch of Trump Tower is kept gleaming, and security is omnipresent but discreet. Shops are chic and tony, among them Cartier, Bucellati, Abercrombie & Fitch, and Asprey.

Returning to Fifth Avenue, cross 57th Street to visit **Bergdorf Goodman,** with its designer boutiques and, across the avenue, a complete men's store. **Van Cleef & Arpels** jewelers is located within Bergdorf's 57th Street corner.

Cross 58th Street to **Grand Army Plaza,** the open space along Fifth Avenue between 58th and 60th streets. The southern block features the Pulitzer Fountain, donated by publisher Joseph Pulitzer of Pulitzer Prize fame. Appropriately enough for this ritzy area, the fountain is crowned by a female figure representing Abundance. When the fountain is dry (as it is much of the time), its rim becomes a perch for tourists and office workers pausing to get a bit of sun. The block to the north holds a gilded equestrian statue of Civil War general William Tecumseh Sherman; beyond it is a grand entrance to Central Park (*see* Tour 7, below).

⑮ Appropriately named **The Plaza,** the famous hotel (*see* Chapter 9) at the western edge of this square is a registered historical landmark built in 1907, now owned by the Trump organization. Its architect, Henry Hardenbergh, was the same man who designed the rather dour Dakota apartment building (*see* Tour 8, below), but here he achieved a sprightly birthday-cake effect with white-glazed brick busily decorated and topped off with a copper-and-slate mansard roof. The hotel has been featured in many movies, from Alfred Hitchcock's *North by Northwest* to more recent films such as *Arthur* and *Crocodile Dundee*. Among the many upper-crust parties that have taken place in the Plaza's ballroom was Truman Capote's Black and White Ball of 1966, attended by everyone who was anyone—all dressed, naturally, in black and white.

Time Out The intimate front bar at **Jean Lafitte** (68 W. 58th St., tel. 212/751–2323) is an unusually relaxed place in this busy area of New York. While waiting for a table at this pleasant French bistro, luxuriate over your drink at the bar.

⑯ Adjacent to Grand Army Plaza stands the **General Motors Building,** a 50-story tower of Georgia marble. One section of the main-floor lobby displays a dozen or so shiny new GM vehicles. The other part of the lobby is the flagship of the legendary **F.A.O. Schwarz** toy store, with its fantastic mechanical clock right inside the front doors. Bigger than it looks from outside, the toy-o-rama offers a vast, wondrously fun selection, although it definitely tends toward expensive imports. Browsing here should bring out the child in everyone, as it did in the movie *Big*, when Tom Hanks and his boss got caught up in tap-dancing on a giant keyboard.

Return to 57th Street and Fifth Avenue, and head east. Stay on the north side of the street to visit **Chanel** (appropriately located at No. 5 E. 57th St.), **Burberrys Ltd.** (9 E. 57th St.), **Hermès,** (11 E. 57th St.), **Louis Vuitton** (51 E. 57th St.), and gizmo shop supreme, **Hammacher Schlemmer** (147 E. 57th St.). In two sleekly art deco subterranean levels, **Place des Antiquaires** (125 E. 57th St.) is an ultra–high-class shopping mall where several dozen of the city's top art and antiques dealers operate out of plate-glass stalls. Some shops have very narrowly defined specialties: Lune, for example, sells almost nothing but antique fans. Whether or not you're in the market for these pricey items, browsing can be fun.

17 At Madison Avenue and 57th Street, look up at the **IBM Building,** a five-sided sheath of dark gray-green granite and glass by Edward Larrabee Barnes. On the ground level there's the entrance to the subterranean **IBM Gallery of Science and Art,** which presents a variety of temporary art shows and the permanent science exhibition *Think,* including lasers, magnets, and superconductors. *Tel. 212/745–3500. Admission free. Open Tues.–Sat. 11–6.*

Time Out At the 56th Street corner, step into IBM's high, cool atrium, one of the most inviting public spaces in town. Small marble-topped tables and wrought-iron chairs are provided, and a small lunchtime café serves those who've come without their brown-bag lunch. The atrium closes at 10 PM.

18 At Madison Avenue and 55th Street, pop into the **AT&T World Headquarters,** designed by architect Philip Johnson. Unlike the sterile ice-cube-tray buildings of Sixth Avenue, AT&T's rose granite columns, its regilded statue of the winged *Golden Boy* in the lobby, and its peculiar "Chippendale" roof have made it an instant landmark for New Yorkers, who consider it the first Post-Modern skyscraper. An adjacent structure houses the **AT&T InfoQuest Center,** a museum of telecommunications technology. Entrants receive an access card on which they encode their names; they then use the card to operate displays on lightwave communication, microelectronics, and computer software. Displays are neither terribly technical nor (on behalf of AT&T) self-serving. Some exhibits—such as those where you program your own music video and rearrange a scrambled picture of your face—are downright entertaining. *Madison Ave. and 56th St., tel. 212/605–5555. Admission free. Open Tues. 10–9, Wed.–Sun. 10–6.*

If you head west on 55th Street, you'll pass a narrow limestone town house that's home to the New York **Friars Club,** a venerable show-biz institution founded in 1956, best known for its banquets at which celebrity guests of honor are mercilessly "roasted" by their peers. Friars have included Frank Sinatra, Milton Berle, Sammy Davis, Jr., and Henny Youngman.

Turn right onto broad Park Avenue to see some of the most important buildings in modern architecture. On the corner of 54th Street, peer to your left (east) toward Lexington Avenue, where you can see the soaring, luminescent white shaft of the

Citicorp Center (1977), designed by Hugh Stubbins & Associates. Its most striking feature is the angled top, originally intended to carry an immense solar-energy collector that was never installed. At street level, the Citicorp Center has a pleasant mall of restaurants and shops.

Directly in front of you, on the west side of Park Avenue between 53rd and 54th streets, is **Lever House,** a 1952 creation by Gordon Bunshaft, of Skidmore, Owings, & Merrill. It's basically a sheer, slim glass box, resting on one end of a one-story-thick shelf that seems to float above the street, balanced on square chrome columns. Because the tower occupies only half of the space above the lower floors, a great deal of air space is left open, and the tower's side wall displays a reflection of its neighbors.

On the other side of Park Avenue, one block south between 52nd and 53rd streets, the **Seagram Building** is the only New York building by German architect Mies van der Rohe, a leading interpreter of the International Style. This, too, is a simple boxlike tower, although the black metal and bronze glass exterior looks more severe than Lever House's cool blue-green. Built in 1958, it created a sense of spaciousness with its ground-level plaza, an innovation at the time that has since become a common element in urban skyscraper design. Inside is one of New York's most venerated restaurants, **The Four Seasons** (*see* Chapter 8).

For a pleasing contrast, walk down to 51st Street, where you'll see **St. Bartholomew's Church** nestled amid the skyscrapers. Built in 1919, it has rounded arches, while its intricate tiled dome is Byzantine. Church fathers have been eager to sell the air space over St. Bart's, to take advantage of the stratospheric property values in this part of town, but landmark preservation forces have so far prevented any such move, thereby protecting this welcome gulf of sky in midtown.

Tour 3: Across 42nd Street

Numbers in the margin correspond with points of interest on the Midtown map.

As midtown Manhattan's central axis, 42nd Street ties together several major points of interest, from the United Nations on the East River, past the Grand Central railroad terminal, to Times Square. (The crosstown bus route continues on to the Jacob K. Javits Convention Center near the Hudson River.) While it's never less than a busy commercial thoroughfare, a few blocks of 42nd Street are downright disreputable, living up to the often-held image of New York as a den of pickpockets, porno houses, prostitutes, and destitutes. An ambitious plan to redevelop Times Square is currently under way, but in the meantime try to imagine West 42nd Street as a scene out of the movie *Taxi Driver*, lyrical in its squalor.

While it may not exactly be the Crossroads of the World, as it is often called, **Times Square** is one of New York's principal energy centers. It's one of many New York City "squares" that are actually triangles formed by the angle of Broadway slashing across a major avenue—in this case, crossing Seventh Avenue at 42nd Street. The square itself is occupied by the former Times Tower, now resheathed in white marble and called **One**

Times Square Plaza. When the *New York Times* moved into its new headquarters on December 31, 1904, it publicized the event with a fireworks show at midnight, thus starting a New Year's Eve tradition. Each December 31, workmen on this roof lower a 200-pound ball down the flagpole by hand, just as they have since 1908. The huge intersection below is mobbed with revelers, and when the ball hits bottom on the stroke of midnight, pandemonium ensues.

The present headquarters of the *New York Times* (229 W. 43rd St.) occupies much of the block between Seventh and Eighth avenues; look for the blue delivery vans lined up along 43rd Street. From 44th to 51st streets, the cross streets west of Broadway are lined with some 30 major theaters (*see* Chapter 10). This has been the city's main theater district since the turn of the century; movie theaters joined the fray beginning in the 1920s. As the theaters drew crowds of people in the evenings, advertisers began to mount huge electric signs here, which gave the intersection its distinctive nighttime glitter. Even the developers who want to change this area intend to preserve the signs, making them bigger and brighter with new technology.

㉓ The northern triangle of the intersection, which reaches up to 47th Street, is named **Duffy Square** after World War I hero Father Francis P. Duffy, the "Fighting Chaplain," who later was pastor of a theater district church on West 42nd Street. Besides the suitably military statue of Father Duffy, there's also one of George M. Cohan, the indomitable trouper who wrote "Yankee Doodle Dandy." Today Duffy Square is an important place to visit for the **TKTS discount ticket booth,** which sells half-price tickets to Broadway and some Off-Broadway shows (*see* Chapter 10). Some days it seems that almost every show in town is up for grabs; at other times there may be nothing available but a few long-running hits and some sleepers. The lines may look long, but they move surprisingly fast.

Until recently, the only live theater on 42nd Street itself was provided for decades by a group of thriving Off-Broadway playhouses, often called **Theatre Row** (*see* Chapter 10), between Ninth and Tenth avenues. As you walk east, peek into No. 330, between Eighth and Ninth avenues, behind the Port Authority Bus Terminal. Originally the McGraw-Hill Building, it was designed in 1931 by Raymond Hood, who later worked on Rockefeller Center. The lobby is an Art Deco wonder of opaque glass and stainless steel. The block between Seventh and Eighth avenues that was once the heart of the theater district is now a sleazy strip of X-rated bookstores, peep shows, and movie theaters; the sidewalks are full of loiterers and panhandlers who drift between here and the Port Authority bus station at 42nd Street and Eighth Avenue. The most prominent vestige of the old 42nd Street is the **New Amsterdam** (214 W. 42nd St.), a designated landmark that opened in 1903. Today the New Amsterdam is "dark"—lying fallow in anticipation of the area's redevelopment—but in its prime it was an opulent two-theater facility that showcased the likes of Eddie Cantor, Will Rogers, Fanny Brice, and the Ziegfeld Girls.

Heading east on 42nd Street, you'll pass **Hotaling's News** (142 W. 42nd St., tel. 212/840–1868), a bustling little shop that carries more than 220 daily newspapers from throughout the United States, most issues only a day or two old. The rear section stocks current newspapers, magazines, and foreign-language books from more than 40 countries.

At Sixth Avenue you'll see steps rising into the shrubbery and ❷❹ trees of **Bryant Park,** named for the poet and editor William Cullen Bryant (1794–1878). This was the site of America's first World's Fair, the Crystal Palace Exhibition of 1853–54; today it's the backyard of the New York Public Library's central research branch. For a while the park was getting rather shaggy, but an elaborate landscape and restoration program should be completed by the time you read this. One reason to enter the park, in any case, is to visit the **Bryant Park Discount Dance and Music Ticket Booth,** which, in a setup similar to TKTS, sells tickets for music and dance performances throughout the city (*see* Chapter 10).

A ground-level passage through the **City University Graduate Center** (33 W. 42nd St.) connects 42nd and 43rd streets; walk through to look at the art exhibits. At the northwest corner of Sixth Avenue and 43rd Street, the International Center of ❷❺ Photography (*see* Tour 5, below) has a newer (1989) branch, **ICP Mid-Town,** which presents several photography shows a year in an ultracontemporary, multilevel space. *Tel. 212/768–4680. Admission: $3 adults, $1.50 students, $1 senior citizens and children under 12. Open Tues., Wed., and Fri.–Sun. 11–6, Thurs. 11–8.*

❷❻ A block north, you'll see the **Algonquin Hotel** (59 W. 44th St.; *see* Chapter 9), which is surprisingly unpretentious considering its history as a haunt of well-known writers and actors. Its most famous association is with a witty group of literary Manhattanites who gathered in its lobby and dining rooms in the 1920s—a clique that included short-story writer Dorothy Parker, humorist Robert Benchley, playwright George S. Kaufman, and actress Tallulah Bankhead. One reason they met here was the hotel's proximity to the former offices of *The New Yorker* magazine (*see* below).

Next door to the Algonquin is the somewhat dingier (and cheaper) **Iroquois Hotel** (49 W. 44th St.), where struggling actor James Dean lived in the early 1950s. Across the street is the **Royalton Hotel** (44 W. 44th St.; *see* Chapter 9), chicly redone by French designer Philippe Starck. You might want to step into its lobby for a peek, but unless your clothes are suitably trendy, you may be hustled along by the staff. Next door, at 42 West 44th Street, is the **Association of the Bar of the City of New York,** with a neoclassical facade resembling the courthouses where its litigating members spend so much of their time.

Back on the north side of the street, at 37 West 44th Street is the **New York Yacht Club,** former longtime home of the America's Cup trophy. Notice its swelling windowfronts, looking just like the sterns of ships, complete with stone-carved water splashing over the sill. The redbrick **Harvard Club** (27 W. 44th St.) echoes the Harvard campus with its modest Georgian-style architecture. Across the street at 28 West 44th Street is the unprepossessing entrance to the building where, until recently, *The New Yorker* magazine originally was put together; now the magazine's unpretentious offices are located at 20 West 43rd Street. At 20 West 44th, the **Mechanics' and Tradesmen's Institute Building,** in a turn-of-the-century prep school building, has a wonderful library in a three-story-high hall; here you'll also find the intriguing **Mossman Collection of Locks,** open free to the public (tel. 212/840–1840; open weekdays 11–1, 2–4, except the first Wed. of every month).

At the corner of Fifth Avenue, look left to notice the large clock on a pedestal set in the Fifth Avenue sidewalk, a relic of an era when only rich people could afford watches. Then turn right and walk south. Between 40th and 42nd streets on Fifth Avenue, you'll find the central research building of the **New York Public Library.** This 1911 masterpiece of Beaux Arts design was financed largely by John Jacob Astor, whose previous library building downtown has since been turned into the Public Theater (*see* Tour 13, below). Its grand front steps are guarded by two crouching marble lions—dubbed "Patience" and "Fortitude" by Mayor Fiorello La Guardia, who said he visited the facility to "read between the lions." After admiring the white marble neoclassical facade (crammed with statues, as is typical of Beaux Arts buildings), walk through the bronze front doors into the grand marble lobby with its sweeping double staircase. Turn left and peek into the Periodicals Room, decorated with trompe l'oeil paintings by Richard Haas commemorating New York's importance as a publishing center. Then take a (quiet) look upstairs at the huge, high-ceilinged main reading room, a haven of scholarly calm, or visit the current exhibition in the art gallery. Among the treasures you might see are Gilbert Stuart's portrait of George Washington, Charles Dickens's desk, and Thomas Jefferson's own handwritten copy of the Declaration of Independence. Free one-hour tours, each as individual as the library volunteer who leads it, are given Monday through Saturday at 11 AM and 2 PM. *Tel. 212/930–0800. Open Mon.–Wed. 10–8:45, Thurs.–Sat. 10–5:45.*

Continue east on 42nd Street to **Grand Central Terminal** (not a "station," as many people call it, since all runs begin or end here). Constructed between 1903 and 1913, this Manhattan landmark was originally designed by a Minnesota architectural firm and later gussied up with Beaux Arts ornamentation. Stop on the south side of 42nd Street to admire the three huge windows separated by columns, and the Beaux Arts clock and sculpture crowning the facade above the elevated roadway (Park Avenue is routed around Grand Central's upper story). Go in the side doors on Vanderbilt Avenue to enter the cavernous main concourse, with its 12-story-high ceiling displaying the constellations of the zodiac. Unfortunately, the terminal has in recent years become a magnet for homeless people, and the once-grand waiting rooms and rest rooms have become shabby indeed. But it's worth a visit, especially at rush hour, when this immense room crackles with the frenzy of scurrying commuters, dashing every which way. *Free tours Wed. at 12:30 PM, tel. 935–3960.*

On the southwest corner of Park Avenue and 42nd Street, directly opposite Grand Central, the **Whitney Museum of American Art at Philip Morris** (120 Park Ave.) occupies the ground floor of the Philip Morris Building. Each year this free branch of the Whitney Museum (*see* Tour 5, below) presents five successive exhibitions of 20th-century painting and sculpture. An espresso bar and seating areas make it a much more agreeable place to rest than anywhere in Grand Central.

The southeast corner of 42nd and Park is a major departure point for buses to the three New York area airports, and upstairs at 100 East 42nd Street you'll find ticket counters for most major U.S. airlines. Next door is the main office of the **Bowery Savings Bank** (110 E. 42nd St.), whose massive arches and 70-foot-high marble columns give it a commanding presence. At the end of the block is the **Chanin Building** (122 E. 42nd St.), notable for the geometric Art Deco patterns that adorn its facade. Across the street you'll see the **Grand Hyatt** (*see* Chapter 9), which was created by wrapping a new black glass exterior around the former Commodore Hotel.

㉙ Ask New Yorkers to name their favorite skyscraper and most will choose the Art Deco **Chrysler Building** at 42nd Street and Lexington Avenue. Although the Chrysler Corporation itself moved out a long time ago, this graceful shaft culminating in a stainless-steel spire still captivates the eye and the imagination. The building has no observation deck, but you can go inside its elegant dark lobby, which is faced with African marble and covered with a ceiling mural that salutes transportation and human endeavor.

㉚ New York's blue-collar tabloid, the *Daily News*, is produced in the **Daily News Building** (220 E. 42nd St.), an Art Deco tower designed with brown-brick spandrels and windows to make it seem loftier than its 37 stories. Step into the lobby for a look at its revolving illuminated globe, 12 feet in diameter; the floor is laid out as a gigantic compass, with bronze lines indicating air mileage from principal world cities to New York. A small gallery displays *News* photos.

㉛ The **Ford Foundation Building** (320 E. 43rd St., with an entrance on 42nd St.) encloses a 12-story, ⅓-acre greenhouse. With a terraced garden, a still pool, and a couple of dozen full-grown trees as centerpieces, the Ford garden is open to the public—for tranquil strolling, not for picnics—weekdays from 9 to 5.

Climb the steps along 42nd Street between First and Second avenues to enter **Tudor City,** a self-contained complex of a dozen buildings featuring half-timbering and lots of stained glass. Constructed between 1925 and 1928, two of the apartment buildings of this residential enclave originally had no east-side windows, lest the tenants be forced to gaze at the slaughterhouses, breweries, and glue factories then located along the East River. Today, however, they're missing a wonderful view of the United Nations Headquarters; you'll have to walk to the terrace at the end of 43rd Street to overlook the UN. This will place you at the head of the **Sharansky Steps** (named for Natan—formerly Anatoly—Sharansky, the Soviet dissident), which run along the **Isaiah Wall** (inscribed "They Shall Beat Their Swords Into Plowshares"); you'll also look down into **Ralph J. Bunche Park** (named for the black American UN undersecretary) and **Raoul Wallenberg Walk** (named for the Swedish diplomat and World War II hero).

㉜ The **United Nations Headquarters** complex occupies a lushly landscaped 18-acre riverside tract just east of First Avenue between 42nd and 48th streets. Its rose garden is especially pleasant to stroll in, although picnicking is strictly forbidden. A line of flagpoles with banners representing the current roster of 159 member nations stands before the striking 550-foot-high slab of the Secretariat Building, with the domed General Assembly Building nestled at its side. The headquarters were

designed in 1947–53 by an international team of architects led
by Wallace Harrison. You can enter the General Assembly
Building at the 46th Street door; the interior corridors overflow with imaginatively diverse artwork donated by member
nations. Free tickets to most sessions are available on a first-
come, first-served basis 15 minutes before sessions begin; pick
them up in the General Assembly lobby. Visitors can take early
luncheon in the Delegates Dining Room (jacket required for
men) or eat anytime in the public coffee shop. *Tel. 212/963–
7713. Open daily 9:15–4:45. 1–hr. tours leave the General Assembly lobby every 15–20 min. Tour admission: $5.50 adults,
$3.50 students. Children under 5 not permitted.*

Tour 4: Murray Hill to Union Square

*Numbers in the margin correspond with points of interest on
the Murray Hill to Union Square map.*

As the city grew progressively north throughout the 19th century, one neighborhood after another had its fashionable heyday, only to fade from glory. But three neighborhoods, east of
Fifth Avenue roughly between 20th and 40th streets, have preserved much of their historic charm, in Murray Hill's brownstone mansions and town houses, Madison Square's classic
turn-of-the-century skyscrapers, and Gramercy Park's Lon-
don-like leafy square. The only "must-see" along this route is
the Empire State Building, but the walk as a whole is worth
taking for the many moments en route when you may feel as if
you've stepped back in time.

❶ Begin on East 36th Street, between Madison and Park avenues, at the **Pierpont Morgan Library.** The core of this small,
patrician museum is the famous banker's own study and library, completed in 1906 by McKim, Mead & White. If you walk
east past the entrance to admire its neoclassical facade, look for
what is believed to be McKim's face on the sphinx in the right-
hand sculptured panel. The rest of Morgan's mansion was torn
down after his death and replaced with exhibition space for his
renowned collection of drawings, manuscripts, and rare books.
(His son, J. P. Morgan, lived in a 45-room brownstone around
the corner, which you can see with a quick stroll to 37th and
Madison; the library bought that mansion and recently opened
it as part of the museum, linked to the library by an indoor garden court, where you can partake of refreshments and the occasional concert.) You enter the library on 36th Street, through
the exhibition wing; whether or not you are interested in the
temporary, often on loan, shows, go down the corridor on your
right to see Morgan's study, its red-damask-lined walls hung
with first-rate paintings, and his majestic personal library with
its dizzying tiers of handsomely bound rare books, letters, and
illuminated manuscripts. *29 E. 36th St., tel. 212/685–0610.
Suggested donation: $3 adults, $1 students and senior citizens.
Open Tues.–Sat. 10:30–5, Sun. 1–5.*

❷ As you proceed south on Madison Avenue, at 35th Street you'll
pass the **Church of the Incarnation,** a broodingly dark brownstone version of a Gothic chapel. Inside, however, there's
enough jewel-like stained glass to counteract the dour effect.
Look especially for the north aisle's 23rd Psalm Window, by the
Tiffany Glass works, or the south aisle's two Angel windows

Tour 4: Murray Hill to Union Square

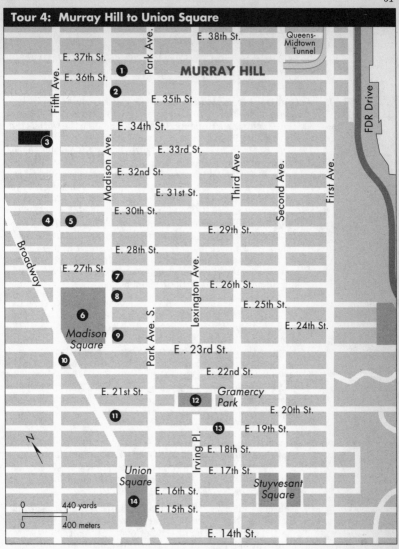

E. 38th St.

Queens-Midtown Tunnel

E. 37th St.

Park Ave.

MURRAY HILL

E. 36th St.

Fifth Ave.

E. 35th St.

FDR Drive

E. 34th St.

Madison Ave.

E. 33rd St.

E. 32nd St.

Third Ave.

Second Ave.

First Ave.

E. 31st St.

E. 30th St.

E. 29th St.

E. 28th St.

Broadway

E. 27th St.

Lexington Ave.

E. 26th St.

E. 25th St.

Madison Square

Park Ave. S.

E. 24th St.

E. 23rd St.

E. 22nd St.

Gramercy Park

E. 21st St.

E. 20th St.

Irving Pl.

E. 19th St.

E. 18th St.

E. 17th St.

Union Square

E. 16th St.

Stuyvesant Square

E. 15th St.

0   440 yards

0   400 meters

E. 14th St.

Appellate Division of the State Supreme Court, **8**

"The Block Beautiful," **13**

Church of the Incarnation, **2**

Church of the Transfiguration, **5**

Empire State Building, **3**

Flatiron Building, **10**

Gramercy Park, **12**

Madison Square, **6**

Marble Collegiate Church, **4**

Metropolitan Life Insurance Tower, **9**

New York Life Insurance Building, **7**

Pierpont Morgan Library, **1**

Theodore Roosevelt Birthplace, **11**

Union Square, **14**

dedicated to infants, which are by the 19th-century English writer-designer William Morris.

At 35th Street and Madison Avenue, veteran globe-trotters will enjoy a stop at **The Complete Traveller Bookstore** (199 Madison Ave., tel. 212/679–4339), a comprehensive shop for travel literature.

Walk west from Madison Avenue to Fifth Avenue and continue south on the west side of the street; at 34th Street, you'll reach the **Empire State Building.** It may no longer be the world's tallest building, but it is certainly one of the world's best-loved skyscrapers. The Art Deco playground for King Kong opened in 1931 after only about a year of construction. The crowning spire was originally designed as a mooring mast for dirigibles, but none ever docked there; in 1951, a TV transmittal tower was added to the top, raising the total height to 1,472 feet. Today more than 16,000 people work in the building, and more than 2.5 million people a year visit the 86th- and 102nd-floor Observatories. At night the top 30 stories are illuminated with colors appropriate to the season (red and green around Christmas; orange and brown for Halloween). In 1956, revolving beacons named the "Freedom Lights" were installed. These lights are illuminated from dusk to midnight.

Pass beneath the stainless-steel canopy on 34th Street to enter the three-story-high marbled lobby, where illuminated panels depicting the Seven Wonders of the World brazenly add the Empire State as the Eighth Wonder. Go to the concourse level to buy a ticket for the observation decks. The 102nd-floor spot is glassed in; the 86th floor is open to the air. In the movie *An Affair to Remember,* Cary Grant waited here impatiently for his rendezvous with Deborah Kerr, unaware that she had just been hit by a car on the busy avenue far below. *5th Ave. and 34th St., tel. 212/736–3100. Admission: $3.50 adults, $1.75 children under 12. Open daily 9:30 AM–midnight.*

Also on the concourse level of the Empire State Building, you'll find the **Guinness World of Records Exhibition,** where clever displays tell the story of various unusual record-holders. *Tel. 212/947–2335. Admission: $5.50 adults, $3.25 children. Open Mon.–Thurs. 9–8, Fri.–Sun. 9 AM–10 PM.*

Continue south on Fifth Avenue to 29th Street and the **Marble Collegiate Church** (1854), a marble-fronted structure built for the Reformed Protestant Dutch Congregation first organized in 1628 by Peter Minuit, the canny Dutchman who bought Manhattan from the native Indians for $24. In recent times its pulpit was occupied by Dr. Norman Vincent Peale *(The Power of Positive Thinking),* Marble Collegiate's pastor from 1932 to 1984.

Go east on 29th Street to the **Church of the Transfiguration** (1 E. 29th St.), which is better known as the Little Church Around the Corner. Set back in a shrub-filled New York version of an old English churchyard, it won its memorable appellation in 1870 when other area churches refused to bury actor George Holland, a colleague of well-known thespian Joseph Jefferson. Jefferson was directed to the "little church around the corner," which did that sort of thing, and the Episcopal institution has welcomed literary and show-biz types ever since. Go inside to see the south transept's stained-glass window, by John

LaFarge, depicting 19th-century superstar actor Edwin Booth in his most famous role, Hamlet.

6 Bordered by Fifth Avenue, Broadway, Madison Avenue, 23rd and 26th streets, **Madison Square** was the site (circa 1845) of New York's first baseball games. On the north end, an imposing 1881 statue by Augustus Saint-Gaudens memorializes Civil War naval hero Admiral Farragut. A somewhat less successful statue at the south end is of William Henry Seward, the Secretary of State who bought Alaska in 1867; the sculptor apparently took a statue he'd made of Lincoln signing the Emancipation Proclamation and simply switched the head for Seward's. The square has recently been rehabilitated with modern sculpture, new benches, and a playground, but there may still be unsavory types about. Many of the once-posh hotels in the neighborhood, having gone to seed, now provide temporary housing for homeless families, and at night, after the office workers have deserted the area, prostitutes ply their trade nearby. It's safe by day, however, and new luxury apartment towers like the one just south of the square are helping to change the neighborhood.

7 The block at 26th Street and Madison Avenue is now occupied by the ornate **New York Life Insurance Building,** designed in 1928 by Cass Gilbert, who also did the Woolworth Building (*see* Tour 17, below). Its birthday-cake top is capped by a gilded pyramid that is stunning when lit at night. Go inside to admire the soaring lobby's coffered ceilings and ornate bronze doors. This was formerly the site of the second (1890–1925) Madison Square Garden, designed by architect and playboy Stanford White, who was shot in the Garden's roof garden by Harry K. Thaw, the jealous husband of actress Evelyn Nesbit—a lurid episode more or less accurately depicted in the movie *Ragtime*.

8 Coincidentally, other scenes in *Ragtime* were filmed in front of the **Appellate Division of the State Supreme Court,** which is at Madison Avenue and 25th Street. The roof balustrade of this imposing white marble Corinthian structure depicts great lawmakers of the past: Moses, Justinian, Confucius, and others, although a statue of Mohammed had to be removed because it offended the Islamic religion to present an image of the prophet.

9 The **Metropolitan Life Insurance Tower** (Madison Ave. between 23rd and 24th Sts.) made this building the world's tallest when it was added in 1909. The 700-foot tower re-creates the campanile of St. Mark's in Venice. The four dials of its clock are each three stories high; wait for the quarter hour to hear it chime. Met Life's North Building, between 24th and 25th streets, is connected by a skywalk. Its Art Deco loggias have attracted many film crews—it appeared in such films as *Eyewitness, After Hours,* and *Radio Days*.

10 The Renaissance-style **Flatiron Building,** by architect Daniel Burnham, occupies the triangular lot formed by Broadway, Fifth Avenue, and 23rd Street. This, too, was the tallest building in the world when it opened (1902). Its rounded front point is only six feet wide, but gentle waves built into the molded limestone-and-terra-cotta side walls soften the wedge effect. Winds invariably swooped down its 20-story height, billowing up the skirts of women pedestrians on 23rd Street, and local traffic cops had to shoo away male gawkers—coining the phrase "23 Skiddoo." Originally named the Fuller Building, it was instantly rechristened by the public because of its resemblance to a flatiron, and eventually the nickname became official. It has also lent its name to the Flatiron District that lies to the south, an area of photographers' studios, residential lofts, and advertising agencies.

Continue south on Broadway and turn east on 20th Street to
⑪ the **Theodore Roosevelt Birthplace,** a reconstruction of the Victorian brownstone where Teddy lived until he was 15 years old. Before becoming president, Roosevelt was New York City's police commissioner and the governor of New York State. The house contains Victorian period rooms and Roosevelt memorabilia; a selection of videos about the namesake of the teddy bear can be seen on request. *28 E. 20th St., tel. 212/260–1616. Admission: $1. Open Wed.–Sun. 9–5; last tour 3:30.*

Time Out   Open 24 hours a day, **Miss Kim's** (270 Park Ave. S) is a combination grocery store, salad bar, and cafeteria of a type that flourishes all over town. You can fill up a container with food from a huge 50-item salad bar or a steam table with hot foods, paying for it by the pound. There's also a pastry counter and sandwich bar; countermen serve hot drinks, including espresso, while cold drinks (including beer) can be taken straight from the cooler. There's seating on a mezzanine, but most people just take their meals outside.

Just east of Park Avenue South between 20th and 21st streets
⑫ lies **Gramercy Park,** a picture-perfect city park complete with flowerbeds, bird feeders, sundials, and cozy benches. It stays nice largely because it's surrounded by a locked cast-iron fence, and only residents of the property around the park can obtain keys. Laid out in 1831 according to a design inspired by London's residential squares, Gramercy Park is surrounded by interesting buildings.

Walk to the northeast corner and head clockwise. The white terra-cotta apartment building at **36 Gramercy Park East** is guarded by concrete knights in silver-paint armor. The turreted redbrick building at **34 Gramercy Park East** was one of the city's first cooperative apartment houses; its tenants have included actors James Cagney, John Carradine, and Margaret Hamilton, who played the Wicked Witch in *The Wizard of Oz*. The austere gray-brown Friends Meeting House at 28 Gramercy Park South became **The Brotherhood Synagogue** in 1974, and a narrow plaza just east of the synagogue contains a Holocaust memorial. Society doyenne Mrs. Stuyvesant Fish, a fearless iconoclast who reduced the time of formal dinner parties from several hours to 50 minutes, resided at **19 Gramercy Park South** in the 1880s.

As you cross Irving Place on the south side of the square, peek inside the park and you'll see a statue of actor Edwin Booth playing Hamlet. Booth lived at No. 16, which he remodeled in the early 1880s to serve as an actors' club, **The Players Club.** Stanford White, the architect for the renovation, was a member of the club, as were many other nonactors. Members over the years have included Mark Twain, Booth Tarkington, John and Lionel Barrymore, Irving Berlin, Winston Churchill, Lord Laurence Olivier, Frank Sinatra, Walter Cronkite, Jack Lemmon, Richard Gere, and Raul Julia.

The **National Arts Club** (15 Gramercy Park S) was once the home of Samuel Tilden, a governor of New York and the Democratic presidential candidate who, in 1876, received more popular votes than Rutherford B. Hayes, although Hayes won the electoral college vote. Calvert Vaux, codesigner of Central Park, remodeled this building in 1874, conjoining two houses. Among its Victorian Gothic decorations are medallions portraying Goethe, Dante, Milton, and Benjamin Franklin.

On the west end of the square, note the row of redbrick Greek Revival town houses, with their fanciful cast-iron verandas looking like something out of New Orleans's French Quarter. Mayor James Harper (elected in 1888) lived at No. 4, behind the pair of street lanterns. The actor John Garfield died in 1952 while staying at No. 3.

Return to Irving Place and head south to 19th Street, where the tree-lined block running to your left, toward Third Avenue, has been called **"The Block Beautiful"** for its fine small 19th-century houses and stables. Silent-film star Theda Bara lived at No. 132; later, so did Mrs. Patrick Campbell, one of George Bernard Shaw's favorite actresses. Painter George Bellows (1882–1925) lived at No. 10.

Time Out **Pete's Tavern** (18th St. and Irving Pl.) claims to be the oldest saloon in New York (1864), and also claims that O. Henry wrote "The Gift of the Magi" while sitting in the second booth to the right. Both facts are disputed, but stop here anyway for a quick burger or a casual beer, and absorb the atmosphere of the Gaslight Era.

O. Henry, whose real name was William Sidney Porter, lived nearby, at 55 Irving Place, although the building he lived in no longer stands. A plaque on the redbrick house at 17th Street and Irving Place proclaims it as the home of Washington Irving, for whom the street is named, but it was his nephew's house, though the famous writer did visit there often. At 40 Irving Place, you'll see a huge bust of the writer outside **Washington Irving High School**, alma mater of Claudette Colbert and Whoopi Goldberg.

Classical music lovers may want to make a detour to 17th Street between First and Second avenues, where at No. 327 the Czech composer Antonin Dvorak lived from 1892 to 1895. It was in this modest brick row house—recently denied landmark status—that Dvorak wrote his most famous symphony, *From the New World*, as well as other renowned works.

At the foot of Irving Place is the **Palladium** (126 E. 14th St.), a former movie palace turned into a cavernous, innovative disco—now well past its brief "in" moment—by Ian Schrager and the late Steve Rubell, of Studio 54 fame, and designed by Arata Isozaki.

Head west to **Union Square,** the area between Park Avenue South and Broadway and 14th and 17th streets. Its name, originally signifying the fact that two main roads merged here, proved doubly apt in the early 20th century when the square became a rallying spot for labor protests and mass demonstrations; many unions, as well as fringe political parties, moved their headquarters nearby. Over the years the area deteriorated into a habitat of drug dealers and kindred undesirables, until a massive renewal program in the 1980s transformed it. If possible, visit on Greenmarket day (Wednesday, Friday, and Saturday), when farmers from all over the Northeast, including some Pennsylvania Dutch and latter-day hippies, bring their goods to the big town: fresh produce, homemade bakery goods, cheeses, cider, New York State wines, even fish and meat. If the prices aren't much lower than those in stores, the quality and freshness are much higher. The benches of Union Square make a great site for a city-style picnic.

Tour 5: Museum Mile

Numbers in the margin correspond with points of interest on the Museum Mile, Upper East Side map.

Once known as Millionaire's Row, the stretch of Fifth Avenue between 79th and 104th streets has been fittingly renamed Museum Mile, for it now contains an impressive cluster of cultural institutions. The connection is more than coincidental: Many museums are housed in what used to be the great mansions of merchant princes and wealthy industrialists. In 1979 a group of 10 Fifth Avenue institutions formed a consortium that, among other activities, sponsors a Museum Mile Festival each June. The Frick Collection and the Whitney Museum of American Art are not officially part of the Museum Mile Consortium, but they're located close enough to be added to this tour.

It would be impossible to do justice to all these collections in one outing; the Metropolitan Museum alone contains too much to see in a day. You may want to select one or two museums to linger in and simply walk past the others, appreciating their exteriors (this in itself constitutes a minicourse in modern architecture). Save the rest for another day—or for your next trip to New York.

Be sure to pick the right day of the week for this tour: Most of these museums are closed on Mondays, but many have free admission during extended hours on Tuesday evenings.

❶ Begin at Fifth Avenue and 70th Street with **The Frick Collection,** housed in an ornate, imposing Beaux Arts mansion built in 1914 for coke-and-steel baron Henry Clay Frick, who wanted the superb art collection he was amassing to be kept far from the soot and smoke of Pittsburgh, where he'd made his fortune. The mansion was designed by architects Carrère and Hastings (also responsible for the Public Library on Fifth Avenue at 40th Street); opened as a public museum in 1935 and expanded in 1977, it still has the appearance of a gracious private home, albeit one with a bona fide masterpiece in almost every room. Strolling through the mansion, one can imagine how it felt to live with Vermeers by the front stairs, Gainsborough and Reynolds portraits in the dining room, canvases by Constable and Turner in the library, and Titians, Holbeins, a Giovanni Bellini, and an El Greco in the living room. Some of the collection's best pieces include Rembrandt's *The Polish Rider* and Jean-Honoré Fragonard's series *The Progress of Love.* Even the resting area is a masterpiece: a tranquil indoor court with a fountain and glass ceiling. *1 E. 70th St., tel. 212/288–0700. Admission: $3 adults, $1.50 students and senior citizens. Children under 10 not admitted. Open Tues.–Sat. 10–6, Sun. 1–6, closed holidays.*

Americas Society, **15**

Asia Society, **16**

Bloomingdale's, **12**

Carl Schurz Park, **19**

Conservatory Garden, **11**

Cooper-Hewitt Museum, **6**

El Museo Del Barrio, **10**

Frick Collection, **1**

Gracie Mansion, **20**

Guggenheim Museum, **4**

Henderson Place Historic District, **18**

International Center of Photography, **8**

Jewish Museum, **7**

Metropolitan Museum of Art, **3**

Museum of the City of New York, **9**

National Academy of Design, **5**

Ralph Lauren, **17**

Seventh Regiment Armory, **14**

Temple Emanu-El, **13**

Whitney Museum of American Art, **2**

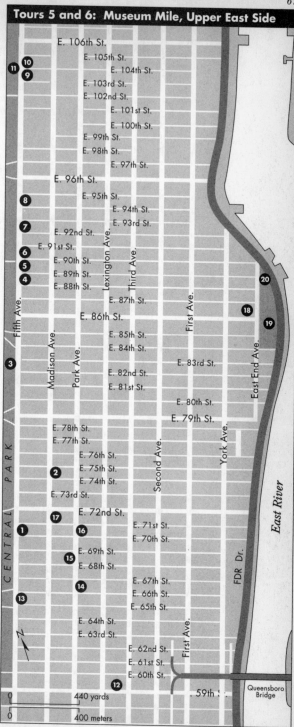

Tours 5 and 6: Museum Mile, Upper East Side

E. 106th St.
E. 105th St.
E. 104th St.
E. 103rd St.
E. 102nd St.
E. 101st St.
E. 100th St.
E. 99th St.
E. 98th St.
E. 97th St.
E. 96th St.
E. 95th St.
E. 94th St.
E. 93rd St.
E. 92nd St.
E. 91st St.
E. 90th St.
E. 89th St.
E. 88th St.
E. 87th St.
E. 86th St.
E. 85th St.
E. 84th St.
E. 83rd St.
E. 82nd St.
E. 81st St.
E. 80th St.
E. 79th St.
E. 78th St.
E. 77th St.
E. 76th St.
E. 75th St.
E. 74th St.
E. 73rd St.
E. 72nd St.
E. 71st St.
E. 70th St.
E. 69th St.
E. 68th St.
E. 67th St.
E. 66th St.
E. 65th St.
E. 64th St.
E. 63rd St.
E. 62nd St.
E. 61st St.
E. 60th St.
59th St.

Fifth Ave.
Madison Ave.
Park Ave.
Lexington Ave.
Third Ave.
Second Ave.
First Ave.
York Ave.
East End Ave.
First Ave.
FDR Dr.

CENTRAL PARK

East River

Queensboro Bridge

N

0   440 yards
0   400 meters

Walk one block east to Madison Avenue and head up to 75th Street to **The Whitney Museum of American Art.** This museum grew out of a gallery in the studio of the sculptor and collector Gertrude Vanderbilt Whitney, whose talent and taste were fortuitously accompanied by the wealth of two prominent families. The current building, opened in 1966, is a minimalist gray granite vault, separated from Madison Avenue by a dry moat; it was designed by Marcel Breuer, a member of the Bauhaus school, which prized functionality in architecture. The monolithic exterior is much more forbidding than the interior, where changing exhibitions offer an intelligent survey of 20th-century American works; a third-floor gallery features a sample of the permanent collection, including Edward Hopper's haunting *Early Sunday Morning* (1930), Georgia O'Keeffe's *White Calico Flower* (1931), and Jasper Johns's *Three Flags* (1958). Alexander Calder's *Circus*, a playful construction he tinkered with throughout his life (1898–1976), stands near the front entrance. The Whitney has also opened branches throughout the city: across from Grand Central Terminal, on Seventh Avenue at 51st Street, and downtown at the Federal Reserve Plaza. *945 Madison Ave. at 75th St., tel. 212/570–3676. Admission: $5 adults, $3 senior citizens; free for students with valid I.D. and children at all times, and for everyone Tues. 6–8. Open Tues. 1–8, Wed.–Sat. 11–5, Sun. noon–6.*

Cut back to Fifth Avenue and walk north to **The American-Irish Historical Society,** in a town house once owned by U.S. Steel president William Ellis Corey, who scandalized his social class by marrying musical comedy star Mabelle Gilman. With its ornamentation and mansard roof, this is another fine example of the French-influenced Beaux Arts style that was so popular at the turn of the century. The society's library holdings chronicle people of Irish descent who became successful in the United States. *991 5th Ave. at 81st St., tel. 212/288–2263. Admission free by appointment. Open Tues.–Fri. 10:30–5, Sat. 10:30–4:30.*

The Metropolitan Museum of Art has valid evidence for billing itself as "New York's number-one tourist attraction"; certainly the quality and range of its holdings make it one of the world's greatest museums. It's the largest art museum in the Western Hemisphere (1.6 million square feet), and its permanent collection of more than 3 million works of art from all over the world includes objects from prehistoric to modern times. The museum, founded in 1870, moved to this location in 1880, but the original redbrick building by Calvert Vaux has since been encased in other architecture. The majestic Fifth Avenue facade, designed by Richard Morris Hunt, was built in 1902 of gray Indiana limestone; later additions eventually surrounded the original building on the sides and back.

The Fifth Avenue entrance leads into the Great Hall, a soaring neoclassical chamber that has been designated a landmark in its own right. Past the admission booths, a vast marble staircase leads up to the European painting galleries, whose highlights include Botticelli's *The Last Communion of St. Jerome*, Pieter Brueghel's *The Harvesters*, El Greco's *View of Toledo*, Johannes Vermeer's *Young Woman with a Water Jug*, and Rembrandt's *Aristotle with a Bust of Homer*. Nearby in the 19th-Century European Painting and Sculpture Galleries, a large central salon full of Impressionist paintings is surrounded by smaller rooms displaying the Impressionists' precursors and successors (with one long gallery devoted to the sculpture of Auguste Rodin).

American art has its own wing, back in the northwest corner; the best approach is on the first floor, where you enter through a refreshingly light and airy garden court graced with Tiffany stained-glass windows, cast-iron staircases by Louis Sullivan, and a marble Federal-style facade taken from the Wall Street branch of the United States Bank. Take the elevator to the third floor and begin working your way down through the rooms decorated in period furniture—everything from a Shaker retiring room to a Federal-era ballroom to the living room of a Frank Lloyd Wright house—and excellent galleries of American painting.

In the realm of 20th-century art, the Met was a latecomer, allowing the Museum of Modern Art and the Whitney to build their collections with little competition until the Metropolitan's contemporary art department was finally established in 1967. The big museum has been trying to make up for lost time, however, and in 1987 it opened the three-story Lila Acheson Wallace Wing, in the southwest corner. Pablo Picasso's 1906 portrait of Gertrude Stein is the centerpiece of this collection.

There is much more to the Met than paintings, however. Visitors with a taste for classical art should go immediately to the left of the Great Hall on the first floor to see the Greek and Roman statuary, not to mention a large collection of rare Roman wall paintings excavated from the lava of Mount Vesuvius. Directly above these galleries, on the second floor, you'll find room after room of Grecian urns and other classical vases. The Met's awesome Egyptian collection, spanning some 3,000 years, lies on the first floor directly to the right of the Great Hall. Its centerpiece is the Temple of Dendur, an entire Roman-period temple (circa 15 BC) donated by the Egyptian government in thanks for U.S. help in saving ancient monuments. Placed in a specially built gallery with views of Central Park to refresh the eye, the temple faces east, as it did in its original location, and a pool of water has been installed at the same distance from it as the river Nile once stood. Another spot suitable for contemplation is directly above the Egyptian treasures, in the Asian galleries: The Astor Court Chinese garden reproduces a Ming Dynasty (1368–1644) scholar's courtyard, complete with water splashing over artfully positioned rocks.

There's also a fine arms and armor exhibit on the first floor (go through the medieval tapestries, just behind the main staircase, and turn right). Or keep going straight from the medieval galleries until you enter the cool skylit white space of the Lehman Pavilion, where the small but exquisite personal collection of the late donor, investment banker Robert Lehman, is displayed in rooms resembling those of his West 54th Street town house. This is one of the lesser-known wings of the Met (perhaps because it's tucked away behind so many other galleries), so it's a good place to go when the other galleries begin to feel crowded.

The new Henry R. Kravis wing creates a new Central Park entrance at the back of the museum. Its first-floor galleries feature the European decorative arts collection, as well as an arcaded courtyard displaying European sculpture.

Although it exhibits only a portion of its vast holdings, the Met offers more than can reasonably be seen in one visit. Choose what you want to see, find a map, and plan your tour accordingly—or, if you're not compulsive about seeing the "major pieces," wander wherever your fancy takes you. Either way, your time will not be wasted. Walking tours and lectures are free with your admission contribution. Tours covering various sections of the museum begin about every 15 minutes on weekdays, less frequently on weekends; they depart from the Tour Board in the Great Hall. Self-guided audio tours can also be rented at a desk in the Great Hall. Lectures, often related to temporary exhibitions, are given frequently. *5th Ave. at 82nd St., tel. 212/535–7710. Suggested contribution: $6 adults, $3 students and senior citizens, children free. Open Tues.–Thurs. and Sun. 9:30–5:15, Fri. and Sat. 9:30–8:45.*

Time Out Across from the Met is the Stanhope Hotel's sidewalk café, **The Terrace** (5th Ave. and 81st St.), open May through October, a convenient spot to take an elegant break after a day at the museum—to sip a cocktail and enjoy light Continental-American fare while you people-watch.

Across from the Met, between 82nd and 83rd streets on Fifth Avenue, one Beaux Arts town house stands its ground amid newer apartment blocks. It now belongs to the Federal Republic of Germany, which has installed a branch of the Goethe Institute here. **Goethe House** (tel. 212/972–3960; call for schedules) offers a changing series of art exhibitions as well as lectures, films, and chamber music concerts; its extensive library (closed in the summer) includes current issues of German newspapers and periodicals. Up at 86th and Fifth, a brightly embellished limestone-and-redbrick mansion, designed by Carrère and Hastings to echo the buildings on the Place des Vosges in Paris, was once the home of Mrs. Cornelius Vanderbilt III. It now houses the **Yivo Institute for Jewish Research** (tel. 212/535–6700; open weekdays 9:30–5:30), with exhibitions focusing on Eastern European and American Jewish history.

④ Frank Lloyd Wright's **Guggenheim Museum** (opened in 1959) is a controversial work of architecture—even many of those who like its assertive six-story spiral rotunda will admit that it does not result in the best space in which to view art. A newly expanded and fully restored Guggenheim Museum is reopening in the early part of 1992 after being closed for almost two years. A new tower and expanded gallery space display the newly acquired Panza Collection of Minimalist art, among other works. Inside, under a 92-foot-high glass dome, a quarter-mile-long ramp spirals down past changing exhibitions of modern art. The museum has especially strong holdings in Wassily Kandinsky, Paul Klee, and Pablo Picasso; the oldest pieces are by the French Impressionists. *1071 5th Ave. at 89th St., tel. 212/360–3513. Admission: $4.50 adults, $2.50 students and senior citizens; free Tues. 5–7:45. Open Tues. 11–7:45, Wed.–Sun. 11–4:45.*

⑤ A block north is **The National Academy of Design,** housed in a stately 19th-century mansion and a pair of town houses on 89th Street. The academy itself, which was founded in 1825, required each elected member to donate a representative work of art, which has resulted in a strong collection of 19th- and 20th-century American art. (Members have included Samuel F. B.

Morse, Winslow Homer, John Singer Sargent, Augustus Saint-Gaudens, and Thomas Eakins.) *1083 5th Ave. at 89th St., tel. 212/369–4880. Admission: $3.50 adults, $2 students and senior citizens; free Tues. 5–8. Open Tues. noon–8, Wed.–Sun. noon–5.*

❻ At 91st Street you'll find the former residence of industrialist Andrew Carnegie, now the home of the **Cooper-Hewitt Museum** (officially the Smithsonian Institution's National Museum of Design). Carnegie sought comfort more than show when he built this 64-room house on what was the outskirts of town in 1901; he administered his extensive philanthropic projects from the first-floor study. (Note the low doorways—Carnegie was only five feet two inches tall.) The core of the museum's collection was begun in 1897 by the three Hewitt sisters, granddaughters of inventor and industrialist Peter Cooper; major holdings include drawings, prints, textiles, furniture, metalwork, ceramics, glass, woodwork, and wall coverings. The Smithsonian rescued their museum from financial ruin in 1963, and the Carnegie Corporation donated the mansion in 1972. The changing exhibitions, which focus on various aspects of contemporary or historical design, are invariably well researched, enlightening, and often amusing. *2 E. 91st St., tel. 212/860–6868. Admission: $3 adults, $1.50 students and senior citizens; free Tues. 5–9. Open Tues. 10–9, Wed.–Sat. 10–5, Sun. noon–5.*

Across 91st Street from the Cooper-Hewitt, the **Convent of the Sacred Heart** is in a huge Italianate mansion originally built in 1918 for financier Otto Kahn, a noted patron of the arts.

Time Out   **Jackson Hole** (Madison Ave. and 91st St.) is a cheerful spot that serves the great American hamburger plus other sandwiches, omelets, chicken, and salads. Ski posters evoke the mood of the eponymous Wyoming resort. Prices are reasonable; beer is available.

---

❼ **The Jewish Museum** (1109 5th Ave. at 92nd St., tel. 212/399–3344), set in a gray stone Gothic-style château built in 1908, usually holds the largest collection of Jewish ceremonial objects in the Western Hemisphere. The museum is closed for renovation through 1992. During this time period, it will present exhibitions at the New-York Historical Society (77th St. and Central Park West; *see* Tour 8, below).

❽ The handsome, well-proportioned Georgian-style mansion on the corner of Fifth Avenue and 94th Street was built in 1914 for Willard Straight, founder of *The New Republic* magazine. Today it is the home of **The International Center of Photography** (ICP), a relatively young institution—founded in 1974—building a strong collection of 20th-century photography. Its changing exhibitions often focus on the work of a single prominent photographer or one photographic genre (portraits, architecture, etc.). The bookstore carries an impressive array of photography-oriented books, prints, and postcards. *1130 5th Ave. at 94th St., tel. 212/860–1777. Admission: $3 adults, $1.50 students, $1 senior citizens and children under 12; free Tues. 5–8. Open Tues. noon–8, Wed.–Fri. noon–5, weekends 11–6.*

As you proceed north on Fifth Avenue, you may want to walk a few paces east on 97th Street to see the onion-domed tower of the **Russian Orthodox Cathedral of St. Nicholas,** built in 1902.

Between 98th and 101st streets, Fifth Avenue is dominated by the various buildings of **Mount Sinai Hospital,** which was founded in 1852 by a group of wealthy Jewish citizens and moved here in 1904. The 1976 addition, the Annenberg Building, is a looming tower of Cor-Ten steel, which has deliberately been allowed to develop a patina of rust.

⑨ **The Museum of the City of New York** traces the course of Big Apple history, from the Dutch settlers of Nieuw Amsterdam to the present day, with period rooms, dioramas, slide shows, and clever displays of memorabilia. An exhibit on the Port of New York illuminates the role of the harbor in New York's rise to greatness; the noteworthy Toy Gallery has several meticulously detailed dollhouses. Weekend programs appeal especially to children. *5th Ave. at 103rd St., tel. 212/534–1672. Suggested contribution: $4 adults; $2 students, senior citizens, and children; $6 family. Open Tues.–Sat. 10–5, Sun. and all legal holidays (not Mon.) 1–5.*

⑩ **El Museo Del Barrio,** founded in 1969, concentrates on Latin culture in general, with a particular emphasis on Puerto Rican art. ("El Barrio" means "the neighborhood," and the museum is positioned on the edge of Spanish Harlem.) The permanent collection includes numerous pre-Columbian artifacts. *1230 5th Ave. at 104th St., tel. 212/831–7272. Suggested contribution: $2. Open Wed.–Sun. 11–5.*

⑪ Having completed this long walk, you may want to reward yourself by crossing the street to Central Park's **Conservatory Garden.** The entrance, at 105th Street, is through elaborate wrought-iron gates that once graced the mansion of Cornelius Vanderbilt II. In contrast to the deliberately rustic effect of the rest of the park, this is a symmetrical, formal garden. The central lawn is bordered by yew hedges and flowering crab apple trees, leading to a reflecting pool flanked by a large wisteria arbor. To the south is a high-hedged flower garden named after Frances Hodgson Burnett, author of the children's classic *The Secret Garden.* To the north is the Untermeyer Fountain, with its three spirited girls dancing at the heart of a huge circular bed where 20,000 tulips bloom in the spring, and 5,000 chrysanthemums in the fall.

Tour 6: The Upper East Side

Numbers in the margin correspond with points of interest on the Museum Mile, Upper East Side map.

The Upper East Side epitomizes the high-style, high-society way of life most people associate with the Big Apple. Between Fifth and Lexington avenues, up to about 86th Street, is an elegant enclave of wealth. Luxury co-ops and condominiums, exquisite town houses, private schools, posh galleries, and international shops line streets where even the sidewalks seem more sparkling clean than any others in Manhattan. You may find the people who live and work in this neighborhood a bit snobbish compared with other New Yorkers, but take it in stride—they treat everybody that way.

A fitting place to begin your exploration of the moneyed Upper East Side is that infamous shrine to conspicuous consumption,
⑫ **Bloomingdale's** (59th St. between Lexington and 3rd Aves., tel. 212/705–2000). This block-long behemoth is noisy, trendy,

and crowded; you'll find everything from designer clothes to high-tech teakettles in slick, sophisticated displays. Not one to shrink from the spotlight, Bloomie's has appeared in more than a few Manhattan movies. Diane Keaton and Michael Murphy shared a perfume-counter encounter here in Woody Allen's *Manhattan;* Robin Williams, playing a Russian musician, defected to the West in *Moscow on the Hudson;* and mermaid Darryl Hannah, in *Splash*, took a crash course in human culture in front of a bank of TVs in the electronics department.

Time Out　On Bloomingdale's sixth floor, frazzled shoppers can take a break at **Le Train Bleu** restaurant (tel. 212/705–2100), decorated like a snappy railroad car and overlooking the 59th Street Bridge. Besides à la carte snacks, it offers one of the best bargains in town for afternoon tea (3–4:30 PM).

Leaving Bloomingdale's, head west on 60th Street toward Fifth Avenue. As you cross Park Avenue, stop for a moment on the wide, neatly planted median strip. Look south toward midtown and you'll see the Pan Am Building, towering over the gilded peaked roof of the Helmsley Building at the foot of the avenue. Then turn to look uptown, and you'll see a thoroughfare lined with massive buildings that are more like mansions stacked atop one another than apartment complexes. As you proceed into the Upper East Side, observe the trappings of wealth: well-kept buildings, children in private school uniforms, nannies wheeling grand baby carriages, dog-walkers, limousines, doormen in braided livery. This is the territory where Sherman McCoy, protagonist of Tom Wolfe's *Bonfire of the Vanities,* lived in pride before his fall.

On the northwest corner of 60th Street and Park Avenue is **Christ Church United Methodist Church** (520 Park Ave.), built during the Depression but designed to look centuries old, with its random pattern of limestone blocks. Inside, the Byzantine-style sanctuary (open Sundays and holidays) glitters with golden handmade mosaics.

Continue west on 60th Street to pass a grouping of very different kinds of clubs. Ornate grillwork curls over the doorway of the scholarly **Grolier Club** (47 E. 60th St.), founded in 1884 and named after the 16th-century French bibliophile Jean Grolier. Its members are devoted to the bookmaking crafts; one of them, Bertram Grosvenor Goodhue, designed this neatly proportioned redbrick building in 1917. The club presents public exhibitions and has a specialized reference library open by appointment only. On the next block over, at 10 East 60th Street, a red canopy shelters the entrance to the **Copacabana**, the once-swanky nightclub commemorated in the Barry Manilow song of the same name. From the time it opened in 1940 until well into the 1950s, the Copa was one of Manhattan's most glamorous night spots, featuring such performers as Ella Fitzgerald, Sid Caesar, Frank Sinatra, Tony Bennett, Sammy Davis, Jr., Nat King Cole, Jimmy Durante, and Lena Horne. The club closed in 1973, although it has since had various comebacks, currently keeping a low profile as a disco and group-function space. Right next door is the exclusive **Harmonie Club** (4 E. 60th St.), one of several private men's social clubs (many of which now admit women) in this area. Built in 1905 by McKim, Mead & White, this pseudo-Renaissance palace, awkwardly stretched to high-rise proportions, is closely guarded by an unfriendly doorman, so it's best to admire it from afar. Across the street is the **Metropolitan Club** (1 E. 60th St.), an even more lordly neoclassical edifice built in 1893, also by McKim, Mead & White. J. P. Morgan established this club when a friend of his was refused membership in the Union League Club; its members today include rulers of foreign countries and presidents of major corporations.

Take a right at Fifth Avenue. On the next block you'll pass **The Pierre** (*see* Chapter 9), a hotel, which opened in 1930; notice its lovely mansard roof and tower. As you cross 62nd Street, take a look at the limestone-and-brick mansion at 2 East 62nd, the home of the **Knickerbocker Club,** another private social club. You may want to detour down this elegant block of town houses; take special note of No. 11, which has elaborate Corinthian pilasters and an impressive wrought-iron entryway.

Two doors west is the **Fifth Avenue Synagogue** (5 E. 62nd St.), a limestone temple built in 1959. Its pointed oval windows are filled with stained glass in striking abstract designs.

⑬ Continue up Fifth Avenue to 65th Street, where you'll see **Temple Emanu-El,** the world's largest Reform Jewish synagogue (it has seats for 2,500 worshipers). Built in 1929 of limestone, it is covered with mosaics and designed in the Romanesque style with Byzantine influences; the building features Moorish and Art Deco ornamentation. *1 E. 65th St., tel. 212/744–1400. Services Mon.–Thurs. 5:30 PM, Fri. 5:15 PM, Sat. 10:30 AM. Guided group tours by appointment.*

Head east across the avenues on 65th Street, taking in their different character. Fifth Avenue, once lined with the mansions of millionaires, is now lined with the co-ops of millionaires. Madison Avenue started out as a commercial street to serve Fifth Avenue patrons, and its somewhat smaller buildings almost all contain shops or businesses at street level. Railroad tracks once ran down the middle of Park Avenue; they were covered with a roadway just after World War I and the grand sweeping street that resulted became a distinguished residential address. Continue on to Lexington Avenue, another commercial street, and you'll see low-rise brownstones whose street-level shops are generally less posh and more practical than those on Madison Avenue.

Between Madison and Park avenues on 65th Street, you'll pass a pair of town houses (45–47 E. 65th St.) built in 1910 for Sara Delano Roosevelt and her son, Franklin, who later became president of the United States. No. 47, where FDR once lay recovering from polio, is now the **Sara Delano Roosevelt Memorial House,** part of Hunter College. Across the street and toward Park Avenue is **Le Cirque** restaurant (*see* Chapter 8), one of the city's gourmet shrines, located in the **Mayfair Regent Hotel** (*see* Chapter 9). On the next block, a pair of fierce, fat stone lions guard the doorway of the **China Institute,** in its pleasant and unpretentious redbrick town house. Changing public exhibitions of Chinese art are held here. *125 E. 65th St., tel. 212/744–8181. Suggested contribution: $1. Open Mon.–Sat. 10–5.*

⑭ Backtrack to Park Avenue and head north toward the red Victorian castle-fortress at 66th Street, the **Seventh Regiment Armory** (643 Park Ave.). This huge structure is still used as a military headquarters (you can see soldiers in camouflage uniforms manning the driveway on Lexington Avenue), but it has plenty of meeting and social space as well, which is used for a tennis arena, a restaurant, a shelter for homeless people, and an exhibit hall that hosts, among other events, two posh annual antiques shows. Both Louis Comfort Tiffany and Stanford White helped design its surprisingly residential interior; go up the front stairs into the wood-paneled lobby and take a look around. Tours are available by appointment (tel. 212/744–2968).

On the west side of Park Avenue, a pair of grand mansions face each other across 68th Street. Though houses have generally been replaced by apartment buildings along Park Avenue, these survivors give you an idea of how the neighborhood once looked. The grandly simple silvery limestone palace on the southwest corner, built in 1920, now houses the prestigious **Council on Foreign Relations** (58 E. 68th St.). The dark-red brick town house on the northwest corner was built in 1909–1911 by McKim, Mead & White for Percy Pyne, the grandson of noted financier Moses Taylor. From 1948 to 1963, this mansion was the Soviet Mission to the United Nations; when the Russians moved out, developers wanted to raze the town house, but in 1965 Marquesa de Cuevas acquired the property and presented it to the Center for Inter-American Relations. Now

⑮ called the **Americas Society**, it has an art gallery that's open to the public. *680 Park Ave., tel. 212/249–8950. Suggested donation: $2. Open Tues.–Sun. noon–6.*

Note how the three houses to the north—built during the following decade, and designed by three different architects—carried on the Pyne mansion's Georgian design to create a unified block. Today these buildings hold the **Spanish Institute** (684 Park Ave.), the **Instituto Italiano di Cultura** (Italian Cultural Institute, 686 Park Ave.), and the **Italian Consulate** (690 Park Ave.).

⑯ Two blocks north, on the east side of Park Avenue, is the **Asia Society**, a museum and educational center in an eight-story red granite building in striking contrast to the older, more traditional architecture of the street. While this is the headquarters of a nonprofit educational society, not technically a museum, it does offer public exhibitions of Asian art, including South Asian stone and bronze sculptures; art from India, Nepal, Pakistan, and Afghanistan; bronze vessels, ceramics, sculpture, and paintings from China; Korean ceramics; and paintings, wood sculptures, and ceramics from Japan. *725 Park Ave., tel. 212/288–6400. Admission: members free, $2 nonmembers, $1 students and senior citizens. Open Tues.–Sat. 11–6, Sun. noon–5.*

New York has been used as a locale for many a movie, and film buffs may enjoy prowling around this neighborhood past some notable location shots. The house at **162 East 70th Street**, near Lexington Avenue, is where mild-mannered Manhattan psychiatrist Dr. Robert Elliot (played by Michael Caine) worked, in the basement office, in Brian DePalma's 1980 suspense film *Dressed to Kill*. A block farther north, at **169 East 71st Street**, the white town house with the green striped awnings was where Holly Golightly (played by Audrey Hepburn) lived in *Breakfast at Tiffany's*. And at **114 E. 72nd Street**, you'll find the modern brick-front apartment tower where Sylvia Miles slipped Jon Voight past the doorman after picking him up on the street in *Midnight Cowboy*.

At this point, shoppers may want to double back to Madison Avenue and get down to shopping business (*see* Chapter 7). The catchphrase "Madison Avenue" no longer refers to the midtown advertising district (most major agencies have moved away from there anyway) but instead to uptown's fashion district: Madison Mile, between 59th and 79th streets, an exclusive area of haute couture designer boutiques, patrician art galleries, and unique specialty stores. For the most part, these shops are small, intimate, expensive—and almost invariably closed on Sundays. Even if you're just window-shopping, it's **(17)** fun to step inside the tony digs of **Ralph Lauren** (867 Madison Ave. at 72nd St.), which hardly seems like a store at all. In fact, it's in the landmark Rhinelander Mansion and has preserved the grand house's walnut fittings, oriental carpets, and family portraits as an aristocratic setting in which to display high-style preppy clothing (it's draped about casually, as though waiting to be put away). Be sure to visit the fourth-floor home furnishings section, where merchandise is arrayed in to-the-manor-born dream suites.

Just east of Madison Avenue, at 35 E. 76th Street, is the **Carlyle Hotel**, one of the city's most elite and discreet properties (*see* Chapter 9). In the early 1960s President John F. Kennedy frequently stayed here; rumor has it that he entertained Marilyn Monroe in his rooms when Mrs. Kennedy was not around. The hotel's current roster of rich-and-famous guests includes Elizabeth Taylor, George C. Scott, Steve Martin, Paul Newman, and Warren Beatty.

West of Madison is the so-called **Gucci Town House** (16 E. 76th St.), the former Gucci family mansion, which in 1988 sold for $7 million, at the time the most ever paid for a New York town house.

Time Out Stop in at the homey, casual **Kalinka Cafe** (1067 Madison at 81st St., tel. 212/472–9656) for a bit of borscht or some chicken Kiev. This narrow restaurant features fresh flowers and delicious Russian entrées ranging from $9 to $20.

Continue north on Madison Avenue past the **Frank E. Campbell Funeral Chapel** (1076 Madison Ave. at 81st St.), *the* place for fashionable funerals since 1898. The somber chocolate-colored edifice has seen massive funeral events for Rudolph Valentino (1926), Robert Kennedy (1968), and Judy Garland (1969), and more recent ceremonies for John Lennon and Rita Hayworth.

If you've still got the energy, head up to 86th Street and walk east all the way over to York Avenue, a far more modest and **(18)** ethnic part of town. In the **Henderson Place Historic District**, you'll find 24 small-scale town houses built in the 1880s in the Queen Anne style, which was developed in England by Richard Norman Shaw. Designed to be comfortable yet romantic dwellings, they combine elements of the Elizabethan manor house with classic Flemish details. Note, especially, the lovely bay windows, the turrets marking the corner of each block, and the symmetrical roof gables, pediments, parapets, chimneys, and dormer windows.

Until the 1830s, when the New York & Harlem Railroad and a stagecoach line began racing through the area, this neighborhood was the quiet, remote hamlet of **Yorkville,** a predominantly German community. Over the years it has also welcomed waves of immigrants from Austria, Hungary, and Czechoslovakia, and local shops and restaurants still bear reminders of this European heritage.

19 When you reach East End Avenue, you'll be facing **Carl Schurz Park,** overlooking the East River. Stand by the railings and look out at the Triborough and Hell's Gate bridges, Ward's and Randall's islands, and, on the other side of the river, Astoria, Queens. During the American Revolution, a house on this promontory was used as a fortification by the Continental army, then was taken over as a British outpost. In more peaceful times, the land became known as East End Park. It was renamed in 1911 to honor Carl Schurz (1829–1906), a famous 19th-century German immigrant who eventually served the United States as a minister to Spain, a major general in the Union Army, and a senator of Missouri. During the Hayes administration Schurz was Secretary of the Interior; he later moved back to Yorkville and worked as editor of the *New York Evening Post* and *Harper's Weekly*.

20 Stroll up Carl Schurz Park to reach one of the city's most famous residences, **Gracie Mansion,** the official home of the mayor of New York. Surrounded by a small lawn and flowerbeds, this Federal-style yellow frame house still feels like a country manor house, which is what it was built as in 1779 by wealthy merchant Archibald Gracie. The Gracie family entertained many notable guests at the mansion, including Louis Philippe (later king of France), President John Quincy Adams, the Marquis de Lafayette, Alexander Hamilton, James Fenimore Cooper, Washington Irving, and John Jacob Astor. The city purchased Gracie Mansion in 1887, and, after a period of use as the Museum of the City of New York (now at Fifth Ave. and 103rd St.—*see* Tour 5, above), Mayor Fiorello H. La Guardia made it the official mayor's residence.

Tour 7: Central Park

Numbers in the margin correspond with points of interest on the Central Park map.

It's amazing that 843 acres of the world's most valuable real estate should be set aside as a park, yet the city's 1856 decision to do so has proved to be marvelous wisdom, for Central Park contributes mightily toward helping New Yorkers maintain their sanity. It provides space large enough to get lost in (the entire principality of Monaco would fit within its borders), space where you can escape from the rumble of traffic to hear a bird sing or watch an earthworm tumble through the soil.

Although it appears to be simply a swath of rolling countryside exempted from urban development, Central Park is in fact one of the most cunningly planned artificial landscapes ever built. When they began in 1858, designers Frederick Law Olmsted and Calvert Vaux were presented with a swampy neighborhood of a few farms, houses, and a church. It took them 16 years, $14 million, and 5 million cubic yards of moved earth to create this playground of lush lawns, thick forests, and quiet ponds. Hills and tunnels artfully conceal transverse roads (65th, 79th, 86th, and 97th streets) so crosstown traffic will not disturb park goers, and a meandering circular drive carries vehicular traffic in the park (the drive is closed to auto traffic on weekends year-round).

Today Central Park hosts just about any activity that a city dweller might engage in outdoors: jogging, cycling, horseback riding, softball, ice skating, croquet, tennis, bird-watching, boating, chess, checkers, theater, concerts, skateboarding, and break dancing. If you're traveling with children, you'll especially appreciate how much there is to do and see. Try to come on a weekend, when local residents gratefully flock here to play—free entertainment is on tap, and the entire social microcosm is on parade.

Weekend crowds also make it safe to go into virtually any area of the park, although even on weekdays you should be safe anywhere along this tour. Despite its bad reputation, Central Park has the lowest crime rate of any precinct in the city—though the spectacularly ugly and frightening attack on a jogger in 1989 has reminded New Yorkers that the wisest course is to stay out of it at night (unless you are attending a free concert along with thousands of others).

Our route covers a lot of territory, but Olmsted and Vaux scattered their attractions so generously that there's something to see or do at almost every turn. One caveat, however: Although there are cafés connected with several attractions, as well as food stands near many entrances, the range of food is limited and predictable. Do as most New Yorkers do and stop beforehand at a deli or gourmet food shop for a picnic to carry in with you. *Tel. 212/397–3156 for general information, 212/360–1333 for a recorded message on city park events, 212/427–4040 for information on weekend walks and talks led by Urban Park Rangers. Bus tours are offered on Tues. and Thurs.*

At Grand Army Plaza, or most intersections of Central Park South (59th Street's name between Fifth and Eighth avenues), you can hire a ride in a horse-drawn carriage. Recently, carriages were restricted by law to ramble only in the park. Carriages operate all year, except in extremely hot or cold weather, and blankets are provided when it's cool. The official rates are $34 for the first 20 minutes and $10 for each additional 15 minutes, although drivers will often try to get more, so be sure to agree on a price in advance. And be forewarned: Only tourists ride in these carriages, so once you get in, you're marked.

To explore the park on foot, begin at Grand Army Plaza. Enter the park along the main road (East Drive), turning down the ❶ first path to your left to the **Pond.** Walk along the shore to the Gapstow Bridge (each of the park's 30 bridges has its own name and individual design), where you can look back at the often-photographed view of midtown skyscrapers reflected in the pond. From left to right, you'll see the peak-roofed brown Sherry-Netherland hotel, the black-and-white General Motors building, the rose-colored "Chippendale" top of the AT&T building, the black glass shaft of Trump Tower, and in front the green gables of the white Plaza Hotel.

❷ Return to the main path and continue north to **Wollman Memorial Rink,** a skating rink that has become a symbol of municipal inefficiency to New Yorkers. Fruitless and costly attempts by the city to repair the deteriorated facility had kept it closed for years, until builder Donald Trump adopted the project and

Bandshell, **8**

Belvedere Castle, **18**

Bethesda Fountain, **9**

Bow Bridge, **11**

Carousel, **4**

Central Park Zoo, **24**

Cherry Hill, **13**

Cleopatra's Needle, **21**

Conservatory Water, **22**

Dairy, **3**

Delacorte Clock, **23**

Delacorte Theater, **17**

Great Lawn, **19**

Loeb Boathouse, **10**

Mall, **6**

Mineral Springs Pavilion, **7**

The Pond, **1**

Ramble, **12**

Shakespeare Garden, **16**

Sheep Meadow, **5**

Strawberry Fields, **14**

Swedish Cottage, **15**

Turtle Pond, **20**

Wollman Memorial Rink, **2**

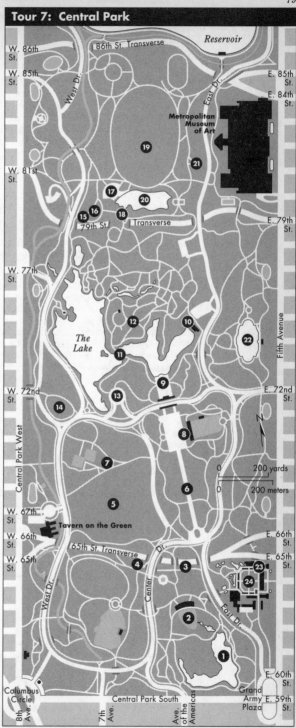

Tour 7: Central Park

quickly completed it. Even if you don't want to join in, you can stand on the terrace here to watch the skaters—ice-skating throughout the winter, roller-skating and miniature golf April to October. The blaring loudspeaker system in this otherwise quiet park makes the rink hard to ignore. *Tel. 212/517–4800. Admission: $5 adults, $2.50 children under 12. Skate rental: $2.50. Open Mon. 10–5, Tues.–Thurs. 10–9:30, Fri. and Sat. 10 AM–11 PM, Sun. 10–9:30.*

From April to October part of the rink becomes the **Gotham Miniature Golf** course, where putters maneuver around scale models of various city landmarks. *Tel. 212/517–4800. Admission: $6 adults, $4 children under age 12. Open Mon. 10–5, Tues.–Thurs. 10–9:30, Fri. and Sat. 10 AM–11 PM, Sun. 10–9:30.*

❸ Turn your back to the rink and you'll see the painted, pointed eaves, steeple, and high-pitched slate roof of the **Dairy,** originally an actual dairy built in the 19th century when cows grazed here. Today it's the park's Visitor Center, offering maps, souvenirs, videos, children's programs, and some very interesting hands-on exhibits. *Tel. 212/397–3156. Open Tues.–Sun. 11–4, Fri. 1–4.*

As you leave the Dairy, follow the path to your right (west) and under the Playmates Arch—aptly named, because it leads to a large area of ballfields and playgrounds. Coming through the
❹ arch, you'll hear the jaunty music of the **Carousel.** Although this isn't the park's original one, it was built in 1908 and later moved here from Coney Island. Its 58 ornately hand-carved steeds are three-quarters the size of real horses, and the organ plays an astonishing variety of tunes, new and old. *Tel. 212/ 879–0244. Admission: 75¢. Open daily 10:30–4:30, weather permitting.*

Climb the slope to the left of the Playmates Arch and walk beside the Center Drive. From here you can choose between two parallel routes: Turn left onto the paved path that runs along-
❺ side the chain-link fence of the **Sheep Meadow,** or go all the way
❻ to the circular garden at the foot of the **Mall.** The broad formal walkway of the Mall called **"The Literary Walk"** is a peaceful spot, lined with the largest group of American elms in the northeast and statues of famous men, including Shakespeare, Robert Burns, and Sir Walter Scott. The other path, however, buzzes on weekends with human activity: volleyball games, roller-skating, impromptu music fests. By contrast, the 15 grassy acres of the Sheep Meadow make an ideal spot for picnicking or sunbathing. It's an officially designated quiet zone, where the most vigorous sports allowed are kite-flying and Frisbee-tossing. This lawn was actually used for grazing sheep until 1934; the nearby sheepfold was turned into the Tavern on the Green restaurant (*see* Tour 8, below).

The gravel path that borders the Sheep Meadow on the north is
❼ heady with the scent of lilacs in spring; it leads to the **Mineral Springs Pavilion,** where there's a snack bar. Behind it are the beautifully manicured **Lawn Bowling Greens** and **Croquet Grounds.** Peer through gaps in the high hedges to watch the players, usually dressed in crisp white. To obtain a permit, call 212/360–8133.

Both the Sheep Meadow path and the Mall eventually lead to
❽ the **Bandshell,** site of summer concerts, speeches, and perfor-

Drive north (cross the drive as soon as possible so you can walk along the lake). Shortly past the lake, you'll see on your right a dark wood chalet that looks like something straight out of Germany's Black Forest. This is the **Swedish Cottage,** where marionette shows have been staged. *Tel. 212/988–9093. Call for schedule.*

Turn right and walk past the cottage to the little-known **Shakespeare Garden,** one of the park's few formal flower plantings, tucked onto terraces on the side of a relatively steep hill. In the garden, you'll find plants that William Shakespeare mentioned in his writings. (It is just one of the many Shakespeare Gardens throughout the world.) The open-air **Delacorte Theater,** where the New York Shakespeare Festival performs each summer, is just around the corner. But for the best view of the Delacorte, head for the top of the hill, aptly called **Vista Rock.**

Vista Rock is dominated by **Belvedere Castle,** built in 1872 of the same gray Manhattan schist that thrusts out of the soil in dramatic outcrops throughout the park. If you step through the pavilion out onto the lip of the rock, you can examine some of this schist, polished and striated by Ice Age glaciers. From here you can look down directly upon the stage of the Delacorte; you can also see the **Great Lawn** stretching beyond, a series of softball fields that hum with action on weekends and most summer evenings. In summer, should you see a few hundred people picnicking in a row around the oval edge of the lawn, you'll know they're waiting to pick up free tickets to a Shakespeare performance at the Delacorte.

The castle itself, a typically 19th-century mishmash of styles— Norman, Gothic, Moorish—was deliberately kept small so that when it was viewed from across the lake, the lake would seem bigger. (The Ramble's forest now obscures the lake's castle view.) Since 1919 it has been a measurement station of the U.S. Weather Bureau; look up to see the twirling meteorological instruments atop the tower. Climb out onto its balconies for a dramatic view, or get a minilesson in geology from the exhibits within. If you've got children with you, visit the ground-floor learning center. *Tel. 212/772–0210. Admission free. Open mid-Feb.–mid-Oct., Tues.–Thur. and weekends 11–5, Fri. 1–5; mid-Oct.–mid-Feb., 1–4.*

From the castle's plaza, take a left (south) and head east above **Turtle Pond,** populated by fish, ducks, and dragonflies, as well as turtles. At the east end of the pond you'll pass a statue of King Jagiello of Poland; groups gather here for folk-dancing on weekends. Follow the path north to nearby **Cleopatra's Needle,** a pollution-worn obelisk covered with hieroglyphics; it was a gift to the city in 1881 from the khedive of Egypt. The copper crabs supporting the huge stone at each corner almost seem squashed by its weight. If you look just past the trees, you can see the glass-enclosed wing of the Metropolitan Museum (*see* Tour 5, above) that holds the Egyptian Temple of Dendur.

Vigorous walkers may want to continue north to the **Reservoir,** popular with New Yorkers for the running track that surrounds it, and, in springtime, for its fragrant flowering trees. The city's main reservoirs are upstate; this one is more or less a holding tank.

Others can return south from Cleopatra's Needle, following the path to the left under Greywacke Arch, which leads around the

mance art. In December 198
nation, thousands of m
ment of silence to p
this area should be
72nd Street transve
nects with the East, C
park just north of here,

9 through a lovely tiled arca
an elaborately patterned
Lake. This ornate, three-tier
lical Bethesda pool in Jerusale
healing powers by an angel (he
center). Perch on the low terrace
tain and watch the rowboaters stro

10 want to get out on the water yourself,
the terrace to **Loeb Boathouse,** where
rowboat (or a Venetian gondola!). The bo
a bike-rental facility and a better-than-a
Boat rental $7 per hr, gondola $30 per 30
2233. Bicycle rental $6 per hr, tandems $12 per
4137.

11 The path to the west of the terrace leads to **Bow Br**
did cast-iron bridge arching over a neck of the lake
from either side is postcard-perfect, with the water re
quintessentially New York image of vintage apartmen
ings peeping above the treetops. If you continue acros
12 bridge, you'll enter the **Ramble,** a heavily wooded 37-acre
laced with twisting, climbing paths. This is prime bird-watc
ing territory; a rest stop along a major migratory route, it shelters many of the 269 species of birds that have been sighted in
the park. Because it is so dense and isolated, however, it may
not be a good place to wander alone.

If you don't venture into the Ramble, recross Bow Bridge and
13 continue west on the lakeside path to **Cherry Hill,** where a circular plaza sets off a wrought-iron-and-gilt fountain that is
smaller, but no less lovely, than Bethesda Fountain. This area
was originally a carriage turnaround and watering area for
horses. The path ahead leads back to the 72nd Street transverse; on the rocky outcrop directly across the road, you'll see a
statue of a falconer gracefully lofting his bird. Turn to the right
and you'll see a more prosaic statue, a pompous bronze figure of
Daniel Webster with his hand thrust into his coat. Cross the
drive behind Webster, being careful to watch for bikes hurtling
around the curve.

14 You've now come to **Strawberry Fields,** the "international peace
garden" memorializing singer John Lennon. Climbing up a hill,
its curving paths, shrubs, trees, and flowerbeds create a deliberately informal pastoral landscape, reminiscent of the English
parks Lennon may have been thinking of when he wrote the
Beatles song "Strawberry Fields." A black-and-white mosaic
set into one of the sidewalks contains simply the word "Imagine," another Lennon song title. Just beyond the trees, at 72nd
Street and Central Park West, is the Dakota (*see* Tour 8, below), where Lennon and his wife Yoko Ono lived at the time of
his death.

Cross the road at the top of Strawberry Fields' hill, turn right
through a rustic wood arbor thickly hung with wisteria vines,
then head back on the path down the hill and follow the West

back corner of the Metropolitan Museum. This side of the park, perhaps in keeping with its proximity to the East Side, has a tamer landscape than the west side, and here you'll see more uniformed nannies and fussy little dogs on leashes. A few minutes' walk will you to one of the park's most formal areas: the symmetrical stone basin of the **Conservatory Water,** where you can watch some very sophisticated model boats being raced each Saturday morning at 10 AM. (Unfortunately, model boats are not for rent here.) At the north end of the pond is one of the park's most beloved statues, José de Creeft's 1960 bronze sculpture of **Alice in Wonderland,** sitting on a giant mushroom with the Mad Hatter, White Rabbit, and leering Cheshire Cat in attendance. Children are encouraged to join in. On the west side of the pond, a bronze statue of **Hans Christian Andersen,** the Ugly Duckling at his feet, is the site of storytelling hours on summer weekends.

Climb the hill at the far end of the Conservatory Water, cross the 72nd Street transverse, and follow the path south to the Children's Zoo. This small but friendly institution—mostly barnyard animals, but a few more exotic critters as well, housed in colorfully designed enclosures that allow the little ones to see up close—was closed at press time for renovations.

Pass under the Denesmouth Arch to the **Delacorte Clock,** a delightful glockenspiel set above a redbrick arch. Every hour its six-animal band circles around and plays a tune, while monkeys on the top hammer their bells.

Just past the clock is the **Central Park Zoo,** reopened in 1988 after years of renovation. Clustered around the central Sea Lion Pool are separate exhibits for each of the Earth's major environments; the Polar Circle features a huge penguin tank and polar-bear floe; the open-air Temperate Territory is highlighted by a pit of chattering monkies; and the Tropic Zone contains the flora and fauna of a miniature rain forest. This is a good zoo for children and adults who like to take time to watch the animals; even a leisurely visit will take only about an hour, for there are only about 100 species on display. Go to the Bronx Zoo (*see* Chapter 4) if you need tigers, giraffes, and elephants— the biggest specimen here is the polar bear. *Tel. 212/439–6500. Admission: $2.50 adults, $1.25 senior citizens, 50¢ children 3–12. No children under 16 allowed in without adult. Open Apr.–Oct., weekdays 10–5, weekends and holidays 11–5:30; Nov.–Mar., daily 10–4:30.*

Tour 8: The Upper West Side

Numbers in the margin correspond with points of interest on the Upper West Side, Columbia map.

The Upper West Side has never been as fashionable as the East Side, despite the fact that it has a similar mix of real estate— large apartment buildings along Central Park West, West End Avenue, and Riverside Drive; and town houses on the shady, quiet cross streets. Once a haven for the Jewish intelligentsia, by the 1960s the West Side had become a rather grungy multiethnic community. In the 1970s gentrification began slowly, with actors, writers, and gays as the earliest settlers. Today, however, this area almost rivals the East Side in attracting high-powered Yuppies who can afford to live anywhere. There seems to be scaffolding everywhere, as landmark brownstones are meticulously restored and new windows installed in huge apartment blocks (a sure sign of impending co-opping). Young families have gravitated to its large apartments; on weekends, the sidewalks are crowded with couples pushing babies around in their imported strollers. Columbus Avenue is a trendy boutique-and-restaurant strip, somewhat hipper and more dynamic than Madison Avenue; Amsterdam Avenue is slowly following suit, although its architecture is still largely tenement-style, its shopfronts an uneasy mix of bodegas and boutiques. Along upper Broadway, new luxury apartment towers are slowly blocking in the horizon. Many longtime Westsiders decry the "yuppification" of their neighborhoods, but the good news is that small businesses now thrive on blocks that a few years ago were not safe to walk on.

1 The West Side story begins at **Columbus Circle,** where a statue of Christopher himself crowns a stately pillar at the intersection of Broadway, Eighth Avenue, Central Park West, and Central Park South. Columbus Circle is a good place to begin any tour of New York, for it is the headquarters of the **New York Convention and Visitors Bureau,** located in a weird pseudo-Moorish structure locally nicknamed "the Lollipop Building." Count on the bureau for brochures; bus and subway maps; hotel, restaurant, and shopping guides; a seasonal calendar of events; free TV-show tickets (sometimes) and discounts on Broadway theater; and sound advice. The New York City Department of Cultural Affairs operates an art gallery on the second floor. *2 Columbus Circle, tel. 212/397–8222. Open weekdays 9–6, weekends 10–6.*

On the southwest quadrant of the circle, the **New York Coliseum,** a blank functional-looking white brick building, was the city's chief convention and trade-show venue before the opening of the Jacob Javits Center. A soaring multiuse complex proposed for the site was bitterly opposed by New Yorkers determined not to let its huge shadow be cast across Central Park; the project was scaled down considerably, and construction may even have begun by the time you read this. On the northeast corner of the circle, an entrance to Central Park is presided over by the Maine Monument, with its florid bronze figures atop a stocky limestone pedestal. The pie-shape wedge of land between Central Park West and Broadway holds the **Paramount Communications Building,** formerly the Gulf & Western Building. The box office of the subterranean Paramount movie theater juts above the ground on the Broadway side of the plaza.

At the world headquarters of the **American Bible Society** (1865 Broadway at 61st St., tel. 212/581–7400), ascend red-carpeted stairs to a little-known second-floor library (open weekdays 9–4:30), which displays, among other things, Helen Keller's massive 10-volume braille Bible, a replica of the original Gutenberg press, and a Torah (Jewish scriptures) from China. Four blocks up the street, the **Mormon Visitors Center** (Broadway and 65th St., tel. 212/595–1825; open daily 10–8) has a free guided tour and films explaining the beliefs of the Church of Jesus Christ of Latter-day Saints.

2 Covering an eight-block area west of Broadway between 62nd and 66th streets, **Lincoln Center** is the home of New York's major-league performing arts institutions. This unified complex of pale travertine marble was built during the 1960s to supplant

American Museum of
Natural History
and Hayden
Planetarium, **8**

Barnard College, **12**

Cathedral of St. John
the Divine, **11**

Columbia
University, **10**

Columbus Circle, **1**

The Dakota, **6**

Grant's Tomb, **14**

Jewish Theological
Seminary, **16**

Lincoln Center, **2**

Museum of American
Folk Art, **3**

New-York Historical
Society, **7**

Riverside Church, **13**

Riverside Park, **9**

Spanish and
Portuguese
Synagogue, Shearith
Israel, **4**

Teachers College, **17**

Union Theological
Seminary, **15**

Verdi Square, **5**

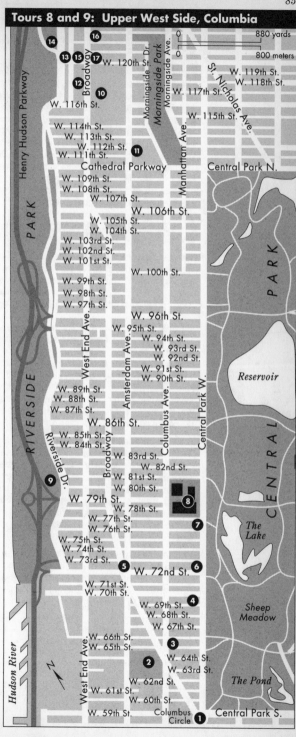

Tours 8 and 9: **Upper West Side, Columbia**

an urban ghetto (*West Side Story* was filmed on the slum's gritty, deserted streets just before the demolition crews moved in). Lincoln Center can seat nearly 18,000 spectators at one time in its various halls (*see* Chapter 10).

Stand on Broadway, facing the central court with its huge fountain, which Mel Brooks fans may recognize as the spot where Zero Mostel and Gene Wilder danced exuberantly in *The Producers.* The three concert halls on this plaza clearly relate to each other architecturally, with their symmetrical bi-level facades, yet each has slightly different lines and different details. To your left, huge honeycomb lights hang on the portico of the **New York State Theater,** home to the New York City Ballet and the New York City Opera. Straight ahead, at the rear of the plaza, is the **Metropolitan Opera House,** its brilliant-colored Chagall tapestries visible through the arched lobby windows; the Metropolitan Opera and American Ballet Theatre perform here. To your right, abstract bronze sculptures distinguish **Avery Fisher Hall,** named after the founder of Fisher Radio and host to the New York Philharmonic Orchestra.

Wander through the plaza, then angle to your left between the New York State Theater and the Metropolitan Opera House into **Damrosch Park,** where summer open-air festivals are often accompanied by free concerts at the **Guggenheim Bandshell.** Angle to your right from the plaza, between the Metropolitan and Avery Fisher, and you'll come to the North Plaza, with a massive Henry Moore sculpture reclining in a reflecting pool. To the rear is the **Library and Museum of the Performing Arts,** a branch of the New York Public Library with an extensive collection of books, records, and scores on music, theater, and dance; visitors can listen to any of 42,000 records and tapes, or check out its four galleries. Next to the library is the wide glass-walled lobby of the **Vivian Beaumont** and **Mitzi E. Newhouse theaters,** officially considered Broadway houses although far removed from the theater district.

An overpass leads from this plaza across 65th Street to the world-renowned **Juilliard School** (for music and theater); its ground floor houses **Alice Tully Hall,** home of the Chamber Music Society of Lincoln Center and the New York Film Festival. Also on 65th Street, between Broadway and Amsterdam, is the newest part of Lincoln Center, the **Walter Reade Theater,** housed in the **Rose Building.** Just opened in the fall of 1991, the auditorium screens five "non-Hollywood"-style films a day, seven days a week.

Visitors can wander freely through the lobbies of all these buildings. A one-hour guided "Take-the-Tour" covers all the grand theaters. *Tel. 212/877–1800, ext. 512, for schedule and reservations. Admission: $6.75 adults, $5.75 students and senior citizens, $3.75 children.*

Conveniently close to Lincoln Center, at the northwest corner of Broadway and 66th Street, you'll find **Tower Records,** the uptown branch of that vast emporium of records, tapes, and CDs.

③ Across the busy intersection, the long-orphaned **Museum of American Folk Art** has found a new home at Columbus Avenue and 66th Street. (This gallery will become an annex once the museum's permanent headquarters on West 53rd Street are completed in 1994.) Its collection includes naïve paintings, quilts, carvings, dolls, trade signs, painted wood carousel horses, and a giant Indian-chief copper weathervane. *2 Lincoln Sq., tel. 212/977–7298. Admission free. Open daily 9–9.*

Turn onto West 67th Street and head toward Central Park along one of the city's most handsome blocks. Many of the apartment buildings here were designed as "studio buildings," with immense windows that make them ideal for artists; look up at the facades and imagine the high-ceilinged spaces within. Also notice the Gothic motifs, carved in white stone or wrought in iron, that decorate several of these buildings at street level. Perhaps the finest apartment building on the block is the **Hotel des Artistes** (1 W. 67th St.), built in 1918, with its elaborate mock-Elizabethan lobby. Its tenants have included Isadora Duncan, Rudolph Valentino, Norman Rockwell, Noël Coward, Fannie Hurst, and contemporary actors Joel Grey and Richard Thomas; another tenant, Howard Chandler Christy, designed the lush, soft-toned murals in the excellent ground-floor restaurant, **Café des Artistes** (*see* Chapter 8), where Louis Malle's *My Dinner with André* was filmed.

Another dining landmark is just inside Central Park at 66th Street, **Tavern on the Green** (*see* Chapter 8). Originally built as a sheepfold, in the days when sheep grazed on the meadows of the park, it was converted into a restaurant in the 1930s. Many of its dining rooms have fine park views, and at night white lights strung through the surrounding trees create an undeniably magical effect.

Movie buffs may want to detour down to 65th Street, where you'll find the Art Deco building that was supposedly "Spook Central" in the movie *Ghostbusters* (55 Central Park West).

4 If you return to Broadway via 70th Street, you'll pass **The Spanish and Portuguese Synagogue, Shearith Israel,** at the southwest corner of 70th and Central Park West, a temple built in 1897 as the fifth home of the oldest Jewish congregation in the United States (founded in 1654). The adjoining "Little Synagogue" is a replica of Shearith Israel's Georgian-style first synagogue; inside are many furnishings from that 1730 temple. On the next block, at 135 West 70th Street, is a startling Egyptian-style facade, built in 1926 as the grand lodge of a fraternal organization, the **Knights of Pythias Temple**. Recently converted into a condo, it has been toned down somewhat from the original multicolored King Tut fantasy.

Cross Broadway at 70th Street and look north to view the uptown skyline. To your right on 71st Street you'll see the **Dorilton**, an ornate redbrick apartment building with an odd buttress flying from one wing to another; this was supposedly the home of the news anchor played by Sigourney Weaver in *Eyewitness*. The **subway kiosk** on the traffic island south of 72nd Street is an official city landmark, a structure with rounded neo-Dutch moldings that was the first express station north of 42nd Street. Rising behind and to the left of it you'll see the white facade and fairy-castle turrets of the **Ansonia Hotel** (73rd St. and Broadway), a turn-of-the-century luxury building whose thick, soundproof walls made it attractive to musicians; once home to Enrico Caruso, Igor Stravinsky, Arturo Toscanini, Florenz Ziegfeld, Theodore Dreiser, and Babe Ruth, today it consists of condominiums. Beyond, at the square's north end, is an imposing gray bank building, now a branch of the Apple Bank for Savings but originally the **Central**

Savings Bank, built to resemble the Federal Reserve Bank downtown.

Time Out For a break, walk back to the east side of this hectic intersection and head up to **Gray's Papaya** (southeast corner of 72nd St. and Amsterdam Ave., tel. 212/799–0243), a New York quasi-institution that pairs the sacred (health-enriching papaya and other natural juices) and the profane (hot dogs smothered in sauerkraut and onions).

⑤ Officially, the triangle south of 72nd Street is **Sherman Square** (named for the Union Civil War general, William Tecumseh Sherman), while the triangle north of 72nd is **Verdi Square** (for Italian opera composer Giuseppe Verdi). In the '70s, however, Verdi Square was better known as "Needle Park" because of the drug addicts who hung out there. While the neighborhood has vastly improved, Verdi Square is still unverdant, but not as unwelcoming as it once was; elderly West Siders now schmooze on the wood benches.

⑥ Head east on 72nd Street, to where the stately **Dakota** presides over the corner of 72nd and Central Park West. Its tenants have included Boris Karloff, Judy Holliday, José Ferrer and Rosemary Clooney, Lauren Bacall, Rex Reed, and Gilda Radner. Soot has darkened the building's yellow brick, stone trim, and copper turrets, and this slightly spooky appearance was played up in the movie *Rosemary's Baby*, filmed here. Stop by the gate on 72nd Street; this is the spot where, in December 1980, a deranged fan shot John Lennon as he came home from a recording session. Lennon is memorialized in Central Park's Strawberry Fields, across the street (*see* Tour 7, above).

Proceed up Central Park West and you'll see several other famous apartment buildings, including **The Langham** (135 Central Park West), where Mia Farrow's apartment was featured in Woody Allen's film *Hannah and Her Sisters;* the twin-towered **San Remo** (145-146 Central Park West), over the years home to Rita Hayworth, Dustin Hoffman, Raquel Welch, Paul Simon, Tony Randall, and Diane Keaton—but not to Madonna, whose application was rejected because of her flamboyant lifestyle; and **The Kenilworth** (151 Central Park West), with its immense pair of ornate front columns, once home to Basil Rathbone, film's quintessential Sherlock Holmes.

⑦ The city's oldest museum, **The New-York Historical Society,** preserves within its stern gray granite home what was unique about the city's past, including the quaint hyphen in "New-York." Along with changing exhibits of American history and art, the museum displays Audubon watercolors, early toys, Tiffany lamps, antique vehicles, and Hudson River School landscapes. *170 Central Park West and 77th St., tel. 212/873–3400. Admission: $3 adults, $2 senior citizens, $1 children under 12; pay what you wish Tues. Open Tues.–Sun. 10–5.*

The Jewish Museum (tel. 212/399–3344) will present exhibits on the first and second floors of The New-York Historical Society through 1992. *Admission: $4.50 adults, $3 senior citizens, $1 children under 12. Sun. and Tues.–Thurs. 10–5, Fri. 10–3.*

⑧ The **American Museum of Natural History,** the attached **Hayden Planetarium,** and their surrounding grounds occupy a four-block tract bounded by Central Park West, Columbus Av-

enue, and 77th and 81st streets. As you approach at 77th
Street, you can see the original architecture in the pink granite
corner towers, with their beehive crowns. A more classical facade was added along Central Park West, with its centerpiece
an enormous equestrian statue of President Theodore Roosevelt, naturalist and explorer.

With a collection of more than 36 million artifacts, the museum
displays something for every taste, from a 94-foot blue whale to
the 563-carat Star of India sapphire. Among the most endur-
ingly popular exhibits are the wondrously detailed dioramas of
animal habitat groups, on the first and second floors just behind the rotunda, and the fourth-floor halls full of dinosaur
skeletons (the Hall of Late Dinosaurs, containing *Tyrannosaurus rex*, will be closed for renovations for nearly three
years). A five-story-tall cast of *Barosaurus* rears on its hind
legs in the Roosevelt Rotunda, protecting its fossilized baby
from a fossil allosaur. In the new Hall of South American Peo-
ples, opened in 1989, bird calls and monkey howls provide a
soundtrack for a look at the Amazon rain forest. The
Naturemax Theater projects films on a giant screen; the
Hayden Planetarium (on 81st Street) has two stories of exhibits, plus several different Sky Shows projected on 22 wrapa-
round screens; its rock-music Laser Shows draw crowds of
teenagers on Friday and Saturday nights. *Museum: tel. 212/
769–5100. Suggested contribution: $5 adults, $2.50 children.
Open Sun.–Tues. and Thurs. 10–5:45; Wed., Fri., and Sat.
10–9. Planetarium: tel. 212/769–5920. Admission: $4 adults,
$3 senior citizens, members, and students; $2 children; $7 for
laser show. Open weekdays 12:30–4:45, Sat. 10–5:45, Sun. 12–
5:45. Naturemax Theater film admission: single feature—$5
adults, $2.50 children; double feature—$7 adults, $3.50 chil-
dren; discounts for members, senior citizens, and groups. Call
212/769–5650 for show times.*

Directly behind the museum is Columbus Avenue, where shoppers may want to forsake this tour for boutique-shopping. If
you do, work your way up one side of the street and back down
the other, going north to 86th Street and south to 67th Street
(*see* Chapter 7).

Return to Broadway via 77th Street to join New Yorkers in a
pilgrimage to some of the city's greatest food shrines, all on the
west side of the street. The fresh produce in the bountiful but
unpretentious **Fairway Market** (2127 Broadway at 74th St.)
practically bursts onto the street. Have a look at the handmade
signs describing the produce and cheeses; they can be as fresh
as the merchandise itself. **Citarella's** fish store at 75th Street
and Broadway features intricate, often absurd arrangements
of seafood on shaved ice in the front window. At the southwest
corner of Broadway and 80th Street, **H & H Bagels** sells several
varieties of huge, chewy bagels hot from the oven, along with
juices, cream cheese, and lox (but no coffee—and they will not
dress your bagel in any way). On the next block, **Zabar's** offers
exquisite delicatessen items, prepared foods, gourmet groceries, coffee, and cheeses; a mezzanine level features cookware,
dishes, and small appliances. Be prepared to muscle a lot of
pushy strangers for elbow room, for Zabar's prides itself on
carrying a vast range of hard-to-get foods, and at prices that
are very reasonable.

Having bought your picnic lunch, you may now want to head west to **Riverside Park,** a long, slender green space along the Hudson River landscaped by Central Park architects Olmsted and Vaux. Enter at 80th Street and Riverside Drive and wander to your right, heading for the **Promenade,** a broad formal walkway with a stone parapet looking out over the river. Before strolling along the Promenade, however, you may want to descend the steps here and go through the underpass beneath Riverside Drive, to reach the **79th Street Boat Basin,** a rare spot in Manhattan where you can walk right along the river's edge, smell the salt air, and watch a flotilla of houseboats bob in the water.

If you walk to the end of the Promenade, you'll see a patch of its median strip exploding with flowers tended by nearby residents. Look up to your right, where the Civil War **Soldiers' and Sailors' Monument,** a tight circle of white marble columns, crests a hill along Riverside Drive. Climb to the monument for a refreshing view of Riverside Park, the Hudson River, and the New Jersey waterfront.

Tour 9: Columbia University and Environs

Numbers in the margin correspond with points of interest on the Upper West Side, Columbia map.

On the high ridge just north and west of Central Park, a cultural outpost grew up at the end of the 19th century, spearheaded by a triad of institutions: Columbia University, which developed the mind; St. Luke's Hospital, which cared for the body; and the Cathedral of St. John the Divine, which tended the soul. Idealistically conceived of as an American Acropolis, the cluster of academic and religious institutions that developed here managed to keep these blocks stable during years when neighborhoods on all sides were collapsing into decay. In the past decade, West Side gentrification has reclaimed the area to the south, while the Harlem areas north and east of here remain problematic. Yet within the gates of the Columbia or Barnard campuses, or inside the hush of the cathedral or Riverside Church, the pace of life seems slower, more contemplative. Being a student neighborhood, the area has a casual atmosphere, hip and yet whole-earth, friendly, and fun.

A logical starting point is on the east side of Broadway at 116th Street, right in front of the campus gates of **Columbia University,** a wealthy, private, coed institution that is New York City's only Ivy League school. The gilded crowns on the black wrought-iron gates serve as a reminder that this was originally King's College when it was founded in 1754, before American independence. Walk along the herringbone patterned brick paths of College Walk into the refreshingly green main quadrangle, dominated by massive neoclassical **Butler Library** to your right (south) and the rotunda-topped **Low Memorial Library** to your left (north). Butler, built in 1934, holds the bulk of the university's 4.5 million books; Low, built in 1895–97 by McKim, Mead & White (who laid out the general campus plan when the college moved here in 1897), is now mostly offices, but on weekdays you can go inside to see its domed, templelike former Reading Room. The steps of Low Library, presided over by Daniel Chester French's statue *Alma Mater*, have been a focal point for campus life, not least during the student riots of

1968. Here Dan Aykroyd and Bill Murray, playing recently fired Columbia research scientists, hit upon the idea of going into business as *Ghostbusters*.

Before Columbia moved here, this land was occupied by the Bloomingdale Insane Asylum; the sole survivor of those days is **Buell Hall,** the gabled orange-red brick house just past Low Library. Just north is **St. Paul's Chapel** (1907), an exquisite little Byzantine-style domed church laid out in the shape of a cross. Step inside to admire the now-renovated tiled vaulting. *Tel. 212/854–6625. Open Sept.–May, Mon.–Fri. 10–4; Sat. 11–2; Sun. for services, 8:30–1 and 5–9. Similar hours June–Aug., but call ahead for Sunday schedule.*

A student-run art gallery has been opened downstairs in the chapel's Postcrypt. *Tel. 212/854–1953. Admission free. Open Tues.–Fri. 2–6 and Sat. 9–12:30 as a coffee house, offering poetry readings and folk music.*

Cross Amsterdam Avenue, either through the second set of campus gates at the other end of College Walk, or by taking the overpass. The rather grim white building on the northeast corner of 116th Street and Amsterdam Avenue features a massive, muscular statue of the Greek prince Bellerophon taming the winged horse Pegasus; this is sculptor Jacques Lipchitz's metaphor for the force of law overcoming disorder, an appropriate sentiment for the front of the **Law School.** Walk east to Morningside Drive, where on your left you'll see the redbrick Georgian-style **President's House** (1912), another McKim, Mead & White design. Across the street you may want to pause on the overlook to gaze into **Morningside Park,** tumbling steeply into a wooded gorge. Designed by Central Park's Olmsted and Vaux, it's a lovely landscape, but bordered as it is by some rough blocks of Harlem, it's not safe to walk in.

As you proceed south on Morningside Drive you'll pass, at 114th Street, the graceful pillared portico of **Eglise de Notre Dame,** a Roman Catholic church that features, behind the altar, a replica of the French grotto of Lourdes; stop in, if possible, during one of the frequent daily services. Around the corner on 113th Street you can still see the baroque 1896 core of **St. Luke's Hospital,** which has grown rather awkwardly into a jumble of newer buildings.

⓫ A chain-link fence runs along 113th Street beside the **Cathedral of St. John the Divine,** New York's major Episcopal church and, when completed, to be the largest cathedral in the world (St. Peter's of Rome is larger, but it's technically a basilica). Here you can have a rare, fascinating look at a Gothic cathedral in progress. Before you go to the main entrance on Amsterdam Avenue, peer into this side lot—the cathedral's **stone-cutting yard,** the only such operation in the United States. This immense limestone-and-granite church has been built in spurts. Its first cornerstone was laid in 1892 and a second in 1925, but with the U.S. entry into World War II, construction came to a "temporary" halt that lasted until 1982. St. John's follows traditional Gothic engineering—it is supported by stonemasonry rather than by a steel skeleton—so new stonecutters had to be trained before the current work could proceed on the two front towers, which will be followed by the transept and, finally, the great central tower. A model in the superb gift shop inside shows what the cathedral might look like when completed, probably quite a few years into the future. The shop (open daily, 9–5), is known for its fine selection of international crafts, jewelry, and ecological literature.

On the wide steps climbing to the Amsterdam Avenue entrance, you'll see five portals arching over the entrance doors; the central one shows St. John having his vision of the Lord in glory, but statuary is still being slowly added to the other portals. Before you go inside, take a closer look at the facade's huge blocks of limestone: Each one carries a pattern of rough chisel marks called "boasting," the individual mason's distinctive signature.

Inside is a vast nave, the length of two football fields, which can seat 5,000 worshipers. The small chapels that border the nave have a surprisingly contemporary outlook. The one immediately to your left celebrates athletes and sports, and just past it is the only **Poet's Corner** in the United States; the right-hand aisle's chapels movingly mourn tragedies such as the Holocaust and the spread of AIDS.

Beneath the 155-foot-high central dome, which could comfortably contain the Statue of Liberty, you can see another quirk of the cathedral: Its original Romanesque-Byzantine design was scrapped in 1907, when architect Ralph Adams Cram took over and instated a Gothic style. Here, where the transept will someday cross the nave, note the rough granite walls of the original scheme (they will eventually be covered with limestone); note also that the side nearer the entrance has a pointed Gothic arch, while the arch near the altar is still rounded Romanesque. The altar area itself expresses the cathedral's interfaith tradition with menorahs, Shinto vases, and golden chests presented by the king of Siam; the church's international mission is represented in the ring of chapels behind the altar, dedicated to various ethnic groups. The **Baptistry**, to the left of the altar, is an exquisite octagonal chapel with a 15-foot-high marble font and a polychrome sculpted frieze commemorating New York's Dutch heritage.

To the south of the cathedral itself is the **cathedral close,** a peaceful precinct of Gothic-style châteaus that include the Bishop's House, the Deanery, and the Cathedral School. A circular plaza just off Amsterdam at 111th Street features the Peace Fountain, which despite its rather grotesque central sculpture is interesting for the outer rim decorated with small bronzes designed by local schoolchildren.

Along with Sunday services (8, 9, 9:30 (in Spanish), and 11 AM, and 7 PM), the cathedral operates a score of community outreach programs and presents a full calendar of nonreligious (classical, folk, winter solstice) concerts. *Amsterdam Ave. and 112th St., tel. 212/316–7400, box office tel. 212/662–2133. Tours Mon.–Sat. 11, Sun. 12:45.*

Time Out On the other side of Amsterdam Avenue, between 110th and 111th streets, you'll find two casual restaurants: **V & T Restaurant** (1024 Amsterdam, tel. 212/663–1708) for spicy pizza and Italian cooking; and the **Hungarian Pastry Shop** (1030 Amsterdam Ave., tel. 212/866–4230) for luscious desserts and coffees.

Walk west to Broadway and back up to 117th Street, where
➌ across from Columbia is its sister institution, **Barnard College,**

established in 1889. One of the former Seven Sisters of women's colleges, Barnard has steadfastly remained a single-sex institution and has maintained its independence from Columbia, although its students can take classes there (and vice versa). The main gates face **Barnard Hall,** its brick-and-limestone design echoing Columbia's buildings. Turn right to follow the path north through the narrow but neatly landscaped campus. The student center and the science tower, a striking pair of modern white limestone buildings, face each other across a short flight of stairs; beyond them is **Milbank Hall,** another stately brick structure in the neoclassical mode. Note the bear (the college's mascot) on the carved stone seal to the left of the central window.

A narrow iron-barred gate to the left (closed on weekends, unfortunately) leads onto Claremont Avenue. Follow either Claremont or Broadway north to 120th Street, where a left-hand turn takes you to Riverside Drive. On your right, **Riverside Church** is a modern (1930) Gothic-style edifice whose smooth, pale limestone walls seem the antithesis of St. John the Divine's rough gray hulk; in fact, it feels more akin to Rockefeller Center, not least because John D. Rockefeller was a major benefactor of the church. While most of the building is refined and restrained, the main entrance, on Riverside Drive, explodes with elaborate stone carving (modeled after the French cathedral of Chartres, as are many other decorative details here). Inside, look at the handsomely ornamented main sanctuary, which seats only half as many people as St. John the Divine does; take the elevator to the top of the 22-story, 356-foot tower (admission: $1), with its 74-bell carillon, the largest in the world. Although affiliated with the Baptist church and the United Church of Christ, Riverside is basically nondenominational, interracial, international, extremely political, and socially conscious. Its calendar includes political and community events, dance and theater programs, and concerts, along with regular Sunday services at 10:45 AM. *Tel. 212/222–5900. Open daily 9–5; Sun. service 10:45.*

Across Riverside Drive, in Riverside Park, stands the General Grant National Memorial Monument, commonly known as **Grant's Tomb,** where Civil War general and two-term president Ulysses S. Grant rests beside his wife, Julia Dent Grant. The white granite mausoleum, with its imposing columns and classical pediment, is much smaller inside than its model Les Invalides in Paris, where Napoleon is buried. Under a small white dome, the Grants' twin black marble sarcophagi are sunk into a deep circular chamber, which you view from above; minigalleries to the sides display photographs and Grant memorabilia. In contrast to this austere monument, the surrounding plaza features wacky 1960s-era mosaic benches, designed by local schoolchildren. *Riverside Dr. and 122nd St., tel. 212/ 666–1640. Admission free. Open Wed.–Sun. 9–5.*

You may want to sit for a moment in Sakura Park, a quiet formal garden on the other side of Riverside Drive, to admire **International House** (1924), an elegant, ornate, pale building that houses many foreign students enrolled in the area. Then walk back east on 122nd Street; across Claremont Avenue, you'll see the prestigious **Manhattan School of Music** in the modern block on your left, and the interdenominational **Union Theological Seminary** in the rough gray collegiate Gothic quadrangle on your right (the main entrance is at Broadway and 120th Street). Founded in 1836, the seminary moved here in 1910; it has one of the world's finest theological libraries.

At the corner of 122nd Street and Broadway, a large blank-walled redbrick tower fronts the intersection at an angle. This **16** is the **Jewish Theological Seminary**, founded in 1887 as a training ground for rabbis, cantors, and scholars of Conservative Judaism. This complex was built in 1930, although the tower, which housed part of the seminary's excellent library, was extensively renovated after a fire in 1966.

As you head back south on Broadway, on your left you'll see the **17** redbrick Victorian buildings of Columbia University's **Teachers College**, founded in 1887 and today the world's largest graduate school in the field of education. Notice the band of stone along the Broadway facade, inscribed with the names of famous teachers throughout history—a fitting comment on this entire academically oriented neighborhood.

Tour 10: Harlem

Numbers in the margin correspond with points of interest on the Harlem map.

Harlem has been the mecca for black American culture and life for nearly a century. Originally called "Nieuw Haarlem" and settled by Dutch farmers, Harlem was a well-to-do suburb in the 19th century; black New Yorkers began settling here in large numbers in about 1900, moving into a surplus of fine apartment buildings and town houses built by real-estate developers for a middle-class white market that never materialized. By the 1920s, Harlem (with one "a") had become the most famous black community in the United States, perhaps in the world. In an astonishing confluence of talent known as the Harlem Renaissance, black novelists, playwrights, musicians, and artists gathered here. Black performers starred in chic Harlem jazz clubs—which, ironically, only whites could attend. Throughout the Roaring Twenties, while whites flocked here for the infamous parties and nightlife, blacks settled in for the opportunity this self-sustaining community represented. But the Depression hit Harlem hard. By the late 1930s, it was no longer a popular social spot for downtown New Yorkers, and many successful black families began moving out to homes in the suburbs of Queens and New Jersey.

By the 1960s, Harlem's population had dropped dramatically, and many of those who remained were disillusioned enough to join in civil rights riots. A vicious cycle of crowded housing, poverty, and crime was choking the neighborhood, turning it into a simmering ghetto. Today, however, Harlem is well on its way to restoring itself. Mixed in with some of the seedy remains of the past are old jewels such as the refurbished Apollo Theatre and such new attractions as the Studio Museum. A great number of Harlem's classic brownstone and limestone homes are being restored and lived in by young families, bringing new life to the community.

Deserted buildings, burned-out shopfronts, and yards of rubble still scar certain parts; although a few whites have begun to move in here, some white visitors may feel conspicuous in what is still a largely black neighborhood. But Harlemites are accus-

tomed to seeing tourists on their streets; only common traveler's caution is necessary during daytime excursions to any of
the places highlighted, although for nighttime outings it's
smart to take a taxi. Bus tours may be a good alternative way to
see Harlem, because they cover more areas than the central
Harlem walk outlined below (*see* Special-Interest Tours in
Chapter 1).

Sunday is a good time to tour Harlem, because that's when you
can listen to gospel music at one of the area's many churches.
Soulful, moving, often joyous, gospel music blends elements
from African songs and chants, American spirituals, and
rhythm and blues. Gospel fans and visitors are welcome at the
① **Canaan Baptist Church of Christ**, where Wyatt Tee Walker is
pastor. *132 W. 116th St., Sun. services 10:45 AM.*

As you head east from the church, notice on the southwest corner of 116th Street and Lenox Avenue the aluminum onion
dome of the **Malcolm Shabazz Mosque** (102 W. 116th St.), a former casino that was converted in the mid-1960s to a black Muslim temple (Malcolm X once preached here). Several Muslim
stores are located nearby.

On weekdays you may want to begin your tour at the next stop,
② **Marcus Garvey Park**, which interrupts Fifth Avenue between
120th and 124th streets. Renamed after Marcus Garvey (1887–
1940), who led the back-to-Africa movement, this rocky plot of
land is interesting less for itself than for the handsome buildings of the surrounding Mount Morris Historic District (Mount
Morris Square was the park's original name). Walk up the west
side of the park to admire the fine town houses facing the park
or on the side streets.

Between the brownstones on 120th Street you'll see **20 West
Home of Black Cinema** (20 W. 120th St., tel. 212/410–2101), a
private, black-owned movie theater that specializes in films
written, produced, and directed by black artists. The owners,
who live in the upper part of the house, have created a cozy
basement theater and a comfortable sitting area where the artists often appear in person to discuss their films after the showing. Call to reserve a seat for one of the nighttime screenings.

Time Out At the other end of Marcus Garvey Park is **La Famille** (2017 5th
Ave., between 124th and 125th Sts., tel. 212/722–9806), a bar
and restaurant that serves great food upstairs and a changing
nighttime menu of jazz downstairs. La Famille offers standard
soul-food fare plus a more Continental menu—although, unfortunately, it's not open for lunch on weekends.

Harlem's main street is **125th Street,** the chief artery of its cultural, retail, and economic life. Real-estate values here have
never come close to those downtown along Fifth Avenue or even
Broadway, and many of the commercial buildings rise only a
few stories. New businesses have been moving in of late, however, bringing smart new shopfronts along a retail row that until recently saw many "For Rent" signs. Among the
revitalization projects is the new National Black Institute of
Communication through Theater Arts on the northeast corner
of Fifth Avenue and 125th Street: Above the street-level stores
is the home of the **National Black Theater** (tel. 212/722–3800),
which produces new works by contemporary black writers.

Abyssinian Baptist
Church, **7**

Apollo Theater, **4**

Black Fashion
Museum, **5**

Canaan Baptist
Church of Christ, **1**

Marcus Garvey
Park, **2**

Schomburg Center for
Research in Black
Culture, **6**

Striver's Row, **8**

The Studio Museum in
Harlem, **3**

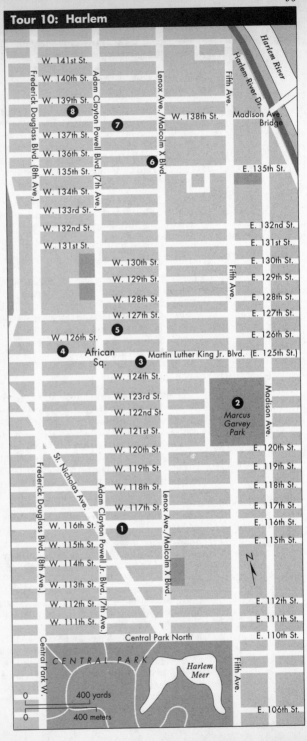

Tour 10: Harlem

Time Out Between 126th and 127th streets is **Sylvia's Soul Food Restaurant** (328 Lenox Ave., tel. 212/996–0660), owned by Sylvia Woods, the self-proclaimed "Queen of Soul Food" in New York. Sylvia has earned that title with such mouth-watering entrées as her spicy barbecued ribs and crispy fried pork chops. On Thursdays, don't miss the juicy peach cobbler for dessert. And if you're an early bird, try the hearty, country-style breakfast.

❸ **The Studio Museum in Harlem**, one of the community's show-places, is a small art museum that houses a large collection of paintings, sculpture, and photographs (including historic photographs of Harlem by James Van DerZee, popular in the 1930s). The museum often offers special lectures and programs, and its gift shop is full of black American and African-inspired books, posters, and jewelry. *144 W. 125th St., tel. 212/865–2420 or 864–4500. Admission: $2 adults; $1 students and children. Free on Wed. for senior citizens. Open Wed.–Fri. 10–5, weekends 1–6.*

The pivotal intersection of 125th Street and Seventh Avenue has been glorified with the name **African Square,** as part of that civic policy that often gives uptown streets different names (Seventh Avenue becomes Adam Clayton Powell, Jr., Boulevard, Eighth Avenue becomes Frederick Douglass Boulevard, Lenox (Sixth) Avenue is called Malcolm X Boulevard) to reflect black heritage. However, just about everybody still uses the streets' former names.

❹ A fantastic restoration brought the **Apollo Theatre**, one of Harlem's greatest landmarks, back to life in 1986. When it opened in 1913 it was a burlesque hall for white audiences only, but after 1934, music greats such as Billie Holiday, Ella Fitzgerald, Duke Ellington, Count Basie, and Aretha Franklin performed here. The theater fell on hard times and closed for a while in the early 1970s. The current Apollo's roster of stars isn't as consistent as it was in the past, but its regular Wednesday night amateur performances are as wild and raucous as they were in the theater's heyday. *253 W. 125th St., tel. 212/749–5838. Call for performance schedules.*

Return to Seventh Avenue and head north to 126th Street,
❺ where the **Black Fashion Museum** is housed in a brownstone. Costumes from black theater and films are displayed, and the work of black fashion designers of the past century is highlighted. *155 W. 126th St., tel. 212/666–1320. Suggested donation: $1.50 adults, $1 students and senior citizens, 50¢ children under age 13. Open weekdays noon–8 by appointment.*

As you head up Seventh Avenue, between 131st and 132nd streets you'll pass what is today the Williams Institutional (Christian Methodist Episcopal) Church. Once this was the **Lafayette Theater,** which presented black revues in the 1920s and housed the WPA's Federal Negro Theater in the 1930s. A tree outside the theater was considered a lucky charm for black actors; having fallen victim to exhaust fumes, it has been replaced by the abstract metal "tree" on the traffic island in the center of Seventh Avenue.

At 135th Street, cross back to Lenox Avenue, where you'll find
❻ the **Schomburg Center for Research in Black Culture**. In 1926 the New York Public Library's Division of Negro History acquired the vast collection of Arthur Schomburg, a scholar of

black and Puerto Rican descent. In 1940, after Schomburg died, this collection, which includes over 100,000 books, documents, and photographs recording black history, was named after him. In 1972, the ever-growing collection was designated a research library and in 1980 it moved into this modern redbrick building from the handsome Victorian one next door (designed by McKim, Mead & White), which is now a branch library. The expansion and renovation of the original Schomburg building was completed in 1991 and includes the new **American Negro Theater**, with seating for 380, and increased gallery space. The center's resources include rare manuscripts, art and artifacts, motion pictures, records, and videotapes. Regular exhibits, performing arts programs, and lectures continue to contribute to Harlem culture. *515 Lenox Ave., tel. 212/491-2200. Admission free. Open Mon.-Wed. noon-8, Fri.-Sat. 10-6.*

7 Founded downtown in 1808, the **Abyssinian Baptist Church** was one of the first black institutions to settle in Harlem when it moved here in the 1920s. The Gothic-style bluestone church was further distinguished by its famous family of ministers—Adam Clayton Powell, Sr., and his son, Adam Clayton Powell, Jr., the first black U.S. congressman. Stop in on Sunday to hear the gospel choir and the fiery sermon of its present minister, Rev. Calvin Butts. *132 W. 138th St. Sun. services 11 AM.*

8 Across Seventh Avenue from the church is a handsome set of town houses known as **Striver's Row** (W. 138th and W. 139th Sts. between 7th and 8th Aves.). Since 1919, black doctors, lawyers, and other middle-class professionals have owned these elegant homes, designed by famous period architects such as Stanford White (his contributions are on the north side of 139th Street). Musicians W. C. Handy ("The St. Louis Blues") and Eubie Blake ("I'm Just Wild About Harry") were among the residents here. The area became known as Striver's Row because less affluent Harlemites felt its residents were "striving" to become well-to-do. These quiet, tree-lined streets are a remarkable reminder of the Harlem that used to be.

Tour 11: Chelsea

Numbers in the margin correspond with points of interest on the Chelsea map.

Like the London district of the same name, New York's Chelsea has preserved its villagelike personality. Both have their quiet nooks where the 19th century seems to live on; both have been havens for artists, writers, and bohemians. Although London's Chelsea is a much more upscale chunk of real estate, New York's Chelsea is catching up, with town-house renovations reclaiming block after block of the side streets. Seventh, Eighth, and Ninth avenues may never be the shopping mecca that King's Road in London's Chelsea has been, but they have plenty of hip, one-of-a-kind boutiques sprinkled among the grubby grocery stores and other remnants of the neighborhood's immigrant tenement past.

Precisely speaking, the New York neighborhood was named not after Chelsea itself but after London's Chelsea Royal Hospital, an old soldiers' home. Running from 14th to 24th streets, from Eighth Avenue west, it was one family's country estate until the 1830s, when Clement Clarke Moore saw the city moving north and decided to divide his land into lots. With an instinctive gift for urban planning, he dictated a pattern of development that ensured street after street of graceful row houses. A clergyman and classics professor, Moore is probably best known for his 1822 poem "A Visit from St. Nicholas," which he composed while bringing a sleigh full of Christmas treats from lower Manhattan to his Chelsea home.

Begin your tour of Chelsea at the corner of Avenue of the Americas (Sixth Avenue) and 18th Street. In the latter part of the 19th century, when the elevated tracks of the Sixth Avenue El train still cast their shadow along this street, the blocks between 18th and 23rd streets were a veritable fashion row. Stand on the west side of the avenue and look across at the elaborately embellished, glazed terra-cotta building just north of **❶** 18th Street. Originally the **Siegel-Cooper Dry Goods Store**, built in 1895, it contains 15½ acres of space, yet it was built in only five months. In its retail heyday, the store's main floor featured an immense fountain—a circular marble terrace with an enormous white-marble-and-brass replica of *The Republic*, the statue Daniel Chester French displayed at the 1883 Chicago World's Fair—which became a favorite rendezvous point for New Yorkers. During World War II, the building was a military hospital. Today it houses the Chelsea Racquet & Fitness Club, a variety of button companies, and a number of graphics and printing firms. Ignore the boarded-up, blacked-out windows on the lower levels and look up at the building's splendid ornamentation: round wreathed windows, Corinthian and Doric pilasters, Romanesque rounded arches, lion heads, and more.

Now cross Sixth Avenue and take a look at the building on the **❷** west side: the original **B. Altman Dry Goods Store**, built in 1876 with additions in 1887 and 1910. Look closely at the exposed columns at the base of the building—it's constructed of cast iron. B. Altman moved out of this giant in 1906 to set up shop in imposing quarters at Fifth Avenue and 34th Street. The latter store closed in 1990.

On the east side of Sixth Avenue at 20th Street is the Gothic-**❸** style **Church of the Holy Communion**, an Episcopal house of worship built in 1846 and designed by architect Richard Upjohn. To the horror of some preservationists, it was converted a few years ago into **Limelight**, a nightclub with state-of-the-art sound and video systems.

On the west side of Sixth Avenue between 20th and 21st streets **❹** stands another former retail palace, the **Hugh O'Neill Dry Goods Store**. Constructed in 1875, this cast-iron building features Corinthian columns and pilasters; its corner towers were once topped off with huge bulbous domes. Look up at the pediment and you'll see the name of the original tenant proudly displayed.

❺ Turn left on 21st Street for a look at **The Third Cemetery of the Spanish & Portuguese Synagogue, Shearith Israel**, a private green oasis with a hardy old ailanthus tree. In use from 1829 to 1851, it is one of three graveyards created in Manhattan by this congregation (*see* Tour 8, above, and Tour 16, below).

Walk back to 20th Street and take a right, heading west. Beginning at Eighth Avenue is the **Chelsea Historic District**, packed with examples of all of Chelsea's architectural periods: Greek and Gothic Revival, Italianate, and 1890s apartment buildings.

B. Altman Dry Goods Store, **2**

Chelsea Hotel, **11**

Church of the Holy Communion (Limelight), **3**

Clement Clarke Moore Park, **9**

Cushman Row, **8**

General Theological Seminary, **7**

Hugh O'Neill Dry Goods Store, **4**

The Joyce Theater, **12**

London Terrace Apartments, **10**

St. Peter's Church, **6**

Siegel-Cooper Dry Goods Store, **1**

The Third Cemetery of the Spanish & Portuguese Synagogue, Shearith Israel, **5**

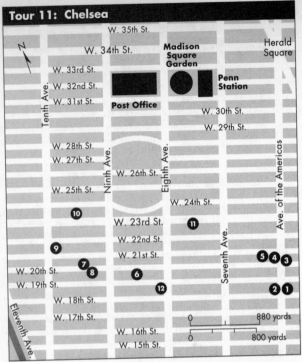

Tour 11: Chelsea

6 At 344 West 20th Street, between Eighth and Ninth avenues, you'll find **St. Peter's Church,** built between 1836 and 1838. The Greek Revival–style **rectory** (1832), to the right of the main church, originally served as the sanctuary. Four years after it was built, the congregation had already laid foundations for a bigger church when, it is said, a vestryman returned from England bursting with excitement over the Gothic Revival that had just taken hold there. The fieldstone **church** that resulted ranks as one of New York's earliest examples of Gothic Revival architecture, although its floor plan is still that of a Greek temple rather than the typical Gothic cross shape. To the left of the church, the brick **parish hall** is an example of the so-called Victorian Gothic style; its churchlike front was added in 1871. The wrought-iron fence framing the three buildings once enclosed St. Paul's Chapel downtown *(see* Tour 17, below).

7 When Clement Clarke Moore divided up his estate, he began by deeding a large section to the **General Theological Seminary,** where he taught Hebrew and Greek. At Ninth Avenue and 20th Street, the Episcopal seminary still occupies a block-long stretch. The stoutly fenced campus is accessible through the modern building on Ninth Avenue; during off hours you can view the grounds from West 20th Street. The **West Building** (1836) is another early example of Gothic Revival architecture in the city. Most of the rest of the complex was completed in 1883–1902, when Eugene Augustus Hoffman, the school's third dean, hired architect Charles Coolidge Haight to design a campus that would rival most American colleges of the day, in the style known as English Collegiate Gothic, which Haight had pioneered. The general campus plan is in an "E" shape, with the spine facing 21st Street. In the center is the **Chapel of the Good Shepherd,** with its 161-foot-high bell tower modeled after the one at Magdalen College, Oxford. **Sherred Hall,** a three-story classroom building flanked by dormitories, expresses beautifully the simple quality and uniform look Haight strove for. **Hoffman Hall,** the refectory-gymnasium, has an enormous dining hall that resembles a medieval knight's council chamber. A 1960s-era building facing Ninth Avenue houses administrative offices and the 210,000-volume **St. Mark's Library,** generally considered the nation's greatest ecclesiastical library; it has the world's largest collection of Latin Bibles. *Tel. 212/243–5150. Open weekdays noon–2:30, Sat. 11–3, Sun. 2–4, and by appointment.*

Across the street from the seminary, at **404 West 20th Street,** is the oldest house in the historic district. Built between 1829 and 1830 in the Federal style, it still has one clapboard side wall, although over the years it acquired a Greek Revival doorway and Italianate windows on the parlor floor, and the roof was raised one story. The houses next door, from 406 to 418 West 20th, are **Cushman Row,** some of the country's most perfect examples of Greek Revival town houses. Built by dry-goods merchant Don Alonzo Cushman, a friend of Clement Clarke Moore who became a millionaire by developing Chelsea, the houses retain such details as the tiny wreath-encircled attic windows, deeply recessed doorways with brownstone frames, and handsome iron balustrades, newels, and fences. Notice the pineapples, a traditional symbol of welcome, atop the newels in front of Nos. 416 and 418.

⑧

Farther down West 20th Street, at **Nos. 446 to 450,** you'll find some exceptional examples of Italianate houses. The arched windows and doorways are hallmarks of this style, which prized circular forms—not least because, being expensive to build, they showed off the owner's wealth.

When you reach Tenth Avenue, turn right and walk north (uptown). Movie buffs might make a quick detour right onto 21st Street to take a peek at **467 West 21st Street,** where, in the 1960s and '70s, Anthony Perkins of *Psycho* was the live-in landlord.

⑨ At 22nd Street, on the east side of Tenth Avenue, is **Clement Clarke Moore Park,** a friendly, understated area of greenery that complements the row-house district.

Time Out | On the northeast corner of this intersection, the **Empire Diner** (210 10th Ave., tel. 212/243–2736), an Art Deco classic with its stainless-steel interior set off by black-and-chrome furnishings, is open 24 hours a day and even features live music. Entrée prices range from $7.95 to $15, but there's plenty on the milk-shake and dessert list for under $5. A full bar is available.

West 22nd Street also has a string of handsome old row houses just east of Tenth Avenue. **No. 435** was the longtime residence of actors Geraldine Page and Rip Torn, who were married in 1961; they nicknamed this Chelsea town house "The Torn Page." In 1987, a year after winning an Oscar for *The Trip to Bountiful,* Page suffered a fatal heart attack here.

⑩ On the block spanning 23rd and 24th streets, between Tenth and Ninth avenues, you can't miss the **London Terrace Apart-**

ments, a huge complex containing 1,670 apartments. When it first opened in 1930, the doormen dressed as London bobbies. It's actually made up of two rows of interconnected apartment buildings, which enclose a block-long private garden. As you walk along 23rd Street, notice the lions on the arched entryways: From the side they look as though they're snarling, but from the front they display wide grins.

The site of the Clarke family manor (where Clement Clarke Moore was born in 1779) was just across 23rd Street here, on what was then a high bluff overlooking the Hudson.

During the 1880s and Gay '90s, 23rd Street was the heart of the entertainment district, lined with theaters, music halls, and beer gardens. Today it is an undistinguished, even rundown, commercial thoroughfare, but there is one relic of its once-proud past: the **Chelsea Hotel**, at 222 West 23rd Street. Built of red brick with lacy wrought-iron balconies and a mansard roof, it opened in 1884 as a cooperative apartment house and became a hotel in 1905, although it has always catered to long-term tenants, with a tradition of broad-mindedness that has attracted many creative types. Its literary roll call of former tenants includes Mark Twain, Eugene O'Neill, O. Henry, Thomas Wolfe, Tennessee Williams, Vladimir Nabokov, Mary McCarthy, Brendan Behan, Arthur Miller, Dylan Thomas, William S. Burroughs, and Arthur C. Clarke (who wrote the script for *2001: A Space Odyssey* while living here). In 1966, Andy Warhol filmed artist Brigid Polk in her Chelsea hotel room, which eventually became *The Chelsea Girls*, considered by many to be Warhol's best film. More recently, the hotel was seen on screen in *Sid and Nancy* (1986), a dramatization of a true-life Chelsea Hotel murder, when drugged punk rocker Sid Vicious accidentally stabbed to death his girlfriend Nancy Spungeon. The shabby, seedy aura of the Chelsea Hotel is part of its allure. Read the commemorative plaques outside and then step into the lobby to look at the unusual artwork, some of it donated in lieu of rent by residents down on their luck.

The performing arts have made a comeback in Chelsea at **The Joyce Theater** (175 8th Ave. at 19th St.), the former Elgin movie house, which was gutted and transformed in 1982 into a sleek art deco/modern theater devoted to dance (*see* Dance in Chapter 10, below). Its presence, which helped revitalize the area, has attracted several good, moderately priced restaurants, especially south of the theater on Eighth Avenue.

Tour 12: Greenwich Village

Numbers in the margin correspond with points of interest on the Greenwich Village and the East Village map.

Greenwich Village, which New Yorkers almost invariably speak of simply as "the Village," enjoyed a raffish reputation for years. Originally a rural outpost of the city—a haven for New Yorkers during early 19th-century smallpox and yellow fever epidemics—many of its blocks still look somewhat pastoral, with brick town houses and low-rises, tiny green parks and hidden courtyards, and a crazy-quilt pattern of narrow, tree-lined streets. In the mid-19th century, however, as the city spread north of 14th Street, the Village became the province of immigrants, bohemians, and students (New York University, today the nation's largest private university, was planted next to

Washington Square in 1831). Its politics were radical and its attitudes tolerant, which is one reason it is home to such a large gay community today.

A lot has changed in the past 20 years, though. Today Village apartments and town houses go for high rents, and several posh restaurants have put down roots. Except for the isolated western fringe, where a string of tough gay bars along West Street attracts some drug traffic and prostitution, the Village is about as safe and clean as the Upper East Side. Nevertheless, something about the tangled street plan and the small buildings encourages anarchy. Shabby shopfronts, hole-in-the-wall restaurants, and nonmainstream arts groups persist and thrive here. There's still a large student population, and several longtime residents remain, paying cheap rents thanks to rent-control laws. The Village is no longer dangerous, but it still feels bohemian.

Several generations of writers and artists have lived and worked here: in the 19th century, Henry James, Edgar Allan Poe, Mark Twain, Walt Whitman, and Stephen Crane; at the turn of the century, O. Henry, Edith Wharton, Theodore Dreiser, and Hart Crane; and during the 1920s and '30s, John Dos Passos, Norman Rockwell, Sinclair Lewis, John Reed, Eugene O'Neill, Edward Hopper, and Edna St. Vincent Millay. In the late 1940s and early 1950s, the Abstract Expressionist painters Franz Kline, Jackson Pollock, Mark Rothko, and Willem de Kooning congregated here, as did the Beat writers Jack Kerouac, Allen Ginsberg, and Lawrence Ferlinghetti. The 1960s brought folk musicians and poets, notably Bob Dylan and Peter, Paul, and Mary.

Begin a tour of Greenwich Village at Washington Arch in ❶ **Washington Square** at the foot of Fifth Avenue. Designed by Stanford White, a wood version of Washington Arch was built in 1889 to commemorate the 100th anniversary of George Washington's presidential inauguration and was originally placed about half a block north of its present location. The arch was reproduced in stone in 1892, and the statues—*Washington at War* on the left, *Washington at Peace* on the right—were added in 1913. Body builder Charles Atlas modeled for *Peace*.

Washington Square started out as a cemetery, principally for yellow fever victims, and an estimated 10,000–22,000 bodies lie below. In the early 1800s it was a parade ground and the site of public executions; bodies dangled from a conspicuous Hanging Elm that still stands at the northwest corner of the square. Later Washington Square became the focus of a fashionable residential neighborhood and a center of outdoor activity.

By the early 1980s, Washington Square had deteriorated into a tawdry place only a drug dealer could love. Then community activism motivated a police crackdown that sent the drug traffic elsewhere and made Washington Square comfortable again for Frisbee players, street musicians, skateboarders, jugglers, stand-up comics, sitters, strollers, and a huge outdoor art fair each spring and fall.

Most of the buildings bordering Washington Square belong to New York University. **The Row,** a series of Federal-style town houses along Washington Square North between Fifth Avenue and University Place, now serves as faculty housing. At 7–13 Washington Square North, in fact, only the fronts were pre-

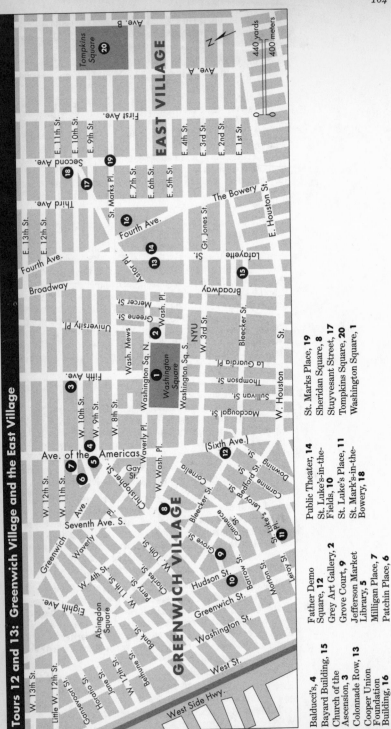

Tours 12 and 13: Greenwich Village and the East Village

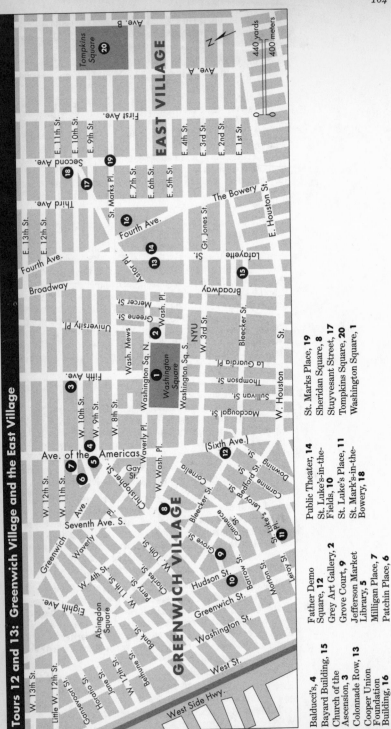

440 yards
400 meters

EAST VILLAGE

GREENWICH VILLAGE

Tompkins Square **20**

Washington Square **1**

Balducci's, **4**
Bayard Building, **15**
Church of the Ascension, **3**
Colonnade Row, **13**
Cooper Union Foundation Building, **16**

Father Demo Square, **12**
Grey Art Gallery, **2**
Grove Court, **9**
Jefferson Market Library, **5**
Milligan Place, **7**
Patchin Place, **6**

Public Theater, **14**
St. Luke's-in-the-Fields, **10**
St. Luke's Place, **11**
St. Mark's-in-the-Bowery, **18**

St. Marks Place, **19**
Sheridan Square, **8**
Stuyvesant Street, **17**
Tompkins Square, **20**
Washington Square, **1**

served, with a large Fifth Avenue apartment building taking over the space behind. Developers were not so tactful when they demolished 18 Washington Square, once the home of Henry James's grandmother, which he later used as the setting for his novel *Washington Square* (Henry himself was born just off the square, in a long-gone house on Washington Place). The house at 20 Washington Square North is the oldest building (1820) on the block. Notice its Flemish bond brickwork—alternate bricks inserted with the smaller surface (headers) facing out—which before 1830 was considered the best way to build stable walls.

On the east side of the square, NYU's main building contains ❷ the **Grey Art Gallery**, whose changing exhibitions usually focus on contemporary art. *33 Washington Pl., tel. 212/998-6780. Suggested donation: $1.50. Open Sept.–May, Tues., Thurs. and Fri. 11–6:30, Wed. 11–8:30, Sat. 11–5; June–Aug., weekdays 11–7.*

On the south side of the square, a trio of red sandstone hulks represents an abortive 1960s attempt to create a unified campus look for NYU, as envisioned by architects Philip Johnson and Richard Foster. At one time, plans called for all of the Washington Square buildings to be refaced in this red stone; fortunately, the cost proved prohibitive. On LaGuardia Place, the undistinguished modern **Loeb Student Center** stands on the site of a famous boardinghouse, nicknamed the House of Genius for the talented writers who had lived there over the years: Theodore Dreiser, Stephen Crane, Willa Cather, O. Henry, and Eugene O'Neill, among others. Across MacDougal Street is the square-towered **Judson Memorial Church** (the tower is now an NYU dormitory), designed by McKim, Mead & White.

Go up Fifth Avenue half a block to **Washington Mews**, a cobblestoned private street lined on one side with the former stables of the houses on The Row. Writer Walter Lippmann and artist-patron Gertrude Vanderbilt Whitney (founder of the Whitney Museum) once had homes in the mews; today it's mostly owned by NYU. A similar Village mews, **MacDougal Alley**, can be found between Eighth Street and the square just off MacDougal Street, one block west.

Eighth Street, the main commercial strip of Greenwich Village, is not the "real" Greenwich Village but a compendium of fast-food purveyors, poster and record shops, and clothing and shoe stores. The people along this street are often the "bridge and tunnel crowd"—a disparaging term Manhattanites use for those who come to the city, via bridge or tunnel, from the other boroughs or suburbs.

On the northwest corner of Fifth Avenue and West 10th Street, ❸ the **Church of the Ascension** is a Gothic-style brownstone designed by Richard Upjohn. Inside, you can admire stained-glass windows by John LaFarge and a marble altar sculpture by Augustus Saint-Gaudens. In 1844, President John Tyler married Julia Gardiner here.

Walk west on **11th Street,** one of the best examples of a Village town house block. One exception to the general 19th-century redbrick look is the modern, angled front window of 18 West 11th Street, usually occupied by a stuffed bear whose outfit changes from day to day. This house was built after the original was destroyed in a 1970 explosion; the owners' radical daughter, Kathy Boudin, had started a bomb factory in the basement with her Weathermen friends. At the time, actor Dustin Hoffman lived next door at No. 16; he was seen on TV news trying to rescue his personal possessions. Hoffman's costar in *The Graduate*, Anne Bancroft, later lived down at 52 West 11th Street with her husband, director Mel Brooks.

On Avenue of the Americas (Sixth Avenue), turn left to sample **④** the wares at **Balducci's** (6th Ave. and 9th St.), a full-service gourmet food store that sprouted from the vegetable stand of the late Louis Balducci, Sr. Along with more than 80 Italian cheeses and 50 kinds of bread, this family-owned enterprise features imported Italian specialties and a prodigious selection of fresh seafood.

Directly opposite, the triangle formed by West 10th Street, Sixth Avenue, and Greenwich Avenue originally held a greenmarket, a jail, and the magnificent towered courthouse **⑤** that is now the **Jefferson Market Library**. Critics variously termed the courthouse's hodgepodge of styles Venetian, Victorian, or Italian; Villagers, noting the alternating wide bands of red brick and narrow strips of granite, dubbed it the Lean Bacon Style. Over the years, the structure has housed a number of government agencies (public works, civil defense, census bureau, police academy); it was on the verge of demolition when public-spirited citizens saved it and turned it into a public library in 1967. Note the fountain at the corner of West 10th Street and Sixth Avenue, and the seal of the City of New York on the east front; inside, look at the handsome interior doorways and climb the graceful circular stairway. If the gate is open, visit the flower garden behind the library, a project run by local green thumbs.

Just west of Sixth Avenue on 10th Street is the wrought-iron **⑥** gateway to a tiny courtyard called **Patchin Place**; around the corner, on Sixth Avenue just north of 10th Street, is a similar **⑦** cul-de-sac, **Milligan Place**, which few New Yorkers even know is there. Both were built around 1850 for the waiters (mostly Basques) who worked at the high-society Brevoort Hotel, long ago demolished, on Fifth Avenue. Patchin Place later became home to several writers, including Theodore Dreiser, e.e. cummings, and Djuna Barnes.

Take Christopher Street, which veers off from the southern end of the library triangle, a few steps to **Gay Street.** A bending lane lined with small row houses circa 1810, Gay Street was originally a black neighborhood and later a strip of speakeasies. Ruth McKinney lived and wrote *My Sister Eileen* in the basement of No. 14, and Howdy Doody was designed in the basement of No. 12.

At the end of Gay Street go west on Waverly Place to the midstreet island occupied by the **Northern Dispensary**, an institution that from 1827 provided health care (first free, then inexpensive) for the needy. In 1988, the debt-ridden clinic, which by then performed only dental services, was heavily fined for refusing to treat two men infected with AIDS and finally had to close its doors. Ironically, the Roman Catholic Archdiocese, which took over the site, decided to turn it into a nursing home for AIDS patients.

Time Out Where Christopher meets Grove and Waverly Place, **Pierre's** (170 Waverly Pl., tel. 212/929–7194) is everyone's favorite little French corner bistro. The sumptuous couscous and the profiteroles are two specialties. Music may include guitar or piano during dinner at this relaxed, friendly place.

As you go west on Christopher Street, you'll pass steps leading down to the **Lion's Head** (59 Christopher St.), a longtime hangout for literary types. Before she found stardom, Jessica Lange was a waitress here. The restaurant faces onto a green triangle that's technically called **Christopher Park,** but it contains a statue of Civil War general Philip Sheridan; this confuses New Yorkers, because there's another triangle to the south (between Washington Place, Barrow Street, and Seventh Avenue) **8** called **Sheridan Square.** Formerly covered with asphalt, Sheridan Square was recently landscaped following an extensive dig by urban archaelogists, who unearthed artifacts dating back to the Dutch and Native American eras.

Sheridan Square was the site of a nasty 1863 riot in which a group of freed slaves were nearly lynched; in 1969, gays and police clashed nearby during a protest march that galvanized the gay rights movement. Across the busy intersection of Seventh Avenue, **Christopher Street** comes into its own as the symbolic heart of New York's gay community. Many bars and stores along here cater to that clientele, although the street is by no means off-limits to other people.

West of Seventh Avenue, the Village turns into a picture-book town of twisting, tree-lined streets, quaint houses, and tiny restaurants. Follow Grove Street from Sheridan Square past the boyhood home of poet Hart Crane (45 Grove St.) to the crossing of Grove and Bedford streets, a secluded intersection that seems to have fallen through a time warp into the 19th century. On the northeast corner stands one of the few remaining clapboard structures in the city (17 Grove St.); wood construction was banned as a fire hazard in 1822, the year it was built. The house has since served many functions; it housed a brothel during the Civil War. Behind it, at 102 Bedford Street, is **Twin Peaks,** an 1835 house that was rather whimsically altered in the 1920s, with stucco, half-timbers, and a pair of steep roof peaks added on.

9 Grove Street curves in front of the iron gate of **Grove Court,** an enclave of brick-fronted town houses from the mid-1800s. Built originally as apartments for employees at neighborhood hotels, Grove Court used to be called Mixed Ale Alley because of the residents' propensity to pool beverages brought from work. It now houses a more affluent crowd: A town house there recently sold for $3 million.

Time Out Don't miss **Patisserie J. Lanciani** (271 W. 4th St., between W. 11th and Perry Sts., tel. 212/929–0739), a tiny black-and-white café where writers gain inspiration as they sample the fresh-baked pastries and the excellent coffee.

The building at 77 Bedford Street is the oldest house in the Village (1799). The place next door, 75½ Bedford Street, has an even greater claim to fame: Not only was it the residence (at different times) of both Edna St. Vincent Millay and John Barrymore, it is also, at 9½ feet wide, New York's narrowest house. The lot was an alley until rising real-estate prices inspired construction in 1873.

Heading west on Commerce Street, you soon reach the **Cherry Lane Theater,** one of the original Off-Broadway houses and the site of American premieres of works by O'Neill, Beckett, Ionesco, and Albee. Across the street stand two nearly identical brick houses separated by a garden. Popularly known as the **Twin Sisters,** the houses were said to have been built by a sea captain for two daughters who loathed each other. Historical record insists that they were built by a milkman who needed the two houses and an open courtyard for his work.

Follow Barrow Street to Hudson Street, so named because this was originally the bank of the Hudson River. The block to the **⑩** northwest is owned by **St. Luke's-in-the-Fields,** built in 1822 as a country chapel for downtown's Trinity Church; its first warden was Clement ("'Twas the Night Before Christmas") Clarke Moore, who figured so largely in Chelsea's history (*see* Tour 11, above). An unadorned structure of soft-colored brick, St. Luke's was nearly destroyed by fire in 1981, but a flood of donations, many quite small, from residents of the West Village financed restoration of the square central tower. A gem of a garden is hidden behind the brick wall; although it is supposed to be open only to residents of the row houses along Hudson Street, which are owned by the church, discreet visitors will not be disturbed—provided they can find their way in past the school behind the church. Bret Harte once lived at 487 Hudson Street, at the end of the row.

Walk south to Leroy Street, which on the east side of Hudson **⑪** becomes **St. Luke's Place,** a row of classic 1860s town houses shaded by graceful gingko trees. Novelist Theodore Dreiser wrote *An American Tragedy* at No. 16; poet Marianne Moore lived at No. 14, playwright Sherwood Anderson at No. 12. Mayor Jimmy Walker (first elected in 1926) lived at No. 6; the lampposts in front are "mayor's lamps," which were sometimes placed in front of the residences of New York mayors. This block is often used as a film location, too: No. 12 is shown as the Huxtables' home on "The Cosby Show" (although the family supposedly lives in Brooklyn), while No. 4 was the setting of the movie *Wait Until Dark*. Before 1890 the playground on the south side of the street was a graveyard where, according to legend, the dauphin of France—the lost son of Louis XVI and Marie Antoinette—is buried.

Across Seventh Avenue, St. Luke's Place becomes Leroy Street again, which terminates in an old Italian neighborhood at Bleecker Street. Amazingly unchanged amid all the Village gentrification, Bleecker between Sixth and Seventh avenues seems more vital these days than Little Italy does. Stop into one of the fragrant Italian bakeries (**Zito's,** 259 Bleecker St., and **Rocco's,** 243 Bleecker St.), or look inside the old-style butcher shops (**Ottomanelli's,** 285 Bleecker St., and **Faicco's,** 260 Bleecker St.). **John's Pizzeria** (278 Bleecker St.) is one of those places that locals swear by. Be forewarned, however: no slices; whole pies only. You may also be tempted to stop in at the **Lafayette Bakery** (298 Bleecker St.); it's French rather than Italian, but the treats are luscious all the same. The activi- **⑫** ty here focuses on **Father Demo Square** (Bleecker St. and 6th Ave.). Across Bleecker Street you'll see the **Church of Our**

Lady of Pompeii, where Mother Cabrini, a naturalized Italian immigrant who became the first American saint, often prayed.

Head up Sixth Avenue to Third Street and check out the playground caged there within a chain-link fence. NBA stars of tomorrow learn their moves on this patch of asphalt, where city-style basketball is played all afternoon and evening in all but the very coldest weather. Across the street, the **Waverly Theater** (323 6th Ave.), a former church converted to a cinema in 1937, is popular with moviegoers for its cult films and midnight shows.

Return along Washington Square South to MacDougal Street and turn right. The **Provincetown Playhouse** (133 MacDougal St.) premiered many of Eugene O'Neill's plays. The two houses at 127 and 129 MacDougal Street were built for Aaron Burr in 1829; notice the pineapple newel posts, a symbol of hospitality. Louisa May Alcott wrote *Little Women* while living at 130-132 MacDougal Street.

At **Minetta Tavern** (113 MacDougal St.), a venerable Village watering hole, turn right onto **Minetta Lane,** which leads to narrow **Minetta Street,** another former speakeasy alley. Both streets follow the course of Minetta Brook, which once flowed through this neighborhood and still bubbles deep beneath the pavement.

The foot of Minetta Street returns you to the corner of Sixth Avenue and Bleecker Street, where you reach the stomping grounds of 1960s-era folksingers (many of them performed at the now-defunct Folk City one block north on West 3rd Street). This area still attracts a young crowd—partly because of the proximity of NYU—to its cafés, bars, jazz clubs, coffeehouses, theaters, and cabarets (*see* Chapter 11), not to mention its long row of unpretentious ethnic restaurants.

Time Out Turn back up MacDougal to stop at the neighborhood's oldest coffeehouse, **Caffe Reggio** (119 MacDougal St., tel. 212/475–9557), where an antique machine steams forth espresso and cappuccino. The tiny tables are close together, but the crowd usually makes for interesting eavesdropping.

Farther east on Bleecker Street, the former **Bleecker Street Cinema** (144 Bleecker St.) was converted from a pair of row houses to a famous 1880s Italian restaurant to a respected repertory cinema. This is the theater where Woody Allen sat rapt in *Crimes and Misdemeanors*, but in 1990 it became one more in a string of rep houses to fall prey to rising New York rents.

Beyond LaGuardia Place (named after the same Mayor Fiorello La Guardia as the airport) loom the modern dorms of New York University. Turn to the left and you're back at Washington Square.

Tour 13: The East Village

Numbers in the margin correspond with points of interest on the Greenwich Village and the East Village map.

The gritty tenements of the East Village—an area bounded by 14th Street on the north, Fourth Avenue or the Bowery on the west, Houston Street on the south, and the East River—provided inexpensive living places for artists, writers, and actors until very recently. Now the East Village can be as costly a place to live as anywhere else south of 96th Street.

In a way, the area has the best of both worlds. New residents have brought in their wake new restaurants, shops, and somewhat cleaner streets, while the old East Villagers maintain the trappings of the counterculture. Longtime iconoclastic theaters such as CSC (Classic Stage Company) Repertory and LaMama (*see* Chapter 10) continue to thrive, although the "hot" art galleries that opened in narrow East Village storefronts a couple of years ago have already deserted this no-longer-a-bargain neighborhood, seeking more floor space in other parts of town.

To explore the East Village, begin at the intersection of East 8th Street, Fourth Avenue, and Astor Place. Sculpture adorns two traffic islands here: One island contains *Alamo*, a massive black cube sculpted by Bernard Rosenthal; another bears an ornate cast-iron replica of a Beaux Arts subway entrance, providing access to the uptown No. 6 line. Go down into the station to see the authentically reproduced wall tiles.

Just west of the intersection, **Astor Wine and Spirits** (12 Astor Pl.) is one of New York's most comprehensive liquor stores, offering good prices on imports and even better deals on house brands. (New York State has unexpectedly restrictive liquor-control laws: Liquor and wine can be sold only in liquor stores, which sell *only* liquor and wine—no beer, soda, ice, or glasses—and must close on Sundays.)

Continue west on Astor Place to **Astor Place Hair Designers** (2 Astor Pl.), where lines of people stretch out to the sidewalk awaiting service. Choose your cut from Polaroids in the window—maybe the Village Cut, a Guido, or a L'il Tony. It costs only $10 for men and $12 for women, and it's open every day.

Continue west to Broadway, where you turn left to hit a trendy downtown shopping strip, especially strong in funky second-hand and surplus clothing stores. Above street level, the old warehouses here have mostly been converted into residential lofts. Walk south to 4th Street, where you'll see **Tower Records** (692 Broadway, tel. 212/505–1500), a very big and very good record-tape-and-CD store that also serves as a mingling place for young hipsters (or would-be hipsters).

Go east on 4th Street to Lafayette Street and turn left. The **⓭** long block ahead of you on your left contains **Colonnade Row** (1833), a grand sweep of four houses (originally nine) fronted by marble Corinthian columns. Although sadly run-down today, in their time these houses were home to millionaires John Jacob Astor and Cornelius Vanderbilt; writers Washington Irving, William Makepeace Thackeray, and Charles Dickens all stayed here at one time or another.

In 1854 Astor opened the city's first free library in the imposing Italian Renaissance–style structure directly across the street, which was renovated in 1967 to serve as the New York Shake-**⓮** speare Festival's **Public Theater**. Under the leadership of producer Joseph Papp, the Public's five playhouses and one cinema present a broad-based repertoire (*see* Chapter 10); the long-running hit *A Chorus Line* had its first performances here, but so have many less commercial plays. The New York Shakespeare Festival is in the midst of a six-year marathon that, for the first time in America, will present in turn all of Shakespeare's plays. *425 Lafayette St., tel. 212/598–7150. Theater tickets: $10–$25 for regular performances, $30 for Shakespeare Marathon productions. Some half-price tickets for most performances available at 6 PM (matinees, 1 PM); the line forms 1–2 hrs earlier, and before that for the most popular shows.*

15 Walk down Lafayette Street to Bleecker Street and turn right. On your left, facing Crosby Street, is the **Bayard Building** (65 Bleecker St.), built in 1898 as the Condict Building and the only structure in New York City designed by Louis Sullivan, one of the Chicago School's leading architects. Its emphatic vertical emphasis and simplicity in its major lines made it radically different from the prevailing, comparatively overadorned Beaux Arts style in New York.

16 Return to Lafayette Street and work north to Astor Place and turn right, heading toward the massive brownstone **Cooper Union Foundation Building.** This college was founded in 1859 by industrialist Peter Cooper, who wanted to provide a forum for public opinion and free technical education for the working class; it still offers tuition-free education and an active public affairs program. Cooper Union was the first structure to be supported by steel railroad rails—rolled in Cooper's own plant. Three galleries present changing exhibitions during the academic year. Walk south along the building to **Cooper Square,** the large open space created where Fourth and Third avenues merge into the Bowery. A statue of Peter Cooper by Augustus Saint-Gaudens presides over the square.

Musicians may want to stop in at the **Carl Fischer Music Store** (62 Cooper Sq., tel. 212/677–1148) to select from the infinitude of sheet music, confer with the knowledgeable staff, and hang out with the musicians there.

A few steps east of Cooper Square on 7th Street, **Surma, The Ukrainian Shop** (11 E. 7th St.) celebrates this neighborhood's tightly knit Ukrainian community. (Across the street, look at the mosaic dome of **St. George's Ukrainian Catholic Church.**) Surma's exotic stock includes Ukrainian books, magazines, and cassette tapes; greeting cards; musical instruments; colorful painted eggs and Surma's own brand of egg coloring; honey; and an exhaustive selection of peasant blouses.

McSorley's Old Ale House (15 E. 7th St.), one of several claimants to the distinction of being New York's oldest bar, is often crammed with collegiate types enticed by McSorley's own brands of ale. McSorley's opened in 1854 but didn't admit women until 1970.

17 Return to Third Avenue and walk north to **Stuyvesant Street,** basically a block-long continuation of Astor Place that angles up toward 10th Street, running through what was once Governor Peter Stuyvesant's "bouwerie," or farm. The house at 21 Stuyvesant Street was built in 1804 as a wedding gift for a great-great-granddaughter of the governor. The redbrick row houses at Nos. 23–35 and 42–46 were added in the 1860s; a similar one around the corner, at 118 East 10th Street, was the childhood home of architect Stanford White.

18 Stuyvesant Street ends in front of **St. Mark's-in-the-Bowery Church,** a 1799 fieldstone country church to which a Greek Revival steeple and a cast-iron front porch have been added. This, the city's oldest continually used church building (Governor Stuyvesant and Commodore Perry are buried here), had to be completely restored after a disastrous fire in 1978. Over the years, St. Mark's has hosted much countercultural activity. In the 1920s a forward-thinking pastor injected the Episcopalian ritual with Native American chants, Greek folk dancing, and Eastern mantras. During the hippie era, St. Mark's welcomed avant-garde poets and playwrights. Today dancers, poets, and performance artists cavort in the main sanctuary, where pews have been removed to accommodate them.

Second Avenue, which borders the church on the east, was known in the early part of this century as the Yiddish Rialto. Between Houston and 14th streets, eight theaters presented Yiddish-language productions of musicals, revues, and heart-wrenching melodramas. Today the theaters are gone; all that remains are Hollywood-style stars that have been embedded in the sidewalk in front of the **Second Avenue Deli** (2nd Ave. and 10th St.) to commemorate Yiddish stage luminaries.

Time Out   For some of the best Italian pastries in the city, try **Veniero Pasticceria** (342 E. 11th St. near 1st Ave., tel. 212/674–7264), a lively café that has rows and rows of incredibly fresh cannolis, fruit tarts, cheesecakes, and other desserts on display. If you can't get in, try **De Robertis Pasticceria** (176 1st Ave., tel. 212/674–7137); it's a more subdued neighborhood hangout.

19   The intersection of Second Avenue and **St. Marks Place** (the name given to 8th Street in the East Village) is the hub of the "hip" East Village. During the 1950s beatniks such as Allen Ginsberg and Jack Kerouac lived and wrote in the area; the 1960s brought Bill Graham's Fillmore East concerts, the Electric Circus, and hallucinogenic drugs. The black-clad, pink-haired or shaven-headed punks followed, and many of them remain today. St. Marks Place between Second and Third avenues is a counterculture bazaar lined with vegetarian restaurants, jewelry stalls, leather shops, haircutters, and stores selling books, posters, and weird clothing; **St. Marks Bookshop** (12 St. Marks Pl.) is excellent for browsing and for getting a sense of the neighborhood. The East Village always manages to get all the styles first; the trend that *Time* magazine will discover in six months is parading down St. Marks Place today.

On the other side of Second Avenue, **Theater 80 St. Marks** (80 St. Marks Pl., tel. 212/254–7400), one of New York's few remaining revival movie houses, shows a different double feature almost daily (the Friday and Saturday bills are the same). The fare includes vintage American and foreign films, some relatively recent finds, and cult classics.

P.S. 122 (150 1st Ave. at 9th St., tel. 212/477–5288) is a former public school building transformed into a complex of spaces for avant-garde entertainment. Shocking, often crude, and predictably unpredictable, P.S. 122 happenings translate the spirit of the streets into performance art. Prices are low, rarely more than $10, except for occasional benefit performances.

East of First Avenue, Manhattan avenues are designated with letters, not numbers, earning this area the nickname Alphabet City. Until relatively recently, Alphabet City also meant a burned-out territory of slums and drug haunts, but colonization by the avant-garde art community changed all that. At the height of the East Village art scene, only a few years ago, there were more than two dozen galleries here, featuring work that was often startling, innovative, or political. The art dealers, however, have either gone out of business or moved to more mainstream (and spacious) sites in SoHo or Greenwich Village.

20 A focal point for the Far East Village is **Tompkins Square**, the leafy park bordered by Avenues A and B and 7th and 10th streets. Although the square itself could use a face-lift (it is currently closed for renovations), the restored brownstones along 10th Street are evidence that Tompkins Square is already smartly gentrified. In the past few years, however, the park has come to symbolize the tension between old and new East Villagers. As police moved to rid the park of vagrants—long a customary feature here—a bloody confrontation broke out in the summer of 1988, and the incident was nearly repeated in the summer of 1989.

Time Out **Jerry's 103** (103 2nd Ave., at 6th St., tel. 212/777–4120) stays open until 2 AM four days a week, and until 4 AM Thurs.–Sat. Its reasonably priced menu (pizzas, pastas, salads, and seafood) and informal atmosphere make it popular at all hours, especially with young artists.

Tour 14: SoHo and TriBeCa

Numbers in the margin correspond with points of interest on the SoHo, TriBeCa, Little Italy, Chinatown map.

Today the names of these two downtown neighborhoods are virtually synonymous with a certain postmodern chic—an amalgam of black-clad artists, hip young Wall Streeters, track-lit loft apartments, new "hot" galleries, and restaurants with a minimalist approach to both food and decor. It's all very urban, very cool, very now. But 25 years ago, they were virtual wastelands. SoHo (so named because it is the district *So*uth of *Ho*uston Street, bounded by Broadway, Canal Street, and Sixth Avenue) was described in a 1962 City Club of New York study as "commercial slum number one." It was saved by two factors: (1) preservationists discovered here the world's greatest concentration of cast-iron architecture, and fought to prevent demolition, and (2) artists discovered the large, cheap, well-lit spaces that cast-iron buildings provide. At first it was technically illegal for artists to live in their loft studios, but so many did that eventually the zoning laws were changed to permit residence.

By 1980, the tide of loft dwellers, galleries, and trendy shops and cafés had made SoHo so desirable a residential area, despite the still-gritty look of the neighborhood, that none but the most successful artists could afford it anymore. Seeking similar space, artists moved downtown to another half-abandoned commercial district, for which a new SoHo-like name was invented: TriBeCa (the *Tri*angle *Be*low *Ca*nal Street, although in effect it goes no farther south than Murray Street and no farther east than West Broadway). The same scenario played itself out again, and TriBeCa's rising rents are already beyond the means of most artists, who have moved instead to Long Island City (*see* Chapter 4) or areas of Brooklyn or New

Jersey. But just because the artists have left doesn't mean that SoHo and TriBeCa aren't still a vital scene.

Perhaps the best introduction to these areas is a walk up Greene Street, where the block between Canal and Grand streets contains the longest continuous row of cast-iron buildings anywhere (Nos. 8–34 Greene St.). The architectural rage between 1860 and 1890, cast-iron buildings were popular because they did not require massive walls to bear the weight of the upper stories. With no need for load-bearing walls, they were able to have more interior space and larger windows. They were also versatile, with various architectural elements produced from standardized molds to mimic any style—Italianate, Victorian Gothic, neo-Grec, to name but a few visible in SoHo. Look, for example, at 28–30 Greene Street, an 1873 **❶** building nicknamed the **Queen of Greene Street**. Besides its pale paint job, notice how many decorative features have been applied: dormers, columns, window arches, and projecting central bays. Handsome as they are, these buildings were always commercial, housing stores and light manufacturing, principally textiles. Along this street notice the iron-loading docks and the sidewalk vault covers studded with glass disks to let light into basement storage areas. In front of 62–64 Greene Street there's one of the few remaining turn-of-the-century bishop's-crook lampposts, with various cast-iron curlicues from the base to the curved top.

❷ At 72–76 Greene Street is the so-called **King of Greene Street**, a five-story Renaissance-style building with a magnificent projecting porch of Corinthian columns. Today the King (now painted yellow) houses three art galleries—**Ariel, Condeso/ Lawler,** and **M-13**—plus **The Second Coming,** which sells vintage clothing, furniture, and other curiosities.

At the northeast corner of Prince and Greene streets, turn to look at the corner diagonally opposite for a rare glimpse of the side of an iron-front building. You'll see the same window pattern and decoration continued, with one window open and a cat sitting on the sill—where it has sat since 1973, when artist Richard Haas first painted this meticulously realistic **mural** on the blank side wall.

Take Prince Street west to Wooster Street, which, like a few other SoHo streets, still has its 19th-century pavement of Belgian blocks, a smoother successor to traditional cobblestones. At 141 Wooster Street, one of several outposts of the DIA Art **❸** Foundation, you can visit the **New York Earth Room,** Walter de Maria's avant-garde 1977 artwork that consists of 140 tons of gently sculpted soil filling a second-floor gallery. *Tel. 212/473–8072. Admission free. Open Wed.–Sat. noon–6.*

Continue west on Prince Street to West Broadway (which, somewhat confusingly, runs parallel to and four blocks west of regular Broadway). This is SoHo's main drag, and on Saturday it can be crowded with smartly dressed uptowners and suburbanites who've come down for a little store- and gallery-hopping (*see* Chapter 7). In the block between Prince and Spring streets alone there are three major art stops: 420 **West Broadway,** with six separate galleries including two of the biggest SoHo names, Leo Castelli and the Sonnabend Gallery; the **Mary Boone Gallery** (417 West Broadway); and another excellent cluster of galleries at **415 West Broadway.** One block south, at **383 West Broadway,** OK Harris has its digs.

Time Out   The crowded, lively **Cupping Room Cafe** (359 West Broadway, tel. 212/925–2898) specializes in comforting soups, muffins, and daily specials, as well as substantial Bloody Marys. A few blocks west you can treat yourself to a three- or five-course lunch ($16–$20) or a five-course dinner ($32) at the student-operated restaurant of The French Culinary Institute, **L'École** (462 Broadway and Grand St., tel. 212/219–8890); you'll get classic French food served in a visually creative presentation.

4   Go east to Broome Street and Broadway where, on the northeast corner, you'll see the sadly unrestored classic of the cast-iron genre, the **Haughwout Building** (488 Broadway), nicknamed the Parthenon of Cast Iron. Built in 1857 to house Eder Haughwout's china and glassware business, the exterior was inspired by a Venetian palazzo. Inside, it contained the world's first commercial passenger elevator, a steam-powered device invented by Elisha Graves Otis.

5   Head north up Broadway, which temporarily loses its SoHo ambience in the midst of discount clothing stores. Just below Prince Street, the 1907 **Singer Building** (561 Broadway) shows the final flower of the cast-iron style, with wrought-iron balconies, terra-cotta panels, and broad expanses of windows. Across the street is one of New York's gourmet shrines, the gleaming **Dean & DeLuca** food market (560 Broadway), whose bread and produce arrangements often are worthy of still-life paintings. The smartly restored **560 Broadway** building also houses a respected multigallery exhibit space; another such space is just up the street at **568 Broadway.**

6   On the west side of Broadway, the **New Museum of Contemporary Art** shows experimental, often radically innovative work by unrecognized artists, none of it more than 10 years old. *583 Broadway between Prince and Houston Sts., tel. 212/219–1222. Suggested donation: $3.50 adults, $2.50 students, senior citizens, and artists. Open Wed., Thurs., and Sun. noon–6; Fri. and Sat. noon–8.*

Go one block west to stone-paved Mercer Street, where the sidewalks may be cluttered with cartons of cloth or leather remnants discarded by the sweatshops upstairs (artists find a lot of good collage material here). Between Broome and Spring streets is **Enchanted Forest** (85 Mercer St., tel. 212/925–6677), with a fanciful selection of stuffed animals, books, and handmade toys that almost deserves to be considered an art gallery. Both kids and adults have a great time here.

7   Two blocks farther south, **The Museum of Holography** has a permanent exhibit on the history of holograms, three-dimensional photographs created by laser beams. This combination science show and art gallery projects a film on holography and has three changing exhibitions a year. The gift shop has a terrific selection of 3-D art and souvenirs. *11 Mercer St. (near Canal St.), tel. 212/925–0581. Admission: $3.50 adults, $2.50 students, children, and senior citizens. Open daily 11–6.*

8   Walk one block to your right on Canal Street, then cross and you're officially in TriBeCa. Go south on Church Street, and turn west on White Street to visit the **Alternative Museum,** a

Alternative Museum, **8**

Chatham Square, **21**

Columbus Park, **22**

Confucius Plaza, **24**

The D & G Bakery, **17**

Duane Park, **9**

First Shearith Israel graveyard, **23**

Grotta Azzurra, **12**

Haughwout Building, **4**

Independence Plaza, **10**

Kam Man, **19**

King of Greene Street, **2**

The Museum of Holography, **7**

New Museum of Contemporary Art, **6**

New York Chinatown History Project, **20**

New York Earth Room, **3**

The Police Building, **16**

Puck Building, **18**

Puglia, **14**

Queen of Greene Street, **1**

San Gennaro Church, **15**

Singer Building, **5**

Umberto's Clam House, **13**

Washington Market Park, **11**

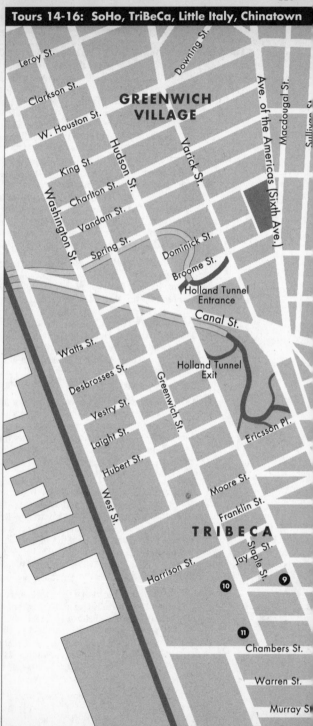

Tours 14-16: SoHo, TriBeCa, Little Italy, Chinatown

gallery that exhibits art with a political or sociopolitical twist. *17 White St., tel. 212/966–4444. Suggested donation: $3. Open Tues.–Sat. 11–6.*

Continue south, down West Broadway, past the life-size iron Statue of Liberty crown above the blue-tiled entrance to **El Teddy's,** a gourmet Mexican restaurant. Stop in for a drink, if only to see how the kitschy decor has been carried out inside.

In the mid-19th century, Worth Street was the equivalent of Seventh Avenue today, the center of the garment trade; the area to the west, near the Hudson River docks, became the heart of the wholesale food business. Turn right onto Duane Street to reach **Duane Park,** preserved since 1800 as a calm, shady triangle; it is still surrounded by cheese, butter, and egg warehouses (note the Land O'Lakes sign facing the south tip of the park).

One block north on Hudson Street, on your right you'll see the Art Deco **Western Union Building** (60 Hudson St.), where 19 subtly shaded colors of brick are laid in undulating patterns. Turn up quiet Jay Street, and pause at narrow Staple Street, little more than an alley, where a green pedestrian walkway overhead links two warehouses. The street is named for the staple products unloaded here by ships in transit that didn't want to pay duty on any extra cargo. Framed at the end of the alley is the redbrick **New York Mercantile Exchange,** its square corner tower topped by a bulbous roof. On the ground floor is an acclaimed restaurant, **Chanterelle** (*see* Chapter 8).

If you continue west on Jay Street, you'll pass the loading docks of a very active food wholesaler, **Bazzini's Nuts and Confections.** Tucked into a corner of its extensive warehouse is its upscale retail shop (corner of Jay and Greenwich Sts.), where you can buy nuts, coffee beans, candies, cookies, and various other delicacies.

On the corner of Greenwich and Harrison streets, a surprising row of early-19th-century town houses is nestled in the side of a huge high-rise apartment complex. These three-story redbrick houses were moved here from various sites in the neighborhood when, in the early 1970s, the food-wholesalers' central market nearby was razed and moved to the Bronx. Walk around the houses to peer into the green yard they enclose.

Time Out The **TriBeCa Grill** (375 Greenwich St., tel. 212/941–3900) is located on the first floor of the old Martinson Coffee Building, which now houses actor Robert De Niro's **Tribeca Film Center,** a movie production complex. The Grill specializes in fresh grilled fish, sumptuous salads, and charcuterie. And that's the old Maxwell Plum's bar in the middle of the restaurant.

The high-rise towers belong to **Independence Plaza,** a pleasant, if somewhat utilitarian, project of the mid-1970s that was supposed to be part of a wave of demolition and construction—until the preservationists stepped in. For several years Independence Plaza remained a middle-class island stranded downtown, far from stores, schools, and neighbors; with TriBeCa's growing chic, however, plus the development of Battery Park City to the south, it has become a much more desirable address.

Movie fans may want to continue north to Moore Street, where a right turn will take you two blocks to 14 Moore Street, the firehouse (still in use) that was filmed as the **Ghostbusters' headquarters** in the movies *Ghostbusters* and *Ghostbusters II*.

⑪ If you go south on Greenwich Street, you'll soon come to the 2½-acre **Washington Market Park**, a much-needed recreation space for this neighborhood. Named after the great food market that once sprawled over this area, it is a green, landscaped oasis with tennis courts, a playground, and even a gazebo. Just across Chambers Street, P.S. 234, a public elementary school, has opened to serve TriBeCa's younger generation. At the corner, a stout little red tower resembles a lighthouse, and iron ship figures are worked into the playground fence—reminders of the neighborhood's long-gone dockside past.

Tour 15: Little Italy

Numbers in the margin correspond with points of interest on the SoHo, TriBeCa, Little Italy, Chinatown map.

Mulberry Street is the heart of Little Italy; in fact, at this point it's virtually the entire body. In 1932 an estimated 98% of the inhabitants of this area were of Italian birth or heritage, but since then the growth and expansion of neighboring Chinatown has encroached on the Italian neighborhood to such an extent that merchants and community leaders of the Little Italy Restoration Association (LIRA) negotiated a truce in which the Chinese agreed to let at least Mulberry remain an all-Italian Street. If you want the flavor of a whole Italian neighborhood, you'd do better visiting Carroll Gardens in Brooklyn or Arthur Avenue in the Bronx (*see* Chapter 4); or rent a video of the Martin Scorsese movie *Mean Streets*, which was filmed in Little Italy back in the very early 1970s.

Start at the intersection of Grand and Mulberry streets. Facing north (uptown), on your right you'll see a series of wide, four-story houses from the early 19th century, built long before the great flood of immigration hit this neighborhood between 1890 and 1924. Turn and look south along the east side of Mulberry Street to see Little Italy's predominant architecture today: tenement buildings with fire escapes projecting over the sidewalks. Most of these are of the late-19th-century New York style known as railroad flats: six-story buildings on 25-by-90-foot lots, with all the rooms in each apartment placed in a straight line like railroad cars. This style was common in the densely populated immigrant neighborhoods of lower Manhattan until 1901, when the city passed an ordinance requiring air shafts in the interior of buildings.

Today Mulberry Street between Broome and Canal streets is crowded with restaurants, cafés, bakeries, imported food shops, and souvenir stores. Especially on weekends, when suburbanites flock here, this is a street for strolling, gawking, and inhaling the aroma of garlic and olive oil. Some restaurants and cafés display high-tech Eurodesign; others seem dedicated to staying exactly as their old customers remember them. One block north, at the southwest corner of Broome and Mulberry streets, stairs lead down through a glass entrance to what seems to be a blue-tiled cave—and, appropriately enough, it is ⑫ the **Grotta Azzurra** (Blue Grotto) restaurant (387 Broome St., tel. 212/925–8775), a longtime favorite for both the hearty food and the very Italian ambience. Across Mulberry Street is **Caffe Roma** (385 Broome St., 212/226–8413), a traditional pastry shop where you can eat cannoli at postage-stamp-size wrought-iron tables. At the corner of Mulberry and Grand, **E. Rossi & Co.** (established in 1902) is an antiquated little shop that sells housewares, espresso makers, embroidered religious postcards, and jocular Italian T-shirts. Down Grand Street is **Ferrara's** (195 Grand St., tel. 212/226–6150), a 100-year-old pastry shop that ships its creations—cannoli, peasant pie, Italian rum cake—all over the world. Another survivor of the pretenement era is at 149 Mulberry Street, formerly the Van Rensselaer House (built in 1816); notice its dormer windows. Today it houses **Paolucci's Restaurant.**

⓭ **Umberto's Clam House** (129 Mulberry St., tel. 212/431–7545) is perhaps best known as the place where mobster Joey Gallo was munching scungili in 1973 when he was fatally surprised by a task force of mob hit men. Quite peaceful now, Umberto's specializes in fresh shellfish in a spicy tomato sauce. Turn onto Hester Street to visit yet another Little Italy institution, ⓮ **Puglia** (189 Hester St., tel. 212/966–6006), a restaurant where guests sit at long communal tables, sing along with house entertainers, and enjoy moderately priced Southern Italian specialties with quantities of homemade wine. (For other Little Italy restaurants, *see* Chapter 8.)

⓯ One street west, on Baxter Street toward Canal Street, stands the **San Gennaro Church** (officially, Most Precious Blood Church, National Shrine of San Gennaro), which each year around September 19 sponsors Little Italy's keynote event, the annual Feast of San Gennaro. (The community's other big festival celebrates St. Anthony of Padua, in June; that church is at Houston and Sullivan streets, in what is now SoHo.) During the feasts, Little Italy's streets are closed to traffic, arches of tinsel span the thoroughfares, the sidewalks are lined with booths offering games and food, and the whole scene is one noisy, crowded, kitschy, delightful party.

Where are the cops when you need them? Certainly not in the former police headquarters, a magnificent 1909 Renaissance-style palazzo that occupies the entire block bounded by Grand, Centre, Baxter, and Broome streets. The police moved to their new quarters, the modern Police Plaza behind the Municipal Building (*see* Tour 18, below) in 1973, and this lavish domed baroque edifice has been converted into a luxury co-op project ⓰ aptly called **The Police Building**. Cross to the far side of Centre Street for a good look at the columns, dome, and statuary around its main entrance, including pediment statues representing each of New York's five boroughs.

Walk up Baxter Street to Spring Street, and turn right to hit ⓱ Mulberry Street. The **D & G Bakery** (45 Spring St.) is one of the last coal-oven bakeries in the United States.

Return to Baxter Street, which soon merges with Lafayette Street. At the corner of Lafayette and Houston streets, on your ⓲ right you'll see the redbrick **Puck Building** (note the gilded figure of Shakespeare's mischievous Puck himself above the entrance). Built in 1885, it was originally headquarters for the 19th-century humor magazine *Puck;* more recently, it was home to New York City's current satire magazine, *Spy.*

Tour 16: Chinatown

*Numbers in the margin correspond with points of interest on
the SoHo, TriBeCa, Little Italy, and Chinatown map.*

Visibly exotic, Chinatown is a popular tourist attraction, but it
is also a real, vital community, where about half of the city's
population of 300,000 Chinese still live. Its main businesses are
restaurants and garment factories; some 55% of its residents
speak little or no English. Theoretically, Chinatown is divided
from Little Italy by Canal Street, the bustling artery that links
the Holland Tunnel (to New Jersey) and the Manhattan Bridge
(to Brooklyn). However, in recent years, an influx of immigrants from the People's Republic of China, Taiwan, and especially Hong Kong has swelled Manhattan's Chinese population,
and Hong Kong residents, anticipating the return of the British colony to PRC domination in 1997, have been investing their
capital in Chinatown real estate. Consequently, Chinatown
now spills over its traditional borders into Little Italy to the
north and the formerly Jewish Lower East Side to the east.

Originally Canal Street was a tree-lined road with a canal running its length. Today the Chinatown stretch of Canal Street is
almost overwhelmed with sidewalk markets bursting with
stacks of fresh seafood and strange-shaped vegetables in extra-
terrestrial shades of green. Food shops proudly display their
wares: If America's motto is "a chicken in every pot," then Chinatown's must be "a roast duck in every window."

19 The slightly less frantic **Kam Man** (200 Canal St.), a duplex supermarket, sells an amazing assortment of fresh and canned
imported groceries, herbs, and the sort of dinnerware and furniture familiar to patrons of Chinese restaurants. Choose from
dozens of varieties of noodles or such delicacies as dried starch
and fresh chicken feet.

Mott Street, the principal business street of the neighborhood,
looks the way you might expect Chinatown to look: narrow and
twisting, crammed with souvenir shops and restaurants in
funky pagoda-style buildings, crowded with pedestrians at all
hours of the day or night. Within the few dense blocks of Chinatown, hundreds of restaurants serve every imaginable type of
Chinese cuisine, from fast-food noodles or dumplings to sumptuous Hunan, Szechuan, Cantonese, Mandarin, and Shanghai
feasts (*see* Chapter 8). Every New Yorker thinks he or she
knows the absolute flat-out best, but whichever one you try, at
8 PM on Saturday, don't be surprised if you have to wait in line
to get in.

As you proceed down Mott Street, take a peek down Pell
Street, a narrow lane of wall-to-wall restaurants whose neon
signs stretch halfway across the thoroughfare.

Time Out   A few steps down Pell Street, turn onto Doyers Street to find
the **Viet-Nam Restaurant** (11 Doyers St., tel. 212/693–0725), an
informal, inexpensive little basement restaurant that serves
spicy, exotic Vietnamese dishes.

At the corner of Mott and Mosco streets stands the **Church of
the Transfiguration.** Built in 1801 as the Zion Episcopal
Church, this imposing Georgian structure with Gothic win-

dows is now a Chinese Catholic church where mass is said in Cantonese and Mandarin.

㉑ The **New York Chinatown History Project** (70 Mulberry St., 2nd floor, tel. 212/619–4785), at the corner of Bayard and Mulberry streets, shows interactive photographic exhibitions on Asian-American labor history. It also has a resource library and bookstore and offers a walking tour of Chinatown.

㉑ At the end of Mott Street is **Chatham Square**, which is really more of a labyrinth than a square: 10 streets converge here, creating pandemonium for cars and a nightmare for pedestrians. A Chinese arch honoring Chinese casualties in American wars stands on an island in the eye of the storm. On the far end of the square, at the corner of Catherine Street and East Broadway, you'll see a branch of the Manhattan Savings Bank, built to resemble a pagoda (in this neighborhood, even some public phone booths have been styled as pagodas).

Skirting Chatham Square, head back to the right to go down Worth Street. The corner of Worth, Baxter, and Park streets was once known as Five Points, the central intersection of a tough 19th-century slum of Irish and German immigrants. To-
㉒ day it has been replaced by **Columbus Park**, a shady, paved urban space where children play and elderly Chinese gather to reminisce about their homelands.

Return to Chatham Square, cross Park Row (on your right) and take a sharp right turn on St. James Place to find two remnants of this neighborhood's pre-Chinatown past. On St. James Place
㉓ is the **First Shearith Israel graveyard** (predecessor of the one in Chelsea, *see* Tour 11, above, connected with the congregation that today worships on the Upper West Side, *see* Tour 8, above). The first Jewish cemetery in the United States, this site was consecrated in 1656, when it was considered to be well outside of town. Walk a half block farther, turn left on James Street, and you'll see **St. James Church,** a stately 1837 Greek Revival edifice where Al Smith, who rose from this poor Irish neighborhood to become New York's governor and a 1928 Democratic presidential candidate, once served as altar boy.

㉔ Go back past Chatham Square and up the Bowery to **Confucius Plaza**, the open area monitored by a statue of Confucius and the sweeping curve of a redbrick high-rise apartment complex named for him. At 18 Bowery, at the corner of Pell Street, stands one of Manhattan's oldest homes, a Federal and Georgian structure built in 1785 by meat wholesaler Edward Mooney. For some exotic shopping, duck into the **Canal Arcade,** a passage linking the Bowery and Elizabeth Street. A few doors down, at 50 Bowery, you'll see the **Silver Palace** restaurant (*see* Chapter 8), worth a peek inside for its Chinese rococo interior, complete with dragons whose eyes are blinking lights.

At the intersection of the Bowery and Canal Street, a grand arch and colonnade mark the entrance to the Manhattan Bridge, which leads to Brooklyn. This corner was once the center of New York's diamond district. Many jewelry dealers have moved uptown to 47th Street between Fifth and Sixth avenues (*see* Off the Beaten Track, below), but a substantial number still occupy shops on the Bowery and the north side of Canal. The selection is pretty good, but don't expect to pay the first price quoted to you.

Tour 17: Wall Street and the Battery

Numbers in the margin correspond with points of interest on the Lower Manhattan map.

Lower Manhattan doesn't cover many acres but it is packed with attractions, for it has always been central to the city's networks of power and wealth. It was here that the New Amsterdam colony was established by the Dutch in 1625; in 1789, the first capital building of the United States was located here. The city did not really expand beyond these precincts until the middle of the 19th century. Today lower Manhattan is in many ways dominated by Wall Street, which is both an actual street and a shorthand name for the vast, powerful financial community that clusters around the New York and American stock exchanges. Visit on a weekday to catch the district's true vitality—but expect to be jostled on the crowded sidewalks if you stand too long, peering at the great buildings that surge skyward on every corner. A different but equally awe-inspiring sight can be found on the tip of the island, as you look out across the great silvery harbor and see enduring symbols of America: the Statue of Liberty and Ellis Island, port of entry for countless immigrants to a new land.

Our tour begins at the southernmost point of Manhattan, at the **Staten Island Ferry Terminal** (for subway riders that's just outside the South Ferry station on the No. 1 line). The **Staten Island Ferry** is still the best deal in town: The 20- to 30-minute ride across New York Harbor provides great views of the Manhattan skyline, the Statue of Liberty, the Verrazano Narrows Bridge, and the New Jersey coast—and it costs only 50¢ one-way. A word of advice, however: While commuters love the ferry service's swift new low-slung craft, the boats ride low in the water and have no outside deck space. Wait for one of the higher, more open old-timers.

To the west of South Ferry lies **Battery Park,** a verdant landfill, loaded with monuments and sculpture, at Manhattan's green toe. The park's name refers to a line of cannons once mounted here to defend the shoreline (which ran along what is currently State Street). Head north along the water's edge to the **East Coast Memorial,** a statue of a fierce eagle that presides over eight granite slabs inscribed with the names of U.S. servicemen who died in the Western Atlantic during World War II. Climb the steps of the East Coast Memorial for a fine view of the main features of **New York Harbor;** from left to right: **Governors Island,** a Coast Guard installation; hilly **Staten Island** in the distance; the **Statue of Liberty** on Liberty Island; **Ellis Island,** gateway to the New World for generations of immigrants; and the old railway terminal in **Liberty Park,** on the mainland in Jersey City, New Jersey.

Continue north past a romantic **statue of Giovanni da Verrazano,** the Florentine merchant who piloted the ship that first sighted New York and its harbor in 1524. The Verrazano Narrows Bridge between Brooklyn and Staten Island—the world's longest suspension bridge—is visible from here, just beyond Governors Island.

Built in 1811 as a defense for New York Harbor, the circular brick fortress now called **Castle Clinton** was, when first built, on an island 200 feet from shore. In 1824 it became Castle Gar-

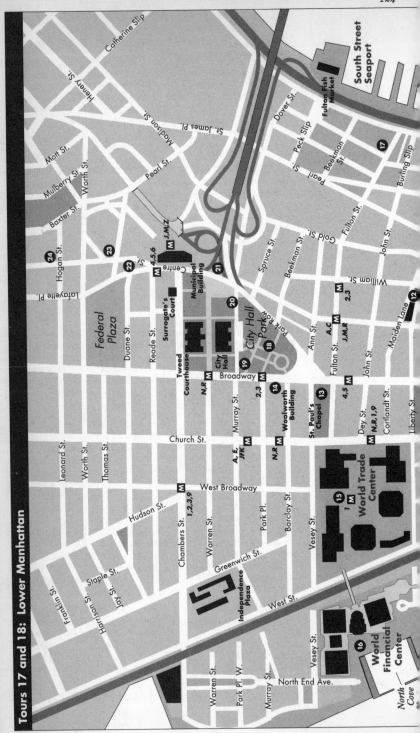

Tours 17 and 18: Lower Manhattan

South Street Seaport

Fulton Fish Market

Catherine Slip

Henry St.

Dover St.

Peck Slip

Beekman St.

Burling Slip

Madison St.

St. James Pl.

Pearl St.

Mott St.

Mulberry St.

Worth St.

Baxter St.

Hogan Pl.

Fulton St.

John St.

Pearl St.

Gold St.

Beekman St.

Spruce St.

William St.

Maiden Lane

17

12

2,3 M

24

23

22

Lafayette Pl.

Federal Plaza

Duane St.

Reade St.

4,5,6 M

Centre St.

Surrogate's Court

Municipal Building

21 M J,M,Z

20

City Hall Park

Park Row

Ann St.

18

Fulton St.

A,C M

John St.

J,M,R M

2,3 M

4,5 M

Tweed Courthouse

City Hall

19 M

Broadway

N,R M

Murray St.

2,3

14

Woolworth Building

13

St. Paul's Chapel

Dey St.

N,R,1,9 M

Cortlandt St.

Maiden Lane

Liberty St.

Leonard St.

Worth St.

Thomas St.

Church St.

A, E M JFK

N,R M

West Broadway

Hudson St.

1,2,3,9 M

Chambers St.

Warren St.

Park Pl.

Barclay St.

Vesey St.

15 M

World Trade Center

Franklin St.

Staple St.

Harrison St.

Jay St.

Independence Plaza

Greenwich St.

West St.

Vesey St.

West St.

Warren St.

Park Pl. W.

Murray St.

North End Ave.

16

World Financial Center

North Cove

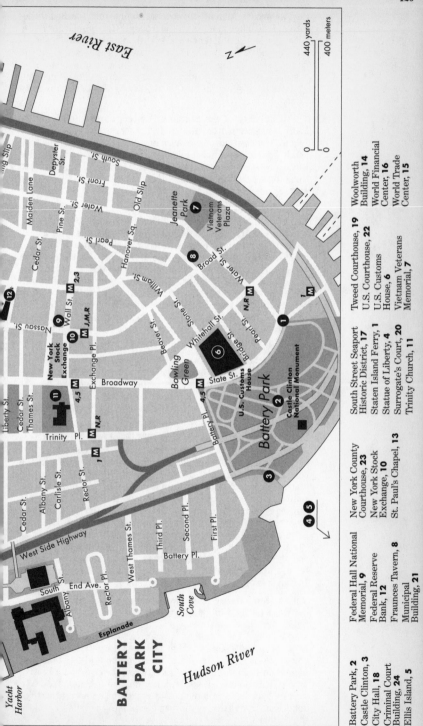

den, an entertainment and concert facility that reached its zenith in 1850 when more than 6,000 people (the capacity of Radio City Music Hall) attended the U.S. debut of the "Swedish Nightingale," Jenny Lind. After landfill connected it to the city, Castle Clinton became, in succession, an immigrant processing center, an aquarium, and now a restored fort, museum, and ticket office for ferries to the Statue of Liberty and Ellis Island.

❹ The popularity of the **Statue of Liberty** surged following its 100th birthday restoration in 1986. After arriving on Liberty Island, you can take an elevator 10 stories to the top of the pedestal. The strong of heart and limb can climb another 12 stories to the crown. Currently you may have to wait in line for up to three hours for the privilege. *Tel. 212/363-3200. Round-trip fare: $6 adults, $3 children. Daily departures on the half hour 9-3; extended hours in summer.*

❺ The price of a ticket to the statue includes a visit to **Ellis Island,** which opened in September 1990 to record crowds after a $140 million restoration, the largest-ever U.S. project of its kind (the fund-raising drive was headed by Chrysler Corporation chairman Lee Iacocca). Now a national monument, Ellis Island was once a federal immigration facility that processed 17 million men, women, and children between 1892 and 1954—the ancestors of more than 40% of Americans living today. *Tel. 212/ 883-1986. Round-trip fare: $6 adults, $3 children 3-17. Daily departures every 45 min. 9:30-3:30. Ellis Island Immigration Museum admission free.*

A broad mall that begins at the landward entrance to Castle Clinton leads back across the park to the **Netherlands Memorial,** a quaint flagpole depicting the bead exchange that bought from the native Indians the land to establish Fort Amsterdam in 1626. Inscriptions describe the event in English and Dutch.

As you leave the park, across State Street you'll see the imposing **U.S. Customs House,** built in 1907 in the ornate Beaux Arts style fashionable at the time. Above the base, the facade features massive columns rising to a pediment topped by a double row of statuary. Daniel Chester French, better known for the statue of Lincoln in the Lincoln Memorial in Washington, DC, sculpted the lower statues, which symbolize various continents (left to right: Asia, the Americas, Europe, Africa); the upper row represents the major trading cities of the world. The Customs House facade appeared in the movie *Ghostbusters II* as the fictional New York Museum of Art. Federal bankruptcy courts are currently housed in the Customs House, and a center of the Smithsonian Institution's Museum of the American Indian is expected to open in early 1993 on the lower floors.

The Customs House faces onto **Bowling Green,** an oval greensward at the foot of Broadway that became New York's first public park in 1733. On July 9, 1776, a few hours after citizens learned about the signing of the Declaration of Independence, rioters toppled a statue of British King George III that had occupied the spot for 11 years; much of the statue's lead was melted down into bullets. In 1783, when the occupying British forces fled the city, they defiantly hoisted a Union Jack to a greased, uncleated flagpole so it couldn't be lowered; patriot John Van Arsdale drove his own cleats into the pole to replace the flag with the Stars and Stripes.

From Bowling Green, head south on State Street. A stunning semicircular office tower in reflective glass hugs the bend of the street at 17 State Street. Next door is the **Shrine of St. Elizabeth Ann Seton** (7-8 State St.). What is now the rectory of the shrine is a redbrick Federal-style town house with a distinctive wood portico shaped to fit the curving street. This house was built in 1793 as the home of the wealthy Watson family; Mother Seton and her family lived here from 1801 to 1803. She joined the Catholic Church in 1805, after the death of her husband, and went on to found the Sisters of Charity, the first American order of nuns. In 1975 she became the first American-born saint. Masses are held here daily.

Continue around onto Water Street, passing on your right **New York Plaza,** a complex of high-tech office towers linked by an underground concourse. Just beyond it is the **Vietnam Veterans Memorial,** where letters from servicemen and -women have been etched into a wall of greenish glass.

❼

❽ Return to Broad Street and go one block inland to **Fraunces Tavern,** a complex of five largely 19th-century buildings housing a museum, restaurant, and bar (*see* Chapter 8). The main building is a Colonial home (brick exterior, cream-colored portico and balcony) built in 1719 and converted to a tavern in 1762. This was the site where, in 1783, George Washington delivered a farewell address to his officers celebrating the British evacuation of New York; later, the building housed some offices of the fledgling U.S. government. Today Fraunces Tavern contains two fully furnished period rooms and other displays of 18th- and 19th-century American history. *Broad and Pearl Sts., tel. 212/425-1778. Admission: $2.50 adults, $1 students, senior citizens, and children. Restaurant open weekdays. Museum open weekdays 10-4.*

Walk through the lobby of the new office building at 85 **Broad Street,** which, paying due homage to urban archaeology, traces the course of the old Dutch Stone Street with a line of brown paving stones. At the side of the building, on Pearl Street, peer through the transparent panel in the sidewalk to see the excavated foundations of the 17th-century Stadt Huis, the old Dutch City Hall.

Time Out The brick plaza behind 85 Broad Street is flanked by a variety of small restaurants. Order a take-out meal or snack and eat it out here on the benches, where you can watch busy office workers milling past.

Head up Pearl Street to **Hanover Square,** a quiet tree-lined plaza that stood on the waterfront when the East River reached Pearl Street. This was the city's original printing house square; on the site of 81 Pearl Street, William Bradford established the first printing press in the colonies. The pirate Captain Kidd lived in the neighborhood, and the brownstone **India House** (1837) used to house the New York Cotton Exchange. Today it holds Harry's of Hanover Square, a vintage Wall Street bar.

Walk inland up Hanover Square to the rounded corner of South William and Beaver streets, where a graceful columned porch marks the entrance to **Delmonico's** restaurant, opened in 1888 on the site of an earlier Delmonico's founded in 1827. A pioneer in serving Continental cuisine, it was *the* place to go at the turn of the century; under different ownership, it is still a restaurant today.

Two blocks farther north, William Street crosses **Wall Street,** so called because it traces the course of a wood wall built across the island in 1653 to defend the Dutch colony against the native Indians. Arguably the most famous thoroughfare in the world, though only a third of a mile long, Wall Street began its financial career with stock traders conducting business along the sidewalks or at tables beneath a sheltering buttonwood tree. Today it's a dizzyingly narrow canyon—look to the right and you'll glimpse a sliver of East River waterfront; look to the left and you'll see the spire of Trinity Church, tightly framed by skyscrapers at the head of The Street.

To learn the difference between Ionic and Corinthian columns, look at the **Citibank Building** to your right (55 Wall St.). The lower stories were part of an earlier U.S. Customs House, built in 1863, and it was literally a bullish day on Wall Street when oxen hauled its 16 granite Ionic columns up to the site. When the National City Bank took over the building in 1907, McKim, Mead & White added a second tier of columns, but made them Corinthian.

One block west on Wall Street, where Broad Street becomes Nassau Street, you'll find on your right a regal statue of George Washington on the steps of the **Federal Hall National Memorial.** This 1883 statue by John Quincy Adams Ward marks the spot where Washington was sworn in as the first U.S. president in 1789. After the capital moved to Philadelphia in 1790, the original Federal Hall became New York's City Hall, then was demolished in 1812 when the present City Hall (*see* Tour 18, *below*) was completed. The clean and simple lines of the current structure, built as (yet another) U.S. Customs House in 1842, were modeled after the Parthenon, a potent symbol for a young nation striving to emulate classical Greek democracy. It's now a museum featuring exhibits on New York and Wall Street. *26 Wall St., tel. 212/264–8711. Admission free. Open weekdays 9–5.*

In building a two-story investment bank at the corner of Wall and Broad streets, J. P. Morgan was in effect declaring himself above the pressures of Wall Street real-estate values. Now **Morgan Guaranty Trust,** the building bears pockmarks near the fourth window on the Wall Street side, created when a bomb in a pushcart exploded in 1920.

⑩ Perhaps the heart of Wall Street is the **New York Stock Exchange,** which has its august Corinthian main entrance around the corner at 20 Broad Street. Compared with the Federal Hall memorial, this neoclassical building is much more elaborately decorated, as befitted the more grandiose national image of 1901, when it was designed. Inside, after what may be a lengthy wait, you can take an elevator to the third-floor visitor center. A self-guided tour, informative slide shows, video displays, and guides may help you interpret the seeming chaos you'll see from the visitors' gallery overlooking the immense (50-foot-high) trading hall. *Tickets available at 20 Broad St., tel. 212/656–5168. Free tickets are distributed at 9:05. Open weekdays 9:20–3:30.*

⑪ **Trinity Church** (Broadway and Wall St.) was established as an Anglican parish in 1697. The present structure (1846), by Richard Upjohn, ranked as the city's tallest building for most of the second half of the 19th century. Its three huge bronze doors were designed by Richard Morris Hunt to recall Ghiberti's doors for the Bapistry in Florence, Italy. Once completely jet black from decades of pollutants, the exterior sandstone is being restored to its original pink color. The church's Gothic Revival interior is surprisingly light and elegant, although you may see derelicts napping in the pews. On the church's south side is a 2½-acre graveyard: Alexander Hamilton is buried beneath a white stone pyramid; and a monument commemorates Robert Fulton, the inventor of the steamboat (he's actually buried in the Livingstone family vault, with his wife). *Tours daily at 2; free 40-min concerts, Tues. 12:45 PM.*

Just north of the church is tiny Thames Street, where a pair of skyscrapers playfully called the **Thames Twins**—the Trinity and U.S. Realty buildings—display early 20th-century attempts to apply Gothic decoration to skyscrapers. Across the street at 120 Broadway, the 1915 **Equitable Building** rises 30 stories straight from its base with no setback; its overpowering shadow on the street convinced the city government to pass the nation's first zoning law. Large public plazas around the bases of skyscrapers have helped to alleviate this problem, and a good example is between Cedar and Liberty streets, where the black-glass **Marine Midland Bank** (1971) features in its street-level plaza a red-and-silver Noguchi sculpture, *Cube*. One block east at William and Pine streets, the plaza surrounding the 65-story **Chase Manhattan Bank Building** holds a striking black-and-white sculpture, *Group of Four Trees*, by Jean Dubuffet.

Liberty Street converges with William Street and Maiden Lane at triangular **Louise Nevelson Plaza,** which contains four black welded-steel abstract Nevelson sculptures, three middle-size pieces and one huge 70-footer. Sit in the plaza and contemplate the **Federal Reserve Bank** directly across the street, which looks like a bank ought to look: gray, solid, imposing, absolutely impregnable—and it had better be, for its vaults reputedly contain a quarter of the world's gold reserves. *33 Liberty St., tel. 212/720–6130. 1-hr tour by advance (at least one month) reservation, weekdays at 10, 11, 1, and 2.*

Across Maiden Lane in Federal Reserve Plaza, with its huge round pillars of sandy brick, you can take an escalator downstairs to see 20th-century art at the **Whitney Museum of American Art Downtown.** *33 Maiden La., tel. 212/943–5655. Admission free. Open weekdays 11–6.*

Continue through the arcade to John Street, where on your right you'll see the **John Street Methodist Church** (44 John St.), on the site of the first Methodist Church in America. Then return to Broadway and head north to **St. Paul's Chapel** (Broadway and Fulton St.), the oldest (1766) surviving church in Manhattan and the site of the prayer service following George Washington's inauguration as president. Built of rough Manhattan stone, it was modeled after London's St. Martin-in-the-Fields. It's open until 4 (Sundays until 3) for prayer and meditation; look in the north aisle for Washington's pew.

Two blocks up Broadway is the so-called "Cathedral of Commerce," the ornate white terra-cotta **Woolworth Building** (Park Pl. and Broadway). When it opened in 1913 it was, at 792 feet, the world's tallest building; it still houses the Woolworth corporate offices. Among its extravagant Gothic-style details are sculptures set into arches in the lobby ceiling; one of them represents old man Woolworth pinching his pennies, while another depicts the architect, Cass Gilbert, cradling in his arms a model of his creation.

Go west on Park Place and turn down Church Street to the **15 World Trade Center,** a 16-acre, 12 million-square-foot complex that contains New York's two tallest buildings (1,350 feet high). To reach the observation deck on the 107th floor of 2 World Trade Center, elevators glide a quarter of a mile into the sky— in only 58 seconds. The view potentially extends 55 miles, although signs at the ticket window disclose how far you can see that day and whether the outdoor deck is open. *Admission: $3.50 adults, $1.75 senior citizens and children, children under 6 free. Open daily 9:30 AM–11:30 PM.*

You can get the same view with a meal at **Windows on the World** (*see* Chapter 8) atop 1 World Trade Center; lighter meals or drinks are available at its **Hors d'Oeuvrerie** (jacket required).

Some 50,000 people work in this seven-building complex, and at street level and underground it contains more than 60 stores, services, and restaurants, as well as the adjacent New York Vista hotel (*see* Chapter 9). There's a TKTS booth selling discount tickets to Broadway and Off-Broadway shows (*see* Chapter 10) in the mezzanine of 2 World Trade Center (open weekdays 11–5:30, Sat. 11–3:30), and on the ninth floor of 4 World Trade Center, a visitors' gallery overlooks the trading floor of the Commodities Exchange (tel. 212/938–2025; open weekdays 9:30–3).

More than a million cubic yards of rock and soil were excavated for the World Trade Center—and then moved across West Street to help beget the 100-acre Battery Park City development, a complete neighborhood built from scratch. Take the pedestrian overpass north of 1 World Trade Center to Battery **16** Park City's centerpiece, the **World Financial Center,** a four-tower complex designed by Cesar Pelli, with some heavy-duty corporate tenants including Merrill Lynch, American Express, and Dow Jones. You'll come out into the soaring **Winter Garden Atrium,** its mauve marble cascade of steps spilling down into a vaulted plaza with 16 giant palm trees, framed by a vast arched window overlooking the Hudson. This stunning space has become a popular venue for free performances by top-flight musicians and dancers (tel. 212/945–0505). Surrounding the atrium are several upscale shops—Godiva chocolatiers, Rizzoli bookshop, clothing stores such as Ann Taylor and Barneys— plus a skylit food court.

Time Out While the courtyard also offers several full-service restaurants, for a quick bite head for **Minters** (tel. 212/945–4455)— and be sure to leave room for their ice-cream cones.

Of the few spots in Manhattan that directly overlook the rivers, **Battery Park City** just may be the best. The outdoor plaza right behind the atrium curls around a tidy little yacht basin; take in the view of the Statue of Liberty and read the stirring quotations worked into the iron railings. Just north of the basin is the terminal for ferry service to Hoboken, New Jersey (tel. 201/463–3779), on the other side of the Hudson River. It's an eight-minute ride to Frank Sinatra's hometown, with a spectacular view of lower Manhattan. The eight-acre North Park, between Chambers and Vesey streets, is scheduled to open in the spring of 1992.

To the south, a longer riverside promenade that eventually will extend to Battery Park accompanies the residential part of Battery Park City, a mix of high rises, town houses, shops, and green squares that does a surprisingly good job of duplicating the rhythms of the rest of the city. Especially noteworthy among the art works populating the esplanade are Ned Smyth's columnated plaza with chessboards; and the South Cove, a collaborative effort, a romantic curved stage set of wood piers and a steel-frame lookout. Slated to open in late 1992 behind South Cove is the **Living Memorial to the Holocaust–Museum of Jewish Heritage** (Battery Pl. between 1st and 2nd Pl., tel. 212/687–9141).

Tour 18: The Seaport and the Courts

Numbers in the margin correspond with points of interest on the Lower Manhattan map.

New York's role as a great seaport is easiest to understand downtown, with both the Hudson River and East River waterfronts within walking distance. While the deeper Hudson River came into its own in the steamship era, the more sheltered waters of the East River saw most of the action in the 19th century, during the age of clipper ships. This era is preserved in the South Street Seaport restoration, centered on Fulton Street between Water Street and the East River. Only a few blocks away, you can visit another seat of New York history: the City Hall neighborhood, which includes Manhattan's magisterial collection of court buildings.

Walk down Fulton Street, named after the ferry to Brooklyn that once docked at its foot (the ferry itself was named after its inventor, Robert Fulton), to Water Street, which was once the shoreline. On the 19th-century landfill across the street is the **17** 11-block **South Street Seaport Historic District,** which was created in 1967 to save this area from being overtaken by skyscrapers. The Rouse Corporation, which had already created slick so-called "festival marketplaces" in Boston (Quincy Market) and Baltimore (Harborplace), was later hired to restore and adapt the existing historic buildings.

The little white lighthouse at Water and Fulton streets is the **Titanic Memorial,** commemorating the sinking of the S.S. *Titanic* in 1912. Beyond it, Fulton Street, cobbled in blocks of Belgian granite, is a pedestrian mall that swarms with visitors, especially on fine-weather weekends; on Friday evenings during summer, young professionals from the Financial District stand shoulder-to-shoulder at cocktail hour. Immediately to your left is the **Cannon's Walk Block,** which contains 15 restored buildings.

At 211 Water Street is **Bowne & Co.,** a reconstructed working 19th-century print shop. Around the corner, a narrow court called Cannon's Walk, lined with shops, opens onto Fulton Street; follow it around to Front Street. Directly across Front Street is the **Fulton Market Building,** a modern building, full of shops and restaurants, that re-creates the bustling commercial atmosphere of the old victual markets that were on this site from 1822 on. On the south side of Fulton Street is the seaport's architectural centerpiece, **Schermerhorn Row,** a redbrick terrace of Georgian- and Federal-style warehouses and countinghouses built in 1811–12. Today the ground floors are occupied by upscale shops, bars, and restaurants, and the **South Street Seaport Museum Visitors Center.** *Tel. 212/669–9424. Admission to ships, galleries, walking tours, Maritime Crafts Center, films, and other seaport events: $6 adults, $5 senior citizens, $4 students, $3 children. Open daily 10–5, longer hours in summer.*

Cross South Street under an elevated stretch of the FDR Drive to **Pier 16,** where the historic ships are docked, including the *Peking,* the second-largest sailing ship in existence; the full-rigged *Wavertree;* and the lightship *Ambrose.* A restored **Pilothouse** is the pierside information center. Pier 16 is also the departure point for the 90-minute **Seaport Line Harbor Cruise.** *Tel. 212/385–0791. The fare is $12 adults, $11 senior citizens, $10 students, $6 children. Combination fares—for the cruise and the other attractions—run $15.25, $13.50, $12, and $7.50.*

To the north is **Pier 17,** a multilevel dockside shopping mall. Its weathered-wood rear decks make a splendid spot from which to sit and contemplate the river; look north to see the Brooklyn, Manhattan, and Williamsburg bridges, and look across to see Brooklyn Heights.

Time Out If you're hungry, head for the fast-food stalls on Pier 17's third-floor **Promenade Food Court.** The cuisine is nonchain eclectic: Seaport Fries, Pizza on the Pier, Wok & Roll, the Yorkville Packing House, the Salad Bowl, or Bergen's Beer & Wine Garden (10 brews on tap). What's really spectacular is the view from the tables in a glass-walled atrium.

As your nose may already have surmised, the blocks along South Street north of the museum complex still house a working fish market, which has been in operation since the 1770s. Although the city has tried to relocate the hundreds of fishmongers of the **Fulton Fish Market** to the South Bronx, the area remains a beehive of activity. Get up early (or stay up late) if you want to see it: The action begins around midnight and ends by 8 AM.

Return to Fulton Street and walk away from the river to Broadway, where St. Paul's Chapel is (*see* Tour 17, above). As you turn right, forking off to your right is **Park Row,** which was known as "Newspaper Row" from the mid-19th to early 20th century, when most of the city's 20 or so daily newspapers had offices there. Today there are only four New York dailies—the *Times,* the *Daily News,* the *Post,* and *Newsday*—and Park Row is an unremarkable commercial strip. In tribute to that past, however, a statue of Benjamin Franklin (who was, after all, a printer) stands in front of Pace University farther up on Park Row.

To the left of Park Row is triangular **City Hall Park,** originally the town common. A bronze statue of patriot Nathan Hale, who was hanged as a spy by the British troops occupying New York City, stands on the Broadway side of the park. In its day this green spot has hosted hangings, riots, and demonstrations; ticker-tape parades up lower Broadway end here, with the honorees receiving keys to the city on the steps of City Hall.

18 **City Hall,** built between 1803 and 1812, is unexpectedly sedate, small-scale, and charming. Its exterior columns reflect the classical influence of Greece and Rome, and the handsome cast-iron cupola is crowned with a statue of Lady Justice. Originally its front and sides were clad in white marble while the back was faced in cheap brownstone, because the city fathers assumed New York would never grow farther north than this! (Limestone now covers all four sides.) The major interior feature is a domed rotunda from which a sweeping marble double staircase leads to the second-floor public rooms. The wood-paneled City Council Chamber in the east wing is small and clubby; the Board of Estimate chamber to the west has colonial paintings and church-pew-style seating; and the Governor's Room at the head of the stairs, used for ceremonial events, is filled with historic portraits and furniture. The mayor's office is on the ground floor. Since the spring of 1989, however, New York City has been busily redefining the roles of these governmental bodies, because the U. S. Supreme Court declared that the city's system violated the Constitution's "one man, one vote" principle.

19 Looming directly behind City Hall is the **Tweed Courthouse,** named after notorious politician "Boss" William Marcy Tweed, under whose corrupt management this building took some $12 million and nine years to build (it was finally finished in 1872, but the ensuing public outrage drove Tweed from office). Although it is imposing, with its columned classical pediment outside and seven-story rotunda inside, almost none of the boatloads of marble that Tweed had shipped from Europe made their way into this building. Today it houses municipal offices; it has also served as a location for several films, most notably *The Verdict.*

20 Across Chambers Street the **Surrogate's Court,** also called the **Hall of Records** (31 Chambers St.), is the most ornate of this City Hall trio. In true Beaux Arts fashion, sculpture and ornament seem to have been added wherever possible to the basic neoclassical structure, yet the overall effect is graceful rather than cluttered. A courtroom here was the venue for *Johnson* v. *Johnson,* where the heirs to the Johnson & Johnson fortune waged their bitter battle.

21 On the east side of Centre Street is the city government's first skyscraper, the **Municipal Building,** built in 1914 by McKim, Mead & White. The "roof" section alone is 10 stories high, bristling with towers and peaks and topped by a gilt statue of Civic Fame. This is where New Yorkers come to pay parking fines and get marriage licenses. An immense arch straddles Chambers Street (traffic used to flow through here); the vaulted plaza in front was the site of a scene in the movie *Crocodile Dundee,* in which the Aussie hunter coolly scares off would-be muggers with his bowie knife.

22 Head north up Centre Street to **Foley Square,** a name that has become synonymous with the New York court system. The **U.S. Courthouse** at 40 Centre Street, designed by Cass Gilbert, has marble steps climbing to a massive columned portico; above this rises a 32-story tower topped by a gilded pyramid, not unlike that with which Gilbert crowned the New York Life building uptown. This courthouse has been the site of such famous recent cases as the tax evasion trial of hotel queen Leona

Helmsley, and Imelda Marcos's acquittal of fraud and racketeering charges.

With its stately columns, pediments, and 100-foot-wide flight **(23)** of marble steps, the **New York County Courthouse,** built in 1926, set the precedent here for neoclassical grandeur. It's actually more eccentric than it looks, having been built in a hexagonal shape to fit an irregular plot of land. That quintessential courtroom drama *Twelve Angry Men* was filmed here, as was the more recent movie *Legal Eagles.*

Turn to look across Foley Square at **Federal Plaza,** which sprawls in front of the gridlike skyscraper of the **Javits Federal Building.** The black glass box to the left houses the **U.S. Court of International Trade.**

Continue up Centre Street past neoclassical civic office build- **(24)** ings to 100 Centre Street, the **Criminal Courts Building,** a rather grim Art Deco tower connected by a skywalk to the detention center known as The Tombs. In *The Bonfire of the Vanities*, Tom Wolfe wrote a chilling description of this court's menacing atmosphere.

In contrast, the **Civil and Municipal Courthouse** across the way at 111 Centre Street is an uninspired modern cube, although it, too, has held sensational trials, including that of subway vigilante Bernhard Goetz. On the west side of this small square is the slick blank granite **Family Court** (60 Lafayette St.), with its off-putting angular facade.

As you walk up Leonard Street, which runs just south of the Family Court, take a look at the ornate Victorian building that runs the length of the block on your left. This is the old New York Life Insurance Company headquarters (346 Broadway), an 1870 building that was remodeled and enlarged in 1896 by McKim, Mead & White. The ornate clocktower facing Broadway is now occupied by the avant-garde **Clocktower Gallery.** After looking at the art on the 13th floor, the adventurous will want to climb a narrow spiral stairway inside the clocktower to see the huge clock's mechanism or step outside on the balcony for a dramatic view of New York City. *108 Leonard St., tel. 212/ 233–1096. Suggested donation: $1. Open Thurs.–Sun. noon–6.*

Manhattan for Free

One of the best, and least expensive, places to be in New York is out on the streets, soaking up the city. That's where you're likely to stumble upon the many free performances—both scheduled and impromptu—given by professionals and amateurs year-round. Music, dance, mime, acting, magic tricks, and more are offered for free or at pass-the-hat prices in parks and plazas all around town (*see* Chapter 10).

Parks and Public Places Another free-but-fascinating New York pastime is people-watching, and one of the best places to go for that is **Central Park** (*see* Tour 7, above), where the Mall and the areas around Bethesda Fountain and the Conservatory Water buzz with activity on weekends and holidays from about noon to dusk. Stroll over to Wollman Rink and watch the skaters, or head up to the Great Lawn to find groups of folk dancers. In the summer, take a picnic, a blanket, and a Frisbee to the Great Lawn in the early afternoon (before noon on weekends) to stake out a spot in line for free tickets to that evening's Shakespeare performance at the Delacorte Theater. While you're waiting, settle back to watch the strollers, joggers, softball teams, and soccer players who congregate in this area. It makes for a long day—tickets aren't handed out until around 6:15 PM, and the plays begin at 8—but the experience is unforgettable.

Another lovely way to spend a day in Central Park is on a walking tour given by Urban Park Rangers, who are knowledgeable about the history, design, geology, wildlife, and botany of the park. Call the Central Park Conservancy (tel. 212/397–3165) for a calendar of free tours, events, exhibitions, family workshops, and other activity ideas.

Rockefeller Center (*see* Tour 1, above) is another good place to enjoy New York for free. In summer, there are various outdoor entertainment programs; in winter, you can watch ice skaters swirl about beneath the giant Christmas tree. **South Street Seaport** (*see* Tour 18, above) offers an assortment of fun free activities year-round: concerts on the pier during summer, a jazz festival in winter, and daily street entertainment.

Historic Sites   For a free guided tour of **Grand Central Terminal,** meet in front of the terminal's Chemical Bank branch at 12:30 PM on Wednesdays. Admission to official meetings of the General Assembly at the **United Nations** is free (pick up tickets at the information desk in the General Assembly lobby, at 46th St. and 1st Ave.).

The **New York Stock Exchange** on Wall Street offers free tours that include a multimedia presentation and a stop in the visitors' gallery overlooking the trading floor. In the same lower Manhattan area (*see* Tour 17, above), you can also arrange in advance for a free tour of the **Federal Reserve Bank** (33 Liberty St., tel. 212/720–6130); explore **Federal Hall** (26 Wall St.), where George Washington was inaugurated as the first president of the United States; and visit **St. Paul's Chapel** (Broadway and Fulton St.), where he worshipped after his inauguration.

Museums   On Tuesday evenings, the main branch of the **Whitney Museum of American Art** (945 Madison Ave. at 75th St.), the **Guggenheim Museum** (1071 5th Ave. at 89th St.), the **Cooper-Hewitt Museum** (2 E. 91st St.), and the **National Academy of Design** (1083 5th Ave. at 89th St.) charge no admission.

The **Metropolitan Museum of Art** (5th Ave. at 82nd St.), the **Museum of the City of New York** (1220 5th Ave. at 103rd St.), the **Cloisters** (Fort Tryon Park, at the northern tip of Manhattan), the **American Museum of Natural History** (Central Park West at 79th St.), the **New Museum of Contemporary Art** (583 Broadway), the **Pierpont Morgan Library** (29 E. 36th St.), and the **Museum of Television and Radio** (1 E. 53rd St.) all have pay-what-you-wish or suggested-donation policies. If all you can spare is a penny, they may not look too happy, but they'll still let you in. You can also pay what you wish to get into the **New-York Historical Society** (170 Central Park West) on Tuesdays and the **Museum of Modern Art** (11 W. 53rd St.) on Thursday evenings.

Television Screenings   For those who love television, free tickets to TV shows are offered from time to time at the **New York Convention and Visitors Bureau** (2 Columbus Circle) and from network personnel buttonholing passersby along Fifth and Sixth avenues.

What to See and Do with Children

New York is as magical a place for children as it is for adults. In fact, there are very few sights or activities in the city that can't be enjoyed from a pint-size perspective. Look for calendars of children's events in *New York* magazine and the *Village Voice* weekly newspaper, available at newsstands. The Friday *New York Times* also has a good listing of children's activities.

Sightseeing   While you're sightseeing with your family, don't miss the **Statue of Liberty** (*see* Tour 17, above) or the **South Street Seaport** (*see* Tour 18, above), both reliable hits with children. Boat rides are also a good way to see the city with youngsters—try the **Circle Line** (Pier 83, west end of 42nd St., tel. 212/563–3200), or, for a shorter, cheaper thrill, the 50¢ ride on the **Staten Island Ferry** (terminal in Battery Park). Another fun, quick way to see the city is to ride the **Roosevelt Island Aerial Tramway** across the East River. Trams board at Second Avenue and 60th Street; the fare is $1.40 in each direction.

Museums   While just about every major museum in New York has something to interest children, certain ones hold special appeal. At the top of the list is the **American Museum of Natural History** (Central Park West at 79th St., tel. 212/769–5100), with its giant dinosaurs (some rooms are off-limits until 1995, when the restoration of the entire collection will be completed), big blue hanging whale, and lifelike dioramas of stuffed beasts. Especially intriguing are the Discovery Room, which features hands-on exhibits for children, and the Naturemax Theater, which shows amazing nature films on its gigantic screen. It's best to savor this building a few halls at a time. The **Hayden Planetarium** (attached to the museum) offers sky shows tailored to seasonal and special events; there is also a preschool show, for which you must make reservations (tel. 212/769–5900). (*See* Tour 8, above.)

The **Children's Museum of Manhattan,** designed for children ages 2–12, offers interactive exhibits organized around common childhood experiences. Children can paint, make collages, try on costumes, pet animals, and generally stay amused for hours on end. *212 W. 83rd St., tel. 212/721–1223. Admission: $4. Open Tues.–Fri. 1–5, weekends 10–5.*

The **Metropolitan Museum of Art** (5th Ave. at 82nd St., tel. 212/535–7710) Uris Center for Education (tel. 212/570–3932) has programs for children: workshops, sketching classes, films, slide talks, drawing lessons, and more, designed for children ages 5 to 12 (*see* Tour 5, above).

Another favorite of the younger generation is the *Intrepid* Sea-Air-Space Museum. This famous World War II aircraft carrier brings to life the history of naval aviation, the modern U.S. Navy, and attempts at space travel. On display are more than 40 aircraft, rockets, and space vehicles, as well as an impressive collection of Congressional Medals of Honor. *Pier 86 at W. 46th St., tel. 212/245–0072. Admission: $7 adults, $6 senior citizens, $4 children ages 6–12. Open Wed.–Sun. 10–5.*

Many of the city's skyscrapers also have ongoing exhibits that will interest youngsters. For instance, **AT&T's InfoQuest Cen-**

ter (Madison Ave. at 56th St., tel. 212/605–5555) has a multilevel interactive museum where, among other activities, children can experiment with robots that respond to hand-clapping or button-pushing (*see* Tour 2, above). On the concourse of the Empire State Building you'll find the **Guinness World of Records Exhibition** (5th Ave. and 34th St., tel. 212/ 947–2335), where children can learn about the biggest, smallest, longest, or shortest world-record holders (*see* Tour 4, above).

If you're willing to venture off the beaten track, you'll find **Aunt Len's Doll and Toy Museum** a real treat. Here Lenon Holder Hoyte will show you her private collection of thousands of dolls of all types, from candy-box to character dolls, plus everything you can think of in the way of accessories. The museum is in Ms. Hoyte's town house, so you must make an appointment. *6 Hamilton Terr. at 141st St. and St. Nicholas Ave., tel. 212/926–4172. Admission $2 adults, $1 children, by appointment only.*

Zoos Central Park's **Children's Zoo** (*see* Tour 7, above), designed with toddlers in mind, features some farm animals and has some great props to climb on, around, and through: Moby Dick, Noah's Ark, a castle, and a rabbit hole, to name a few. The zoo was closed at press time for renovations. A few steps away is the more traditional **Central Park Zoo,** which was recently refurbished. Only 100 or so species are on display, so it can be toured in a reasonable amount of time, but older children may be disappointed that it has no really big animals, as the Bronx Zoo does (*see* Chapter 4).

Parks and The obvious first choice is **Central Park,** where children can
Playgrounds ride bicycles, play tennis, row boats, go horseback riding, ice-skate, roller-skate, skateboard, jog, fly kites, feed ducks, throw Frisbees—the list goes on and on (*see* Chapter 6). Children age 12 and under will enjoy the nostalgic **Carousel** (mid-park at 65th St., tel. 212/879–0244), complete with painted horses that prance up and down to jaunty organ music; it costs only 75¢ a ride. **Belvedere Castle** offers an inviting hands-on learning center with an emphasis on natural science. *Mid-park at 79th St., tel. 212/772–0210. Admission free. Open mid-Oct.–mid-Feb., Tues.–Thurs. and weekends 11–5, Fri. 1–5; mid-Oct.–mid-Feb., closes at 4.*

There are also child-oriented activities in the **Dairy** (mid-park at 65th St., tel. 212/397–3156). Hand-puppet shows are presented at the **Heckscher Puppet House** (mid-park at 62nd St., tel. 212/397–3162 for schedule and reservations), while marionette productions appear at the **Swedish Cottage Theater** (mid-park at 79th St., tel. 212/988–9093 for schedule and reservations).

Central Park has several excellent adventure playgrounds, in which weathered-wood structures, often underlaid with soft sand, support slides, swings, bridges, ladders, monkey bars, and other devices that safely encourage active play. Playgrounds can be found along the park's western edge at 68th Street, 81st Street, 85th Street, 93rd Street, and 100th Street; along the eastern edge at 67th Street, 71st Street, 77th Street, 85th Street, and 95th Street; and at the large Heckscher playground mid-park at 62nd Street.

Other good public playgrounds can be found at **Battery Park City** (West St. south of Vesey St.), **Washington Square** (at the foot of 5th Ave., between Waverly Pl. and W. 4th St.),

Abingdon Square (at the triangular junction of Hudson, Bleecker, and Bank Sts. in the West Village), **John Jay Park** (east of 1st Ave. between 76th and 78th Sts.), and **Riverside Park** (west of Riverside Drive; playgrounds at 82nd and 89th Sts.).

Entertainment   Madison Square Garden (7th Ave. between 31st and 33rd Sts., tel. 212/563–8300) offers, besides sports events (*see* Chapter 6), some extravaganzas that especially appeal to children. There are major **ice shows** in winter, and each spring brings the **Ringling Bros. Barnum & Bailey Circus.** (Check local newspapers for dates, times, and ticket information.) Another favorite New York spectacle is the **Big Apple Circus** (tel. 212/268–3030), which performs in Lincoln Center October through January.

For theater groups catering to children, *see* Chapter 10.

Storytelling   **Eeyore's Books for Children** (2212 Broadway at 79th St., tel. 212/362–0634, or 25 E. 83rd St., tel. 212/988–3404), a wonderful children's bookstore, has storytelling on Sundays (11 AM on the West Side, 12:30 on the East Side, except July–Aug.). **Storyland** (1369 3rd Ave., tel. 212/517–6951) has a weekly story hour on Sundays at 1. In summer, the **Hans Christian Andersen Statue** at the Conservatory Water in Central Park (at 74th St.) is the site for storytelling on Saturdays from 11 AM to noon. Pick up the monthly "Events for Children" brochure at branches of the **New York Public Library** to find out about library story hours, as well as child-oriented film programs. Branch libraries with particularly good children's rooms include the Donnell (20 W. 53rd St.), the Jefferson Market (425 6th Ave. at 10th St.), and the St. Agnes (444 Amsterdam Ave. at 82nd St.).

Shopping   Besides toy stores (*see* Chapter 7), children—especially older ones—may want to investigate the following shops. **Village Comics** (163 Bleecker St., 2nd floor, and 227 Sullivan St., tel. 212/777–2770) and **Funny Business Comics** (656 Amsterdam Ave., tel. 212/799–9477) carry a delightful, esoteric stock of old and new comic books. **Forbidden Planet** (821 Broadway at 12th St., tel. 212/473–1576, and 227 E. 59th St., tel. 212/751–4386) has everything the science-fiction or fantasy fanatic could ever want, including stuffed animals, coloring books, comic books, and collectibles.

Restaurants   At the East Village's **Two Boots** (37 Ave. A, between 2nd and 3rd Sts., tel. 212/505–2276), young customers are provided with crayons and coloring books. TV monitors tend to make the waiting easier at the East Side and West Side locations of **Border Cafe** (244 E. 79th St., tel. 212/535–4347, and 2637 Broadway at 100th St., tel. 212/749–8888). Good hamburgers are served in a casual, fun atmosphere at **Hamburger Harry's** in TriBeCa (157 Chambers St. between Hudson and Greenwich Sts., tel. 212/267–4446) and in midtown (145 W. 45th St., tel. 212/840–2756). At South Street Seaport, Pier 17's **Promenade Food Court** offers a wide variety of quick foods to eat in a wide-open space.

Off the Beaten Track

Public Spaces   Under the city's zoning laws, new office buildings can receive a variance—to add extra stories, for example—by designing and maintaining a portion of interior or exterior space for public use. Such spaces are a boon for city dwellers and visitors:

They provide clean, safe, attractive areas where you can sit, relax, read a newspaper, and people-watch. Most are planted with greenery, from potted plants to towering trees, or have some form of falling water to muffle the sounds of the city. Many have snack bars, working telephones, and—what can be very difficult to find elsewhere in Manhattan—clean public rest rooms. The following public spaces are listed from lower Manhattan up.

In the modernistic atrium of the **Continental Insurance Building** (180 Maiden La. at Front St.) just two blocks south of the South Street Seaport Museum, benches surround copious foliage amid an ultramodern structure that looks as if it's made out of Tinker Toys. *Near Tours 17 and 18.*

ChemCourt (272 Park Ave. between 47th and 48th Sts.) in the Chemical Bank Building provides benches around plantings of exotic shrubs, all informatively labeled in English and Latin. A glass roof lets the sunshine into the ground floor of the 50-story silver-gray tower. *Near Tour 2.*

On the mezzanine and basement floors of 875 **Third Avenue** (between 52nd and 53rd Sts.), tables and chairs are set in a lobby surrounded by an array of fast-food establishments selling pizza, bagels, muffins, Chinese food, sandwiches, and salads. The basement also connects with the 53rd Street subway station (E, F lines). *Near Tour 2.*

A boon to midtown's weary, **Paley Park** (3 E. 53rd St.) was the first of New York's "pocket parks" to be inserted among the high-rise behemoths, placed on the site of the former society night spot the Stork Club. A waterfall blocks out traffic noise, and feathery honey locust trees provide shade. There's a snack bar that opens when weather permits. *Near Tour 1.*

Another pocket park, **McGraw-Hill Park** (6th Ave. between 48th and 49th Sts.) behind the McGraw-Hill Building, has a stunning walk-through wall of water. *Near Tour 1.*

Nice Places to Live Many of the loveliest residential areas of the city remain so precisely because they *are* off the beaten track, and hence out of the commercial flow. New Yorkers all eventually find their own dream blocks, where they intend to move as soon as they hit the lottery. Here, from south to north, is an utterly subjective sampling, uptown and down.

The city's longest stretch of redbrick town houses preserved from the 1820s and 1830s runs along the north side of **Charlton Street** (west of 6th Ave.), with high stoops, paneled front doors, leaded-glass windows, and narrow dormer windows all intact. While you're here, stroll along parallel King and Vandam streets for more fine Federal houses. This quiet enclave was once an estate called Richmond Hill, whose various residents included George Washington, John and Abigail Adams, and Aaron Burr. *Near Tours 12 and 14.*

Sniffen Court (off 36th St. between Lexington and 3rd Aves.) is an easily overlooked cul-de-sac of 19th-century brick stables converted into town houses, with an atmosphere that's equal parts old London and New Orleans. Sniffen Court was for many years the home of sculptor Malvina Hoffman. *Near Tour 4.*

In the exclusive East Side neighborhood known as Turtle Bay, the secluded two-block-long **Beekman Place** (east of 1st Ave.

between 49th and 51st Sts.) has an aura of unperturbably elegant calm. Residents of its refined town houses have included the Rockefellers, Alfred Lunt and Lynn Fontanne, Ethel Barrymore, and Irving Berlin. Go down the steps at 51st Street to reach a walkway along the East River. *Near Tour 2.*

Roosevelt Island (East River, 48th to 85th Sts.) is a 2½-mile-long East River island that was taken over by a residential complex in the 1970s, although only half of the high-rise buildings originally planned have been built. Some fragments remain of the asylums and hospitals once clustered here, when it was known as Welfare Island. Walkways along the edge of the island provide fine river views, and it's surprisingly quiet, compared with the city so near. The real treat, however, is the 3½-minute ride over on an aerial tram that looks like an oversize Fisher-Price toy. The one-way fare is $1.40. *Near Tour 6.*

Pomander Walk (94th to 95th Sts., between Broadway and West End Ave.) is a surprising hidden slice of Merry Olde England, inspired by the stage sets for an American version of a 1911 British play, *Pomander Walk.* Peep through the locked gate on 94th Street to see Tudor-style houses, window boxes, and neatly trimmed hedges. *Near Tours 8 and 9.*

Built at the turn of the century, the white Beaux Arts town houses lining **West 105th Street** (between West End Ave. and Riverside Dr.) are like a vision of Paris. The apartment building at the northeast corner of Riverside Drive now belongs to the American Buddhist Academy; go around the corner to see its immense bronze Buddha. Marion Davies, mistress of William Randolph Hearst, once lived in the house at 331 Riverside Drive. *Near Tours 8 and 9.*

Commercial Districts The tendency in New York is for merchants in similar trades to cluster together in certain neighborhoods, where their customers can hop from one office to another. As you walk about the streets, you'll come upon sudden thickets of fur dealers, hat makers, button sellers, or flower suppliers, to name just a few. These three districts are particularly large and vibrant:

Gansevoort Market (around Gansevoort and Greenwich Sts.) features otherwise undistinguished warehouse buildings that each morning become the meat market for the city's retailers and restaurants. Racks of carcasses make a fascinating if not very pretty sight. Action peaks on weekdays from 5 to 9 AM. *Near Tours 11 and 12.*

The **Garment District** (7th Ave. between 31st and 41st Sts., also called "Fashion Avenue") teems with warehouses, workshops, and showrooms that manufacture and finish mostly women's and children's clothing. On weekdays the streets are crowded with trucks and the sidewalks swarm with daredevil deliverymen wheeling garment racks between factories and specialized subcontractors. *Near Tour 3.*

The relatively unglitzy jewelry shops at street level in the **Diamond District** (47th St. between 5th and 6th Aves.) are just the tip of the iceberg; upstairs, millions of dollars' worth of gems are traded, and skilled craftsmen cut precious stones. Wheeling and dealing goes on at fever pitch, all rendered strangely exotic by the presence of a host of Hasidic Jews in severe black dress, beards, and curled sidelocks. *Near Tour 1.*

4 Exploring the Other Boroughs

Many visitors to Manhattan notice the four outer boroughs—Brooklyn, Queens, the Bronx, and Staten Island—only from a Circle Line cruise, leaving those areas to remain ciphers, part of the city yet not. *Don't fall asleep on the subway,* the unschooled tourist tells himself, *or you may end up in the Bronx!*

Manhattanites themselves, many driven over the river by astronomical rents, have only recently begun to discover the outer boroughs. They've found sky, trees, and living space among the 19th-century brownstones, converted industrial lofts, Art Deco apartment palaces, and tidy bungalows. They've also found fascinating ethnic enclaves and a host of museums, parks, and gardens.

The reality is that Manhattan is only a small part of New York City. Its population of 1.487 million is smaller than that of either Brooklyn (2.3 million) or Queens (1.95 million), and only slightly larger than that of the Bronx (1.203 million). Staten Island may be less populous (379,000), but it's 2½ times the size of Manhattan.

There are things to see and do in the outer boroughs that you simply won't find in Manhattan and most are just a subway ride away from midtown.

Manhattanites may try to put you off such a journey, but don't be daunted. After a couple of beers, those same people may rave about their favorite place for cheesecake (Junior's on Flatbush Avenue in Brooklyn), or a great outdoor barbecue they had at their sister-in-law's suburban-style house (in Forest Hills Gardens, Queens); you may even have to listen to a story about their life's peak experience—found in the bleachers of Yankee Stadium in . . . the Bronx!

Brooklyn

Tour 19: Brooklyn Heights

Numbers in the margin correspond with points of interest on the Brooklyn Heights map.

"All the advantages of the country, with most of the conveniences of the city." So ran the ads for a real-estate development that sprang up in the 1820s just across the East River from downtown Manhattan. Brooklyn Heights—named for its enviable hilltop position—was New York's first suburb, linked to the city first by ferry and later by the Brooklyn Bridge. Feverish construction quickly transformed the airy heights into a fashionable upper-middle-class community. Happily, some 600 buildings more than 100 years old remain intact today, making Brooklyn Heights a kind of picture book of 19th-century American architecture.

This walking tour actually begins in lower Manhattan near City Hall (take the Lexington Avenue IRT to City Hall or the Seventh Avenue IRT to Park Place). From there you'll approach the Heights in grand fashion, via the pedestrian walkway over the **Brooklyn Bridge.** The Great Bridge promenade takes little more than an hour to walk and is a New York experience on a par with the Statue of Liberty trip or the Empire State Building ascent. Even if you haven't the time to poke around the Brooklyn side, take the unforgettable walk across the bridge.

(You can catch a ride back to Manhattan on the No. 2 or 3 subway at the Clark Street station, just a few blocks southwest of the walkway terminus.)

Before this bridge was built, Brooklynites had to rely on a ferry that connected Manhattan's Fulton Street to Brooklyn—a charming way to travel, surely, but unreliable in the fog and ice of winter. (Today there is talk of reinstating ferry service, though the armies of Wall Street nine-to-fivers commuting from Brooklyn manage just fine riding the subway or taking an invigorating morning constitutional over the bridge.)

After some 50 years of talk about a bridge, John Augustus Roebling, a respected engineer, was handed a bridge construction assignment in 1867. As the project to build the first steel suspension bridge slowly took shape over the next 15 years, it captured the imagination of the city; on its completion in 1883, it was called the Eighth Wonder of the World. Its twin Gothic-arched towers rise 268 feet from the river below. The roadway is supported by a web of steel cables, hung from the towers and attached to block-long anchorages on either shore. It is hardly the longest suspension bridge in the world anymore; the George Washington Bridge over the Hudson River has twice its span. But it remains a symbol of what man can accomplish and is a beautiful monument as well—in Walt Whitman's words, "the strong, light work of engineers."

In 1884 P. T. Barnum took 21 elephants across the bridge, just to prove it was sound, and motion picture directors have capitalized on it for photo opportunities: Gene Kelly danced across it in *On the Town;* Meryl Streep quaffed champagne there in *Sophie's Choice;* and in *Tarzan's New York Adventure*, Johnny Weismuller used it as a diving board.

As you look south from the walkway, the pinnacles of downtown Manhattan loom on your right, Brooklyn Heights stands sentinel on your left, and before you yawns the harbor, with Lady Liberty showing herself in profile. Turn about for a fine view up the East River, spanned within sight by the Manhattan and Williamsburg bridges. You don't need binoculars to enjoy the vistas, but you'd do well to bring a hat or scarf, because the wind whips through the cables like a dervish.

When the walkway splits, take the left fork, descend the steps, turn right, and pass under the bridge. This spills you out into Breukelen—as the founding Dutch first called this part of Long Island—at Cadman Plaza West, where a not-too-inviting park surrounds a conglomeration of government buildings, including the **New York Supreme Court** (former domain of fighting U.S. Attorney Rudolph Giuliani) and Brooklyn's **Borough Hall.** There's little reason to linger here, so head back alongside the bridge, descending toward the riverbank on Old Fulton Street.

2 As you approach the **Fulton Ferry Landing,** in the shadow of the Brooklyn Bridge, you'll pass the solid-looking expanse of the bridge's eastern Anchorage, which is the setting for occasional performance-art extravaganzas and art exhibitions. Along this route you'll also cross under a noisy ramp of the Brooklyn–Queens Expressway. The pavement frequently gives way to cobblestone, a reminder of the past century, and Cadman Plaza takes on another name, Old Fulton Street.

144

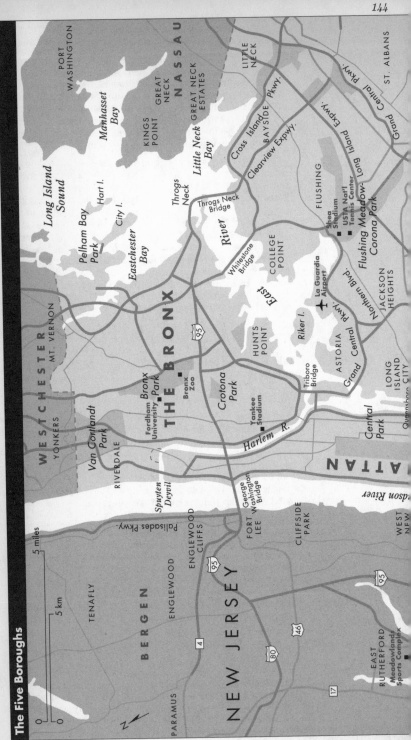

The Five Boroughs

NEW JERSEY

PARAMUS

TENAFLY

BERGEN

ENGLEWOOD

ENGLEWOOD CLIFFS

CLIFFSIDE PARK

FORT GEORGE LEE WASHINGTON BRIDGE

EAST RUTHERFORD

Meadowlands Sports Complex

WEST NEW

Palisades Pkwy.

Hudson River

Spuyten Devil

RIVERDALE

Van Cortlandt Park

Fordham University

Bronx Park

Bronx Zoo

THE BRONX

Crotona Park

Harlem R.

Yankee Stadium

WESTCHESTER

YONKERS

MT. VERNON

Eastchester Bay

Pelham Bay Park

Hart I.

City I.

Long Island Sound

PORT WASHINGTON

Manhasset Bay

KINGS POINT

GREAT NECK ESTATES

GREAT NECK

NASSAU

LITTLE NECK

Throgs Neck

Throgs Neck Bridge

East River

Whitestone Bridge

COLLEGE POINT

Little Neck Bay

Cross Island Pkwy.

Clearview Expwy.

BAYSIDE

FLUSHING

Shea Stadium

USTA Nat'l Tennis Center

Flushing Meadow-Corona Park

La Guardia Airport

Riker I.

HUNTS POINT

Triboro Bridge

ASTORIA

Grand Central Pkwy.

JACKSON HEIGHTS

Northern Blvd.

Long Island Expwy.

Grand Central Pkwy.

ST. ALBANS

LONG ISLAND CITY

Queensboro

Central Park

MANHATTAN

5 miles

5 km

144

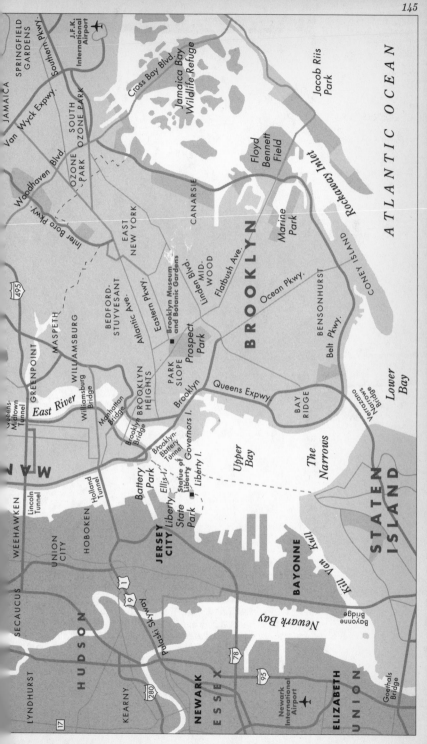

Brooklyn Bridge, **1**

Brooklyn Heights
Promenade, **6**

Brooklyn Historical
Society, **8**

Church of St. Ann and
the Holy Trinity, **7**

Fulton Ferry
Landing, **2**

Grace Church, **10**

Our Lady of Lebanon
Maronite Cathedral, **9**

Plymouth Church of
the Pilgrims, **4**

24 Middagh Street, **3**

Willow Street, **5**

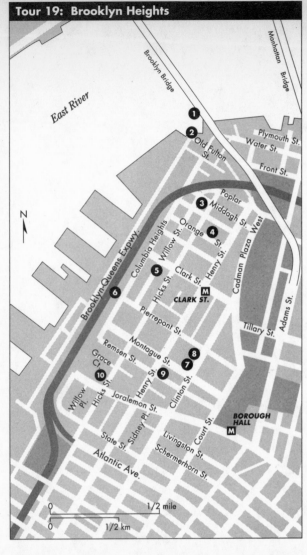

Tour 19: Brooklyn Heights

At first glance the Old Fulton Street area will seem dark and depressing, shadowed by ancient warehouses whose contents one can only speculate on. But look up and around. Several blocks north you'll notice the **Walentas Building** (1 Main St.), a handsomely be-towered and -clocked, post–Civil War structure erected by a corrugated-box magnate. On the south side of Fulton Street is the **Eagle Warehouse** (28 Old Fulton St.), with its striking round-arched Romanesque Revival entryway, enhanced by bronze lettering and fancy ironwork. The first office of the *Brooklyn Eagle* newspaper, it is now a residential co-op.

A few blocks down Front Street, you can visit the sites of **Gleason's Boxing Arena** (now a parking garage at 21–29 Front St.) and **Gym** (still at 75 Front St.), which moved here from

Manhattan's West Side. For 50 years, boxing greats such as Muhammad Ali, Roberto Duran, and Jake LaMotta put up their dukes and trained at Gleason's.

At the foot of Old Fulton Street is the **Fulton Ferry Terminal,** a self-possessed yellow-shingled tower that lists slightly. Walk out onto the **Ferry Pier** for a surprisingly pleasant whiff of the river and a worm's-eye view of the bridge. A plaque by the rail will help you identify the buildings of the downtown Manhattan skyline you'll see. Nearby, a former Erie Lackawanna coffee barge is moored to the pier. Dubbed Bargemusic (tel. 718/624–4061) by its operators, it is the setting for a series of Thursday and Friday evening and Sunday afternoon chamber-music concerts.

At 1 Water Street you'll find the **River Café** *(see* Chapter 8), which looks like a mobile home beached beside the river, though clusters of festive white Christmas lights on the surrounding trees liven up this excellent restaurant.

The Ferry Landing is a much-neglected place, although plans exist for full-scale reclamation—for instance, turning the tobacco warehouse next to the River Café into a museum and mall. For those who venture there now, the place is genuinely atmospheric, with none of the finished corners of South Street Seaport.

Go back up Old Fulton Street and take a right on Everit Street, which after a block becomes Columbia Heights, to climb toward Brooklyn Heights. On your way you'll pass the world headquarters of **Jehovah's Witnesses,** located in the Heights since 1909. The church published more than 71.5 million Bibles between 1926 and 1990.

❸ Turn left onto Middagh Street (pronounced *mid*-awe) and continue on until you arrive at **No. 24,** the oldest home in the neighborhood—a Federal-style wood residence with a mansard roof. Peer through a door in the wall on Willow Street for a glimpse of the cottage garden and carriage house in the rear.

Carry on along Middagh, turning right at Henry Street, a happy commercial avenue of restaurants and greengrocers, then turn again onto Orange Street. On the north side of the block between Henry and Hicks streets is a formidable institution: **❹** the **Plymouth Church of the Pilgrims,** which was the vortex of abolitionist sentiment in the years before the Civil War, thanks to the stirring oratory of Brooklyn's most eminent theologian, Henry Ward Beecher. In the Underground Railroad that smuggled slaves to freedom, Plymouth Church was more or less "Grand Central Station." Beside the church is a courtyard (locked, alas) with a statue of Beecher. His house, a prim Greek Revival brownstone, lies around the corner at **22 Willow Street.**

Turn left off Orange onto Willow Street, crossing Pineapple and Clark. (Street names in the Heights are an eccentric collection, reportedly created by a certain Miss Middagh, who despised the practice of naming streets for the town fathers and **❺** preferred instead various fruits.) **Willow Street,** between Clark and Pierrepont, is one of the prettiest and most architecturally varied blocks in the Heights. Note Nos. 108–112, built in the blend of terra-cotta reliefs, bay windows, and towers known as the Shingle or Queen Anne style. Farther down the block, on the other side, stand three distinguished brick Federal row houses allegedly part of the Underground Railroad.

As you turn right onto Pierrepont Street, heading toward the river, glance down Columbia Heights to your right, where Nos. 210–220 comprise a brownstone grouping often cited as the most graceful in New York. Norman Mailer lives on this street—lucky Mr. Mailer—and from a rear window in No. 111, John Roebling's son Washington (who in 1869 succeeded his father as chief engineer for the Brooklyn Bridge) directed the building of the bridge from his sickbed.

❻ Pierrepont Street ends at the **Brooklyn Heights Promenade,** a sliver of park one-third of a mile long, hanging over the ferry district like one of Babylon's fabled gardens. Cantilevered over two lanes of the Brooklyn–Queens Expressway and a service road, this quiet esplanade area is lined with benches offering front-row seats for the Manhattan skyline show. Circling gulls squawk, tugboats honk, and the city seems like a vision from another planet.

As you leave the Promenade (via Montague Street), look left to see Nos. 2 and 3 **Pierrepont Place,** two brownstone palaces built in the 1850s by a China trader and philanthropist, and used as a location for John Huston's film *Prizzi's Honor* (the frightful Mafia chieftain Don Corrado lived here). On your right lies **Montague Terrace,** where Thomas Wolfe lived when he finished *You Can't Go Home Again.* In the 1940s and 1950s, the neighborhood was said to be home to the city's largest number of writers outside Greenwich Village, among them Carson McCullers, W. H. Auden, Arthur Miller, and Truman Capote.

As you head east, Montague Street turns into a commercial district often disparaged for its homogeneous Yuppie character. Still, restaurants here feature everything from Hungarian to Japanese food, and window shopping can be fun. On the last block before Cadman Plaza West (north side), note an interesting row of banks: the Art Deco **Municipal Credit Union** (No. 185); a **Citibank** (No. 183) that looks like a latter-day Roman temple; and **Manufacturers Hanover Trust Company** (No. 177), a copy of the Palazzo della Gran Guardia in Verona, Italy.

❼ The **Church of St. Ann and the Holy Trinity** lies at the northwest corner of Montague and Clinton streets. Its historic stained-glass windows—the first made in the United States—are currently being restored. In recent years, the church has become a performing arts and film series center frequented by downtown Manhattan types. *157 Montague St., tel. 718/858–2424. Box office open Tues.–Sat. noon–6.*

A block north, at the corner of Clinton and Pierrepont, is the **❽** **Brooklyn Historical Society,** with its 1989 Shellens Gallery. The collection includes Brooklyn Dodgers' bats and balls, trick mirrors from Coney Island, and a 300-pound cast-zinc eagle saved from the offices of the *Brooklyn Eagle.* The society's library on the second floor—with its rich carved-wood bookcases and lustrous stained-glass windows—is a showcase for late 19th-century interior design; it also holds 10,000 rare photographs and 100,000 books. *128 Pierrepont St., tel. 718/624–0890. Library admission: $2.50. Open Tues.–Sat. 10–4:45. Shellens Gallery admission: $2.50 adults, $1 children; Tues. free. Open Tues.–Sun. noon–5.*

Return south along Clinton Street, then turn right onto Remsen Street. At the corner of Remsen and Henry streets, stop to take in the Romanesque Revival **Our Lady of Lebanon Maronite Cathedral** (113 Remsen St.), designed by prolific architect Richard Upjohn. It features the Shrine of St. Sharbel Makhlouf and doors salvaged from the 1943 wreck of the ocean liner *Normandie*. Turn left onto Hicks Street to visit another Upjohn creation, **Grace Church** (254 Hicks St.). Built in Gothic Revival style, it is shaded by an 80-foot elm tree. Across Hicks Street is **Grace Court Alley,** a traditional mews with a score of restored carriage houses.

The extreme southwest corner of Brooklyn Heights, encompassing the west ends of Joralemon Street and Willow and Columbia places, is a quiet, leafy, untrammeled area, rich in architectural pleasures. Along the north side of Joralemon, 25 **Greek Revival brownstones** (Nos. 29–75) delicately sidestep their way down the hill toward the river and the piers. Peek into Columbia Place to see an early attempt at humane, low-cost housing, the **Riverside tenements** (4–30 Columbia Pl.), dating from the 1870s. Then follow **Willow Place** south along the peaceful block between Joralemon and State streets; in late afternoon, the houses take on the colors of a faded quilt. Shrinking back from the street is an old chapel (26 Willow Pl.), now home to an amateur theater group.

Time Out **Camille's** (311 Henry St., near Atlantic Ave.) is a cozy and inexpensive spot, with antique counters and no more than 10 tables. The muffins, challah bread, and cakes are homemade, as are the soups. Imagine Berkeley come to Brooklyn and you've got the picture.

To return to Manhattan from here, go back west along Joralemon Street until you reach the Borough Hall subway station at Court Street. To explore more of nearby Brooklyn, however, you may want to head up **Atlantic Avenue,** with its exotic Syrian and Lebanese shops and, farther east, a string of antiques stores crammed with relatively reasonable buys. Or go south along Court Street to **Carroll Gardens,** the Italian brownstone neighborhood pictured in the 1987 film *Moonstruck.* The **Cammareri Brothers Bakery** (502 Henry St.) is where Nicolas Cage worked in that film; in real life, the bakery turns out staff-of-life-like Italian loaves and dense cheesecake. The food stores in the neighborhood are in general an Italian cook's dream.

Tour 20: Park Slope

Numbers in the margin correspond with points of interest on the Park Slope map.

This neighborhood, which grew up in the late 1800s on the west side of Prospect Park, is today one of Brooklyn's most sought-after sections. Many families have moved in to renovate the handsome brownstones that line its blocks—beware the heavy traffic in baby strollers!

Begin on **Seventh Avenue,** the area's main commercial street, accessible by the D, Q, 2, or 3 subway trains. Here, among other interesting shops, you'll find a wine store of real distinction, **Leon Paley Ltd.** (88 7th Ave.), as well as three diet-defying bakeries: **Cousin John's** (70 7th Ave.); **Faith's** (around the corner at 169 Lincoln Pl.); and the **New Prospect At Home** (52 7th Ave.). The corner of Seventh Avenue and Sterling Place was the site of a horrendous plane crash in 1960, which leveled several buildings around the intersection; down the street, the **Brownstone Gallery** (76 7th Ave.) keeps a photograph of the grounded plane on display.

Turn east on Lincoln Place to find the Slope's most venerable edifice, the **Montauk Club** (25 8th Ave.), an 1891 mansion modeled on Venice's Ca' d'Oro. Notice the friezes of Montauk Indians and the private side entrance, built especially for members' wives in the 19th century.

Make your way south along Eighth Avenue, sampling the brownstones on various streets along the way (President and Carroll streets are especially handsome), until you reach **Montgomery Place**, a block-long street between Eighth Avenue and Prospect Park West. This is considered by many to be the neighborhood's finest block, lined by a picturesque variety of town houses designed by the Romanesque Revival genius C.P.H. Gilbert.

Return along Prospect Park West to **Grand Army Plaza**, a geographic star from which radiate Prospect Park West, Eastern Parkway, and Flatbush and Vanderbilt avenues. At its center stands the **Soldiers' and Sailors' Memorial Arch**, patterned on the Arc de Triomphe in Paris. Three heroic sculptural groupings adorn the arch: atop, a four-horsed chariot by Frederick MacMonnies, so dynamic that it almost seems on the verge of catapulting off the arch; to the sides, the victorious Union Army and Navy of the Civil War. Inside are bas-reliefs of Presidents Abraham Lincoln and Ulysses S. Grant, sculpted by Thomas Eakins and William O'Donovan, respectively. A secret doorway leads to a spiral staircase and, ultimately, the arch's top (it's open April 29–June 17, weekends 11–4:30). To the northwest, Neptune and a passel of debauched tritons leer over the edges of the **Bailey Fountain**, where tulle-drenched brides and grooms in technicolor tuxes come to pose after exchanging vows.

To the southeast of the plaza is the main entrance to **Prospect Park**, a 536-acre urban playground designed by Frederick Law Olmsted and Calvert Vaux, who considered it superior to their earlier creation, Central Park, because no streets divided it and no bordering skyscrapers would break its rural illusion. Woods, water, and meadows remain the park's three basic thematic elements. Inside the entrance is the 90-acre **Long Meadow**, full of picnickers and kite-fliers on weekends, and the site of free New York Philharmonic and Metropolitan Opera performances in the summer. Follow the circular drive to the right, and at the entrance at Prospect Park West and 3rd Street you'll see the **Litchfield Villa**, an Italianate mansion built in 1857. It now holds the park's administrative offices, but visitors are welcome to step inside and view the interior. Across the main drive is the **Picnic House** (tel. 718/788–0055), stage for a year-round schedule of drama, dance, music, storytelling, and puppetry.

If you follow the drive to the left of the main entrance, you'll come to the **zoo**, scheduled to reopen in 1992 as a children's zoo. Just beyond the zoo is a restored 1912 **carousel** (50¢ a ride) and the **Lefferts Homestead**, a gambrel-roofed Dutch colonial farm-

Boathouse, **8**
Brooklyn Botanic Garden, **11**
The Brooklyn Museum, **12**
Brooklyn Public Library, **10**
Garden Terrace, **9**
Grand Army Plaza, **3**
Lefferts Homestead, **6**
Litchfield Villa, **4**
Montauk Club, **1**
Montgomery Place, **2**
Quaker Cemetery, **7**
Zoo, **5**

Tour 20: Park Slope

house (1783) that holds a museum of period home furnishings and changing exhibitions. *Tel. 718/965–6505. Admission free. Open May–Sept., Wed.–Sat. noon–4, Sun. noon–5; Oct.–Dec. and Apr., Wed.–Sun. noon–4; Jan.–Mar., weekends noon–4.*

7 The middle of the park is a forested ravine, cut by a stream and dotted with bridges. Follow the central drive, which bisects the park here, to the **Quaker Cemetery**, where you will find Montgomery Clift's quiet grave. If you stay on the circular drive, **8** you'll soon pass the terra-cotta **Boathouse** (tel. 718/287–3474), styled after the Library of St. Marks in Venice; today it houses a visitor center, art exhibitions, and a café. Farther down the path is the giant, gnarled **Camperdown Elm**, which Marianne Moore immortalized in a poem in the 1960s. Moore became one of the park's chief advocates, a labor she termed "my only mor- **9** tal entanglement." South of here is a formal **garden terrace**, near the shore of a 60-acre **lake** inhabited by a fleet of ducks and swans.

10 If you return to Grand Army Plaza, to the east of the park's main entrance, you will find the main branch of the **Brooklyn Public Library**. Built in 1941, it applies Art Deco streamlining to the grand neoclassical look of Beaux Arts public buildings. Notice the bas-relief carvings and the inscription picked out in gold above the entrance. Step inside to admire the murals in the lobby. *Tel. 718/780–7700. Open Tues.–Thurs. 9–8, Fri. and Sat. 10–6, Sun. 1–5.*

Eastern Parkway, which runs from Grand Army Plaza past the library, mimics the grand sweep of the boulevards of Paris and

Vienna. Every Labor Day weekend the parkway hosts the biggest and liveliest carnival outside the Caribbean—a cacophony of calypso, steel band, and reggae music, with plenty of conch curry, spice bread, and meat patties to go around.

⓫ A couple of hundred yards along the parkway is an entrance to the **Brooklyn Botanic Garden,** which occupies 52 acres across Flatbush Avenue from Prospect Park. The garden exudes a beguiling Oriental atmosphere, due to the presence of a **Japanese Garden,** complete with a blazing red torii gate and a pond laid out in the shape of the Chinese character for "heart." The Japanese cherry arbor turns into a heart-stopping cloud of pink every May. Wander through the **Cranford Rose Garden** (5,000 bushes, 1,200 varieties); the **Fragrance Garden,** designed especially for the blind; the **Shakespeare Garden,** featuring plants immortalized by the bard; and **Celebrity Path,** Brooklyn's answer to Hollywood's famous sidewalk, with the names of homegrown stars—including Mel Brooks, Woody Allen, Zero Mostel, Barbara Stanwyck, and Mae West—inscribed on stepping-stones. In May 1988, the garden gained a complex of handsome greenhouses called the **Steinhardt Conservatory,** which holds thriving desert, tropical, temperate, and aquatic vegetation, as well as a display charting the evolution of plants over the past 140 million years. The **C.V. Starr Bonsai Museum** in the Conservatory grows about 75 miniature Japanese plants. The Botanic Garden Shop is a fine place to stop, particularly if you're a gardener yourself. *1000 Washington Ave., tel. 718/ 622–4433. Admission to garden free. Admission to Steinhardt Conservatory Nov.–Mar. free; Apr.–Oct., $2 adults, $1 senior citizens and children 3–12. Garden open Apr.–Sept., Tues.– Fri. 8–6, weekends and holidays 10–6; Oct.–Mar., Tues.–Fri. 8–4:30, weekends and holidays 10–4:30. Closed Thanksgiving, Dec. 25, and Jan. 1. Conservatory open Apr.–Sept., Tues.– Sun. 10–5; Oct.–Mar., Tues.–Sun. 10–4.*

⓬ **The Brooklyn Museum,** designed by the McKim, Mead & White team in 1897, sports huge Daniel Chester French statues of Brooklyn and Manhattan (as classical ladies) on its Eastern Parkway front. With over 2 million objects, the Brooklyn collection is the seventh largest in the country. The museum's renovation and expansion project by Japanese architect Arata Isozaki and New York firm James Stewart Polshek includes a new auditorium with a wavelike ceiling, and new galleries in the oldest part of the building, slated to open in the fall of 1992. Look especially for its **Egyptian Art** collection (third floor), considered the best of its kind anywhere outside London or Cairo, or the African and Pre-Columbian Art (first floor), another collection recognized worldwide. In the gallery of **American painting and sculpture** (fifth floor) you'll find *Brooklyn Bridge* by Georgia O'Keeffe, as well as striking works by Winslow Homer, John Singer Sargent, and Gilbert Stuart. The **Period Rooms** (fourth floor) include the complete interior of the Jan Martense Schenck House, built in the Brooklyn Flatlands section in 1675, as well as a suite of rooms decorated in Moorish style from the 54th Street mansion of John D. Rockefeller. Outdoors, the **Frieda Schiff Warburg Memorial Sculpture Garden** features relics from "lost New York," such as a lion's head from Coney Island's Steeplechase Park. The museum also offers excellent special exhibitions, a treasure chest of a gift shop, and dramatic views of Manhattan from its Eastern Parkway-Washington Avenue corner. *200 Eastern Pkwy., tel. 718/638–5000.*

Suggested contribution: $4 adults, $1.50 senior citizens, $2 students with valid ID, children under 12 free. Open Wed.–Sun. 10–5.

Queens

Tour 21: Long Island City and Astoria

Numbers in the margin correspond with points of interest on the Long Island City and Astoria map.

In the 1800s, along the East River in Queens, a string of neighborhoods thrived due to their ferry links with Manhattan. One of the busiest ferries connected a finger of land called Hunters Point with East 34th Street, Manhattan. Here, a business district known as Long Island City burgeoned. (Queens is, after all, on the western end of Long Island, as is Brooklyn.) Factories, boardinghouses, municipal buildings, and restaurants clustered around the intersection of Vernon Boulevard and Jackson Avenue, while north along Vernon Boulevard tycoons built summer homes, with boathouses and lawns that reached gracefully to the banks of the river. Today the community has found new life as a mecca for artists, who've migrated with their paint pots and welding tools to airy, low-rent studios.

A 10-minute ride on the No. 7 subway from Times Square or Grand Central Terminal will take you to the 45th Road Court House Square station. This noisy intersection is a fine introduction to this part of Queens, where the dark, clanking hulk of the El keeps the sunlight from penetrating to the street.

Long Island City's streets puzzle cartographers and visitors alike; you'll find numbered streets running north and south, and numbered avenues, roads, and drives going east–west. Consider 45th Avenue: To its south lies 45th Road, and to its north is 44th Road, 44th Avenue, and 44th Drive. But bear with this confusion and turn east onto 45th Avenue, where you'll

❶ find the **Hunters Point Historic District,** full of immaculate row houses with their original stoops and cornices. Their fine condition is due partly to their having been faced in resilient Westchester stone. At 21st Street, a small park offers benches (for pigeons and people) and a setting for a large metal sculpture called *Bigger Bird* by Daniel Sinclair. The warehouses surrounding the park are a warren of artists' studios; above their low roofs there's an unimpeded view of Manhattan.

❷ On 21st Street, between 46th Road and 46th Avenue, is **P.S.1,** a contemporary art museum housed in what was originally a Ward 1 school. The founders of P.S.1 were the first of the art-conscious to see the possibilities in the area; back in 1976 they turned the old school into lecture rooms, studio space for artists, and wide white galleries. On display are special exhibitions and a number of permanent works, including James Turrell's sky piece *Meeting* and Alan Saret's *Fifth Colar Chthonic Wall Temple* (1976). *46–01 21st St., tel. 718/784–2084. Admission free. Open Wed.–Sun. noon–6.*

The intersection of **Jackson Avenue** and **Vernon Boulevard** is still the commercial center of the neighborhood, as it was when the ferry operated from the foot of Borden Avenue. Modest shingled homes, butcher shops, diners, and the Vernon–Jack-

American Museum of
the Moving Image, **9**

Court House Square, **5**

Hunters Point Historic
District, **1**

International Design
Center, **6**

LaGuardia Community
College, **7**

P.S. 1, **2**

St. Demetrios
Cathedral, **8**

Silvercup Studios, **4**

Water's Edge
Restaurant, **3**

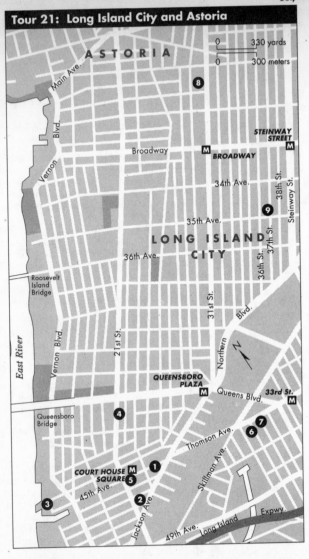

son subway stop crowd together beneath the huge, four-bar-
reled stacks of the old Pennsylvania Railroad generating plant.
(Schwartz Chemicals, as the structure is identified on its eastern face, was a later occupant; today the behemoth contains an
assortment of smaller manufacturing firms and some indoor
tennis courts.) At 49th Avenue and Vernon Boulevard, the
steeple of **St. Mary's Roman Catholic Church** rises more spirit-
ually into the sky than the stacks of old Schwartz.

Vernon Boulevard, originally called the Williamsburg Turnpike Road, was Queens's first true highway, leading to the
mansions along the river, all now demolished. The area to the
west of Vernon is slated to change dramatically once again,
when the Hunters Point Development plan turns 70 acres of

riverfront and 20 acres of landfill between the Midtown Tunnel and Queensboro Bridge into a sprawling apartment complex and commercial mall.

Time Out Only locals know about **Café Vernon** (46–18 Vernon Blvd., tel. 718/784–8518), a tiny, unassuming Italian restaurant at Vernon Boulevard and 46th Road. Don't let its modesty fool you, though, because it offers splendid, filling repasts of Italian sandwiches, soups, and pastas. Prices are moderate; the atmosphere is homey.

③ A white concrete block of a building rises at the foot of 44th Drive. Another warehouse? Hardly. This is the **Water's Edge Restaurant,** a Queens dining spot where in summertime gay umbrellas sprout up on the dock, and boaters check in for quick vodka tonics. Inside is an elegant restaurant that charges Manhattan prices, bringing in its sophisticated clientele via a complimentary ferry service from the city's 23rd Street Marina Tuesday–Saturday. From the pier outside you can survey the **Queensboro Bridge,** which extends 7,000 feet, from Manhattan's East 60th Street to Crescent Street, Queens. Finished in 1909, its construction claimed the lives of 50 workers. A detour north on Vernon Boulevard will take you to the bridge's base at Queens Plaza, where there's a riverfront park and a lonely remnant of the past century, the old **New York Architectural Terra Cotta Company,** complete with Tudor Revival adornments and chimney pots.

It's ironically appropriate that the sometimes tatty western section of Queens should have become an outpost for America's glitziest industry, the motion pictures. In Long Island City, filmmakers began to gather in 1983 to make movies and commercials at a 3-block-long complex, converted from a bakery **④** into 14 soundstages. **Silvercup Studios** (42–25 21st St.) can be reached by walking west from Vernon to the intersection of 21st Street and 43rd Avenue. Here you might catch a glimpse of Bill Cosby punching in for work on his latest commercial. Such movies as *Godfather III, Sea of Love, and When Harry Met Sally* were also shot within the walls of old Silvercup.

⑤ Now hike back down 21st Street to 45th Avenue, which will bring you to **Court House Square.** Notice first—you probably couldn't fail to—the towering green **Citicorp Building.** What's Citicorp doing in Long Island City? Currently, Manhattan office space is running at $40–$95 per square foot, while in Queens you can rent at a cool $17–$27. I. M. Pei is responsible for the building's basic design, which carries over some general themes from its sister across the river, the Citicorp Building at East 53rd Street and Lexington Avenue.

Much more modest is the 1908 Beaux Arts **New York State Supreme Courthouse** (25–10 Court House Sq.) across from Citicorp, the scene of a number of sensational trials both real and fictional—the courthouse is frequently used as a location by neighborhood movie studios.

Thomson Avenue will lead you—perilously, due to roaring traffic alongside—over the mind-boggling mesh of the Long Island Railroad tracks. Just past here, Thomson Avenue merges into **Queens Boulevard,** one of the borough's chief transverses.

To your right lie the shells of several once-thriving industries: the **Sunshine Biscuit Company** (Skillman between 29th St. and 30th St.), **American Eveready Building** (29–10 Thomson Ave.), **Adams Chewing Gum Factory** (30–30 Thomson Ave.), and **White Motor Company Factory** (31–10 Thomson Ave.), all built between 1914 and 1920 in a delightful mix of the practical and the ornamental. The **International Design Center** (tel. 718/937–7474), completed in 1985, now occupies the former three structures. This vast marketplace (1 million square feet) for the products of interior designers was built at a cost of more than $125 million. Peek inside to see the ballooning central atrium, surrounded by showrooms ad infinitum. Gigantic elevators for unloading train cars occupied those central spaces back in the days when these buildings still turned out crackers, bubble gum, and auto parts.

❼ Next door is **LaGuardia Community College,** whose **Archives** (31–10 Thomson Ave., tel. 718/482–5065) contain the papers of the city's most colorful mayor, Fiorello H. La Guardia. New York's "Little Flower," as La Guardia came to be called, presided over the metropolis during the Depression.

Walk three blocks west to the 33rd Street station of the No. 7 subway—which *could* take you back into Manhattan, or, better still, a bit farther into Queens. Travel one stop to Queensboro Plaza, then change for the N train, getting off three stops later at Broadway to visit **Astoria,** one of New York's most vital ethnic neighborhoods. It was originally German, then Italian, but today you're likely to hear more Greek spoken. Astoria's business district along Broadway bustles with curiosities. The **K & T Meat Market** (37–11 Broadway) sends 500 whole lambs to city kitchens every week. Greek pastry shops (*xaxaroplasteion*) and coffeehouses (*kaffenion*) shoot heady smells onto the avenue. The house specialty at the **Roumeli Taverna** (33–04 Broadway) is *mezedakia,* or Greek hors d'oeuvres. Late into the night the **Grecian Cave** nightclub (next to the Oyster Bay Restaurant and Crystal Palace complex at 31–01 and 31–11 Broadway) resounds with Greek crooners and bouzouki music. But

❽ Astoria's heart is the Greek Orthodox **St. Demetrios Cathedral** (30–11 30th Dr.), a brick building with a red tile roof and the largest Orthodox congregation outside Greece.

In the 1920s, such stars as Gloria Swanson, Rudolph Valentino, and the Marx Brothers came to this neighborhood to work at "the Big House," Paramount's movie-making center in the east. Today the 13-acre **Kaufman Astoria Studios** (34–12 36th St.), with its monumentally columned entrance, remains a principal player in the movie biz. Since 1977, scores of pictures have been produced here, including *The Cotton Club, The Verdict, Arthur, The Wiz,* and *The World According to Garp.*

❾ A visit to the **American Museum of the Moving Image** next door should satisfy almost any film fan's cravings. Opened in September 1988, the museum houses a 195-seat theater and a 60-seat screening room where fascinating film series flicker by— among them a John Ford program and tributes to leading Hollywood cinematographers. Galleries feature exhibitions such as "Behind the Screen: Producing, Promoting Motion Pictures and Television" and those studying the technological aspects of film (including hands-on displays that allow visitors to try their skills at editing). Commissioned artworks are on display, such as the Red Grooms and Lysiane Luong theater, *Tut's Fever,* a metaphorical recapitulation of Egyptian-style picture palaces of the 1930s (you'll find lifelike figures of Theda Bara at the ticket booth and Mae West serving up popcorn); and Korean Nam June Paik's video installation, "The Getaway Car," a commentary on movies. The museum's collection of movie memorabilia includes 70,000 items; in the costume display you might find outfits worn by Rudolf Valentino or Bette Davis. *35th Ave. at 36th St., tel. 718/784–0077. Admission: $5 adults, $4 senior citizens, $2.50 students and children. Open Tues.–Fri. noon–4, Sat. and Sun. noon–6.*

Tour 22: Flushing

Numbers in the margin correspond with points of interest on the Flushing map.

There are two quite different reasons to visit the Flushing neighborhood of Queens: to view a historic section that played an instrumental role in the fight for religious freedom in America, and to cavort in Flushing Meadows Corona Park, with its many sports facilities. Surrounding these two focal points is a multiethnic community that is increasingly dominated by Asians; it's a bubbling melting pot rarely visited by New Yorkers themselves.

Take the No. 7 subway to its final stop, the Main Street–Flushing station. Main Street and its two parallel neighbors, Prince and Union streets, serve up a banquet for Korean, Chinese, and Indian gourmands. Browse in them for exotic tastes of this "Little Asia," as it is sometimes called. At Main Street and 39th Avenue you will pass a Gothic-style church built of brownstone and native Manhattan schist: this is **St. George's Episcopal Church,** built in 1854. One of the signers of the Declaration of Independence, Francis Lewis, was vestryman in the church's earlier building.

Continue to Northern Boulevard and turn right. At 137–16 Northern Boulevard is the wood-shingled, tiny-windowed **Friends Meeting House,** New York City's oldest place of worship. Built in 1694, it's still used for the Quakers' 11 AM Sunday-morning services.

Turn right on Bowne Street to see where the Quakers first met, in the **Bowne House,** one of the oldest standing residences in the city. John Bowne and his family joined the English settlers in Flushing—then called by its Dutch name, Vlissigen—in 1655; this house was built in 1661. Governor Peter Stuyvesant had banned the Quakers in 1657; they met secretly in the woods until Bowne, a Quaker convert, invited them to gather in his house. Stuyvesant imprisoned and then exiled Bowne for his defiance, but Bowne convinced the Dutch West India Company to order the colony's governor to tolerate all religious groups, a right preserved more than 100 years later in the U.S. Constitution. The Bowne House is now a museum of decorative arts and household furnishings, including those used by nine generations of the family, who lived there until 1947. *37–01 Bowne St., tel. 718/359–0528. Admission: $2 adults, $1 children under 12. Open Tues., Sat., Sun. 2:30–4:30; last tour, 4:10.*

Across Bowne Street, in front of the entrance to a large apartment house at no. 36-40, is the **Fox Oaks Rock,** marking the site of an impassioned sermon delivered in 1672 by George Fox,

Bowne House, **2**

Friends Meeting House, **1**

Kingsland Homestead, **3**

New York Hall of Science, **8**

Queens Museum, **6**

Queens Zoo, **7**

Shea Stadium, **4**

U.S. Tennis Association National Tennis Center, **5**

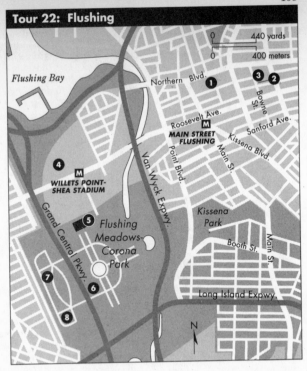

Tour 22: Flushing

founder of the Quaker sect. Scheduled to address the society inside Bowne's house, Fox had to move the meeting outside because of the huge turnout.

③ Pass through the park north of Bowne House to view the **Kingsland Homestead,** a gambrel-roofed wood farmhouse built circa 1785. Its original owner was a Quaker farmer; his son-in-law, the dashing sea captain Joseph King, gave it its name. The house was moved to this site in 1968 to escape demolition. Now home to the Queens Historical Society, it contains several exhibits about local history. *143–35 37th Ave., tel. 718/939–0647. Admission: $2 adults, $1 students, senior citizens, and children. Open Tues., Thurs., and weekends 2:30–4:30.*

In the park beside the Kingsland Homestead is the **Weeping Beech,** a huge beech tree with trailing branches, planted from a cutting brought by Samuel Parsons from Belgium in 1847 and recently declared a historical landmark. Parsons's nursery supplied many other unusual species of trees still standing in Flushing, as well as in Central and Prospect parks. The site of the nursery is now the 235-acre **Kissena Park,** in southwest Flushing.

Eight blocks south on Bowne Street is the **Hindu Temple of North America** (45–47 Bowne St.), an intricately decorated pavilioned temple erected in the 1970s by Indian artisans.

Return to the Main Street–Flushing station and take the No. 7 train one stop, to Willets Point–Shea Stadium. This will bring you to **Flushing Meadows Corona Park,** a stretch of greenery running from Flushing Bay to the Grand Central Parkway.

Recreation facilities here include a marina, boats, a carousel, bicycling paths, an indoor ice-skating rink, picnic grounds, a swimming pool, and theaters and museums. Just north of the park, and linked to it by a wide wood walkway (onto which you ❹ will emerge from the station), is **Shea Stadium,** home of the New York Mets baseball team. At the other end of the ❺ walkway, at the park's northern tip, is the **U. S. Tennis Association National Tennis Center** (tel. 718/592–8000), host since 1978 to the annual U.S. Open tennis tournament. Its courts are available for play outside of tournament time (*see* Chapter 6).

The park was the site of both the 1939 and 1964 World's Fair, and several structures from those expositions remain, including the landmark **Unisphere,** a 380-ton steel globe. At the end of ❻ the fairground mall is the **Queens Museum,** housed in what was the New York Pavilion for the 1939 fair. Its most notable exhibit is the Panorama, an 18,000-square-foot architectural model of New York City's five boroughs. *Tel. 718/592–2405. Suggested donation: $2 adults, $1 senior citizens, students, and children over 5. Open Tues.–Fri. 10–5, weekends noon–5.*

The west section of the park contains the refurbished **Queens** ❼ **Zoo,** (scheduled to be reopen in 1992), which focuses on North American animals in their natural habitats. *Admission: $2.50 adults, $1.25 senior citizens, 50¢ children under 12. Open Nov.–Mar. daily 10–4:30; Apr.–Oct., weekdays 10–5, weekends 10–5:30.*

❽ Children enjoy the park's **New York Hall of Science,** where they can interact with hands-on exhibits on such topics as color and illusion, the atom, self-sensory machines, and microorganisms. *Tel. 718/699–0005. Admission: $3.50 adults, $2.50 senior citizens and children. Open Wed.–Sun. 10–5.*

The Bronx

Tour 23: Fordham and the Zoo

Numbers in the margin correspond with points of interest on the Fordham and the Bronx Zoo map.

The only borough attached to the North American mainland, the Bronx was first settled by Dutch, French, English, and Swedish country squires, who established manorial holdings there while fighting off Indians. The Village of Fordham was founded by John Archer in the mid-1600s, although little now remains from the colonial era. But the area does dramatically illustrate another aspect of Bronx history—the influx of immigrant groups from the 1840s onward: first the Irish, then Germans, Italians, and Jews. Later waves included blacks and Hispanics, and today there are new infusions of Albanian and Cambodian immigrants.

To reach the old Village of Fordham, ride the D subway to the Kingsbridge Road station, where you'll alight alongside a fine stretch of that Bronx Champs Elysées, the **Grand Concourse.** Here you get a sense of the roadway as engineer Louis Riis envisioned it—a 4-mile-long "speedway," facilitating excursions into the country—as well as a view to the west of the **Kingsbridge Armory,** built in 1912, one of the largest such structures in the world.

Poe Park, at East Kingsbridge Road and the Grand Concourse, ❶ is so named because it contains the **Edgar Allan Poe Cottage,** whose white wood siding and green shutters recall earlier, more idyllic days. Here Poe and his wife, Virginia, sought refuge from Manhattan and from the vicissitudes of the writerly life between 1846 and 1849. He wandered the countryside on foot and listened to the tintinnabulation of the church bells at nearby St. John's College Church (now Fordham University). His rocking chair and the bed his wife died in can be seen in the cottage today. Among the works he completed during this period are the poems "Ulalume," "The Bells," "Eureka," and "Annabel Lee." *Tel. 212/881–8900. Admission: $2. Open Wed.– Fri. 9–5, Sat. 10–4, Sun. 1–5.*

A couple of blocks south is the intersection of Fordham Road and the Grand Concourse, the Times Square of the Bronx. **Alexander's** department store, at the very top of the Fordham Road hill, once produced the largest number of sales per square foot of any department store in the country. Venture south on ❷ the Grand Concourse to **Loew's Paradise Theatre** (2413 Grand Concourse), which many claim is the best remaining 1930s-style movie house. The exterior ornamentation looks like a claymation fantasy; inside, a sloping, tiled entryway leads to a gorgeously garish Baroque-style lobby. Tell the ticket-taker that you're an architecture student and you may be able to get in without paying for the latest kung fu movie. John Eberson, the dean of bijou-builders, designed this gem in 1929; happily, he wasn't alive to see it converted to a quadplex in 1981.

Don't stroll farther south on the Grand Concourse from the Paradise—the neighborhood swiftly declines. Instead, turn ❸ west on East 188th Street to peek at the **Creston Avenue Baptist Church** (114 E. 188th St.), built in 1905 and looking like it belongs not among the commercial chaos of Fordham Road, but in Merry Old England.

The Bx 12 bus will take you east along Fordham Road to Arthur Avenue; if you prefer the hike, you'll pass myriad coffee shops and discount stores, the Metro North train's Fordham stop, 1 Fordham Plaza (a modern green-and-white birthday-cake-like construction), and the looming Theodore Roosevelt High School.

Belmont, the neighborhood surrounding the intersection of Arthur Avenue and East 187th Street, has come to be called "The Bronx's Little Italy"—although actually it's a bigger Little Italy than the one in Manhattan. It really lights up after the sun sets, but it's also a daytime place, where some 14,500 families socialize, shop, work, and eat fabulously. Along Arthur Ave- ❹ nue you'll pass **Ciccarone Playground,** sporting a huge painted Italian flag. Indeed, as you study the surrounding two-story frame homes and tenements, the neighborhood begins to seem tinted exclusively in shades of white, red, and green: Italy's colors. A left turn onto East 187th Street takes you into an Italian commercial panoply; on one stellar block between Hughes and Belmont avenues you'll find **Egidio's Pastry Shop** (622 E. 187th St.), **Danny's Pork Store** (626 E. 187th St.), **Catholic Goods** (630 E. 187th St.), which sells Italian greeting cards, **Borgatti's Ravioli & Egg Noodles** (632 E. 187th St.), and the **Roma Luncheonette** (636 E. 187th St.). Across the street, resi- ❺ dents' spiritual lives are tended to at **Our Lady of Mt. Carmel Roman Catholic Church** (627 E. 187th St.). The church, built in

Bronx Zoo, **9**

Ciccarone
Playground, **4**

Creston Avenue
Baptist Church, **3**

Edgar Allan Poe
Cottage, **1**

Enrico Fermi Cultural
Center, **6**

Fordham University, **7**

Loew's Paradise
Theatre, **2**

New York Botanical
Garden, **8**

Our Lady of Mount
Carmel Roman
Catholic Church, **5**

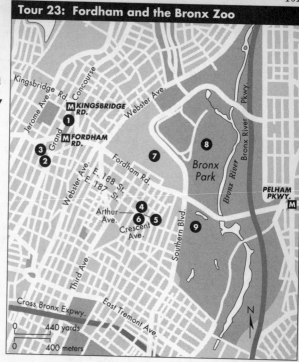

Tour 23: Fordham and the Bronx Zoo

1907, is an imposing brick structure with columned arches and four jutting flagpoles; inside, amid the marble columns and the intricate stained-glass windows, there is an indescribable smell of old religion, as well as many more saints. Drop a quarter into a slot to light a votive candle, or sit and contemplate this symbol of stability in an immigrant world.

6 A block south is the **Enrico Fermi Cultural Center/Belmont Branch New York Public Library** (610 E. 186th St.), where the Heritage Collection contains several volumes outlining the contributions of Italians and Italian-Americans. Nearby the **Arthur Avenue Retail Market** (2344 Arthur Ave.), a skylit shopping mart, offers 70 stalls, where Italian sausages and cheeses hang from on high.

Time Out **Dominick's** (2335 Arthur Ave., tel. 212/733–2807) enjoys a reputation as Belmont's best restaurant. Here there are no menus, no wine lists—just hearty Italian food, savored at congested common tables, and cooked by members of a family that's been at Dominick's for 30 years. Finish off your meal with an espresso laced with sambucco.

7 Return to Fordham Road to explore the 85-acre campus of **Fordham University**, built around the site of the old Rose Hill Manor House (1838). Begun in 1841 as a Jesuit college, Fordham now has an undergraduate enrollment of 7,500, and an auxiliary campus near Lincoln Center.

Enter the grounds via Bathgate Avenue and you'll find yourself in an enclave of Collegiate Gothic architecture, shady trees, and green turf. Maps are posted around the campus or are available in the admissions office at Dealy Hall; use them to locate such highlights as the **Old Rose Hill Manor Dig;** the **University Church,** with its stained glass donated by King Louis Philippe of France (1773–1850); the pleasant **Edward's Parade;** and **Keating Hall,** sitting like a Gothic fortress in the center of things. After meandering through Fordham, make your way to the university's main entrance, fronting on Bronx (or, properly, New York Zoological) Park.

❽ Of all reasons to make a trip to The Bronx, **The New York Botanical Garden** is perhaps the best. The Fordham entrance leads into this serene but extraordinarily varied treasury, the dream of a husband-and-wife botanical team, Dr. Nathaniel Lord and Elizabeth Britton. After visiting England's Kew Gardens in 1889, they returned full of fervor to create a similar haven in New York. In 1991, the New York Botanical Garden celebrated its centennial.

The garden stretches for 250 acres around the dramatic gorge of the Bronx River. It holds the historic **Lorillard Snuff Mill,** built by two French Huguenot snuff manufacturers in 1840 to power the grinding of tobacco for snuff. Nearby, the Lorillards grew roses to supply fragrance for their blend. The snuff mill now houses a café, open daily 10–5. A walk along the Bronx River from the mill leads the visitor to the botanical garden's 40-acre **Forest,** the only uncut woodland in New York City. Outdoor plant collections include the **Erpf Compass Garden,** where cobblestones denoting the points of a compass are surrounded by a riotous display of flowers. Inside the luminous **Enid A. Haupt Conservatory** are displays of ferns, tropical flora, and Old and New World deserts. At the **Museum Building,** there's a gardening shop, a library, and a world-renowned herbarium holding 5.5 million dried plant specimens. *Bronx Park, tel. 212/ 220–8700. Garden admission is by voluntary contribution. Open Nov.–Mar., Tues.–Sun. and Mon. holidays 10–6; Apr.– Oct., Tues.–Sun. and Mon. holidays 10–7. Apr.–Oct. Conservatory admission free Sat. 10–12; other times $3.50 adults, $1.25 senior citizens and students. Children under 6 free. Open Nov.–Mar., Tues.–Fri. and Mon. holidays 10–4, Sat.–Sun. 10–5; Apr.–Oct., Tues.–Fri. and Mon. holidays 10–5, Sat.– Sun. 10–6. Last admission one hour before closing. Parking: $4.*

❾ Also in Bronx Park is the **Bronx Zoo,** the nation's largest urban zoo. It deserves nearly an entire day's visit on its own; if you want to return on another day, you can take the BxM11 bus that runs up Madison Avenue ($3.50).

At the Bronx Zoo you'll see two different historical methods of wild-animal keeping. The turn-of-the-century zoological garden houses monkeys, sea lions, and elephants (among many others) in fancy Beaux Arts–style edifices at **Astor Court.** It's being gradually replaced by the animal-in-habitat approach used in the **World of Birds,** with its capacious walk-through indoor natural habitats; in **Jungleworld,** an indoor tropical rain forest complete with five waterfalls, millipedes, flowering orchids, and pythons; and in the new **Baboon Reserve.** The **Children's Zoo** (open Apr.–Oct.) features many hands-on learning activities, as well as a large petting zoo. At the **Zoo Center,** visitors will find a rare Sumatran rhino. The zoo as a whole has more than 4,000 animals representing 667 species. *Bronx Park,* *tel. 212/367–1010. Admission: Fri.–Mon. $4.75 adults, $2 children under 12 (Nov.–Mar. $2.50 adults, $1 children), free senior citizens and children under 2; Tues.–Thurs., voluntary contribution; open weekdays 10–5, weekends and holidays 10–5:30.*

Staten Island

Tour 24: Snug Harbor and Richmondtown

Numbers in the margin correspond with points of interest on the Staten Island map.

Even though Staten Island is officially a borough of New York City, many Staten Islanders (as do the rest of the bridge and tunnel crowd) refer to Manhattan as "The City." Perhaps that's because farms and vast woodlands have distinguished it from the more crowded and developed Manhattan since 1661, when Staten Island was permanently settled as a farming community by the Dutch (after several fatal battles with the Native American tribes who already inhabited the area). When oystering became a thriving industry in the early 1800s, farmers brought free blacks up from Maryland to help plant new oyster beds. The black community on the south shore became known as "Sandy Ground"; descendants of the first black oystermen still live there. Factories came later, as did shipbuilding.

Today Staten Island still feels more residential than the other boroughs. Getting around can be somewhat difficult for visitors because the various attractions are so spread out, but bus service is convenient.

The greatest way to introduce yourself to Staten Island is by taking the 20-minute ride across New York Harbor on the **1** **Staten Island Ferry,** which leaves regularly from the southern tip of Manhattan (*see* Tour 17 in Chapter 3). On the boats with outer decks, passengers can get a better look at the spectacular views of lower Manhattan's skyscrapers and the splendidly restored Ellis Island and Statue of Liberty.

2 From the ferry terminal, a seven-minute ride on the S40 bus or on a special trolley will take you to the **Snug Harbor Cultural Center,** which on a warm summer afternoon might be hosting a New York Philharmonic concert, an art show, or an old-fashioned flea market. Once part of a sprawling farm, then a home for "aged and decrepit sailors," the center is based around a row of five columned Greek Revival temples, built between 1831 and 1880, facing onto the Kill Van Kull, a wide stream that flows into Upper New York Bay. The former chapel is now the 210-seat **Veterans Memorial Hall,** site of many indoor concerts and gatherings. Among several newer institutions on the 80-acre grounds is the **Newhouse Center for Contemporary Art,** which features changing exhibitions (open Wed.–Sun. noon–5; voluntary contribution). A variety of cultural events are held throughout the year in this tranquil setting. *1000 Richmond Terr., tel. 718/448–2500. Admission free. Open 8 AM–dusk. Guided tours weekends 2 PM; suggested donation $2.*

The **Staten Island Botanical Gardens,** also on the Snug Harbor grounds, feature a perennial garden, a greenhouse, 10 acres of natural marsh habitat, a fragrance garden for the blind, and a

Tour 24: Staten Island

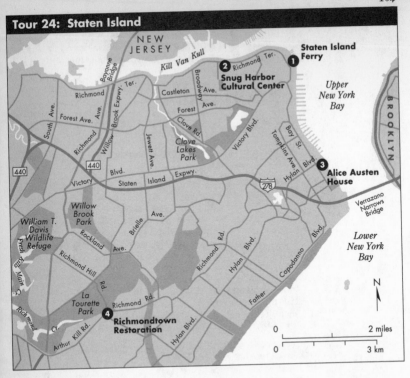

bonsai collection. *1000 Richmond Terr., tel. 718/273–8200. Admission free. Open 8 AM–dusk.*

The **Staten Island Children's Museum,** which moved to the complex back in 1986, offers four revolving hands-on exhibitions to introduce children to such diverse topics as news and media, storytelling, and insects. *1000 Richmond Terr., tel. 718/273–2060. Admission: $2, children under 3 free. Open Wed.– Fri. 1–5, weekends 11–5.*

❸ Return to the ferry terminal and catch the S51–Bay Street bus for the 2-mile ride to Hylan Boulevard and the **Alice Austen House.** Photographer Alice Austen (1866–1952) defied tradition when, as a girl of 10, she received her first camera as a gift from an uncle and promptly began taking pictures of everything and everyone around her. Austen went on to make photography her lifetime avocation, recording on film a vivid "social history" of Staten Island in the early part of the century. The cozy, ivy-covered Dutch-style cottage she lived in for almost all her life has been restored, and many of her photographs are on exhibit. *2 Hylan Blvd., tel. 718/816–4506. Suggested donation: $2 adults. Open Thurs.–Sun. noon–5.*

❹ Take the S74–Richmond Road bus from the ferry terminal to the **Richmondtown Restoration,** a unique museum village on the site of Staten Island's first permanent settlement founded in 1685. The 26 historic buildings on this 96-acre complex have been restored inside and out; some were here originally, while others were relocated from other spots on the island. Many of the buildings, such as the Greek Revival courthouse that serves as the **Visitors Center,** date from the 19th century; other architectural styles on site range from Dutch Colonial to Victorian Gothic Revival. The **Voorlezer's House,** built in 1695, is the oldest elementary schoolhouse in the United States; it looks like the mold from which all little red schoolhouses were cast.

During the warmer months, costumed interpreters demonstrate early American crafts and trades such as printing, tinsmithing, and baking. The **Staten Island Historical Society Museum,** built in 1848 as the second county clerk's and surrogate's office, now has in its archives American china, furniture, toys, and tools, plus a collection of Staten Island photographs, including some 7,000 works by Alice Austen.

During a summer visit, you might want to make reservations for the 19th-century dinner, cooked outdoors and served with utensils of the period. The Autumn Celebration shows off craftspeople demonstrating their skills; the annual Encampment in May is a re-creation of a Civil War battle. Richmondtown regularly hosts other fairs, flea markets, and tours of the historic buildings. *Tel. 718/351–1611. Admission: $4 adults, $2.50 senior citizens and children 6–18. Open Wed.–Fri., Sun. 1–5.*

What to See and Do with Children

Museums
For children who really love hands-on involvement, the place to go is the **Brooklyn Children's Museum.** Its exhibits cover everything from the environment to nature, science, and more; and its attractions include tunnels, water, bubbles, animals, steam, and neon lights. *145 Brooklyn Ave., tel. 718/735–4432. Suggested donation: $2. Open June–Aug., Wed–Sun. noon–5; Sept.–May, Wed.–Fri., 2–5, weekends and holidays noon–5.*

Hands-on exhibits are a feature of the **Staten Island Children's Museum** (*see* Tour 24, above), part of the Snug Harbor Cultural Center. Your children may also be interested in the **Staten Island Historical Society** in the **Richmondtown Restoration** (*see* Tour 24, above), which has a Museum of Childhood with displays of antique dolls, toys, and children's furnishings.

For science, the **New York Hall of Science,** in Flushing Meadows Corona Park, Queens (*see* Tour 22, above), has touchable exhibits on—what else?—science and technology.

Queens is also the place for the movie mavens in your family. The **American Museum of the Moving Image** (*see* Tour 21), the only museum in the United States devoted to film and television, has a collection of 70,000 artifacts, a state-of-the-art theater, and an experimental video screening room.

Parks and Zoos
New York is lucky enough to have the largest zoo of any city in the United States: the **Bronx Zoo** (*see* Tour 23, above). This is not a place of cramped cages and pacing beasts: Most of the animals live in replicas of their natural habitats. In the Children's Zoo area (open Apr.–Oct.), kids can wander along trails through woods and marshes and pet the animals.

Adjacent to the Bronx Zoo, the **New York Botanical Garden** (*see* Tour 23, above) is one of the world's largest botanic gardens. Its

Enid A. Haupt Conservatory is a crystal palace of ever-changing plant exhibits; there are also 12 outdoor display gardens, walking trails, and some 40 acres of New York City's original forest.

The **Staten Island Zoo** (Barrett Park, 614 Broadway, Staten Island, tel. 718/442–3100) is small but of very high quality, featuring one of the world's finest collections of reptiles, as well as a separate **Children's Zoo.**

Brooklyn's **Prospect Park Zoo** (*see* Tour 20, above) and the **Queens Zoo** (*see* Tour 22, above) are both being refurbished; the former reopens in 1992, and the latter should be done by press time. Children may also enjoy the **Queens County Farm Museum** (73–50 Little Neck Pkwy., Floral Park, Queens, tel. 718/347–3276), a restored, 200-year-old working farm. Although it's open only on weekends, the museum does offer interesting programs.

Stroll through the **Brooklyn Botanic Garden** (*see* Tour 20, above), whose 52 lush acres feature a hill-and-pond Japanese garden; gardens devoted to fragrant plants, roses, and herbs; a conservatory with tropical, desert, and temperate pavilions; and a bonsai museum.

Nearly 300 different varieties of fish are on display in Brooklyn at the **New York Aquarium** (Surf Ave. at W. 8th St., Coney Island, tel. 718/265–FISH). Children will marvel at the performance by dolphins, sea lions, and electric eels.

Off the Beaten Track

Brooklyn **Coney Island.** It's the home of the hot dog, "the king of roller coasters" (the Cyclone), the Wonder Wheel, suntan lotion, crowds, fried clams, girls and boys necking under the boardwalk, and old men staring vacantly out to sea. While it may have declined from its glory days early in this century—when visitors lunched at an ocean-side hotel built in the shape of an elephant, glided across the nation's biggest dance floor at Dreamland, or toured a replica of old Baghdad called Luna Park—Coney Island still has a boardwalk, a 2.7-mile-long beach, and a huge amusement park. The **New York Aquarium** (tel. 718/265–FISH) keeps watery beasts—sharks, black-footed penguins, octopuses, piranhas, and Beluga whales, who show off their swimming skills at feeding time—on view nearby. Two blocks away is **Brighton Beach Avenue,** the main street of a community of some 30,000 Soviet émigrés, where inexpensive restaurants serving up Soviet Georgian cuisine abound. D, Q, N, B, and F subways serve the Coney Island–Brighton Beach area.

Green-Wood Cemetery (25th St. and 5th Ave.). Built in the 1840s, the cemetery features a stately Gothic Revival gatehouse, designed by Richard Upjohn, that still moves visitors to a sublime pitch of melancholy. The 478 acres contain 5 lakes, 22 miles of lanes, and 209 paths named for bushes, flowers, and trees. Among the illustrious—or infamous—citizens interred there are Samuel F.B. Morse, Boss Tweed, and Peter Cooper. It's open daily 8–4; call the superintendent (tel. 718/768–7300) for permission to tour.

Queens **The Isamu Noguchi Garden Museum** (32–37 Vernon Blvd., tel. 718/204–7088). East of Astoria, near riverside Rainey Park, the Japanese sculptor Isamu Noguchi took studio space in a photo-engraver's factory some 30 years ago. Part of it now holds 12 galleries that offer Noguchi devotees a concentration of the sculptor's evocative work in stone, garden, and stage-set design, along with videos documenting his long career. A small sculpture garden adjoins the museum. Across Vernon Boulevard lies the **Socrates Sculpture Park** (Vernon Blvd. at Broadway, tel. 718/956–1819), 4.2 acres of large, abstract artworks that first appear almost as an urban hallucination. *Saturday bus service to Noguchi Museum leaves every hour on the half hour, 11:30–3:30, from the Asia Society, Park Ave. and 70th St. in Manhattan. Fare: $5; Suggested contribution: $2. Museum open Apr.–Nov. Wed. and Sat. 11–6.*

Bronx **Riverdale.** This is perhaps the Bronx's most attractive neighborhood; wide-open territory for outer-borough explorers, it's best visited by car, taking the Kappock Street exit from the Henry Hudson Parkway. Manhattan millionaires built summer homes here, with stirring views of the New Jersey Palisades across the Hudson River, in the early part of this century. A drive along Palisade Avenue, picturesque Sycamore Avenue above West 252nd Street, and Independence Avenue between West 248th and 254th streets will take you past some of Riverdale's handsomest mansions. Alas, only **Wave Hill** (249th St. and Independence Ave., tel. 212/549–3200) is open to the public, but a visit to this 28-acre estate will conjure up the image of Riverdale's wealthy past. Built in 1844, then lavishly added onto by J. P. Morgan's partner George Perkins, the estate offers splendid views of the Hudson, a greenhouse, a sweeping lawn with giant elm and maple trees, and old-fashioned herb and flower gardens. *Admission: weekends, $2 adults, $1 senior citizens and students; children under 6 free. Free weekdays. Open Sept.–Apr., daily 10–4:30, May–Aug., Sun.–Tues. and Thurs.–Fri., 10–5:30, Sat. and Wed. 10–7.*

City Island. At the extreme west end of the Bronx is a bona fide island measuring 230 acres wide—a little bit of Cape Cod come to the metropolis. Back in 1761, a group of the area's residents planned a port to rival New York's, but when that scheme hit the shoals, they returned to perennial maritime pursuits such as fishing and boat building. City Island-produced yachts have included a number of America's Cup contenders. Connected to Pelham Bay Park by bridge, City Island offers visitors a maritime atmosphere and good seafood restaurants with names like Sammy's Fish Box and Johnny's Reef. City Island also has the **North Wind Undersea Museum** (610 City Island Ave., tel. 212/885–0701).

5 Sightseeing Checklists

The following checklists organize New York City's attractions by category, so you can supplement sights from the walking tours with related places of interest throughout the five boroughs. They may also help you choose walking tours by showing you which routes include sites that may be related to your own special interests. Attractions that have already been covered in Chapters 3 or 4 include nothing more than a reference to the walking tour in which they appear. Attractions that appear here only are followed by a brief description and useful information.

Museums and Galleries

Abigail Adams Smith Museum. Once the converted carriage house of the home President John Adams built for his daughter Abigail, this 18th-century treasure is now owned by the Colonial Dames of America. Nine rooms display furniture and articles of the Federal period, and an adjoining garden is designed in 18th-century style. *421 E. 61st St., tel. 212/838–6878. Admission: $2 adults, $1 senior citizens, students, and children under 12. Open weekdays noon–4, Sun. 1–5. In June and July, closed Sun., open Tues. evenings until 8. Closed Aug.*

Afro Arts Cultural Centre. Artifacts from East, West, North, and Central Africa are on exhibit. *2191 Adam Clayton Powell, Jr., Blvd. (7th Ave.), tel. 212/996–3333. Suggested contribution: $3.75 adults, $2.75 children. Open daily 9–5.*

American Craft Museum. *See* Tour 1 in Chapter 3.

American Museum of the Moving Image. *See* Tour 21 in Chapter 4.

American Museum of Natural History. *See* Tour 8 in Chapter 3.

American Numismatic Society. The society, founded in 1858, displays its vast collection of coins and medals, including many that date back to ancient civilizations, in one of several museums in the Audubon Terrace complex. *Broadway at 155th St., tel. 212/234–3130. Admission free. Open Tues.–Sat. 9:30–4:30, Sun. 1–4.*

Americas Society. *See* Tour 6 in Chapter 3.

Asia Society Galleries. *See* Tour 6 in Chapter 3.

The AT&T InfoQuest Center. *See* Tour 2 in Chapter 3.

Black Fashion Museum. *See* Tour 10 in Chapter 3.

Brooklyn Children's Museum. *See* What to See and Do with Children in Chapter 4.

Brooklyn Historical Society. *See* Tour 19 in Chapter 4.

Brooklyn Museum. *See* Tour 20 in Chapter 4.

Bronx Museum of the Arts. Founded in 1971, this museum displays changing exhibitions of contemporary and modern art. Caution is very much advised in visiting this neighborhood. *1040 Grand Concourse, Bronx, tel. 212/681–6000. Suggested donation: $2 adults, $1 children. Open Mon.–Thurs., and Sat. 10–4:30, Sun. 11–4:30.*

Children's Museum of Manhattan. *See* What to See and Do with Children in Chapter 3.

China House Gallery (China Institute). *See* Tour 6 in Chapter 3.

City Gallery. Above the New York Convention and Visitors Bureau, the gallery shows changing exhibitions by mostly local artists in all media. *2 Columbus Circle, tel. 212/974–1150. Admission free. Open weekdays 10–5:30.*

City Island Historical Nautical Museum. Tucked away on the tiny island at the end of the Bronx, this museum celebrates the area's nautical heritage. *190 Fordham St., City Island, Bronx.*

Admission: $2 adults, $1 children and senior citizens. Open Sun. 2–5.

Clocktower Gallery (Institute for Contemporary Art). *See* Tour 18 in Chapter 3.

The Cloisters. Perched atop a wooded hilltop near Manhattan's northernmost tip, the Cloisters houses the Metropolitan Museum of Art's medieval collection in the style of a medieval monastery. Colonnaded walks connect authentic French and Spanish monastic cloisters, a French Romanesque chapel, a 12th-century chapter house, and a Romanesque apse. An entire room is devoted to a superb set of 15th- and 16th-century tapestries depicting a unicorn hunt. The view of the Hudson River and the New Jersey Palisades (an undeveloped Rockefeller family preserve) enhances the experience. The No. 4 "Cloisters-Fort Tryon Park" bus provides a lengthy but scenic ride; catch it along Madison Avenue below 110th Street, or Broadway above; or take the A subway to 190th Street. *Fort Tryon Park, tel. 212/923–3700. Suggested donation: $6 adults, $3 senior citizens and students, children 12 and under free. Open Tues.– Sun. 9:30–5:15. Closes at 4:45 Nov.–Mar.*

Cooper-Hewitt Museum (Smithsonian Institution's National Museum of Design). *See* Tour 5 in Chapter 3.

Dezerland's Dream Car Collection. The world's largest collection of American classic convertibles from the 1950s is displayed, alongside nostalgic exhibits. Also here are an indoor drive-in movie theater featuring seating in vintage convertibles, and a gallery that sells one-of-a-kind furniture created from auto parts. *270 11th Ave., tel. 212/564–4590. Admission: $15. Open Tues.–Sun. 10 PM–4 AM, Fri. 6 PM–4 AM.*

Federal Hall National Memorial. *See* Tour 17 in Chapter 3.

Forbes Magazine Galleries. On permanent exhibit, the late publisher Malcolm Forbes's collection includes 500 toy boats, and 12,000 toy soldiers, plus rotating exhibitions of paintings, presidential papers, and Fabergé Imperial Easter eggs. *62 5th Ave., tel. 212/206–5548. Admission free. Open Tues.–Wed., Fri.–Sat. 10–4. Call 212/206–5549 for group tour reservations.*

Fraunces Tavern Museum. *See* Tour 17 in Chapter 3.

Frick Collection. *See* Tour 5 in Chapter 3.

Garibaldi Meucci Museum. Housed in an altered Federal farmhouse, this museum offers letters and photographs describing the life of fiery Italian patriot Guiseppe Garibaldi; it also documents Antonio Meucci's indisputable claim to having invented the telephone before Alexander Graham Bell did. *420 Tompkins Ave., Staten Island, tel. 718/442–1608. Admission free. Open Tues.–Fri. 9–5, weekends 1–5.*

Grolier Club of New York. *See* Tour 6 in Chapter 3.

Guggenheim Museum. *See* Tour 5 in Chapter 3.

Guinness World of Records Exhibition *See* Tour 4 in Chapter 3.

Harbor Defense Museum of New York City. Located at the Brooklyn end of the Verrazano-Narrows Bridge, this museum features small arms, uniforms, artillery equipment dating to the 18th century, and an array of military miniatures. *Fort Hamilton, Brooklyn, tel. 718/630–4349. Admission free. Open Mon., Thurs., and Fri. 1–4, Sat. 10–5, Sun. 1–5.*

Hayden Planetarium. *See* Tour 8 in Chapter 3.

Hispanic Society of America. An extensive collection of ancient and modern Hispanic paintings, sculpture, and decorative arts is housed in a richly appointed building. *Broadway at 155th St., tel. 212/926–2234. Admission free. Open Tues.–Sat. 10–4:30, Sun. 1–4. Closed holidays.*

IBM Gallery of Science and Art. *See* Tour 2 in Chapter 3.

ICP Mid-Town. *See* Tour 3 in Chapter 3.

International Center of Photography. *See* Tour 5 in Chapter 3.

***Intrepid* Sea-Air-Space Museum.** *See* What to See and Do with Children in Chapter 2.

Isamu Noguchi Garden Museum. *See* Off the Beaten Track in Chapter 4.

Jamaica Arts Center. An Italian Renaissance Revival building, built in 1898, showcases a variety of multiethnic arts ranging from the Yueh Lung Shadow Theatre to Olu Dara and the Natchezsippi Band. *161–04 Jamaica Ave., Queens, tel. 718/658–7400. Admission free. Open Tues.–Sat. 10–5.*

Japan Society Gallery. This wonderfully serene setting holds exhibitions from well-known Japanese and American museums, as well as private collections. Also offered are movies, lectures, classes, concerts, and dramatic performances. *333 E. 47th St., tel. 212/832–1155. Suggested donation: $2.50. Open Tues.–Sun. 11–5, but only when shows are installed.*

Jewish Museum. *See* Tours 5 and 8 in Chapter 3.

Library and Museum of the Performing Arts (New York Public Library at Lincoln Center). *See* Tour 8 in Chapter 3.

Lower East Side Tenement Museum. America's first urban "living-history" museum preserves and interprets the life of immigrants and migrants in New York's Lower East Side. Gallery exhibits, walking tours, and dramatic performances are offered. *97 Orchard St., tel. 212/431–0233. Tours: $12 adults, $6 students. Open Tues.–Fri. 11–4.*

Marchais Center of Tibetan Art. One of the largest private, non-profit collections of Tibetan sculpture, scrolls, and paintings outside of Tibet is displayed in a museum resembling a Tibetan temple. *338 Lighthouse Ave., Staten Island, tel. 718/987–3478. Admission: $2.50 adults, $2 senior citizens, $1 children. Open April–Nov., Wed.–Sun. 1–5. By appointment Wed.–Fri. the remainder of the year.*

Metropolitan Museum of Art. *See* Tour 5 in Chapter 3.

Museo del Barrio. *See* Tour 5 in Chapter 3.

Museum of American Folk Art. *See* Tour 8 in Chapter 3.

Museum of Television and Radio. *See* Tour 1 in Chapter 3.

Museum of the City of New York. *See* Tour 5 in Chapter 3.

Museum of Holography. *See* Tour 14 in Chapter 3.

Museum of Modern Art. *See* Tour 1 in Chapter 3.

National Academy of Design. *See* Tour 5 in Chapter 3.

National Museum of the American Indian. What began as the private collection of George G. Heye has grown into the largest grouping of Native American materials in the world. Various exhibits are devoted to North, Central, and South American Indians. Soon this collection will be moved, part to the Smithsonian Institution in Washington, DC, part downtown to the U.S. Customs House (*see* Tour 17 in Chapter 3). *Broadway at 155th St., tel. 212/283–2497. Admission: $3 adults, $2 students and senior citizens. Open Tues.–Sat. 10–5, Sun. 1–5.*

New Museum of Contemporary Art. *See* Tour 14 in Chapter 3.

New York City Fire Museum. Hand-pulled and horse-drawn apparatus, engines, sliding poles, uniforms, and fireboat equipment are featured in this comprehensive collection of authentic fire-fighting tools from the 18th, 19th, and 20th centuries. *278 Spring St., tel. 212/691–1303. Suggested donation: $3 adults, 50¢ children. Open Tues.–Sat. 10–4. Closed Sun., Mon., and holidays.*

New York City Transit Museum. A converted 1930s subway station displays 18 restored classic subway cars and has an operating signal tower. *Boerum Pl. at Schermerhorn St., Brooklyn Heights, tel. 718/330–3060. Admission: $2 adults, $1.50 senior citizens, $1 children. Open Tues.–Fri. 10–4, Sat. 11–4.*

New-York Historical Society. *See* Tour 8 in Chapter 3.

New York Hall of Science. *See* Tour 22 in Chapter 4.

Nicholas Roerich Museum. Housed in an Upper West Side town house (built in 1898), this small, eccentric museum displays the work of the Russian artist who, among many other things, designed sets for Diaghilev ballets. Vast paintings of the Himalayas are a focal point of the collection. *319 W. 107th St., tel. 212/864–7752. Admission free. Open Tues.–Sun. 2–5.*

North Wind Undersea Museum. Displays are devoted to marine mammal rescue and deep-sea diving. *610 City Island Ave., Bronx, tel. 212/885–0701. Admission: $3 adults, $2 children. Open weekdays 10–5, weekends noon–5.*

Pierpont Morgan Library. *See* Tour 4 in Chapter 3.

Police Academy Museum. The second floor of the city's police academy is full of law-enforcement memorabilia—uniforms, firearms, batons, badges, even counterfeit money—dating back to the time of the Dutch. *235 E. 20th St., tel. 212/477–9753. Admission free. Open weekdays 9–3, large groups by appointment.*

P.S. 1 Museum (Institute for Contemporary Art). More than a dozen galleries in a former public school in Long Island City, Queens, often feature experimental and innovative works by emerging artists. *46–01 21st St., tel. 718/784–2084. Admission $2. Open Wed.–Sun. noon–6.*

Queens County Farm Museum. *See* What to See and Do with Children in Chapter 4.

Queens Museum. *See* Tour 22 in Chapter 4.

Schomburg Center for Research in Black Culture (New York Public Library). *See* Tour 10 in Chapter 3.

Snug Harbor Cultural Center. *See* Tour 24 in Chapter 4.

Society of Illustrators Museum of American Illustration. A 1,000-piece collection features contemporary and historical works. Solo, group, and themed shows are exhibited. *128 E. 63rd St., tel. 212/838–2560. Admission free. Open weekdays 10–5, Tues. 10–8.*

South Street Seaport Museum. *See* Tour 18 in Chapter 3.

Staten Island Children's Museum. *See* Tour 24 in Chapter 4.

Staten Island Historical Society Museum. *See* Tour 24 in Chapter 4.

Studio Museum in Harlem. *See* Tour 10 in Chapter 3.

Ukrainian Museum. This small East Village institution celebrates the cultural heritage of the Ukraine, displaying ceramics, jewelry, hundreds of brilliantly colored Easter eggs, and an extensive collection of Ukrainian costumes and textiles. *203 2nd Ave. between 12th and 13th Sts., tel. 212/228–0110. Admission: $1 adults, 50¢ students and senior citizens, children under 6 free. Open Wed.–Sun. 1–5.*

Urban Center. Exhibits on architecture, urban design, and historic preservation are housed in the north wing of the Villard Houses, at the foot of the Helmsley Palace Hotel. *457 Madison Ave. between 50th and 51st Sts., tel. 212/935–3960. Admission free. Open Mon.–Wed., Fri. and Sat. 11–5.*

Whitney Museum of American Art. *See* Tour 5 in Chapter 3.

Whitney Museum of American Art at Equitable Center. In this pair of galleries in the grand lobby of the Equitable Building (itself a showcase for some fine large artworks), changing exhibitions highlight 20th-century art from the Whitney's main collection. *787 7th Ave. between 51st and 52nd Sts., tel. 212/554–1113. Admission free. Open Mon.–Wed. and Fri. 11–6, Thurs. 11–7:30, Sat. noon–5.*

Whitney Museum Downtown at Federal Reserve Plaza. *See* Tour 17 in Chapter 3.

Whitney Museum at Philip Morris. *See* Tour 3 in Chapter 3.

Architectural Landmarks

American Telephone & Telegraph Building (1983, Philip Johnson and John Burgee). *See* Tour 2 in Chapter 3.

Bayard Building (1898, Louis Sullivan). *See* Tour 13 in Chapter 3.

Bowery Savings (1923, York & Sawyer). *See* Tour 3 in Chapter 3.

Carnegie Hall (1891, William B. Tuthill). Outside it's a stout, square brown building with a few Moorish-style arches added, almost as an afterthought, to the facade. Inside, however, is a simply decorated, 2,804-seat auditorium that is considered one of the finest in the world, although some critics say the acoustics haven't been the same since a recent renovation. Tours are available on Tuesdays and Thursdays *at 11:30, 2, and 3. W. 57th St. at 7th Ave., tel. 212/247–7800.*

Chrysler Building (1929, William Van Alen). *See* Tour 3 in Chapter 3.

Citicorp Center (1977, H. Stubbins & E. Roth). *See* Tour 2 in Chapter 3.

City Hall (1812, Mangin, McComb). *See* Tour 18 in Chapter 3.

Dakota Apartments (1884, Henry J. Hardenbergh). *See* Tour 8 in Chapter 3.

Empire State Building (1931, Shreve, Lamb, Harmon). *See* Tour 4 in Chapter 3.

Flatiron Building (1902, Daniel H. Burnham). *See* Tour 4 in Chapter 3.

Ford Foundation Building (1967, Roche & Dinkeloo). *See* Tour 3 in Chapter 3.

GE Building, formerly the **RCA Building** (1933, Raymond Hood). *See* Tour 1 in Chapter 3.

Grand Central Terminal (1913, Warren & Wetmore, Reed & Stem). *See* Tour 3 in Chapter 3.

Guggenheim Museum (1959, Frank Lloyd Wright). *See* Tour 5 in Chapter 3.

Haughwout Building (1856, John P. Gaynor). *See* Tour 14 in Chapter 3.

Jacob K. Javits Convention Center (1986, I. M. Pei). The largest center of its kind in the Western Hemisphere, the center contains 1.8 million gross square feet set on a 22-acre-by-5-block site. The glassed-in entry lets in lots of sky, earning it the nickname "the Crystal Palace." *11th Ave. at 35th St.*

Lever House (1952, Skidmore, Owings & Merrill). *See* Tour 2 in Chapter 3.

Low Memorial Library (1897, McKim, Mead & White). *See* Tour 9 in Chapter 3.

New York Public Library (1911, Carrere & Hastings). *See* Tour 3 in Chapter 3.

Pan Am Building (1963, Emery Roth & Sons, Pietro Belluschi, and Walter Gropius). The waves of protest that greeted this building's construction over the north end of Grand Central Terminal were largely responsible for Grand Central's receiving protected landmark status in 1965. This 59-story monolith, with its faceted walls of precast concrete, towers over the foot of Park Avenue. *200 Park Ave. at 45th St.*

Plaza Hotel (1907, Henry J. Hardenbergh). *See* Tour 2 in Chapter 3.

Seagram Building (1958, Mies van der Rohe with Philip Johnson). *See* Tour 2 in Chapter 3.

United Nations (1953, Wallace K. Harrison and international committee). *See* Tour 3 in Chapter 3.

U.S. Customs House (1907, Cass Gilbert). *See* Tour 17 in Chapter 3.

Villard Houses (1886, McKim, Mead & White). Now part of the Helmsley Palace hotel, these three brownstone mansions, conceived by newspaper publisher Henry Villard, form an early Italian Renaissance-style courtyard set off by elaborate ironwork. Many of the original interior spaces remain in prime condition. *Madison Ave. at 50th St.*

Woolworth Building (1913, Cass Gilbert). *See* Tour 17 in Chapter 3.

World Financial Center (1989, Cesar Pelli). *See* Tour 17 in Chapter 3.

World Trade Center (1977, Yamasaki & Roth). *See* Tour 17 in Chapter 3.

Historical Sites

Bartow-Pell Mansion. This Greek Revival restoration—with sunken gardens, period furnishings, paintings, and a 200-volume library was built in 1842. *Shore Rd. N., Pelham Bay Park, Bronx, tel. 212/885–1461. Admission: $2; children under 12 free. Open Wed., weekends, noon–4.*

Castle Clinton. *See* Tour 17 in Chapter 3.

Edgar Allan Poe Cottage. *See* Tour 23 in Chapter 4.

Ellis Island. *See* Tour 17 in Chapter 3.

Fraunces Tavern. *See* Tour 17 in Chapter 3.

Gracie Mansion. *See* Tour 6 in Chapter 3.

Morris-Jumel Mansion. In 1776 George Washington spent a month at this hilltop house, built in 1765. His office can still be seen. *1765 Jumel Terr., tel. 212/923–8008. Admission: $3 adults, $2 senior citizens and students; children under 12 free. Open Tues.–Sun. 10–4.*

New York Stock Exchange. *See* Tour 17 in Chapter 3.

Old Merchant's House. Built in 1830, this Federal-style house was home to the Tredwell family from 1835 to 1933, when the last of the elderly Tredwell sisters died. The original furnishings and architectural features remain intact, offering a rare glimpse of family life in the mid-19th century. *29 E. 4th St., tel. 212/777–1089. Admission: $3 adults, $2 students and senior citizens. Open Sun. 1–4 and at other, varying times. Closed Aug.*

Radio City Music Hall. *See* Tour 1 in Chapter 3.

Richmondtown Restoration. *See* Tour 24 in Chapter 4.

South Street Seaport. *See* Tour 18 in Chapter 3.

Theodore Roosevelt Birthplace. *See* Tour 4 in Chapter 3.

Van Cortlandt House. Recently renovated, this 1748 house is full of furnishings and household goods that reflect both its Dutch and British owners. It's now run by the National Society of Colonial Dames. *Broadway at 246th St., Bronx, tel. 212/543–3344. Admission: $2 adults, $1 senior citizens and students; children under 14 free. Open Tues.–Fri. 11–3, Sun. 1–5.*

Wave Hill. George Walbridge Perkins, an early conservationist and partner of J. P. Morgan, bought this 28-acre estate in 1903, adding greenhouses, gardens, and a second mansion (an 1844 fieldstone manor house already occupied the site). In its time, the main house's residents have included Theodore Roosevelt, Mark Twain, and conductor Arturo Toscanini; at one time it was the official residence of the United Kingdom's ambassador to the United Nations. *249th St. and Independence Ave., Bronx, tel. 212/549-3200. Admission: weekends, $2 adults, $1 senior citizens and students; children under 6 free. Free weekdays. Open Sept.–Apr., daily 10–4:30; May–Aug., Sun.–Tues. and Thurs.–Fri., 10–5:30, Sat. and Wed. 10–7.*

Churches and Temples

Abyssinian Baptist Church (Baptist). *See* Tour 10 in Chapter 3.

Cathedral of St. John the Divine (Episcopal). *See* Tour 9 in Chapter 3.

Central Synagogue (Reform Jewish). Built in 1872, this Moorish-style temple is the oldest continually used synagogue building in the city. Note its onion-domed exterior and colorfully stenciled interior. *652 Lexington Ave., at 55th St.*

Church of Our Lady of Pompeii (Roman Catholic). *See* Tour 12 in Chapter 3.

Fifth Avenue Synagogue (Orthodox Jewish). *See* Tour 6 in Chapter 3.

Friends Meeting House, now the **Brotherhood Synagogue** (Conservative Jewish). *See* Tour 4 in Chapter 3.

Grace Church (Episcopal). This fine mid-19th-century example of an English Gothic Revival church, the site of many society weddings, is set in a small green yard in Greenwich Village. Topped by a finely ornamented octagonal marble spire, this design by James Renwick, Jr., has some excellent pre-Raphaelite stained-glass windows inside. *802 Broadway, at E. 10th St.*

John Street Methodist (United Methodist). *See* Tour 17 in Chapter 3.

Little Church Around the Corner (Church of the Transfiguration) (Episcopal). *See* Tour 4 in Chapter 3.

Marble Collegiate (Reformed). *See* Tour 4 in Chapter 3.

Riverside Church (Interdenominational). *See* Tour 9 in Chapter 3.

Spanish & Portuguese Synagogue, Shearith Israel (Orthodox Jewish). *See* Tour 8 in Chapter 3.

St. Bartholomew's (Episcopal). *See* Tour 2 in Chapter 3.

St. Luke's-in-the-Fields (Episcopal). *See* Tour 12 in Chapter 3.

St. Mark's-in-the-Bowery (Episcopal). *See* Tour 13 in Chapter 3.

St. Patrick's Cathedral (Roman Catholic). *See* Tour 2 in Chapter 3.

St. Paul's Chapel (Episcopal). *See* Tour 17 in Chapter 3.

St. Paul's Chapel at Columbia University (Nondenominational). *See* Tour 9 in Chapter 3.

St. Thomas (Episcopal). *See* Tour 2 in Chapter 3.

Temple Emmanu-El (Reform Jewish). *See* Tour 6 in Chapter 3.

Trinity Church (Episcopal). *See* Tour 17 in Chapter 3.

Parks and Gardens

Battery Park. *See* Tour 17 in Chapter 3.
Battery Park City Esplanade. *See* Tour 17 in Chapter 3.
Brooklyn Botanic Gardens. *See* Tour 20 in Chapter 4.
Bryant Park. *See* Tour 3 in Chapter 3.
Carl Schurz Park. *See* Tour 6 in Chapter 3.
Central Park. *See* Tour 7 in Chapter 3.
Clement Clarke Moore Park. *See* Tour 11 in Chapter 3.
Columbus Park. *See* Tour 16 in Chapter 3.
Flushing Meadows Corona Park. *See* Tour 22 in Chapter 4.
Fort Tryon Park. At the northern tip of Manhattan, high over the Hudson, this park offers stunning views of the Palisades, plus an attractive though somewhat wild garden. It also contains the Cloisters (*see* Museums and Galleries, above).
Gramercy Park. *See* Tour 4 in Chapter 3.
Jamaica Bay Wildlife Refuge (Crossbay Blvd., Broad Channel, Queens, tel. 718/474–0613). Nearly as big as the whole of Manhattan, this refuge offers temporary accommodations for migrating birds, plus nature trails around ponds and wooded uplands and through marshes. Open dawn to dusk.
Kissena Park (tel. 718/520–5359). Located in southwest Flushing, Queens, this park protects precious acres of original Long Island forests and marshland, demonstrating to visitors what the area looked like 100,000 years ago. Visitors can enjoy the new walking trails.
Madison Square. *See* Tour 4 in Chapter 3.
Marcus Garvey Park. *See* Tour 10 in Chapter 3.
New York Botanical Garden. *See* Tour 23 in Chapter 4.
Pelham Bay Park (tel. 212/430–1890). With more than 2,000 acres, this Bronx park is the largest in the city. Purchased by Thomas Pell from the Indians in 1654, its facilities include a mile-long beach, nature paths, a canoe launch, bridle path and riding academy, fishing, picnic grounds, and tennis courts.
Prospect Park. *See* Tour 20 in Chapter 4.
Riverside Park. *See* Tours 8 and 9 in Chapter 3.
Staten Island Botanical Gardens. *See* Tour 24 in Chapter 4.
Union Square. *See* Tour 4 in Chapter 3.
United Nations Rose Garden. *See* Tour 3 in Chapter 3.
Van Cortlandt Park (tel. 212/430–1890). Located on 2 square miles of the north-central Bronx, this park includes facilities for tennis, swimming, running, baseball, soccer, cricket, and rugby. The nation's oldest municipal golf course is here, as is Van Cortlandt House (*see* Historical Sites, above).
Washington Market Park. *See* Tour 14 in Chapter 3.
Washington Square. *See* Tour 12 in Chapter 3.

Statues, Monuments, and Fountains

Alice in Wonderland, Central Park (José de Creeft). *See* Tour 7 in Chapter 3.
Alma Mater, Columbia University (Daniel Chester French). *See* Tour 9 in Chapter 3.
Atlas, Rockefeller Center (Lee Lawrie). *See* Tour 1 in Chapter 3.
Bethesda Fountain, Central Park (Emma Stebbins). *See* Tour 7 in Chapter 3.

Clock Sculpture Facade, Grand Central Terminal (Jules Coutan). *See* Tour 3 in Chapter 3.

Cube, Marine Midland Bank (Isamu Noguchi). *See* Tour 17 in Chapter 3.

Delacorte Clock, Central Park (Andrea Spadini). *See* Tour 7 in Chapter 3.

General Grant National Memorial, W. 122nd St. and Riverside Dr. (John Duncan). *See* Tour 9 in Chapter 3.

General Sherman, Grand Army Plaza (Augustus Saint-Gaudens). *See* Tour 2 in Chapter 3.

George Washington, Federal Hall National Memorial (John Q. Adams Ward). *See* Tour 17 in Chapter 3.

Group of Four Trees, Chase Manhattan Plaza (Jean Dubuffet). *See* Tour 17 in Chapter 3.

Hammarskjold Plaza Sculpture Garden (Don Gummer). Huge sculptures and lots of space at Second Avenue between 46th and 47th streets.

Hans Christian Andersen, Central Park (Georg Lober). *See* Tour 7 in Chapter 3.

Lincoln Center Fountain (Philip Johnson). *See* Tour 8 in Chapter 3.

Lions, New York Public Library's central research building (E. C. Potter). *See* Tour 3 in Chapter 3.

Louise Nevelson Plaza. *See* Tour 17 in Chapter 3.

Prometheus, Rockefeller Center's lower plaza (Paul Manship). *See* Tour 1 in Chapter 3.

Pulitzer Fountain, Grand Army Plaza (Carrere & Hastings) with **Abundance** facade (Karl Bitter). *See* Tour 2 in Chapter 3.

Reclining Figure, Lincoln Center (Henry Moore). *See* Tour 8 in Chapter 3.

Soldiers' and Sailors' Memorial Arch, Grand Army Plaza, Park Slope, Brooklyn (John H. Duncan). *See* Tour 20 in Chapter 4.

Statue of Liberty, New York Harbor (Frederick A. Bartholdi). *See* Tour 17 in Chapter 3.

Statues on the Mall, Central Park. *See* Tour 7 in Chapter 3.

Unisphere, Flushing Meadows Corona Park, Flushing, Queens (Peter Muller-Munk, Inc.) *See* Tour 22 in Chapter 4.

Vietnam Veterans Memorial, Water Street (William Fellows and Peter Wormser). *See* Tour 17 in Chapter 3.

Washington Square Arch, Washington Square (Stanford White). *See* Tour 12 in Chapter 3.

Zoos

Bronx Zoo & Children's Zoo. *See* Tour 23 in Chapter 4.

Central Park Zoo & Children's Zoo. *See* Tour 7 in Chapter 3.

New York Aquarium. *See* What to See and Do with Children in Chapter 4.

Prospect Park Zoo. *See* Tour 20 in Chapter 4.

Queen's Zoo. *See* Tour 22 in Chapter 4.

Staten Island Zoo. *See* What to See and Do with Children in Chapter 4.

6 Sports, Fitness, Beaches

by Karen Cure

A resident of New York's Upper West Side, Karen Cure is the author of Fodor's Sunday in New York.

Never known for turning their backs on trends, New Yorkers— who were always sports-mad as spectators—have caught the fitness bug. Though surrounded by concrete, they have discovered that the out-of-doors is a wonderful place, and they are stopped by nothing in their passion for their sports: You can see them jogging in the park when it's sleeting, or heading for the tennis bubble on the most blustery of Sunday winter afternoons. From boccie to croquet, no matter how esoteric the sport, there's a place to pursue it in New York. You'll find oases of greenery you'd never imagine here (13% of the city, in fact, is parkland). And if you strike up a conversation while waiting to rent a boat or a bike at the Loeb Boathouse, or while stretching before a jog around the Reservoir in Central Park, you'll discover a friendly, relaxed side of New Yorkers that you might not otherwise get the chance to see.

Just one word before you set out: Now that fitness is so popular here, weekends are very busy. If you need to rent equipment or secure specific space—for instance, a tennis court—go very early or be prepared to wait.

Spectator Sports

Many events described below take place at **Madison Square Garden** (7th Ave. between 31st & 33rd Sts.); tickets can be ordered by phone through the box office (tel. 212/465–6000) or Ticketmaster (tel. 212/307–7171). Even when events are sold out, you can often pick up a pair of tickets on the day of the game outside the venue, either from a scalper or from a fellow sports fan whose guests couldn't make it at the last minute. Ticket agencies, listed in the Manhattan yellow-pages phone directory, can be helpful—for a price.

Baseball

The **New York Mets** play at Shea Stadium (tel. 718/507–8499), at the penultimate stop on the No. 7 subway in Flushing, Queens. Watching them play to the cry of "Let's Go Mets!" is today's mania. Yankee Stadium (tel. 212/293–6000), accessible by the No. 4, D, or C subways to the 161st Street station in the Bronx, is the home of the **New York Yankees.** Baseball season runs from April to October.

Basketball

Only recently have the **New York Knickerbockers** (the "Knicks") aroused any hometown passion, but the team turnaround has made tickets for home games, played late October– April at Madison Square Garden, hard to come by. For up-to-date game roundups, phone the New York Knickerbockers Hot Line (tel. 212/751–6310).

Boxing and Wrestling

The *Daily News*'s annual Golden Gloves **boxing** bout and other major competitions are staged in Madison Square Garden. **Wrestling**, a more frequent Garden presence, is stagy and outrageous, drawing a rowdy but enthusiastic crowd.

Football

The **New York Giants** play September–December at Giants Stadium in East Rutherford, New Jersey (tel. 201/935–8111), as do the **New York Jets** (tel. 516/838–6600). All seats for Giants games and most for Jets games are sold on a season-ticket basis, and there's a waiting list for those; remaining Jets tickets for scattered singles are snapped up almost as soon as they go on sale in August.

Hockey

The **New York Rangers** play at Madison Square Garden; the **New York Islanders** at Nassau Veterans Memorial Coliseum in Uniondale, Long Island (tel. 516/794–4100); and the **New Jersey Devils** at the Brendan Byrne Arena in East Rutherford, New Jersey (tel. 201/935–6050). Tickets are usually available at game time; the season runs from October to April.

Horse Racing

Thoroughbreds Modern **Aqueduct Racetrack** (Rockaway Blvd., Ozone Park, Queens, tel. 718/641–4700), with its spate of new lawns and gardens, holds races late October–early May; the track is closed Tuesdays.

Belmont Park (Hempstead Turnpike, Elmont, Long Island, tel. 718/641–4700), the grande dame of New York racing, is home of the third jewel in horse racing's triple crown, the Belmont Stakes. Horses run here May–July and late August–October, but never on Tuesdays.

The **Meadowlands** (East Rutherford, NJ, tel. 201/935–8500), generally a trotting venue, also has a flat track season from Labor Day to December.

Standardbreds **Yonkers Raceway** (Central Ave., Yonkers, NY, tel. 212/562–9500) features harness racing daily year-round.

The **Meadowlands** (East Rutherford, NJ, tel. 201/935–8500) runs both trotters and pacers January–mid-August.

Running

The **New York City Marathon,** which has taken place annually in late October or early November since 1970, may be won by the Grete Waitzes, Bill Rodgerses, and other stars of the worldwide running circuit, but New Yorkers love to cheer on the pack of 22,000 (some 16,000 of them finish). Racewalkers, "jogglers," oldsters, youngsters, and disabled competitors help to make this what former Olympic Organizing Committee president Peter V. Ueberroth called "the best sporting event in the country." Spectators line rooftops and sidewalks, promenades, and terraces all along the route—but don't go near the finishing line in Central Park unless you relish mob scenes.

Tennis

The annual **U.S. Open,** held from late August through early September at the U.S.T.A. National Tennis Center, is one of the high points of the tennis buff's year, and tickets to watch the late rounds are some of the hottest in town. Early round matches are entertaining, too, and with a stadium court ticket you can also view matches in outlying courts—where the bleachers are so close you can almost count the sweat beads on the players' foreheads—and in the grandstand, where bleacher seating is first-come, first-served. During early rounds, ushers may help you move down to better seats in the stadium court or the grandstand (in exchange for a gratuity of $5 or $10). Wherever you sit, the attractive crowd of casual visitors, tennis groupies, and celebrities makes for terrific people-watching. The U.S. Tennis Association (Flushing Meadows-Corona Park, Flushing, NY 11368, tel. 718/271–5100) sells tickets by mail beginning in May; from June on, call Teletron (tel. 212/947–4840 or 800/922–2030).

The tennis year winds up in Madison Square Garden with the **Virginia Slims Tournament** in mid-November (tel. 212/563–8954), with tickets on sale beginning in September.

Track and Field

The **Millrose Games** take place at Madison Square Garden every year in February.

The **New York Track and Field Games** are held in late July at Wein Stadium, Columbia University. For information, contact the New York Road Runners Club (9 E. 89th St., 10128, tel. 212/860–4455).

Participant Sports

Bicycling

Although it's a problem to keep a bicycle in most Manhattan apartments, that doesn't affect the popularity of the sport here. A sleek pack of dedicated racers zooms around Central Park at dawn and at dusk daily, and on weekends, parks swarm with recreational cyclists. **Central Park**'s circular drive is closed to traffic from 10 AM to 3 PM and 7 to 10 PM on weekdays, and from 7 PM Friday to 6 AM Monday. On holidays, it's closed from 8 PM the night before until 6 AM the day after. In **Riverside Park,** the promenade between 72nd and 110th streets, with its Hudson River view, gets a more easygoing crowd. Other good bets: the **Wall Street** area, deserted on weekends; the Hudson-view **Battery Park Esplanade;** or the winding roads in Brooklyn's **Prospect Park,** also closed to cars.

Bike Rentals Expect to leave a deposit or a credit card at the following: **AAA Bikes in Central Park** (Loeb Boathouse, mid-park near East 74th St., tel. 212/861–4137); **Bicycles Plus** (204 E. 85th St., tel. 212/794–2201); **Gene's Bicycles** (242 E. 79th St., tel. 212/249–9218); **Metro Bicycles** (1311 Lexington Ave. at 88th St., tel. 212/427–4450); or **Pedal Pusher** (1306 2nd Ave. between 68th and 69th Sts., tel. 212/288–5592). Some rent only 3-speeds; others have 10-speeds as well.

Group Trips For organized rides with other cyclists, contact: **Central Park Cycling & Sports Association** (tel. 212/956–5920); **Hungry Pedalers Gourmet Bicycle Tours,** visiting destinations of culinary interest (771 West End Ave., tel. 212/989–8851); or the **Staten Island Bicycling Association** (Box 141016, Staten Island 10314, tel. 718/273–0805).

Billiards

It used to be that pool halls were dusty, grimy, sticky places—and there are still a few of those around. But they've been joined by a group of oh-so-chic spots with deluxe decor, high prices, and even classical music or jazz in the background.

Amsterdam Billiard Club, (344 Amsterdam Ave., between 76th and 77th Sts., tel. 212/496–8180).

Billiard Club (220 W. 19th St., tel. 212/206–7665).

Chelsea Billiards (54 W. 21st St., tel. 212/989–0096).

Julian's Billiards (138 E. 14th St., tel. 212/475–9338).

Society Billiards (10 E. 21st St., tel. 212/529–8600).

Tekk Billiards (75 Christopher St., tel. 212/463–9282).

21 Billiards (2121 Broadway at 75th St., tel. 212/721–1909).

Bird-watching

Manhattan's green parks and woodlands provide habitat for thousands of birds, everything from summer tanagers and fork-tailed flycatchers to Kentucky warblers and common nighthawks. Since the city is on the Atlantic flyway, a major migratory route, you can see birds that nest as far north as the High Arctic. May is the best season, since the songbirds are in their freshest colors—and so many are singing at once that you can hardly distinguish their songs. To find out what's been seen where, call the Rare Bird Alert (tel. 212/832–6523).

Good bets include 1,146-acre **Van Cortlandt Park** (tel. 212/548–7070) in the Bronx, with its freshwater marshes and upland woods. In Brooklyn there are 526-acre **Prospect Park** (tel. 718/788–8549) and **Green-Wood Cemetery** (tel. 718/783–8776). The Ramble in Manhattan's **Central Park** (tel. 212/397–3091) is another prime spot. In Queens, try **Jamaica Bay Wildlife Refuge,** 9,155 acres of salt marshes, fresh and brackish ponds, and open water (tel. 718/474–0613). In Staten Island, head for the fairly undeveloped 317-acre **Wolfe's Pond Park** (tel. 718/984–8266), where the pond and the nearby shore can be dense with geese and ducks during the annual migrations.

Guided Walks The **New York City Audubon Society** (71 W. 23rd, tel. 212/691–7483) has occasional bird-watching outings. Also check with the **Urban Park Rangers,** a uniformed division of the Parks Department that organizes frequent outdoor walks. Each borough has its own troop: Manhattan (tel. 212/408–0209); the Bronx, (tel. 212/430–1800); Brooklyn, (tel. 718/965–8900); Queens (tel. 718/520–5900); and Staten Island, (tel. 718/390–8000).

Boating

The boating available on New York City's ponds and lakes conjures up 19th-century images of a parasol-twirling lady being rowed by her swain. But there's a huge demand for this activity, and on weekends you'd better go early or be prepared to wait.

In **Central Park,** the boats are rowboats (plus one Venetian gondola) and the rowing terrain is the 18-acre Central Park Lake. Rent your boat at **Loeb Boathouse** (tel. 212/517–2233), near 74th Street, from spring through fall.

In **Prospect Park,** pedal-powered two- and four-seater boats
scuttle across the 60-acre Prospect Lake and Lullwater. Rentals are available at **Pelican Boat Rentals** (tel. 718/287–9824),
near the Wollman Skating Rink.

Boccie

This Italian version of bowling thrives in New York, with 100
city courts in the five boroughs. The easiest to get to from midtown are at 96th Street and First Avenue; at East River Drive
and 42nd Street; and at the Thompson Street Playground (at
Houston St.) in Greenwich Village. There's also a boccie court
at Il Vagabondo, a vintage Italian restaurant east of Bloomingdale's (351 E. 62nd St., tel. 212/832–9221).

Bowling

The closing of several major lanes recently has left Manhattan
with just one bowling alley, **Bowlmor** (110 University Pl., tel.
212/255–8188). This funky 44-lane operation can't compare to
modern layouts on TV (or in your own hometown). But you can't
beat the colorful Village crowd—or the intensity of the competition.

Chess and Checkers

Central Park's Chess & Checkers House is picturesquely situated atop a massive stone outcrop. Ten tables are available for
indoor play on weekends, 11:30–4:30, and 24 outdoor tables are
available during all daylight hours. Pick up playing pieces at
the Dairy (mid-park at 64th St., tel. 212/397–3165); there is no
charge, but a deposit is required.

Downtown in Greenwich Village, the **Village Chess Shop** (230
Thompson St., tel. 212/475–9580) is always an active spot. Uptown, the **Manhattan Chess Club** (154 W. 57th St., tel. 212/333–
5888) sponsors tournaments and exhibitions; instruction is
available on both beginning and intermediate levels.

Fencing

The oldest fencing salle in the Western Hemisphere, the **Fencers Club** (154 W. 71 St., tel. 212/865–9800), has been the sparring ground for scores of U.S. Olympians since its opening in
1883. Evening jousting sessions make a swashbuckling sight
through the street-level windows. Other clubs include **Santelli
Salle D'Armes** (40 W. 27 St., tel. 212/683–2823) and **Blade** (212
W. 15 St., tel. 212/620–0144).

Fishing

The smell of fish and saltwater entrances New Yorkers, and it's
not far away by car or subway. No license is necessary for saltwater angling. Brooklyn's **Sheepshead Bay,** where turn-of-the-century swells like Diamond Jim Brady summered, is the main
center for party boats; its fleet is among the country's largest,
with some 28 boats going out every day year-round. The piers
are on Emmons Avenue, and departure times are posted locally—typically 6, 7, and 8 AM for full-day trips, and 8 AM and 1 PM
for half-day outings. Tackle rentals and bait are provided. Call

Mike's Tackle & Bait Shop (tel. 718/646–9261) for additional information.

On quaint City Island, a Bronx bastion of the salty life, **Jack's Bait & Tackle** (Cross St. and City Island Ave., Bronx, tel. 212/ 885–2042) rents boats with 6 HP motors to go out for flounder, stripers, bluefish, porgy, eel, and blackfish.

Flounder, fluke, small blues, porgy, and bass make for good shore fishing at **Pelham Bay Park**'s Orchard Beach (tel. 212/ 885–2275) in the Bronx; at **Breezy Point Jetty** and **Canarsie Pier** in the Gateway National Recreation Area (tel. 718/474–4600) in Brooklyn; and at **Rockaway Beach** (tel. 718/318–4000) in Queens.

Golf

Although New York golf courses don't measure up to those in world golf meccas such as Scotland, many New Yorkers are avid golfers, and on weekends they jam the handful of verdant, well-kept city courses.

Bethpage State Park, in the Long Island town of Bethpage, about one hour and 20 minutes from Manhattan, is home to five golf courses, including its 7,065-yard par-71 Black, generally ranked among the nation's top 25 public courses. Reservations for tee times are not accepted; on weekends and Monday, the line starts forming at midnight for the Black course's tee time tickets to go on sale at 4 AM. It's not so congested on other days, or on the other four courses on the property.

Of the 13 city courses, the 6,492-yard Split Rock in **Pelham Bay Park,** the Bronx, is considered the most challenging (tel. 212/ 885–1258; 718/225–4653 for tee times). **Van Cortlandt Park** has the nation's first municipal golf course, established in 1895— the hilly 6,052-yard Van Cortlandt (tel. 212/543–4595). Queens has a 5,431-yard course at **Forest Park** (Forest Park W. Dr. and 80th St., tel. 718/296–0999); Staten Island has the 5,891-yard **Silver Lake** (915 Victory Blvd. near Forest Ave., tel. 718/447– 5686; 718/225–4653 for tee times).

Driving Range In midtown Manhattan you can practice your swing in netted cages, with bull's-eye backdrops, at the **Richard Metz Golf Studio** (425 Madison Ave. at 49th St., 3rd floor, tel. 212/759–6940). A spectacular new driving range with 110 stalls, 36 miniature golf holes, and 18 batting cages opens on Randall's Island this year (tel. 212/225–9187).

Miniature Golf Putting courses are at **Gotham Miniature Golf** (at Wollman Rink, Central Park near 64th St., tel. 212/517–4800), where putters maneuver around scale models of city landmarks, and at yuppyish **Putter's Paradise** (48 W. 21st St., tel. 212/727– 7888).

Horseback Riding

A trot on the bridle path around Central Park's Reservoir, renovated in 1987, provides a pleasant look at New York. Experienced English-saddle riders can rent mounts at the carefully run **Claremont Riding Academy** (173–177 W. 89th St., tel. 212/ 724–5100), the city's oldest riding academy and the only riding stable left in Manhattan. Private lessons, including dressage, are available at beginner through advanced levels, for $32 per half hour; horse rentals are $30 per hour.

Hotel Health Clubs

Although space is tight in Manhattan hotels, most of them offer some kind of fitness facility, even if it's just an arrangement enabling guests to use a nearby health club (*see* Chapter 9). These hotels have some of the better on-premises workout centers:

Doral Park Avenue (70 Park Ave., tel. 212/687–7050), with one-on-one training and aerobic and Nautilus equipment at the Doral Fitness Center (also available to guests of the **Doral Court, Doral Tuscany,** and **Doral Inn**).

Le Parker Meridien (118 W. 57th St., tel. 212/245–5000), featuring a rooftop pool and a basement-level workout center.

The Peninsula (700 5th Ave., tel. 212/247–2200), with a pool on the 22nd floor, plus exercise machines and a dining terrace.

U.N. Plaza (1 United Nations Plaza, tel. 212/355–3400), combining a handsome top-floor pool with a roomful of exercise machines. It's also the only hotel in New York with an indoor tennis court.

Vanderbilt YMCA (224 E. 47th St., tel. 212/755–2410), which offers guests free access to the Y's athletic facilities—pools, gym, running track, weight room, machines, and exercise classes.

New York Vista (3 World Trade Ctr., tel. 212/938–9100), with a pool, an exercise area, and a running track.

Ice Skating

Each of the city's rinks has its own character, but all have scheduled skating sessions, with the surfaces tended between times. Lockers, skate rentals, music, and snack bars complete the picture. Major rinks include the one in **Rockefeller Center** (50th St. at 5th Ave., lower plaza, tel. 212/757–5730), postage-stamp size and utterly romantic; **Sky Rink** (450 W. 33rd St., 16th floor, tel. 212/695–6555 or, for lessons, 212/239–8385), the city's biggest indoor skating spot and its only year-round rink, where dancer Mikhail Baryshnikov tutored Olympic skater Debi Thomas; and the beautifully situated **Wollman Memorial Rink** (Central Park near 64th St., tel. 212/517–4800). Be prepared for crowds on weekends.

Jogging and Racewalking

In New York, lawyers jog, doctors jog, investment bankers jog, antiques dealers jog, and mothers jog (sometimes pushing their toddlers ahead of them in speedy Baby Jogger strollers). Publicity notwithstanding, crime is not a problem as long as you jog when and where everybody else does.

In Manhattan, **Central Park** is the busiest spot, specifically along the 1.58-mile track circling the **Reservoir,** New York Road Runners' Club President Fred Lebow's favorite running ground. A runners' lane has been designated along the park roads, which are closed to traffic weekdays 10–3 and 7–10, and from 7 PM Fridays to 6 AM Mondays in summer, weekends only in winter. A good 1.72-mile route starts at Tavern on the Green along the West Drive, heads south around the bottom of the park to the East Drive, and circles back west on the 72nd Street park road to your starting point. **Riverside Park,** along the Hudson River bank in Manhattan, is glorious at sunset. You can cover 4½ miles by running from 72nd to 116th streets and back. There are eight laps to a mile on the park's outdoor track near 74th Street. In Manhattan, figure 20 north–south blocks per mile.

Other favorite Manhattan circuits are around **Gramercy Park** (⅛ mile), **City Hall Park** (½ mile), **Washington Square Park** (½ mile), the **Battery Park City Esplanade** (about 2 miles), and **Roosevelt Island** (3.6 miles). In Brooklyn, try the **Brooklyn Heights Esplanade,** facing the Manhattan skyline, or the roads in **Prospect Park.**

Races and Group Runs A full, year-round schedule is organized by the **New York Road Runners Club** (9 E. 89th St., tel. 212/860–4455), including group runs at 6:30 PM and 7:30 PM Monday through Friday, starting at the club headquarters, and at 10 AM Saturdays at 90th Street and Fifth Avenue in Central Park.

Roller Skating

While roller skating is no longer the mania it once was, there are certain New Yorkers who ignore that; wearing headphones, they whirl and twirl to music that they alone can hear. A prime spot, particularly on weekends, is in **Central Park** between the Mall and Bethesda Fountain. **Wollman Rink** (midpark at 63rd St., tel. 212/517–4800) converts to a roller rink during warm months, and rentals are available. You can also rent at **Blades West** (105 W. 72nd St., tel. 212/787–3911, and 160 E. 86th St., tel. 212/996–1644).

Swimming

Municipal pools such as the **Carmine Street Pool** (7th Ave. S and Clarkson St., tel. 212/397–3107) are great places to mix with a real cross-section of native New Yorkers. The **U.N. Plaza, Parker Meridien,** and **New York Vista** hotels (*see* Chapter 9) all have good swimming pools for use by their guests (*see* also Beaches, below). The **YWCA** has a sparkling 75-foot lap pool available at $5 per half hour to members of all YWCAs (610 Lexington Ave. at 53rd St., tel. 212/755–4500).

Tennis

The New York City Parks Department maintains scores of tennis courts. The most scenic are the 24 in **Central Park** (mid-park near 94th St., tel. 212/397–3190), set in a thicket of trees with the skyline beyond. Modestly priced, same-day, single-play admissions are available at the Tennis House adjoining the courts. Lessons are given on four hard courts (tel. 212/289–3133).

You can also play where John McEnroe and Ivan Lendl do: at the **U.S.T.A. National Tennis Center** (tel. 718/592–8000) in Flushing Meadows-Corona Park, Queens, site of the U.S. Open tournament. The center has 29 outdoor and 9 indoor courts, all Deco Turf II. Reservations are accepted up to two days in advance. If a $150 million expansion goes according to schedule, 15 new courts open to the public and three new stadiums will be added to the center, with construction starting in 1992.

Local clubs and private courts include:

Boulevard Gardens Tennis Club (51–26 Broadway, Woodside, Queens, tel. 718/545–7774), whose six good red-clay courts, bubble-covered in winter, are very easy to get to by car from Manhattan.

Crosstown Tennis (14 W. 31st St., tel. 212/947–5780), with four indoor hard courts that are air-conditioned in summer.

HRC Tennis (Piers 13 and 14, East River at Wall St., tel. 212/422–9300), with eight Har-Tru courts under two bubbles, which are air-conditioned in summer.

Manhattan Plaza Racquet Club (450 W. 43rd St., tel. 212/594–0554), on whose five courts Virginia Slims and U.S. Open players have been known to practice.

Beaches

Fine weather brings sun-worshiping New Yorkers out in force. Early in the season, the nearest park or even a rooftop is just fine for catching rays, but later on everyone heads for New York City beaches. Call before you go to check on swimming conditions.

Long Island

New Yorkers' favorite strand may be **Jones Beach** (tel. 516/785–1600), one of the great man-made beaches of the world, built during the era of the famous parks commissioner Robert Moses. Up the shore is another good beach at **Robert Moses State Park** on Fire Island (tel. 516/669–0449). The Long Island Railroad (tel. 718/217–5477) runs regular transportation in the summer from Penn Station to Jones Beach, Robert Moses State Park, and Long Beach.

City Beaches

The most popular spot is just a subway ride away: the 7½-mile Atlantic strand in Queens's **Rockaways** (tel. 718/318–4000), site of some of the city's best surf.

Jacob Riis Park (tel. 718/474–4600), part of the Gateway National Recreation Area in Brooklyn, has a boardwalk stretching a full mile along the surfy Atlantic. On Staten Island, there are terrific Atlantic-surf beaches at **Wolfe's Pond Park** (tel. 718/984–8266) and along the 7,500-foot **Franklin D. Roosevelt Boardwalk,** from Miller Field in the Gateway National Recreation Area (tel. 718/351–8700) to Fort Wadsworth.

7 Shopping

by Karen Cure

Shopping in New York is theater, architecture, and people-watching all rolled into one. Big stores and small ones, one-of-a-kinds and chains together present an overwhelming array of "Things." There are fabulous department stores, with something for everyone, and tiny specialists: You can find a store full of balloons (**Toy Balloon**, 204 E. 38th St., tel. 212/682-3803), and others offering Japanese-style screens (**Tonee Corp.**, 108 Wooster St., tel. 212/966-4213), personal and business security equipment (**Counter Spy Shop**, 675 3rd Ave., tel. 212/557-3040; by appointment only), and kayaks and folding boats (**Hans Klepper Corp.**, 35 Union Sq. W., tel. 212/243-3428).

Another important lure of Manhattan shopping is the bargain. Major intersections are instant markets as street peddlers hawk fake Gucci and Cartier watches at $15–$25 each. (These may just possibly last a year or two.) There are thrift shops and resale shops where, it's whispered, Jackie O sends her castoffs and Catherine Deneuve snaps up antique lace. At off-price and discount stores, mark-offs are, as locals say, "to die for," and the sales are even better. Designers' showroom sales allow you to buy cheap at the source; auctions promise good prices as well.

Shopping Hours   Stores are generally open Monday–Saturday from 10 AM to 5 or 6 PM, but neighborhood peculiarities do exist. In midtown and lower Manhattan, shops are often closed all weekend. Most stores on the Lower East Side close on Friday afternoon and all day Saturday for the Jewish Sabbath, while keeping normal hours on Sunday. Sunday hours, also common on the West Side and in the Village, are the exception on the Upper East Side.

Sales   Sales take place in August (for summer merchandise) and in December and January (for winter wares); these sales are announced in the papers. Sales of special merit may end up in *New York* magazine's "Sales and Bargains" column. These often include sales in manufacturers' showrooms that are otherwise never promoted to the public. If your visit is planned for April or October, when most take place, you might phone your favorite designer and ask whether one is in the offing. Find out before you go whether the seller requires cash or accepts credit card or checks (whether local or out-of-state).

Shopping Neighborhoods

New York shops are collected in neighborhoods rather than in malls, so there's nothing more pleasant than shop-crawling when the weather is fine. Locations, if not included here, can be found in store listings below.

South Street   The Seaport's shops are located along the cobbled, pedestri-
Seaport   ans-only extension to Fulton Street; in the Fulton Market building, the original home of the city's fish market; and on the three levels of Pier 17. You'll find some of the best of the country's upscale retailers: **Ann Taylor** and **Laura Ashley** for women's clothing, **Brookstone** for fancy gadgets and hardware, **Coach** for handbags, **Caswell-Massey** for fragrances, and **Sharper Image** for high-tech gimmickry. The big catalogue house **J. Crew** chose the Seaport as the location for its first retail outlet. There are also few-of-a-kind shops, notably the **Strand** bookstore, where second-hand volumes overflow into sidewalk bins; **Mariposa** for butterflies; and **Hats in the Belfry**

A & S Plaza, **14**

Alexander's, **2**

575 Fifth Avenue, **10**

Barneys New York, **15**

Bergdorf Goodman, **4**

Bloomingdale's, **1**

Century 21, **19**

Henri Bendel, **5**

Herald Center, **13**

Lord & Taylor, **11**

Lower East Side
(Orchard Street), **16**

Macy's, **12**

Manhattan Art and
Antiques Center, **7**

Place des
Antiquaires, **3**

Rockefeller Center, **8**

Saks Fifth Avenue, **9**

South Street
Seaport, **20**

Trump Tower, **6**

World Financial
Center, **17**

World Trade
Center, **18**

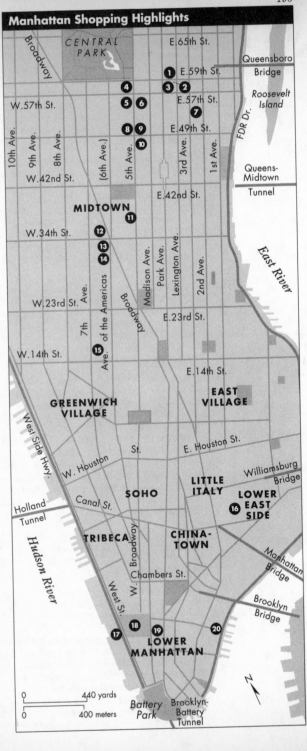

Manhattan Shopping Highlights

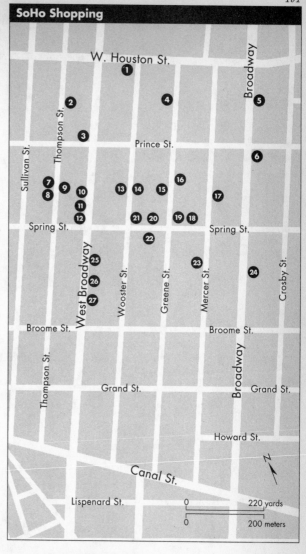

Ad Hoc Softwares, **12**
Alaïa New York, **17**
Back Pages Antiques, **4**
Bébé Thompson, **9**
Betsey Johnson, **2**
Canal Jean, **24**
Comme des Garçons, **14**
D.F. Sanders, **27**
Dean & DeLuca, **6**
Ecco, **7**
Enchanted Forest, **23**
Gallery 121, **19**
Harriet Love, **10**
Irish Books and Graphics, **5**
Joovay, **11**
La Rue des Reves, **21**
Mano à Mano, **5**
Multiple Impressions, **22**
Norma Kamali O.M.O., **18**
O.K. Harris, **25**
Parachute, **13**
Paula Cooper, **1**
Penny Whistle Toys, **20**
Peter Fox, **8**
Think Big!, **26**
Untitled, **3**
Wolfman-Gold & Good Company, **16**
Zona, **15**

for inexpensive hats. Business is brisk, especially on fine summer days and on weekends.

World Financial Center Although the nearby World Trade Center bills its concourse as the city's busiest shopping center, the World Financial Center in Battery Park City is a shopping destination to reckon with, thanks to stores such as **Barneys New York** for clothing, **Godiva Chocolatier** for chocolates, **Mark Cross** for leather goods, **Ann Taylor,** and **Caswell-Massey.** The **Gallery of History** sells original historical documents as works of art. **State of the Art** has home and office accessories, **Il Papiro** offers hand-marbled Italian paper products, and **CD Street** strives to be the ultimate compact disc store. Most are open on Sundays.

57th Street / 5th Avenue Shopping

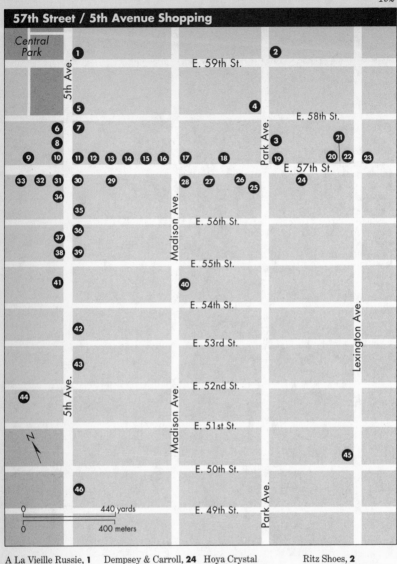

A La Vieille Russie, **1**

André Emmerich Gallery, **18**

Beltrami, **38**

Bergdorf Goodman, **6, 7**

Bijan, **26**

Buccellati, **35**

Bulgari, **31**

Burberry, **12**

Cartier, **43**

Chanel, **11**

Charivari 57, **32**

Charles Jourdan, **35**

Ciro, **39**

Dempsey & Carroll, **24**

Doris Leslie Blau, **12**

Doubleday Bookshop, **8**

F.A.O. Schwarz, **5**

Fortunoff, **42**

Galeries Lafayette New York, **29**

Gazebo, **21**

Godiva Chocolatier, **41, 45**

Hammacher Schlemmer, **23**

Harry Winston, **37**

Hermès, **13**

Hoya Crystal Gallery, **25**

Israel Sack, **14**

J.N. Bartfield Books, **33**

James Robinson, **14**

Kenneth Jay Lane, **35**

Laura Ashley, **16**

Louis, Boston, **22**

Martha, **3, 35**

Matsuda, **19**

Morrell & Company, **40**

Pace Gallery, **28**

Place des Antiquaires, **20**

Ritz Shoes, **2**

Saks Fifth Avenue, **46**

Salvatore Ferragamo, **34**

Sheridan, **17**

Steuben, **36**

Susan Bennis Warren Edwards, **9**

T. Anthony, **4**

Tiffany & Co., **30**

Traveller's Bookstore, **44**

Van Cleef & Arpels, **10**

Victoria's Secret, **27**

Wally Findlay Gallery, **15**

Lower East Side Once home to millions of Jewish immigrants from Russia and Eastern Europe, this area is New Yorkers' bargain beat. The center of it all is narrow, unprepossessing Orchard Street, which is crammed with tiny, no-nonsense clothing and shoe stores ranging from kitschy to elegant. Don't expect to schmooze with salespeople, especially on Sunday, the busiest day of the week. Start at Houston Street, walk down one side as far as Canal Street, then walk back up. Essential stops include **Fine & Klein** for handbags; **Forman's** for women's clothing; and **Lace-Up Shoes**. Grand Street (off Orchard St., south of Delancey St.) is chockablock with linens, towels, and other items for the home; the Bowery (between Grand St. and Delancy St.), with lamps and light fixtures.

SoHo On West Broadway, SoHo's main drag, and on Broadway and Wooster, Greene, Mercer, Prince, Spring, Broome, and Grand streets, major art galleries keep company with chic clothing stores such as **La Rue des Rêves** and **Victoria Falls**. Well-known stops include decorative-items specialist **Wolfman-Gold & Good Company** and Southwest-themed **Zona;** gourmet food emporium **Dean & DeLuca;** and **D.F. Sanders**, where accessories and housewares are sleekly, stunningly contemporary. Many stores in SoHo close on Mondays.

Herald Square Reasonable prices prevail at this intersection of 34th Street and Avenue of the Americas (Sixth Avenue). Giant **Macy's** is the linchpin. Opposite, in glittering Herald Center (the former E. J. Korvette—the original Saks & Company), the chief draw is Manhattan's first **Toys "Я" Us**. Next door on Sixth Avenue, the new **A&S Plaza** atrium-mall is anchored by the Manhattan outlet of the Brooklyn-based A&S department store, which makes for wonderful browsing, as do **Lechter's**, for home furnishings, and **Mouse N' Around,** for cartoon-emblazoned togs. The concentration of shops in a small area makes it a good bet in nasty weather.

Midtown Near Grand Central The biggest men's clothiers are here on and just off the stretch of Madison Avenue nicknamed "Trad Avenue": **J. Press; Brooks Brothers; Paul Stuart; F. R. Tripler;** and **Wallachs**. Most also handle women's clothing in dress-for-success styles.

Fifth Avenue The boulevard that was once home to some of the biggest names in New York retailing is not what it once was, that role having been usurped by Madison Avenue north of 57th Street. But Fifth Avenue from Central Park South to Rockefeller Center still shines with **F.A.O. Schwarz** and **Bergdorf Goodman** (both the main store and **Bergdorf Goodman Men** are at 58th St.), **Tiffany** and **Bulgari** jewelers (at 57th St.), the various luxury stores in **Trump Tower** (at 56th St.), **Henri Bendel**, across the street, **Steuben** glassware and **Ferragamo** shoes (at 55th St.), **Cartier** jewelers (at 52nd St.), and so on down to **Saks Fifth Avenue** (at 50th St.). **Rockefeller Center** itself provides a plethora of shops. To the south (at 47th St.) is the shiny 575 atrium mall, named for its Fifth Avenue address.

57th Street The thoroughfare of Carnegie Hall, the Russian Tea Room, and the Hard Rock Café supports stores that sell everything from remaindered books to $50,000 diamond-and-platinum bracelets. Begin at the **Compleat Strategist** game store (between 8th and 9th Aves.) and head eastward, via the **Pottery Barn, Coliseum Books,** and **Jerry Brown** and **Paron** fabric stores. As you approach Fifth Avenue, you're in the creamiest New York retail territory, with **Bergdorf Goodman's** flagship store. East of Fifth you'll find the new **Galeries Lafayette New York,** a branch of the famous French department store, and such exclusive stores as **Chanel; Burberrys; Louis, Boston;** and the **Place des Antiquaires** antiques shop complex. Above and alongside these stores are top art galleries such as **André Emmerich** and **Wally Findlay.**

Columbus Avenue Between 66th and 86th streets, this former tenement district is now home to some of the city's glitziest stores. Shops are mostly modern in design, upscale but not top-of-the-line. Clothing runs the gamut from preppy for men and women (**Frank Stella Ltd.**) to high funk (**Betsey Johnson**) and high style (**Charivari**). It's a good source for fine costume jewelry (**Ylang Ylang**). Children will enjoy stops at **The Last Wound-Up, Mythology,** and **Penny Whistle Toys.**

Upper East Side Along Madison and Lexington avenues, roughly between 57th and 72nd streets, New York branches of world-renowned designer emporiums are joined by a group of spirited retailers who fill their stores with the unique and the stylish. Items for the home, fine antiques, and wonderful clothing predominate—and the prices aren't always sky-high.

Blitz Tours

Get your subway tokens ready, and save enough cash for cab fare to lug all your packages home from these shopping itineraries. They're arranged by special interest; addresses, if not included here, can be found in the store listings below.

Antiques Spend two hours at the **Manhattan Art & Antiques Center** (1050 2nd Ave. at 55th St.), then swing over to 57th Street to the **Place des Antiquaires** and spend two hours there. Stroll westward across 57th Street, stopping at **James Robinson** and **Israel Sack.** Then head up Madison to **America Hurrah** (at 65th St.), **Didier Aaron** (on 67th St.), **Thomas K. Woodard** (near 69th St.), **Hirschl & Adler Folk** (at 70th St.), **Leigh Keno** (on 74th St.), **Stair & Company** (near 74th St.), **DeLorenzo** and **Leo Kaplan** (near 75th St.), **David A. Schorsch** (on 76th St.), **Florian Papp** (at 76th St.), and **Barry Friedman** (at 83rd St.).

Bargains Start early at **Century 21** or **Syms** (its motto: "an educated consumer is our best customer"). Take a cab to Hester and Orchard streets and shop along Orchard to Houston Street. (Prowl along Grand Street if you're more interested in soft goods for your home than in clothing.) Leave at 2:30 and take a cab to **S&W** in Chelsea; then take the subway uptown to **Loehmann's** in the Bronx, which is open until 9. Pick up snacks at street vendors and nosh as you whiz from one spot to the next. But remember: On Saturdays, things are closed on the Lower East Side.

Children If your kids have stamina, start with **Louis Tannen's,** the magic store, which opens at 9, or **Forbidden Planet,** which opens at 10. Then take a cab uptown and do Columbus Avenue, beginning with **Penny Whistle Toys** (at 81st St.), and on to **Mythology** (at 77th St.), **The Last Wound-Up** (at 73rd St.), and **Star Magic** (Amsterdam Ave. at 73rd St.). Stop at **Steve's Ice Cream** (Columbus Ave. at 73rd St.) for an ice-cream cone with mix-ins, then go visit the creatures at the American Museum of Natural History (Central Park West at 77th St.).

Acker Merrall & Condit, **31**

Ann Taylor, **36**

Aris Mixon & Company, **18**

Avventura, **6**

The Ballet Shop, **38**

Betsey Johnson, **33**

The Cat Store, **2**

Charivari, **4, 11, 15, 34**

Conran's, **14**

Contre-Jour, **35**

Descamps, **5**

Ecco, **24**

Eeyore's Books for Children, **19**

Endicott Booksellers, **7**

Frank Stella Ltd., **8**

Greenstones and Cie, **9**

Gryphon Record Shop, **28**

HMV, **29**

The Last Wound-Up, **26**

Laura Ashley, **16**

Murder Ink, **1**

Mythology, **21**

Only Hearts, **17**

P.S. 44 Market, **22**

Penny Whistle Toys, **10**

Peter Fox, **20**

Pottery Barn, **27**

Putumayo, **23**

Shakespeare & Company, **12**

Star Magic, **30**

To Boot, **32**

Tower Records, **37**

West Side Kids, **3**

Ylang Ylang, **25**

Zabar's, **13**

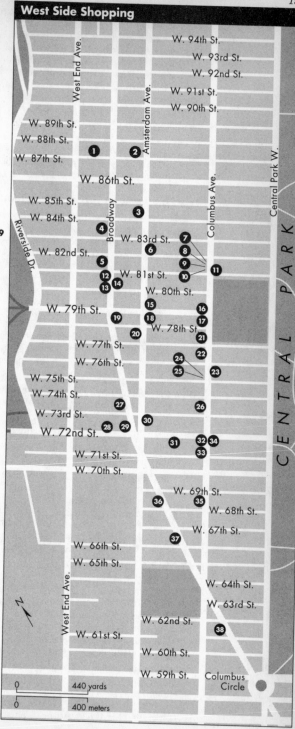

West Side Shopping

Cook's Tour Browse in **Zabar's** for a couple of hours beginning at 8 AM; then go across town to **Kitchen Arts & Letters** bookstore (1435 Lexington Ave., between 93rd & 94th Sts., tel. 212/876–5550) and proceed down to **Bridge Kitchenware** (214 E. 52nd St., tel. 212/688–4220). Head downtown to hit **Balducci's** in the Village, **Dean & DeLuca** in SoHo, and, if there's time before 6, **Kam-Man** in Chinatown. If not, head up to **Macy's** Cellar area. If you live in an inland state, make your last stop in New York **Citarella** (2135 Broadway at 75th St., tel. 212/874–0383), and have some great fish packed in ice to go.

Luxury Spend 90 minutes at **Saks Fifth Avenue,** then stroll up Fifth. Leave **Trump Tower** by 2:30. Visit **Tiffany** and **Bergdorf Goodman** before closing time. On Monday or Thursday, windowshop your way across 57th Street and north on Lexington Avenue to **Bloomingdale's,** which doesn't close until 9 PM. On other nights, take a cab downtown to **Barneys New York** for a finale.

Home Furnishings Start at **Barneys New York,** which opens at 10, and visit its Chelsea Passage. Then take a cab to SoHo and stroll around, making sure not to miss **D. F. Sanders, Wolfman-Gold & Good Company,** and **Zona.** When things there close—at 6 or 7—take the No. 6 subway to **Bloomingdale's,** if it's Monday or Thursday, or the Q or R train to **Macy's,** which is open late Mondays, Thursdays, and Fridays.

Department Stores

Most of these stores keep regular hours on weekdays and are open until 8 at least one night a week. Many have personal shoppers who can walk you through the store at no charge.

Alexander's (Lexington Ave. between 58th and 59th Sts., tel. 212/593–0880). This store has a dual personality: half polyester paradise, half bastion of high style at a discount.

A&S (33rd St. and 6th Ave., tel. 212/594–8500). The old Gimbel's, a block south of Macy's, lives again as home to A&S Plaza, whose nine floors are anchored by Abraham & Straus, well established in the outer boroughs.

Barneys New York (106 7th Ave. at 17th St., tel. 212/929–9000). Founded as a menswear discounter some 60 years ago, Barneys is now the place to see what's hot. The still-extensive selection of menswear ranges from made-to-measure and European and American couture to mass-market natural-shouldered suits; the women's store, in an adjacent group of brownstones, is a showcase of current women's fashion. The Chelsea Passage area can be counted on for distinctive and one-of-a-kind accessories for the home.

Bergdorf Goodman (754 5th Ave., between 57th and 58th Sts., tel. 212/753–7300). Good taste reigns in an elegant and understated setting. The Home Department is room after exquisite room of wonderful linens, tabletop items, and gifts. The expanded men's store, across the street, occupies the former home of the giant F.A.O. Schwarz toy store.

Bloomingdale's (1000 3rd Ave. at 59th St., tel. 212/355–5900). Its main floor is a stupefying maze of mirrors and black walls, elsewhere the racks are overfull, salespeople overworked, and the departments constantly on the move. Still, selections are dazzling at all but the lowest price points, and the markdowns

Aberbach Fine Art, **8**

America Hurrah, **37**

Baccarat, **48**

Barry Friedman, **3**

Bottega Veneta, **47**

Caviarteria, **45**

Cerutti, **28**

Christie's, **46**

Coe Kerr, **4**

D.F. Sanders, **9**

David Schorsch, **14**

DeLorenzo, **10**

Descamps, **38**

Didier Aaron, **36**

E. Braun, **39**

Eeyore's Books for Children, **2**

Emanuel Ungaro, **29**

Encore, **1**

Erica Wilson, **40**

Florian Papp, **11**

Floris, **41**

Giorgio Armani, **27**

Givenchy, **12**

Godiva, **30**

Hirschl & Adler Folk, **20**

Isselbacher, **7**

Koos van den Akker, **31**

Lederer, **49**

Leigh Keno American Furniture, **16**

Leo Kaplan Ltd., **13**

The Limited, **42**

Mabel's, **21**

Madison Avenue Bookshop, **23**

Maud Frizon, **24**

Michael's Resale, **5**

Mishon, Mishon, **17**

Missoni, **25**

Montenapoleone, **35**

North Beach Leather, **34**

Polo/Ralph Lauren, **18**

Second Act Children's Wear, **6**

Sherry Lehman, **43**

Sonia Rykiel, **33**

Stair & Company, **15**

T. Anthony, **50**

Teuscher Chocolates, **44**

Thomas K. Woodard, **22**

Valentino, **26**

Ylang Ylang, **32**

Yves St. Laurent Rive Gauche, **19**

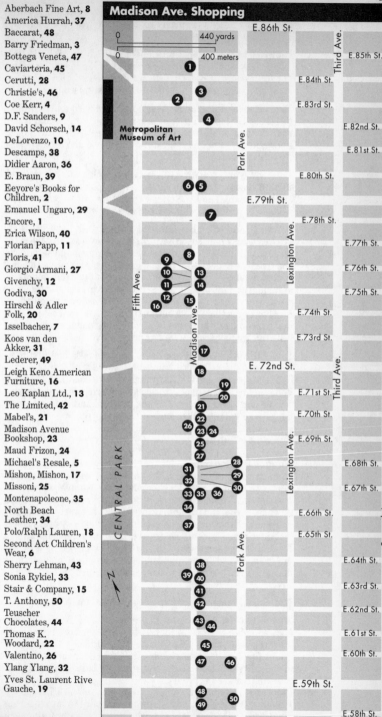

Madison Ave. Shopping

on top-of-the-line designer goods extremely rewarding. Exotic special promotions regularly fill the store with the goods of a single country or region.

Galleries Lafayette New York (4–10 E. 57th St., tel. 212/259–2870). This new branch of the French fashion store, occupying the former site of Bonwit Teller, carries mostly French labels in an upscale assortment of better and designer apparel.

Henri Bendel (712–716 5th Ave., between 55th and 56th Sts., tel. 212/247–1100). Though under new ownership and a new roof (having moved from West 57th Street), Bendel's is still known for its savvy buying, stylish displays, and sophisticated little boutiques.

Lord & Taylor (424 5th Ave., between 38th and 39th Sts., tel. 212/391–3344). This store can be relied upon for the wearable, the fashionable, and the classic in clothes and accessories for women. It's refined, well-stocked and never overwhelming.

Macy's (Herald Sq., Broadway at 34th St., tel. 212/695–4400). No less than a miracle on 34th Street, Macy's main store is the largest retail store in America and the biggest on earth. Over the past two decades, it has grown chic enough to rival Bloomingdale's in the style department, but its main floor is reassuringly traditional. The latest trends are represented in almost every area the store covers. Estate Jewelry offers an excellent selection of fine antique pieces. And for cooking gear and housewares, the Cellar nearly outdoes Zabar's, with which it has an annual year-end caviar price war.

Saks Fifth Avenue (611 5th Ave., between 50th and 51st Sts., tel. 212/753–4000). This wonderful store still embodies the spirit of service and style with which it opened in 1926. Saks believes in good manners, the ceremonies of life, and dressing for the part; the selection for men, women, and children—now doubled by recent expansion—reflects this quality.

Specialty Shops

Antiques Antiquing is fine sport in Manhattan, and goods run the gamut from rarefied museum-quality to wacky, way-out, and eminently affordable. Premier shopping areas are on Madison Avenue north of 57th Street, and on 57th Street east of Fifth Avenue. Around 11th and 12th streets, between University Place and Broadway, a tantalizing array of settees, tables, bedsteads, and rocking chairs overflow onto the sidewalks in front of wholesalers with "To The Trade" signs on their doors; however, a card from your hometown architect or decorator may be all you need to get inside. Saturdays are the best time to find most dealers open.

Many small dealers cluster in two antiques "malls":

Manhattan Art & Antiques Center (1050 2nd Ave., between 55th and 56th Sts., tel. 212/355–4400). More than 100 dealers stocking everything from paisley and Judaica to satsuma, scientifica, and samovars jumble the three floors here. The level of quality is not, as a rule, up to that of Madison Avenue, but then neither are the prices.

Place des Antiquaires (125 E. 57th St., tel. 212/758–2900). From its 30-foot-high marble-paved entrance to its glittering glass-walled shops, this is a lavish place. Its dealers offer such high-end goods as 17th-century tapestries, export porcelain, American folk art, and Chinese textiles.

American and English **America Hurrah** (766 Madison Ave., between 65th and 66th Sts., 3rd floor, tel. 212/535–1930). Superb American patchwork quilts and other Americana can be found here.
David A. Schorsch (30 E. 76th St., No. 11A, tel. 212/439–6100). New York's Shaker specialist works by appointment only.
Florian Papp (962 Madison Ave., between 75th and 76th Sts. tel. 212/288–6770). This store has an unassailed reputation among knowledgeable collectors.
Hirschl & Adler Folk (851 Madison Ave., between 70th and 71st Sts., tel. 212/988–3655). This offshoot of the Hirschl & Adler Modern gallery is devoted to the best in Americana.
Hyde Park Antiques (836 Broadway, between 12th and 13th Sts., tel. 212/477–0033). This store features English decorative arts, William and Mary through Regency periods.
Israel Sack (15 E. 57th St., tel. 212/753–6562). This is widely considered one of the very best places in the country for 18th-century American furniture.
Leigh Keno American Furniture (19 E. 74th St., 1st floor, tel. 212/734–2381). Before he was 30, Leigh Keno set a new auction record in the American antiques field by paying $2.75 million for a hairy-paw-foot Philadelphia wing chair. He has a good eye and an interesting inventory, including some more-affordable pieces.
Steve Miller American Folk Art (17 E. 96th St., tel. 212/348–5219). This gallery is run by one of the country's premier folk art dealers, the author of *The Art of the Weathervane*.
Thomas K. Woodard (835 Madison Ave., between 69th and 70th Sts., 2nd floor, tel. 212/794–9404). Americana and antique quilts are among the specialties of this prestigious dealer.

Eclectic **Elliott Galleries** (155 E. 79th St., tel. 212/861–2222). Furniture and large accessories are upstairs; reproduction furniture—at lesser prices—below.
Newel Art Galleries (425 E. 53rd St., tel. 212/758–1970). Located in the heart of the East Side's interior design district, this six-story gallery, the city's biggest antiques store, has a huge collection that roams from the Renaissance to the 20th century.

European **Artisan Antiques** (81 University Pl. at 11th St., tel. 212/751–5214). Art Deco chandeliers come in merry profusion, along with lamps, sconces, and other lighting fixtures from France.
Barry Friedman (1117 Madison Ave., between 83rd and 84th Sts., tel. 212/794–8950). Wiener Werkstätte, Bauhaus, De Stijl, Russian Constructivist, and other European avant-gardists star.
Brass Antique Shop (32 Allen St., tel. 212/925–6660). Candlesticks, chandeliers, andirons, teapots, and other objects in brass, sterling, and copper fill the shelves and teeter on the tables in this old Lower East Side shop.
DeLorenzo (958 Madison Ave., between 75th and 76th Sts., tel. 212/249–7575). Come here to explore the sinuous curves, strongly articulated shapes, and highly polished surfaces of French Art Deco furniture and accessories at their best.
Didier Aaron (32 E. 67th St., tel. 212/988–5248). This highly esteemed gallery specializes in superb 18th- and 19th-century furniture and paintings.
Leo Kaplan Ltd. (967 Madison Ave., between 75th and 76th

Sts., tel. 212/249–6766). The impeccable items here include Art Nouveau glass, pottery, and porcelain from 18th-century England, stunning antique and modern paperweights, and Russian artworks, including creations by Fabergé.

Malmaison Antiques (253 E. 74th St., tel. 212/288–7569). This gallery has the country's largest selection of Empire furniture and decorative arts.

Pierre Deux Antiques (369 Bleecker St., tel. 212/243–7740). The company that brought French Provincial to America still offers an excellent selection.

Stair & Company (942 Madison Ave., between 74th and 75th Sts., tel. 212/517–4400). Period rooms stylishly show off fine 18th- and 19th-century English mahogany here.

Fun Stuff **Back Pages Antiques** (125 Greene St., tel. 212/460–5998). To acquire an antique juke box or slot machine, just drop in.

Darrow's Fun Antiques (309 E. 61st St., tel. 212/838–0730). The first of the city's nostalgia shops, the store is full of whimsy.

Apothecary and Fragrance Shops **Caswell-Massey** (518 Lexington Ave. at 48th St., tel. 212/755–2254). The original store displays its fragrant toiletries in polished old cases; branches are in the World Financial Center and South Street Seaport.

Essential Products Company (90 Water St., tel. 212/344–4288). This company, established in 1895, sells knockoffs of famous fragrances at a fraction of the original price tags.

Floris (703 Madison Ave., between 62nd and 63rd Sts., tel. 212/935–9100). Floral English toiletries beloved of such beauties as Cher, Sophia Loren, and Catherine Deneuve fill this re-creation of the cozy London original.

Art Galleries America's art capital, New York has numerous wealthy collectors, so many galleries are minimuseums (*see* also Auctions, below).

Aberbach Fine Art (980 Madison Ave., between 76th and 77th Sts., tel. 212/988–1100). Exhibits here include paintings and sculptures by various modern and contemporary artists.

André Emmerich Gallery (41 E. 57th St., tel. 212/752–0124). Located in the Art Deco Fuller Building, this gallery displays major works by major modern artists.

Art in General (79 Walker St., tel. 212/219–0473). This gallery exhibits works in a variety of mediums (including painting, sculpture, and photography), by emerging contemporary artists.

A Clean, Well-Lighted Place (363 Bleecker St., tel. 212/255–3656). Prints by well-known artists, including Sean Scully, Susan Rothenberg, Robert Motherwell, and David Hockney, are displayed here.

Coe Kerr (49 E. 82nd St., tel. 212/628–1340). The collection here spans 19th- and 20th-century American paintings.

Fred Dorfman, Inc. (123 Watts St., tel. 212/966–4611). This gallery has a reputation for being a place where dealers and collectors go to discover new pieces. You'll find paintings and graphics by Keith Haring, Roy Lichtenstein, Andy Warhol, and Mark Kostabi.

Gagosian (980 Madison Ave., between 76th and 77th Sts., tel. 212/744–2313). Works on display are by such artists as Richard Serra, Willem De Kooning, Jasper Johns, Frank Stella, Warhol, David Salle, and Philip Taaffe.

Gallery 121 (121 Spring St., tel. 212/925–4331). Featured are paintings, graphics, and sculptures by such artists as Erté,

Peter Max, Salvador Dali, Haring, Joan Miró, James Rizzi, and Warhol.

Isselbacher (41 E. 78th St., tel. 212/472–1766). This gallery offers prints by late-19th- and 20th-century masters such as Henri Toulouse-Lautrec, Henri Matisse, Marc Chagall, Miró, Pablo Picasso, and Edvard Munch.

Multiple Impressions (128 Spring St., tel. 212/925–1313). Twentieth-century American, European, and South American paintings and prints are offered here at reasonable prices.

O. K. Harris (383 W. Broadway, tel. 212/431–3600). The oldest gallery in SoHo, opened in 1969, O. K. Harris showcases paintings, sculpture, and photography by contemporary artists.

Pace Gallery (32 E. 57th St., tel. 212/421–3292). This gallery features such well-known modern and contemporary artists as Picasso, Alexander Calder, and Julian Schnabel.

Paula Cooper (149 and 155 Wooster St., tel. 212/674–0766). Exhibits include contemporary paintings and sculpture.

SoHo Photo (15 White St., tel. 212/226–8571). In the heart of TriBeCa, this gallery exhibits various photographers' work.

Wally Findlay Gallery (17 E. 57th St., tel. 212/421–5390). The specialty here is 20th-century art.

Books With so many of the country's publishing houses, magazines, and writers based here, there is an abundance of book shops, small and large. Of course, all the big national chains are here—Barnes & Noble, B. Dalton, Brentano's, Doubleday, Waldenbooks—with branches all over town.

Biography Bookshop (400 Bleecker St., tel. 212/807–8655). Diaries, letters, and other biographical and autobiographical material from small and large publishers worldwide fill this tidy, well-organized store.

Books & Company (939 Madison Ave., between 74th and 75th Sts., tel. 212/737–1450). A comfy sofa invites lingering here.

Coliseum Books (1771 Broadway at 57th St., tel. 212/757–8381). This supermarket of a bookstore has a huge, quirky selection of remainders, best-sellers, and scholarly works. Its late hours are worth knowing about.

Endicott Booksellers (450 Columbus Ave., between 81st and 82nd Sts., tel. 212/787–6300). This intelligent, wood-paneled bookstore features evening readings.

Gotham Book Mart (41 W. 47th St., tel. 212/719–4448). The late Frances Steloff opened this store years ago with just $200 in her pocket, half of it on loan. But she helped launch D. H. Lawrence and Henry Miller and is now legendary among bibliophiles, as is her bookstore, an oasis for those who truly love to read. Solid fiction and nonfiction are emphasized in the collection of nearly a quarter of a million books and 50,000 magazines. Though organization may seem haphazard, the knowledgeable staff can help you find what you want.

Irish Books & Graphics (580 Broadway at Prince St., tel. 212/274–1923). Here you'll find the country's widest selection of books about Ireland, both current and out-of-print titles.

Librairie de France/Libraria Hispanica (610 5th Ave., in Rockefeller Ctr., tel. 212/581–8810; 115 5th Ave. at 19th St., tel. 212/673–7400). These huge collections of foreign-language books, periodicals, and records are among the country's largest.

Madison Avenue Bookshop (833 Madison Ave., between 69th and 70th Sts., tel. 212/535–6130). Serious stuff is sold here in pleasant surroundings.

Rizzoli (31 W. 57th St., tel. 212/759–2424; 454 West Broadway, tel. 212/674–1616; World Financial Center, tel. 212/385–1400). An elegant marble entrance, oak paneling, chandeliers, and classical music accompany a stock of records and books on art, architecture, dance, design, foreign language, and travel uptown; the selection downtown, strong on business and children's titles, comes without the fin-de-siècle frills.

Shakespeare & Company (2259 Broadway at 81st St., tel. 212/580–7800). The stock here represents what's happening in publishing today in just about every field. Late hours are a plus.

Children's Books **Books of Wonder** (464 Hudson St., tel. 212/645–8006; 132 7th Ave. at 18th St., tel. 212/989–3270). This store offers an excellent stock of children's books for all reading levels. Oziana is a specialty, and the 18th Street branch offers antique books as well as new publications.

Eeyore's Books for Children (2212 Broadway, between 78th and 79th Sts., tel. 212/362–0634; 25 E. 83rd St., tel. 212/988–3404). The large, shrewd selection here should delight any young reader. Weekend story hours and author appearances please the under-6 crowd.

Maps **Hagstrom Map and Travel Center** (57 W. 43rd St., tel. 212/398–1222). This may be the ultimate map store.

Rand McNally Map & Travel (150 E. 52nd St., tel. 212/758–7488). The excellent selection covers the world.

Music **Joseph Patelson Music House** (160 W. 56th St., tel. 212/582–5840). A huge collection of scores has long made this the heart of the music lover's New York.

Mystery and Suspense Whodunits are the specialty at: **Foul Play** (302 W. 12th St. at Bank St., tel. 212/675–5115; 1465 2nd Ave., between 76th and 77th Sts., tel. 212/517–3222); **Murder Ink** (271 W. 87th St., tel. 212/362–8905); and **Mysterious Bookshop** (129 W. 56th St., tel. 212/765–0900).

Rare and Used Books **Argosy Bookstore** (116 E. 59th St., tel. 212/753–4455). This sedate nook keeps a scholarly stock of books and autographs.

J. N. Bartfield Books (30 W. 57th St., 3rd floor, tel. 212/245–8890). This legend in the field offers old and antiquarian books distinguished by binding, author, edition, or content.

Pageant Print and Book Shop (109 E. 9th St., tel. 212/674–5296). Michael Caine browsed in this relic of old New York in Woody Allen's *Hannah and Her Sisters*.

Strand (828 Broadway at 12th St., tel. 212/473–1452). Eight miles of shelves house more than two million books at this biggest of Manhattan's used-book stores. Among them are antiquarian books, fiction, nonfiction, how-to, and history—remainders and reviewer's copies, as well as secondhand titles.

Travel Books **Complete Traveller Bookstore** (199 Madison Ave. at 35th St., tel. 212/685–9007). Old and new titles are sold here.

Traveller's Bookstore (22 W. 52nd St., tel. 212/664–0995). The stock includes essays and novels, as well as maps and guides.

Cameras and Electronics **Bi-Rite** (15 E. 30th St., tel. 212/685–2130). Once your turn comes, this tiny discounter's Hasidic salesmen offer good service, great prices. Take model numbers; there's no showroom.

47th Street Photo (67 W. 47th St., 115 W. 45th St., and other locations; tel. 212/398–1410). Prices can be better elsewhere, but these stores manned by Hasidic Jews are a heavyweight among electronics discounters. Note Friday and Saturday closings.

Harvey Electronics (2 W. 45th St., tel. 212/575–5000). A well-informed staff offers top-of-the-line audio equipment.

Willoughby's (110 W. 32nd St., tel. 212/564–1600). Calling itself the world's largest camera store, Willoughby's rates high among amateurs and pros for selection and service.

220V Appliances **Dembitzer Brothers** (5 Essex St., tel. 212/254–1310) and **Thor Export Sales Company** (1225 Broadway at 30th St., Suite 706, tel. 212/679–0077) offer products wired for international eletrical wiring.

Children's Clothing **Bébé Thompson** (98 Thompson St., tel. 212/925–1122). Downtown style is evident here: plenty of black-and-white and jungle prints among the embroidered treasures.

Cerutti (807 Madison Ave., between 67th and 68th Sts., tel. 212/737–7540). This is where Nanny takes her Little Princess, and Yoko Ono shopped for Sean Lennon when he was a tyke.

Citykids (130 7th Ave., between 17th and 18th Sts., tel. 212/620–0120). This busy store carries colorful, fun clothing and accessories. Don't miss the hand-painted T-shirts and sweatshirts with New York themes.

Greenstones & Cie (442 Columbus Ave., between 81st and 82nd Sts., tel. 212/580–4322). Catering to junior Yuppies, this store offers some handsome clothes, particularly sweaters.

Wicker Garden and Wicker Garden's Baby (1318 and 1327 Madison Ave., near 93rd St., tel. 212/410–7000). Top-of-the-line pretties for boys, girls, babies, and their rooms are sold here.

Resale Shops **Once Upon A Time** (171 E. 92nd St., tel. 212/831–7619) and **Second Act Children's Wear** (1046 Madison Ave. at 80th St., tel. 212/988–2440) offer gently worn children's wear, sizes 0–14.

Crystal Three peerless sources are: **Baccarat** (625 Madison Ave., between 58th and 59th Sts., tel. 212/826–4100); **Hoya Crystal Gallery** (450 Park Ave., between 56th and 57th Sts., tel. 212/223–6335); and **Steuben** (717 5th Ave. at 56th St., tel. 212/752–1441).

Food For food lovers, New York's gourmet specialty shops are a truly moveable feast: Much of the food can travel home with you.

Caviar **Macy's** and **Zabar's** (*see* below) feature good deals on caviars; **Caviarteria** (29 E. 60th St., tel. 212/759–7410) and **Petrossian** (182 W. 58th St., tel. 212/245–2217) are specialists.

Chocolate and Candy **Elk Candy Company** (240 E. 86th St., tel. 212/650–1177). This is a marzipan fantasy and a chocoholic's sweet dream.

Godiva Chocolatier (Madison Ave. at 67th St., tel. 212/249–9444; 701 5th Ave., between 54th and 55th Sts., tel. 212/593–2845; 560 Lexington Ave. at 50th St., tel. 212/980–9810; 85 Broad St., tel. 212/514–6240). This famous maker features cleverly molded chocolates—and oh, those embossed gold boxes!

Li-Lac Chocolates (120 Christopher St., tel. 212/242–7374). This unpretentious nook feeds the Village's sweet tooth.

Neuchatel Chocolates (2 W. 59th St., in the Plaza Hotel, tel. 212/751–7742; 55 E. 52nd St., in Park Avenue Plaza between Park and Madison, tel. 212/759–1388). Velvety chocolates come in five dozen varieties here—all made in New York to approximate the Swiss chocolates.

Teuscher Chocolates (620 5th Ave., in Rockefeller Ctr., tel. 212/246–4416; 25 E. 61st St., tel. 212/751–8482). Fabulous chocolates made in Switzerland are flown in weekly for sale in these jewel-box shops, newly decorated each season.

Coffee **Empire Coffee and Tea Company** (592 9th Ave., between 42nd and 43rd Sts., tel. 212/586–1717). The selection here numbers almost 90 different beans.

McNulty's Tea & Coffee Company (109 Christopher St., tel. 212/242–5351). Antique wood paneling says "Old New York"; the barrels of beans say "Timor," "Java," or "New Guinea."

Porto Rico Importing Company (201 Bleecker St., tel. 212/477–5421). This dark, old-fashioned, and highly aromatic store has been a local coffee source since 1907.

Gourmet Markets **Balducci's** (424 6th Ave. at 9th St., tel. 212/673–2600). In this former mom-and-pop food shop, now one of the city's finest food stores, mounds of baby carrots keep company with frilly lettuce, feathery dill, and superlative meats, fish, cheeses, chocolates, baked goods, pastas, vinegars, oils, crackers, and prepared foods.

Dean & DeLuca (560 Broadway at Prince St., tel. 212/431–1691). This huge SoHo trendsetter, splendidly bright white, has an encyclopedic selection, from the austere cheese counter to the shelves of crackers and the display cases of prepared foods.

Kam-Man (200 Canal St., tel. 212/571–0330). The city's premier Chinese market, Kam-Man is stuffed with bizarre exotic foods. The staccato sound of Chinese and the mysterious smells make a stop here like an instant trip to Asia.

Zabar's (2245 Broadway at 80th St., tel. 212/787–2000). Visit here not so much to snap up everything in sight—Zabar's now sells by mail order, too—as to enjoy the atmosphere of one of New York's favorite feeding troughs. As you're exploring the possibilities among the jams and jellies from a dozen makers and several countries, or checking out the barrels of coffees or the wonderful array of teas, keep an eye peeled for celebrities—perhaps the first violinist with the New York Philharmonic or the villainness on a long-running soap opera. Dried herbs and spices, dried fruits, chocolates, and assorted bottled foods are downstairs, along with a fragrant jumble of fresh breads and the cheese, meat, and smoked-fish counters. Upstairs is one of New York's largest selections of kitchenware.

Wine **Acker Merrall & Condit** (160 W. 72nd St., tel. 212/787–1700). Known for its selection of red burgundies, this store has knowledgeable, helpful personnel.

Garnet Liquors (929 Lexington Ave., between 68th and 69th Sts., tel. 212/772–3211). Its fine selection includes champagne at prices that one wine writer called "almost charitable."

Morrell & Company (535 Madison Ave., near 54th St., tel. 212/688–9370). Peter Morrell is a well-regarded and very colorful figure in the wine business.

Sherry Lehmann (679 Madison Ave., between 61st and 62nd Sts., tel. 212/838–7500). It's a New York institution.

Sokolin (178 Madison Ave., between 33rd and 34th Sts., tel. 212/532–5893). Knowledgeable oenophiles shop here.

Goldstar (103–05 Queens Blvd., Forest Hills, Queens, tel. 718/459–0200). This may be tops in the country for Italian wine.

Fun and Games These are stores by adults, for adults, but with such humor and whimsy that kids will like them, too.

Compleat Strategist (11 E. 33rd St., tel. 212/685–3880; 320 W. 57th St., tel. 212/582–1272). All kinds of strategy games are supplied for the serious enthusiast.

Darts Unlimited (30 E. 20th St., tel. 212/533–8684). English darts and boards are exquisitely crafted at this specialist.

Game Show (474 6th Ave., between 11th and 12th Sts., tel. 212/633–6328). The mix here includes board games, box games, and card games.

Little Rickie (49½ 1st Ave. at 3rd St., tel. 212/505–6467). This fun spot is packed with wacky novelties and vintage treasures that baby-boomers remember from childhood.

Louis Tannen's (6 W. 32nd St., 4th floor, tel. 212/239–8383). You'll find sword chests, dove-a-matics, magic wands, and crystal balls, not to mention the all-important top hats with rabbits, at this six-decades-old magicians' supply house.

Marion & Company (315 W. 39th St., 16th floor, tel. 212/594–1848). Playing cards come in all shapes and sizes here.

Mouse N' Around (A&S Plaza, 7th floor, tel. 212/947–3954). Clothing for kids and grownups here all comes emblazoned with cartoon favorites like Mickey, Minnie, and the Jetsons.

Mythology (370 Columbus Ave., between 77th and 78th Sts., tel. 212/874–0774). This store stocks nearly everything with a sense of the fanciful, from robots to antique toys.

Only Hearts (386 Columbus Ave. at 79th St., tel. 212/724–5608). Romance is the theme. Heart-shaped waffle irons, anyone?

Star Magic (743 Broadway, between 8th St. and Astor Pl., tel. 212/228–7770; 275 Amsterdam Ave. at 73rd St., tel. 212/769–2020; 1256 Lexington Ave., between 84th and 85th Sts., tel. 212/988–0300). Astronomy meets New Age in a clutter of crystals, star charts, and other celestial playthings.

The Cat Store (562 Amsterdam Ave. at 87th St., tel. 212/595–8728). Everything's coming up cats here.

The Last Wound-Up (290 Columbus Ave., between 73rd and 74th Sts., tel. 212/787–3388; 889 Broadway at 19th St., tel. 212/529–4197). "If it winds up, it winds up here" is one motto of this store. The other is "Don't postpone joy."

Think Big! (390 West Broadway, between Broome and Spring Sts., tel. 212/925–7300). Huge replicas of various ordinary objects stock this amusing store.

Gizmos and Whatchamacallits

Hammacher Schlemmer (147 E. 57th St., tel. 212/421–9000). The store that offered America the first pop-up toaster, the first automatic steam iron, and the first telephone answering machine and microwave oven still ferrets out the outrageous, the unusual, and the best-of-kind.

Sharper Image (Pier 17, South St. Seaport, tel. 212/693–0477; 4 W. 57th St., tel. 212/265–2550). This retail outlet of the catalogue company stocks gifts for the pampered executive who has everything.

Home Decor and Gifts

Aris Mixon & Company (381 Amsterdam Ave., between 78th and 79th Sts., tel. 212/724–6904). The intrigue here is in the mix of newly manufactured, handmade, and antique.

Avventura (463 Amsterdam Ave., between 82nd and 83rd Sts., tel. 212/769–2510). Glory in Italian design in all its streamlined beauty here. Tabletop items and accessories are all stunning.

Be Seated (66 Greenwich Ave., between 11th St. and 7th Ave., tel. 212/924–8444). Manhattan's source for the world's best basketwork is redolent of rattan and raffia.

Charlotte Moss & Company (1027 Lexington Ave., between

73rd and 74th Sts., tel. 212/772–3320). Within what looks like a vine-wrapped, chintz-cozy English country house, you'll find English country-house-style treasures.

Cherchez (862 Lexington Ave., between 64th and 65th Sts., tel. 212/737–8215). Potpourri and dried flowers keep company with antique linens in this vision of the sweetly scented good life.

Conran's (2–8 Astor Pl., tel. 212/505–1515; 160 E. 54th St. in Citicorp Ctr., tel. 212/371–2225; 2248 Broadway at 81st St., tel. 212/873–9250). This outpost of the British Habitat store features components of a stylish yet not-too-expensive life.

Contre-Jour (190 Columbus Ave., between 68th and 69th Sts., tel. 212/877–7900). Don't miss it to see whatever's au courant in blown glass and sculpted wood, teapots, and tableware.

D. F. Sanders (386 West Broadway, tel. 212/925–9040; 952 Madison Ave., between 75th and 76th Sts., tel. 212/879–6161). The sleek, postmodern items on display at these design centers are destined to be classics.

Dot Zero (165 5th Ave. at 22nd St., tel. 212/533–8322). The spirit of this store is ultracontemporary, but often playful.

Gazebo (127 E. 57th St., tel. 212/832–7077). Quilts and wicker overflow this bastion of American style.

Jenny B. Goode (1194 Lexington Ave., between 80th and 81st Sts., tel. 212/794–2492; 11 E. 10th St., tel. 212/505–7666). Charming china serving pieces and bibelots star.

Mabel's (849 Madison Ave., between 70th and 71st Sts., tel. 212/734–3263). Enchanting animal lovers is the business of this Noah's Ark of knickknacks in animal shapes.

Pottery Barn (117 E. 59th St., tel. 212/753–5424; 2109 Broadway, between 73rd and 74th Sts., tel. 212/595–5573; 250 W. 57th St., tel. 212/315–1855; 231 10th Ave., between 23rd and 24th Sts., tel. 212/206–8118; and other locations). The emphasis here is on setting the oh-so-chic table. Overstocks are discounted at Tenth Avenue.

Wolfman-Gold & Good Company (116 Greene St., tel. 212/431–1888). Half antique and half contemporary in spirit, this chic SoHo shop, a major New York trendsetter, is all white, with touches of blond wood and wicker. Tableware is the focus.

Zona (97 Greene St., tel. 212/925–6750). SoHo's airy, high-ceilinged bastion of the Southwestern look offers Solieri bells, earth-toned textiles, and terra-cottas, all artfully displayed.

Linens Luxurious linens enchant at **D. Porthault** (18 E. 69th St., tel. 212/688–1660), **E. Braun** (717 Madison Ave., between 63rd and 64th Sts., tel. 212/838–0650), **Frette** (779 Madison Ave., between 67th and 68th Sts., tel. 212/988–5221), and **Pratesi** (829 Madison Ave. at 69th St., tel. 212/288–2315). Chic prevails at lower prices at **Ad Hoc Softwares** (410 West Broadway at Spring St., tel. 212/925–2652), **Descamps** (723 Madison Ave., between 63rd and 64th Sts., tel. 212/355–2522, and 454 Columbus Ave. at 82nd St., tel. 212/874–8690), and **Sheridan** (595 Madison Ave. at 57th St., tel. 212/308–0120). For bargains, check out the Lower East Side's dry goods merchants (most on Grand St.) and **Century 21** (12 Cortlandt St. between Broadway and Church St., tel. 212/227–9092).

Jewelry, Watches, and Silver Most of the world's premier jewelers have retail outlets in New York, and the nation's jewelry wholesale center is on 47th Street.

A La Vieille Russie (781 5th Ave., between 59th and 60th Sts., tel. 212/752–1727). Stop here to behold, up close, bibelots by

Fabergé and others, encrusted with jewels or exquisitely enameled.

Buccellati (725 5th Ave., between 56th and 57th Sts. in Trump Tower, tel. 212/308–5533). The oversize Italian jewelry here makes a statement. Silver is around the corner (46 E. 57th St., tel. 212/308–2507).

Bulgari (730 5th Ave. at 57th St., and 2 E. 61st St., in the Pierre Hotel, tel. 212/486–0086). The expertly crafted jewelry here has an understated, tailored look.

Cartier (2 E. 52nd St., tel. 212/753–0111). Simple but superb pieces are displayed in the former mansion of the late yachtsman and society king Morton F. Plant.

David Webb (455 Park Ave., at 57th St., tel. 212/421–3030) features gem-studded pieces, often enameled and in animal forms. Anything but understated.

Fortunoff (681 5th Ave., between 53rd and 54th Sts., tel. 212/758–6660). Good prices on gold and silver jewelry, flatware, and hollowware draw crowds to this large store.

Harry Winston (718 5th Ave. at 56th St., tel. 212/245–2000). The moneyed clientele here appreciates this store's oversized stones and impeccable quality.

H. Stern (645 Fifth Ave., between 50th and 51st Sts., tel. 212/688–0330). Colored gemstones in contemporary settings are the specialty of this Brazilian firm. A boutique on the second floor sells objets d'art in semiprecious stones.

James Robinson (15 E. 57th St., tel. 212/752–6166). This family-owned business features wonderful new and antique silver, fine estate jewelry, and table accessories.

Jean's Silversmiths (16 W. 45th St., tel. 212/575–0723). Where to replace the butter knife missing from your great-aunt's set? Try this dusty, crowded shop.

Tiffany & Co. (727 5th Ave., at 57th St., tel. 212/755–8000). A shiny robin's egg blue box from this venerable New York jeweler announces the contents as something very special. Along with the $50,000 platinum-and-diamond bracelets, there is a great deal that's affordable on a whim.

Van Cleef & Arpels (744 5th Ave. at 57th St., tel. 212/644–9500). The jewelry here is sheer perfection.

Costume Jewelry Fabulously faux wares can be found at **Ciro** (711 5th Ave. at 56th St., tel. 212/752–0441, and other locations); **Kenneth Jay Lane** (725 5th Ave., in Trump Tower, tel. 212/751–6166); **Mishon Mishon** (899 Madison Ave., between 72nd and 73rd Sts., tel. 212/288–7599); and **Ylang Ylang** (806 Madison Ave., between 67th and 68th Sts., tel. 212/879–7028; 324 Columbus Ave., between 75th and 76th Sts., tel. 212/496–0319; and 4 W. 57th St., tel. 212/247–3598).

Luggage and Leather Goods **Beltrami** (711 5th Ave., between 55th and 56th Sts., tel. 212/838–4101). Italian leathers are this store's stock in trade.

Bottega Veneta (635 Madison Ave., between 59th and 60th Sts., tel. 212/319–0303). The superb goods here are for people who know real quality.

Crouch & Fitzgerald (400 Madison Ave. at 48th St., tel. 212/755–5888). Since 1839, this store has offered a terrific selection in hard- and soft-sided luggage, plus handbags.

Fine & Klein (119 Orchard St., tel. 212/674–6720). Fabulous handbags are discounted here.

Lederer (613 Madison Ave. at 58th St., tel. 212/355–5515). The excellent selection here includes exotic skins.

North Beach Leather (772 Madison Ave. at 66th St., tel. 212/

772–0707). High fashion leather wear comes in many colors here.

T. Anthony (480 Park Ave. at 58th St., tel. 212/750–9797). This store's hard- and soft-sided luggage of coated fabric with leather trim has brass fasteners that look like precision machines.

Menswear Because New York is home to movie moguls, architects, writers, and international lawyers, bankers, and businessmen, its department and specialty stores offer a number of looks.

Alan Flusser Shop (14 E. 52nd St., tel. 212/888–7100). Fans come here for the designer's unusual traditional look.

Brooks Brothers (346 Madison Ave. at 44th St., tel. 212/682–8800). The bare travertine underfoot, high ceilings overhead, and undecorated showcases on the ground floor suggest a New England spareness at this institution in American menswear. Styles are conservative, and tailoring standards are extremely high—as they have always been.

Frank Stella Ltd. (440 Columbus Ave. at 81st St., tel. 212/877–5566; 1382 6th Ave., between 56th and 57th Sts., tel. 212/757–2295). Classic clothing with subtle variations is offered here.

F. R. Tripler (366 Madison Ave. at 46th St., tel. 212/922–1090). Oxxford, Hickey Freeman, and other top-notch manufacturers are represented here. The styles are a bit less conservative than at Brooks Brothers.

J. Press (7 E. 44th St., tel. 212/687–7642). This store emphasizes the oxford-cloth shirt, the natural-shoulder suit, the madras-patch Bermuda shorts, and the amusing club tie.

Louis, Boston (131 E. 57th St., tel. 212/308–6100). Luxurious conservative fashions from this estimable New England clothier have garbed four generations of Harvard men.

Mano à Mano (580 Broadway, between Houston and Prince Sts., tel. 212/219–9602). SoHo chic prevails here.

Paul Smith (108 5th Ave. at 16th St., tel. 212/627–9770). Dark mahogany Victorian cases display downtown styles.

Paul Stuart (Madison Ave. at 45th St., tel. 212/682–0320). In this celebrated retailer, the fabric selection is interesting, the tailoring superb, and the look traditional but not stodgy.

Saint Laurie, Ltd. (897 Broadway, between 19th and 20th Sts., tel. 212/473–0100). This family-owned business sells suits manufactured on the premises in styles ranging from the boxy to the Italianate in lovely fabrics. Prices are lower than for comparable garments elsewhere, but still not cheap.

Wallachs (555 5th Ave. at 46th St., tel. 212/687–0106). Here you'll find good service and a sound collection of reasonably priced classics.

Discounts New York men looking for bargains rely on **BFO** (149 5th Ave. at 21st St., 6th floor, tel. 212/254–0059); **Eisenberg and Eisenberg** (85 5th Ave. at 16th St., tel. 212/627–1290); **Moe Ginsburg** (162 5th Ave. at 21st St., tel. 212/242–3482); **Rothman's** (200 Park Ave. S at 17th St., tel. 212/777–7400); and **Syms** (42 Trinity Pl., tel. 212/797–1199; cash only).

Men's Shoes **Church English Shoes** (428 Madison Ave. at 49th St., tel. 212/755–4313). This store has been selling beautifully made English shoes since 1873; the fitters are especially knowledgeable.

To Boot (256 Columbus Ave., between 71st and 72nd Sts., tel. 212/724–8249). Here you'll find stylish shoes and boots for a more fashionable business look.

Needlecraft
Fabric

Seamstresses prize the selection and prices at shops in the upper 30s between Broadway and Eighth Avenue, such as **C&B** (250 W. 39th St., tel. 212/354–9360). Luxurious imports fill **Jerry Brown** (37 W. 57th St., tel. 212/753–3626), **Paron** (60 W. 57th St., tel. 212/247–6451), **Paron II** (56 W. 57th St.), which discounts remnants, and **Weller** (54 W. 57th St., tel. 212/247–3790). **Liberty of London** (630 5th Ave. at 51st St., tel. 212/459–0080) stocks the famous English florals and paisleys.

Trimming

Dingy 38th Street between Fifth and Sixth avenues is a treasure chest. Jewels include **Hyman Hendler & Sons** (67 W. 38th St., tel. 212/840–8393), the ribbon king, since 1900; and **Tinsel Trading** (47 W. 38th St., tel. 212/730–1030), for new and antique trims and tassels. Uptown, buttons cram **Tender Buttons** (143 E. 62nd St., tel. 212/758–7004).

Yarns

Erica Wilson (717 Madison Ave., between 63rd and 64th Sts., 2nd floor, tel. 212/832–7290). The eponymous British-born needlepoint authority is a top resource.

New York Yarn Center (1011 6th Ave., between 37th and 38th Sts., 2nd floor, tel. 212/719–5648). There's a huge selection of yarns here to suit many purposes.

Pamela Duval (833 Lexington Ave., between 63rd and 64th Sts., tel. 212/751–2126). Look for the needlepoint canvases with funny quotations.

Paper, Greeting Cards, Stationery

Dempsey & Carroll (110 E. 57th St., tel. 212/486–7508). Supplying New York's high society for a century, this firm is always correct, but seldom straitlaced.

Kate's Paperie (8 W. 13th St., tel. 212/633–0570). This wonderful spot features fabulous wrapping papers, some handmade; bound blank books; and more.

Untitled (159 Prince St., tel. 212/982–2088). The stock here includes thousands of tasteful greeting cards and postcards.

Performing Arts Memorabilia

The Ballet Shop (1887 Broadway, between 62nd and 63rd Sts., tel. 212/581–7990). This balletomane's delight near Lincoln Center showcases dance ephemera and artifacts.

Drama Book Shop (723 7th Ave., between 48th and 49th Sts., tel. 212/944–0595). The comprehensive stock here includes scripts, scores, and libretti.

Memory Shop (109 E. 12th St., tel. 212/473–2404). Movie stills and posters by the million are on sale here.

Motion Picture Arts Gallery (133 E. 58th St., 10th floor, tel. 212/223–1009). Vintage posters enchant collectors here.

Movie Star News (134 W. 18th St., tel. 212/620–8160). The film memorabilia emphasizes Hollywood glamour.

One Shubert Alley (Shubert Alley, between 44th and 45th Sts. west of Broadway, tel. 212/944–4133). Show-biz souvenirs reign at this Theater District shop.

Richard Stoddard (18 E. 16th St., Room 305, tel. 212/645–9576). This veteran dealer offers out-of-print books, back issues of magazines, old programs, and other printed matter.

Theatrebooks (1600 Broadway, between 48th and 49th Sts., Room 1009, tel. 212/757–2834). This is a good place to schmooze and browse.

Triton Gallery (323 W. 45th, between 8th and 9th Aves., tel. 212/765–2472). Theatricals!

Posters

Posteramerica (138 W. 18th St., tel. 212/206–0499). Victorian to 20th-century posters are displayed in this renovated carriage house, the country's oldest store of its type.

Records The city's best record stores match its music scene: diversified, esoteric, and very in-the-know. They also provide browsers with a window to New York's hipper subcultures.

Bleecker Bob's Golden Oldies (118 W. 3rd St., tel. 212/475–9677). The staff sells punk, new wave, progressive rock, reggae, and R&B until the wee hours.

Footlight Records (113 E. 12th St., tel. 212/533–1572). Stop here to browse through New York's largest selection of old musicals and movie soundtracks.

Gryphon Record Shop (251 W. 72nd St., 2nd floor, tel. 212/874–1588). *New York* magazine called this the city's best rare-record store, citing its 40,000 out-of-print and rare LPs.

HMV (2081 Broadway at 72nd St., tel. 212/721–5900, and 1280 Lexington Ave. at 86th St., tel. 212/348–0800). The tidal wave of the Manhattan music scene in 1990, these state-of-the-art record superstores stocking 800,000 disks, tapes, and videos are giving Tower Records a run for its money.

House of Oldies (35 Carmine St., tel. 212/243–0500). The specialty here is records made between 1950 and the present—45s and 78s, as well as LPs; there are more than a million titles.

Jazz Record Center (135 W. 29th St., 12th floor, tel. 212/594–9880). Here is the city's only jazz-record specialist.

J&R Music World (23 Park Row, tel. 212/732–8600). This store offers a huge selection with good prices on major releases.

Midnight Records (263 W. 23rd St., tel. 212/675–2768). This rare rock specialist stocks obscure artists from the '50s on.

Tower Records (692 Broadway at 4th St., tel. 212/505–1500; 1965 Broadway at 66th St., tel. 212/799–2500). The founder's objective here—to offer every record in the world—has been complicated by the onslaught of CDs and tapes, but it does suggest the broad scope of selection in all three mediums. The scene is pure New York; at the Village branch, the black leather usually goes with pink, green, or tiger-striped hair in bizarre cuts; the Upper West Side outlet has good selection but less local color.

Souvenirs of New York City Ordinary Big Apple souvenirs can be found in and around major tourist attractions. More unusual items can be found at:

Accent New York (489 5th Ave., between 41st and 42nd Sts., tel. 212/599–3661). This store features every possible variation of the New York souvenir T-shirt, mug, key chain, etc.

Citybooks (61 Chambers St., tel. 212/669–8245). Come here for photo calendars, maps, books, seals, subway token tietacks and letter openers, traffic signs ("Don't Even Think of Parking Here"), Sanitation Department T-shirts, and even teddy bears wearing miniature versions of the above.

New York Bound Bookshop (50 Rockefeller Plaza, tel. 212/245–8503). Old or rare New York books and prints are the specialty in this delightfully knowledgeable store.

Think New York (875 7th Ave., between 55th and 56th Sts., tel. 212/957–8511). New York City stars on mugs, aprons, and many other objects, some surprising and unusual.

Toys Many toy companies are headquartered here, and the windows of the Toy Center at 23rd Street and Fifth Avenue display the latest thing, especially during February's Toy Week, when all the out-of-town buyers come to place orders for the Christmas season (*see also* Fun and Games, above).

Enchanted Forest (85 Mercer St., tel. 212/925–6677). Fancy reigns in this shop's stock of unique handmades.

F.A.O. Schwarz (767 5th Ave. at 58th St., tel. 212/644–9400). You will be hooked on this sprawling two-level children's store from the minute you walk through the door and one of the costumed staff members—a donkey, a clown, a cave woman, or a mad scientist—extends a welcome. In front of you is a wonderful mechanical clock with many dials and dingbats; beyond are all the stuffed animals in the world, dolls large and small, things to build with (including blocks by the pound), things to play dress-up with, computer things, games, toy cars (including a multi-thousand-dollar Ferrari), and much more.

Penny Whistle Toys (132 Spring St., tel. 212/925–2088; 448 Columbus Ave., between 81st and 82nd Sts., tel. 212/873–9090; 1283 Madison Ave., between 91st and 92nd Sts., tel. 212/369–3868). Meredith Brokaw, wife of newscaster Tom Brokaw, has developed an intriguing selection of quality toys here.

West Side Kids (498 Amsterdam Ave., at 84th St., tel. 212/496–7282). The shrewd selection here mixes educational toys with a grab bag of fun little playthings.

Dolls and Miniatures **Dollhouse Antics** (1343 Madison Ave. at 94th St., tel. 212/876–2288). This is a miniaturist's paradise, with infinitesimal accessories such as a small *New York Times*.

Toy Soldiers **The Soldier Shop** (1222 Madison Ave. at 88th St., tel. 212/535–6788). Lead soldiers old and new parade by the hundreds here.

Trains and Models Railroad aficionados will be dazzled by the vast selections at: **America's Hobby Center** (146 W. 22nd St., tel. 212/675–8922); **Polk Hobby** (314 5th Ave., tel. 212/279–9034); **Red Caboose** (16 W. 45th St., 4th floor, tel. 212/575–0155); and **Train Shop** (23 W. 45th St., basement level, tel. 212/730–0409).

Umbrellas and Canes **Stanley Novak** (115 W. 30th St., Room 400, tel. 212/947–8466). The cane's the thing, and there are hundreds here.
Uncle Sam Umbrella (161 W. 57th St., tel. 212/247–7163). The city's top umbrella dealer offers both basics and oddball stuff.

Women's Clothing The department stores' collections are always good: **Saks** for its designers; **Macy's** for its breadth; **Bloomingdale's** for its extremes; **Barneys** for its trendy chic; and **Lord & Taylor** for its classicism. The following add another dimension.

Trendsetters **Charivari** (2315 Broadway, between 83rd and 84th Sts., tel. 212/873–1424). Since Selma Weiser founded this store on the Upper West Side, she has made a name for herself internationally for her eagle eye on the up-and-coming and avant-garde. The branches, too, take a high-style, if pricey, approach: **Charivari Sport** (201 W. 79th St., tel. 212/799–8650); **Charivari Workshop** (441 Columbus Ave. at 81st St., tel. 212/496–8700); **Charivari 72** (257 Columbus Ave. at 72nd St., tel. 212/787–7272); and **Charivari 57** (18 W. 57th St., tel. 212/333–4040).
Parachute (121 Wooster St., tel. 212/925–8630). The SoHo styles here are what you need for your next club date.
Patricia Field (10 E. 8th St., tel. 212/254–1699). This store collects the essence of the downtown look.
La Rue des Rêves (139 Spring St., tel. 212/226–6736). Stylish clothing for stylish women who like either an elegant, understated look or Tina Turner styles.

Salons Members of New York's charity-ball set drop more on a single dress than most of us spend on a year's wardrobe at **Sara**

Fredericks (508 Park Ave., between 59th and 60th Sts., tel. 212/759–1254); **Martha** (475 Park Ave. at 58th St., tel. 212/753–1511; 725 5th Ave., in Trump Tower, tel. 212/826–8855) and **Martha International** (473 Park Ave., between 57th and 58th Sts., tel. 212/371–7400), where the look is more youthful.

Designer Showcases
Alaïa New York (131 Mercer St., tel. 212/941–1166). The Paris-based designer shows his body-conscious clothing here.

Betsey Johnson (130 Thompson St., tel. 212/420–0169; 248 Columbus Ave., between 71st and 72nd Sts., tel. 212/362–3364). The look here is still hip.

Chanel (5 E. 57th St., tel. 212/355–5050). The classic designs here never go out of style.

Comme des Garçons (116 Wooster St., tel. 212/219–0660). A SoHo shop showcases this Japanese designer.

Emanuel Ungaro (803 Madison Ave., between 67th and 68th Sts., tel. 212/249–4090). The style here is body-conscious but it's never flashy.

Emporio Armani (110 5th Ave., between 16th and 17th Sts., tel. 212/727–3240). The Italian designer's casual line is featured.

Giorgio Armani (815 Madison Ave., between 68th and 69th Sts., tel. 212/988–9191). In this lofty blond-and-beige space with grand, arched windows and doors, Armani's high-end line looks oh-so-chic.

Givenchy (954 Madison Ave. at 75th St., tel. 212/772–1040). This designer is famous for timeless elegance.

Hermès (11 E. 57th St., tel. 212/751–3181). Patterned scarves and Grace Kelly bags are hallmarks.

Koos van den Akker (34 E. 67th St., tel. 212/249–5432). Collage meets couture in the home of the Dutch-born former Dior designer once known as the Rembrandt of ready-to-wear.

Lanvin (831 Madison Ave. at 69th St., tel. 212/472–9436). These clothes are classics.

Matsuda (156 5th Ave., between 20th and 21st Sts., tel. 212/645–5151, and 461 Park Ave. at 57th St., tel. 212/935–6969). Kudos go out for wonderful cuts and fine muted hues.

Missoni (836 Madison Ave. at 69th St., tel. 212/517–9339). Wonderfully textured knits, suits, and sportswear stand out.

Norma Kamali O.M.O. (11 W. 56th St., tel. 212/957–9797). The look here ranges from sweatshirts to evening gowns.

Polo/Ralph Lauren (867 Madison Ave. at 72nd St., tel. 212/606–2100). Lauren's flagship store is not only the ultimate expression of the Ralph Lauren way of life, but it's also one of New York's most distinctive shopping experiences, in a grand, carefully renovated turn-of-the-century town house.

Sonia Rykiel (792 Madison Ave., at 67th St., tel. 212/744–0880). Signature knits for day and evening pack the racks.

Valentino (825 Madison Ave., between 68th and 69th Sts., tel. 212/744–0200). The mix here is at once audacious and beautifully cut, with the best of France and Italy on its racks.

Yves St. Laurent Rive Gauche (855 Madison Ave., between 70th and 71st Sts., tel. 212/988–3821). The looks range from chic to classic for day and evening.

Classicists
Ann Taylor (2017 Broadway, near 69th St., tel. 212/873–7344; 25 Fulton St., tel. 212/608–5600; 805 3rd Ave. at 50th St., tel. 212/308–5333; 3 E. 57th St., tel. 212/832–2010). These stores provide what the elegant young woman with a sense of style needs for work and play.

Burberry's (9 E. 57th St., tel. 212/371–5010). The look is classic and conservative—and nobody does a better trench coat.

Romantics **Laura Ashley** (21 E. 57th St., tel. 212/752–7300; 398 Columbus Ave. at 79th St., tel. 212/496–5110; 4 Fulton St., tel. 212/809–3556). Old-fashioned English frocks abound here.
Victoria Falls (451 West Broadway, tel. 212/254–2433). The romantic clothes here are antique or made just yesterday.

Ethnic Looks **Putumayo** (857 Lexington Ave., between 64th and 65th Sts., tel. 212/734–3111, 341 Columbus Ave., between 76th and 77th Sts., tel. 212/595–3441; and 147 Spring St., tel. 212/966–4458). There's cool cotton clothing here, much of it crinkly and easy to pack.

Hip Styles **Canal Jean** (504 Broadway, between Spring and Broome Sts., tel. 212/226–1130). Casual funk draws hip shoppers.
Reminiscence (74 5th Ave., between 13th and 14th Sts., tel. 212/243–2292). The theme is strictly '50s and '60s, in vintage and new clothing.
The Limited (691 Madison Ave. at 62nd St., tel. 212/838–8787). Considering the address, prices are moderate for well-styled, though not outrageous clothing, much of it casual.
Trash and Vaudeville (4 St. Mark's Pl., tel. 212/777–1727). Black, white, and electric colors are the focus here.
Unique Clothing Warehouse (726 Broadway at Waverly Pl., tel. 212/674–1767). Where the young and hip have been dressing themselves to look just like their friends for two decades, Unique is also around the corner from a flea market where student-entrepreneurs hawk baseball caps and boxer shorts with trendy images.

Vintage **Harriet Love** (412 West Broadway, tel. 212/966–2280). This is the doyenne of the city's vintage clothing scene.
Screaming Mimi's (22 E. 4th St., tel. 212/677–6464). Old clothes go avant-garde here.

Lingerie Exquisite little things in silk and lace, both naughty and nice, are found at **Joovay** (436 West Broadway, tel. 212/431–6386); **Montenapoleone** (789 Madison Ave. at 67th St., tel. 212/535–2660); and **Victoria's Secret** (34 E. 57th St., tel. 212/758–5592).

Discount **Aaron's** (627 5th Ave., between 17th and 18th Sts., Brooklyn, tel. 718/768–5400). A half hour on the R train and a one-block walk access high-end clothing at a savings.
Bolton's (225 E. 57th St., tel. 212/755–2527; other locations). The styles won't stop traffic, but you can count on finding basics at moderate prices.
Century 21 (22 Cortlandt St., between Broadway and Church St., tel. 212/227–9092). Spiffy quarters make bargain-hunting a pleasure, and there are fabulous buys on very high fashion. Note that there are no try-ons, but items may be returned within 12 working days after purchase.
Daffy's (111 5th Ave. at 18th St., tel. 212/529–4477; 335 Madison Ave. at 44th St., tel. 212/557–4422). Cheap stuff is priced cheaper, and pricey stuff is marked way down.
Forman's (82 Orchard St., tel. 212/228–2500). This is an unexpectedly attractive longtime mainstay of the Lower East Side.
Loehmann's (236th St. and Broadway, The Bronx, tel. 212/543–6420). The flagship store of this premier off-price outlet is an institution among shopaholics.
Ms., Miss or Mrs./Ben Farber (462 7th Ave., between 35th and 36th Sts., 3rd floor, tel. 212/736–0557). This Garment Center fixture is known to canny shoppers for 30% to 60% discounts.

S&W (165 W. 26th St., tel. 212/924–6656). Prices here are good to great on coats, furs, lingerie, handbags, and accessories.
The Gap Outlet (60 W. 34th St., in Herald Sq., tel. 212/643–8960). Lower-than-sale prices prevail on Gap classics.

Women's Shoes **Charles Jourdan** (725 5th Ave., in Trump Tower, tel. 212/644–
Designer Shoes 3830; 769 Madison Ave. at 66th St., tel. 212/628–0133). Shoes feature quirky heels and extravagant colors or patterns.
Maud Frizon (19 E. 69th St., tel. 212/249–5368). These extravagant styles come in outrageous shapes and sizzling colors.
Peter Fox (105 Thompson St., tel. 212/431–7426 and 431–6359; 378 Amsterdam Ave. at 77th St., tel. 212/874–6399). Looks here are outside the fashion mainstream—really fun.
Salvatore Ferragamo (717 5th Ave. at 56th St., tel. 212/759–3822). No stylistic gimmicks here, just beautiful shoemaking.
Susan Bennis Warren Edwards (22 W. 57th St., tel. 212/755–4197). Here you'll find alligator, silk, satin, suede, canvas, and buttery-soft leather exquisitely worked.

Moderately Priced The shoes at these stores tend toward the classic, in a good
Shoes range of colors and styles: **Ecco** (324 Columbus Ave., between 75th and 76th Sts., tel. 212/799–5229; 94 7th Ave., between 15th and 16th Sts., tel. 212/675–5180; 111 Thompson St., tel. 212/925–8010); **Galo** (825 Lexington Ave. at 63rd St., tel. 212/832–3922; 692 Madison Ave., between 62nd and 63rd Sts., tel. 212/688–6276); **Joan & David** (805 3rd Ave., between 49th and 50th Sts., tel. 212/486–6740); **Maraolo** (782 Lexington Ave., between 60th and 61st Sts., tel. 212/832–8182); and **Ritz** (309A Columbus Ave., between 74th and 75th Sts., tel. 212/595–1492; 14 W. 8th St., between 5th and 6th Aves., tel. 212/228–4137; 505 Park Ave. at 59th St., tel. 212/838–3319).

Discount and Discounters dot Reade Street between Church and West
Lower-Priced Shoes Broadway, including **Anbar** (93 Reade St., tel. 212/227–0253). Several Orchard Street stores discount uptown shoe styles; try **Lace-Up Shoes** (110 Orchard St., tel. 212/475–8040) for moderate discounts on very high-style shoes.

Secondhand Shops

Thrift Shops Affluent New Yorkers donate castoffs to thrift shops run for charity. And oh, such castoffs! Often they're supplemented by closeouts from major stores. Hours are limited, so call ahead.

Arthritis Foundation Thrift Shop (121 E. 77th St., tel. 212/772–8816).
Council Thrift Shop (767 9th Ave., between 51st and 52nd Sts., tel. 212/757–6132).
Everybody's Thrift Shop (261 Park Ave. S, between 20th and 21st Sts., tel. 212/355–9263).
Girls Club of New York Thrift Shop (202 E. 77th St., tel. 212/535–8570).
Irvington Institute for Medical Research Thrift Shop (1534 2nd Ave. at 80th St., tel. 212/879–4555).
Memorial Sloan-Kettering Cancer Center Thrift Shop (1440 3rd Ave., between 81st and 82nd Sts., tel. 212/535–1250).
New York Hospital Auxiliary Thrift Shop (439 E. 71st St., tel. 212/535–0965).
Spence-Chapin Corner Shop (1430 3rd Ave., between 80th and 81st Sts., tel. 212/737–8448).

Resale Shops When the oh-so-social women of New York have clothing too good to give away, they consign it to their local resale shop. To find top-of-the-line designs at secondhand prices, try: **Encore** (1132 Madison Ave., between 84th and 85th Sts., upstairs, tel. 212/879–2850); **Exchange Unlimited** (563 2nd Ave. at 31st St., tel. 212/889–3229); **Michael's Resale** (1041 Madison Ave., between 79th and 80th Sts., tel. 212/737–7273); and **Renate's** (235 E. 81st St., tel. 212/472–1698).

Auctions

New York's lively auction scene means regular sales from internationally known houses. Fine art sells for millions, but for almost everything else, prices are often a steal. Sales are advertised in the *New York Times*, particularly in Friday's "Weekend" and Sunday's "Arts & Leisure" sections. If you note a sale of interest, attend the exhibition to inspect the wares, peruse the catalogue, discuss possible payment methods, and find out whether you'll need a paddle for bidding.

Christie's (502 Park Ave. at 59th St., tel. 212/546–1000, 212/371–5438 for recorded schedules). This 200-year-old London firm is the oldest of its kind in the world; it's had an American presence for a decade. The annex is **Christie's East** (219 E. 67th St., tel. 212/606–0400).

Sotheby's (1334 York Ave. at 72nd St., tel. 212/606–7000, 212/606–7245 for recorded schedules). This is Christie's chief rival, also originally from London. On the premises is the **Arcade**, where interesting and well-priced also-rans go on the block.

William Doyle Galleries (175 E. 87th St., tel. 212/427–2730, 212/427–4885 for recorded schedules). The charismatic and amazingly energetic William Doyle has turned his instinct for accumulation into a major force on the New York auction scene. Sales here are always entertaining.

Smaller houses include: **Gotham Galleries** (80 4th Ave., between 10th and 11th Sts., tel. 212/677–3303); **Greenwich Auction Room** (110 E. 13th St., tel. 212/533–5930); **Guernsey's Auction** (108½ E. 73rd St., tel. 212/794–2280); **Lubin Galleries** (30 W. 26th St., tel. 212/924–3777); **Swann Galleries** (104 E. 25th St., tel. 212/254–4710); and **Tepper Galleries** (110 E. 25th St., tel. 212/677–5300).

Flea Markets

The season runs from March or April to November or December at these markets in school playgrounds and parking lots.

Annex Antiques Fair and Flea Market (6th Ave. at 25th St., tel. 212/243–5343), Saturdays and Sundays.

P.S. 44 Market (Columbus Ave., between 76th and 77th Sts., tel. 212/947–6302 evenings), Sundays.

P.S. 41 (Greenwich Ave. at Charles St., tel. 212/752–8475), Saturdays.

P.S. 183 Market (67th St., between York and 1st Aves., tel. 212/737–8888), Saturdays.

Tower Market (Broadway, between W. 4th and Great Jones Sts., tel. 718/273–8702), Saturdays and Sundays.

8 Dining

by John F.
Mariani and Peter
D. Meltzer

John F. Mariani
is food and travel
correspondent for
Esquire, *food
writer for* USA
Today, *and host of
the PBS television
series "Crazy for
Food." Peter D.
Meltzer is
editor-at-large for*
Food Arts, *wine
columnist for*
Ultra, *and author
of* The Wine
Spectator's *"Grand
Award" restaurant
wine listing.*

In much the same way that New York has long been considered America's financial and artistic capital, it has also become the nation's—some might even say the world's—gastronomic epicenter. The sheer quantity of New York restaurants is staggering: There are some 16,000 establishments in all if you count corner coffee shops and diners.

More important are the variety and the quality. Within its few square miles, the island of Manhattan contains dozens of culinary cultures—including Brazilian, Cuban, Greek, Hungarian, Mexican, and Japanese, to mention a few—all enriched by a pragmatic American style and a very hip gloss. The city also offers the finest French food outside of Paris, the most authentic Italian specialties outside of Bologna, the most varied styles of Chinese cuisine outside of Hong Kong, and the spiciest Thai dishes outside of Bangkok. This is the place that gave the world lox, fettuccine primavera, negimaki, Delmonico steak, and a number of other dishes one might have thought originated in Europe or Asia. And when it comes to steak houses, New York created and defines the genre.

But the past year has been a watershed for New York City's restaurants due to the general downturn of the economy, the shrinking of expense accounts, and a trend toward more casual dining habits. Ironically, all of this has been a boon for the person who wants to eat out in New York. Not only have prices in many of the most expensive restaurants dropped, but many others are now offering special fixed-price menus at bargains unthinkable a year or two ago.

While last year witnessed a number of splashes on the restaurant scene like Remi, TriBeCa Grill, Cocopazo, and Le Comptoir, the economic turmoil has also produced a wide range of charming "downscale" restaurants such as Vince & Eddie's, Mesa Grill, and Prix Fixe, where main courses run under $20 and they don't hassle you if you only order a glass of wine and an entrée and split a dessert.

New restaurants such as Carmine's on the Upper West Side have taken the town by offering enormous portions of food served family style for very moderate prices, while trattorias and bistros in TriBeCa, SoHo, and the Village are opening with a minimum of decor, a maximum of noise, short menus, and low prices.

With so much to pick from, choosing where to dine in New York may be exasperating. Probably the best strategy is to select your restaurant on the basis of your budget and the neighborhood you're visiting; after that, you can decide which type of cuisine and what atmosphere you prefer. We've set this chapter up first by region and then by cost, giving choices for every price range within each neighborhood.

Prices New York may not be the most expensive city in the world when it comes to dining out (Tokyo probably takes that honor), and prices are lower in many new eateries, but by and large, New York restaurants are quite a bit more expensive than those in most American cities. It has become increasingly difficult to find a good meal for under $20 a head. And while you might

All restaurant reviews in this chapter have been adapted from Passport to New York Restaurants *(Passport Press, Ltd.), a pocket guide by John F. Mariani and Peter D. Meltzer.*

spend $100 per person in Boston, Los Angeles, or Washington, DC, you can easily spend that much in New York, even at lesser restaurants where all too often you're paying for a false sense of chic, a panorama, or a valued table. We've skirted such restaurants in favor of places we think represent true value, even for those for whom money is no object. Highly recommended restaurants in each category are indicated by a star ★.

Category	Cost*
Very Expensive	over $60
Expensive	$40–$60
Moderate	$20–$40
Inexpensive	under $20

per person, excluding drinks, service, and sales tax (8¼%)

The following credit card abbreviations are used: AE, American Express; DC, Diners Club; MC, MasterCard; and V, Visa.

It's worth noting that lunch prices tend to be much lower than dinner prices at the better spots; you can dine regally at the most deluxe restaurants in town for less than $40 per person at lunch, eating the same meal that would cost you $75–$100 at dinner. Be aware, however, that most of the top-flight restaurants are not open for lunch on Saturday.

Many haute cuisine restaurants offer three-course, fixed-price menus, which usually cost a bit less than meals ordered à la carte, but be wary of the ubiquitous supplements and surcharges on such menus. Some fixed-price meals are called "tasting menus" or, in French, *menus dégustation*. These offer a sampling of anywhere from five to 10 dishes—usually at quite a high price—and give you a very good indication of a kitchen's strengths, since they include the best the chef is making that night.

Even with fixed-price meals, coffee and after-dinner beverages are almost never included, so if a waiter suggests an item, ask whether it is complimentary or additional. A waiter who asks, "Would you like a soufflé for dessert?" does not necessarily mean that it's a giveaway—it may cost you plenty on top of your bill. If a waiter says, "The owner would like to buy you a drink," however, you should not have to pay for that drink. Check your bill accordingly.

In many restaurants, your waiter may come to your table to recite a long list of the evening's specials, often without quoting prices. If you're tempted, don't be bashful about asking a dish's price—you don't want to discover when the bill arrives that you've paid for the ingredients' airfare from Alaska!

Wine Some of the best wine cellars in the country are to be found here at grand restaurants such as Le Cirque, Lutèce, and The Four Seasons. You'll find equally great wines at Felidia, Sparks, Smith & Wollensky, and the Grand Central Oyster Bar. While it's possible to spend upwards of $100 per bottle at these places, good value often lurks at the lower end of the list. As a general rule, plan on spending at least the equivalent of a dinner entrée on your bottle. Unless budget requires, however, don't go for the cheapest listing you find because it's probably no bargain:

An $18 bottle usually bears a much higher markup than a $28 one.

Dress Codes For men, a jacket and tie (and very often a suit) are never out of place and always welcome at New York restaurants; many specifically require them. For women, it's always safe to be "dressy." There are, however, a large number of restaurants where "casual" dress is acceptable—as long as it's neat and carries a certain amount of taste. Blue jeans might be all right in Chinatown or a pizza parlor, but slacks and a sweater or tweed jacket will put you in better stead elsewhere. Cutoffs and shorts are worn only in the heat of summer, and then only at very casual restaurants.

Reservations Even though the past season has witnessed a decline in restaurant business, that doesn't mean you can show up at any hour and expect to be seated immediately. Reservations are always a good idea and, more often than not, essential at our top-rated restaurants. Weekdays are easier than weekends, and lunch easier still. You'd also be surprised how many times no-shows open up a table even on a Saturday night, so it's worth a last-minute call to find out. Another ploy to snare an otherwise booked table is to make a very early (say, 6 PM) or quite late (9:30 PM) reservation. Even the best restaurants often have tables at those hours. Sometimes you may be asked for a confirmation telephone number. Always phone when you intend to cancel.

Smoking New York City law now stipulates that restaurants with more than 50 seats must set aside nonsmoking sections. Make your preference known when you reserve.

Dining Hours Most New Yorkers dine out at approximately 8 PM. Pretheater dining can be a lot of fun, but expect it to be rushed: You'll want to be out by 7:45, and restaurants that cater to the theater crowd will make sure you are. If you prefer to wait until after the show to eat, you'll find that New York restaurants take good care of hungry night owls who want something more than diner food.

Seating Many people worry about the "seating game"—who gets the best tables and how to avoid being placed in what's known as "Siberia"—in deluxe or trendy restaurants. The best tables are customarily doled out to regulars or high-powered celebrities. Don't assume that not getting an *A* table is a deliberate slight. If you are seated at a table you find truly awful—next to the rest room, the kitchen, or service station, for instance—politely request another. If space allows, the maître d' will happily place you elsewhere—perhaps not at the window table, but at a better one. Whatever you do, DO NOT "grease the palm" of the maître d': It may work, but it'll mark you as a patsy, ready to be gouged by the rest of the staff.

Tipping If you have received good service and liked where the maître d' seated you, on the way out you may want to give him a tip (anywhere from a few dollars to $10 or more iᴸ you wish to be remembered), but it is in no way mandatory. As for tipping others, remember that most service staffs pool their tips at the end of each evening (busboys and bartenders are given a share), so it is not necessary to provide a separate tip for everyone who serves you. If you do want to separate your tip in a deluxe restaurant, give 15% to the waiter and 5% to the captain. Otherwise, just leave behind 15%–20% in one lump sum.

Wine stewards are tipped only when they perform special services, such as decanting rare wines or advising you throughout a multicourse meal, in which case a tip of a few dollars is in order. Coat-check attendants usually get $1 per coat; parking valets get about the same per car. If you're just ordering drinks, a tip of $1 on a $5–$10 order is just fine.

A quick way to figure your tip is to double the tax you've been charged: that would equal 16½%, a perfectly adequate amount.

Lower Manhattan

Expensive   **Fraunces Tavern.** A good, evocative American restaurant inside a historic structure (where Washington bade farewell to his troops in 1783), Fraunces Tavern is one of the last bits of Colonial New York remaining, and the museum upstairs is delightful. Downstairs there's a barroom that fills up at midday and after 5 PM with the bulls and bears of Wall Street. The main dining room is a cheery spot in antique style where you can enjoy everything from a hearty breakfast of oatmeal and eggs to lunches and dinners that focus on such classic American dishes as steak, chops, and seafood. The pies and cakes are fitting endings. *54 Pearl St. (at Broad St.), tel. 212/269–0144. Reservations required at lunch, advised at dinner. Jacket and tie advised. AE, DC, MC, V. Closed Sat. and Sun.*

Hudson River Club. The opening of the World Financial Center has resulted in some splendid new restaurants within the last year. One of the most attractive is the Hudson River Club, which looks out over the mouth of the Hudson River. This is real corporate dining style—golden woods, lots of brass, thick carpeting—and the ambience is civil if not exciting. The service is neither, and you may wait forever to be greeted and served. The menu, under chef Wally Malouf, features the products and ingredients of the Hudson River Valley in season—such as, Millbrook Farms venison loin and rib chops, New York foie gras, cheeses from New York farms, and Millbrook Chardonnay. While the food is quite good, it's unfortunately not very special. A tasting menu is available at $55. *4 World Financial Center, tel. 212/786–1500. Reservations advised. Jacket and tie required. AE, V. Closed for lunch weekends.*

★ **Le Pactole.** Romeo DiGobbi, former maitre d' at Le Cirque, and Willy Krause, former owner of Le Perigord Park, spent a long time and a lot of money fashioning this large, formal dining room with a grand panorama of the Hudson River, and it's the best restaurant of the dozen or so in the World Financial Center. The food is what is called "retro cuisine," which is an attempt to bring back classic dishes that had become clichés but that now taste new again. The menu is very large, but the kitchen does most things very well. There's even a good cheese tray. Any of the terrines and pâtés, sole Murat, and the gratin de fruits are especially recommended. The prix fixe dinner is $32.50. Le Pactole has excellent banquet facilities. *2 World Financial Center, tel. 212/945–9444. Reservations advised. Jacket and tie advised. AE, DC, MC, V.*

★ **Windows on the World.** Perched on the 107th floor of the World Trade Center, with a spectacular view of the city unfolding beneath, this restaurant is one of the country's most awesome. Remember, however, that window tables are hard to get, and you may feel disappointed if you go on a rainy or foggy night. The simpler food items—such as paillard of chicken or veal, rack of lamb, and American chocolate cake—are often the best choices. Pretheater dinners range from $28 to $39. The wine list at Windows is one of the most extensive in the country, with tremendous breadth of choice and very fair prices. In fact, Windows is so committed to wine that it actually offers a special dining experience for oenophiles at **Cellar in the Sky,** a compact, enclosed dining room in which a seven-course menu is served with carefully matched wines at a fixed price of $80. *1 World Trade Center, tel. 212/938–1111. Reservations required. Jacket and tie required. AE, DC, MC, V. Closed to public weekday lunch.*

Moderate **Bridge Cafe.** Just a couple of blocks north of the South Street Seaport and one block south of the Brooklyn Bridge, this tiny, affable eatery with red-checked tablecloths is housed in the oldest wood-frame building in New York. It's the best choice in the neighborhood for solid contemporary cooking, including fried calamari, hearty soups, and roast duck. *279 Water St. (at Dover St.), tel. 212/227–3344. Reservations advised. Dress: casual. AE, DC, MC, V. Closed Sat. lunch.*

South Street Seaport. This is not a restaurant but an impeccably restored 19th-century historic district (*see* Tour 18) stretching from Water Street to John Street. Its attractions include many restaurants that make pleasant places for lunch or dinner. A host of fast-food restaurants serve a wide variety of ethnic cooking. One good bet is **Sloppy Louie's,** a very old place specializing in seafood and antique charm, though it's a bit touristy. *92 South St., tel. 212/509–9694. Reservations advised. Dress: casual. AE, DC, MC, V.*

SoHo and TriBeCa

Very Expensive **Bouley.** This is a modern restaurant whose truly genteel roots
★ are reflected in every piece of furniture, as well as in the arched ceilings, the impressionistic landscapes on the walls, and the sedate lighting. David Bouley, a very sensible cook who never strays from good taste, offers a bargain ($65 for dinner, $32 for lunch) tasting menu of many courses, along with a regular à la carte menu. The food is exciting without ever being trendy. Bouley does beautiful sea scallops with sea urchins in an herb broth, salmon braised in Bandol wine, monkfish with tomato-coriander sauce, sturgeon with summer squash, and sorbet "soup"; he is justly famous for his hot dessert soufflés. His staff has good and bad nights, however, and waits between courses may turn into lapses. *165 Duane St. (near Hudson St.), tel. 212/608–3852. Reservations required. Jacket and tie required. AE, DC, MC, V. Closed Sat. lunch and Sun.*

Chanterelle. The place is intentionally very stark, with bare walls and one massive floral arrangement. Chef-owner David Waltuck's menus, limited and ever-changing, offer a few meals each night at a prix fixe of $68 for three courses and $87 for a tasting menu of six courses. The prix fixe lunch costs $30. Recommended dishes include cold lobster consommé, foie gras and papaya salad, rabbit loin with chanterelles, sweetbreads and morels, and beef fillet in red wine sauce. Desserts are somewhat disappointing, but not the Armagnac and prune ice cream. An extensive but expensive wine list is available. *2 Harrison St. (near Hudson St.), tel. 212/966–6960. Reservations advised. Jacket and tie advised. AE, DC, MC, V. Closed Sun. and Mon.*

Manhattan Dining (Uptown)

Al Amir, **20**
Alcala, **9**
Alo Alo, **29**
Amerigo's, **1**
Amsterdam's Bar and
Rotisserie, **7**
Anatolia, **15**
Arizona 206, **28**
Aureole, **30**
Bangkok Cuisine, **45**
Barbetta, **48**
Cabana Carioca, **46**
Café des Artistes, **34**
Café Luxembourg, **11**
Ca' Nova, **32**

Carmine's, **5**
Chez Josephine, **51**
Docks, **6**
The Ginger Man, **36**
Gallagher's, **44**
Hard Rock Café, **38**
J.G. Melon, **10, 23**
Joe Allen, **47**
La Cité, **43**
Lattanzi, **50**
Le Bernardin, **42**
Le Cirque, **26**
Le Régence, **25**
Mark's Restaurant, **19**

Mazzei, **17**
Mezzaluna, **22**
Mocca Hungarian
Restaurant, **16**
Orso, **49**
Parioli
Romanissimo, **13**
Petrossian, **39**
Pig Heaven, **18**
Poiret, **8**
Post House, **31**
Remi, **41**
Russian Tea Room, **40**
San Domenico, **37**
Sette Mezzo, **24**

Sidewalkers, **12**
Sign of the Dove, **27**
Sylvia's, **2**
Table d'Hote, **3**
Tavern on the
Green, **33**
The Terrace, **4**
Vašata, **21**
Vico Ristorante, **14**
Vince & Eddie's, **35**

Manhattan Dining (Downtown)

Acme Bar & Grill, **25**
Alison on Dominick Street, **32**
America, **10**
An American Place, **3**
Angelo's, **41**
Bouley, **34**
Bridge Cafe, **53**
Cafe Iguana, **12**
Cafe Loup, **18**
Capsouto Freres, **33**
Chanterelle, **37**
Chefs and Cuisiniers Club, **6**
The Coach House, **24**

El Teddy's, **39**
Florent, **19**
Fraunces Tavern, **50**
Giorgio, **11**
Gotham Bar & Grill, **20**
Hudson River Club, **47**
Il Cortile, **43**
Indochine, **23**
Jerry's, **30**
Katz's Delicatessen, **26**
Kwong and Wong, **46**
La Colombe D'Or, **4**
Le Madri, **9**
Le Pactole, **48**
Lola, **7**

Mesa Grill, **14**
Montrachet, **40**
Noodle Town, **42**
The Odeon, **38**
Omen Restaurant, **29**
Park Bistro, **5**
Periyali, **16**
Price Fixe, **15**
Provence, **28**
Quatorze, **17**
Rojas-Lombardi Ballroom, **2**
Rose Cafe, **21**
Silver Palace, **44**

Siracusa Gourmet Café, **22**
Soho Kitchen and Bar, **31**
South St. Seaport, **51**
Tommy Tang, **35**
Tribeca Grill, **36**
Union Square Café, **13**
Villa Mosconi, **27**
Windows on the World, **49**
Wong Kee, **45**
World Yacht Cruises, **1**
Zig Zag Bar & Grill, **8**

Expensive

★ Alison on Dominick Street. This small and intimate restaurant is one of the best in the neighborhood; owner Alison Price really enjoys making her customers feel right at home. The low-key dining rooms featuring white walls, blue banquettes, and entertaining black-and-white photographs help make this a congenial spot. Chef Thomas Valenti's excellent Provençal-inspired menu includes braised beef with white beans, vegetable tart, skate with cabbage and bacon, and chocolate hazelnut mousse with pistachio cream. *38 Dominick St. (near Hudson St.), tel. 212/727–1188. Reservations required. Jacket advised. AE, DC, MC, V.*

★ Montrachet. Set in a quaint TriBeCa location and presided over by the dedicated Drew Nieporent, Montrachet has proved to be one of the most consistently satisfying restaurants in New York City. Its chef, Debra Ponzek, is serious about the essential flavors of her ingredients, and care is shown in the preparation of every dish. The wines are very carefully chosen, too, so rely on sommelier Daniel Johnnes's advice. Montrachet is priced somewhat below comparable establishments. Prices for the three fixed-price meals—$25, $32, and $45—are extremely reasonable. Signature dishes include sautéed foie gras, red snapper with red peppers and lemon, roast chicken with sweet garlic, salmon with lentils, pheasant with olives, and banana tart. *239 W. Broadway (near White St.), tel. 212/219–2777. Reservations advised. Dress: casual. AE. Closed Sun., and Mon.– Thurs. and Sat. lunch.*

Moderate

★ Capsouto Freres. Its setting in a glorious old landmark building, its view of the Hudson, and its own soaring architectural design make this a stand-out restaurant in TriBeCa. The brothers Capsouto were among the first in the city to offer Mediterranean and Provençal cuisine, and they do it very well indeed. The soft-shell crabs *à la meunière* are superb, and the Provençal dishes—especially terrine Provençale, roasted lotte and lobster in sauternes, and steak with mixed peppercorns—are terrific, as is the blueberry crumble cake. The weekend brunch is very popular. *451 Washington St. (near Canal St.), tel. 212/966–4900. Reservations advised. Dress: casual. AE, DC. Closed Mon. lunch.*

El Teddy's. Lots of glitter and tile—the legacy of restaurants past—provide one of the city's more offbeat interiors. This is also one of the few spots in New York where margaritas are made to measure with your choice of several different tequilas. The promising menu includes updated Mexican specialties, such as masa tarts with chicken and chile, cactus salad with jicama, portobello mushrooms with salsa verde, shrimp marinated in lime and tequila, and charred tuna steak with salsa fresca. *219 W. Broadway (between Franklin and White Sts.), tel. 212/941–7070. Reservations advised. Dress: casual. AE, DC, MC, V.*

★ The Odeon. Housed in a 1930s Art Deco cafeteria, this was the first notable restaurant in the TriBeCa neighborhood. Popularized by the SoHo art set, who still make it one of their chief stomping grounds after midnight, it's a great place to plug into the "scene" in this very artsy district. Everybody seems to wear black, look slightly world-weary, and recognize each other. The food is high-quality bistro/brasserie fare with changing specials. Try the butternut squash ravioli with escarole, and the braised lamb shank with lentils. The triple-chocolate pudding is a soothing finale. The set menu lunch is $14.50.

145 W. Broadway (at Thomas St.), tel. 212/233–0507. Reservations advised. Dress: casual. AE, DC, MC, V. Closed Sat. lunch.

Provence. An authentic bistro, of the kind that dot the Riviera, this spot has become very popular for its unprepossessing decor, its decent prices, and its commendable Provençal food. The seafood dishes are especially good, from the *pissaladiere* (a kind of French pizza) to the bourride. The early crowd at dinner are locals; the later crowd, artists and gallery owners from the area. The restaurant attracts a very artsy-literary bunch, as shown in the scene filmed here for the movie *Crossing Delancey*. The front room on the street is charming, but the rear is rather plain. *38 MacDougal St. (near Prince St.), tel. 212/475–7500. Reservations advised. Dress: casual. AE.*

Tommy Tang. This Hollywood transplant to TriBeCa has traveled well. Still going very strong, it attracts home-bound Wall Streeters in the early evening and a mixed bag of area residents and fans of Thai cuisine later on. Its high-ceilinged, geometric design and attractive young staff create a lively backdrop for some serious eating. You might want to share a variety of appetizers to sample a wide array of the kitchen's output: Start with chicken saté, "naked" shrimp, or spicy chicken wontons. For a main course, try blackened whole chili fish, grilled breast of chicken, Original Tommy Duck, or any of a number of spicy Thai pasta dishes. For dessert, a homemade sorbet serves as a refreshing finale. *323 Greenwich St. (near Reade St.), tel. 212/334–9190. Reservations advised. Dress: casual chic. AE, DC, MC, V. Closed Sat. lunch and Sun.*

★ **TriBeCa Grill.** With Robert De Niro, Mikhail Baryshnikov, Christopher Walken, Bill Murray, and other celebs as partners, TriBeCa Grill wouldn't need to serve more than burgers and chili to be a hit, but partner Drew Nieporent, owner of the renowned Montrachet nearby, has made sure the kitchen, under chef Don Pintabona, is first rate and that all customers are treated equally, even on the craziest nights. The large brick dining room, with its grand bar salvaged from Maxwell's Plum, has well-separated tables and real vitality, as do dishes such as lobster gazpacho, cavatelli with pecorino cheese, lobster in a broth of vegetables and scallions, potato pancakes Vonnas, and lemon crème brûlée with poppy-seed crust. *375 Greenwich St. (near Franklin St.), tel. 212/941–3900. Reservations advised. Dress: casual. AE, DC, MC, V.*

Inexpensive **Jerry's.** The decor at this lively spot might be described as updated diner. Although the ambience is relaxed, the kitchen is far from laid back in its diligent preparation of American specialties. You can expect an eclectic repertoire, including grilled peasant bread with gorgonzola, spiced steak with onion jam, peppercorn-seared salmon with chive butter and horseradish mashed potatoes, and wholesome sandwiches. Don't miss the superb french fries. *101 Prince St. (between Mercer and Greene Sts.), tel. 212/966–9464. Dinner reservations advised. Dress: casual. AE, MC, V. Closed Sun. dinner.*

Katz's Delicatessen. This is a long-standing favorite of New Yorkers who like to shop for bargains on Orchard Street, then repair to Katz's for big, fat pastrami or corned beef sandwiches, knishes, brisket, garlicky franks, dripping pickles, terrific french fries, and cream soda. This is an original Jewish deli (you can buy wonderful salami and cold cuts to go, and the restaurant ships anywhere in the world) with a 1950s atmosphere that includes lots of schmoozing and yelling. Food is served cafeteria style: You move along the line, shout your order, and then sit down. You've got to know what you want because the counter men can make sandwiches faster than you can say "pastrami-on-rye." *205 E. Houston St. (near Orchard St.), tel. 212/254–2246. Reservations unnecessary. Dress: casual. AE.*

Soho Kitchen and Bar. This characteristic and special SoHo eatery has a great deal of spaciousness, good music, a casual-but-well-groomed crowd, plenty of laughter, and good, basic fare at decent prices. Soaring ceilings are a fit halo for the giant artwork here, and one of the main draws is the oversize bar offering at least 100 wines by the glass on any given night. The wines are often served in sequences of eight selections at a time. Try the crisp-edged pizzas and any of the pasta dishes. *103 Greene St. (near Prince St.), tel. 212/925–1866. Reservations advised. Dress: casual. AE, DC, MC, V.*

Chinatown and Little Italy

Moderate **Angelo's.** A very old-fashioned Italian-American spot, smack in the middle of Little Italy, this is certainly better than most of the tourist traps that surround it. Angelo's has a homey feel, with its simple decor and black-and-white tile floors. The pasta is very good, especially the perciatelli with vegetable sauce, and the chicken with garlic is as fine as you'll find in the neighborhood. Go with the whole family—this place welcomes kids. *146 Mulberry St., tel. 212/966–1277. Reservations advised weekends. Dress: casual. AE, DC, MC, V. Closed Mon.*

★ **Il Cortile.** Easily the best restaurant in Little Italy, Il Cortile is a tad more refined than some of the other storefront operations in the neighborhood, and its menu is far more interesting. The garden room in back is lovely, and there are a couple of coveted window tables up front. The management really cares about every customer here, and they take reservations and credit cards—not everyone in this area does. The waiters gladly help you with the menu, and if you ask for the wine list, your waiter will say, "I'm the wine list." Trust him, but ask the price. Then tuck into a greaseless *spiedino alla romana* (fried mozzarella and bread with anchovy sauce), a plate of potato *gnocchi* (dumplings) with rosemary and fresh *porcini* mushrooms, or a beautifully cooked San Pietro fish with wine and oil. *125 Mulberry St. (near Hester St.), tel. 212/226–6060. Reservations advised. Dress: casual. AE, DC, MC, V.*

★ **Kwong and Wong.** This unassuming Chinatown spot has fast become one of the most highly regarded restaurants for seafood (a live-fish tank is on the premises), and the big portions of dishes like geoduck clams or whole fish are meant to be shared. Skip the menu and go with the specials. *11 Division St., (near Bowery), tel. 212/941–7411. Reservations advised. Dress: casual. AE, V.*

Inexpensive **Noodle Town.** Despite the ridiculous name and premises that might charitably be called "quaint," this Chinatown noodle parlor in the Hong Kong tradition of "sit-'em-serve-'em-move-'em" offers absolutely scrumptious food at very low prices. The half duck for $8.50 is the most expensive item here. Don't miss the Hong Kong noodles, the luscious, brimming soups, the pan-fried noodles with black beans, or just about anything else you can point to on the enormous menu. *28½ Bowery (near Bayard St.), tel. 212/349-0923. Dress: casual. No credit cards.*

Silver Palace. A vast hall in which waiters rush about with trays full of dim-sum dumplings, this is a great place to go for weekend lunch. Food is served all day and the crowds are a fun-loving bunch. You pay by the plate—just point to what you want and be adventurous. Although the service can be quite rude, the dumplings are irresistible—everyone orders too much, but you'll find it difficult to spend more than $15 per person. *52 Bowery (near Canal St.), tel. 212/964-1204. No reservations. Dress: casual. No credit cards.*

Wong Kee. Here is a clean, bright, and completely uncluttered Chinese restaurant that has the added virtue—rare in Chinatown—of being consistent and dependable. It's a cliché to say you should order what the Orientals are ordering, but here it is true: Look around you and ask for whatever everybody else seems to be eating that day—duck with star anise, perhaps, or beef with sour cabbage. The bare-bones decor and fast service are part of the fun. If you don't make a reservation, be prepared for a wait on weekends. *113 Mott St. (near Canal St.), tel. 212/226-9018. Reservations advised. Dress: casual. No credit cards.*

Greenwich Village

Expensive
★
The Coach House. Owner Leon Lianides opened The Coach House in the late 1940s, and American cooking has never had higher standards to meet than those he's set here for generations of diners. The premises are exquisitely set, with antiques and fine paintings on old, wood-paneled walls. A lovely passage about The Coach House in Pat Conroy's novel *Prince of Tides* points out that a restaurant such as this one puts you in touch with New York's unique greatness. You can't go wrong with anything on the menu, from the corn sticks to the famous black-bean soup. The rack of lamb is superlative, as is the fish cooked in bouillon, and the desserts are nonpareil, especially the quince tart and the pecan pie. The place is traditionally popular on Sunday evenings. Fixed-price menus range from $32 to $38. *110 Waverly Pl. (near Ave. of the Americas), tel. 212/777-0303. Reservations required weekends. Jacket advised. AE, DC, MC, V. Closed Mon.*

★
Gotham Bar & Grill. Chef Alfred Portale has brought the Gotham into the front ranks of New York City restaurants. It was always beautiful, with high ceilings, a pink-marble bar, a striking pink-green-black color scheme, and a crowd of attractive diners, but the food is now up to par with the decor. Portale, a careful chef, draws out flavors and combines tastes with true panache, making this a major stop on the gourmet circuit. He's at his best with Italian and Provençal-style items, such as quail salad with shiitake mushrooms, ravioli stuffed with rabbit, warm skate salad, roast squab with saffron, flourless chocolate cake, and warm raspberry gratin. *12 E. 12th St. (near 5th Ave.), tel. 212/620-4020. Reservations recommended. Dress: casual. AE, DC, MC, V. Closed lunch weekends.*

Moderate
Cafe Loup. This is a casual and inviting Village restaurant where you can sit down to a full-course meal or order from an array of light entrées, such as tuna pasta or smoked chicken, called "small plates." For regular appetites, consider the pâté forestière or carrot soup, followed by delectable roast chicken

and succulent french fries, and raspberry walnut tart. *105 W. 13th St. (near 6th Ave.), tel. 212/255–4746. Reservations advised. Dress: casual. AE, MC, V.*

Florent. This is absolutely, positively one of the hippest restaurants in lower Manhattan, not for its food—which is only passable French bistro fare (grilled flank steak, sausages, onion soup, and vegetable gratinés)—but for the retro neighborhood it's in (the meat market district), its decor (barely converted diner), and the late-night crowd that comes here (Madonna, the Talking Heads, and a lot of other musicians). The waiters are friendly enough, however, so if you can get a table after 9 PM, just inhale the atmosphere and have a good time. It won't cost you much. A prix fixe dinner is $14.95 before 7:30 PM, $16.95 after. Do take a taxi (and have one waiting outside when you exit). *69 Gansevoort St. (between Greenwich and Washington Sts.), tel. 212/989–5779. Reservations advised. Dress: casual. No credit cards. Open 24 hrs.*

Indochine. Tucked away opposite the Public Theater is this exotic Vietnamese restaurant, complete with a banana-leaf motif on its walls. Convenient as it is for theatergoers, Indochine has developed a certain cachet and draws an interesting crowd from all over town. The menu features good shrimp beignets, marinated beef salad, and chicken wings. *430 Lafayette St. (near Astor Pl.), tel. 212/505–5111. Reservations advised. Dress: casual. AE, DC, MC, V. Dinner only.*

★ **Quatorze.** Although the location of this attractive French bistro, loosely modeled on Paris's celebrated Brasserie Lipp, lacks the élan of the Boulevard St. Germain, staples such as *saucisson de Lyon* (garlic sausage), *salade aux lardons* (chicory lettuce with bacon), creamy pâté, *coq au vin* (chicken in red wine sauce), calf's liver, and *choucroute garnie* (sausages and ham on a bed of sauerkraut) are worthy of the real thing. You'll also find here one of the best apple tarts in the city, as well as a very good wine list. A fixed-price lunch is offered for $10. *240 W. 14th St. (off 7th Ave.), tel. 212/206–7006. Reservations advised. Dress: casual. AE. Closed for lunch Mon.*

Rose Cafe. Chef-owner Richard Krause, who formerly owned the pricey restaurant Melrose, offers a menu of some enticing, moderately priced dishes that seems a judicious balance of the old and the new. Right on Fifth Avenue, the premises are open, relaxed, and unpretentious; the service is quite the same. Ask for a window table and watch the passing parade of Greenwich Village nightlife. Krause is at his best with full-flavored meats (such as rabbit with basil-tomato cream), pear and gorgonzola salad, wild mushrooms in a salad, and candy-sweet desserts. His Peking duck Chinois with scallion pancakes is particularly delightful. *24 5th Ave. (at 9th St.), tel. 212/260–4118. Reservations advised. Dress: casual. AE, DC, MC, V.*

Siracusa Gourmet Café. Although the ambience is friendly and ultrasimple, there is nothing unassuming about the cuisine at this popular little Village haunt close to Cooper Union. Ignore the nondescript decor and focus instead on the menu: an enticing array of antipasti—fried vegetables, superb charcuterie—and excellent pastas, such as *pasticciotto* (pasta stuffed with zucchini, mushrooms, and pignoli nuts), and tagliarini *campagna* with sausage and tomato. There is a take-out counter up front featuring many of the menu highlights, plus wonderful *biscotti* (Italian cookies) to go. *65 4th Ave. (near 10th St.), tel. 212/254–1940. Reservations advised. Dress: casual. AE. Closed Sat. lunch and Sun.*

Villa Mosconi. Here's a pleasant, old-fashioned Greenwich Village trattoria, the kind they don't often make any more. You come here to eat heartily at a fair price and to be treated like an old friend by owner Peter Mosconi; you'll get a good feeling of the way the Village used to be a decade or so ago. The warm, comfortable premises have the requisite Italian landscapes and still lifes on the walls. Among the good and gutsy food, the tagliatelle (flat-ribboned egg pasta) al pesto, *zuppa pesce* (mixed seafood in a tomato sauce) and the veal alla giardiniera (with vegetables) are especially recommended. *69 MacDougal St. (near Houston St.), tel. 212/673–0390. Reservations advised. Dress: casual. AE, DC, MC, V.*

Inexpensive **Acme Bar and Grill.** ★ Here's an authentic, down-home Cajun joint, complete with corrugated tin ceilings, exposed beams, and every conceivable type of hot sauce ever produced, lined up along an enormous interior wall. Deep-fried oyster po' boys, Cajun shrimp, and collard greens are just a few of the regional specialties offered at this casual and ever-lively Louisiana transplant. *9 Great Jones St. (near Broadway), tel. 212/420–1934. No reservations. Dress: casual. No credit cards.*

Chelsea, Gramercy, Murray Hill

Expensive **An American Place.** ★ Located in stunning Art Deco quarters (nearly three times as large as its former Lexington Avenue space), An American Place continues to maintain the very high standards that won it so many accolades in the past. Although he has changed his menu, chef Larry Forgione has preserved several signature dishes, such as terrine of American three-smoked fish. Pleasing additions to his roster of appetizers include a napoleon of house-smoked salmon and potato crisp, and a dobo-style barbecued duck with cilantro cream and toasted pignoli nuts. Winning main courses worth considering include sautéed breast of free-range chicken and charred fillet of steak with herbed whipped potatoes. For dessert, be sure to try the chocolate brownie with vanilla sauce. If you dine between 5:30 and 7:30 PM, you can take advantage of the prix fixe specials from $29 to $32. *2 Park Ave. (entrance on 32nd St.), tel. 212/684–2122. Reservations advised. Dress: casual. AE, DC, MC, V. Closed Sun.*

★ **Le Madri.** Certainly one of the most highly publicized Italian restaurants in New York, this establishment has succeeded not due to the hype but because of its good food. A very beautiful crowd of regulars from the fashion and publishing world may be seen here. Owner Pino Luongo brings in talented Italian women home cooks on a rotating basis to advise the chef on family regional specialties. The pizzas can be terrific, the pastas remain true to the best in Italy, and the steak alla fiorentina is unsurpassed. Don't miss the tempting desserts, either. Expect a crush, wobbly service, and too often a wait, but this is a great spot to go for lunch after shopping at Barneys across the street. *168 W. 18th St. (on 7th Ave.), tel. 212/727–8022. Reservations advised. Jacket advised. AE. Closed for lunch Sat. and Sun.*

★ **World Yacht Cruises.** A three-hour yacht cruise around Manhattan gives you more spectacle than Windows on the World, the Rainbow Room, and The River Café combined. Add to this some above-average Continental cuisine, dancing to a good band, and gratuities (but not drinks)—and you'll still pay only $59–$64.50 per person ($24.75 for lunch; $37.50 for brunch).

You can experience the thrill of the stars, the water, and the lights of New York over lunch, dinner, or Sunday brunch. *Pier 62, W. 23rd St. (on the Hudson River), tel. 212/929–7090. Reservations required. Jacket required. AE, MC, V. Jan.–Apr., cruises Fri.–Sun. only.*

Moderate   **The Ballroom.** This popular cabaret also has the city's first tapas restaurant—serving plates and platters of Spanish "snacks" that range from anchovies in grape leaves to squid, pork, chorizo, ceviche, and everything else in between. Chef-owner Felipe Rojas-Lombardi is also a master of main courses, though there is some inconsistency in his presentations. This is a quaint spot for unusual food and entertainment, not too far from Madison Square Garden. The cabaret can be cramped. *253 W. 28th St. (near 8th Ave.), tel. 212/244–3005. Reservations advised. Dress: casual. AE, DC, MC, V. Closed Sun. dinner, and Mon.*

Cafe Iguana. As fast-paced as a roadrunner, this big, sprawling bar-restaurant, often packed tight with singles and vibrating with music, is a gregarious Mexican eatery. Its fans are legion; witness the number who purchase the T-shirts and other Iguana memorabilia in the upstairs gift shop. The wild decor features lots of variations on its lizard namesake. The fajitas and chicken Tijuana are excellent, and a good Sunday brunch and children's special meals are also available. This can be a good spot to take the family early in the evening. *235 Park Ave. S (at 19th St.), tel. 212/529–4770. Reservations advised. Dress: casual. AE, DC, MC, V. Closed Sat. lunch.*

Chefs and Cuisiniers Club. "CCC," as it's called, is a worthwhile idea well realized: Several of New York City's most notable chefs, such as Rick Moonen of the Water Club and Charles Palmer of Aureole, opened this pleasant little bistro as an after-service refuge where confreres can get together to eat, swap stories, and blow off steam (the kitchen is open until 2 AM nightly except Sundays). The public is also welcome to enjoy Chef Peter Assue's restrained Mediterranean food, which is a bit underseasoned but nonetheless satisfying. Although the premises are spare, the blue jeans on the waiters slovenly, and the wine list minimal, this is a good neighborhood spot and cannot help but intrigue those who follow the comings and goings of New York's stellar chefs. *36 E. 22nd St. (off Broadway), tel. 212/228–4399. Reservations advised. Dress: casual. AE, MC, V. Closed for lunch weekends.*

★ **La Colombe D'Or.** For years this has been a paragon of French bistros, serving up good Provençal food with some modern touches under the supervision of the Studley family. It's very cozy, both downstairs and upstairs (though the bar gets smoky), thanks to printed fabrics, brick walls, and the ring of laughter from people enjoying a night out. The food is pure Provençal—excellent bouillabaisse, cannelloni of Provençal beef stew with braised leeks, semicured cod with fresh beans, smoked salmon with seasonal relish, rich cassoulet, and luscious walnut torte, for example—and the well-priced wine list has chosen bottlings to complement the food. *134 E. 26th St. (near Lexington Ave.), tel. 212/689–0666. Reservations advised. Dress: casual. AE, DC, MC, V. Closed Sat. lunch and Sun.*

Lola. Boisterous, seductive, and very "hot," Lola is one of the most convivial restaurants in this area. The food, a blend of Southern, Caribbean, and French cooking, is overseen by Lola herself, whose style is mirrored in the glow of the lighting, the beautiful bar, and the flowers that deck the large, open room. The noise level can be a bit deafening, though. This is a great spot for brunch on Sunday, when live music is performed. Lola's "100 spice" chicken is renowned, and the onion crisps are simply terrific. Specials include chicken sausage and shrimp curry, grilled halibut with roasted red-pepper vinaigrette and black bean salad, and grapefruit and orange sorbet. *30 W. 22nd St. (near 6th Ave.), tel. 212/675-6700. Reservations advised. Dress: casual. AE. Closed Sun. dinner.*

Mesa Grill. This cavernous space, for the past several years a homage to seafood known as Sofi, has been transmogrified by owners Jerry Kretchmer and Jeff Bliss and Chef Bobby Flay into a Southwestern extravaganza. Attractive lighting fixtures and colorful banquettes create a festive mood. Would that the soundproofing could contain the resultant noise! Most diners seem unperturbed by the din as they sample Flay's largely successful menu full of spices and textures, such as salmon cakes with pineapple tomatillo salsa, swordfish with peppers and pesto, and lamb chops with jalapeño preserves. *102 5th Ave. (at 15th St.), tel. 212/807-7400. Reservations advised. Dress: casual. AE, DC, MC, V.*

★ **Park Bistro.** In look and feel, this is one of Manhattan's best approximations of a French bistro. Leather banquettes, posters, and photographs create the right ambience, and a trio of Frenchmen at the helm assures that everything will be *comme il faut.* Chef Jean-Michel Diot's Provençe-inspired cooking is a delight. Be sure to sample a signature appetizer consisting of slices of potato smothered in grilled goat cheese, radicchio, and an olive vinaigrette dressing. You might start your meal with *petatou* (warm potato salad with goat cheese). For a main course, consider the skate with cocoa beans or lamb with eggplant. *414 Park Ave. S (near 28th St.), tel. 212/689-1360. Reservations advised. Jacket advised. AE, DC.*

Periyali. This enticing Greek restaurant does some out-of-the-ordinary cooking that clearly appeals to its regular crowd. The food is nicely seasoned and amply portioned. If you're in the mood for Greek cooking—albeit not of the classic variety—Periyali (which means seashore) is the place to go. Specialties include grilled lamb chops, grilled shrimp with herbs, and charcoal-grilled octopus. Don't overlook the cinnamon ice cream. *35 W. 20th St. (near 6th Ave.), tel. 212/463-7890. Reservations advised. Dress: casual. AE, MC, V. Closed Sun.*

Prix Fixe. While the name is inelegant, the concept is solid: Take over the premises of a grand café (most recently Il Palazzo), do it up with style, put a brilliant young chef named Terrance Brennan (formerly of the Polo) in the kitchen, and offer menus at $21 and $36, and wines in three price categories. The quality of the food is generally good, but we do hear complaints that the kitchen is not up to feeding a full house with any consistency. Salmon tartare with marinated fennel, rack of lamb with Moroccan spices and curried ratatouille wontons, and chocolate banana "burst" with banana ice cream and candied walnuts are some of the more dependable choices. *18 W. 18th St. (near 5th Ave.), tel. 212/675-6777. Reservations advised. Dress: casual. AE, DC, MC, V. Closed Sat. lunch.*

★ **Union Square Café.** Owner Danny Meyer and chef Michael Romano have created an unusual and attractive scene for animated dining. Oysters Union Square are a signature appetizer; sour-dough *bruschetta*, grilled with tomato, basil, and olive oil is another sure bet. You can count on good beef, lamb, roast loin of rabbit, and grilled marinated tuna. Don't overlook the nightly pasta specials, such as porcini gnocchi. The wine list is one of the city's most innovative. Desserts are irresistibly rich; try the chocolate stuffed soufflé cupcake with espresso custard sauce. *21 E. 16th St. (near Broadway), tel. 212/243–4020. Reservations advised. Jacket advised. AE, DC, MC, V. Closed Sun.*

Inexpensive   **America.** This cavernous and lively spot tends to attract a youngish crowd, many of whom are content to hang out at the enormous and inviting bar and simply watch the scene. Noise levels can be problematic. Not surprisingly, America serves up an ambitious but often inconsistent array of American favorites and specials, from po' boy sandwiches to burgers and fajitas. *9 E. 18th St. (near 5th Ave.), tel. 212/505–2110. Reservations advised. Dress: casual. AE, MC, V.*

Giorgio. This pleasant trattoria bristles by day with a smattering of publishing and advertising types and takes on a more relaxed, neighborhood feeling by night. Regardless of the hour, its kitchen churns out a good angel-hair pasta salad with fresh marinated tomatoes and basil, excellent brick-oven pizzas, pasta specials, and tasty sandwiches, such as smoked salmon and mozzarella. *245 Park Ave. S (between 19th and 20th Sts.), tel. 212/460–9100. Reservations advised. Dress: casual. AE, DC, MC, V. Closed for lunch weekends.*

Zig Zag Bar & Grill. More a bar than a grill and more a hangout than a fine restaurant, this popular Chelsea establishment hosts a cross-section of New York City's artists, photographers, stylists, and other nightcrawlers who come here all dressed in black to meet their friends and to gossip about each other. You'll easily enter into the spirit of it all, for the long bar is a friendly one, and the food is actually much more than you might expect—big sandwiches of red peppers and salami, juicy hamburgers, and good, gloppy desserts. Skip the barbecued ribs. *206 W. 23rd St. (near 7th Ave.), tel. 212/645–5060. Reservations advised for 5 or more. Dress: casual. AE.*

Midtown East

Very Expensive   **The Four Seasons.** One of the city's most important and beauti-
★   fully designed restaurants, this place never rests on its laurels, thanks to co-owners Paul Kovi and Tom Margittai and the outstanding team they have assembled. The food is simple and elegant in the Pool Room, where you can dine on shrimp in three-fruit-and-mustard sauce, fresh pheasant or venison in season, or on offerings of the highly popular Spa Cuisine. The Grill Room is a powerhouse at lunch; at dinner, a menu with imaginative borrowings from Oriental cuisine takes over. There's a stellar wine list and the service is superb. The pretheater dinner costs $41.50. *99 E. 52nd St. (near Park Ave.), tel. 212/754–9494. Reservations required. Jacket required. AE, DC, MC, V. Closed Sat. lunch and Sun.*

La Côte Basque. Here's a restaurant with a history of revival: It was opened some decades ago by the legendary Henri Soulé, foundered when he died, and was restored to eminence by current owner Jean-Jacques Rachou. The place still looks very glamorous—with butter-colored walls, sprightly murals, dark beams, and a glittering bar—but the greeting at the door may be indifferent to newcomers, and the service abrupt. This is an

Midtown East Dining

Alfredo's the Original
of Rome, **21**

American Festival
Café, **25**

Aquavit, **8**

Billy's, **35, 39**

Brasserie, **22**

Bukhara, **31**

Chin Chin, **30**

China Grill, **9**

Dawat, **16**

Docks, **42**

The Edwardian
Room, **3**

Extra! Extra!, **41**

Felidia, **17**

The Four Seasons, **23**

Grand Central Oyster
Bar & Restaurant, **40**

Hatsuhana, **28**

Il Nido, **20**

La Caravelle, **4**

La Côte Basque, **7**

La Reserve, **26**

Le Cygne, **11**

Le Perigord, **36**

Lutèce, **33**

Manhattan Ocean
Club, **2**

Michael's, **5**

Mickey Mantle's, **1**

Nippon, **29**

Palm, **37**

Pentop Bar, **6**

The Quilted
Giraffe, **12**

The Rainbow
Room, **27**

Rosa Mexicano, **19**

Sandro's, **18**

Scarlatti, **24**

Serendipity, **15**

Shun Lee Palace, **13**

Smith & Wollensky, **32**

Sparks Steak
House, **38**

The "21" Club, **10**

Yellowfingers, **14**

Zarela, **34**

institution, however, and the food, which comes out of the kitchen lickety-split, is hearty, classic, elaborate, and satisfying. The scallops in cream and the crème brûleé are textbook perfect, as is the breast of chicken Gismonda. The extensive and inordinately expensive wine lists can be irritating, since there are no vintages given for many white wines. Still, you can't go wrong with the veal chop and mushrooms or the sky-high soufflés, and the set-menu lunch ($32) and dinner ($55) offer considerable savings. *5 E. 55th St. (near 5th Ave.), tel. 212/688-6525. Reservations required. Jacket and tie required. AE, DC, MC, V. Closed Sun.*

★ **Lutèce.** Lutèce is widely considered the finest French restaurant in New York City, a fact attested to by an up-to-three-week wait for a reservation. Spruced up by design maven Sam Lopata a few years ago, this East Side town house looks better than ever. But regulars come here not for dazzle but for perfection. Chef-owner André Soltner is a brilliant and highly dedicated cook who frets over every dish; ask him to choose your meal and you will never forget the experience. The repertoire ranges from terrine of cod in aspic, crêpes filled with home-smoked salmon and crabmeat, and red snapper *goujonettes* (slender strips) in red pepper sauce, to caramelized rack of lamb, roast guinea hen, foie gras en brioche, and gratin of chestnuts with *crème anglaise*. The wine list is extensive and expensive. The prix fixe lunch costs $38, $60 for the pre-theater dinner. *249 E. 50th St. (near 2nd Ave.), tel. 212/752-2225. Reservations required. Jacket and tie required. AE, DC, MC, V. Closed Mon. and Sat. lunch, all day Sun., and Aug.*

The Quilted Giraffe. Owners Barry and Susan Wine brought fresh ideas to modern cuisine some 10 years ago in the original Quilted Giraffe on Second Avenue, then moved into this stunningly designed new space in the AT&T building. There is continuous evolution in the food, which may range from a box of beautifully composed sushi to a "chocolate delirium" for dessert. The food can be either breathtaking or so quirky that you wonder whether it's worth the astronomical price ($45 for lunch, $75 for dinner, prix fixe menus only), especially since portions are on the small side. (This may well be the most expensive restaurant in the country.) Mr. Wine delights in creating such dishes as wasabi tuna pizza, but you may also sup with pleasure on classic confit of duck, sweetbreads with caramel sauce, or grilled salmon with sweet-hot mustard. *550 Madison Ave. (off 55th St.), tel. 212/593-1221. Reservations advised. Jacket required. AE, DC, MC, V. Closed Sat. lunch, Sun., and Mon.*

★ **The Rainbow Room.** This is still the most talked-about rehab on the Manhattan restaurant beat. Together, restaurateur-cum-impresario Joe Baum and architect Hugh Hardy marshaled a $25 million budget to renovate and revitalize one of the city's greatest institutions. The result is a dramatic setting towering over midtown and serving up an unusual array of dishes. Some, such as tournedos Rossini and baked Alaska, are redolent of a bygone era; others, such as sautéed foie gras, are very contemporary. An extensive wine list, full of vintage treasures, enables you to order anything from a '28 claret to an '82 cabernet sauvignon. The musical entertainment changes regularly. Go with a group, dress festively, and don't forget your dancing shoes. *30 Rockefeller Plaza (at 50th St.), tel. 212/632-5000.*

Reservations required (6 wks. in advance). Jacket and tie required. Closed Mon. AE.

The "21" Club. One of the most famous restaurants in the world, the "21" Club originally opened as a speakeasy during Prohibition and flourished well into the 1980s, when it started to seem both stuffy and scruffy to many. Since its renovation in 1987, "21" has improved its food 100%. However, it has gone through several changes in the kitchen, and the main dining room is still not as crowded as it once was. The greeting at the door is friendlier than it used to be. Moreover, the place looks just great with its period paintings, Remington bronzes, and eclectic array of bric-a-brac ranging from beer steins and football helmets to vintage toys suspended from the ceiling. The club's challenge will be to lure back some of its old-guard clientele, or at least their sons and daughters, and establish a new breed of regulars. If you go, try the "21 burger" or the crab cakes and, in the spirit of Hemingway and Bogart, have a drink at that great downstairs bar. *21 W. 52nd St. (near 5th Ave.), tel. 212/582–7200. Reservations advised. Jacket and tie required. AE, DC, MC, V. Closed Sun.*

Expensive **Aquavit.** This is a splendid-looking Scandinavian restaurant (it's about time!) set on three levels in Nelson Rockefeller's former town house, where soaring walls, a waterfall, a smorgasbord bar, a wonderful selection of iced aquavits, and delicious food set the mood. At night the lighting is particularly dramatic, turning the main room into a unique dining spot. By day cool gray tones dominate, making this a good place for a business lunch. The menu is weighted towards seafood specialties: assorted smoked fish, gravlax, and salmon. Don't overlook the arctic venison in juniper-and-apple sauce, or the Swedish pancakes. The fixed-price menu is $60, with a pretheater dinner of $19 (two courses) and $38 (three courses); an à la carte menu upstairs is good for a fast bite. *13 W. 54th St. (near 5th Ave.), tel. 212/307–7311. Reservations required downstairs. Jacket required. AE, DC, MC, V. Closed Sun.*

The Edwardian Room. The splendor of this dining room in the Plaza Hotel is unmatched by any other restaurant in New York, thanks to Ivana Trump's restoration of this dowager dining room to its former grandeur. Executive chef Kerry Simon is slowly developing the menu to balance standard Continental dishes with some new ones that are lighter and more modern, such as foie gras wrapped in potato with truffle vinaigrette, salmon tartare with curry oil, roast duck with lentils and mint, and squid lasagna with lobster and goat cheese. A dessert of banana slices with coconut ice cream is spectacular. This is a wonderful spot for a romantic twilight dinner or a quiet, uninterrupted business lunch. *59th St. and 5th Ave., tel. 212/759–3000. Reservations advised. Jackets required (jacket and tie at dinner). AE, DC, MC, V. Closed for Mon. dinner.*

★ **Felidia.** Lidia and Felix Bastianich have long led the movement for authentic *cucina Italiana* in New York City, and have had tremendous influence across the country thanks to their unbridled enthusiasm, their attentiveness to detail, and their spectacular wine list. The food is usually great, refined but homey, full of delicacy and flavor, and always cooked with fervor. The only flaw is the crush at the bar from people waiting for reserved tables. The brick and blanched-wood decor is very cozy. Choose from a wide array of daily specials, or go with such standbys as cold antipasti, ziti with lamb sauce, *pappardelle* (wide noodles) with broccoli di rape, salmon with mustard sauce, or pineapple and strawberries with balsamic vinegar. Felidia's wine cellar is one of the country's finest, and Lidia herself will be happy to instruct you on the latest estate bottlings from Italy. *243 E. 58th St. (near 2nd. Ave.), tel. 212/758–1479. Reservations required. Jacket and tie required. AE, DC, MC, V. Closed Sat. lunch and Sun.*

★ **Grand Central Oyster Bar & Restaurant.** Opened in 1912, this granddaddy of American seafood restaurants is renowned for its extraordinary offerings of oysters and every kind of fish that swims into the Fulton Fish Market downtown. Located underneath Grand Central Terminal's Great Hall, it's an astounding space to eat in; it's always crowded at lunchtime (less so for dinner), but there's a quieter rear room, as well as that famous oyster bar. Don't try coming late for your reservation or you'll lose it. The range of offerings here—chowders, grilled and poached fish, smoked salmon—is the best you'll ever see, and everything is prepared with great integrity. The white wine list is one of the most interesting in the United States. *Grand Central Terminal, tel. 212/490–6650. Lunch reservations required, dinner reservations advised. Dress: casual. AE, DC, MC, V. Closed weekends.*

★ **Il Nido.** This is a major player in Northern Italian (specifically, Tuscan) cuisine, and it's constantly jammed with expense-accounters who'll pay a hefty tab for some of the best food in New York. The dining room is sophisticated without being studied: a mix of dark wood beams, white walls, plaid carpet, and a sea of white tablecloths. The regulars know what they like—a sampling of three pastas on one plate, massive veal chops with wild mushrooms, and the delicious *tiramisù* (mascarpone and sponge cake), the classic Italian dessert—but ask owner Adi Giovanetti what he'd suggest and you should be very happy. The wine list is long and impressive. *251 E. 53rd St. (near 2nd Ave.), tel. 212/753–8450. Reservations required. Jacket and tie required. AE, DC, MC, V. Closed Sun.*

★ **La Caravelle.** Owner André Jammet has restored this great classic restaurant to eminence, bringing the Jean Pages murals of Paris back to pristine condition, keeping the atmosphere both bright and genteel, and appointing a talented young chef—a move that ensures La Caravelle's position as one of the most consistently rewarding dining experiences in New York City. Many of the classic dishes remain, but the chef has been encouraged to innovate, and every week he changes his menu dégustation (priced at $70), which is offered on request. Less expensive options are the prix fixe lunch ($33), pretheater dinner ($37), and prix fixe dinner ($59). Go for his specials: Enjoy the fresh foie gras, the light crab ravioli, and, for dessert, the tour de force coconut soufflé. The wine list is very fine, the service staff is affable. *33 W. 55th St. (near 5th Ave.), tel. 212/586–4252. Reservations required. Jacket and tie required. AE, DC, MC, V. Closed Sat. lunch and Sun.*

La Reserve. Catty-corner to Rockefeller Center is this airy, stylish restaurant, which serves a good balance of classic, nouvelle, and regional French cuisine. The large front dining room is decorated with rural murals, the lighting is cheerful, and the staff, under owner Jean-Louis Missud, is admirably professional. The large rear room, however, lacks personality. The menu changes to suit the seasons; specialties include salmon with lentils, raviolli with scallops and beurre blanc, and apple tart. This is a very fine place—and far more friendly than many of the French deluxe establishments. The wine list is solid. Prix fixe meals are available at lunch ($31) and dinner ($40 for pretheater, otherwise $49). *4 W. 49th St. (near 5th Ave.), tel. 212/247–2993. Reservations advised. Jacket and tie required. AE, DC, MC, V. Closed Sat. lunch and Sun.*

Le Cygne. At this charming French restaurant, the beautiful pastel interior and conscientious service are appropriate complements to such notable dishes as timbale of poached egg and lobster roe, *croustillant de salmon* (fresh salmon atop a potato pancake), duck confit, breast of chicken with leek and truffle, and ravioli of lobster and wild mushrooms. Leave room for such luscious desserts as cassis delight. The fixed-price lunches are $30 and $37; the fixed-price dinners are $45 and $58. *55 E. 54th St. (near Madison Ave.), tel. 212/759–5941. Reservations required. Jacket and tie required. AE, DC, MC, V. Closed Sat. lunch and Sun.*

★ **Le Perigord.** This deluxe French restaurant is a perfect example of how classicism can be renewed successfully and maintain its vibrancy year after year. Le Perigord, under owner Georges Briguet, has long been one of Manhattan's finest dining spots, but with the addition of chef Antoine Bouterin a few years ago, its kitchen has become truly inspired. With its soft lighting, pretty flowered accents, and superb staff, this is a very romantic place, and there is no better host than Mr. Briguet for making a newcomer feel right at home. Your best bet is to put yourself in Bouterin's hands or go with his specials—items such as beef with truffles on a potato galette (a bed of thinly sliced potatoes) and passion fruit mousse. His halibut in court bouillon is great. A prix fixe lunch costs $29; the set-menu dinner is $49. *405 E. 52nd St. (near 1st Ave.), tel. 212/755–6244. Reservations advised. Jacket and tie required. AE, DC, MC, V. Closed Sun.*

Michael's. Owner Michael McCarty has re-created his Santa Monica hit in midtown Manhattan, and in the main, it travels well. The greeting from the peripatetic McCarty couldn't be friendlier, and the modern-art–festooned interior provides an attractive backdrop to Michael's French–American menu. While the food may not be on the cutting edge of new American cooking, the menu reads very well. Highlights such as graavlax with mustard sauce, seafood cassoulet, grilled saddle of rabbit, scallops in a chardonnay cream sauce, and trio of five sorbets, coupled with a well-conceived wine list, make the experience quite memorable nonetheless. *24 W. 55th St. (near 5th Ave.), tel. 212/767–0555. Reservations advised. Jacket and tie advised. AE, DC, MC, V.*

★ **Palm.** Since 1926, Palm has been known as the New York steak house par excellence—though hardly for its decor: The floors are covered with sawdust; the walls with the discolored murals of favorite customers. You'll probably have to wait in the much-too-smoky, cramped bar if your reservation is anytime after 6 PM. The waiters don't hold much truck with amenities, but they're not really brusque, just robotic. You come here for 16-ounce aged steaks, gargantuan lobsters, great cheesecake, and anything else on the menu (well, the spaghetti's not so good). The wine list is a joke. Palm Too, right across the street, is just as good though not as antique. *837 2nd Ave. (near 45th St.), tel. 212/687–2953. Lunch reservations required, dinner reservations for 4 or more. Dress: casual. AE, DC, MC, V. Closed Sat. lunch and Sun.*

Scarlatti. Owner Lello Arpaia has made this peach-colored dining room with its formal accents into one of the best Italian restaurants in midtown. The best specialties are in the Southern Italian mode, but this is not your "red sauce" kind of place: It offers authentic Italian cookery of a very high order. The staff can sometimes be too mannered (as in, "Let me suggest a nice veal chop for the young lady"), but Lello is a dedicated restaurateur who really wants you to have a great meal and some good wine. Try the malfatti pasta with artichokes, penne with smoked cheese and tomato, sea bass roasted with herbs, or the mezzaluna ravioli with cream and saffron sauce. A pretheater dinner is offered for $32. *34 E. 52nd St. (near Madison Ave.), tel. 212/753-2444. Reservations required. Jacket required. AE, DC, MC, V.*

★ **Smith & Wollensky.** Here is a very large, handsome, oak-floored steak-and-seafood house; it may not have Palm's historic dowdiness, but its food can be just as good. The steaks are unassailably among the best anywhere; the breads, veal chops, lobsters, stone crabs, and apple brown betty are all recommended; and the wine list is quite extraordinary, especially for cabernet sauvignon and vintage claret. Service is brisk and adequate to the job, although the place is jammed with businesspeople day and night, before theater and after work. This is a smooth operation, very much a "New York joint." *201 E. 49th St. (at 3rd Ave.), tel. 212/753-1530. Reservations advised. Jacket advised. AE, DC, MC, V.*

★ **Sparks Steak House.** This mock colonial dining room is paradise for the oenophile—or even the amateur wine buff—who's curious about sampling mature vintages of French, Italian, Spanish, or California wine. Indeed, owner Pat Cetta can lay claim to the biggest collection of fine and rare wines in the city. What's more, his markups are reasonable. Opt for Sparks's signature steak au fromage, accompanied by a magnum of '73 Mayacamus cabernet sauvignon. (Beef is hardly de rigueur; you can choose from a wide array of fish, fowl, lamb, and veal dishes.) Cap off the evening with a late-harvest Riesling or a Château d'Yquem '81 with luscious cheesecake. *210 E. 46th St. (near 3rd Ave.), tel. 212/687-4855. Reservations required. Jacket and tie advised. AE, DC, MC, V. Closed Sun.*

Moderate **Alfredo's the Original of Rome.** Despite the hoopla about its links to the glamorous Alfredo's of Rome, and despite its tucked-away location in the Citicorp building, this popular place happens to serve Italian food of a very high order. Owner Guido Bellanca and his sons work hard to maintain an authentic level of cooking, as do the chefs regularly imported from Italy. You won't go wrong with any of the pastas, especially the famous fettuccine Alfredo, the risotto with mascarpone and spinach, or the panzotti with walnuts and herbs. Recommended for dessert are the tiramisù and the gelati. There's a bargain lunch on Sunday with good jazz and a daily prix fixe lunch priced at $24.95. *153 E. 53rd St. (near 3rd Ave.), tel. 212/371-3367. Reservations advised. Dress: casual. AE, DC, MC, V.*

American Festival Café. If you have time for just one dining stop in New York with your family, this should be it. Set right next to the Rockefeller Center skating rink, the restaurant offers a view of the Prometheus statue, the row of flags from all nations, and majestic skyscrapers. The dining room is decorated with fine folk art in a casual, amiable way, and the food sticks to American classics, with a few modern touches. You won't go wrong with prime rib, crab cakes with cole slaw, or Sedutto's ice cream. This is a great place for pretheater dining, and the $21.95 prix fixe dinner is a bargain. At Christmastime, when the plaza's giant tree is lighted, it's the most festive spot in the city. *20 W. 50th St. (in Rockefeller Center), tel. 212/246–6699. Reservations required. Dress: casual. AE, DC, MC, V.*

Brasserie. At any hour, 24 hours a day, you can find something warm and good to eat at the Brasserie, which can come in handy after a long evening at the opera or a brisk early morning walk. The subterranean dining room is bright and cheerful, and it serves a good rendering of French bistro classics. There's a rectangular counter where you can sit for a quick or solitary meal, and the place always draws a friendly crowd. Try such items as the cassoulet or the roast chicken. Desserts are homey and good, too. *100 E. 53rd St. (near Park Ave.), tel. 212/751–4840. Reservations unnecessary. Dress: casual. AE, DC, MC, V.*

Bukhara. Bukhara stands out for specializing in the cuisine of the North-West Frontier of India. Especially savory are the barbecued meats and luscious tandoori specials. You'll eat these Indian regional dishes with your fingers amid a sedate dining room full of glistening copper pots and colorful Bukhara rugs. Don't miss the pork spareribs, the Seekh kebab, or the Sikandari raan. You won't find this kind of food in too many other cities. The prices here are fair ($16.95 for the set menu lunch, $24.95 at dinner) and the service is courteous. A good Sunday brunch is also available. *148 E. 48th St. (near Lexington Ave.), tel. 212/838–1811. Reservations advised. Dress: casual. AE, DC, MC, V.*

China Grill. This is a vast and handsome, kite-festooned dining room that fills the ground floor of the CBS building (known to locals as "Black Rock"). In concept, the China Grill is essentially a California transplant à la Wolfgang Puck's Chinois on Main in Los Angeles (though he has no connection with China Grill). The menu features a variety of grilled fare with Oriental flavorings and leans toward seafood dishes. All are beautifully presented. It's a very popular place, and can be quite noisy, but the standards have been kept up. It's great for lunch and pre- or post-theater dinners; the latter is priced at $32. *52 W. 53rd St. (off 6th Ave.), tel. 212/333–7788. Reservations advised. Jacket advised. AE, DC, MC, V. Closed Sun.*

Chin Chin. Vintage photographs snapped in the Far East at the turn of the century, combined with bleached walls, plush banquettes, and dramatic lighting, create a sleek, stark look at this beguiling but noisy Chinese café. Happily, the kitchen's output equals the drama of the decor, making this an excellent midtown outpost for Chinese fare. It serves good pork dumplings, fried squid, three-glass chicken (a glass each of water, soy sauce, and wine are added to the sauce), orange beef, sesame noodles, and scallion pancakes. *216 E. 49th St. (near 3rd Ave.), tel. 212/888–4555. Reservations advised. Dress: casual. AE, DC, MC, V. Closed weekend lunch.*

★ **Dawat.** Unquestionably the city's most attractive Indian restaurant, Dawat specializes in authentic and unusual regional dishes. Veteran Indian-food-lovers make this their second home. The fixed-price lunches, $11.95 and $12.95, are excellent values. Whether you fancy chicken tikka, fish or goat stew, *baghari jhinga* (spiced shrimp), or such vegetable preparations as baked eggplant, green beans in coconut, or *kheer* (yogurt with shredded cucumber), you will not be disappointed. Try the Taj Mahal beer. *210 E. 58th St. (near 3rd Ave.), tel. 212/*

355–7555. Reservations advised. Dress: casual. AE, DC, MC, V. Closed Sun. lunch.

★ **Hatsuhana.** This is considered New York City's best sushi restaurant. There are two locations: The original on 48th Street is pleasant enough, but the newer Park Avenue branch (actually wedged off the avenue between the streets) is prettier, with a greenhouse dining room. At both you'll find Japanese businesspeople at the sushi bar or the tables, challenging the *itamae* (master sushi chef) to come up with something interesting. He always does—from mackerel and pickled ginger to broiled squid feet! The sashimi is perfectly fresh; the service, fast-paced. *237 Park Ave. (on 46th St.), tel. 212/661–3400; 17 E. 48th St. (near Madison Ave.), tel. 212/355–3345. Reservations required. Jacket and tie advised. AE, MC, V. Closed Sat. and Sun.*

★ **Manhattan Ocean Club.** A sleek and stylish interior adorned with Picasso ceramics makes this two-tiered restaurant one of the most attractive spots for seafood dining. The new chef, Jonathan Parker, has added some fine dishes to the menu while maintaining traditional favorites. Try the lobster salad with couscous and Moroccan spices, monkfish with lentils, and rosemary-crusted red snapper, plus standbys such as glistening fresh oysters, good poached salmon, grilled swordfish, fillet of sole, blackened redfish, and the warm chocolate tart. *57 W. 58th St. (near 6th Ave.), tel. 212/371–7777. Reservations advised. Jacket and tie advised. AE, DC, MC, V. Closed weekend lunch.*

Mickey Mantle's. You can practically conjure up the whole scenario before setting foot in this fun midtown restaurant: Oversize television screens throughout are tuned to (what else?) baseball games past and present; ball club paraphernalia—bats, gloves, antique uniforms—abound. The food is hearty and the portions, whether of burgers, fries, or salads, are very large. What's more, Mickey Mantle himself actually drops in from time to time. This place is great for kids, both little and big. *42 Central Park S (near 6th Ave.), tel. 212/688–7777. Reservations advised. Dress: casual. AE, DC, MC, V.*

★ **Nippon.** One of the first modern Japanese restaurants in the United States, Nippon has long been a pioneer in everything from fine decor and tatami rooms to bringing sushi and sashimi to the attention of the American public. At this large and bright place, the negimaki roll was created to satisfy Americans' taste for beef with a Japanese accent. The staff has remained cordial to all its customers. It's best to allow the chef to prepare a special dinner for you, featuring everything from imaginative sushi to exotic main courses; your meal will be unforgettable. The tatami rooms are for parties. *155 E. 52nd St. (near Lexington Ave.), tel. 212/355–9020. Reservations advised. Jacket advised. AE, DC, MC, V. Closed Sat. lunch and Sun.*

Pentop Bar. In the era before air-conditioning, rooftop restaurants were quite common in Manhattan. Weather permitting, the Pentop restaurant, located on the 23rd floor of the Peninsula Hotel, revives the experience. Grilled fare prevails for dinner, and at lunch you can choose from a cold buffet of charcuterie and light salads, and roast chicken or leg of lamb. There's an enclosed bar area in case of inclement weather. *700 5th Ave. (at 55th St., in the Peninsula Hotel), tel. 212/903–3902. Reservations advised for dinner. Jacket advised. AE, DC, MC, V.*

Rosa Mexicano. This is a good choice for classic regional Mexican fare, served up in attractive stucco-and-wood surroundings. Marvelous margaritas and excellent guacamole are prepared tableside to your taste; spicy sausage, beef, and chicken are cooked on an open grill. Other specialties include stuffed peppers, *carnitas* (morsels of meat), and *helados* (ice cream). *1063 1st Ave. (near 58th St.), tel. 212/753–7407. Reservations advised. Dress: casual. AE, DC, MC, V.*

★ **Sandro's.** Nowhere will you find a more ebullient chef than Sandro Fioriti, who bounds *ex culina* and slaps down whatever it is that strikes his fancy that night—roast pork *alla romana*, with fennel and rosemary, roast chicken, luscious *bruschetta* (toast) with tomato, or fresh-from-the-oven lemon cookies. There is a menu, but go with Sandro's suggestions and you'll have hearty food, full of flavor. The gelati are among the best in the city. The staff is amiable, and everything is on the upswing here. The premises are effectively modern and simple, ideal for large parties or groups. *420 E. 59th St. (near 1st Ave.), tel. 212/355–5150. Reservations advised. Jacket advised. AE, DC, MC, V.*

★ **Shun Lee Palace.** One of the problems with most Chinese restaurants is their lack of consistency from month to month and year to year. Shun Lee's owner Michael Tong, however, shows what can be done when restaurateur and customer have the same standards. The result is the most reliably satisfying Chinese food in New York City, from the Peking duck and the beautifully orchestrated banquet dishes to the pork wontons and the tuna steak. The premises, though cramped, are visually exciting; the staff can be either helpful or not, depending on your captain. *155 E. 55th St. (off Lexington Ave.), tel. 212/371–8844. Reservations advised. Jacket advised. AE, DC, MC, V.*

Zarela. This is one of the city's best spots for sophisticated Mexican cuisine served in comfortable surroundings. Owner Zarela Martinez (formerly of Café Marimba) continues to innovate and change her menu according to the seasonal availability of ingredients. Her trademark dishes include chicken Chilaquiles (chicken prepared with layers of fried tortillas), *calamar a la Veracruzana* (fried squid in a spicy tomato, onion, green olive, and jalapeño sauce), fajitas, whole grilled trout, and tuna with mole sauce. Sample the fried plantains, and try to leave room for the luscious desserts, especially the maple walnut pumpkin cheesecake. *953 2nd Ave. (near 50th St.), tel. 212/644–6740. Reservations advised. Dress: casual. AE, DC. Closed weekend lunch.*

Inexpensive **Billy's.** Charging a fair price for a fair meal, this neighborhood pub has been serving up seafood, steaks, chops, burgers, and corned beef hash—a house specialty—for the better part of the century, and numbers many a devoted regular. The old New York decor is completely apt for a pleasant lunch or early dinner. *948 1st Ave. (near 52nd St.), tel. 212/355–8920. Reservations advised for 3 or more. Dress: casual. AE, DC, MC, V.*

Extra! Extra! Located in the *Daily News* building, this restaurant has an interior that really is black and white and red all over. The menu sports such eclectic offerings as alligator sausage, mustard chicken, and fried calamari with Thai chili sauce. It's a friendly and lively spot, for lunch in particular. *767 2nd Ave. (at 41st St.), tel. 212/490–2900. Reservations advised. Dress: casual. AE, DC, MC, V. Closed weekend lunch.*

Serendipity 3. Looking as bright as when it opened in the 1960s,

Serendipity 3 is as good as its name—a swell little place where you'll find all sorts of surprises, from campy gifts, postcards, and paraphernalia to some very tasty food: chili, burgers, and scrumptious desserts like frozen hot chocolate. The people who eat here range from Brooke Shields to prom queens; from East Side artists to Scarsdale matrons and children of all ages. *225 E. 60th St. (near 2nd Ave.), tel. 212/838–3531. Reservations advised on weekends. Dress: casual. AE, DC, MC, V.*

Yellowfingers. This bright, lively corner restaurant is especially convenient to Bloomingdale's and perfect for a light bite after a movie (several cinemas are located nearby). You'll find quality food here, including a good Caesar salad and onion rings that are offered as a first course. An enticing array of entrées ranges from sandwiches, such as grilled tuna steak with parsley and red onion on *foccacia* (puffy pizza bread), to homemade herbed sausages. You'll also have a nice selection of wines by the glass. *1009 3rd Ave. (at 60th St.), tel. 212/751–8615. No reservations. Dress: casual. AE, DC, MC, V.*

Theater District

Very Expensive **Le Bernardin.** This commodious and elegant dining room has
★ dazzled the most demanding gourmets since its opening. With his light, flavorful sauces and tasteful creativity, Gilbert LeCoze is a true master of form and substance, and his sister Maguy greets customers with a French chic found nowhere else in New York. The service is usually impeccable, though there can sometimes be a wait for a confirmed table. The wine list is very good, but quite expensive. Creative appetizers include black bass tartar with caviar, marinated cod with ginger, and shrimp and basil beignets. Among the entrées, the poached halibut with rosemary and onion confit vies in excellence with another version prepared with capers and a warm vinaigrette. The fish carpaccios are excellent, and the trademark roast monkfish with cabbage is a must. At $42 and $68, respectively, the prix fixe lunch and dinner are relative bargains. *155 W. 51st St. (near 7th Ave.), tel. 212/489–1515. Reservations required. Jacket and tie required. AE, DC, MC, V. Closed Sun.*

Expensive **Barbetta.** This is New York's oldest Italian restaurant and an
★ elegant beauty run by Laura Maioglio. Every great musician and actor has eaten here, including Toscanini. The premises are set in a lovely town house, with a delightful garden for warm-weather dining; upstairs are elegant private dining rooms. The pretheater crowd is a bit rushed here, but you won't find better food in the neighborhood. Specialties include linguine with black-olive paste, sensational risotto with rosé champagne, and sturgeon with olives and fennel. There is a six-course pretheater menu priced at $39 and a seven-course tasting menu at $55. *321 W. 46th St. (near 8th Ave.), tel. 212/246–9171. Reservations advised. Jacket advised. AE, DC, MC, V. Closed Sun.*

La Cité. Owner Alan Stillman's (of Smith & Wollensky, The Post House, and Manhattan Ocean Club) latest creation evokes the image of a grand Franco-American restaurant; close attention has been paid to interior design. Chef Frederick Perrier does wonderful Alsatian brasserie classics like *choucroute garnie, frise aux lardons* (chicory lettuce with bacon), and *confit de canard* (preserved duck), with nightly specials that are equally appealing. You'll also find good grilled mustard-coated chicken and excellent *frites*. The interesting wine list includes several French country wines. Prices are generally higher, however, than you'd expect for such relatively simple fare, and service can sometimes be agonizingly slow. *120 W. 51st St. (near 6th Ave.), tel. 212/956–7100. Reservations advised. Dress: casual. AE, DC, MC, V.*

Gallagher's. The best of the West Side steak houses, this spot has a lot of tradition and Broadway razzle-dazzle about it. The place has always been a big hangout for sports figures, and there are photos of all the great ones on the walls. The meat—unquestionably fine aged prime—hangs in the window, and the whole place buzzes with masculine guffaws. If you like that kind of environment, this is an enticing place, especially before or after the theater. Stay with the steaks, lobster, onion rings, and cheesecake, and you'll be happy as a clam. *228 W. 52nd St. (off Broadway), tel. 212/245–5336. Reservations advised. Dress: casual. AE, DC, MC, V.*

Petrossian. Here's a special spot for fanciers of fine caviar and smoked fish in every manifestation imaginable. At the New York outpost of his famed Parisian emporium, Armen Petrossian has imposed a highly stylized, updated-deco interior to set the stage for a unique evening, exotic lunch, or unusual theater outing. The fixed-price menus ($37.50 for the pretheater dinner and postpheater dinner, $60 for the regular dinner) include tastings of most delicacies and, at today's prices, actually represent very good value. Indulge yourself in a trio of sevruga, osetra, and beluga caviar, or sample the superb seared salmon with smoked salmon ravioli. There's also a good champagne list. *182 W. 58th St. (near 7th Ave.), tel. 212/245–2214. Reservations advised. Jacket and tie advised. AE, DC, MC, V. Closed Sun.*

★ **Russian Tea Room.** Justly famous for its longevity, its polished Imperial Palace decor, and its endless parade of celebrities (a scene from the movie *Tootsie* was filmed here), the RTR is legendary—and well it should be. Of course, if you're not Dustin Hoffman or Luciano Pavarotti, you probably won't get an "A" table downstairs, but upstairs is just as bright and shining, especially at holiday time. The food has improved measurably over the past year or two, since noted chef Jacques Pepin began consulting here. Enjoy the blini with caviar, the chicken Kiev, full of butter, and the delicious borscht soup. A set-menu dinner is offered for $39.50. *150 W. 57th St. (near 7th Ave.), tel. 212/265–0947. Reservations advised. Jacket required at dinner. AE, DC, MC, V.*

Moderate **Chez Josephine.** Quintessential French bistro fare—quail,
★ roast chicken, *pommes frites*—is served in a setting designed to pay homage to the late nightclub singer Josephine Baker (the owner is her adopted son). The place is decked out with paintings and posters from the period when Baker was all the rage in Paris. Even the famed piano on which she used to practice has been restored; it is now occupied by a modern-day chanteuse who evokes a bygone era. This place is great fun. *414 W. 42nd St. (near 9th Ave.), tel. 212/594–1925. Reservations advised. Dress: casual. AE, MC, V. Closed Sun. and lunchtime.*

Lattanzi. Despite its insipid decor and cramped quarters, a service staff that always seems distracted, and one of New York's most absurdly priced and dull wine lists, when Lattanzi does get the food out of the kitchen it can be delicious and full flavored. The place is jammed pretheater, so book after 8 PM, when a second menu featuring dishes favored by Rome's Italian Jewish community is proffered and the staff is not quite so harried. Particularly noteworthy are the artichokes *alla Giudea* (deep-fried), ravioli with porcini, fettuccine with stracotto beef, and snapper with raisins and vinegar. *361 W. 46th St. (near 9th Ave.), tel. 212/315–0980. Reservations advised. Jacket and tie not required. AE. Closed Sun.*

★ **Orso.** By far, this is the most popular restaurant in the Theater District; it's even tough to get a table after the theater. The reasons are not hard to find: The atmosphere is unpretentious, the greeting at the door warm (and apologetic if they can't fit you in), the price is extremely fair, and the rustic trattoria fare is very good indeed. It gets its fair share of celebrities, too. Recommended are the ravioli with potato and sage butter, grilled chicken with beans and garlic, and polenta with cheese and lentils. *322 W. 46th St. (near 8th Ave.), tel. 212/489–7212. Reservations advised. Dress: casual. MC, V.*

★ **Remi.** Designer-owner Adam Tihany has created a stunning interior, replete with flying buttresses and a larger-than-life Venetian mural. He already draws a smart crowd who really know their Italian food. Chef-partner Francesco Antonucci is a master of Venetian cuisine, and, if Remi continues on its present course, this should be one of the great ones within a year. Check out the grappa selection. *Bigoli* (spaghetti) with mushrooms and speck, goose carpaccio, risotto with cuttlefish, ravioli with fresh tuna and ginger, roast squab, *fegato veneziana* (calf's liver Venetian style), cheesecake, and crème brûlée are just some of superb dishes offered. *145 W. 53rd St. (near 7th Ave.), tel. 212/581–4242. Reservations advised. Dress: casual. AE, DC, MC, V. Closed weekend lunch.*

Inexpensive **Bangkok Cuisine.** New York doesn't have the number of good Thai restaurants many smaller cities have, but Bangkok Cuisine is one of the oldest and best. It doesn't look like much—rather dark and bare-bones with a fish tank in the dining room—but the food is delicious and (on request) as hot as you can stand it. The pad Thai noodles and shrimp is a great dish here, as are the crispy mee krob noodles and the whole fried fish. *885 8th Ave. (near 53rd St.), tel. 212/581–6370. Reservations advised. Dress: casual. AE, MC, V. Closed Sun. lunch.*

Cabana Carioca. It may seem dingy—you follow the music up a flight of stairs to a thickly varnished, rather weird-looking dining room—but Cabana Carioca serves the best Brazilian food in New York: great platters and pots steaming with black beans, manioc flour, *feijoada* (the Brazilian national stew), and seafood. All of it is lusty and filling, and nothing is particularly expensive. *123 W. 45th St. (near 7th Ave.), tel. 212/581–8088. Reservations advised. Dress: casual. AE, DC, MC, V.*

Hard Rock Café. People come here not so much for dinner or lunch as for a lift. Music blares from noon until the wee hours. The decor aptly consists of a collection of guitars belonging to celebrated musicians. You can count on decent hamburgers, sandwiches, and french fries. There is *always* a line to get in, even at 11:30 in the morning; they don't take reservations, so be prepared for a wait. *221 W. 57th St. (near Broadway), tel. 212/459–9320. No reservations. Dress: casual. AE, DC, MC, V.*

Joe Allen. A longtime hangout for theatergoers and actors, Joe Allen (there's a Los Angeles and a Paris branch) has no pretensions and serves decent, simple food. The ribs and burgers are dependable, the service is affable (often by actors between jobs), and the place buzzes with a certain theatrical history. It's a good spot for before or after the show. *326 W. 46th St. (near 8th Ave.), tel. 212/581-6464. Reservations required. Dress: casual. MC, V.*

Upper East Side

Very Expensive **Le Cirque.** Here is the international restaurant par excellence.
★ Glamorous, extravagant, studded nightly with famous names from every walk of life, Le Crique glitters under the ownership of Sirio Maccioni, and Daniel Boulud is one French chef every other chef in town watches for his never-ending array of great dishes, which may be sea scallops with black truffles, a homey pot-au-feu, or a grandiose baby lamb of unsurpassed succulence. A multitude of signature dishes, including pasta primavera, is available on request. Desserts are always a delight, from the famouus crème brûlée to the spun-sugar fantasies. The prix fixe lunch of $36 is a great way to sample this splendid fare. The ever-expanding, ever-innovative wine list remains one of the city's best and most moderately priced. *58 E. 65th St. (near Park Ave.), tel. 212/794-9292. Reservations required. Jacket and tie required. AE, DC, Closed Sun.*

Le Régence. Located in the glorious Plaza Athenée Hotel, this very formal restaurant is an elaborate exercise in *ancien regime* decor. It's ideal for business entertaining, with tables spaced widely apart. The fabulous food is overseen by France's noted Rostang family (Jo, Philippe, and Michel), who cook here on rotation while a superlative chef mans the kitchens day to day. This place is for serious eating: pompano with black olive crust, salmon rillettes with sour cream, lobster ravioli, figs with coulis of fruit, and several other delicacies you won't find elsewhere in this country. There's a good wine list, too. The $25.50 prix fixe lunch is a great value, as is the Sunday prix fixe dinner, at $59.50. *37 E. 64th St. (near Madison Ave.), tel. 212/ 606-4647. Reservations required. Jacket and tie required. AE, DC, MC, V.*

★ **Parioli Romanissimo.** The reserved beauty of Parioli, set in a town house off Fifth Avenue, makes this a very romantic spot, but it is the food that draws well-heeled customers here year after year. Owner Rubrio Rossi serves up exquisite Northern Italian cooking. You may feast on *cotechino* (fresh pork sausage) with white truffles, risotto with wild mushrooms, or an enormous rack of lamb with rosemary. Leave room for a selection from the finest cheese cart in the city. Prices are very, very high, but you do get value—except on the wine list, which is not particularly extensive but is exorbitantly priced. *24 E. 81st St. (off 5th Ave.), tel. 212/288-2391. Reservations required. Jacket and tie required. AE, DC. Closed for lunch and Sun.*

Expensive **Alo Alo.** Executive chef Matthew Kenney has done miracles with the menu here; if only someone else would do the same with the decibels. This highly popular, whimsically designed trattoria has become a staple of the singles set, and from the sounds of it, most of them appear to work on the trading floor of the Stock Exchange. Kenney's innovations such as duck pizza with goat cheese and rosemary, marinated artichoke with toasted walnuts and Parmesan, grilled veal chop with mandarin glaze and risotto, and seared red tuna with caramelized shallot vinaigrette and crispy beet chips have elevated the once-passable food to pleasing new levels. So bring your earplugs and sample the fare. *1030 3rd Ave. (at 61st St.), tel. 212/838–4343. Reservations advised. Dress: casual. AE, DC, MC, V.*

Arizona 206. Despite its casual atmosphere and piercing noise level, this remains a dynamic restaurant for Southwestern cuisine. At lunchtime be sure to sample the smoked sturgeon quesadilla with chayote papaya relish, the grilled tuna steak burger with ancho chips and smoked chili ketchup, or the Creole pecan arugula salad with pear-nectar vinaigrette and blue goat cheese. At dinner, try the black-bean cakes with dandelion greens and Cajun crawfish, warm lobster tostada salad with chili avocado sauce, or loin of venison with white bean-broccoli rabe succotash and pistachio pesto. For a super-rich finale, treat yourself to the truffle cake of devil's food and Mexican chocolate. (The adjacent Arizona Café, a no-reservation, less-expensive sibling, features innovative grilled specials and can be a lively alternative.) *206 E. 60th St. (near 3rd Ave.), tel. 212/838–0440. Reservations advised. Dress: casual. AE, DC, MC, V. Closed Sun. lunch.*

★ **Aureole.** Since its promising debut in November 1988, Aureole continues to impress and delight. Magnificent floral arrangements against a bas-relief backdrop make this one of the city's most charming restaurants. Chef Charlie Palmer is forever innovating, with appetizers such as smoked quail *waterzootje* (in vegetable broth); charred lamb salad; carpaccio of yellowfin tuna, tomato and onion tarte; and home-made mozzarella with eggplant; and entrées such as grilled breast of capon on a bed of leeks; roast squab smothered in a blanket of crisp potatoes; charcoal-grilled salmon on a bed of ratatouille; and applewood–cured mallard. Desserts are excellent, especially the Aureole's bittersweet chocolate timbale or pear and pistachio tort with warm pear fritters. There is a prix fixe dinner for $55. *34 E. 61st St. (near Madison Ave.), tel. 212/319–1660. Reservations required. Jacket and tie required. AE, DC, MC, V. Closed Sun.*

★ **Ca' Nova.** Owner Corrado Muttin himself admits that Ca' Nova always had style but little to distinguish it from other East Side Italian restaurants. So he hired Ali Fathalla to transform a mediocre kitchen into one of unique Mediterranean tastes, and now this is fast becoming one of the city's most delectable destinations. The premises are quite romantic, and the crowd is definitely chic. You can't go wrong with the sweet pepper and basil soup, grilled quail with sage and mushroom polenta, rigatoni with eggplant and ricotta, sliced rack of lamb Provençal, and flan of cheesecake with pistachio sauce. *696 Madison Ave. (near 63rd St.), tel. 212/838–3725. Reservations advised. Jacket and tie advised. AE, DC, MC, V.*

Mark's Restaurant. Chef Philippe Boulot is one of this year's brightest new stars of the culinary firmament. His technique, acquired via Joel Robuchon and Alain Senderens, is impeccable, his ideas sound, and his food full of flavor. Boulot's wife, Susan, creates pastries that match up with his menus. Curiously enough, the lighter lunch dishes are not nearly so appetizing, and the premises are overly formal, which the staff compensates for by making the service extremely smooth. Fixed-price meals are offered at lunch ($24) and dinner ($45, $60 with wine). Specialties such as baked potato with spinach and lobster, napoleon of asparagus and wild mushroom ragout, braised duck leg, and nectarine and blueberry crisp make this much more than a "hotel restaurant." *77th St. at Madison Ave. (in the Mark Hotel), tel. 212/879–1864. Reservations advised. Jacket and tie advised. AE, DC, MC, V.*

★ **Mazzei.** Named after the 18th-century Italian who was a diplomat for the fledgling United States, Mazzei is the scene of kitchen politics that are clearly as astute as the ambassador would expect. A concise but carefully conceived menu includes gnocchi in a wild mushroom sauce, sautéed calamari in a tomato sauce, superb Cornish hen with peperoncini, roast pheasant, and scallops with peas; the zabaglione is spectacular. The premises are warm and comfortable—definitely the setting for some first-rate dining. *1564 2nd Ave. (near 81st St.), tel. 212/628–3131. Reservations advised. Jacket and tie not necessary. AE, MC, V.*

Post House. Here's a lively and engaging spot for both lunch and dinner, with a sleek checkerboard interior complemented by an eclectic array of Americana artifacts. Such standbys as Caesar salad, crab cakes, grilled sirloin, and addictive cottage fries vie with such creative new additions as venison chili, lobster pot pie, and Cajun beef. All can be paired with selections from a stellar wine list. *28 E. 63rd St. (near Madison Ave.), tel. 212/935–2888. Reservations advised. Jacket and tie advised. AE, DC, MC, V. Closed weekend lunch.*

★ **Sette Mezzo.** In the space of a year, this restaurant has become the Upper East Side's trattoria of record, attracting a very posh uptown crowd. The menu is similar to Vico, its older sibling *(see below)*, with such signature dishes as homemade stuffed mozzarella, fried zucchini, red snapper with balsamic vinegar, and penne with sausage and broccoli rappe (bitter Italian broccoli). The flattened breaded veal chop is another must; alternatively, try the paillard of veal with olives and tomatoes. For dessert, sample the excellent *tiramisù* or *tartufo* ice cream. *969 Lexington Ave. (near 70th St.), tel. 212/472–0400. Reservations required. Dress: casual. No credit cards.*

★ **Sign of the Dove.** For years this place was the quintessential celebration restaurant, known for its lavish decor, its outrageous prices, and the lineup of limos outside its door. Today the decor is somewhat toned down but still luxurious, and the prices are still high ($52.50 for the set menu dinner)—but the food is better than ever. Clearly owner Joe Santo has brought this old bird back to life, so there's good reason for romance to take hold again. Go with Chef Andrew D'Amico's Muscovy duck confit with pumpkin pancakes, baked fig chutney, and roast pears, the perfect roast loin of lamb, and the chocolate and banana mousse *gâteau*. *1110 3rd Ave. (at 65th St.), tel. 212/861–8080. Reservations required. Jacket required. AE, DC, MC, V. Closed Mon. lunch.*

Moderate **Al Amir.** This comfortable and cheerful spot specializes in Mid-
★ dle Eastern cuisine. Because such a tantalizing array of cold and hot appetizers is available, you might consider dispensing with a main course altogether. The starters include excellent *hummos* (mashed chick peas and sesame paste), *baba ghannouj* (broiled eggplant with sesame cream), *makanek* (spicy lamb meat sausage), and *falafel* (crushed fava beans and chick peas). Charcoal-broiled *chich taouk* (marinated chicken), *kafta* (grilled ground lamb meat), or *gambari* (grilled jumbo shrimps) make worthwhile entrées. Leave room for the excel-

lent homemade pastries. You might also try a bottle of Château Masur, a superb red wine from Lebanon. *1431 2nd Ave. (near 74th St.), tel. 212/737–1800. Reservations advised. Jacket advised. AE, DC, MC, V. Closed for lunch Mon.–Sat.*

Anatolia. Faux marble columns, striking abstract light fixtures, and a trace of traditional Turkey (an antique samovar and tray) make for an unusual, effective setting. Go with an appetite because you'll want to eat at least three full courses. Superb appetizers include zucchini "pancakes" stuffed with feta cheese, dill, and scallions; baked vine leaves stuffed with pilaf; and Turkish meat and arugula pie. For the main course, try the skewers of grilled quail in grape leaves or "Sultan's Bliss"— lamb in a tomato sauce, served on a bed of roasted eggplant. For dessert, you can choose from an irresistible selection of baklava (both traditional and contemporary) and custards; there's also a delectable rendering of apricots in light cream. If you can manage an early dinner, try the pretheater special for $15. *1422 3rd Ave. (between 80th and 81st Sts.), tel. 212/517–6262. Reservations advised. Dress: casual. AE, DC, MC, V. Closed Sun. lunch (and dinner in summer).*

Mezzaluna. The walls are decked out with dozens of artful interpretations of the two-handled chopping device for which the restaurant is named. This bristling trattoria is alive until the wee hours and is still populated by a trendy European crowd. The menu's highlights include carpaccio, insalata Mezzaluna, fresh tortellini (filling varies seasonally), pasta specials, and superb brick-oven pizzas. *1295 3rd Ave. (near 74th St.), tel. 212/535–9600. Reservations for 4 or more. Dress: casual. No credit cards.*

Mocca Hungarian Restaurant. If you're feeling low, head straight for Mocca Hungarian, where you'll find some well-made, though not particularly refined, Hungarian specialties such as *gulyas* (a classic stew), chicken paprikas, and dessert crêpes. Drink the robust red Hungarian wine, Egri Bikaver, and you'll soon feel very happy. This is a real neighborhood restaurant, with very little in the way of decor but a great deal of warmth. *1588 2nd Ave. (near 83rd St.), tel. 212/734–6470. Reservations advised. Dress: casual. No credit cards.*

Pig Heaven. This place is great fun for its piggy decor—dancing pigs, ceramic pigs, all kinds of porcine jokes. But it's also one of the neighborhood's most interesting Chinese restaurants, specializing in barbecued pork and other dishes that will make you wonder what you ever saw in egg rolls. The place is always crowded and boisterous, but no one seems to mind. Begin with the light dumplings, sample the Cantonese suckling pig, and try the special three-glass chicken. It's open late on weekends. *1540 2nd Ave. (near 80th St.), tel. 212/744–4887. Reservations advised on weekends. Dress: casual. AE, DC, MC, V.*

★ **Table d'Hôte.** With a total of only nine tables, this tiny, antique-festooned restaurant qualifies as one of the smallest eateries in New York. Yet it is an ideal spot to retreat to after an evening at one of the Upper East Side museums or when your travels take you to the neighborhood. Here you can count on very well-prepared American/Continental fare, with first courses such as snails in puff pastry, black bean soup with jalapeño cream, or goat cheese fritters. Entrées include grilled chicken breast with wild rice, carrots, and cabbage; lamb; and salmon. End your meal with good tarte tartin. Nine wines are offered by the glass. The prix fixe dinner of $25 is an excellent value. *44 E.*

92nd St. *(near Madison Ave.), tel. 212/348–8125. Reservations advised. Dress: casual. AE.*

Vašata. This is one of the few remaining Czech restaurants in a neighborhood that was once full of Eastern European places. Vašata is still a solid and very friendly little spot where you get good value for the dollar and you'll never leave hungry. Sample the menu—roast goose, dumplings, apricot crêpes—everything is wonderful and filling. The atmosphere is very Old World, and the owners are delighted you paid them a visit. *339 E. 75th St. (near 1st Ave.), tel. 212/988–7166. Reservations advised. Dress: casual. AE, MC, V. Closed Mon.*

★ **Vico Ristorante.** This intimate, white-walled silver of a space has become a hit. Bordering on boisterous, this neighborhood trattoria more than offsets the noise level with wonderful homespun pastas and innovative creations such as wilted radicchio with grilled smoked mozzarella, expertly fried zucchini and baby artichokes, country sausage with broccoli, flattened breaded veal chop, and delicious tiramisù. *1603 2nd Ave. (near 83rd St.), tel. 212/772–7441. Reservations advised. Dress: casual. No credit cards. Closed lunch.*

Inexpensive
★ **J. G. Melon.** This popular neighborhood pub bristles with activity well past midnight. The casual decor is enlivened by paintings and prints of—what else?—the melon in myriad manifestations. Melon attracts a diverse uptown crowd and gives the first-time visitor an instant slice of neighborhood life. (There's also a West Side branch at 74th and Amsterdam Avenue.) Both serve excellent bacon cheeseburgers, club sandwiches, and cottage fries, and have great bars. *1291 3rd Ave. (at 74th St.), tel. 212/744–0585. No reservations. Dress: casual. No credit cards.*

Lincoln Center

Expensive
★ **Café des Artistes.** The history surrounding Café des Artistes goes back to just after World War I, when the apartment building it's in was home to many of the finest artists and musicians of the day—including Howard Chandler Christy, who painted the restaurant's celebrated murals of young girls romping in a primeval forest that looks a little like Central Park. The paintings give this beautiful dining room a romance few other restaurants possess, but owner George Lang also demands high standards in the food, from the fine bistro fare, the pâtés, and the terrines to the chocolate Ilona torte. After a Lincoln Center performance, expect to see some of the city's most notable notables dining here. A set menu lunch is offered weekdays ($19.50), the dinner ($32.50) daily. *1 W. 67th St. (near Central Park W), tel. 212/877–3500. Reservations required. Jacket required at dinner. AE, DC, MC, V.*

★ **San Domenico.** This bellwether restaurant replicates its famed namesake in Imola, Italy. Owner Tony May shows that Italian food can be as good here as over there. The premises are deluxe but not overly formal, jarred only by orange tablecloths. The wine list is extraordinary in its Italian offerings, and the service staff is most attentive. Both a prix fixe lunch ($35) and dinner (pretheater, $42.50; otherwise $55) are available. Have the signature ravioli with egg and truffles, the lusty *pappa al pomodoro* (a broth of tomato, onion, garlic, and bread), the lobster fricasee with artichokes, and finish off with mascarpone cream with espresso sauce. *240 Central Park S (off Columbus*

Circle), tel. 212/265–5959. Reservations required. Jacket required. AE, DC, MC, V. Closed Sat. lunch and Sun.

Tavern on the Green. Just about every tourist has heard of this fanciful restaurant, and most come here to stare at its flamboyant decoration. But New Yorkers come, too, because Tavern is undeniably lively and fun. Warner LeRoy's fantasy of lights and antiques in this sumptuous Central Park setting works brilliantly; he does more banquet business here than anyone in the city. You may feast on such dishes as spaghetti with tomato, basil, and roasted duck sausage, and rack of veal with wild mushrooms. The wine list is quite good, and prix fixe menus are available at a variety of prices. *Central Park W (at 67th St.), tel. 212/873–3200. Reservations advised. Jacket advised. AE, DC, MC, V.*

Moderate

★ **Café Luxembourg.** Still stylish, but now a lot less boisterous than it was, Café Luxembourg remains one of the West Side's better bistros—and is priced accordingly (although the $28 pretheater dinner is a bargain). Its original chef has departed, but you can still expect a solid menu and satisfying specials. Go for the seafood appetizers, baby lamb, steak au poivre, and crème brûle. *200 W. 70th St. (near Amsterdam Ave.), tel. 212/873–7411. Reservations advised. Dress: casual chic. AE, DC, MC, V. Closed weekday and Sat. lunch.*

Inexpensive

The Ginger Man. There's little to recommend the food at The Ginger Man, which serves up rather humdrum burgers, french fries, and other staples, but its proximity to Lincoln Center makes this an ideal spot to grab a bite before or after a performance. And you never know who might be coming through the door next—quite possibly a celebrity or a whole corps de ballet. *51 W. 64th St. (off Broadway), tel. 212/399–2358. Reservations required. Dress: casual. AE, DC, MC, V.*

★ **Vince & Eddie's.** One of the most charming new American restaurants to debut this season, Vince & Eddie's is named after owners Vincent Orgera (who tends bar) and Eddie Schoenfeld, former maitre d'/impresario at Auntie Yuan's and Shun Lee. The attractive, modified country look was orchestrated by Sam Lopata. The menu is devoid of gimmickry; it simply works well. Try the onion tart, fried calamari salad, calf's liver with apples and onion rings, mashed turnip with crisped shallots, red snapper with walnuts, and apple tureen. There's garden dining in season. *70 W. 68th St. (between Central Park W and Columbus Ave.), tel. 212/721–0068. Reservations advised. Dress: casual. AE, DC, MC, V.*

Upper West Side

Expensive

★ **The Terrace.** Perched atop a Columbia University dorm (though not associated with the school), this elegant dining room, with its panoramic view of Manhattan and the Hudson River, is packed most nights but remains unknown to most people. It should be better known: The food is every bit the equal of the view, with prices slightly below those of comparable downtown menus. There is a new chef here, but you may expect expertly conceived French and Continental classics such as quail with caramelized squash, red snapper with cilantro and tomato-onion confit, and profiteroles for dessert, executed with considerable flourish. The prix fixe dinner is $46. *400 W. 119th St. (near Amsterdam Ave.), tel. 212/666–9490. Reservations required.*

Jacket and tie required. AE, DC, MC, V. Closed Sat. lunch, Sun., and Mon.

Moderate **Alcala.** An innovative Spanish restaurant-cum-tapas-bar, this place is designed for conservative uptown tastes. The decor is unassuming (the ubiquitous brick-and-brass look) and at times the food can be equally restrained. Good tapas include empanadas and wild mushrooms with chorizo; the seafood paella can be garlicky, and the grilled tuna can be bland. *349 Amsterdam Ave. (near 76th St.), tel. 212/769–9600. Reservations advised. Dress: casual. AE, DC, MC, V. Dinner only.*

Amsterdam's Bar and Rotisserie. This modest eatery and bar lacks all pretension, yet it is an important watering hole for Westsiders, who flock here to eat and drink with their good-looking friends. It's high-ceilinged and decorated with minimal effort, throwing the burden of showmanship on the customers, who dress up in the latest styles and wait at the bar for tables. The food is good, substantial, and low in price. You can't go wrong with the steaks or the well-regarded roast chicken and french fries. Desserts are gooey and worth every calorie. *428 Amsterdam Ave. (near 80th St.), tel. 212/874–1377. No reservations. Dress: casual. AE, DC, MC, V.*

Carmine's. Those who wouldn't deign to set foot in Little Italy or have never eaten in the Bronx, Brooklyn, or Queens, have made Carmine's the retro-chic restaurant of the year—a big, new, sprawling, loud, red-sauce, family place with old-fashioned Italian-American food served in double portions at very fair prices. Not that Carmine's is any better than dozens of other Italian-American restaurants in New York; it's just that it's caught on, and people wait an hour or more in a smoke-engulfed bar to gorge here on rubbery calamari, very good pastas, and nice garlicky chicken *scarpariello.* Volume business means volume cooking and slow service. *2450 Broadway (near 91st St.), tel. 212/362–2200. Reservations advised. Dress: casual. AE. Closed for lunch.*

Docks. This highly popular spot for seafood is contemporary in look but has the charm of an old-time seafood house. You dine on two separate levels separated by stairs and a gleaming brass rail. A blackboard lists the daily oyster specials and the catch of the day (which will also be rattled off by your waiter). Such staples as grilled scallops or salmon can be found on the regular menu along with grilled halibut. *2427 Broadway (near 89th St.), tel. 212/724–5588; also at 633 3rd Ave. (near 40th St.), tel. 212/986–8080. Reservations advised. Dress: casual. AE, DC, MC, V.*

★ **Poiret.** White walls with a floral motif, candlelit tables, and a handsome flower-festooned vitrine create an airy ambience at this popular French spot. The only flaw in the design is the soundproofing, but the first-rate bistro fare more than compensates, even when you have to raise your voice a tad to be heard over the beautifully seasoned and flavorful Mediterranean soup. Try the warm shrimp mousse and frisé salad. Whether you order the filet mignon or steak bearnaise, be sure to request a side dish of pommes frites. For dessert, Poiret makes an admirable crème brûlée. *474 Columbus Ave. (between 82nd and 83rd Sts.), tel. 212/724–6880. Reservations advised. Dress: casual. AE, DC, MC, V. Closed Sat. lunch.*

Sidewalkers. This is one of New York's few Maryland crab houses, where you drink beer while you pound and pick away at spiced blue crab claws. The huge dining room, which appears once to have been a lobby, is jammed with casually dressed Westsiders. The Creole gumbo is excellent, but the rest of the dishes just aren't up to those crabs. *12 W. 72nd St. (near Central Park W), tel. 212/799–6070. Reservations advised. Dress: casual. AE, DC, MC, V. Closed for lunch.*

Worth a Special Trip

Brooklyn
Very Expensive
★

The River Café. The beauty of the water, the Brooklyn Bridge, and the Manhattan cityscape make this a must-go for a unique sense of New York City's majesty. Chef David Burke has real talent and creates some innovative cuisine, such as a sautéed quail appetizer with sweetbread homefries and quail eggs, and seared salmon with ginger and a cracked-pepper crust and lotus chips. The dining room has no bad tables, but those smack at the window do not come cheap—expect a wait even with a reservation. All dinners are $55; there is a six-course tasting menu for $75. *1 Water St., tel. 718/522–5200. Reservations required. Jacket required. AE, DC, MC, V.*

Harlem
Moderate

Sylvia's. If you're craving great barbecue, down-home soul food, and something uniquely New York, catch a cab to Harlem (and have one waiting outside when you exit) and stop in at Sylvia's, a marvelous and justly famous restaurant serving up huge portions of great ribs, pork chops, candied sweet potatoes, and pecan pies. Bring an appetite and expect to take something home. It's good for Sunday lunch. *328 Lenox Ave. (near 126th St.), tel. 212/996–0660. Reservations required. Dress: casual. No credit cards.*

The Bronx
Moderate
★

Amerigo's. In the safe Bronx neighborhood of Throgs Neck, this has been an institution for half a century; under owners Tony and Anna Cortese, it gets better every year. There are two dining rooms: one casual, the other a bit more refined, with low lighting, sculpture, and a spacious bar. The Italian-American menu offers everything from rich, lusty *spiedino* (mozzarella fried in bread-crumb batter, with anchovy sauce) and gnocchi with a verdant pesto to terrific prime steaks, chops, and fresh lobsters. The osso buco is among the best in New York City. The Italian wine list is comprehensive in all regions, and prices for enormous portions are fair indeed. *3587 E. Tremont Ave., tel. 212/792–3600. Reservations required weekends. Jacket suggested in main dining room. AE, DC, MC, V. Closed Mon.*

Queens
Moderate

The Water's Edge. Easily as enchanting as The River Café in Brooklyn, this aptly named dining room just south of the 59th Street Bridge is spacious and very convivial, both at the bar and in the dining room. There's been a recent change of chefs here, so our rating is on the conservative side, but we don't expect radical changes in the basically solid Continental menu. Singer-pianist Larry Woodard is one of the best in the business, and for once music truly enhances one's enjoyment of the meal. There is even ferry service (except in winter) every hour from 6 PM to 10 PM Tuesday–Saturday from the 34th Street Landing. *44th Dr. at the East River, tel. 718/482–0033. Reservations advised. Jacket required. AE, DC, MC, V. Closed Sun.*

9 Lodging

by Jane Hershey

A New York-based freelance writer whose work has appeared in Good Housekeeping, US, *and* Elle, *Jane Hershey is a long-time contributor to various Fodor's guides.*

If any single element of your trip to New York City is going to cost you a lot of money, it'll be your hotel bill. European cities may offer plenty of low-priced—albeit undistinguished—lodgings, but New York doesn't. Real estate is at a premium here, and labor costs are high, so hoteliers start out with a lot of expenses to cover. And there are enough well-heeled visitors to support competition at the premium end of the spectrum, which is where the profits are. Considering the healthy occupancy rate, market forces are not likely to drive current prices down. Fleabags and flophouses aside, there's precious little here for under $100 a night. We have noted a few budget properties, but on the sliding scale of Manhattan prices even our "Inexpensive" category includes hotels that run as high as $125 for one night's stay in a double room.

Once you've accepted that you must pay the going price, though, you'll have plenty of choices. In general, Manhattan hotels don't measure up to those in other U.S. cities in terms of room size, parking, or outside landscaping. But, this being a sophisticated city, New York hotels usually compensate with fastidious service, sprucely maintained properties, and restaurants that hold their own in a city of very knowledgeable diners. Besides, where else can you sleep in Frank Lloyd Wright's former apartment, swim with a view of the Empire State Building, or eat breakfast in bed while watching sea lions at play?

Price is by no means the perfect indicator of impeccable service, pleasant surroundings, or delicious cuisine, so we've tried to indicate the shortcomings of various properties, as well as their strong points. Common sense should tell you not to anticipate the same kind of personal service from even a top-flight convention hotel, such as the New York Hilton, as you would from a smaller, sedate property like the Doral Tuscany, even though both have rooms in the same price range. Know your own taste and choose accordingly. If you like bright lights, a lively lobby, and a central location, a residential-style hotel could disappoint you, no matter how elegant it is.

Basic rules of decorum and dress are observed at the better hotels. With few exceptions, jackets (and frequently ties) are required in formal dining and bar areas after 5 or 6 PM. Bare feet or beach sandals are not allowed, and an overall sloppy appearance won't encourage good service.

Women on their own, even at upscale hotels like the Waldorf-Astoria or the Helmsley Palace, should be aware that they may be accosted in public areas, either by male guests trying to find companions or by hotel staff trying to chase away the hookers who transact business in hotel lobbies. Because these "working girls" often look quite respectable, any single woman may be suspect. You might want to ask the concierge to point out places where you'll feel comfortable relaxing or waiting on your own. Many female travelers find VIP floors, with their concierge-controlled lounges and complimentary beverages and snacks, a boon for avoiding such situations.

Most Manhattan hotels are in the midtown area, so we have categorized them by price range rather than location. Exact prices could be misleading: Properties change their so-called "rack rates" seasonally, and most hotels offer weekend packages that include such tempting extras as complimentary meals, drinks, or tickets to events. Your travel agent may have brochures about such packages; also look for advertisements in travel magazines or the Sunday travel sections of major newspapers such as the *New York Times*, the *Washington Post*, or the *Los Angeles Times*. Note: Many hotels offer corporate rates to regular customers if they ask.

Visitors can also take advantage of reputable discount booking services such as **Express Hotel Reservations.** This Boulder, Colorado company offers savings of 20–30% on superior rooms at a variety of New York hotels, along with travel advice and other information. There is no charge for any of the company's services (it is used frequently by major companies, such as Hallmark and The Limited). Participating hotels include the New York Hilton, Le Parker Meridien, and several of the Doral properties. Call 800/356–1123 for further information.

Highly recommended lodgings in each price category are indicated by a star ★. Though not *every* acceptable hotel has been included, enough ground has been covered to help you find a good match.

Category	Cost*
Very Expensive	over $260
Expensive	$180–$260
Moderate	$125–$180
Inexpensive	under $125

All prices are for a standard double room, excluding 21¼% city and state sales tax.

The following credit card abbreviations are used: AE, American Express; DC, Diners Club; MC, MasterCard; V, Visa.

Reservations New York is constantly full of vacationers, conventioneers, and business travelers, all requiring hotel space. Try to book your room as far in advance as possible, using a major credit card to guarantee the reservation; you might even want to work through a travel agent. Because this is a tight market, overbooking can be a problem, and "lost" reservations are not unheard of. Most properties, especially those that are part of national or worldwide chains or associations (i.e. Marriott or Leading Hotels of the World), are cooperative and generous when a reservation is lost, but guaranteed reservations usually prevent any problems. When signing in, take a pleasant but firm attitude; if there is a mix-up, chances are the outcome will be an upgrade or a free night.

Hotels with famous restaurants appreciate it when guests who want to use those facilities book tables when they make their room reservations.

Services Unless otherwise noted in the individual descriptions, all the hotels listed have the following features and services: private baths, central heating, air-conditioning, private telephones, on-premises dining, valet and room service (though not necessarily 24-hour or short notice), TV (including cable and pay-per-view films), and a routine concierge staff. Larger hotels will generally have video or high-speed checkout capability.

New York City has finally allowed liquor minibars to be installed in rooms. Most hotels have added this much-anticipated amenity—at least in their more expensive units.

Pools are a rarity, but most properties have fitness centers; we note only those that are on the premises, but other hotels usually have arrangements for guests at nearby facilities.

We've already warned you against bringing a car to Manhattan, but here's another reason: the lack of hotel parking. Many properties in all price ranges *do* offer parking facilities, but they are often at independent garages that charge up to $20 or more per day.

Very Expensive

★ **The Carlyle.** Located in one of the city's finest residential areas, this beautifully appointed traditional hotel is considered one of New York's finest. The mood is English manor house; larger rooms and suites, many of them decorated by the famous interior designer Mark Hampton, have terraces, pantries, and antique furnishings. Baths, though more subdued than others in town, are marbled and chock-full of de rigueur amenities such as hair dryers, fine toiletries, and makeup mirrors. Most visitors have heard about the famous Café Carlyle, where performers such as Bobby Short entertain. But the hotel also contains the charming Bemelman's Bar, with whimsical animal murals on the walls and live piano music at night, and the formal Carlyle Restaurant, with French cuisine and old-fashioned courtly service. This is one of the few grand hotels where European elegance and American friendliness really mix; you don't have to be a famous face to get a smile or good treatment. The concierge service is especially excellent. *35 E. 76th St. (at Madison Ave.), 10021, tel. 212/744–1600, fax 212/717–4682. 185 rooms. Facilities: restaurant, café, bar, lounge, VCRs and stereos, fax machines, kitchenettes and pantries in larger units, fitness center, meeting rooms. AE, DC, MC, V.*

The Lowell. Think how nice it would be to arrive in New York and find that a rich uncle had offered you the run of his elegant pied-à-terre—that's the feeling you'll get at The Lowell. There's no lobby in the true sense, just a regal front-desk area with a few chairs and newspapers. Upstairs, on the second floor, is a picture-perfect tea-and-lunch-room in the English-country-house style; adjacent is a first-rate steak restaurant, the Post House (*see* Chapter 8). The guest rooms, mostly suites, are at once fashionable and homey: Furnishings are an eclectic mix of traditional pieces with surprisingly modern accents. Bathrooms have good lighting and generous Saks Fifth Avenue amenities. Some rooms have wood-burning fireplaces, a relative rarity in the city. There's even one super suite with its own fitness center. This is not a hotel for hunting down celebrities, although it has become a favorite of many, such as George Michael and David Bowie, who prize its amiable but utterly discreet service. *28 E. 63rd St., 10021, tel. 212/838–1400 or 800/345–3457, fax 212/319–4230. 60 rooms. Facilities: restaurant, small meeting room, some kitchenettes. AE, DC, MC, V.*

The Mark. Just one block north of the Carlyle, the former Madison Avenue Hotel has recently been completely redone by its new owner, Rafael Hotels; it could provide its neighbor with some healthy competition in terms of price and amenities. Even

Algonquin, 44

Beekman Tower, 31

Best Western, 23

Carlyle, 5

Doral Court, 50

Doral Inn, 30

Doral Park Ave., 50

Doral Tuscany, 49

Drake, 16

Dumont Plaza, 53

Embassy Suites, 39

Excelsior, 2

Grand Hyatt, 47

Helmsley Middletowne, 33

Helmsley Palace, 28

Holiday Inn Crowne Plaza, 24

Hotel Edison, 37

Hotel Esplanade, 3

Hotel Wentworth, 41

Inter-Continental, 34

Iroquois, 43

Journey's End, 48

Le Parker Meridien, 18

Loews New York, 26

Lowell, 8

The Mark, 4

Marriott Marquis, 40

Mayfair Regent, 7

Milford Plaza, 46

Morgans, 51

N.Y. Hilton, 21

N.Y. Int'l Youth Hostel, 1

New York Vista, 56

Paramount, 38

Peninsula, 17

Pickwick Arms, 25

Pierre, 12

The Plaza, 14

Radisson Empire, 10

Ramada Inn, 36

The Regency, 11

Rihga Royal, 20

Ritz-Carlton, 13

Roger Smith Winthrop, 35

Royalton, 45

San Carlos, 27

Shelburne, 52

Sheraton New Yorker, 22

Sloane YMCA, 54

Southgate Tower, 55

Surrey Hotel, 6

U.N. Plaza, 42

Vanderbilt YMCA, 32

Waldorf-Astoria, 29

Wellington, 19

West Side YMCA, 9

Wyndham, 15

Manhattan Lodging

86th St.

Metropolitan Museum of Art

Museum of Natural History

E. 79th St.

Fifth Ave.

E. 72nd St.

Central Park W

Columbus Ave.

Central Park

Central Park S.

Columbus Circle

W. 57th St.

E. 57th St.

Third Ave.

Second Ave.

First Ave.

Ninth Ave.

Sixth Ave. (Avenue of the Americas)

Rockefeller Center

Madison Ave.

Park Ave.

Lexington Ave.

FDR Dr.

Port Authority Bus Terminal

W. 42nd St.

Times Square

Fifth Ave.

Grand Central Terminal

E. 42nd St.

Public Library

Empire State Building

Eighth Ave.

Seventh Ave.

Broadway

Herald Square

W. 34th St.

E. 34th St.

Park Ave. S.

Lexington Ave.

Madison Square Garden

Penn Station

Madison Sq.

W. 23rd St.

E. 23rd St.

Gramercy Park

Union Sq.

Stuyvesant Sq.

W. 14th St.

E. 14th St.

660 yards

600 meters

the least expensive rooms have high-quality TVs and VCRs, and its bathrooms feature art deco tiles or marble, deep tubs, *and* separate stall showers. Most rooms have pantries, too. Color schemes are warm to reflect the Italian neoclassical motif. Women will feel comfortable in the discreet public areas. Mark's, a cozy and elegant restaurant and lounge, features the unique French-American cuisine of chef Philippe Boulot. **Mr.** Rafael came from Regent Hotels International, and the current manager came from the Mayfair Regent—two highly promising omens for ensuring the hotel's future success. *25 E. 77th St., 10021, tel. 212/744–4300 or 800/THE–MARK, fax 212/744–2749. 185 rooms. Facilities: restaurant, café, lounge, meeting rooms, VIP suites with terraces. AE, DC, MC, V.*

★ **The Mayfair Regent.** General manager Dario Mariotti adds a cheery Italian influence to this low-key, gracious hotel. Locals know it for its traditional tea lounge and its always-white-hot restaurant, Le Cirque (*see* Chapter 8). Even the smallest of the guest rooms have marble baths and traditional-style, peach-tone decor with up-to-date extras such as dual-line telephones and outlets to accommodate portable computers and facsimile machines. Service is super-efficient; guests are offered umbrellas, room humidifiers, customized pillow selection, and the ingenuity of longtime concierge Bruno Brunelli, who can usually conjure up impossible tickets or reservations. While its overall appearance isn't quite as glitzy as that of some other hotels in this price category, The Mayfair Regent more than makes up for its slightly lived-in feel (which many guests, incidentally, prefer) with friendliness and an always-lively atmosphere. At press time, there were rumors that the hotel would be sold. *610 Park Ave. (at 65th St.), 10021, tel. 212/288–0800 or 800/545–4000, fax 201/737–0538. 150 rooms. Facilities: restaurant, lounge, meeting rooms, unlimited local phone calls. AE, DC, MC, V.*

The Peninsula. The former Gotham Hotel on Fifth Avenue has gone through more changes in the past five years than the plot of a TV soap opera. After being magnificently renovated as the Hotel Maxim, it is now owned and operated by the respected Peninsula Group of Hong Kong. The new owners have wisely left the Maxim's furnishings intact, including the sumptuous (by New York or any standards) marble baths. Even the smaller rooms have graceful sculpted art nouveau headboards, desks, and armoires; some also have the same sweeping views down Fifth Avenue as the more expensive suites. Many bathrooms feature Jacuzzi tubs; all have bidets and Lanvin toiletries. The acclaimed (and very pricey) Adrienne restaurant, and its less lofty café and bar serve high-style French cuisine. The new rooftop health club, with state-of-the-art exercise machines, a decent-size pool, massage and facial services, and a dining area with a terrace, is a knockout. The only drawback is the sometimes indifferent attitude of the staff. *700 5th Ave., 10019, tel. 212/247–2200 or 800/262–9467, fax 212/903–3949. 250 rooms. Facilities: restaurant, café, lounge, meeting rooms, pool, fitness center. AE, DC, MC, V.*

★ **The Pierre.** The Four Seasons, a Canadian hotel group, has made a specialty of "freshening up" classic properties, and the Pierre is one of their notable successes. One might expect haughtiness along with the creamy, oriental-carpeted halls and bright chandeliers, but you won't find that here: The staff has a sense of fun about working in these posh surroundings. Rooms, most of which have been recently refurbished, are traditionally decorated in soft floral patterns, with quilted bedspreads and fine wood furniture. Bathrooms have recently been upgraded and are generously stocked with Four Seasons' amenities. The Boudoir suites, overlooking the Central Park Zoo and Wollman Ice Rink, are worth the extra price. Café Pierre can hold its own against many of the city's best spots; the Bar features low-key jazz piano in the evenings, and formal afternoon tea is served under the blue cherubim-filled dome of the Rotunda. There are no gimmicks here—just good old-fashioned style and service. *5th Ave. at 61st St., 10021, tel. 212/838–8000 or 800/ 332–3442, fax 212/940–8109. 204 rooms. Facilities: restaurant, bar, tearoom, meeting rooms, manned elevators, packing service upon request, hand-laundry service. AE, DC, MC, V.*

The Plaza. When real-estate developer and casino operator Donald Trump purchased this National Historic Landmark in 1988, locals shuddered a bit, but there is actually much to applaud. (Trump's fortunes have since waned, and by now The Plaza might be under new ownership.) This former haunt of F. Scott Fitzgerald, George M. Cohan, Frank Lloyd Wright, and the Beatles is ready to receive a relatively demanding public. Prices have edged up, but so has the quality of even the least expensive rooms. New color schemes are in burgundy or teal blue; fresh, floral-patterned quilted spreads grace the large beds. Furnishings, though still "hotel-like" in most units, are of high quality. Bathrooms, even those not yet fully redone, have fluffy new towels and French toiletries. One real advantage here is the size of guest rooms—only a handful of other classic properties can offer similar spaciousness in nearly all accommodations. Food-and-beverage service has made major strides throughout the property. Current executive chef Kerry Simon (formerly of Lafayette and Lutèce) will certainly earn plaudits here. The Edwardian Room and the Oak Room, always known for elegant atmosphere, now offer food to match. Even the scones at the Palm Court, that gracious, classic lobby lounge, seem fresher. The last word was that Trader Vic's bar—renowned for its elaborate exotic drinks—will stay open, although the space formerly occupied by its restaurant will possibly be turned into a health club. *5th Ave. at 59th St., 10019, tel. 212/759–3000 or 800/228–3000, fax 212/753–1468. 807 rooms. Facilities: 2 restaurants, 2 bars, café, art gallery, handicapped-guest rooms, meeting rooms, packing service upon request, large concierge staff. AE, DC, MC, V.*

Rihga Royal. Right behind the New York Hilton on West 54th Street is Manhattan's first all-suite luxury hotel. Japanese in ownership and largely European in staff, The Rihga suffers a bit from lack of local recognition, though its Halcyon restaurant is beginning to gain a following. Suites are truly gracious, featuring subdued, modern furnishings and lavish marble baths, most with tubs and stall showers. Many units have fax machines and VCRs. While regular prices are very expensive, on weekends and during slow seasons, these generous accommodations are often deeply discounted, so ask before you book. *151 W. 54th St., 10019, tel. 212/307–5000 or 800/937–5454, fax 212/765–6530. 500 suites. Facilities: restaurant, bar, lounge, meeting rooms, business center. AE, DC, MC, V.*

The Ritz-Carlton. This property—once hot, then lukewarm—has recently been brought under genuine Ritz-Carlton management, and overall service should soon be raised to the company's high standards. Guest rooms have been refurbished in the R-C manner: brocade bedspreads, marble baths, and rich wood accents. The rooms with Central Park views are definitely preferable, but all accommodations are identical in decor and amenities. The relatively understated atmosphere manages not to be stuffy. The hotel's most notable guests of late include rock group U2 and Ed Begley, Jr. In fact, bartender Norman Bukofzer in the Jockey Club draws a coterie of convivial celebrities. *112 Central Park S, 10019, tel. 212/757–1900 or 800/241–3333, fax 212/757–9620. 210 rooms. Facilities: restaurant, bar, meeting rooms, complimentary limousine service to Wall Street. AE, DC, MC, V.*

Expensive

Doral Court, Doral Park Avenue, and **Doral Tuscany.** Doral has created a cozy enclave of three hotels in the East 30s Murray Hill district. Guests at any one property can sign for meals and drinks at all three; they also have complimentary access to the Doral Saturnia Fitness Center at 90 Park Avenue. The Doral Tuscany and its adjacent neighbor, the Doral Court (which has slightly lower prices that actually put it in the "Moderate" category), have attractive, traditionally furnished guest rooms and suites; the Tuscany's baths and bedrooms are more formal and elegant, though both properties are well maintained. The Doral Park Avenue has recently been refurbished by designer Sarah Lee. The atmosphere in both public and guest room areas echoes the Saturnia property in Florida. All three have good restaurants, the best and most acclaimed being the Tuscany's Time and Again, which features a changing menu of American nouvelle specialties. The Park Avenue's new restaurant, Saturnia, has spa cuisine, while the Doral Court's Courtyard Café offers one of the city's nicer outdoor dining spaces. *Doral Court, 130 E. 39th St., 10016, tel. 212/685–1100 or 800/624–0607, fax 212/889–0287. 248 rooms. Facilities: café, meeting rooms, complimentary parking on all weekend packages. AE, DC, MC, V. Doral Park Avenue, 70 Park Ave. (at 38th St.), 10016, tel. 212/687–7050 or 800/847–4135, fax 212/808–9029. 220 rooms. Facilities: 2 restaurants, bar, café, meeting rooms, fitness center, complimentary parking on all weekend packages. AE, DC, MC, V. Doral Tuscany, 120 E. 39th St., 10016, tel. 212/686–1600 or 800/847–4078, fax 212/779–7822. 119 rooms. Facilities: restaurant, lounge, meeting rooms, complimentary parking on all weekend packages. AE, DC, MC, V.*

The Drake. Swissôtel took over this former Loews property in 1981; it is favored by many business travelers from here and abroad for its solid service and highly desirable location, just off Park Avenue at 56th Street. The hotel recently remodeled its public areas. Guest rooms have been refreshed with improved furnishings and a more contemporary look; the same goes for the well-stocked bathrooms. The advantage here is room size: The prewar building was originally designed as an apartment house, so the rooms have enough space for refrigerators and other homey touches. Where this lodging truly shines is in its dining services—this is the home of the acclaimed French restaurant Lafayette. Reservations are difficult to get, but the agreeable hotel staff will do their utmost to get hotel guests in. For a good deal less money, the Café Suisse is a pleasant surprise—many locals enjoy its Swiss specialties and hard-to-find Swiss wines, and its desserts are made by the Lafayette pastry chef. There's more comfort here than spit and polish, but the prices and the quality of the food-and-beverage service more than make up for any lapses. *440 Park Ave., 10022, tel. 212/421–0900 or 800/63–SWISS, fax 212/371–4190. 600 rooms. Facilities: restaurant, café, bar, meeting rooms, complimentary limousine service to Wall Street, luggage check-in for Swissair passengers. AE, DC, MC, V.*

Embassy Suites. Another welcome addition to the Times Square area, this familiar name's new flagship has far more flair than anticipated. The elevated lobby is done up in modern art deco style; color schemes and furnishings are bold and contemporary. Suites have coffeemakers, small microwave ovens, refrigerators, and even complimentary sodas and snacks. Guest rooms, though hardly elegant, are cheerful and comfortable. All rates include free full breakfast, and daily cocktails in a private lounge area. There's also a regular restaurant and bar, featuring well-priced grills and salads. At press time there were plans to have live entertainment in the evening. Those skeptical of this chain's ability to keep prices in line while moving up to New York's more sophisticated tastes should be pleasantly surprised. The staff seems eager to please, too. Meanwhile, Embassy will have to beef up its street-level security; the block continues to be somewhat unsavory. *1568 Broadway at 47th St., 10036, tel. 212/719–1600 or 800/EMBASSY, fax 212/921–5212. 460 suites. Facilities: restaurant, bar, meeting rooms, complimentary use of nearby health club and pool. AE, DC, MC, V.*

Grand Hyatt New York. What was formerly the Commodore is now a glittering marble-and-chrome edifice managed by Hyatt. Sports fans will enjoy gawking at their favorite athletes in the lobby—almost all the pro teams stay here when in town. Like other towering midtown hotels, this one's designed primarily for business travelers. Guests have remarked at the odd shapes of certain rooms, but the savvy staff tries to avoid using these when the hotel is not full. Color schemes are blessedly soft, running to teal blue, gray, and rose. Regency Club rooms on the 31st and 32nd floors are worth the extra money if you require extra pampering and service; otherwise, they are nearly identical with regular units. The lounge is truly gracious, and the free treats taste as good as they look. The hotel's food in general is superior to that of many other Hyatt properties. Trumpet's, the formal dining room, serves better-than-average nouvelle cuisine and has a truly impressive wine list for a commercial hotel. Service throughout the hotel is pleasant, if not as polished as that of smaller New York properties. As with many other chains, it's quite easy to book a room or even a suite here at reduced rates. *Park Ave. at Grand Central Terminal (at 42nd St.), 10017, tel. 212/883–1234 or 800/233–1234, fax 212/697–3772. 1,400 rooms. Facilities: restaurant, café, lounge, ballroom, meeting rooms, VIP floor. AE, DC, MC, V.*

The Helmsley Palace. This glass monolith with a landmark palazzo at its feet is many visitors' vision of the ideal New York hotel: big, slightly overwrought, and always busy. Palace rooms are generous by Manhattan standards, and those on the higher floors have views of St. Patrick's Cathedral and the East Side. Furnishings are cookie-cutter plush: padded and gilded headboards, reproduction chairs and tables, and pseudo-brocade bedcovers. Smaller suites are cramped and not worth the extra money. Public rooms, many of them located in the original 100-year-old Villard Houses, contain valuable pieces of art and lovely architectural details. The hotel has a variety of bars and eating spots; skip all meals except the posh afternoon tea.

The staff is friendly and the location can't be beat for those who want to shop on Fifth Avenue or have business in midtown. *455 Madison Ave., 10022, tel. 212/888-7000 or 800/221-4982, fax 212/355-0820. 963 rooms. Facilities: restaurant, 2 lounges, tearoom, meeting rooms, kitchenettes in suites. AE, DC, MC, V.*

Holiday Inn Crowne Plaza. The new deluxe flagship of the famous commercial hotel chain, a towering roseate stone edifice, has been built on the exact site of the original music publishing company of Irving Berlin—he wrote the music for the movie *Holiday Inn*, from which the chain took its name. Public areas with a rose and beige color scheme are softer and more opulent than those of its neighboring competitor, The Marriott Marquis. Upstairs, the decent-size rooms continue the rose color scheme, this time with a touch of teal blue. Guest rooms start at the 16th floor so that everyone gets an eyeful from the panoramic windows. Bathrooms are beyond basic, though the amenities found within could be more lavish. Another minor drawback is the serious lack of closet space, even in the suites. An attractive, surprisingly sophisticated lobby restaurant, Samplings, features appetizer- and full-size dishes, salads, and desserts, and there's also a larger restaurant, The Broadway Grill. The health club includes a shallow (3½ feet deep throughout) lap pool, run by the same company that built the Vista's well-regarded facility. New Yorkers are divided on the hotel's Vegas-style neon nighttime facade, though it may just be what's needed to restore one's confidence in the wild West Side. *1605 Broadway (at 49th St.), 10019, tel. 212/977-4000 or 800/HOLI-DAY, fax 212/333-7393. 770 rooms. Facilities: 3 restaurants, café, lounge, fitness center, pool, ballroom, meeting rooms, business center. AE, DC, MC, V.*

The Inter-Continental New York. The stately old Barclay was bought by this reputable worldwide company a few years ago but, happily, not much has changed. The warmly lit traditional lobby, with its faded Persian carpets and aviary, still stands, as does the rather old-fashioned American restaurant. Rooms, alas, could use some updating, as could the charmless bathrooms. Some suites have been nicely refurnished, but even these have somewhat less panache than those of other hotels in this price category. Some businesspeople swear by the hotel's service, though a few recent reports have not been as favorable. The new on-premises workout and massage facility is attractive and well-designed, as are the redecorated banquet and meeting rooms on the same level. One can only hope that the Inter-Continental's new owners, the Japanese Saison Group and SAS airlines, will get busy and spruce this place up—it has the potential to shine. *111 48th St. (E. of Park Ave.), 10017, tel. 212/755-5900 or 800/327-0200, fax 212/644-0079. 680 rooms. Facilities: restaurant, bar, meeting rooms, fitness center, complimentary parking on weekends. AE, DC, MC, V.*

Le Parker Meridien. This dramatic, modern French hotel, whose soaring blond-wood lobby links 56th and 57th streets, is within a short stroll of some of the city's finest stores and cultural spots. This is one of the best luxury bets for fitness-minded visitors: It has an airy rooftop swimming pool and a state-of-the-art basement-level workout center—both complimentary to guests. Its main drawback is that its guest rooms lack the stylish touches one might anticipate from a French-managed property. Fortunately, a complete room redecorating plan should be well underway by this year, along with a modernization of the pool area. Baths are on a par with the rooms, though there are luscious Lanvin soaps. The hotel's service is anything but snooty. The fabled Maurice restaurant is back, this time with lower prices and simpler dishes; chef Marc Salonsky, formerly of Petrossian, is at the helm. *118 W. 57th St., 10019, tel. 212/245–5000 or 800/543–4300, fax 212/307–1776. 700 rooms. Facilities: restaurant, café, bar, meeting rooms, voice mail, fitness center, pool, accompanied jogging. AE, DC, MC, V.*

The Marriott Marquis. This five-year-old giant is one of the places New Yorkers love to hate: It's obvious, brash, bright, and definitely geared to conventions and groups. Still, anything that brings new life and light to the Times Square area is welcome. As at other Marriotts, the help is ultrafriendly and informative, if not terribly polished. Rooms (though Marriott claims otherwise) are *not* the largest in town, but they're large enough; their color schemes are restful and their bathrooms perfectly adequate and modern. Some rooms have dramatic urban views. Good news for those with a fear of heights: The glass-walled atrium elevators have been slowed down considerably. There's a revolving restaurant, The View, on the 46th floor, and a second revolving lounge on the 8th-floor lobby level. Most patrons have booked here on some sort of reduced or group rate. Note: Marriott has refurbished the former Halloran House (now The New York Marriott East Side) at 48th Street and Lexington Avenue. The atmosphere here is more traditional. *1535 Broadway (at 45th St.), 10036, tel. 212/398–1900 or 800/228–9290, fax 212/704–8930. 1,877 rooms. Facilities: 3 restaurants, café, 3 lounges, several meeting rooms, theater, VIP floor, business center. AE, DC, MC, V.*

Morgans. There's no hotel sign outside; savvy guests—many of them from the film, fashion, and recording industries—are expected to know about this chic, private, unconventional property, the conceit of renowned French designer Andree Putman. Guests who want to be cuddled by the past will hate this ultramodern, high-tech statement in black and white, but those who appreciate understated chic and want to be on the cutting edge of fashion will find nothing more suitable. Walls are covered with gray bird's-eye maple and sprayed with Zolatone. There are chrome miniblinds, ecru Roman shades, limited-edition Robert Mapplethorpe photographs, bud vases with tropical flowers, down comforters, and some of the softest sheets you've ever slept on. Bathrooms are lined with Putman's signature black and white tile, with poured granite floors, stainless steel cruise-ship sinks and laboratory-style fixtures. The small lobby of glass and bronze, with an Escher-like carpet, is a place *not* to be seen. Frequent guests include Julia Roberts and Cher, who rented the penthouse for a full year. The staff is as attractive and helpful as any in the country. *237 Madison Ave. (between 37 and 38th Sts.), tel. 212/686–0300, fax 212/779–8352. 113 rooms. Facilities: 24-hour room service, VCRs, parking service, 24-hour fitness room, Continental breakfast.*

The New York Hilton. In a sense, this is the city's premier hotel for professional meetings, large and small. It has a special conference center, a business center run by the *Wall Street Journal*, and loads of multilingual help. Hilton spends vast sums on keeping it trim, and it shows: There's a distinctive landscaped driveway, and the modern lobby, with its new fountain, sparkles with well-kept furnishings. Considering the size of this property (more than 2,000 rooms), guest areas are surprisingly well maintained, if not always spacious or terribly fashionable. Even the smaller rooms are tastefully arranged and have many modern touches, such as alarm clock/radios and remote-control TVs. Guests who pay extra for recently refurbished Tower Level accommodations get slightly larger rooms and use of a stylish lounge with a separate boardroom and complimentary drinks and snacks. The new Grill 53 restaurant has better-than-average hotel fare. If you don't expect high levels of personal attention or unfaltering elegance, this well-run machine will usually satisfy. *1335 6th Ave. (at 53rd St.), 10019, tel. 212/ 586–7000 or 800/HILTONS, fax 212/315–1374. 2,034 rooms. Facilities: restaurant, nightclub, 2 cafés, bar, several meeting rooms, multilingual desk, VIP floor, fitness center, business center, American Express desk. AE, DC, MC, V.*

The New York Vista. Managed by Hilton International, this striking downtown property has been the only significant hotel below 34th Street since it opened nine years ago. There is, however, a new Marriott on West Street, with other competitors to follow. This new competition should eventually force the Vista up to par. Until then, try to book a redecorated room. Guest rooms have nice views of nearby Battery Park City and the new World Financial Center on the Hudson River, but they are otherwise undistinguished. However, the hotel has a dramatic health club, with a swimming pool that sits in the center of a multifunction exercise area, under a running track. In addition, the hotel's dining rooms offer above-average American cuisine. The best-known is The American Harvest, which features a seasonaly changing menu of domestic meats, seafood, and produce. *3 World Trade Center, 10048, tel. 212/938–9100, fax 212/321–2107. 829 rooms. Facilities: 2 restaurants, 2 lounges, meeting rooms, pool, fitness center, VIP floor, free parking with weekend packages. AE, DC, MC, V.*

★ **The Regency.** Loews' upper-echelon property is a favorite for power breakfasts and fancy press events (the working rich-and-famous enjoy its discreet and surprisingly relaxed atmosphere). The stately, chandeliered lobby is reminiscent of the kind of private apartment house that comes with a personal staff to help with every need. Guest rooms and suites feature high-quality dark-wood furniture and brocade bedspreads. Bathrooms are of marble, and some have tiny TVs. Service is paramount at this property, where the King—Loews Hotel's president Jonathan Tisch—really does stand guard (and eats breakfast every day). *540 Park Ave., 10021, tel. 212/759–4100 or 800/223–2356, fax 212/826–5674. 400 rooms. Facilities: restaurant, lounge, meeting rooms, fitness center. AE, DC, MC, V.*

The Royalton. Former Studio 54 disco kings Ian Schrager and the late Steve Rubell, in their quest for a second career as New York hotel moguls, completely rehabilitated this once-shabby property directly across from the Algonquin (*see* Moderate, below) on West 44th Street off Fifth Avenue. The Royalton, with its witty art moderne design by French decorator Philippe Starck, has a plush but slightly spooky atmosphere: The halls are narrow and dark, as are some of the strangely shaped rooms. Still, the beds and other furnishings are quite comfy, and the bathrooms are decidedly fun—they all have either oversize slate shower stalls or giant circular tubs (a few have botn). Toiletries are elegant, and so is the service. The on-premises Restaurant 44 has excellent cuisine and a full liquor license (note: guests cannot purchase alcoholic beverages anywhere else on the property, including through room service). This could be a delightful spot for a romantic theater weekend for two people with a sense of the absurd. *44 W. 44th St., 10036, tel. 212/869–4400 or 800/635–9013, fax 212/869–8965. 205 rooms. Facilities: restaurant with bar, meeting rooms, game and library areas, VCRs, stereos. AE, DC, MC, V.*

★ **U.N. Plaza-Park Hyatt.** It's easy to miss the entrance to this favorite among the business and diplomatic set—it's on a quiet side street near (naturally) the United Nations. The small but striking lobby gives the illusion of endless space, thanks to clever designs in dark marble and mirrors; Japanese floral arrangements add warmth and drama. What makes this place really special, though, are the guest rooms, all with breathtaking views of Manhattan's East Side, and the delightful rooftop pool, where one can do laps while watching jets bank along the skyline. This is also the only hotel in New York that boasts its own on-premises tennis court. The decor is modern but not overpoweringly sterile, and the color schemes are soothing. The burgundy-hued Ambassador Grill has a new menu, featuring grilled game in season; prices are still reasonable by hotel standards. Service throughout the hotel is first-rate. Families with young children will especially appreciate the nearby U.N. park and the hotel's safe location. Recently, this property became a member of the distinctive Park Hyatt group of hotels, which can only mean that high standards will be continued. *1 United Nations Plaza, 10017, tel. 212/355–3400 or 800/223–1234, fax 212/702–5051. 444 rooms. Facilities: restaurant, 2 lounges, meeting rooms, pool, fitness center, tennis court, complimentary limousine service to Wall Street and theater district. AE, DC, MC, V.*

The Waldorf-Astoria. Along with the Plaza (*see* Very Expensive, above), this Art Deco masterpiece personifies New York at its most lavish and powerful. Hilton, its owner, has spent a fortune on refurbishing both public areas and guest rooms. Original murals and mosaics, elaborate plaster ornamentation, fine old-wood walls and doors—all look fresh and new. In the guest rooms, some of which start at the low end of this category, there are new bedspreads, carpets, and other signs of upgrading. Bathrooms throughout are old but beautifully kept up and rather spacious by today's standards. Everyone from the Duchess of York to the honeymoon couple from Miami or the salesman from Omaha gets the same amenities; of course, in the very private Tower section, everything becomes just that much grander. There has been a move to modernize the menu at Peacock Alley, where Waldorf salad first made news. Service in the dining areas, however, can be pokey and rude, especially outside of regular meal times. The hotel's richly tinted, hushed lobby serves as an interior centerpoint of city life; it's nice to see the rest of the place looking proud, too. *301 Park Ave., 10022, tel. 212/355–3000 or 800/HILTONS, fax 212/421–8103. 1,692 rooms. Facilities: 3 restaurants, coffee shop, tearoom, lounge, ballroom, meeting rooms. AE, DC, MC, V.*

Moderate

★ **The Algonquin.** While this landmark property's English-drawing-room atmosphere and burnished-wood lobby are being kept intact, its working parts (the plumbing, for instance) are being improved under new Japanese owners. Management is also redecorating, restoring the old mahogany doors and trim, improving the telephone service, and creating a conference and business area. This much-beloved hotel, where the Round Table group of writers and wits once met for lunch, still shelters many a celebrity, particularly literary types visiting nearby publishing houses or the *New Yorker* magazine offices. Late-night performances go on as usual at the Oak Room, with singers such as Julie Wilson and Andrea Marcovicci. Bathrooms and sleeping quarters retain Victorian-style fixtures and furnishings, only now there are larger, firmer beds, modern TVs, VCRs (upon request), computerized phones, and Caswell-Massey toiletries. Tubs, tiles, and sinks are being relined as needed. Personal service, especially for repeat customers, continues to be excellent. Even if you choose another hotel to sleep in, stop by the Algonquin for afternoon tea or a drink in its cozy, clubby lobby. *59 W. 44th St., 10036, tel. 212/840–6800 or 800/548–0345, fax 212/944–1419. 165 rooms. Facilities: restaurant, 2 lounges, meeting rooms, complimentary parking on weekends, business center. AE, DC, MC, V.*

The Doral Inn. While this Doral is far more modest in decor and commercial in feeling than the others discussed above, it is nonetheless a good value among the many hotels along Lexington Avenue. Rooms are average in size and cheerful, if not inventive, in decor; there are some surprisingly impressive terrace suites. A small workout area is connected to a squash club, and guests can also use the Doral Park Avenue's Saturnia Fitness Center. *541 Lexington Ave. (at 50th St.), 10022, tel. 212/755–1200 or 800/223–5823, fax 212/319–8344. 700 rooms. Facilities: 2 restaurants, meeting rooms, fitness center, squash club, self-service laundry. AE, DC, MC, V.*

The Helmsley Middletowne. It may be hard to believe that this low-key residential-style retreat is managed by the same flamboyant folks who run the Helmsley Palace (*see* Expensive, above). Tucked away on East 48th Street near Lexington Avenue, the Helmsley Middletowne is a more than serviceable money-saver for those who can take care of their own business and social needs: There's no lobby, no restaurant, and no room service, but the area is packed with dining options. Most units are suites or oversize doubles, and many are large enough for families. The decor is homey traditional; most units have been redone, though there are still some signs of wear and tear in the bathrooms. Most rooms have pantries and dual-line telephones. *148 E. 48th St., 10017, tel. 212/755–3000 or 800/221–4982, fax 212/832–0261. 192 rooms. AE, DC, MC, V.*

Journey's End. This Canadian chain's first Manhattan property is what the demanding bargain hunter has been waiting for. No-nonsense, clean, attractive rooms and baths are at one fixed price. Most accommodations come with queen-size beds; all have modern TVs and telephones with long cords. Guests can use a small lounge area for complimentary coffee and newspapers. There were plans at press time for an independently owned Italian restaurant to open on the premises. At night, this part of midtown is somewhat quiet and therefore prone to street crime. However, security at the hotel appears to be superior. Another plus—it's just a few blocks away from the airport bus departure area on Park Avenue near Grand Central Terminal. *3 E. 40th St., 10016, tel. 212/447–1500 or 800/668–4200. 189 rooms. Facilities: lounge, independent on-premises restaurant, business services on request. AE, DC, MC, V.*

Loew's New York Hotel. Loews' moderate-price New York property has an impersonal style, but most of its regulars—

business travelers—don't mind because the hotel generally runs quite well. Rooms, most of them recently refurbished, are comfortable and well-designed. Deluxe units (only slightly higher in price than standard) come with goodies, such as Godiva chocolates and complimentary liquor miniatures. The new Lexington Avenue Grill is a vast improvement over Maude's, as is the striking new maroon art deco carpeting and wood-tone lobby. Note: During low occupancy periods, guests can actually book rooms here for the upper end of Inexpensive prices; even suites come down below the $200 range. Loews takes care of its properties, so the hotel can more than hold its own with some of its neighbors. *Lexington Ave. (at 51st St.), 10022, tel. 212/752–7000, fax 212/758–6311. 766 rooms. Facilities: restaurant, lounge, meeting rooms, fitness center. AE, DC, MC, V.*

★ **Manhattan Suites East.** Here's a group of good-value properties for the traveler who likes to combine full hotel service with independent pied-à-terre living. These nine midtown hotels have different characters and varying prices, though all fall within the Moderate category. The four best are the recently redone **Beekman Tower** (3 Mitchell Pl.), near the United Nations and on the edge of a trendy East Side residential area; the **Dumont Plaza** (150 E. 34th St.), especially convenient for convention goers with its location on a direct bus line to the Javits Center; the **Surrey Hotel** (20 E. 76th St.), in the neighborhood of Madison Avenue art galleries and designer boutiques; and the **Southgate Tower** (371 7th Ave.), the most attractive and secure place to sleep within close range of Madison Square Garden and Penn Station. Except for the modern style at the Dumont, all have traditional guest-room decor; the Surrey's rooms border on the truly elegant. Most accommodations have pantries, and larger units have dining areas with full-size tables. Other hotels in this group tend to be more residential, except for the full-service **Shelburne** (303 Lexington Ave.); many top corporations use them as interim lodgings for newly relocated executives. The Beekman, Surrey, Shelburne, and Dumont Plaza have restaurants (Harold's at the Dumont Plaza and the Zephyr Grill at the Beekman are trying hard, though not always succeeding), which can also be used for room service. The Dumont, Southgate, and the Shelburne have on-premises fitness centers. The older hotels in the group do have some disappointing rooms, but overall these properties are outstanding for the price, considering their convenience, location, and space. Their weekend package rates are hard to beat. *Sales office, 505 E. 75th St., 10001, tel. 212/772–2900 or 800/ME–SUITE. AE, DC, MC, V.*

Radisson Empire Hotel. This old hotel recently changed ownership, so it's a matter of time before one knows what's what, but since the new owner is media mogul John Kluge, the Empire should only gain in luster. The lobby is warm and inviting; halls are decorated in soft gray with elegant lamps. Rooms and suites are a bit like small boxes, but nicely furnished; special room features include high-tech electronics, and the small but immaculate baths have heated towel racks. Although this hotel's prices have gone up, it's still one of the city's better buys in terms of quality and location, right across the street from Lincoln Center. At press time there was no room service, but no matter: The neighborhood is loaded with all-hours dining options. *Broadway (at 63rd St.), 10023, tel. 212/265–7400, 800/ 221–6509, or 800/223–9868, fax 212/315–0349. 368 rooms. Facilities: restaurant, voice mail. AE, DC, MC, V.*

The Roger Smith Winthrop. Don't be put off by the dusty, faded lobby—the hotel is in the process of a gradual redecoration. The lobby and public areas of this sleeper have been remodeled. The guest rooms upstairs are clean, well decorated, and spacious, and special units have small but luxurious marble baths with Jacuzzis. All rooms have pantries, and there's a complimentary Continental breakfast. Guests also receive free passes (one per person) to the Museum of Modern Art. A tea lounge and a new full-service restaurant are in the works. This is a homey, attractive place to return to at the end of a busy day in midtown. *501 Lexington Ave., 10017, tel. 212/755–1400 or 800/241–3848, fax 212/319–9130. 200 rooms. Facilities: restaurant, meeting room. AE, DC, MC, V.*

The San Carlos. This small, residential-style property offers basic hotel service, clean modern rooms, and a neighborly atmosphere. Larger suites come with kitchenettes, making them a good choice for families. The small wood-paneled lobby is gracious and well lit; women travelers can feel quite secure here. *150 E. 50th St., 10022, tel. 212/755–1800 or 800/722–2012. 140 rooms. Facilities: restaurant. AE, DC, MC, V.*

The Sheraton New Yorker Hotel & Towers, Sheraton Manhattan. Readers know that these properties have not been among our favorites. We've been informed that by spring, 1992, both hotels will have undergone a multimillion-dollar transformation in anticipation of the Democratic National Convention. At press time, the plans looked promising, but prices were also due for a "readjustment," so ask questions before booking rooms. *811 7th Ave., 10019, tel. 212/581–1000 or 800/325–3535, fax 262–4410. 1,835 rooms. Facilities: restaurant, café, coffee shop, disco, ballroom, several meeting rooms. AE, DC, MC, V.*

The Wyndham. This genteel treasure sits across from The Plaza and adjacent to the Helmsley Park Lane. The savvy, independent traveler who cares more about gracious rooms and a friendly atmosphere than about imposing lobbies and hand-to-mouth service might well choose this spot over its neighbors. Owner and general manager John Mados keeps prices down by not offering room service or fancy amenities; what he does provide are some of the prettiest and most spacious accommodations in Manhattan. Even the least expensive double room has fresh floral-print bedspreads, comfortable chairs, and decorator wall coverings. A slight drawback is the old-fashioned, white-tile bathrooms. Suites (all of which come with pantries) start as low as $160 per night; they are painted in sunny shades and fitted with antique furniture, tasteful Chinese rugs, and an eclectic mix of everything else. The small lobby is unusually secure—a doorman controls the "in" buzzer 24 hours a day. The limited staff is pleasant, and they can be extra attentive once they get to know you. This hotel is a favorite of stars such as Carol Burnett and media personalities Leonard Maltin and Barbara Walters. However, some of our readers have reported less-than-perfect service and hospitality. *42 W. 58th St., 10019, tel. 212/753–3500, fax 212/754–5638. 201 rooms. Facilities: restaurant. AE, DC, MC, V.*

Inexpensive

★ **Chatwal Inns.** This latest welcome group addition to the Big Apple hotel scene features six properties, located mostly in the Broadway-midtown area, that provide clean, attractively designed rooms at relatively unpainful prices. All guests receive a complimentary Continental breakfast. Some of the larger properties, like the Best Western affiliate (234 W. 48th St.), have on-premises full-service restaurants as well. Rooms, though relatively small throughout all six hotels, are immaculate and have all the basic amenities travelers have come to expect, including bathroom toiletries, modern telephones, and TVs. Since many of the buildings were, until recently, rather dilapidated, don't be put off by the dingy facades of Chatwal properties like **The Quality Inn Midtown** (157 W. 47th St.) or **The Chatwal Inn** (132 W. 45th St.); their interiors are among the chain's nicest. Sant S. Chatwal, owner of Bombay Palace restaurants, is to be applauded for his restoration and pricing efforts. *Tel. 800/826–4667; in Canada: 800/621–4667. Facilities: restaurants, small meeting rooms, lounges, depending on the property. AE, DC, MC, V.*

The Excelsior. New York's Upper West Side has become a sort of "Left Bank" area. The only missing Parisian element is the wide choice of quality small hotels. The Excelsior is very much like those dependable second-class European properties. A great location (right across from the American Museum of Natural History and the Hayden Planetarium), clean, pleasant rooms, a helpful staff, and low prices make this a find. Furnishings are relatively new; baths are old but in good condition. Rooms on higher floors have lovely views of Central Park. There is frequent bus and subway service nearby. Great for younger travelers, but more mature visitors will enjoy saving money here, too. *45 W. 81st St., 10024, tel. 212/362–9200 or 800/368–4575, fax 212/721–2994. 120 rooms. Facilities: coffee shop, kitchenettes in suites. AE, DC, MC, V.*

Hotel Edison. A popular budget stop for tour groups from here and abroad, this offbeat old hotel is getting a face-lift. A gruesome murder scene for *The Godfather* was shot in what is now Sophia's restaurant, and the pink plaster coffee shop has become a hot place to eavesdrop on show-business gossip thanks to such celebrity regulars as Jackie Mason. Guest rooms are brighter and fresher than the dark corridors seem to hint. There's no room service, but this part of the theater district has so many restaurants and delis that it doesn't matter much. The crowd here is perfectly wholesome, so save money on your room and spend the big bucks on better theater seats. *228 W. 47th St., 10036, tel. 212/840–5000. 1,000 rooms. Facilities: restaurant, coffee shop, bar. AE, DC, MC, V.*

Hotel Esplanade. This handsome prewar structure is a block from the busiest section of upper Broadway. The immediate neighborhood, West End Avenue, is pleasant—less so the somewhat dingy rooms and suites. Though the Esplanade is still largely a residential property, management encourages the transient traveler with some group and long-stay rates. There's a laundry room, a small fitness center, and an attractive independent restaurant on the premises. While the accommodations are spacious, we saw peeling wallpaper and exposed wiring in some units. Try elsewhere first, but keep this hotel in mind if the Upper West Side is a must location. *305 West End Ave. (at 74th St.), 10023, tel. 212/874–5000 or 800/367–1763,* *fax 212/496–0367. 200 rooms. Facilities: restaurant, laundry room, fitness center, discounted parking. AE, DC, MC, V.*

Hotel Iroquois. On the same block as the Algonquin and the Royalton, this shabby but friendly hotel is becoming popular with Soviet visitors. Halls are a bit dark, with some exposed stairwells, but the rooms are presentable for the price. Suites, some with kitchens, can be real bargains during slow periods. Jan Wallman's supper club is next door. What makes the whole scene okay is the fact that this part of 44th Street is always busy long into the night. *49 W. 44th St., 10036, tel. 212/840–3080 or 800/332–7220, fax 212/827–0464. 135 rooms. No facilities. AE, DC, MC, V.*

Hotel Wentworth. This relatively small prewar hotel is on a midtown street that's usually pulsating with South American atmosphere—some of the city's best-known Brazilian restaurants are right outside the door. Don't be put off by the grim lobby; upstairs you'll find perfectly acceptable bedrooms and modern bathrooms. The atmosphere is similar to that of many second-class European hotels. This is a popular stop for South Americans, although one frequently sees well-dressed U.S. businessmen, too. Single women might find the area a bit eerie at night. *59 W. 46th St., 10036, tel. 212/719–2300 or 800/223–1900. 250 rooms. No facilities. AE, DC, MC, V.*

The Milford Plaza. A Best Western affiliate, this old hotel has modernized its entire interior, but the decor doesn't help alleviate the gloomy atmosphere, and the guest rooms are still closet-size. In the bright public areas, security appears to be tight, as well it should be in this somewhat seedy section of Eighth Avenue. Restaurants include Mamma Leone's Italian restaurant, a popular spot with tourists. The theater-district location is this hotel's main draw, but be forewarned: Many guest rooms are truly claustrophobic, though new wall coverings offer some relief. *270 W. 45th St., 10036, tel. 212/869–3600, 800/221–2690 or, in NY, 800/522–6449; fax 212/819–1433. 1,300 rooms. Facilities: 3 restaurants, meeting rooms. AE, DC, MC, V.*

New York International Youth Hostel. American Youth Hostels recently opened this ambitious facility on Manhattan's Upper West Side. Here, in a renovated 19th-century Gothic-style building, you'll find dormitory accommodations at rock-bottom prices. In addition, the hostel provides conference areas, kitchens, and dining rooms. There are no private baths; rooms hold up to six beds; guests can rent sheets. All ages are welcome, but there is a limit of one week per stay. Although the immediate neighborhood is still a bit rough, the location is convenient to Columbia University, Harlem, and new stores and eating spots on upper Broadway and Columbus and Amsterdam avenues. This is a welcome alternative for the self-sufficient traveler. At press time, the hostel was going through an early shakedown period, so call in advance about exact prices and available amenities. *891 Amsterdam Ave. (at 103rd St.), 10025, tel. 212/932–2300. 90 rooms. Facilities: dining area, patio, kitchen, self-service laundry, travel service desk, conference rooms for nonprofit groups. AE, DC, MC, V.*

★ **Paramount.** What used to be the dowdy Century Paramount is the latest transformation by the same team that owns The Royalton (*see* Expensive, above) and Morgans (*see* Expensive, above). In many ways, this property is both the best buy and most fun of the three. The lobby is dramatic; there's a single wide stairway leading to the mezzanine-level dining area. The public area seating groups are at once homey and high style. Even if you don't dress like David Byrne or Madonna, you'll feel welcome. Rooms are, as rumored, rather small, but all of the singles contain queen-size beds and can certainly be used by two people. Philippe Starck's furnishings, in keeping with Ian Schrager's concepts, are offbeat; the old bathrooms have been fixed up with disco touches like conical steel sinks, and storage areas take a few minutes to decipher. Larger units are out of the Inexpensive price range, but can be used by up to six people at a time. There are several dining options, including a branch of Dean & DeLuca for gourmet take-out fare. Again, as with all properties in this company, the liquor license is at issue, but guests can bring their own wine or spirits to meals. At press time there were plans to reopen the Billy Rose Diamond Horseshoe nightclub. While the Paramount is not for the old-at-heart, it's definitely a category standout. *235 W. 46th St., 10019, tel. 212/764–5500 or 800/225–7474, fax 212/354–5237. 610 rooms. Facilities: two restaurants, take-out food shop, fitness center, children's playroom, business center, VCRs in rooms. AE, DC, MC, V.*

Pickwick Arms Hotel. This convenient East Side establishment charges $80 a night for standard renovated doubles but has older singles with shared baths for as little as $50. The marble-clad lobby is small but brightly lit, and the staff is friendly. Guest rooms have been comfortably furnished in white bamboo. Guests have access to a roof garden; although there is no restaurant, the neighborhood is loaded with places to eat, and a café on the ground floor sells sandwiches, snacks, and a great cup of coffee. This is an acceptable budget alternative in a good area. *230 E. 51st St., 10022, tel. 212/355–0300 or 800/ PICKWIK, fax 212/755–5729. 400 rooms. No facilities. AE, MC, V.*

Ramada Hotel. Another of Loews' budget properties, this motel-style building has an outdoor rooftop swimming pool and lounge area with snack bar. Rooms and suites were recently upgraded. Daily garage rates are reasonable. This is a good bet for theater-bound families during the summer months. *48th St. and 8th Ave., 10019, tel. 212/581–7000 or 800/2–RAMADA, fax 212/974–0291. 366 rooms. Facilities: restaurant, lounge, pool, meeting room. AE, DC, MC, V.*

Vanderbilt YMCA. Of the various Manhattan Ys offering accommodations, this is the best as far as location and facilities are concerned. Although rooms hold up to four people, they are little more than dormitory-style cells—even with only one or two beds to a room, you may feel crowded. Each room does have a late-model TV, however. There are no private baths; communal showers and toilets are clean. Guests are provided with basics such as towels and soap. Besides the low price, this Y offers instant free membership to its on-premises pool, gym, running track, exercise rooms, and sauna. Many of the athletic and public areas, including the pool, have been remodeled. An informal cafeteria and a friendly hospitality desk encourage travelers to mix with one another. The Turtle Bay neighborhood is safe, convenient, and interesting (the United Nations is a few short blocks away). Other YMCAs in town include the 561-room **West Side Y** (5 W. 63rd St., 10023, tel. 212/787–4400), which may be hard to get into but is in the desirable Lincoln Center area; and the 1,490-room **Sloane House YMCA** (356 W. 34th St., 10001, tel. 212/760–5860), which is in a gritty and somewhat unsafe neighborhood. *224 E. 47th St., 10017, tel. 212/*

755–2410. 430 rooms. Facilities: cafeteria, meeting rooms, self-service laundry, gift shop, luggage storage, pool, fitness center. No credit cards.

Wellington Hotel. A large, old-fashioned property whose main advantages are reasonable prices and a midtown location, the Wellington attracts many budget-conscious Europeans. Rooms are small but clean and reasonably cheery; baths are serviceable. Standard hotel services are available upon request. The brightly lit lobby provides a reassuring welcome for late-night returns. *871 7th Ave. (at 55th St.), 10019, tel. 212/247–3900 or 800/652–1212, fax 212/768–3477. 700 rooms. Facilities: restaurant. AE, DC, MC, V.*

Bed-and-Breakfasts

Hundreds of rooms are available on a bed-and-breakfast basis in Manhattan and the outer boroughs, principally Brooklyn. B&Bs almost always cost well below $100 a night; some singles are available for under $50.

New York B&Bs, however, are not the quaint old mansions you find in other localities. They fall largely into two categories: (1) *Hosted apartments*, a bedroom in an apartment where the host is present; (2) *unhosted apartments*, entire apartments that are temporarily vacant. The unhosted option is scarcer and somewhat more expensive.

Along with saving money, B&Bs permit you to mingle with New Yorkers and stay in "real" neighborhoods rather than in tourist enclaves. The disadvantages are that accommodations, amenities, service, and privacy may fall short of what you get in hotels. Sometimes you really do get breakfast and sometimes you don't. And you usually can't pay by credit card.

Here are a few reservation agencies that book B&B accommodations in and near Manhattan. There is no fee for the service, but they advise you to make reservations as far in advance as possible. It's a good idea to find out something about the city before you contact them, and then to request accommodations in a neighborhood that you prefer.

Bed and Breakfast Network of New York (134 W. 32nd St., Suite 602, 10001, tel. 212/645–8134).

City Lights Bed and Breakfast, Ltd. (Box 20355, Cherokee Station, 10028, tel. 212/737–7049).

New World Bed and Breakfast (150 5th Ave., Suite 711, 10011, tel. 212/675–5600 or 800/443–3800).

Urban Ventures (306 W. 38th St., 10018, tel. 212/594–5650).

10 The Arts

by Susan Spano Wells

Brooklyn resident Susan Spano Wells writes about travel for The New York Times, Ladies' Home Journal, *and* Woman's Day. *She is the author of a young adult novel and a frequent contributor to the book review pages of* Newsday.

On a bad day in New York—when it's raining and a cab can't be engaged for blood or money, the subways are flooded, and the line at the cash machine stretches to Poughkeepsie—many New Yorkers may feel as if they'd sell the city back to the Indians for two bits. But in the end, they put up with the urban hassles for at least one obvious reason: New York's unrivaled artistic life. Despite the immense competition and the threat of cuts in city aid to the arts, artists from all disciplines continue to come to the city to find their compatriots and to produce their work. Audiences can only benefit.

There are somewhere between 250 and 300 legitimate theaters in New York, and many more ad hoc venues—parks, churches, universities, museums, lofts, galleries, streets, and rooftops—where performances ranging from Shakespeare to sword-dancing take place. The city is, as well, a revolving door of festivals and special events: Summer jazz, one-act play marathons, international film series, and celebrations of music from the classical to the avant-garde are just a few.

In New York, the arts routinely make the headlines. Pick up a week's worth of newspapers and you'll learn of casting disputes at the Metropolitan Opera, prima ballerinas with bruised knees, big Broadway musicals whose directors are replaced hours before opening, and the constant entertaining haggles between backers, artists, and critics. It's chaos. What a town!

New York's most renowned centers for the arts are tourist attractions in themselves:

Lincoln Center (W. 62nd to 66th Sts., Columbus to Amsterdam Aves., tel. 212/877–2011) is a 14-acre complex that houses the Metropolitan Opera, the New York Philharmonic, the Juilliard School, the New York City Ballet, the American Ballet Theatre, the New York City Opera, the Film Society of Lincoln Center, the Walter Reade Theater, the Chamber Music Society of Lincoln Center, the Lincoln Center Theater, the School of American Ballet, and the New York Public Library's Library and Museum of the Performing Arts. Tours of Lincoln Center are available (tel. 212/877–1800; *see* Tour 8 in Chapter 3).

Carnegie Hall (W. 57th St. at 7th Ave., tel. 212/247–7800) is a premier hall for concerts. An old joke says it all: A tourist asks an old guy with a violin case, "How do you get to Carnegie Hall?" His reply: "Practice, practice." Music masters such as Rudolph Serkin, Leonard Bernstein, Judy Collins, Isaac Stern, and Frank Sinatra, along with great orchestras and debuting talents, have comprised the Carnegie bill. Performances are held in both its main auditorium (opened in 1891 with a concert conducted by Tchaikovsky) and in Weill Recital Hall. Recent restorations brought a face-lift to the building's facade, an enlarged lobby at street level, and a modernized backstage. However, critics still dispute whether the restoration damaged the main auditorium's famed acoustics. From August 1990 to May 1991, Carnegie pulled out all stops to celebrate its centennial.

Radio City Music Hall (1260 6th Ave., tel. 212/632–3100), an Art Deco gem, opened in 1932 with 6,000 seats, a 60-foot-high foyer, two-ton chandeliers, and a powerful Wurlitzer organ. Here you'll find everything from Grateful Dead concerts to Christmas and Easter extravaganzas (featuring the perennial Rockettes kickline), restored movie classics, and star-studded

TV specials. Tours (tel. 212/632–4041) are conducted most days, departing from the main lobby (*see* Tour 1 in Chapter 3).

City Center (131 W. 55th St., tel. 212/581–7907), under its eccentric, tiled Spanish dome (built in 1923 by the Ancient and Accepted Order of the Mystic Shrine and saved from demolition in 1943 by Mayor Fiorello La Guardia) hosts dance troupes, such as Alvin Ailey, Paul Taylor, and Merce Cunningham. Recently, the Manhattan Theatre Club also took up residence there, bringing along its highly touted bill of innovative contemporary drama.

Madison Square Garden (W. 31st to W. 33rd Sts. on 7th Ave., tel. 212/465–6000), camped atop Penn Station, includes a 20,000-seat arena, and the 5,600-seat Forum, which should have completed its $200 million renovation and expansion in the fall of 1991. Sports events such as ice hockey and boxing, plus big-draw pop music concerts and music shows keep it rocking. There's even room for the Knicks and the Rangers to call it home. Should your favorite rock band not be appearing at the Garden, check out its suburban sister halls: the **Nassau Coliseum** (Long Island, tel. 516/794–9300 or 212/307–7171) and the **Meadowlands Arena** (New Jersey, tel. 201/935–3900).

Brooklyn Academy of Music (BAM; 30 Lafayette Ave., Brooklyn, tel. 718/636–4100) is America's oldest performing arts center (begun in 1859), but its reputation is decidedly contemporary thanks to feistily innovative dance, music, opera, and theater productions. The present building, a white Renaissance Revival palace, was built in 1908. In 1987 BAM opened its **Majestic Theatre,** a partly restored vaudeville house, around the corner; The Helen Owen Carey Playhouse and the Lepercq Space are also part of BAM.

Other important arts centers include **Town Hall** (123 W. 43rd St., tel. 212/840–2824) for, among other things, concert versions of lost Broadway musicals; **Merkin Concert Hall** (129 W. 67th St., tel. 212/362–8719), which features mainly classical chamber music; **Symphony Space** (Broadway at 95th St., tel. 212/864–5400), a cavernous converted movie theater with an eclectic offering that ranges from Chinese opera to short stories read by stars; the **92nd Street Y** (1395 Lexington Ave., tel. 212/996–1100), known for its classical music concerts, readings by famous writers, and the Lyrics and Lyricists series; and **The Kitchen** (512 W. 19th St., tel. 212/255–5793), a showcase for "downtown," avant-garde videos, music, performance art, dance, and films.

Getting Tickets

Much has been made of the ballooning cost of tickets, especially for Broadway shows—though major concerts and recitals don't come cheap in New York, either. *Miss Saigon* nudged top Broadway ticket prices into the three-figure zone. Members of the League of American Theaters and Producers would be quick to remind frustrated play goers that the rise in ticket prices hasn't been out of line with the rise in the cost of everything else. But that's cold comfort when you're faced with an astronomical expenditure for one night's entertainment.

On the positive side, tickets for New York City's arts events aren't hard to come by—unless, of course, you're dead set on seeing the season's hottest, sold-out show. Generally, a theater or concert hall's box office is the best place to buy tickets, since in-house ticket sellers make it their business to know about their theaters and shows and don't mind pointing out (on a chart) where you'll be seated. For advance purchase, send the theater or hall a certified check or money order, several alternate dates, and a self-addressed stamped envelope.

You can also pull out a credit card and call **Tele-Charge** (tel. 212/239–6200), **Ticketron** (tel. 212/246–0102), **HIT-TIX** (tel. 212/564–8038), or **Ticketmaster** (tel. 212/307–7171) to reserve tickets—newspaper ads generally will specify which you should use for any given event. A small surcharge ($1–$3) will be added to the total, and your tickets will be waiting for you at the theater.

For those willing to pay top dollar to see that show or concert everyone's talking about but no one can get tickets for, try a ticket broker. Recently tickets to the long-sold-out *Phantom of the Opera* began at $75 plus commission through brokers; had the same seat been available at the box office, it would have sold for $50. A few brokers to try are **Union Tickets** (tel. 800/234-TIXS), **N.Y. Theatre Tickets** (tel. 201/392–0999), **Golden/Leblangs Ticket Service** (tel. 212/944–8910). Also, check the lobbies of major hotels for ticket broker outlets.

You may be tempted to buy from the ticket scalpers who frequently haunt the lobbies of hit shows. But beware: Last year they were reportedly selling tickets to *Les Misérables* for $100–$150, when seats were still available at the box office for a fraction of that price.

Off- and Off-Off-Broadway theaters have their own joint box office called **Ticket Central** (416 W. 42nd St., tel. 212/279–4200). While there are no discounts here, tickets to performances in these theaters are less expensive than Broadway tickets—Ticket Central prices average $8–$20 per person—and they cover an array of events, including legitimate theater, performance art, and dance. Because Ticket Central is located on Theatre Row (42nd St. between 9th and 10th Aves.), the emphasis is on selling nearby Off-Broadway theaters, such as Playwrights' Horizons or The Harold Clurman Theatre, which send their most successful offerings on to Broadway.

Discount Tickets   The best-known discount source may be the **TKTS booth** in Duffy Square (47th St. and Broadway, tel. 212/354–5800), a venerable institution operated by the Theatre Development Fund that sells tickets for Broadway and some Off-Broadway plays at half price (plus a $2 surcharge per ticket) on the same day of the performance. The names of shows available on that day are posted on boards in front of the booth. If you're interested in a Wednesday or Saturday matinee, go to the booth between 10 and 2, check out what's offered, and then wait in line. For evening performances, the booth is open 3–8; for Sunday matinee and evening performances, noon–8. One caution: TKTS accepts only cash or traveler's checks—no credit cards. The wait is generally pleasant (weather permitting), as the bright lights and babble of Broadway surround you. You're likely to meet friendly theater lovers eager to review shows they've recently seen; often you'll even meet struggling actors who can give you the inside scoop. By the time you get to the booth, you may be willing to take a gamble on a show you would otherwise never have picked, and it just might be more memorable than one of the long-running hits.

So successful has TKTS proved (last year it sold nearly 1.7 million seats), that auxiliary booths have opened in the Wall Street area (2 World Trade Center) and in Brooklyn Heights (near the intersection of Court and Montague Sts.). The World Trade Center branch is open weekdays 11–5:30, Saturday 11–1; for matinees and Sundays, 11–closing the day before the performance; for Off-Broadway evening performances, 11–1. In Brooklyn, evening-performance tickets are on sale weekdays 11–5:30, Saturday 11–3:30; tickets for matinees and Sundays are sold a day ahead; Off-Broadway tickets are sold until 1. The lines at these TKTS outstations are shorter than those at Duffy Square, though occasionally the offerings are somewhat limited.

A setup similar to TKTS has arisen in the **Bryant Park Music and Dance Discount Ticket Booth,** located on 42nd Street next to Bryant Park, just west of the New York Public Library. This booth sells discounted tickets for music and dance events (including performances at Lincoln Center, City Center, Carnegie Hall, and even a few nightclubs). It's open Tuesday, Thursday, and Friday noon–2 and 3–7; Wednesday and Saturday 11–2 and 3–7; Sunday noon–6. Unlike TKTS, the Bryant Park booth has a telephone information line (tel. 212/382–2323).

A newcomer to Grand Central Terminal, **Star*Tix Grand Central,** next to the Amtrak ticket counter, offers both hard-to-get Broadway tickets (for a maximum of $19.50 plus the full ticket price) and discount Broadway tickets ($7 surcharge per ticket) plus discount tickets for concerts and dance events ($7 surcharge per ticket), vouchers for discount tickets for Off- and Off-Off-Broadway plays ($2.50 surcharge per voucher), and free-admission vouchers for cabaret and comedy clubs ($2.50 surcharge per voucher). Tickets and vouchers can be purchased up to one month before the performance. Credit cards are accepted for full-price advance sale tickets only; other payments must be made in cash or traveler's checks. Star*Tix Grand Central is open weekdays 8–7; Saturday 11–3. You can call the 24-hour Star*Tix Hotline to find out what events are available (tel. 212/932–1000).

Discounts on big-name, long-running shows (such as *Cats* and *Les Misérables*) are often available if you can lay your hands on a couple of "twofers"—discount ticket coupons found on various cash registers around town, in line at TKTS, at the New York Visitors and Convention Bureau (at 2 Columbus Circle), and at the office of their producer, the **Hit Show Club** (630 9th Ave., 8th floor, tel. 212/581–4211; open weekdays 9:15–3:45).

The Public Theater (425 Lafayette St., tel. 212/598–7150) regularly sets aside tickets for sale at a discount through its **Quiktix.** If you're interested in sampling Joe Papp's current offerings (*see* Theater, Beyond Broadway, below), join the Quiktix line anytime before 6 PM for evening performances, and before 1 PM for matinees. Tickets are sold on a first-come, first-served basis.

A slew of ticket clubs exist to serve repeat theatergoers, so if you plan to be in the city for a long time, they may be worth investigating. The newest is **Advance Entertainment New York** (tel. 212/239–2570), essentially a telemarketing firm whose phones are manned by "resting" actors and actresses. For $95 a year, members receive constant updates on what's hot and free ticket procurement—sometimes at a discount and with special attention paid to getting good seats. AENY can be used on a one-time, no obligation-to-join basis. Other ticket groups include **Stubs Preview Club** (tel. 212/398–8370), $35 a year, specializing in preview showings; and the **Theatre Development Fund** (1501 Broadway, tel. 212/221–0885), whose TDF vouchers are available for $3 to students, union members, teachers, performing arts professionals, and members of volunteer groups, among others. When redeemed at the box office, the vouchers are worth $5 off the cost of a ticket for dance, theater, and musical events at Off-Off-Broadway theaters.

Finding Out What's On

To find out who or what's playing where, your first stop should be the newsstand. The *New York Times* isn't a prerequisite for finding out what's going on around town, but it comes in pretty handy, especially on Fridays with its "Weekend" section. On Sundays, the *Times*'s "Arts and Leisure" section features longer "think pieces" on everything from opera to TV—and lots more ads, plus a calendar of cultural events for the upcoming week.

If your tastes are more adventurous, try the weekly paper *The Village Voice;* its club listings are unrivaled, its "Choices" section reliable. When its club-tattler-cum-critic Michael Musto talks (in a column called "La Dolce Musto"), night prowlers and club pixies listen. The *Voice* is published on Wednesdays.

Some of the most entertaining listings can be found in *The New Yorker* magazine. "Goings On About Town" heads off each weekly issue with ruthlessly succinct reviews ("a crass actor who seems to dote on the sound of his own voice"; "a long, rambling bar and restaurant with a white-trash-chicken-shack theme") of theater, art, music, film, and nightlife. *New York* magazine's "Cue listings" and "Hot Line" section are useful, too. The *New York Native* and *Outweek* cover the gay scene.

The League of New York Theatres and Producers and Playbill magazine publish a bimonthly *Broadway Theatre Guide,* available in hotels and at the Visitors and Convention Bureau offices. For information on the lower Manhattan cultural scene, write for a *Downtown Arts Activities Calendar* (Lower Manhattan Cultural Council, 1 World Trade Ctr., Suite 1717, New York, NY 10048).

You can also get updated information by phone from NYC/ON STAGE, the Theatre Development Fund's 24-hour information service (tel. 212/768–1818).

Theater

Almost everyone who visits New York ends up spending several hours in a theater seat. The theater—not the Statue of Liberty or South Street Seaport—is the city's number-one tourist attraction; though pundits would have you believe it's a doomed beast, if it is, it's putting on a surprisingly lively, not to mention prolonged, death scene. Theater folk continue to make

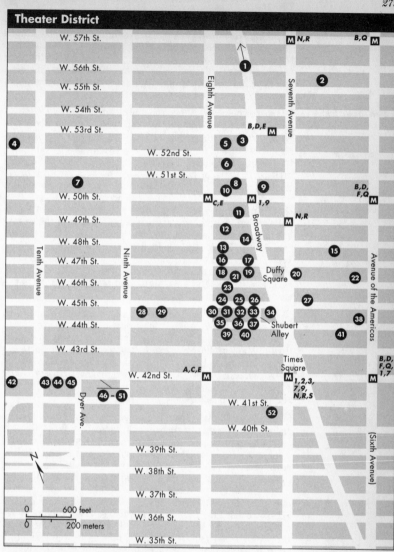

Ambassador, **11**

American Place, **22**

Ethel Barrymore, **17**

Belasco, **38**

Biltmore, **16**

Booth, **33**

Broadhurst, **36**

Broadway, **3**

Brooks Atkinson, **18**

Circle in the Square, **10**

Cort, **15**

Cubiculo, **7**

Douglas Fairbanks, **45**

Edison, **19**

Ensemble Studio, **4**

Eugene O'Neill, **12**

45th Street and William Redfield, **28**

Gershwin, **8**

Golden, **30**

Harold Clurman, **50**

Helen Hayes, **40**

INTAR, **48**

Imperial, **24**

John Houseman, **43**

Judith Anderson, **47**

Kaufman, **42**

Lamb's, **41**

Lincoln Center Theater: Vivian Beaumont, Mitzi E. Newhouse, **1**

Longacre, **13**

Lunt-Fontanne, **21**

Lyceum, **27**

Majestic, **35**

Manhattan Theatre Club (City Center), **2**

Marquis, **26**

Martin Beck, **29**

Minskoff, **34**

Music Box, **25**

Nat Horne, **44**

Nederlander, **52**

Neil Simon, **6**

Palace, **20**

Playwrights Horizons, **49**

Plymouth, **32**

Richard Rogers, **23**

Royale, **31**

Samuel Beckett, **51**

St. James, **39**

Shubert, **37**

South Street, **46**

Virginia, **5**

Walter Kerr, **14**

Winter Garden, **9**

their rounds, combining business and art to produce their crazy stew. Delicate little ladies tottering about in their pillbox hats are really theatrical grande dames, with fast answers to the flashers on Eighth Avenue; shifty-looking guys toting battered briefcases turn out to be famous directors; and the girls and boys scuttling through stage doors are chorus members rushing to exchange their Nikes for tap shoes.

Broadway Theater District
To most people, New York theater means Broadway, that region bounded by 42nd and 53rd streets, between Sixth and Ninth avenues, where bright, transforming lights shine upon porn theaters and jewel-box playhouses alike (*see* Theater District map). Although the area's busy sidewalks contain more than their share of hustlers and pickpockets, visitors brave them for the playhouses' plentiful delights. Extravagant plans for redevelopment of the Times Square area continue to ricochet from marquee to marquee; amid the grunge, major hotels keep springing up in this area. With every thud of the wrecker's ball, theater devotees pray for the survival of the essential character of Broadway—as Paul Goldberger put it in the *New York Times*, "the world of memory, the magical Times Square of old, the lively, glittering district of theaters, restaurants, cabarets, hotels, and neon signs that was in many ways the city's symbolic heart."

Historically speaking, the nation's entertainment capital was once composed of almost 50 theaters, which sprang up between 1899 and 1925 near the intersection of Broadway and 42nd Street. Many of those original showplaces have been gutted or turned into movie houses. The legitimate theaters that remain are squeezed into side streets in such tight spaces that from the outside it's often hard to imagine that there's room inside for an audience, much less a stage.

Some of the old playhouses are as interesting for their history as for their current offerings: the **St. James** (246 W. 44th St.) is where Lauren Bacall served as an usherette in the '40s, and a sleeper of a musical called *Oklahoma!* woke up as a hit; the **Lyceum** (149 W. 45th St.) is New York's oldest still-functioning theater, built in 1903 with a posh apartment on top that now holds the Shubert Archive (open to scholars by appointment only); the **Shubert Theatre** (225 W. 44th St.) is where Barbra Streisand made her 1962 Broadway debut, and the long-run record-breaker, *A Chorus Line*, played for 15 years; and the **Martin Beck Theatre** (302 W. 45th St.), built in 1924 in Byzantine style, is the stage that served up premieres of Eugene O'Neill's *The Iceman Cometh*, Arthur Miller's *The Crucible*, and Tennessee Williams's *Sweet Bird of Youth*.

As you stroll around the theater district, you may also see: **Shubert Alley,** a shortcut between 44th and 45th streets where theater moguls used to park their limousines, today site of a jam-packed Great White Way memorabilia store called One Shubert Alley; **Actors' Equity** (165 W. 46th St.), home of the stage actor's union, and a crashing place for auditionees between cattle calls; **Manhattan Plaza,** a largely subsidized apartment complex at Ninth Avenue and 42nd Street inhabited primarily by theater people, whose rent in hard times is assessed at 30% of their income (whatever that comes to); **Theatre Row** (42nd St. between 9th and 10th Aves.), a convivial collection of small Off-Broadway theaters; and **Restaurant Row** (46th

St. between 8th and 9th Aves.), which offers plenty of choices for dining before or after a show. For a deeper drink of the district, join a **Backstage on Broadway talk** (tel. 212/575–8065), hosted by a professional actor, director, stage manager, or designer.

Recent seasons have brought their requisite gloomy speculation about the future of commercial theater. British imports, sessions with stand-up comics, and revivals of old standards often seem to outnumber riskier productions of new plays. Serious drama still has a hard time finding serious audiences, but has been faring pretty well of late with the recent successes of the Pulitzer Prize-winning *The Heidi Chronicles* and *The Piano Lesson*, as well as the Steppenwolf production of *The Grapes of Wrath* and Lincoln Center's *Six Degrees of Separation*. Can Broadway compete with the new fad for "Sensurround drama" (*Tony 'n' Tina's Wedding*), in which dinner is offered along with the play? Is the American musical gone with the wind from London, which blew in hits like *The Phantom of the Opera* and *Miss Saigon*? While the answers to such questions wait in the wings, New York's splendid invalid, the Broadway theater, carries on.

In determining which Broadway show to see, first consider the long-running hits: *Cats*, *Les Misérables*, *The Phantom of the Opera*, *The Fantasticks* (downtown), and others, which most magazine and newspaper listings helpfully point out. Then look beyond the marquees for both tomorrow's hits and today's resounding flops. Remember, there's something special about catching a show in previews or seeing a harshly reviewed play before it bites the dust. A lousy review can quickly close a show, even though discriminating audience members often disagree with the critics.

Beyond Broadway Ten years ago it was relatively simple to categorize the New York stage beyond Broadway. It was divided into Off-Broadway and Off-Off-Broadway, depending on a variety of factors that included theatrical contract type, location, and ticket price. Today such distinctions seem strained, as Off-Broadway prices have risen and the quality of some Off-Off-Broadway productions has improved markedly. Off- and Off-Off-Broadway is where Eric Bogosian and Laurie Anderson make their home. It's the land where *Driving Miss Daisy* was conceived and such plays as *Nunsense* and *Other People's Money* enjoy long runs. To complicate matters further, scores of established companies hop from one theater to another, or go underground for a season or two and then reemerge in new quarters. Unremitting rent hikes have become the bane of such smaller theaters' existence. As a study undertaken by the Alliance of Resident Theatres/New York recently pointed out, small theaters often venture into marginal neighborhoods and revivify them, only to be forced out by gentrification.

Name actors appear in top-flight productions at **Lincoln Center's** two theaters: the **Vivian Beaumont** and the more intimate **Mitzi E. Newhouse** (65th St. and Broadway, tel. for both 212/362–7600). Strong management there led by Gregory Mosher (to be succeeded by Andre Bishop in January 1992) has scored some startling successes—witness the long runs of John Guare's *The House of Blue Leaves* and the vintage Cole Porter musical *Anything Goes*. Downtown at the **Public Theater** (425 Lafayette St., tel. 212/598–7150) New York's premier *homme* *de theatre*, Joseph Papp, mounts new and classic plays, along with film series, dance concerts, and musical events. His Shakespeare marathon, scheduled to last six years, will present all the Bard's works with a roster of big-name stars. In the summertime, Papp's Shakespeare Festival raises its sets in Central Park's open-air Delacorte Theater, while the **Festival Latino** takes over the building at Astor Place.

One of the major Off-Broadway enclaves is **Theatre Row,** a collection of small houses (100 seats or less)—such as the John Houseman and Douglas Fairbanks theaters, Playwrights Horizons, or the Harold Clurman Theatre—on the downtown side of 42nd Street between Ninth and Tenth avenues. Another Off-Broadway neighborhood lies in Greenwich Village, around Sheridan Square. Its theaters include **Circle Rep** (99 7th Ave. S, tel. 212/924–7100), a showcase for new playwrights; **Circle in the Square Downtown** (159 Bleecker St., tel. 212/254–6330); the **Lucille Lortel Theater** (121 Christopher St., tel. 212/924–8782); the **Cherry Lane Theater** (38 Commerce St., tel. 212/989–2020); and the **Provincetown Playhouse** (133 MacDougal St., tel. 212/477–5048). Other estimable Off-Broadway theaters are flung across the Manhattan map: the **Promenade Theatre** (Broadway at 76th St., tel. 212/580–1313); the **Roundabout** (100 E. 17th St., tel. 212/420–1883), specializing in revivals of the classics; and the **Manhattan Theatre Club** (at City Center, 131 W. 55th St., tel. 212/581–7907).

Here are a few other Off- and Off-Off-Broadway theater groups to keep your eye on:

The Classic Stage Company (136 E. 13th St., tel. 212/677–4210), providing a showcase for the classics—some arcane, others European—in new translations and adaptations.
The Ensemble Studio Theatre (549 W. 52nd St., tel. 212/247–4982), with its tried-and-true roster of players, stressing new dramatic works.
The Jewish Repertory Theatre (344 E. 14th St., tel. 212/505–2667), begun in 1972, producing plays about Jewish life; one recent offering, *Crossing Delancey*, was turned into a hit film.
Manhattan Punch Line (410 W. 42nd St., tel. 212/239–0827), devoted to comedy since 1979.
Musical Theatre Works (St. Peter's Church, corner of 54th St. and Lexington Ave., tel. 212/677–0040), for musical comedy experiments.
The Negro Ensemble Company (Theatre Four, 155 W. 46th St., tel. 212/575–5860), for high-caliber black drama.
The New Theatre of Brooklyn (465 Dean St., Brooklyn, tel. 718/230–3366), off Flatbush Avenue (on the outskirts of Park Slope), offering new plays and neglected classics.
The Pan Asian Repertory Theatre (Playhouse 46, 423 W. 46th St., tel. 212/245–2660), a center for Asian and Asian-American artists, producing new works or adapted Western plays.
Perry Street Theatre Co. (31 Perry St., tel. 212/255–7190), presenting innovative new plays as well as concerts.
Repertorio Español (Gramercy Arts Theatre, 138 E. 27th St., tel. 212/889–2850), an Obie-award-winning Spanish arts repertory theater whose productions are in Spanish.
Riverside Shakespeare Company (Playhouse 91, 316 E. 91st St., tel. 212/369–2273), a troupe that, since 1977, has been performing the Bard's works and other classic plays in parks throughout the five boroughs, and is now in residence on 91st Street.

Second Stage (McGinn/Cazale Theatre, 2162 Broadway at W. 76th St., tel. 212/873–6103), producing recent plays that may not have been given a fair shake their first time around.

The Soho Rep (46 Walker St., below Canal St. between Broadway and Church St., tel. 212/977–5955), dedicated to contemporary plays on controversial issues.

Theatre for a New Audience (220 E. 4th St., tel. 212/505–8345) performs both Shakespearean productions and new plays by important contemporary playwrights.

TWEED (496 Hudson St., tel. 212/777–0536), a decidedly downtown company that explores contemporary themes through various theatrical forms.

Avant-Garde   Last, but not at all least, is New York's fabled theatrical avant-garde. The "experimental theater" movement's founders may no longer be the long-haired hippies they were when they first started doing mixed-media productions and promoting off-center playwrights (such as Sam Shepard) in the '60s, but they continue at the forefront. Take Ellen Stewart, also known, simply and elegantly, as "LaMama." Over the past two decades, her East Village organization has branched out to import European innovators and has grown physically as well. **La MaMa E.T.C.** (74A E. 4th St., tel. 212/475–7710) now encompasses a First Floor Theater, an Annex theater, and a club. At these you'll see African fables, New Wave opera, reinterpretations of the Greeks (assisted by the likes of director Andrei Serban and composer Elizabeth Swados), and novels adapted for the stage.

Another chief player in the theatrical avant-garde is **Mabou Mines** (150 1st Ave., tel. 212/473–0559), a peripatetic troupe whose trademarks are the innovative use of stage technology and the repeated exploration (some call it "deconstruction") of Samuel Beckett's texts. A recently expanded four-theater cultural complex is home to the experimentalist **Theater for the New City** (155 1st Ave., tel. 212/254–1109), which also sponsors a street-theater program, arts festivals, and Christmas and Halloween spectacles. Still thriving is the **Ridiculous Theatrical Company** (1 Sheridan Sq., tel. 212/691–2271). This theater has been around since 1972, honing its unique performance style: a blend of classical acting—usually in drag—and high camp.

Performance Art   At the vanishing point of the avant-garde is that curious mélange of artistic disciplines known as performance art. Intentionally difficult to categorize, it blends music and sound, dance, video and lights, words, and whatever else comes to the performance artist's mind, to produce events of erratic success—sometimes fascinating, sometimes deadening. Performance art is almost exclusively a downtown endeavor, though it is also showcased in the outer boroughs, especially Brooklyn, where the **Brooklyn Academy of Music** (30 Lafayette Ave., Brooklyn, tel. 718/636–4100) has built its considerable reputation on its annual Next Wave Festival, which features many performance works. To BAM have come the performance-art elite, including Philip Glass, Laurie Anderson, and David Byrne.

Other performance-art showcases are:

Franklin Furnace (112 Franklin St., tel. 212/925–4671), since 1976 a supporter of off-center arts—this is where Eric

Bogosian (seen in the movies *Funhouse* and *Talk Radio*) got his start.

The Kitchen (512 W. 19th St., tel. 212/255–5793) in new Chelsea digs, perhaps *the* Manhattan center for performance art, although video, dance, and music have their moments here, too.
Performance Space 122, or **P.S. 122** (150 1st Ave., tel. 212/477–5288), called by *The Village Voice* "the petri dish of downtown culture." Occupying a former public school that was comedian George Burns's alma mater, P.S. 122 presents exhibitions and productions that come and go quickly but seldom fail in freshness. Look especially for its annual marathon in February, in which scores of dazzling downtowners take part.
BACA Downtown (111 Willoughby St., Brooklyn, tel. 718/596–2222), another Brooklyn outpost of the avant-garde, featuring up-and-comers and imported acts.
P.S. 1 (46–01 21st St., Queens, tel. 718/784–2084), a contemporary art museum in lively Long Island City, Queens, featuring occasional theatrical events.

Music

"Gentlemen," conductor Serge Koussevitzky once told the assembled Boston Symphony Orchestra, "maybe it's good enough for Cleveland or Cincinnati, but it's not good enough for New York." That's New York's place in the musical world, in a nutshell; quite simply, it's the top, for performers and music lovers alike.

New York possesses not only the country's oldest symphony, the New York Philharmonic, but also three renowned conservatories—The Juilliard School, The Manhattan School of Music, and Mannes College of Music—plus myriad musical performance groups. Since the turn of the century, the world's great orchestras and soloists have made Manhattan a principal stopping point. In recent years, live TV and radio broadcasts have brought the music played in New York to millions more listeners across the North American continent.

To those who visit the city for its music, New York opens like a Stradivarius case. In an average week, between 50 and 150 events—everything from zydeco to Debussy, Cole Porter, Kurt Weill, and reggae—appear in newspaper and magazine listings, and weekly concert calendars are published in all of the major newspapers. Record and music shops, such as the cavernous **Tower Records** (692 Broadway, tel. 212/505–1500, and 1965 Broadway, tel. 212/799–2500), **J & R Music World** (23 and 33 Park Row, tel. 212/732–8600), the reliable **Bleecker Bob's Golden Oldies** (118 W. 3rd St., tel. 212/475–9677), and the classy **Patelson's** (160 W. 56th St., tel. 212/582–5840), serve as music information centers, too, as do the city's radio stations. WNYC (FM 93.9 and AM 820) and WQXR (FM 96.3 and AM 1560) update listeners on current musical events, and WNCN (FM 104) does the same; WNCN's "Café 104" (Fridays, noon–1 PM) is a good source for info on weekend concerts and cultural events. The **Bryant Park Music and Dance Discount Ticket Booth** (42nd St. just east of 6th Ave., tel. 212/382–2323) also lists music around town.

In recent seasons, the city has been fevered by a mania for composer marathons. Early music, often performed on historic instruments, has caught the New York public's ear, too. Up from downtown wafts the sound of New Music, played by such masters as saxophonist John Zorn, the Kronos Quartet, and Peter Gordon's Love of Life Orchestra, and, increasingly, the uptown establishment halls, including Carnegie and Avery Fisher, are expanding their repertoires to accommodate them. Recently, infusions of Third World music—the Big Apple calls it World Beat—have thickened the city's musical stew, with smaller concert halls and alternative venues featuring the melodies of Cuba, Ghana, and other countries you'd need an atlas to locate.

Classical Music **Lincoln Center** (W. 62nd St. and Broadway) remains the city's musical nerve center, especially when it comes to the classics. The 150-year-old **New York Philharmonic,** led by new musical director Kurt Masur, performs at Avery Fisher Hall (tel. 212/874–2424). In summer, the popular **Mostly Mozart** concert series presents an impressive roster of classical performers. Avery Fisher, designed by Max Abramovitz, opened in 1961 as Philharmonic Hall, but underwent drastic renovation in 1976 to improve the acoustics (at a price tag of $5 million). The result is an auditorium that follows the classic European rectangular pattern. To its stage come the world's great musicians; to its boxes, the black-tie-and-diamond-tiara set.

A note for New York Philharmonic devotees: The orchestra rehearses Thursday mornings at 9:45. In season (September–June), and when conductors and soloists are amenable, rehearsals are open to the public for $5. Call 212/874–2424 for information.

Near Avery Fisher is Alice Tully Hall (tel. 212/362–1911), an intimate "little white box," considered as acoustically perfect as concert houses get. Here the **Chamber Music Society of Lincoln Center** tunes up, along with promising Juilliard students and famous soloists and concert groups. Lincoln Center's outdoor Damrosch Park, and Bruno Walter Auditorium (in the Library of the Performing Arts, tel. 212/870–1630) often offer free concerts; two summer programs, **Serious Fun** and **Classical Jazz,** have been added in recent years to the Lincoln Center bill as well.

While Lincoln Center is only 30 years old, another famous classical music palace—**Carnegie Hall** (W. 57th St. at 7th Ave., tel. 212/247–7800)—recently celebrated its 100th birthday. This is the place where the great pianist Paderewski was attacked by ebullient crowds (who claimed kisses and locks of his hair) after a performance in 1891; where young Leonard Bernstein, standing in for New York Philharmonic conductor Bruno Walter, made his triumphant debut in 1943; where Jack Benny and Isaac Stern fiddled together and where the Beatles played one of their first U.S. concerts. When threats of the wrecker's ball loomed large in 1960, a consortium of Carnegie loyalists (headed by Isaac Stern) rose to save it; an eventual multi-million-dollar renovation in 1986 worked cosmetic wonders, but many critics believe that the face-lift damaged the Main Concert Hall's celebrated acoustics. Public tours are conducted on Tuesdays and Thursdays at 11:30, 2, and 3; for information, call 212/247–7800.

Other prime classical music locales are:

Aaron Davis Hall at City College (W. 135th St. at Convent Ave., tel. 212/650–6900), uptown scene of world music events and a variety of classical concerts and dance programs.

Grace Rainey Rogers Auditorium at the Metropolitan Museum of Art (5th Ave. at 82nd St., tel. 212/570–3949), providing classical music in classic surroundings.

Merkin Concert Hall at the Abraham Goodman House (129 W. 67th St., tel. 212/362–8719), almost as prestigious as the concert halls at Lincoln Center.

Kaufman Concert Hall at the 92nd St. Y (1395 Lexington Ave., tel. 212/415–5440), with the New York Chamber Symphony in residence, plus star recitalists and chamber music groups.

Bargemusic at the Fulton Ferry Landing in Brooklyn (tel. 718/624–4061), with chamber music bubbling from an old barge and a fabulous skyline.

Brooklyn Academy of Music (30 Lafayette Ave., tel. 718/636–4100), ever experimenting with new and old musical styles, and still a showcase for the Brooklyn Philharmonic.

Outdoor Concerts   Weather permitting, the city's great out-of-doors becomes one wide concert hall. Each August, the plaza around Lincoln Center explodes with the **Lincoln Center Out-of-Doors** series. In the summertime, both the **Metropolitan Opera** and the **New York Philharmonic** decamp to municipal parks, rocking the greenswards with the trills of *La Bohème* or the thunder of the *1812 Overture*. These occasions are free, which explains why on one balmy summer night in 1986, the Philharmonic made *The Guinness Book of World Records* by entertaining a crowd of 800,000. (For information call Lincoln Center, tel. 212/877–2011, or the City Parks Events Hotline, tel. 212/360–1333). The Museum of Modern Art hosts free Friday and Saturday evening concerts of 20th-century music in their sculpture garden as part of the **Summergarden** series (tel. 212/708–9850). A **Jazzmobile** (tel. 212/866–4900) trucks jazz and Latin music to parks throughout the five boroughs, and Prospect Park comes alive with the sounds of its annual **Celebrate Brooklyn Concert Series** (tel. 718/788–0055). Starlit Saturday evenings at South Street Seaport turn Pier 16 into **Summerpier** (tel. 212/669–9400), featuring a range of musical styles.

Lunchtime   During the work week, more and more lunchtime concerts pro-
Concerts   vide musical midday breaks at public atriums all over the city. Events are generally free, and bag-lunching is encouraged. Check out the **Continental Insurance Atrium** (180 Maiden La.); the **World Financial Center's Winter Garden Atrium** (across the West Side Highway from the World Trade Center); and the **Citicorp Center Marketplace** (54th St. and Lexington Ave.). And, of course, everywhere—in parks, on street corners, and down under in the subway—aspiring musicians of all kinds hold forth, with their instrument cases thrown open for contributions. True, some are hacks, but others are bona fide professionals: moonlighting violinists, Broadway chorus members indulging their love of the barbershop quartet, or horn players prowling up from clubs to take in the fresh air.

Downtown, the venerable **Trinity Church** (Broadway and Wall St., tel. 212/602–0747) presents free lunchtime concerts of mostly classical music. On Tuesdays, concerts are at 12:45; on Mondays and Thursdays, they're at 12:10 up the street in St. Paul's Chapel (Fulton St. and Broadway).

A midtown music break can be found at **St. Peter's Lutheran Church** (619 Lexington Ave., at the Citicorp Ctr., tel. 212/935–2200), with its Wednesday series of lunchtime jazz at 12:30 and its Sunday jazz vespers at 5.

Opera

Recent decades have sharply intensified the public's appreciation for grand opera—partly because of the charismatic personalities of such great singers as Placido Domingo and Beverly Sills, and partly because of the efforts of New York's magnetic **Metropolitan Opera.** A Met premiere draws the rich and famous, the critics, and the connoisseurs. At the Met's elegant Lincoln Center home, with its Marc Chagall murals and weighty Austrian-crystal chandeliers, the supercharged atmosphere gives audiences a sense that something special is going to happen, even before the curtain goes up. Luciano Pavarotti put it best: "When it comes to classical music, New York can truly be called a beacon of light—with that special quality that makes it *'unico in mondo,'* unique in the world."

The Metropolitan Opera (tel. 212/362–6000) performs its vaunted repertoire from September to mid-April, and though tickets can cost as much as $115 apiece, standing room is available for far less. Standing room tickets for the week's performance go on sale on Sunday.

Meanwhile, the **New York City Opera,** which performs in Lincoln Center's New York State Theater (tel. 212/870–5570), has faced the departure of its famous general director, Beverly Sills. But with conductor Christopher Keene at the helm, it persists in its "tradition of taking chances on unfamiliar works, old and new" (in the words of *New York Times* critic Donal Henahan) and in nurturing young American stars-to-be. City Opera recently widened its repertoire to include several classic musical comedies, such as *Brigadoon, South Pacific,* and *The Sound of Music,* and it continues its ingenious practice of "supertitling"—electronically displaying, above the stage, line-by-line translations into English for foreign-language operas. Recent seasons have included such time-tested favorites as *Candide, Madama Butterfly,* and *Rigoletto.*

Opera aficionados should also keep track of the **Carnegie Hall** schedule (tel. 212/247–7800) for debuting singers and performances by the Opera Orchestra of New York, which specializes in presenting rarely performed operas in concert form, often with star soloists. Pay close attention to new developments at the **Brooklyn Academy of Music** (tel. 718/636–4100), which kicked off its BAM Opera project in 1989 with the Welsh Opera's production of *Falstaff;* it scheduled the American premiere of John Adams' *The Death of Klinghoffer* for the 1991 season.

Other city opera groups include:

Amato Opera Theatre (319 Bowery, tel. 212/228–8200), a showcase for rising singers.
New York Gilbert and Sullivan Players (251 W. 91st St., Apt. 4C, tel. 212/769–1000), performing G & S classics at Christmas and other times.
Opera Ebony (2109 Broadway, Suite 1418, tel. 212/874–7245), a black company performing major and minor works.
Repertorio Español (138 E. 27th St., tel. 212/889–2850), whose performers sing in Spanish.

True devotees might consider a New York opera theme tour— several days of concentrated immersion, usually conducted by an expert. Check *Opera Monthly* magazine (Box 816, Madison Square Station, 10159, tel. 212/627–2120) for the names of tour firms.

Dance

Ballet Visiting balletomanes live out their dreams in New York, where two powerhouse companies—the New York City Ballet and the American Ballet Theatre—continue to please and astonish.

The **New York City Ballet,** a hallmark troupe for over 40 years, recently presented a festival of Jerome Robbins's ballets, highlighting some of the successful choreographer's best works. NYCB has long been famous for its repertoire of George Balanchine works, and now Peter Martins is breaking new ground with his series of dances inspired by the avant-garde music of Michael Torke. The company performs in Lincoln Center's New York State Theater (tel. 212/870–5570). Its season runs from November to February—with December set aside for the beloved annual production of *The Nutcracker*—and from April to June.

Founded by Lincoln Kirstein and Balanchine in 1948, NYCB continues to stress dance as a whole above individual ballet stars, though that hasn't stopped a number of prima ballerinas (such as Patricia McBride, Suzanne Farrell, and Darci Kistler) from standing out. The company contains 110 dancers altogether, and maintains a repertoire of 20th-century works unmatched in the world.

Across the plaza at Lincoln Center, the Metropolitan Opera House (tel. 212/362–6000) is home to the **American Ballet Theatre,** noted especially for its brilliant renditions of story ballets and its lyrical style, as well as its world-renowned featured dancers. Its season opens in April, when the opera season closes, and runs through June.

Part of Lincoln Center's dance vitality is accounted for by the presence of the **School of American Ballet,** the focus for the dreams of young dancers across the country. Some 2,000 of them vie for spots in SAB's summer session, and a talented handful of the 200 who make it into the summer group go on to join the school. Here the Balanchine legacy lives on, and soulful-eyed baby dancers are molded into professional performers. You can see SAB students dashing across 66th and Broadway with leotard-stuffed bags slung over their shoulders, or congregating in **The Ballet Shop** (1887 Broadway, tel. 212/581–7990).

When the ABT and NYCB take a break from performing, Lincoln Center acts as impresario for dozens of world-renowned companies, such as the Bolshoi and Royal Danish ballets.

The varied bill at **City Center** (131 W. 55th St., tel. 212/581–7907) often includes touring ballet companies; recently the Matsuyama Ballet from Japan performed there.

Modern Dance At City Center (131 W. 55th St., tel. 212/581–7907), the moderns hold sway. In seasons past, the New York-based **Martha Graham Dance Company,** the **Paul Taylor Dance Company,** the **Dance Theater of Harlem,** and the **Merce Cunningham Dance Company** have performed here. The **Brooklyn Academy**

of Music (30 Lafayette Ave., tel. 718/636–4100) features contemporary dance as a component of its **Next Wave Festival** every fall.

A growing modern dance center is the **Joyce Theater** (175 8th Ave., tel. 212/242–0800), permanent home of **Feld Ballets/NY,** founded in 1974 by an upstart ABT dancer who went on to become a principal fixture on the dance scene. The loony acrobats of **Pilobolus** and the avant-garde **ZeroMoving Company** have also performed at the Joyce, which is housed in a former Art Deco movie theater. At Symphony Space (2537 Broadway, tel. 212/864–1414), the bill features ethnic dance.

Here's a sampling of other, mostly experimental and avant-garde, dance forums:

Dance Theater Workshop (219 W. 19th St., tel. 212/691–6500), one of New York's most successful laboratories for new dance.
Danspace Project (at St. Mark's-in-the-Bowery Church, 10th St. and 2nd Ave., tel. 212/529–2318), with a series of avant-garde and historical choreography that runs from October to June.
P.S. 122 (150 1st Ave., tel. 212/477–5288), where dance events border on performance art; among others, Meredith Monk occasionally cavorts here.
Repertorio Español (138 E. 27th St., tel. 212/889–2850), oft-visited by the famed Spanish stylist Pilar Rioja.
Washington Square Church (135 W. 4th St., tel. 212/777–2528), for modern dance and dance theater.

Film

On any given week, New York City seems a kind of film archive featuring all the major new releases, classics renowned and arcane, unusual foreign offerings, small independent flicks, and cutting-edge experimental works. Because you don't usually need to buy tickets in advance, movie-going is a great spur-of-the-moment way to rest from the rigors of sightseeing. You may have to stand a while in a line that winds around the block, but even that can be entertaining—conversations overheard in such queues are generally just as good as the previews of coming attractions. Note, however, that these lines are generally for people who have already bought their tickets; be sure, as you approach the theater, to ask if there are separate lines for ticket *holders* and ticket *buyers*.

Festivals New York's numero uno film program remains the **New York Film Festival,** conducted by the Film Society of Lincoln Center every September and October at Alice Tully and Avery Fisher halls (tel. 212/362–1911). Its program includes 25–50 hot movies, most of them never seen before in the United States; the festival's hits usually make their way into local movie houses over the following couple of months. This festival has presented the U.S. premieres of such memorable movies as Martin Scorsese's *Mean Streets*, François Truffaut's *Day For Night*, Lawrence Kasdan's *The Big Chill*, and Akira Kurosawa's *Ran*. In March the Film Society joins forces with the Museum of Modern Art to produce a **New Directors/New Films** series, where the best works by up-and-coming directors get their moment to flicker. This series is held at MOMA's Roy and Niuta Titus theatres (11 W. 53rd St., tel. 212/708–9490).

Museums The **American Museum of the Moving Image** (35th Ave. at 36th St., Queens, tel. 718/784–0077 or 784–4520), housed in a building belonging to the historic Kaufman Astoria Studios, offers multiple galleries that are a movie buff's paradise, as are its 195-seat Riklis Theatre and 60-seat Warner Communications Screening Room. The museum presents more than 700 programs annually, including major artist-oriented retrospectives, Hollywood classics, experimental videos, and TV documentaries.

In midtown Manhattan, the **Museum of Television and Radio** (25 W. 52nd St., tel. 212/752–7684) has a gigantic collection of 40,000 radio and TV shows, including everything from *The Patty Duke Show* to *Soap*, *Cheers*, and *Taxi*. The museum's library provides 96 consoles, where you can watch whatever you wish for up to an hour at a time. It also offers noontime "comedy breaks," featuring classic side-splitters from radio and TV, and a series of Saturday morning screenings for children.

First-Run Houses Film traditionalists rue the current multiplexing craze that has turned the city's big-screen, single-show theaters into warrens where as many as six movies play concurrently; a firm called Cineplex Odeon seems to be moving toward a monopoly in this area. Just in 1989, multiscreen complexes opened up all over town: at Worldwide Plaza (320 W. 50th St.), in Chelsea (260 W. 23rd St.), in the Union Square area (890 Broadway at Loew's 19th St.), on the Upper East Side (123 E. 86th St.), and in SoHo (Houston and Mercer Sts.)—whose construction moved the *New York Times* to wonder, "Is a multiplex just too, shudder, suburban for SoHo?" In 1990–91, multiscreen houses opened in the East Village (2nd Ave. at 12th St. and 3rd Ave. at 11th St.). Whether this increase in the number of cinemas will ease lines at the box office remains to be seen. Extensive first-run film information can be obtained by dialing 212/777–FILM, the Movie Phone sponsored by WPLJ and *New York* magazine.

In 1989, lavish restorations of the big-screen movie classics *Lawrence of Arabia* and *Gone with the Wind* were brought to the two New York theaters, respectively, best equipped to handle such extravaganzas: The **Ziegfeld** (141 W. 54th St., west of 6th Ave., tel. 212/765–7600), with its awesome sound system, and **Radio City Music Hall** (1260 6th Ave., tel. 212/247–4777), with its 34-foot-high screen and 4,500-watt projector.

The Times Square area is still a movie mecca, though action flicks prevail on 42nd Street, and viewers should be warned to sit tight and hold on to their purses. Posh East Side first-run theaters line Third Avenue between 57th and 60th streets and continue up Second Avenue into the 60s. Other groups are clustered around East 34th Street and West 23rd Street.

Midnight Movies At a handful of Greenwich Village theaters, midnight madness continues with late and late-late showings of eccentric classics such as *King of Hearts*, *The Rocky Horror Picture Show*, and *The Texas Chainsaw Massacre*. **East Side Cinema** (3rd Ave. at 55th St., tel. 212/755–3020), the **Quad Cinema** (13th St. between 5th and 6th Aves., tel. 212/255–8800), the **Angelika Film Center** (Houston and Mercer Sts., tel. 212/995–2000), and the **Waverly Twin** (6th Ave. at W. 3rd St., tel. 212/929–8037) are the theaters to check out for these.

Revival Houses Cineplex Odeon ignited a firestorm of protest in 1988 when it transformed one of New York's most cherished old revival houses, the **Regency** (Broadway at 67th St., tel. 212/724–3700) into a first-run theater. When it threatened to do the same thing to the **Biograph Cinema** (225 W. 57th St., tel. 212/582–4582), 30,000 signatures were gathered to block the conversion. Today, the Biograph remains a revival island in a sea of first-run theaters. America's first revival repertory cinema, the **Thalia,** closed in 1987, and a downtown version bit the dust not long after. But revivals can still be found at:

Cinema Village (3rd Ave., between 12th and 13th Sts., tel. 212/505–7320), often offering as many as three sets of double features a week.

Film Forum (209 W. Houston St., tel. 212/727–8110) in a brand-new building, has series based on movie genres, directors, and other film artists.

Theatre 80 St. Marks (80 St. Marks Pl., tel. 212/254–7400), small and shabby but convivial, sports double-features from the '30s and '40s and a welcoming coffee bar.

Foreign Films New York film lovers are used to reading subtitles. Between the interest generated by the Film Festival, the city's population of foreign executives and diplomats, and a large contingent of cosmopolitan *cinéastes*, there's always an audience here for foreign films. New Yorkers saw the French *Three Men and a Cradle* long before it was Americanized into *Three Men and a Baby;* such recent movies as the Swedish *My Life As a Dog*, the Japanese *Tampopo*, and the Italian *Cinema Paradiso* were long-running hits in this city. The following cinemas more or less specialize in foreign films:

Carnegie Screening Room (887 7th Ave. between 56th and 57th Sts., tel. 212/757–2131), an adjunct of the tony Carnegie Hall Cinema.

The Plaza (42 E. 58th St., tel. 212/355–3320), a showcase for some of the most talked-about foreign entries.

Lincoln Plaza (Broadway between 62nd and 63rd Sts., tel. 212/757–2280), three subterranean cinemas playing long-run foreign hits.

68th Street Playhouse (3rd Ave. at 68th St., tel. 212/734–0302), with exclusive extended runs of foreign discoveries.

Quad Cinema (13th St. between 5th and 6th Aves., tel. 212/255–8800), with first-run Hollywood, art, and foreign films.

Foreign films also run at art societies and museums around town, including:

Asia Society (725 Park Ave. at 70th St., tel. 212/517–2742).

Florence Gould Hall (55 E. 59th St., tel. 212/355–6160) is the site for French films sponsored by the French Institute-Alliance Française.

Goethe House (1014 5th Ave., between 82nd and 83rd Sts., tel. 212/972–3960).

International Center of Photography (1130 5th Ave. at 94th St., tel. 212/860–1777).

Japan Society (333 E. 47th St., tel. 212/752–3015).

The Museum of Modern Art (11 W. 53rd St., tel. 212/708–9490).

Avant-Garde Films The **Public Theater** (425 Lafayette St., tel. 212/598–7171) is one of the city's most reliable forums for experimental and independent film. Many of its series focus on politics and social issues, or are tributes to nonmainstream artists. **The Collective for Living Cinema** (41 White St., tel. 212/925–2111), **Anthology Film Archives** (32–34 2nd Ave., tel. 212/477–2714), **Millennium Film Workshop** (66 E. 4th St., tel. 212/673–0090), and **Walter**

Reade Theater (70 Lincoln Center Plaza, tel. 212/875–5000), showcase more off-center works, old and new, American and foreign.

Readings and Lectures

New York is, of course, the center of the American publishing world, and as a result most writers—however reclusive—eventually find reason to come here. The Writers Guild headquarters and the U.S. offices of P.E.N. International are in Manhattan; the National Book Awards are presented here annually in the grand foyer of the New York Public Library.

If you're interested in the written word (and in stealing a look at the people who create it), a New York fiction or poetry reading is a good idea. They spring up all over the city— in bookstores, libraries, museums, bars, and legitimate theaters—drawing some of the top names in contemporary literature, writers such as Russell Banks, Kurt Vonnegut, Tom Wolfe, Mary Gordon, Louise Ehrdrich, and Margaret Atwood, as well as debuting talents.

A major reading and talk series held at the **Lincoln Center Library for the Performing Arts** (tel. 212/870–1630) specializes in musicians, directors, singers, and actors. In fact, the entire **New York Public Library** system (tel. 212/930–0571) is a wide-open field for reading events, as is the **Brooklyn Public Library** network (tel. 718/780–7700).

At the **Metropolitan Museum of Art** (5th Ave. at 82nd St., tel. 212/535–7710 or 570–3949), seasonal lectures regularly draw sell-out crowds. Artist such as David Hockney hold forth here, as do the world's eminent art historians.

Authors, poets, lyricists, and travelogue-spinners take the stage at the **92nd St. Y** (1395 Lexington Ave., tel. 212/996–1100), while the **West Side YMCA** (5 W. 63rd St., tel. 212/787–6557) offers readings by major novelists, poets, and humorists in a series called "The Writer's Voice."

Many Manhattan bookstores organize evening readings by authors or recently published books. Best bets are **Books & Co.** (939 Madison Ave. near 74th St., tel. 212/737–1450), **Endicott Booksellers** (450 Columbus Ave. near 81st St., tel. 212/787–6300), **Three Lives and Co.** (154 W. 10th St., tel. 212/741–2069), and the **Pomander Bookshop** (955 West End Ave. at 107th St., tel. 212/866–1777).

The Arts for Kids

In the seemingly endless argument over whether or not to raise kids in this city, New York parents consistently point out the advantages of being able to expose their offspring to the city's cultural treasures. Precocious Manhattan toddlers cut their teeth on outings to the Metropolitan Museum, puppet plays in Central Park, holiday spectaculars at Radio City, and traditional Christmas performances of *The Nutcracker* ballet. Many performing arts groups cater specifically to children, including:

The Big Apple Circus (35 W. 35th St., tel. 212/268–3030), whose escapades charm the toughest New Yorkers throughout the five boroughs during the summer months and at Lincoln Center from October through January.

Don Quijote Experimental Children's Theatre (Lincoln Square Theater, 250 W. 65th St., tel. 212/496–8009), which exposes city kids to realistic theater exploring topics such as literacy and aging.

52nd St. Project (549 W. 52nd St., tel. 212/245–1350), presenting plays that are collaborations between inner-city kids and professional theater artists.

4th Wall Repertory Company (Truck & Warehouse Theater, 79 E. 4th St., tel. 212/254–5060), producers of musical shows, with plenty of audience participation.

Hartley House Theatre (413 W. 46th St., tel. 212/666–1716), featuring adaptations of classic fairy tales and such.

Henry Street Settlement Louis Abrons Arts Center (466 Grand St., tel. 212/598–0400), founded by a nurse to care for the sick and disadvantaged, now bringing the arts to kids and families with the Arts for Family series every Sunday.

The Little Orchestra Society (220 W. 42nd St., tel. 212/704–2100), with concert series that introduce classical music concepts to children ages three–five at Florence Gould Hall (55 E. 59th St.) or ages six–12 at Lincoln Center.

Little People's Theatre Company (The Courtyard Playhouse, 39 Grove St., tel. 212/765–9540), where audiences participate in such classics as *Hansel and Gretel*, Sundays at 1:30 and 3 PM.

The Open Eye: New Stagings for Youth (270 W. 89th St., tel. 212/769–4143), offering both classic and new plays.

The Paper Bag Players (tel. 212/362–0421), for children four–nine, have a winter season at Symphony Space, where they perform original plays such as *I Won't Take a Bath*.

Theatreworks/USA (at the Promenade Theatre, Broadway and 76th St., tel. 212/677–5959), for their polished productions about historical figures and events.

Thirteenth Street Repertory Company (50 W. 13th St., tel. 212/675–6677), which directs its performances to children ages four and up.

Vineyard Theater (108 E. 15th St. and 309 E. 26th St., tel. 212/353–3366), presenting children's events during the winter holiday season.

11 Nightlife

by Susan Spano
Wells

Okay, so you've taken the Staten Island Ferry, you've lunched at the Plaza, and you've visited the Met. But don't tuck yourself in just yet. Instead, get yourself truly attuned to the Big Apple's schedule, which runs more by New York nocturnal than by eastern standard time. Even if you're not a night owl by habit, it's worth staying up late at least once, for by night, Manhattan takes on a whole new identity.

Clubs and Entertainment

New York nightlife really started to swing in 1914, when a pair of ballroom dancers, Florence and Maurice Walton, took over management of the Parisian Room, in what is today's theater district. At Chez Maurice, as the new club was called, the city's café society learned a sensual dance at "Tango Teas." Then came the Harlem Renaissance of the 1920s and '30s, and the New York jazz scene shifted north of 110th Street. In the 1950's night spots mushroomed in Greenwich Village and the East 50s. Along 52nd Street in those years, recalls columnist Pete Hamill, "you could walk down a single block and hear Art Tatum, Billie Holiday, and Charlie Parker. And you could go to the Latin Quarter and see girls running around with bananas on their heads. On the other hand, Babe Ruth doesn't play for the Yankees anymore, either."

Well, maybe not, but Dwight Gooden does play for the Mets, and the old Copacabana Club has been reincarnated now as a discotheque. *Plus ça change* . . . In truth, the current nightclub scene is probably more varied and vital than it ever was, but in different ways. To begin with, it has moved downtown—along with just about everything else—to dead-looking East Village dives that come alive nightly, to classic jazz joints in the West Village, to sleekly decorated TriBeCa see-and-be-seen traps, and to preppy hangouts around Wall Street.

There are enough dedicated club-hoppers here to support night spots for almost every idiosyncratic taste. But keep in mind that *when* you go is just as important as where you go in clubland. Clubs vary their themes every night of the week. Depending on where you go, an appropriate costume for a night on the town could include anything from blue suede shoes to an Armani coat to a Balenciaga gown; anything from an orange fright wig to leather and chains to a vintage pink poodle skirt.

That doesn't mean that "anything goes," however, for exclusivity is the name of the game. At certain clubs, gimlet-eyed door staff zealously guard the barrier of velvet rope outside, selecting customers according to arbitrary standards. For a new crop of gypsy clubs, only those in the know can even find out where the group is meeting this week.

On Friday, *the New York Times*'s "Weekend" section carries a "Sounds Around Town" column that can give you a picture of what's in the air, as can the *Village Voice*, which probably has more nightclub ads than any rag in the world. Or stop by Tower Records (692 Broadway, tel. 212/505–1500, and 1695 Broadway, tel. 212/799–2500), where fliers about coming events and club passes are stacked outside. You may also get good tips from your cab driver or waitress—they hear and see more than most people do—or from a suitably au courant hotel concierge. Just remember that what's hot and what's not changes almost weekly in this city, so visitors are at a distinct disadvantage. We've tried to give you a rounded sample of reliable hangouts—establishments that are likely to be still in business by the time you use this book—but clubs come and go as fast as spawning tsetse flies, so phone ahead to make sure your target night spot hasn't closed or turned into a polka hall. Most will charge a cover of at least $10 a head; some go as high as $20–$50 (nobody said catting around was going to be cheap!). Take cash because many places don't accept plastic. *Et maintenant, mesdames et messieurs*, what's your choice?

Putting On the Ritz

You and your date are wearing Oscar de la Renta and Armani finery; your transport's a white stretch limo; and you've just come from dinner at Lutèce. Just remember to hide this guidebook in your tux pocket or your rhinestone clutch so people won't guess you're not regulars at:

The Ballroom (253 W. 28th St., tel. 212/244–3005). This very hip Chelsea spot has an extensive tapas bar and a nightclub where some of the great chanteuses—including Peggy Lee and Helen Schneider—rhapsodize.

Café Society (915 Broadway at 21st St., tel. 212/529–8282). Whoosh through the revolving doors to astonishment: soaring ceilings, pink art deco decor, a long, inviting bar, and dinner dancing. The quixotic entrepreneur who owns Café Society also runs Society Billiards next door.

The Carlyle (35 E. 76th St., tel. 212/744–1600). The hotel's discreetly sophisticated Café Carlyle is where Bobby Short plays when he's in town; Bemelmans' Bar, with murals by the author of the Madeleine books, regularly stars jazz pianist Barbara Carroll.

Nell's (246 W. 14th St., tel. 212/675–1567). Back in vogue, Nell Campbell (of *Rocky Horror* fame) reintroduced sophistication to nightlife with her club. The tone in the upstairs jazz salon is Victorian; downstairs is for tête-à-têtes and dancing.

The Oak Room (at the Algonquin Hotel, 59 W. 44th St., tel. 212/840–6800). Please don't gawk at the famous writers as you come in. Just head straight for the long, narrow club-cum-watering hole; at the piano you'll find, perhaps, singer Julie Wilson, the hopelessly romantic Andrea Marcovicci, or heart-throb jazzman Harry Connick, Jr.

The Rainbow Room and **Rainbow and Stars Club** (30 Rockefeller Plaza, tel. 212/632–5000). You can find two kinds of heaven high up on Rockefeller Center's 65th floor. The Rainbow Room serves dinner (*see* Chapter 8), and dancing to the strains of a live orchestra takes place on a floor right out of an Astaire/Rogers musical. At the intimate new Rainbow and Stars Club, singers such as Tony Bennett and Liliane Montevecchi entertain, backlit by a view of the twinkling lights of the city.

The Russian Tea Room (150 W. 57th St., tel. 212/265–0947). This latest entrant into the cabaret scene features seasoned performers such as Sylvia Syms and Margaret Whiting as well as newcomers on Sunday evenings on the second floor.

Stringfellows (35 E. 21st St., tel. 212/254–2444). At this British import for the jet-and-blank-check set, you can order from an extensive, and expensive, selection of champanges At 11, mirrored panels unveil a dance floor, where commodities traders,

TV commentators, and famous fashion designers invade each other's personal space.

Boogie and Be Seen

The city's busiest dance floors are seeing all kinds of styles revived, from "voguing" to the Twist to bebop swings and lifts. Revelers come to socialize, to find romance, to scream business deals over the music, to show off their glad rags, or to be photographed rubbing shoulders with stars.

Dukie's (in the Gold Bar, 345 E. 9th St., no phone). This classic East Village neighborhood bar is transformed into a dance club on Friday nights. Interior design is not Dukie's trademark—unless you're inspired by the silver toilet seat over the bar. The crowd is interesting; the music, discs from the past.

Juke Box NYC (304 E. 39th St., tel. 212/685–1556). Nineteen-fifties and early '60s nostalgia is offered here in what looks like a high school gym. The mood is that of a nonstop giddy graduation prom, where guests revive their teenage selves, happily singing and bopping along to a variety of rock 'n' roll.

Limelight (47 W. 20th St., tel. 212/807–7850). In this transformed Chelsea church, the stained-glass windows endure amid catwalks, spiral staircases, and energetic dancers getting down. Although it's no longer at the cutting edge in terms of its pretty-people draw, this is still a great place for garrulousness and gyration.

M.K. (204 5th Ave., tel. 212/779–1340). Located across from the Flatiron building, the SoHo-chic design attracts a celebrity crowd to this supper club noted for its number of film premiere parties.

Mars (10th Ave. at 13th St., tel. 212/691–6262). Since late 1989, this hot spot has been known as *the* place to go. Take your pick among five levels here (the basement theme is "Afrotech"). The door staff is *very* particular.

Private Eyes, Inc. (12 W. 21st St., tel. 212/206–7770). This quality video palace caters to a varied but generally hip Manhattan crowd. The dance floor is smallish, but the style is never cramped.

The Red Zone (440 W. 54th St., tel. 212/582–2222). Opened in January 1989, this 14,000-square-foot disco features huge movie screens where images of water-lapped beaches and the Wild West are projected. Upstairs is a restaurant and bar.

Roseland (239 W. 52nd St., tel. 212/247–0200). This famous old ballroom-dance floor is still open Thursday through Sunday, but you should call in advance to make sure it hasn't been taken over for the evening by a concert or a private party.

Roxy (515 W. 18th St., tel. 212/645–5156). This place wins the award for the city's most cavernous club to date. Although the design is plain, the club remains enjoyable and popular.

Second Story (415 E. 91st St., tel. 212/410–1360). The East Side coat-and-tie crowd let down their hair here (while managing, even in the heat of the moment, to remain impeccably coiffed). Abundant mahogany; rock 'n' roll from the '60s to the '90s.

Shout! (124 W. 43rd St., tel. 212/869–2088). In the converted Henry Miller Theater, the disc jockey spins '60s hits from the orchestra seats. This is the place for serious dancing. Thursdays through Saturdays, professional dancers enliven the action every half-hour.

20 West (27 W. 20th St., tel. 212/924–0205). Offering dance workouts for the over-25 crowd, this "fun food drinkery" features Top-40 hits from the '60s through the '80s, and snacks from a low-priced "munchie menu."

Woody's in the Village (82 E. 4th St., tel. 212/982–3686). Rolling Stone Ron Wood's place is fast becoming an East Village landmark for rockers. The adjacent gallery for musicians-turned-artists is a must-see.

Jazz Notes

Jazz players always come home to Manhattan. Somehow, the city evokes their sound. Greenwich Village is still the mecca, with more than 12 jazz nightclubs, although plenty of others are strewn around town. Here are some classics:

The Angry Squire (216 7th Ave., tel. 212/242–9066). This Chelsea jazz outpost cooks with live jazz seven nights a week.

Arthur's Tavern (57 Grove St., tel. 212/675–6879). The place starts to cook late (say 1 or 2 AM) and eschews all fancy trappings. It attracts a mixed crowd and offers jazz on the steamy side.

Birdland (2745 Broadway, tel. 212/749–2228). Although way up on the West Side (at 105th St.), this spot is still close to the Village at heart. You'll find lots of up-and-coming groups here, as well as the requisite thick atmosphere.

The Blue Note (131 W. 3rd St., tel. 212/475–8592). This club may be the jazz capital of the world. Just an average week could bring Irma Thomas, the Modern Jazz Quartet, and Dizzy Gillespie. If jazz is your thing, make a beeline to the Blue Note.

Bradley's (70 University Pl., tel. 212/228–6440). With brighter-than-usual lighting and, generally, jazz piano, this is a spot for serious fans of jazz and blues.

Carlos I (432 6th Ave., tel. 212/982–3260). Another major Village jazz establishment, this club offers everything from boogie-woogie to blues.

Dan Lynch's Blues Bar (221 2nd Ave., tel. 212/677–0911). This jazz surprise in the East Village bustles, with jam sessions on Saturday and Sunday afternoons.

Fat Tuesday's (190 3rd Ave., tel. 212/533–7902). Two sets are played here every night but Monday in an intimate basement; there's a popular restaurant/bar upstairs.

Fortune Garden Pavilion (209 E. 49th St., tel. 212/753–0101). Jazz and Chinese food create the Fortune Garden's celestial duo. Music every night of the week.

Indigo Blues (221 W. 46th St., tel. 212/221–0033). A club that opens headlining Miles Davis is serious about its booking policy. This one doesn't disappoint. The stylishly decorated room seats 200.

The Kitchen (512 W. 19th St., tel. 212/255–5793). The home of the downtown arts features jazz mixed with a little New Music and World Beat.

The Knitting Factory (47 E. Houston St., tel. 212/219–3055). It looks seedy on the outside, but inside there's often fine avant-gardish jazz.

Red Blazer Too (349 W. 46th St., tel. 212/262–3112). Roaring '20s, Dixieland, and above all swing music are on tap here. It's a hot spot for after the theater.

Sweet Basil (88 7th Ave. S, tel. 212/242–1785). A little ritzy, though reliable, this night spot presents a range that runs from swing to fusion.

Tramps (45 W. 21st St., tel. 212/727–7788). The place has been on the scene for two decades now, with the likes of Albert Collins and Buster Poindexter. Come here for a little Chicago blues in the big city.

Upstairs at Greene Street (105 Greene St., tel. 212/925–2415). The restaurant has smashing surroundings converted from a three-story parking garage. Greene Street spent a long time looking for its niche, but it seems to have found it with free jazz and ultracool environs.

The Village Gate (Bleecker and Thompson Sts., tel. 212/475–5120). This is another of the classic Village jazz joints. Music starts at 9:30 PM. Upstairs there's a cabaret theater.

The Village Vanguard (178 7th Ave. S, tel. 212/255–4037). This old Thelonius Monk haunt lives on in a smoky cellar until recently presided over by the late jazz impresario Max Gordon. It's pricey, but worth every penny.

Rock Around the Clock

The roots of rock may lie in America's heartland, but New York has added its own spin. Crowds at the Big Apple's rocketerias are young, enthusiastic, and hungry; the noise is often deafening, but you can catch many a rising star in this lively scene. Here's where to go:

The Bitter End (147 Bleecker St., tel. 212/673–7030). This old Village standby still serves up its share of new talent, as it once did Joan Armatrading and Warren Zevon.

The Cat Club (76 E. 13th St., tel. 212/505–0090). Another place with a big dance floor, this one specializes in heavy metal music, but on Sundays it throws in swing—just to keep you on your toes.

CBGB & OMFUG (315 Bowery, tel. 212/982–4052). American punk rock was born here, in this long black tunnel of a club featuring bands with inventive names: Blind Idiot God, Rude Buddhas, Chemical Wedding. Repair your ears and your appetites at the Pizza Boutique next door.

Maxwell's (1039 Washington St., Hoboken, NJ, tel. 201/798–4064). If you're adventurous enough to cross the Hudson, take the PATH train to Hoboken, a once-low-rent outpost for young artistic types that's been gentrified. Musicians know Maxwell's, even if most Manhattanites don't; it offers up a mix of New Music and rock. At press time, it was rumored that the ownership would be changing; so might the future of Maxwell's.

101 Avenue A (101 Ave. A, tel. 212/420–1590). Dancing transvestites might greet you at the bar of this mainly gay hangout; in the back, different kinds of music are played every night, all at a decibel level high enough to qualify as rock.

Palladium (126 E. 14th St., tel. 212/473–7171). Here you'll find the world's biggest dance floor, fashioned from the gutted hulk of a theater, along a New Wave/Oriental '60s-psychedelic theme. Home to the V.I.P. Mike Todd room, Lambada fever, and Club MTV, it is no longer the hot ticket it was a few years ago; still, this place is to clubland what Macy's is to shopping.

The Ritz (254 W. 54th St., tel. 212/541–8900). There must be something magical about the former site of Studio 54; this club is just as popular but not quite as infamous as its predecessor. Weeknight shows begin at 9 PM; the main floor is for dancing, with seating in the balcony. The Ritz turns into a nightclub called Clubland after concerts or on nonconcert evenings.

The Rock 'n' Roll Café (149 Bleecker St., tel. 212/677–7630). A week's worth of band names should clue you in: War Babies, Mixed Media, the Down Town Boys, and Hell Hounds.

Spo-Dee-O-Dee (565 W. 23rd St., tel. 212/206–1990). This Chelsea haunt alternates jazz and rock performances in a cozy, publike setting.

Wetlands Preserve (161 Hudson St., tel. 212/966–4225). Billed as a "watering hole for activists," this relative newcomer specializes in psychedelic rock. There are Grateful Dead nights on Tuesdays, and "Eco-Saloons" on Sundays.

The Latin and Island Beat

Next to dependable jazz, Latin music is the sound of the moment in New York clubs. Salsa, samba, merengue—all offer an exotic counterpoint to the city's rhythms, and Big Apple musicians have found ways to integrate the Latin strain with indigenous styles. Check them out at:

Club Broadway (2551 Broadway, tel. 212/864–7600). This Upper West Side club is a tradition on the Latin music scene.

15 Waverly (15 Waverly Pl., tel. 212/533–3048). This tropical Village club features Brazilian, Caribbean, and African music.

Island Club (285 W. Broadway, tel. 212/226–4598). This is another reliable place to hear reggae music.

Kilimanjaro (531 W. 19th St., tel. 212/627–2333). S.O.B.'s (*see* below) has got major competition with this large club, which opened in 1989, riding on the success of the DC original; it features world beat music.

S.O.B.'s (204 Varick St., tel. 212/243–4940). Since 1982, this has been the—and we mean *the*—place for reggae, Trinidadian carnival, zydeco, African, and Caribbean funk. The initials stand for Sounds of Brazil, just in case you wondered. The decor is à la Tropicana; the favored drink, a Brazilian *caipirinha*.

The Village Gate (Bleecker and Thompson Sts., tel. 212/475–5120). Monday at this jazz club is Latin night from February through November; the line starts forming early to hear the likes of Reuben Blades.

Down-Home Sounds

The Bottom Line (15 W. 4th St., tel. 212/228–6300). Clubs come and go, but this granddaddy has stayed around since 1974. Its reputation is for showcasing talents on their way up, as it did for both Stevie Wonder and Bruce Springsteen. There's no way to categorize the Bottom Line bill, except to say that folk has headlined consistently. The sound system is swell, but don't go for the first set and expect to stay for the next—they round up all you little dogies and herd you out through the door.

Delta 88 (332 8th Ave., tel. 212/924–3499). This Chelsea joint was described by *The New Yorker* as having a "white-trash-chicken-shack theme." R & B is the mainstay, along with a dash of hillbilly, zydeco, and blues.

Eagle Tavern (355 W. 14th St., tel. 212/924–0275). Come here for Irish folk music, plus a little bluegrass and comedy.

The Lone Star Roadhouse (240 W. 52nd St., tel. 212/245–2950). In the heart of the theater district, this offspring of a recently closed downtown landmark is an anomaly—but a welcome one.

Inhabiting a heady two-story space, it has a long bar for picking up long drinks. The food runs to chili and deep-fried crayfish; the music from doo-wop to gospel.

O'Lunney's (12 W. 44th St., tel. 212/840–6688). Green table-cloths and the smell of stale beer accompany live music—contemporary, folk, country/western—Monday–Saturday.

Rodeo Bar (375 3rd Ave., tel. 212/683–6500). This night spot lets loose jamming fiddles and accordions, as well as a comic country band called the Surreal McCoys.

Speakeasy (107 MacDougal St., tel. 212/598–9670). Pure folk is found here, every night.

Comic Relief

The *Village Voice* covers the comedy scene well, and it's worth checking its listings because lots of music clubs book comedians for periods between sets. Some cabarets and music spots that often bring in stand-ups are Eighty-eight's, Michael's Pub, the Duplex (*see* The Show's the Thing, below), and the Village Gate (*see* Jazz Notes, above). Several clubs, however, are exclusively devoted to comedy acts:

The Boston Comedy Club (82 W. 3rd St., tel. 212/477–1000). Beantown comedians come here to test their stuff in the Big Apple.

Catch a Rising Star (1487 1st Ave., tel. 212/794–1906). Johnny Carson got his start here, and his talent scouts still show up to test the comic current. This place is neither trendy nor cutting edge, but it is reliable.

Chicago City Limits (351 E. 74th St., tel. 212/772–8707). This troupe's been doing improvisational comedy for a long time, and it seldom fails to whip its mostly youngish audiences into a laughing frenzy. Chicago City Limits performs in an East Side church and is very strong on audience participation.

Comedy Cellar (117 MacDougal St., tel. 212/254–3630). This spot has been running for some years now beneath the Olive Tree Café, with a bill that's a good barometer of who's hot.

The Comic Strip (1568 2nd Ave., tel. 212/861–9386). The atmosphere here is strictly corner bar. The stage is brilliantly lit but minuscule (8 by 10 feet); the bill, unpredictable but worth checking out.

Dangerfield's (1118 1st Ave., tel. 212/593–1650). Since 1969, this has been an important showcase for prime comic talent. It's owned and frequently visited by comedian Rodney Dangerfield himself.

The Improvisation (358 W. 44th St., tel. 212/765–8268). The Improv is to comedy what the Blue Note is to jazz. Lots of now-famous comedians got their first laughs here, among them Richard Pryor and Robin Williams. It gets crowded, especially on weekends; there are two shows on Fridays and three on Saturday nights.

Stand Up N.Y. (236 W. 78th St., tel. 212/595–0850). A 175-seat Upper West Side option for comedy devotees, this club books lots of bright faces coming off recent TV gigs, and occasional drop-ins by stars. Monday is political-satire night.

The Show's the Thing

Cabaret takes many forms in New York City, from a lone crooner at the piano to a full-fledged song-and-dance revue. Various night spots have stages; here are some of the most consistently entertaining.

Danny's Skylight Room (346 W. 46th St., tel. 212/265–8133). Danny's is housed in the Grand Sea Palace, a fixture on Restaurant Row. It offers a little bit of everything: jazz, crooners, ivory-tinklers, and monologuists.

Don't Tell Mama (343 W. 46th St., tel. 212/757–0788). At this convivial theater district spot, composer/lyricist hopefuls show their stuff. Extroverts will be tempted by the open mike policy of the piano bar in front.

The Duplex (61 Christopher St., tel. 212/255–5438). This longtime Village favorite has moved to great new digs on the corner of Sheridan Square. Catch a singing luminary-on-the-rise in the upstairs cabaret, or join the happy crowd downstairs by the piano for a Broadway sing-along.

Eighty-eight's (228 W. 10th St., tel. 212/924–0088). Come here to hear songs by the best of Broadway's tunesmiths (among other things) and inventively assembled programs.

Jan Wallman's (49 W. 44th St., tel. 212/764–8930). Located in the lobby of the Hotel Iroquois, this club is known for singing pianists in the Michael Feinstein mold.

Michael's Pub (211 E. 55th St., tel. 212/758–2272). Guess which underweight, bespectacled Jewish comedian-writer-actor-director often moonlights on the clarinet here on Monday nights? On other evenings, other fine performers such as Mel Tormé take the stage. The crowd is very monied, very uptown.

One Fifth (1 5th Ave., tel. 212/260–3434). This New York steak house serves up other choice cuts as well—comedians, musicians, and singers, such as the multitalented Phoebe Légère.

Steve McGraw's (158 W. 72nd St., tel. 212/595–7400). This West Side supper club and bar presents sophisticated comedy revues.

West Bank Café (407 W. 42nd St., tel. 212/695–6909). In an attractive bistro-type restaurant across from Theatre Row, moonlighting musical-comedy triple threats (actor/singer/dancers) show off; on occasion, new plays are read.

Bars

While the health-club craze may have hit New York hard, there's little danger that Manhattanites will abandon their bars. Drinking establishments thrive and multiply, particularly in TriBeCa, where it appears bar design has become a minor art. The city's liquor laws allow bars to stay open until 4 AM, so it's easy to add on a watering stop at the end of an evening's merriment.

Vintage Classics

The Algonquin Hotel Lounge (59 W. 44th St., tel. 212/840–6800). This is a venerable spot, not only because it was the site of the fabled literary Round Table, but also for its elegant tone. A fabulous grandfather clock tolls the passing hours, while noted writers still come and go (*see also* The Oak Room in Putting on the Ritz, above).

Café des Artistes (1 W. 67th St., tel. 212/877–3500). This restaurant, as well known for its glorious Beaux Art murals as for its food (*see* Chapter 8), has a small, warm bar where interesting strangers tell their life stories and the house drink is pear champagne.

Elaine's (1703 2nd Ave., tel. 212/534–8103). The food's nothing special, and you will be relegated to an inferior table, but go to crane your neck and gawk. Woody Allen's favorite table is by the cappuccino machine. It's best to visit late, when the stars rise in Elaine's firmament.

The Four Seasons (99 E. 52nd St., tel. 212/754–9494). Miró tapestries greet you as you enter this power bar through the Grill Room (*see* Chapter 8). Watch for Kissingers and Trumps.

The Jockey Club (112 Central Park S, tel. 212/757–1900). Dressy and traditional, this is a slice of upper-crust New York in the lobby of The Ritz-Carlton. It's a very double-martini sort of place.

The Oak Bar (at the Plaza Hotel, 5th Ave. and 59th St., tel. 212/759–3000). With its plummy, dark-wood furnishings, this old favorite continues to age well. Its great location draws sophisticates and high rollers, shoppers, tourists in the know, and stars.

The River Café (1 Water St., Brooklyn, tel. 718/522–5200). An eminently romantic spot, hidden at the foot of the Brooklyn Bridge, this restaurant offers smashing views of Wall Street and the East River. Tables are set up on a terrace when it's warm (*see* Chapter 8).

Top of the Tower (3 Mitchell Pl., tel. 212/355–7300). There are other, higher hotel-top lounges, but this one on the 26th floor of the Beekman Hotel still feels like it's halfway to heaven. The atmosphere is elegant and subdued, with piano arpeggios in the background.

"21" Club (21 W. 52nd St., tel. 212/582–7200). Famous for its old-time club atmosphere even before it was filmed in *All About Eve*, this isn't exactly a swinging joint, but its conservative environs evoke a sense of connections, power, and prestige. It's tough to get in unless you plan to eat here, too (*see* Chapter 8).

Windows on the World (1 World Trade Center, tel. 212/938–1111). To borrow Cole Porter's words: "You're a Botticelli, you're Keats, you're Shelley . . . you're the top." Here, you'll be 107 stories up, drinking in your favorite poison and the outstanding view (*see* Chapter 8).

Drinking Spots Around Town

South of Houston Street

The Bridge Café (279 Water St., tel. 212/227–3344). This busy little fish restaurant flanks the Brooklyn Bridge, a hop, skip, and a jump from South Street Seaport. The bar is abridged, but between lunch and dinner you can pass a pleasant afternoon sipping a good selection of wines at a table.

Ear Inn (326 Spring St., tel. 212/226–9060). There's nothing fancy here, though it inhabits an 1817 Federal house. It's the artsy crowd that makes the place, along with Saturday afternoon poetry readings—they call them "lunch for the ear."

Fanelli's (94 Prince St., tel. 212/226–9412). This is a casual SoHo neighborhood bar, where many come on Sundays with the fat *New York Times* under their arms.

I Tre Merli (463 W. Broadway, tel. 212/254–8699). The sound of happy drinkers spills out of the massive doors of this wide, inviting restaurant/bar. Wine by the glass is a favorite here—16 different varieties are offered.

The Manhattan Brewery Restaurant (42 Thompson St., tel. 212/219–9250). Manhattan's only brewery opened in 1981 and includes a bar that attracts a cheerful, noisy crowd. Try a "brown and tan"—half amber, half light ale.

Raoul's (180 Prince St., tel. 212/966–3518). The decor is 1950s chic; the clientele, upscale downtown.

South Street Seaport (Water and Fulton Sts.) There's no dearth of drinking opportunities at this major New York attraction: **Fluties, Roebling's,** the **Fulton Street Café,** and **McDuffy's Irish Coffee House,** to mention only a few. On warm Friday evenings, the Seaport is transformed into a gigantic college mixer, where apprentice Wall Streeters go to meet others from the Ivy League.

The Sporting Club (99 Hudson St., tel. 212/219–0900). Lots of TV monitors here stay tuned to the evening's major sports event. Aficionados come in after punching out on Wall Street.

Spring Street Bar and Restaurant (162 Spring St., tel. 212/219–0157). At the heart of trendy SoHo, this spot possesses a sleek bar with Japanese overtones and an artsy clientele.

Chelsea and the Village

America (9–13 E. 18th St., tel. 212/505–2110). Outside, a lone neon star tells you you've found the place. Inside, there's a vast and stunning skylit room, with an oval bar situated beyond and above the tables.

Bayamo (704 Broadway, tel. 212/475–5151). If you can't get in at the Caliente Cab Company (*see* below), try this handsome, paper-palm-shaded spot nearby. The food is Chinese-Cuban.

Cadillac Bar (15 W. 21st St., tel. 212/645–7220). A full Chelsea block long, this lively bar has graffiti-slathered walls, Tex-Mex food, and many warm bodies happily packing in margaritas.

Caliente Cab Company (61 7th Ave. S, tel. 212/243–8517). The party never seems to stop at this roomy Tex-Mex restaurant/bar. You'll find pleasant outside seating and plenty of tequila.

Cedar Tavern (82 University Pl., tel. 212/243–9355). Here's a very informal, warm spot for a post-double-feature beer. Years ago, this was the hangout of choice for a generation of New York painters.

Chumley's (86 Bedford St., tel. 212/675–4449). There's no sign to help you find this place—they took it down during Chumley's speakeasy days. A fireplace warms this relaxed spot where the burgers are hearty, and the kitchen stays open past 10 PM.

Downtown Beirut I (158 1st Ave., tel. 212/777–9011). This electrified East Village hangout attracts artists and student types.

Downtown Beirut II (157 E. Houston, tel. 212/614–9040). This club picks up where I left off with live entertainment.

Ed Debevic's (661 Broadway, tel. 212/982–6000). Your drinks will be served up in high-camp style in this imitation 1950s diner, a recent offshoot of the Chicago original.

Harvey's Chelsea House (108 W. 18th St., tel. 212/243–5644). Here is one of the last remaining traditional enclaves in this increasingly trendy neighborhood. Booths and a long bar offer solace and booze downstairs.

McSorley's Old Ale House (15 E. 7th St., tel. 212/473–9148). One of New York's oldest saloons (opened in 1854), this place has its own satisfying label of ale. Weekend nights are boisterous; on Sunday afternoons McSorley's offers quaint surroundings for reading the paper and munching on a plate of the house specialty, onions and cheese.

Peter MacManus Café (152 7th Ave., tel. 212/929–9691). It's known simply as MacManus's to the regulars, who like this bar's unpretentiousness. Among them are lots of actors, fresh from acting classes in the neighborhood.

Metropolis Café (31 Union Sq. W, tel. 212/675–2300). Soaring ceilings and lots of white marble distinguish this pretty Yuppie drink palace—it's so pretty, in fact, that it's often used as a backdrop for movies and commercials.

Old Town Bar and Restaurant (45 E. 18th St., tel. 212/473–8874). Tawdry and proudly unpretentious, this bar posts signs announcing "quiche not served here," and "the coffee is only four hours old." The Old Town has been around since 1897, long before the trendy set discovered Chelsea.

Peculier Pub (145 Bleecker St., tel. 212/353–1327). Here, in the heart of the Village, you'll find 275 brands of beer, from Aass to Zyweic.

Pete's Tavern (129 E. 18th St., tel. 212/473–7676). This saloon is famous as the place where O. Henry wrote "The Gift of the Magi." These days, it's ever crowded with noisy, friendly souls.

The White Horse Tavern (567 Hudson St., tel. 212/243–9260). Famous among the literati, this is the place where Dylan Thomas drained his last cup to the dregs. From April to October, there's outdoor café drinking.

Midtown and the Theater District

Barrymore's (267 W. 45th St., tel. 212/391–8400). This is a pleasantly downscale theater-district spot, with the requisite show posters on the wall. Listen in to the conversations at the bar and you'll hear the tawdry, true stories of what goes on behind gilt prosceniums.

Café Un Deux Trois (123 W. 44th St., tel. 212/354–4148). This old hotel lobby, charmingly converted, is chicly peopled. The bar itself is small, but it's a hot spot after the theater.

Century Café (132 W. 43rd St., tel. 212/398–1988). An immense vintage neon sign lights up the bar at this trendy, friendly theater-district bistro.

Charley O's (on Shubert Alley, between 44th and 45th Sts., tel. 212/840–2964). Its seemingly endless bar is conveniently located for quick intermission pit stops during dull shows.

Hard Rock Café (221 W. 57th St., tel. 212/459–9230). Embraced by the kids of stars—in fact, its clientele seems eternally prepubescent—this place is big, popular, and far too noisy for talk.

Houlihan's (49th St. and 7th Ave., tel. 212/575–2012). Great happy hours attract a congenial, post-college crowd. This is a safe bet for before- and after-showtime fare.

Joe Allen (326 W. 46th St., tel. 212/581–6464). At this old reliable on Restaurant Row, everybody's en route to or from a show.

The Landmark Tavern (626 11th Ave., tel. 212/757–8595). This aged pub (opened in 1868) is blessed by the glow of warming fireplaces.

Raga (57 W. 48th St., tel. 212/757–3450). In this fine midtown Indian restaurant, a comfortable, deep-chaired lounge hosts a pleasant happy hour.

Sardi's (234 W. 44th St., tel. 212/221–8440). If you care for the theater, don't leave New York without visiting this establishment, which is as much a fixture in the theater district as the playhouses themselves. Looking like some grande dame of the theater, this recently renovated landmark has beefed up its wine list and added "light" cuisine to its menu, but continues to serve venerable dishes that are all but extinct, amidst its caricature-covered walls.

Top of the Sixes (666 5th Ave., tel. 212/757–6662). This bar has an impressive nighttime view, from 39 stories up above Fifth Avenue.

East Side **Ciao Bella** (1311 3rd Ave., tel. 212/288–2555). This postmodern Italian restaurant/bar, like its well-heeled clients, keeps trying very hard to be in style, and generally succeeds.

Jim McMullen's (1341 3rd Ave., tel. 212/861–4700). A young, quintessential Upper East Side watering hole, McMullen's has a large, busy bar decked with bouquets of fresh flowers. Here you'll find lots of Gold Cards, tennis talk, and alumni fund gathering.

La Famille (2017 5th Ave., tel. 212/722–9806). The cuisine is southern at this longtime Harlem favorite, where you'll find a warm drinking lounge downstairs.

P.J. Clarke's (915 3rd Ave., tel. 212/759–1650). New York's most famous Irish bar, this bar comes complete with the requisite mirrors and polished wood. Lots of after-workers like unwinding here, in a place that recalls the days of Tammany Hall.

The Polo Lounge (at the Westbury Hotel, 15 E. 69th St., tel. 212/535–9141). This place is, in a word, classy; it's frequented by European royalty and Knickerbocker New York.

Rusty's (1271 3rd Ave., tel. 212/861–4518). This casual restaurant, owned by former Mets right fielder Rusty Staub, is beloved by members of the Big Apple's professional teams and Central Park leagues alike. The ambience is pleasant enough to win you, even if baseball is not your thing.

The Water Club (500 E. 30th St., tel. 212/683–3333). Right on the East River, with a pleasing outside deck, this is a special-occasion kind of place—especially for those who've already been to all the special landlocked spots in town.

The Terrace (at the Hotel Inter-Continental, 111 E. 48th St., tel. 212/421–0836). A gilded, gargantuan birdcage greets you as you enter. To your left is a spacious lounge, with a pianist reinforcing the sophisticated atmosphere.

Third Avenue Sports Bar (497 3rd Ave., tel. 212/686–8422). This pub is popular with the same crowd that spends Saturday afternoons glued to "The Wide World of Sports." Mets posters cover the walls, and there are TVs galore.

West Side **The Conservatory** (at the Mayflower Hotel, 15 Central Park West, tel. 212/581–1293). Furnished, perhaps, out of a Bloomingdale's window, this is reputedly the haunt of Hollywood movie barons in town to cut deals. Beyond all that, it's a pleasant, quiet place in which to talk and drink.

Dublin House (225 W. 79th St., tel. 212/874–9528). Above the door glows a small neon harp; inside you'll find lots of very young professionals, Columbia students, and softball teams throwing back two-bit drafts.

The Ginger Man (51 W. 64th St., tel. 212/399–2358). This old reliable in the Lincoln Center area offers a seemingly endless warren of rooms, handsome Tiffany lamps, and famous faces from ABC-TV (several blocks uptown).

J. G. Melon (340 Amsterdam Ave., tel. 212/877–2220). A quiet corner pub at the intersection of 76th Street and Amsterdam, this spot has a small but comfortable bar and additional table space in the back room. Pictures of melons—the fruit—are everywhere you look. The East Side branch is at 1291 Third Avenue.

Lucy's Restaurant (503 Columbus Ave., tel. 212/787–3009). This Southern California-Mex hangout is a hit with young Upper Westsiders, who pack themselves into the bar area and sometimes even manage to dance. The decor is playful Gulf beach hut.

Museum Café (366 Columbus Ave., tel. 212/799–0150). Trendy, overdesigned joints on Columbus Avenue come and go, but this one across from the American Museum of Natural History endures thanks to nice streetside windows and high, airy ceilings. Split a homemade pizza as you drink.

The Saloon (1920 Broadway, tel. 212/874–1500). The menu goes on and on; the bar is large and informal; and the waitresses and waiters cruise around on roller skates. It may be gimmicky, but the spirit of fun is infectious.

Gay Bars

The Bar (68 2nd Ave., tel. 212/674–9714). This classic East Village gay bar is a bit seamy to look at, but an unforced and convivial atmosphere prevails. Late weekend nights—after 1 AM—are best.

Crazy Nanny (21 7th Ave. S., tel. 212/366–6312). Even in wide-open New York, women's bars aren't easy to find. This one's small, but that doesn't discourage the die-hard jukebox dancers.

The Eagle's Nest (142 11th Ave., tel. 212/691–8451). The hormones are always running at this favorite cruise bar, attracting a balanced mix of types, including pool players and dancing fools (there's a DJ on board).

Julius (159 W. 10th St., tel. 212/929–9672). Warm, friendly, and low-key, Julius was one of the first bars on the gay scene; it's renowned for its beefy "Julius Burger." The crowd's a little older now, but the place still offers respite from more frenetic atmospheres.

Marie's Crisis (59 Grove St., tel. 212/243–9323). You've got to love it for its name, and for its ecstatic piano sing-alongs— everybody seems to know all the words to Stephen Sondheim's musical *Sunday in the Park with George*.

Uncle Charlie's Downtown (56 Greenwich Ave., tel. 212/255–8787). This extremely popular Village gay bar is visited by stylish young men and distinguished-looking professionals. Happy hour on weeknights between 5 and 8 packs them in.

12 Excursions from New York City

by David Laskin

Freelance writer David Laskin is the author of Eastern Islands: Accessible Islands of the Atlantic East Coast. *His articles about travel and other subjects have appeared in the* New York Times, Travel & Leisure, *and* Esquire.

The pleasures of New York may be inexhaustible, but the city itself can be exhausting, and after a few days of full-tilt touring you may need a break from the concrete, the noise, the hubbub, and the congestion. Here are three destinations within easy striking distance of Manhattan: a beach resort at the eastern end of Long Island; a quintessential New England village near the coast of Connecticut; and two historic mansions overlooking the Hudson River. In any of these spots, you will find clean air, lots of space in which to wander, green and rural landscapes, and escape from the pressures of the city. Each is close enough to the city to be seen in a day trip, but you may prefer an overnight or weekend visit to explore these towns at greater leisure.

Montauk

As the easternmost point in New York State, the last village of the Hamptons, and the tip of fish-shaped Long Island's tail, Montauk has the double allure of extremity and the sea. To get as far out into the ocean as you can without leaving dry land, make the trip not only to Montauk Village, but out to Montauk Point, where the 1795 lighthouse decreed by George Washington confronts the raging Atlantic from an eroding bluff.

Montauk is often lumped together with the trendy Hamptons, but actually it is quite distinct both in history and in atmosphere from that string of South Shore towns to its west. Named for the Montaukett Indians, Montauk (old-timers put the accent on the second syllable, but most people emphasize the first) was America's first ranch, serving as the open cattle range for South Shore farmers from Colonial days until the late 19th century. There was really no settlement here, aside from the three houses built for the cattle keepers. In stark contrast to East Hampton with its elegant Colonial homes and inns, Montauk is a 20th-century village, dominated by beach motels, undistinguished storefronts, and 1950s suburban-style housing.

But then, you don't go to Montauk for the architecture—you go for the beaches; the wild, rolling moors of Hither Hills; and the lighthouse at the Point. Despite the oceanfront development of the past two decades, Montauk retains the feel of the open range it used to be, and has the delightful bonus of miles and miles of superb white sand beaches on the Atlantic.

Tourist Information
The **Montauk Chamber of Commerce** (tel. 516/668–2428) is located on Main Street, on the Plaza in the center of town.

Getting Around
Although you can get to Montauk from New York City by train (the Long Island Railroad from New York's Penn Station, tel. 516/822–5477) or by bus (the Hampton Jitney from 41st St. between Lexington and 3rd Aves., tel. 212/936–0440 or 516/283–4600; reservations required), a car gives you the most freedom and flexibility for a day trip. From New York City, the Midtown Tunnel will take you to the Long Island Expressway (Rte. 495); follow it to Exit 70 (Manorville Rd.), then follow the signs to Route 27 (Sunrise Hwy.). Route 27 changes its name to the Montauk Highway and goes all the way out to Montauk Point. You can park your car on the street in town or at the IGA parking lot on the western edge of town.

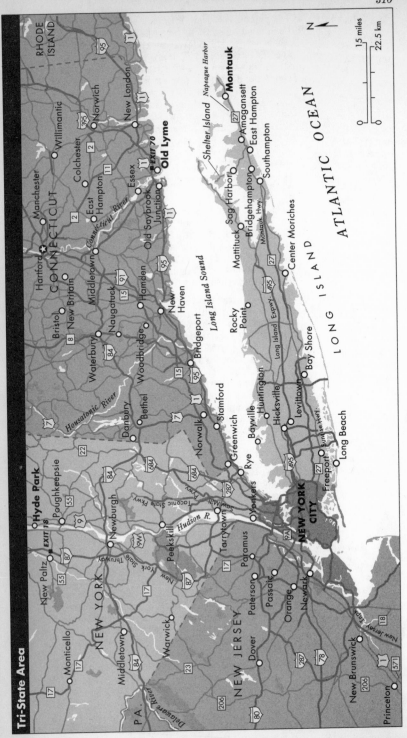

Tri-State Area

Exploring The landscape between Amagansett and Montauk is almost lu-
The Village nar: flat, windswept, and scrubby, with glimpses of ocean to
the south and Napeague Harbor to the north. You know you're
approaching Montauk Village when beach motels featuring the
inevitable watery names—Wavecrest, Driftwood, Seascape,
Seacrest—start coming thick and fast beside the road.

Just east of the convergence of Montauk Highway and Old Montauk Highway, you come to the **Second House,** Montauk's oldest standing dwelling, which was built in 1797 to replace a
house built in 1746. (The First House, near the entrance to
Hither Hills Park, burned down in 1909; the Third House, 3 miles east of the village at Montauk County Park, dates from
1804.) Originally the home of summertime livestock herders,
the Second House is now a museum run by the Historical Society, with exhibits of antique tools and furniture. *Rte. 27, tel.
516/668–5340. Admission: $1 adults, 50¢ children. Open daily
in summer 10–2:30.*

At the center of Montauk Village is a traffic circle known as the
Plaza. Here stands Montauk's most bizarre and incongruous
building—a seven-story Tudor-style office tower that looks
about as much at home in Montauk as a sand dune would look on
Fifth Avenue. This and the palatial Montauk Manor off Edgemere Avenue are about all that remain of developer Carl Fisher's elaborate (and fortunately failed) scheme in the 1920s to
turn Montauk into "the Miami of the North." Fisher built the
tower as his office building; it was recently converted to
condos.

Time Out **Plaza Restaurant** (on the Plaza, tel. 516/668–4687) serves
breakfast all day, along with burgers, salads, sandwiches, and
desserts.

If you follow Edgemere Avenue from the Plaza out of town until
it runs into Flamingo Road, and then follow that until it inter-
sects with West Lake Drive, you'll arrive at **Montauk Harbor** on
Lake Montauk, headquarters for a large commercial fishing
fleet as well as charter fishing boats. The deck at Gosman's
Dock (*see* Dining, below) is a choice spot to nurse a drink and
watch the fishermen come home to port with swordfish, tuna,
bluefish, cod, and pollack.

From the harbor, take West Lake Drive south past Star Island,
site of the posh Montauk Yacht Club and the U.S. Coast Guard
Station, until you hit Montauk Highway again. Turn left and
drive to the highway's end at Montauk Point. Here, at the edge
of the ocean, stands the **Montauk Lighthouse,** Long Island's
oldest, commissioned by President George Washington in 1790
and built of red sandstone in 1796. When the light was first kin-
dled in 1797, the lighthouse stood nearly 300 feet from the
ocean; today, the ocean nibbles at the shore within 50 feet of the
base. A small museum housed in the old keeper's quarters displays photographs and maps as well as the immense Fresnel
lenses that once refracted the light. For years the tower was
closed to visitors, but today you can climb up the 137 steps for a
sweeping view on a clear day of the East End, Gardiners Island, the distant shore of Connecticut, and Block Island off the
coast of Rhode Island. *Rte. 27, tel. 516/668–2544. Admission:
$2 adults, $1 children 6–12. Open Martin Luther King and
Washington's Birthday weekends 11–4; March–Apr., week-*

*ends and May, Fri.–Mon. 10:30–4:30; June, weekdays 10:30–
4:30, weekends 10:30–6: July and Aug., Sun.–Fri. 10:30–6,
Sat. 10:30–8; Sept., weekdays 10:30–4:30, weekends 10:30–6;
Oct. Fri.–Mon., Nov. weekends, and Thanksgiving weekend
10:30–4:30. Closed Dec.*

The 724-acre state park surrounding the lighthouse has hiking
trails, surf fishing, picnic tables, and a refreshment stand;
there are beaches on both the ocean and Long Island Sound,
but heavy surf and submerged rocks make swimming hazard-
ous here. *Open daily, sunrise–sunset.*

The Beaches Montauk has some of the finest beaches on an island renowned
for fine beaches, but the trick is getting access to them. If
you've come by car, your best bet is **Hither Hills State Park,** a
1,750-acre oceanfront park a few miles west of Montauk Village; this is the only official public beach in Montauk where you
can park without a town permit. Hither Hills has a bathhouse,
surf fishing, oceanfront camping, a picnic area, hiking through
pitch pine and scrub oak forests, a central shower building, a
playground, and a refreshment stand and store that are open in
summer. *Rte. 27, tel. 516/668–2493. Admission: $4 per car (free
after Labor Day and until Memorial Day). Open first week of
Apr.–mid-Oct., daily sunrise–sunset; Camping by advance
reservation only (tel. 800/456–CAMP).*

You can also reach the ocean by walking to the south end of just
about any street in town. The roar of the surf drowns out the
sound of the highway traffic, the dunes block out most of the
town buildings, and the breeze brings you the heady salt scent
of the sea.

Dining *Price categories are the same as in the Dining chapter for New
York City.*

★ **Gosman's.** Gosman's has everything you could ever hope for in a
classy fish restaurant: a spectacular location at the entrance to
Montauk Harbor, indoor and outdoor dining, and the freshest
possible fish, since Gosman's is also a wholesale and retail fish
supplier. The one catch is its size—it seats 400 between its indoor dining room, two deck dining areas, and waterside patio.
It is hugely popular, though, and since it takes no reservations,
you may have to wait some time to be seated in peak season.
Try the broiled fluke, which is not available at many places outside Montauk, or the broiled tuna. The Cajun-style blackfish
and weakfish are both excellent, and lobster is very popular.
The chocolate torte dessert was designed expressly for
chocoholics. *West Lake Dr., tel. 516/668–5330. No reservations. Dress: casual (no jogging shorts). MC, V. Closed mid-
Oct.–mid-Apr. Closed Tues. mid-Apr.–Memorial Day and
Labor Day–mid-Oct. Moderate.*

The Inn at Napeague. Despite its tacky-looking building, this
restaurant actually serves some of the best seafood and Continental dishes in town, including bouillabaisse, grilled mako,
swordfish, and tuna, and steak au poivre. The cozy, unpretentious dining room has a nautical theme, with shiny wood tables
and fish nets hanging from the ceiling. *Montauk Hwy. at
Napeague Harbor, tel. 516/267–3332. Reservations advised.
Dress: casual. AE. Dinner only; closed Nov.–mid-Apr. Moderate.*

Windjammer Restaurant. One of the few restaurants in Montauk Village that is open year-round, the Windjammer has a

dining room that feels about as big as a football field (but much more comfortable), with tables set well apart and spectacular views of Fort Pond through large picture windows. Specialties include flounder baked in parchment, poached salmon with lobster caviar, bouillabaisse, and such Continental dishes as sautéed breast of chicken with artichoke, and veal with crabmeat and hollandaise sauce. *Edgemere Rd., tel. 516/668–2872. Reservations suggested. Dress: casual. AE, DC, MC, V. Closed Tues. mid-Nov.–mid-Mar. Moderate.*

Lodging The following chart establishes price categories for all of the lodgings listed in this chapter. In towns such as Montauk that have a "season" (generally Memorial Day to Labor Day), these categories reflect in-season prices; off-season prices are considerably lower.

Highly recommended accommodations are indicated by a star ★

Category	Cost*
Very Expensive	over $120
Expensive	$90–$120
Moderate	$50–$90
Inexpensive	under $50

*All prices are for a standard double room; excluding tax and gratuities.

The following credit card abbreviations are used: AE, American Express, DC, Diners Club; MC, MasterCard; V, Visa.

★ **Gurney's Inn Resort and Spa.** This resort has long been popular for its fabulous location high on a bluff overlooking 1,000 feet of private ocean beach; in recent years it has become even more famous for the International Health and Beauty Spa at Gurney's Inn—one of America's only Marino therapeutic spas, a European therapy that features the use of seawater and sea plants. The large, luxurious rooms, all with ocean views, have refrigerators and room service, and guests have the choice of modified-American meal plans (breakfast and dinner) or spa cuisine (also breakfast and dinner). The oceanview restaurant features French cuisine, and spa cuisine is served in a separate oceanview dining room. The indoor pool, nearly Olympic size, has heated sea water. *Old Montauk Hwy., 11954, tel. 516/668–2345. 125 rooms with bath. Facilities: restaurant, bar, health club, exercise equipment and classes, Roman bath, recreation room, indoor pool, meeting rooms, golf and tennis nearby. AE, DC, MC, V. Very Expensive.*

Shepherd's Neck Inn. This country inn gives you a real feel for the simple, unpretentious seagoing style that sets Montauk apart from the trendier Hamptons to the west. Located in a residential area, it has 5 acres of quiet grounds and the rooms are spacious. Furnishings are simple—a step up from motel-drab but with no valuable antiques or breakables—so the inn is well suited for families and groups. Guests choose between two meal plans: bed-and-breakfast or modified American (breakfast and dinner). Golf, beaches, and boats are nearby. *Second House Rd., Box 639, 11954, tel. 516/668–2105. 70 rooms with bath. Facilities: restaurant, bar, heated pool, tennis, AV and*

VCR equipment, meeting rooms, card room, movie room with nightly features. MC, V. Expensive–Very Expensive.

Old Lyme

With its classic white Congregational church, clapboard mansions, and gracious country inns, **Old Lyme** is redolent of the old Yankee spirit of New England. Situated near Long Island Sound, at the mouth of the Connecticut River, the town rose to prominence as a shipbuilding center in the mid-19th century, but it declined with the advent of steamships in the late 1880s (the local waters were too shallow for the deeper-draft steam-powered vessels). Old Lyme's loss was our gain, for the town remains much as it was in the days of the clipper ships, when as many as 60 sea captains lived in its fine Federal, Georgian, and Greek Revival houses. Many of these homes still stand on Lyme Street, their tall arched windows and fanlighted doors gazing serenely down on wide lawns and tidy gardens. Behind them runs the marshy Lieutenant River, part of which is protected as a nature reserve for waterfowl.

Old Lyme achieved new prominence as an art colony around 1900, when Florence Griswold, daughter of a sea captain, opened her father's mansion as a boardinghouse for artists. For nearly three decades, the leading painters of the American Impressionist school came to stay with Miss Florence and paint in the open air.

Tourist Information Contact the **Selectman's Office** in the Old Lyme Town Hall (Lyme Street, 06371, tel. 203/434–1605).

A brochure outlining a self-guided walking (or driving) tour of historic Old Lyme is available at the Griswold Museum (*see* Exploring, below).

Getting Around The only way to travel directly from New York to Old Lyme is by car. Take I–95 north to Exit 70; at the bottom of the ramp turn left, and at the first traffic light make a right onto Route 1. After about half a mile, you'll come to another light: This is Lyme Street. A left turn here takes you to the inns and the Griswold Museum; a right turn leads you to the Town Hall and the Congregational church.

Amtrak (tel. 800/872–7245) has frequent service out of Penn Station to Old Saybrook Junction, Connecticut, a 20-minute taxi ride from Old Lyme.

Exploring A tour of Old Lyme should begin at the **Florence Griswold Museum,** an imposing lemon-yellow mansion built in 1817 with a broad portico supported by four white columns. Miss Florence opened the house to artists around 1900, and her generous support made it a kind of summer headquarters for the American Barbizon and Impressionist movements. Such painters as Childe Hassam, Henry Ranger, William Chadwick, and Walter Griffin came here to capture the soft, bright Connecticut landscape.

Today the Griswold Museum gives visitors a wonderful opportunity to see paintings exhibited in the house where the artists resided. Some of the best works were painted *on* the house—to repay Miss Florence for her hospitality, artists decorated her wood paneling and doorways. The dining room panels have some especially fine landscapes. The downstairs of the house, furnished with period pieces, contains such masterpieces as Charles Ebert's *Monhegan Headlands* and William Chadwick's *On the Porch*, as well as exhibits of birdcages, dollhouses, and toys. Upstairs are galleries with changing displays of the works of painters who worked in Old Lyme. *96 Lyme St., tel. 203/434-5542. Admission: $2 adults, children under 12 free. Open Nov.-May, Wed.-Sun. 1-5; June-Oct., Tues.-Sat. 10-5 and Sun. 1-5.*

Next door to the Griswold Museum is the **Lyme Art Association,** founded by members of the Old Lyme art colony in 1914 and housed in a simple shingled building designed by Charles Platt in 1921. The association galleries present changing art shows. *90 Lyme Street, tel. 203/434-7802. Suggested donation: $3. Open May-Oct., Tues.-Sat. noon-5, Sun. 1-5.*

A walk up and down Lyme Street will take you past a number of fine old homes. A few doors north of the Griswold Museum is the **Ely-Noyes House,** which has wide eaves, a flat roof, a columned porch, and large barns on well-maintained grounds. South of the museum you'll find the **John Sill House,** a nobly proportioned late-Georgian structure sitting behind a formal wrought-iron gate, and now the home of the **Lyme Academy of Fine Arts** (open weekdays 9-4:30). Walk a few steps farther to the **Deming-Avery House,** built in 1726 with a low gambrel roof, black shutters, and a white rail fence.

The **First Congregational Church** is a replica of the 1817 church designed by Samuel Belcher that burned down in 1907 (an even earlier church on the site was hit by lightning in 1815). It is a picture-postcard New England church, with a grand portico supported by four soaring white columns, a square clock tower, and a tapering steeple surmounted by a weather vane.

Time Out Head east on Route 156 to find the **Hall Mark Ice Cream Place,** noted for its fresh-made ice cream; sandwiches and snacks are also available (open May-Oct.).

To reach the Old Lyme beach on Long Island Sound, follow Route 156 about 1½ miles south of town to Hartford Avenue, where you turn right and continue to the public parking lot, on the right.

Dining and *For price categories, see the Montauk lodging price chart,*
Lodging *above.*

The Old Lyme Inn. Occupying an 1850 farmhouse, with a new wing added in 1985, the Old Lyme Inn is a touch more formal than the Bee and Thistle (*see* below), and it feels less rural and secluded, being set rather close to the road and next to I-95. But the Old Lyme Inn compensates with the size of its guest rooms, particularly the eight rooms in the new wing, which combine modern bathrooms with antique furniture, including canopied beds, Victorian cut-velvet love seats, and mirrored gentlemen's dressers. The inn's formal main dining room has a high ceiling hung with Victorian etched-glass globes; blue plush chairs, gold brocade wallpaper, and massive oil paintings recall the stately grandeur of the French Empire style. The cuisine is innovative American, and the seasonally changing menu features fresh poached salmon in potato crust, veal with Roquefort butter and braised celery, and, in winter, venison with red-currant sauce. There is also a less formal Grill Room serving a lighter menu. *85 Lyme St., tel. 203/434–2600. 13 rooms. Facilities: restaurant, bar, grill, private dining rooms. AE, DC, MC, V. Closed first 2 wks Jan. Expensive–Very Expensive.*

★ **The Bee and Thistle.** In this quintessential country inn, a 1756 mansion, both public rooms and guest rooms have been furnished with period antiques. The two downstairs parlors have flower-print Chippendale sofas, comfy wing chairs, and working fireplaces. Each bedroom has a different flowery wallpaper and antique quilts, and many have four-poster beds with hand-knotted fishnet canopies. The Innkeepers' Cottage, a small outbuilding sleeping two that opened in 1990, offers extra privacy and such amenities as sliding glass doors, kitchen, and outdoor decks. The 5 acres of rustically landscaped grounds stretch to the Lieutenant River, and the gardens are full of flowers in spring and summer. Four small, cheerful dining rooms overlooking the garden serve a changing menu of sophisticated American country cooking: for lunch there might be chowders, English sausages, crab cakes, and gorgonzola ravioli; dinner standouts may include quail stuffed with sausage and apples, venison with port and cranberry sauce, and rainbow trout grilled with garlic sausage and honey tarragon. *100 Lyme St., tel. 203/434–1667. 11 rooms, 9 with bath. Children under 12 not allowed. Facilities: restaurant, bar. AE, DC, MC, V. Closed Dec. 24–25, first 2 wks. Jan. Moderate–Expensive.*

Hyde Park

The Hudson River is often compared to Germany's Rhine—though its history is not as long, its scenery is just as spectacular: mountains rise from its shores, vineyards are tucked away in the folds of its hills, and lordly estates crown its picturesque promontories. The village of Hyde Park, on the east side of the Hudson, is graced with two of these estates, the Vanderbilt Mansion and the Franklin D. Roosevelt National Historic Site, both owned and operated by the National Park Service. Magnificent houses in their own right, both are also fascinating for their historic importance.

Tourist Information The **Dutchess County Tourism Promotion Agency** is at 532 Albany Post Road in Hyde Park (Box 2025, Hyde Park, NY 12538, tel. 914/229–0033). A regional tourist information center runs May–October in the Carriage House at the FDR home. For more information about either historic house, contact the **National Park Service** (519 Albany Post Rd., 12538, tel. 914/229–9115).

Getting Around The only direct way to reach the Hyde Park historic homes from New York City is to drive. Take the New York State Thruway to Exit 18, New Paltz, and follow signs to the mid-Hudson Bridge. Cross the bridge and pick up Route 9 north. The Roosevelt home is 5 miles north on the left-hand side, the Vanderbilt mansion is 2 miles farther north, also on the left.

An alternative is to take the Henry Hudson Parkway (Rte. 9A) to the Saw Mill River Parkway, and follow that to the Taconic State Parkway. Get off at the exit for Route 55 west (Poughkeepsie), and follow Route 55 to Route 9. Proceed 5 miles north to the Roosevelt house.

Exploring
The FDR
Historic Site

Springwood, the house where Franklin Delano Roosevelt, the nation's 32nd president, was born, was purchased by Roosevelt's father in 1867. In 1915 FDR and his mother, Sara, enlarged the circa 1826 frame house that stood on the grounds, stuccoing over the central section and adding two native blue fieldstone wings; they also added the white colonnaded portico over the front entrance and the balustrade around the terrace, Georgian-style touches that give the house an air of quiet elegance. The house contains the original furniture that FDR's parents collected, including an 18th-century grandfather clock, Chinese porcelains, and the delicate Dresden chandelier and mantel set in the formal Dresden room, which was used as a music room. The office (which FDR called the "Summer White House") is where he and Winston Churchill signed an agreement to pursue the development of the atomic bomb in 1942; his bedroom upstairs still contains his books, family photos, and the blanket and leash of Fala, his famous Scottie.

On the grounds of the Roosevelt estate are the hemlock-hedged rose garden where Eleanor and Franklin Roosevelt are buried and, in a separate building, the Franklin D. Roosevelt Library and Museum, which holds the president's personal papers, books, and some of his ship models. A nature trail winds down the steep slopes that rise above the Hudson.

Though Eleanor lived at Hyde Park after her marriage to Franklin, the house remained very firmly under the control of her steely mother-in-law; Eleanor escaped Sara's rule for picnics at the nearby property of Val-Kill, where in the 1920s she built a stone Dutch-style cottage to a design made by her husband. After FDR's death, Eleanor retired to a small stucco-and-fieldstone building there, now open as the Val-Kill Museum. Visitors to Val-Kill can view a film about Mrs. Roosevelt and the property and tour her cottage, with its knotty pine walls and scores of photographs of family and friends (among them such world leaders as Haile Selassie, Jawaharlal Nehru, and Marshal Tito). *FDR Historic Site, tel. 914/229–9115. Admission: $3.50, children under 16 and senior citizens over 62 free. Open Nov.–Mar., Thurs.–Mon. 9–5; Apr.–Oct., daily 9–5. Closed Thanksgiving, Christmas, New Year's Day. Val-Kill admission free. Open Apr.–Oct., daily 9–5, Mar. and Nov.–Dec., weekends 9–5.*

The Vanderbilt
Mansion

The Vanderbilt Mansion, a 54-room Renaissance-style palace encased in brilliant Indiana limestone, is a grand monument of the gilded age. Completed in 1898 to a design by the renowned architectural firm McKim, Mead and White, it was built for Commodore Vanderbilt's grandson Frederick, who came here with his wife Louise in the spring and autumn to pursue his hobbies of gardening, farming, and raising purebred livestock. Though smaller than the Breakers, which was built for Frederick's brother at Newport, Rhode Island, this house is far grander, more formal, and to some minds more pretentious than the Roosevelt home down the road. The interior has a dizzying gilt-and-marble opulence, for Mr. and Mrs. Frederick Vanderbilt ransacked the Orient, the Near East, and Europe to decorate their home. Don't miss Mrs. Vanderbilt's Louis XV–style bedroom, which, like the bedchambers of French queens, has a carved railing around the bed and painted medallions of languidly elegant pastel figures set into the wood-paneled walls. The meticulously landscaped formal parterre garden features a loggia, a pergola, a rose garden, and symmetrical flower beds. Views of the Hudson from the grounds are breathtaking; a road through the 211-acre property leads to a picnic area on the river. *Tel. 914/229–9115. Admission: $2, children under 16 and senior citizens over 62 free. Open Apr.–Oct., daily 9–5; Nov.–March, Thurs.–Mon. 9–5. Closed Thanksgiving, Christmas, New Year's Day.*

Dining *Price categories are the same as in the Dining chapter for New York City.*

★ **Culinary Institute of America.** This renowned school for chefs, housed in a former Jesuit seminary just a short drive from the Roosevelt and Vanderbilt mansions, has four dining rooms where students prepare and serve meals as the grand finale of their 21 months of training. The *Escoffier Room*, named for the great French culinary artist Auguste Escoffier, features classic French cooking in an elegant maroon-and-rose dining room with black chandeliers, cushioned chairs and banquettes, and a window through which you can watch the students cooking. The offerings change every season, and the prix fixe menu ($20 lunch, $40 dinner) changes daily. Entrées might include beef fillet with mushrooms and wine, grilled salmon on a bed of lentils, strips of veal and fillet of sole with dill cream, and couscous with clams. The *American Bounty* dining room, which pioneered the return to regional American cooking a few years back, has a warm and friendly decor with green-cushioned wood chairs, arched windows overlooking a courtyard, and a wonderful display of fresh-baked breads and the local produce in front of the small kitchen, where you can watch students at work on the desserts and pastries. Menus change daily, but entrées might include stuffed breast of chicken with pecans and Kentucky bourbon, fillet of mahimahi in macadamia nuts with fresh pineapple salsa, scallop salad, and shrimp and Cajun sausage with pecan rice. The less expensive menu at the casual *St. Andrew's Café* features nutritionally balanced, low-calorie, low-cholesterol meals in a cheerful 65-seat room enlivened with hanging plants. The smaller *Caterina de Medici* dining room, featuring northern Italian cooking, is primarily for staff and family members of CIA students. The public is welcome to book any remaining tables by calling the school on Tuesday morning at 8:30; reservations are taken three weeks in advance. Typical entrées include braised stuffed veal shank with vegetable sauce, and fillet of sea bass with saffron and basil. Smoking is prohibited in all the restaurants. *Rte. 9, tel. 914/471–6608. Reservations required, booked on a quarterly basis. Jacket required (casual dress only for St. Andrew's Café). AE, DC, MC, V. Escoffier and American Bounty closed Sun. and Mon.; St. Andrew's and Caterina de Medici closed weekends. Inexpensive–Expensive.*

Coppola's Restaurant. Located a half mile from the FDR home, this restaurant features an extensive selection of southern Italian standards along with steaks, chops, and seafood dishes. The decor is exactly what you'd expect from a family-oriented Italian restaurant: crystal chandeliers, red-and-white tablecloths, and pictures and murals of Italy. Popular dishes include veal marsala and Italian seafood plate with clams, mussels, calamari, and shrimp on linguine; there is also a children's menu. The same family runs the adjacent Dutch Patroon Inn, a 34-room motel. *Rte. 9, tel. 914/229–9113. Dress: casual. AE, DC, MC, V. Inexpensive.*

Pepe's. This nice, cozy Italian restaurant convenient to the historic homes may have the inevitable red-checked tablecloths and posters of historic Italy, but it features some imaginative dishes at good prices. Standouts include the linguine topped with fish and shellfish, stuffed artichoke, and fettuccine carbonara. The homemade cheesecake is recommended for dessert. *108 Albany Post Rd., tel. 914/229–9050. Dress: casual. MC, V. Inexpensive.*

Lodging *For price categories, see Montauk lodging price chart.*

Village Victorian Inn. Built as a private home in 1860 in an Italianate Victorian style, this pale yellow house was converted to a small inn in 1987. It's furnished throughout with Victorian antiques, including canopy beds, French armoires, marble-topped dressers, and a walnut Hepplewhite dressing table. Full breakfast (included) is served in the cozy dining room, where a fire is lit in winter, and there is tea in the afternoon. The inn hosts mystery weekends and holds advance reservations at the Culinary Institute (*see* above). *31 Center St., Rhinebeck, 12572, tel. 914/876–8345. 5 rooms. AE, MC, V. Very Expensive.*

The Beekman Arms. A few miles north of the historic homes, this Rhinebeck landmark claims to be the oldest inn in America, dating to 1766, though it has been expanded over the years and now includes several 19th-century buildings. Rooms in the old section feature pine floors and reproductions of Colonial furniture; many have four-poster beds. The Delamater House, down the street, is a Victorian-Gothic-style cottage with an inviting front porch. The furnishings here are reproductions of Victorian pieces, and 20 additional rooms, all with working fireplaces, are located in the newer Delamater Courtyard buildings. Just opened this summer, the Gables is a Gothic Revival cottage with four nonsmoking rooms, all furnished with spanking-new Victorian reproductions. The hotel's cozy, low-ceilinged Beekman 1776 Tavern was recently taken over by Larry Forgioni, the chef and creator of New York's An American Place. Forgioni's celebrated spins on traditional American fare should give the Culinary Institute some stiff competition. *4 Mill St., Rhinebeck, 12572, tel. 914/876–7077. 59 rooms. Facilities: restaurant, bar. AE, DC, MC, V. Moderate–Expensive.*

The Super 8 Motel. This Hyde Park branch of the nationwide chain is conveniently located near the entrance to the FDR house and a quarter-mile from the Vanderbilt Mansion. Although clean and new (it was built four years ago), the Super 8 has little to distinguish it from the standard roadside offering. Free Continental breakfast is served. *Rte. 9, Hyde Park, 12538, tel. 914/229–0088. 61 rooms. AE, DC, MC, V. Inexpensive–Moderate.*

Index

A&S (department store), *196*

Aaron Davis Hall, *285*

Abigail Adams Smith Museum, *169*

Abyssinian Baptist Church, *98*

Acme Bar and Grill, *229*

African-Square, *97*

Afro Arts Cultural Centre, *169*

Al Amir (restaurant), *247–248*

Alcala (restaurant), *251*

Alexander's (department store), *160, 196*

Alfredo's the Original of Rome (restaurant), *238*

Algonquin Hotel, *57, 265–266*

Alice Austen House, *164*

Alice Tully Hall, *86, 284*

Alison on Dominick Street (restaurant), *224*

Alo Alo (restaurant), *245–246*

Alternative Museum, *115, 118*

American Ballet Theatre, *288*

American Bible Society, *84*

American Craft Museum, *51*

American Festival Cafe, *238–239*

American-Irish Historical Society, *68*

American Museum of Natural History, *88–89, 136, 137*

American Museum of the Moving Image, *156–157, 165, 289, 290*

American Negro

Theater, *98*

American Numismatic Society, *169*

America (restaurant), *232*

American Place, An (restaurant), *230*

Americas Society, *75*

Amerigo's (restaurant), *252*

Amsterdam's Bar and Rotisserie, *251*

Anatolia (restaurant), *248*

Angelo's (restaurant), *226*

Ansonia Hotel, *87*

Antiques shops, *194, 198–200*

Apollo Theatre, *97*

Apothecary shops, *200*

Appellate Division of the State Supreme Court, *63*

Aquavit (restaurant), *235*

Arizona 206 (restaurant), *246*

Arriving and departing, *17–23*

Art galleries, *200–201*

Arts, *274–292*

centers for, *274–275*

and children, *292–293*

dance, *288–289*

film, *289–292*

information on, *277*

music, *284–287*

opera, *287–288*

readings and lectures, *292*

theater, *278–284*

tickets for, *275–278*

Asia Society Gallery, *75*

Astoria, *156–157*

Astor Place Hair Designers, *110*

AT&T Infoquest Center (museum), *54, 136–137*

AT&T World Headquarters, *54*

Atlantic Avenue, *149*

Aureole (restaurant), *246*

Auctions, *215*

Aunt Len's Doll and Toy Museum, *137*

Avant-Garde Films, *291–292*

Avery Fisher Hall, *86*

B. Altman Dry Goods Store, *99*

Backstage on Broadway tour, *279*

Balducci's (gourmet shop), *106*

Ballet, *288*

Ballet Shop, *288*

Ballroom, The (restaurant), *230*

Bangkok Cuisine (restaurant), *244*

Bargains, *194*

Barbetta (restaurant), *242*

Bargemusic, *147, 286*

Barnard College, *92–93*

Barneys New York (department store), *196*

Bars

Chelsea and the Village, *304–305*

classics, *302–303*

East Side, *306*

gay bars, *307*

Midtown and Theater District, *305–306*

SoHo, *303–304*

West Side, *306–307*

Bartow-Pell Mansion, *174*

Baseball, *179*

Basketball, *179*

Battery, *123–128*

Battery Park, *123*

Battery Park City, *129–130, 137*

Bayard Building, *111*

Bazzini's Nuts and Confections, *118*

Beaches, *187, 312*

Bed-and-breakfasts, *271*

Bee and Thistle (inn), *316*

Beekman Arms (inn), *319*

Beekman Place, *139–140*

Beekman Tower (hotel), *267*

Belmont, *160–161*

Bergdorf Goodman (department store), *53, 196*

Bicycling, *181*

Big Apple Circus, *138*

Billiards, *182*

Billy's (restaurant), *241*

Bird-watching, *182*

Black Fashion Museum, *97*

Bleecker Street Cinema, *109*

Bloomingdale's, *72–73, 196, 198*

Boathouse (Prospect Park), *151*

Boating, *182–183*

Boccie, *183*

Bookstores, *201–202*

Borough Hall (Brooklyn), *143*

Bouley (restaurant), *223*

Bowling, *183*

Bowling Green, *126*

Bowne House, *157*

Boxing, *179*

Brasserie (restaurant), *239*

Bridge Cafe (restaurant), *223*

Brighton Beach Avenue, *166*

British travelers, tips for, *3–4*

Bronx, *159–163*

children's activities, *165–166*

Fordham, *159–163*

off the beaten track, *167*

restaurants, *252*

Bronx Museum of the Arts, *169*

Bronx Zoo, *162, 163,* 165

Brooklyn, *142–153*

Brooklyn Heights, *142–143, 146–149*

children's activities, *165–166*

off the beaten track, *166*

Park Slope, *149–153*

restaurants, *252*

Brooklyn Academy of Music, *275, 286, 287*

Brooklyn Botanic Garden, *152, 166*

Brooklyn Bridge, *142–143*

Brooklyn Children's Museum, *165*

Brooklyn Heights, *142–143, 146–150*

Brooklyn Heights Promenade, *148*

Brooklyn Historical Society, *148*

Brooklyn Museum, *152–153*

Brooklyn Public Library, *151*

Bryant Park, *57*

Bryant Park Discount Dance and Music Ticket Booth, *57, 277*

Bukhara (restaurant), *239*

Burberry's Ltd. (boutique), *54*

Cabana Carioca (restaurant), *244*

Cabaret, *301–302*

Café des Artistes, *87, 249*

Cafe Iguana (restaurant), *230*

Cafe Loup (restaurant), *227–228*

Cafe Luxembourg, *250*

Café Vernon, *155*

Caffe Reggio, *109*

Caffe Roma, *120*

Cameras, *202–203*

Camille's (restaurant), *149*

Cammareri Brothers Bakery, *149*

Camperdown Elm, *151*

Canaan Baptist Church of Christ, *95*

Cannon's Walk Block, *131*

Ca'Nova (restaurant), *246*

Capsuoto Freres (restaurant), *224*

Carl Fischer Music Store, *111*

Carl Schurz Park, *77*

Carlyle Hotel, *76, 256*

Carmine's (restaurant), *251*

Carnegie Hall, *173, 274, 285, 287, 288–289*

Car rentals, *21–22*

Carroll Gardens, *149*

Cartier, Inc., *52*

Cash machines, *9–10*

Castle Clinton, *123, 126*

Cathedral of St. John the Divine, *91–92*

Central Park, *77–83, 134–135, 137*

Alice in Wonderland statue, *83*

Bandshell, *80–81*

Belvedere Castle, *83, 137*

Bethesda Fountain, *81*

Bow Bridge, *81*

Carousel, *80, 137*

Cherry Hill, *81*

Children's Zoo, *84*

Cleopatra's Needle, *83*

Conservatory Water, *83*

Dairy, *80, 137*

Delacorte Clock, *83*

Delacorte Theater, *82*

Gotham Miniature Golf, *80*

Great Lawn, *82*

Hans Christian Andersen statue, *83, 138*

Heckscher Puppet House, *137*

Lawn Bowling Greens and Croquet Grounds, *80*

Loeb Boathouse, *81*

Mall, *80*

Mineral Springs Pavilion, *80*

Pond, *78*

Ramble, *81*

Reservoir, *82*

Shakespeare Garden, *82*

Sheep Meadow, *80*

Strawberry Fields, *81*

Swedish Cottage Theater, *82, 137*

Turtle Pond, *82*

Vista Rock, *82*

Wollman Memorial Rink, *78, 80*

Zoo, *83, 137*

Central Synagogue, *175*

Chanel (boutique), *54*

Chanin Building, *59*

Channel Gardens, *47*

Chanterelle (restaurant), *223*

Charlton Street, *139*

Chatham Square, *122*

Chatwal Inns, *269*

Chefs and Cuisiniers Club (restaurant), *230*

Chelsea, *98–102*

bars, *304–305*

restaurants, *229–232*

Chelsea Historic District, *99–102*

Chelsea Hotel, *102*

ChemCourt, *139*

Cherry Lane Theater, *108*

Chess and checkers, *183*

Chez Josephine (restaurant), *243*

Children, *10–12*

and arts, *292*

Manhattan activities, *136–138*

other boroughs, activities in, *165–166*

shopping for, *194*

Children's clothing stores, *203*

Children's Museum of Manhattan, *136*

Children's zoos, *83, 137, 162, 167*

China Grill, *239*

China Institute, *74*

Chinatown, *121–122*

restaurants, *226–227*

Chin Chin (restaurant), *239*

Christ Church United

Methodist Church, *73*

Christopher Street, *107*

Chrysler Building, *59*

Churches, *175–176*

Church of Our Lady of Pompeii, *108–109*

Church of St. Ann and the Holy Trinity, *148*

Church of the Ascension, *105*

Church of the Holy Communion, *99*

Church of the Incarnation, *60–61*

Church of the Transfiguration (Chinatown), *121–122*

Church of the Transfiguration (Murray Hill), *62–63*

Ciccarone Park, *160*

Circle Line, *136*

Citibank Building, *128*

Citicorp Building (Queens), *155*

Citicorp Center (Manhattan), *54–55*

City Center, *275, 288*

City Gallery, *169*

City Hall, *133*

City Island, *167*

City Island Historical Nautical Museum, *169–170*

Classical music, *284–285*

Clement Clarke Moore Park, *101*

Clocktower Gallery, *134*

Cloisters, *135, 170*

Closing times. *See* Opening and closing times

Coach House (restaurant), *227*

Colonnade Row, *110*

Columbia University area, *90–94*

Columbus Avenue, shopping on, *194*

Columbus Circle, *84*

Columbus Park, *122*

Comedy clubs, *300*

Complete Traveller Bookstore, *62*

Coney Island, *166*
Confucius Plaza, *122*
Conservatory Garden (Central Park), *72*
Continental Insurance Building, *139*
Cooper-Hewitt Museum, *71*, *135*
Cooper Square, *111*
Cooper Union Foundation Building, *111*
Copacabana, *73*
Coppola's Restaurant, *318*
Costs, *9*
Council on Foreign Relations, *75*
Country music clubs, *300–301*
Court House Square, *155*
Creston Avenue Baptist Church, *160*
Crime, *24*
Criminal Court Building, *134*
Crystal shops, *203*
Culinary Institute of America, *318*
Cupping Room Cafe, *115*
Cushman Row, *101*

D&G Bakery, *120*
Daily News Building, *59*
Dakota (apartments), *88*
Damrosch Park, *86*
Dance
ballet, *288*
modern, *288–289*
Dance clubs, *297–298*
Dawat (restaurant), *239–240*
Days Inn, *268*
Dean & DeLuca (gourmet shop), *115*
Delmonico's (restaurant), *127–128*
Deming-Avery House, Old Lyme, CT, *315*
Department stores, *196*, *198*
De Robertis Patisserie (cafe), *112*

Dezerland's Dream Car Collection, *170*
Diamond District, *140*
Dining. *See* Restaurants
Disabled travelers, hints for, *12–13*
Discount tickets, *276–278*
Docks (restaurant), *251*
Dominick's (restaurant), *161*
Doral Court (hotel), *260*
Doral Inn, *266*
Doral Park Avenue (hotel), *260*
Doral Tuscany (hotel), *260*
Dorilton (apartments), *87*
Drake (hotel), *260–261*
Dress codes, *219*
Duane Park, *118*
Duffy Square, *56*
Dumont Plaza (hotel), *267*
Dutchess County Tourist Office, *316*

Eagle Warehouse, *146*
East Side bars, *306*
East Village, *109–113*
Edgar Allan Poe Cottage, *160*
Edwardian Room (restaurant), *235*
Eglise de Notre Dame (church), *91*
Eighth Street, *106*
Electronics, *202–203*
Eleventh Street, *106*
Ellis Island, *126*
El Museo Del Barrio, *72*
El Teddy's (restaurant), *118*, *224*
Ely-Noyes House, Old Lyme, CT, *315*
Embassy Suites (hotel), *261*
Empire Diner, *101*
Empire State Building, *62*
Enchanted Forest

(toy store), *115*
Enid A. Haupt Conservatory, *162*
Enrico Fermi Library and Cultural Center, *161*
Excelsior (hotel), *269*
Extra! Extra! (restaurant), *241*

F.A.O. Schwarz (toy store), *53–54*
Father Demo Square, *108*
Federal Hall National Memorial, *128*, *135*
Federal Plaza, *134*
Federal Reserve Bank, *129*, *135*
Feld Ballet, *289*
Felidia (restaurant), *235–236*
Fencing, *183*
Ferrara (café), *120*
Festivals, *5–8*
Fifth Avenue, shopping on, *193*
Fifth Avenue Presbyterian Church, *52*
Fifth Avenue Synagogue, *74*
Fifty-seventh Street, shopping on, *193–194*
Film, *289–292*
avant-garde, *291–292*
festivals, *289*
first-run houses, *290*
foreign, *291*
midnight movies, *290*
museums, *290*
revival houses, *290–291*
Film (camera), *10*
First Congregational Church, Old Lyme, CT, *315*
First Shearith Israel, *122*
Fishing, *183–184*
Flatiron Building, *63–64*
Flea markets, *215*
Florence Griswold Museum, Old Lyme, CT, *314–315*
Florent (restaurant), *228*

Flushing, *157–159*
Flushing Meadows Corona Park, *158–159*
Foley Square, *133*
Food shops, *203*, *204*
Football, *180*
Forbes Magazine Galleries, *170*
Ford Foundation Building, *59*
Fordham University, *161–162*
Foreign films, *291*
Fort Tryon Park, *176*
Forty-second Street, *55–60*
Fountains, *176–177*
Four Seasons (restaurant), *55*, *232*
Fox Oaks Rock, *157–158*, *233*
Fragrance shops, *200*
Franklin D. Roosevelt Boardwalk, *187*
Franklin D. Roosevelt National Historic Site, *317*
Fraunces Tavern, *127*, *220*
Free activities, *134–135*
Friars Club, *54*
The Frick Collection, *66*
Frieda Schiff Warburg Sculpture Garden, *152*
Friends Meeting House, *157*
Fulton Ferry Landing, *143*
Fulton Ferry Terminal, *147*
Fulton Fish Market, *132*
Fulton Market Building, *131–132*
Fun/fantasy shops, *204–205*

Gadget stores, *205*
Gallagher's (restaurant), *243*
Galleries Lafayette New York, *198*
Gansevoort Market, *140*
Gardens, *176*

Garibaldi Meucci
  Museum, *170*
Garment District, *140*
Gay bars, *307*
Gay Street, *106*
GE Building, *47, 50*
General Motors
  Building, *53*
General Theological
  Seminary, *100*
Getting around,
  25–30
Ginger Man, The
  (restaurant), *250*
Giorgio (restaurant),
  232
Gleason's Boxing
  Arena and Gym,
  146–147
Goethe House
  (German
  library/museum), *70*
Golf, *184*
Gosman's
  (restaurant), *312*
Gotham Bar & Grill,
  227
Governors Island, *123*
Grace Church, *149,
  175*
Grace Rainey Rogers
  Auditorium, *286*
Gracie Mansion, *77*
Gramercy Park,
  64–65
  restaurants, *229–232*
Grand-Army Plaza
  (Brooklyn), *150*
Grand Army Plaza
  (Manhattan), *53*
Grand Central Oyster
  Bar & Restaurant,
  236
Grand Central
  Terminal, *58, 135*
Grand Concourse,
  159–160
Grand Hyatt New
  York (hotel), *59, 261*
Grant's Tomb, *93*
Gray's Papaya King,
  88
Greek Revival
  brownstones, *149*
Greenwich Village,
  102–109
  bars, *304*
  restaurants, *227–229*
Green-Wood
  Cemetery, *166*

Grey Art Gallery, *105*
Grotta Azzurra
  (restaurant),
  119–120
Grolier Club, *73*
Grove Court, *107*
Gucci (boutique), *52*
Guggenheim
  Bandshell, *86*
Guggenheim
  Museum, *70, 135*
Guided tours, *30–31*
Guinness World
  Records Exhibit
  Hall, *62, 137*
Gurney's Inn Resort
  and Spa, *313*

Hammacher
  Schlemmer (store),
  54
Hammarskjold Plaza
  Sculpture Garden,
  177
Hanover Square, *127*
Harbor Defense
  Museum of New
  York City, *170*
Hard Rock Cafe, *244*
Harlem, *94–98*
  restaurants, *252*
Harmonie Club,
  73–74
Harry Winston
  (jeweler), *52*
Hatsuhana
  (restaurant), *240*
Haughwout Building,
  115
Hayden Planetarium,
  88–89, 136
Helmsley
  Middletowne (hotel),
  266
Helmsley Palace
  (hotel), *261–262*
Henderson Place
  Historic District, *76*
Henri Bendel
  (department store),
  52, 198
Herald Square,
  shopping in, *193*
Hermès (boutique),
  54
Hindu Temple of
  North America, *158*
Hispanic Society of
  America, *170*
Historic sites, *135,*

174–175, 316–317
Hither Hills State
  Park, *312*
Hockey, *180*
Holiday Inn Crowne
  Plaza, *262*
Home decor shops,
  205–206
Hors d'Oeuvrerie
  (restaurant), *130*
Horseback riding,
  184–185
Horse racing, *180*
Hostels, *270*
Hotaling's News,
  56–57
Hotel des Artistes, *87*
Hotel Edison, *269*
Hotel Esplanade,
  269–270
Hotel health clubs,
  185
Hotel Pierre, *74*
Hotels, *254–272*
  bed-and-breakfasts,
  272
  Hyde Park, *319*
  Montauk, *313–314*
  Old Lyme, CT,
  315–316
  reservations, *255*
  services, *255–256*
Hotel Wentworth, *270*
Hudson River Club
  (restaurant), *220*
Hugh O'Neill Dry
  Goods Store, *99*
Hunters Point
  Historic District,
  153
Hyde Park, *316–319*
  exploring, *317–318*
  hotels, *319*
  restaurants, *318–319*
  tourist information,
  316
  transportation to, *316*

IBM Building, *54*
IBM Gallery of
  Science and Art, *54*
Ice skating, *185*
ICP Mid-Town, *57*
Il Cortile
  (restaurant), *226*
Il Nido (restaurant),
  236
Independence Plaza,
  118
India House, *127*

Indochine
  (restaurant), *228*
Inn at Napeague, *312*
Inter-Continental
  New York (hotel),
  262
International
  Building, *47*
International Center
  of Photography, *71*
International Design
  Center, *156*
International House,
  93
Intrepid Sea-Air
  Space Museum, *136*
Iroquois Hotel, *58,
  270*
Isamu Noguchi
  Garden Museum,
  167

Jackson Avenue,
  153–154
Jacob K. Javits
  Convention Center,
  173
Jacob Riis Park, *187*
Jackson Hole
  (restaurant), *71*
Jamaica Arts Center,
  171
Jamaica Bay Wildlife
  Refuge, *176*
Japan Society
  Gallery, *171*
Javits Federal
  Building, *134*
Jazz clubs, *298–299*
Jean Lafitte
  (restaurant), *53*
Jefferson Market
  Library, *106*
Jehovah's Witness
  headquarters, *147*
Jerry's (restaurant),
  225
Jerry's 103
  (restaurant), *113*
Jewelers, *206–207*
Jewish Museum, *71,
  88*
Jewish Theological
  Seminary, *94*
J. G. Melon
  (restaurant), *249*
Joe Allen
  (restaurant),
  244–245
Jogging, *185–186*

John Sill House, Old
Lyme, CT, *315*
John Street
Methodist Church,
129
Jones Beach, *187*
Journey's End
(hotel), *266*
Joyce Theatre, *102*,
289
Judson Memorial
Church, *105*
Juilliard School of
Music, *86*

Kalinika Cafe, *76*
Kam Man
(supermarket), *121*
Katz's Delicatessen,
225–226
Kaufman Astoria
Studios, *156*
Kaufman Concert
Hall, *286*
Kenilworth
(apartments), *88*
King of Greene
Street (building),
114
Kingsbridge Armory,
159
Kingsland
Homestead, *158*
Kissena Park, *158*,
176
The Kitchen
(performance
center), *275*
Knickerbocker Club,
74
Knights of Pythias
Temple, *87*
Kwong and Wong
(restaurant), *226*

La Caravelle
(restaurant), *236*
La Cité (restaurant),
242–243
La Colombe D'Or
(restaurant), *230*
La Côte Basque
(restaurant),
232–233
Lafayette Theater, *97*
La Famille
(restaurant), *95*
LaGuardia
Community College
Archives, *156*

Langham
(apartments), *88*
La Reserve
(restaurant),
236–237
Latin music
nightclubs, *300*
Lattanzi
(restaurant),
243–244
Leather goods,
207–208
Le Bernardin
(restaurant), *242*
Le Cirque
(restaurant), *245*
Le Cygne
(restaurant), *237*
L'Ecole (restaurant),
115
Lefferts Homestead,
150
Le Madri
(restaurant), *229*
Le Pactolel
(restaurant), *220*
Le Parker Meridien
(hotel), *262–263*
Le Perigord
(restaurant), *237*
Le Regence
(restaurant), *245*
Le Train Bleu, *73*
Lever House
(building), *55*
Librairie de France,
47
Library and Museum
of the Performing
Arts, *86*
Lincoln Center, *84*,
86
arts, *274*, *281*, *285*
restaurants, *249–250*
Lion's Head
(restaurant), *107*
Litchfield Villa, *150*
Little Italy, *119–120*
Living Memorial to
the Holocaust-
Museum of Jewish
Heritage, *131*
Lodging. *See* Hotels
Loeb Student Center,
105
Loews Paradise
Theater, *160*
Loews New York

Hotel, *266*
Lola (restaurant),
230–231
London Terrace
Apartments,
101–102
Long Island City,
153–156
Lord & Taylor
(department store),
198
Louise Nevelson
Plaza, *129*
Louis Vuitton
(leather goods), *54*
Lowell (hotel), *256*
Lower East Side,
shopping on, *193*
Lower East Side
Tenement Museum,
171
Lower Manhattan,
restaurants, *220*, *223*
Low Memorial
Library, *90–91*
Luggage, *9*, *207–208*
Lunchtime concerts,
286
Lutèce (restaurant),
233
Lyceum Theater, *279*
Lyme Academy of
Fine Arts, *315*
Lyme Art
Association, *315*

MacDougal Alley,
105
McGraw-Hill
Building, *51*
McGraw-Hill Park,
139
McSorley's Old Ale
House, *111*
Macy's, *199*
Madison Mile, *76*
Madison Square, *63*
Madison Square
Garden, *179*, *275*
Majestic Theatre, *275*
Malcolm Shabazz
Mosque, *95*
Manhattan
arts, *274–293*
Central Park, *77–83*
Chelsea, *98–102*
children's activities,
136–138
Chinatown, *121–122*
Columbia University

area, *90–94*
East Village, *109–113*
Forty-second Street, .
55–60
free activities,
134–135
Greenwich Village,
102–109
Harlem, *94–98*
hotels, *254–272*
Little Italy, *119–120*
Midtown, Fifth to
Park avenues, *52–55*
Murray Hill to Union
Square, *60–66*
Museum Mile, *67–72*
nightlife, *294–307*
off the beaten track,
138–140
orientation, *44–46*
restaurants, *217–252*
Rockefeller Center,
46–52
Seaport and the
Courts, *131–134*
SoHo and TriBeCa,
113–119
Upper East Side,
72–77
Upper West Side,
83–90
Wall Street and the
Battery, *123–131*
Manhattan Ocean
Club (restaurant),
240
Manhattan School of
Music, *93*
Manhattan Suites
East (hotels), *267*
Marble Collegiate
Church, *62*
Marchais Center of
Tibetan Art, *171*
Marcus Garvey Park,
95
Mark (hotel), *256*,
258
Mark's (restaurant),
246
Marriott Marquis
(hotel), *263*
Martin Beck
Theatre, *279*
Mayfair Regent
Hotel, *74*, *258*
Mazzei (restaurant),
247
Meadowlands Arena,
275

Men's shoes, *208–209*
Menswear, *208*
Merkin Concert Hall, *286*
Mesa Grill (restaurant), *231*
Metropolitan Club, *74*
Metropolitan Life Insurance Tower, *63*
Metropolitan Museum of Art, *68–70, 135, 136*
Metropolitan Opera, *86, 286, 287*
Mezzaluna (restaurant), *248*
Michael's (restaurant), *237*
Mickey Mantle's (restaurant), *240*
Midtown East, *52–55*
restaurants, *232–242*
shopping, *193*
Milford Plaza (hotel), *270*
Milligan Place, *106*
Minetta Lane, *109*
Minters, *130*
Miss Kim's, *64*
Mitzi E. Newhouse theater, *86, 281*
Mocca Hungarian Restaurant, *248*
Modern dance, *288–289*
Money changing, *25*
Montague Terrace, *148*
Montauk, *309–314*
beaches, *312*
exploring, *311–312*
hotels, *313–314*
restaurants, *312–313*
tourist information, *309*
transportation to, *309*
Montauk Chamber of Commerce, *309*
Montauk Club, *150*
Montauk Harbor, *311*
Montauk Lighthouse, *311–312*
Montgomery Place, *150*
Montrachet (restaurant), *224*
Monuments, *176–177*
Morgan Guaranty Trust, *128*
Morgans (hotel), *263*

Mormon Visitors Center, *84*
Morningside Park, *91*
Morris-Jumel Mansion, *174*
Mossman Collection of Locks, *58*
Mott Street, *121*
Mount Sinai Hospital, *72*
Municipal Building, *133*
Murray Hill, *60–66*
restaurants, *229–232*
Museum Mile, *67–72*
Museum of American Folk Art, *86–87*
Museum of Holography, *115*
Museum of Modern Art, *51, 135*
Museum of Television and Radio, *51–52, 135, 290*
Museum of the City of New York, *72, 135*
Museums, *169–173*
children's, *136–137, 165*
free, *135*
Manhattan, *66–72*
Music, *284–286*
classical, *285–286*
lunchtime concerts, *286*
outdoor concerts, *286*

Nassau Coliseum, *275*
National Academy of Design, *70–71, 135*
National Arts Club, *65*
National Black Theater, *95*
National Museum of the American Indian, *171*
Needlecraft, *209*
Netherlands Memorial, *126*
New Amsterdam (theater), *56*
New Directors/New Films, *289*
Newhouse Center for Contemporary Art, *163*
New Museum of Contemporary Art, *115, 135*

New York Aquarium, *166*
New York Botanical Garden, *162, 165–166*
New York Chinatown History Project, *122*
New York City. See also Bronx; Brooklyn; Manhattan; Staten Island
the Bronx, *159–163*
Brooklyn, *142–153*
Manhattan, *44–140*
Queens, *153–159*
Staten Island, *163–165*
New York City Ballet, *288*
New York City Fire Museum, *171*
New York City Opera, *287*
New York City Transit Museum, *171–172*
New York Coliseum, *84*
New York Convention and Visitors Bureau, *84, 135*
New York County Courthouse, *134*
New York Earth Room (soil sculpture), *114*
New York Film Festival, *289*
New York Hall of Science, *159, 165*
New York Harbor, *123*
New York Hilton (hotel), *263–264*
New York Historical Society, *88, 135*
New York International Youth Hostel, *270*
New York Life Insurance Building, *63*
New York Mercantile Exchange, *118*
New York Philharmonic, *285, 286*
New York Plaza, *127*

New York Public Library, *58*
New York State Supreme Courthouse, *155*
New York State Theater, *86*
New York Stock Exchange, *128, 135*
New York Supreme Court, *143*
New York Times Building, *56*
New York Vista (hotel), *264*
New York Yacht Club, *57*
Nicholas Roerich Museum, *172*
Nightclubs, *296–297*
Nightlife, *295–307*
bars, *302–307*
cabaret, *301–302*
comedy clubs, *301*
country music, *300–301*
dancing, *297–298*
elegant clubs, *296–297*
gay bars, *307*
jazz clubs, *298–299*
Latin and Island music, *300*
rock and roll, *299–300*
92nd Street Y, *275*
Nippon (restaurant), *240*
Noodle Town (restaurant), *226–227*
North Wind Undersea Museum, *167, 172*

Odeon (restaurant), *224–225*
Off-Broadway theaters, *281–283*
Older travelers, hints for, *13–15*
Old Lyme, CT, *314–316*
exploring, *314–315*
hotels and restaurants, *315–316*
tourist information, *314*
transportation to, *314*
Old Lyme Inn, *315–316*

Old Merchant's
House, *174*

Olympic Tower, *52*

One Times Square
Plaza, *55–56*

Opening and closing
times, *24–25*

Opera, *287–288*

Orso (restaurant),
244

Our Lady of Lebanon
Roman Catholic
Church, *149–150*

Our Lady of Mt.
Carmel Roman
Catholic Church,
160

Outdoor concerts,
286

Package deals, *3*

Packing for trip, *8–9*

Paley Park, *139*

Palm (restaurant),
237

Pan Am Building,
173–174

Paramount (hotel),
270–271

Paramount
Communications
Building, *84*

Parioli Romanissimo
(restaurant), *245*

Park Bistro, *231*

Park Row, *132*

Parks, *176*

Manhattan, *77–83*,
134–135, 137

other boroughs,
*150–151, 158,
165–166*

Park Slope, *149–153*

Partenope
(restaurant), *156*

Patchin Place, *106*

Patisserie Lanciani,
107

Pelham Bay Park,
176

Peninsula (hotel), *258*

Pentop Bar
(restaurant), *240*

Pepe's (restaurant),
318–319

Performance art,
283–284

Performing arts
memorabilia, *209*

Periyali (restaurant),

231

Pete's Tavern, *65*

Petrossian
(restaurant), *243*

Pickwick Arms
Hotel, *271*

Pier 16, *132*

Pier 17, *132*

Pierpont Morgan
Library, *60, 135*

Pierre (hotel),
258–259

Pierre's (bistro), *107*

Pig Heaven
(restaurant), *248*

Pilobolus, *289*

Place des Antiquaires
(shopping mall), *54*

Players Club, *64*

Playgrounds,
137–138

Plaza (hotel), *53, 259*

Plymouth Church of
the Pilgrims, *147*

Poiret (restaurant),
251

Police Academy
Museum, *172*

Police Building, *120*

Pomander Walk, *140*

Posters, *209*

Post House
(restaurant), *247*

Prix Fixe
(restaurant), *231*

Promenade Food
Court, *132*

Prometheus (statue),
47

Prospect Park,
150–151

Prospect Park Zoo,
166

Provence
(restaurant), *225*

Provincetown
Playhouse, *109*

Public spaces,
138–140

Public Theater,
110–111, 281–282

Puck Building, *120*

Puglia (restaurant),
120

Quaker Cemetery,
151

Quality Inn
Midtown, *269*

Quatorze

(restaurant), *228*

Queen of Greene
Street (building), *114*

Queens, *153–159*

Astoria, *156–157*

children's activities,
166, 167

Flushing, *157–159*

Long Island City,
153–156

off the beaten track,
167

restaurants, *252*

Queensboro Bridge,
155

Queens Boulevard,
155–156

Queens County Farm
Museum, *166*

Queens Museum, *159*

Queens Zoo, *159, 166*

Quilted Giraffe
(restaurant), *233*

Racewalking,
185–186

Radio City Music
Hall, *50–51, 274–275*

Radisson Empire
Hotel, *267*

Rainbow Room
(restaurant), *50,
234–235*

Ralph Lauren
(boutique), *76*

Ramada Hotel, *271*

Reading materials,
15–16

Readings, *291–292*

Records, *210*

Regency (hotel), *264*

Restaurant Row, *279*

Restaurants, *217–252*

Bronx, *252*

Brooklyn, *252*

Chelsea, Gramercy
Park, Murray Hill,
229–232

children's, *138*

Chinatown and Little
Italy, *226–227*

dining hours, *219*

dress codes, *219*

Greenwich Village,
227–229

Harlem, *252*

Hyde Park, *318–319*

Lincoln Center,
249–250

lower Manhattan, *220,*

223

Midtown East,
232–242

Montauk, *312–313*

Old Lyme, CT,
314–316

prices, *217–218*

Queens, *252*

reservations, *219*

seating, *219*

SoHo and TriBeCa,
223–226

Theater District,
241–245

tipping, *219–220*

Upper East Side,
245–249

Upper West Side,
250–252

wine, *218–219*

Rest rooms, *24*

Revival houses (film),
290–291

Richmondtown
Restoration,
164–165

Rihga Royal (hotel),
259

Ringling Bros.
Barnum & Bailey
Circus, *138*

Ritz-Carlton (hotel),
259–260

River Cafe, The *147,
252*

Riverdale, *167*

Riverside Church, *93*

Riverside Park, *90*

Riverside tenements,
149

Robert Moses State
Park, *187*

Rock and roll clubs,
299–300

Rockaways, *187*

Rockefeller Center,
46–52, 135

Roger Smith
Winthrop (hotel),
267

Roller skating, *186*

Roosevelt Island, *140*

Roosevelt Island
Aerial Tramway,
136

Rosa Mexicano
(restaurant), *241*

Rose Cafe, *228*

Royalton Hotel, *57,
264–265*

Running, *180*
Russian Orthodox
Cathedral of St.
Nicholas, *71*
Russian Tea Room
(restaurant), *243*

St. Bartholomew's
Church, *55*
St. Demitrios
Cathedral, *156*
St. George's
Episcopal Church,
157
St. James Church,
122
St. James Theater,
279
St. Luke's-
in-the-Fields, *108*
St. Luke's Place, *108*
St. Mark's-
in-the-Bowery
Church, *111–112*
St. Mark's Library,
101
St. Marks Place, *112*
St. Mary's Roman
Catholic Church,
154
St. Patrick's
Cathedral, *52*
St. Paul's Chapel, *91*
St. Paul's Chapel
(Wall Street), *129,
135*
St. Peter's Church,
100
St. Thomas Church,
52
Saks Fifth Avenue
(department store),
52, 198
San Carlos (hotel),
268
San Domenico
(restaurant),
249–250
Sandro's
(restaurant), *241*
San Gennaro
Church, *120*
San Remo
(apartments), *88*
Scarlatti
(restaurant),
237–238
Schermerhorn Row,
132
Schomburg Center

for Research in
Black Culture,
97–98
School of American
Ballet, *288*
Seagram Building, *55*
Seaport Harbor Line
Cruise, *132*
Seasonal events, *5–8*
Secondhand shops,
214–215
Second House,
Montauk, *311*
Selectman's Office,
Old Lyme, CT,
314–316
Serendipity
(restaurant),
241–242
Sette Mezzo
(restaurant), *247*
Seventh Avenue (Park
Slope), *149–150*
Seventh Regiment
Armory, *74–75*
Seventy-ninth Street
Boat Basin, *90*
Shea Stadium, *159*
Shelburne (hotel),
267
Shepherd's Neck Inn,
313–314
Sheraton Centre &
Towers (hotel), *268*
Sheraton Manhattan
(hotel), *268*
Sheridan Square, *107*
Sherman Square, *88*
Shopping, *189–215*
auctions, *215*
department stores,
196, 198
flea markets, *215*
hours for, *189*
itineraries for, *194,
196*
neighborhoods for,
189–194
sales, *189*
secondhand shops,
214–215
specialty shops,
198–214
Shrine of St.
Elizabeth Ann
Seton, *127*
Shubert Alley, *279*
Shubert Theater, *279*
Shun Lee Palace
(restaurant), *241*

Sidewalkers
(restaurant),
251–252
Siegel-Cooper Dry
Goods Store, *99*
Sign of the Dove
(restaurant), *247*
Silvercup Studios,
155
Silver Palace
(restaurant), *122,
227*
Singer Building, *115*
Siracusa Gourmet
Cafe, *228*
Sloane House YMCA,
271
Sloppy Louie's
(restaurant), *223*
Smith & Wollensky
(restaurant), *238*
Sniffen Court, *139*
Snug Harbor
Cultural Center, *163*
Society of
Illustrators Museum
of American
Illustration, *172*
Socrates Sculpture
Park, *167*
SoHo, *113–119*
bars, *303–304*
restaurants, *223–226*
shopping, *193*
SoHo Kitchen and
Bar, *226*
Soldiers' and Sailors'
Memorial Arch, *150*
Soldiers' and Sailors'
Monument, *90*
Southgate Tower
(hotel), *267*
South Street Seaport,
131–132, 135, 136
restaurants, *223*
shopping, *189, 191*
Souvenir shops, *210*
Spanish and
Portuguese
Synagogue, Shearith
Israel, *87*
Sparks Steak House,
238
Specialty shops,
198–214
Sports, *179–187*
Staten Island,
163–164
children's activities,
165, 166

Richmondtown,
164–165
Snug Harbor, *163–164*
Staten Island
Botanical Gardens,
163–164
Staten Island
Children's Museum,
164, 165
Staten Island Ferry,
123, 136, 163
Staten Island
Historical Society
Museum, *165*
Staten Island Zoo,
166
Stationery, *209*
Statue of Liberty,
126
Steuben Glass, *52*
Storytelling, *138*
Striver's Row, *98*
Studio Museum in
Harlem, *97*
Stuyvesant Street,
111
Subway kiosk, 72nd
St., *87*
Super 8 Motel, *319*
Surma, The
Ukranian Shop,
111
Surrey Hotel, *266*
Surrogate's Court
(Hall of Records),
133
Swimming, *186*
Sylvia's (restaurant),
97, 252
Symphony Space,
275

Table d'Hôte
(restaurant),
248–249
Tavern on the Green,
87, 250
Teachers College, *94*
Telephones, public,
23–24
Television screenings,
175
Temperature
averages, monthly,
5
Temple Emanu-el, *74*
Temples, *175–176*
Tennis, *180–181,
186–187*
Terrace (café), *70*

The Terrace
(restaurant),
250–251
Thames Twins
(buildings), *129*
Theater, *278–284*
avant-garde, *283*
Broadway, *280–281*
information, *278*
Off-Broadway,
281–283
performance art,
283–284
Theater 80, *112*
Theater District
bars, *305–306*
Broadway theaters,
280–281
restaurants, *242–245*
Theatre Row, *56,
280, 282*
Theodore Roosevelt
Birthplace, *64*
Third Cemetery of
the Spanish and
Portuguese
Synagogue, Shearith
Israel, *99*
Ticket clubs, *277–278*
Tickets, *275–278*
Tiffany & Co., *52–53*
Time-Life Building,
51
Times Square, *55–56*
Tipping, *219–220*
Titanic Memorial, *131*
TKTS discount ticket
booth, *56, 276–277*
Tommy Tang
(restaurant), *225*
Tompkins Square, *113*
Tour groups, *2–3*
Tourist information
Hyde Park, *316*
Montauk, *309*
New York City, *2, 22*
Old Lyme, CT, *314*
Tower Records, *86,
110*
Town Hall, *275*
Toy stores, *210–211*
Track and field, *181*
Transportation
to Hyde Park, *316*
to Montauk, *309*
New York City,
arriving and
departing, *16–23*
New York City,
getting around,

25–30
to Old Lyme, *314*
TriBeCa, *113–119*
restaurants, *223–226*
TriBeCa Grill and
Film Center, *118,
225*
Trinity Church,
128–129
Trump Tower, *53*
Tudor City, *59*
Tweed Courthouse,
133
Twenty-one Club
(restaurant), *235*
Twenty West (Home
of Black Cinema), *95*
Twin Peaks (house),
107
Twin Sisters
(houses), *108*

Ukranian Museum,
172
Umberto's Clam
House, *120*
Umbrellas, *211*
Union Square, *65–66*
Union Square Cafe,
231–232
Union Theological
Seminary, *93–94*
Unisphere, Flushing
Meadows Park, *159*
United Nations
Headquarters,
59–60, 135
University Club, *52*
U.N. Plaza-Park
Hyatt (hotel), *265*
Upper East Side,
72–77
restaurants, *245–249*
shopping, *194*
Upper West Side,
83–90
restaurants, *250–252*
U.S. Courthouse, *133*
U.S. Court of
International Trade,
134
U.S. Customs House,
126
U.S. Tennis
Association
National Tennis
Center, *159*

Van Cleef & Arpels
(jeweler), *53*

Van Cortlandt
Mansion, *174*
Van Cortlandt Park,
176
Vanderbilt Mansion,
317–318
Vanderbilt YMCA,
271
Vasata (restaurant),
249
Veniero Pasticceria
(cafe), *112*
Verdi Square, *88*
Vernon Boulevard,
153–155
Veterans Memorial
Hall, *163*
Vico Ristorante, *249*
Viet-Nam
Restaurant, *121*
Vietnam Veterans
Memorial, *127*
Villa Mosconi
(restaurant), *229*
Village Victorian
Inn, *319*
Villard Houses, *174*
Vince and Eddie's
(restaurant), *250*
Visitor information,
2
Vivian Beaumont
theater, *86, 281*
Voorlezer's House,
165

Waldorf-Astoria, *265*
Walentas Building,
146
Wall Street, *128–131*
Washington Market
Park, *119*
Washington Mews,
105
Washington Square,
103, 105, 137
Water's Edge
Restaurant and East
River Yacht Club,
155, 252
Wave Hill, *167, 175*
Waverly Theater, *109*
Weather, *5*
Weeping Beech, *158*
Wellington Hotel, *271*
Western Union
Building, *118*
West Side bars,
306–307
West Side Y, *271*

Whitney Museum of
American Art, *68*
Whitney Museum of
American Art
Downtown, *129,
172–173*
Whitney Museum of
Art at Philip
Morris, *58*
Willow Street,
147–148
Windjammer
Restaurant, *312–313*
Windows on the
World (restaurant),
130, 220, 223
Wine cellars, *218–219*
Winter Garden
Atrium, *130*
Wolfe's Pond Park,
187
Women's clothing,
211–214
Women's shoes, *214*
Wong Kee
(restaurant), *227*
Woolworth Building,
129–130
World Financial
Center, *130*
shopping in, *191*
World Trade Center,
130
World Yacht Cruises
(restaurant),
229–230
Wrestling, *179*
Wyndham (hotel), *268*

Yellowfingers
(restaurant), *242*
Yivo Institute for
Jewish Research,
70
YMCAs, *271–272*
Yorkville, *76–77*

Zabar's (gourmet
shop), *89, 204*
Zarela's (restaurant),
241
Zero Moving
Company, *289*
Zig Zag Bar & Grill,
232
Zoos, *83, 137, 150,
159, 162–163, 165,
166, 177*

Personal Itinerary

Departure *Date*

Time

Transportation

Arrival *Date*   *Time*

Departure *Date*   *Time*

Transportation

Accommodations

Arrival *Date*   *Time*

Departure *Date*   *Time*

Transportation

Accommodations

Arrival *Date*   *Time*

Departure *Date*   *Time*

Transportation

Accommodations

Personal Itinerary

Arrival   *Date*   *Time*

Departure   *Date*   *Time*

Transportation

Accommodations

Arrival   *Date*   *Time*

Departure   *Date*   *Time*

Transportation

Accommodations

Arrival   *Date*   *Time*

Departure   *Date*   *Time*

Transportation

Accommodations

Arrival   *Date*   *Time*

Departure   *Date*   *Time*

Transportation

Accommodations

Addresses

Name	*Name*
Address	*Address*
Telephone	*Telephone*
Name	*Name*
Address	*Address*
Telephone	*Telephone*
Name	*Name*
Address	*Address*
Telephone	*Telephone*
Name	*Name*
Address	*Address*
Telephone	*Telephone*
Name	*Name*
Address	*Address*
Telephone	*Telephone*
Name	*Name*
Address	*Address*
Telephone	*Telephone*
Name	*Name*
Address	*Address*
Telephone	*Telephone*
Name	*Name*
Address	*Address*
Telephone	*Telephone*

Fodor's Travel Guides

U.S. Guides

Alaska
Arizona
Boston
California
Cape Cod, Martha's
  Vineyard, Nantucket
The Carolinas & the
  Georgia Coast
The Chesapeake
  Region
Chicago
Colorado
Disney World & the
  Orlando Area
Florida
Hawaii

Las Vegas, Reno,
  Tahoe
Los Angeles
Maine, Vermont,
  New Hampshire
Maui
Miami & the
  Keys
National Parks
  of the West
New England
New Mexico
New Orleans
New York City
New York City
  (Pocket Guide)

Pacific North Coast
Philadelphia & the
  Pennsylvania
  Dutch Country
Puerto Rico
  (Pocket Guide)
The Rockies
San Diego
San Francisco
San Francisco
  (Pocket Guide)
The South
Santa Fe, Taos,
  Albuquerque
Seattle &
  Vancouver

Texas
USA
The U. S. & British
  Virgin Islands
The Upper Great
  Lakes Region
Vacations in
  New York State
Vacations on the
  Jersey Shore
Virginia & Maryland
Waikiki
Washington, D.C.
Washington, D.C.
  (Pocket Guide)

Foreign Guides

Acapulco
Amsterdam
Australia
Austria
The Bahamas
The Bahamas
  (Pocket Guide)
Baja & Mexico's Pacific
  Coast Resorts
Barbados
Barcelona, Madrid,
  Seville
Belgium &
  Luxembourg
Berlin
Bermuda
Brazil
Budapest
Budget Europe
Canada
Canada's Atlantic
  Provinces

Cancun, Cozumel,
  Yucatan Peninsula
Caribbean
Central America
China
Czechoslovakia
Eastern Europe
Egypt
Europe
Europe's Great Cities
France
Germany
Great Britain
Greece
The Himalayan
  Countries
Holland
Hong Kong
India
Ireland
Israel
Italy

Italy 's Great Cities
Jamaica
Japan
Kenya, Tanzania,
  Seychelles
Korea
London
London
  (Pocket Guide)
London Companion
Mexico
Mexico City
Montreal &
  Quebec City
Morocco
New Zealand
Norway
Nova Scotia,
  New Brunswick,
  Prince Edward
  Island
Paris

Paris (Pocket Guide)
Portugal
Rome
Scandinavia
Scandinavian Cities
Scotland
Singapore
South America
South Pacific
Southeast Asia
Soviet Union
Spain
Sweden
Switzerland
Sydney
Thailand
Tokyo
Toronto
Turkey
Vienna & the Danube
  Valley
Yugoslavia

Wall Street Journal Guides to Business Travel

Europe

International Cities

Pacific Rim

USA & Canada

Special-Interest Guides

Bed & Breakfast and
  Country Inn Guides:
  Mid-Atlantic Region
  New England
  The South
  The West

Cruises and Ports
  of Call
Healthy Escapes
Fodor's Flashmaps
  New York

Fodor's Flashmaps
  Washington, D.C.
Shopping in Europe
Skiing in the USA &
  Canada

Smart Shopper's
  Guide to London
Sunday in New York
Touring Europe
Touring USA